BORLAND C++ HANDBOOK, SECOND EDITION

Chris H. Pappas
William H. Murray, III

Osborne McGraw-Hill

Berkeley New York St. Louis San Francisco
Auckland Bogotá Hamburg London Madrid
Mexico City Milan Montreal New Delhi Panama City
Paris São Paulo Singapore Sydney
Tokyo Toronto

Osborne **McGraw-Hill**
2600 Tenth Street
Berkeley, California 94710
U.S.A.

For information on translations or book distributors outside of the U.S.A., please write to Osborne **McGraw-Hill** at the above address.

Borland C++ Handbook, Second Edition

1234567890 DOC 998765432

ISBN 0-07-881779-X

BORLAND C++ HANDBOOK, SECOND EDITION

To Mary and Sharon
                    —Chris H. Pappas

To my son Paul
                    —William H. Murray

Publisher

Kenna S. Wood

Acquisitions Editor

Frances Stack

Associate Editor

Jill Pisoni

Technical Editor

Robert Goosey

Project Editor

Madhu Prasher

Copy Editor

Margaret Flynn

Proofreading Coordinator

Factotum Rags

Proofreader

Colleen Paretty

Indexers

Chris H. Pappas
William H. Murray

Director of Electronic Publishing

Deborah Wilson

Production Supervisor

Barry Bergin

Production Assistant

George Anderson

Computer Designers

Stefany Otis
Fred Lass

Cover Designers

Bay Graphics, Inc.
Mason Fong

CONTENTS

ACKNOWLEDGMENTS

First and foremost, we would like to thank Jeff Pepper, Editor-in-Chief at Osborne/McGraw-Hill, for his help in the preparation of this book. The production groups at Osborne/McGraw-Hill have done an exceptional job in typesetting and formatting this text. Osborne professionals have always been top-notch people to work with.

We would like to thank the people at Borland International who have been so positive about this project. In particular, Nan Borreson helped greatly with beta copies of software and technical literature.

Thanks to the programmers at Borland who built such a fine compiler. Programmers everywhere will praise you for the easy-to-use integrated programming environment and mouse support. Special recognition must go to those unsung technical writers at Borland responsible for preparing the documentation for the package components—you have done an outstanding job.

PREFACE

This book highlights Borland's C++ compiler package, which includes the C++ compiler, Assembler, Debugger, and Profiler. You don't have to be a professional programmer to use this book. This book teaches you C, C++, and assembly language from the ground up and was designed for either the novice or professional who owns Borland's sophisticated programming package, as well as for those interested in learning more about procedure-oriented and object-oriented programming. The *Borland C++ Handbook* is a multifaceted book designed with you, the programmer, in mind. We will guide you through many traps and potential pitfalls encountered by program developers. By the time you reach the end of this book, you will be able to efficiently use your C++ package and write and debug sophisticated C, C++, and assembly language code. We have made every effort to make this book readable and to help form a foundation for future study.

HOW THIS BOOK IS ORGANIZED

This book can be used in a variety of ways depending on your background and programming needs. The book can be divided into six major sections:

- Chapters 1, 2, 3, and 4 introduce you to the programming tools contained in the Borland C++ compiler package.

- Chapters 5, 6, 7, 8, 9, 10, 11, and 12 cover the foundations of programming concepts in the C and C++ languages. These are procedure-oriented chapters teaching traditional programming concepts.

- Chapters 13 and 14 build upon the ideas introduced in earlier C chapters, to teach you the concepts and definitions of object-oriented programming. Here you will learn how procedure-oriented and object-oriented programs differ and how to write a simple object-oriented program. The object-oriented program developed in Chapter 14 is similar to earlier programs using the procedure-oriented approach.

- Chapters 15 and 16 show you how to utilize the various C and C++ libraries provided by Borland. Here you will learn of features that allow you to control your computer's hardware and also use extensive graphics routines.

- Chapters 17, 18, and 19 teach assembly language programming fundamentals. Learn to use high-speed assembly language code to control your computer's keyboard and screen options. You will also learn how to combine C code with assembly language routines, pass arguments, and even interface with external hardware circuits.

- Chapters 20, 21, 22, 23, 24, and 25 introduce you to Microsoft Windows concepts and show you how to use the Borland C++ compiler to develop applications that include GDI primitives, cursors, icons, menus, dialog boxes, and how to use the Debugger to explore Windows code. These are successive chapters that will give you a quick start in developing Windows code.

Chapter 1 will help you choose specific sections of this book if you are interested in a selective study of C, C++, or assembly language. For the novice programmer, we of course recommend starting with Chapter 1 and ending with Chapter 25. The ability to write advanced C, C++, assembly language, and Microsoft Windows code is the reward for diligent work and an honest programming effort.

CONVENTIONS USED IN THIS BOOK

The following conventions have been used throughout this book:

- When referring to something that applies equally to C and C++, the reference will be to C.

- Function names and other reserved words appear in **boldface** type.

- Keywords, variables, and constants appear in *italic* type.

- Program listings are shown in typewriter-style text.

- Text for you to enter from the keyboard is printed in **boldface**.

- The first time a technical term is mentioned, it is printed in *italic* type.

I

INTRODUCTION

1

THE SUM OF THE PARTS
MAKES THE WHOLE

Have you ever found yourself in a hardware store, ready to make a purchase, and been faced with a decision between two possible tools? One tool is marked *general purpose* and the other is marked *professional*. Our experience has been that general-purpose tools are great for occasional use, but in the long run, they don't hold up under extended use. On the other hand, professional quality tools are usually built better, contain additional features, and will weather the storm of constant heavy-duty use. Which tool do you buy? Your decision is usually based on price, features, quality, and intended use.

When you purchased the Borland C++ package, you were probably looking for a programming tool, or set of tools, that offers flexibility and performance and that will hold up under heavy-duty use. This package of tools should not become outdated as your programming skills increase. You made the right decision. You don't have to be a professional programmer in order to use the Borland C++ package.

This book attempts to do three basic things. First, it helps you explore and understand the definitions and uses for the individual components in your Borland C++ package. Second, it is a complete C, C++, and assembly language text. It teaches you the definitions and skills for writing programs in C, C++, and assembly language. By the end of this book, you should

have learned the skills that can move you from a beginning to an intermediate level of programming in each of these languages. Third, this book will
show you how to integrate the components of the compiler package so that
you can blend C, C++, and assembly language into the best possible finished program.

In this chapter you'll be introduced to the Borland C++ package with all
of its components, and you'll find out how to install and run the package
on your computer.

THE LAYOUT OF THE BORLAND C++ PACKAGE

The Borland C++ package can be overwhelming when you first take it out
of the box. Don't be intimidated, however. Just separate manuals, disks, and
literature into different piles. Set the disks and literature aside for now and
examine the stack of manuals. You can separate this stack into two categories: user's guides and reference guides. The user's guides contain the
installation instructions for each component in the package. (Installation is
covered a little later in this chapter.) They also contain detailed information
for all of the features of each component. The reference guides, on the
other hand, contain reference information for each language. They include
detailed information on function calls and other mnemonics. Never lose
these manuals.

Now separate the manuals into three categories: C++, assembly language, and the Debugger/Profiler. The following sections explain what
these three products are, what they do, and how they are used.

The C and C++ Compiler

You use the components of the C++ package to write stand-alone programs
in C or C++. The C language provides a general-purpose programming
environment that is structured, modular, and compiled. C is quickly becoming a required language for systems programmers and beginners alike.
When you install your C++ software, you will have the option of working
in a fully integrated development environment or using the compiler in a
command-line mode.

The C++ compiler converts program code into object code. When you write C or C++ programs, your source code name will usually end with a *.c* or *.cpp* extension. Here are some sample source code names:

myfirst.c
mysecond.cpp
counter.c
multiplier.cpp

After successful compiling, your disk will also contain object files, for example:

myfirst.c
mysecond.cpp
counter.c
multiplier.cpp
myfirst.obj
mysecond.obj
counter.obj
multiplier.obj

Object files contain a translation of the original source code that the computer can read directly. To get the final executable file, the object code is linked with the Linker. The Linker sets the memory addresses where the executable code will be located when the program is executed. The Linker usually produces files with the *.exe* extension. When the object files are linked, your disk will contain the following:

myfirst.c
mysecond.cpp
counter.c
multiplier.cpp
myfirst.obj
mysecond.obj
counter.obj
multiplier.obj
myfirst.exe
mysecond.exe
counter.exe
multiplier.exe

You can run the executable files by typing their names at the command-line prompt. You will learn how to enter and execute simple C and C++ code in Chapter 2, "Getting Started with the Borland C++ Compiler."

The Assembler

You can use the components of the Assembler package to write stand-alone programs in assembly language. Assembly language is machine specific (microprocessor) and, as a result, is not nearly as portable as C code. The Borland Assembler will allow you to develop code for the Intel family of microprocessor chips. These currently include the 8086, 8088, 80186, 80286, 80386, and 80486.

Assembly language is a cryptic programming language that permits you to write code closely associated with the actual machine code of the computer. While many programmers judge it harder to learn and program with, assembly language offers the skillful programmer the advantages of speed and complete hardware control. You can write stand-alone assembly language programs with the Borland editor, and then assemble and link them.

The Assembler converts program code into object code. When you write assembly language programs, your source code name will usually end with the *.asm* extension. Here are some assembly language source code names:

scrclear.asm
timer.asm

After successful assembly, your disk will also contain object files, for example:

scrclear.asm
timer.asm
scrclear.obj
timer.obj

Object files from assembly language also contain a translation of the original source code that the computer can read directly. To get the final executable file, the object code is linked with the Linker. When the object files from the assembly language programs are linked, your disk will contain the following:

scrclear.asm
timer.asm
scrclear.obj
timer.obj
scrclear.exe
timer.exe

You can run the executable files just by typing their names at the command-line prompt. You will learn how to enter and execute simple assembly language code in Chapter 3, "Getting Started with Borland's Assembler."

The Debugger and the Profiler

When you write C, C++, or assembly language programs, you will eventually make mistakes. The errors you make can be divided into two broad categories: syntax errors and programming errors. Syntax errors are reported to you when you compile or assemble program code. If the errors are serious enough, the compiler or Assembler will abort the process and no executable file will be produced. To repair this type of error, enter the editor and fix the code at the designated line. The Borland reference guides will be invaluable for this. Syntax errors are often the easiest errors to fix. (Editing and code correction will be discussed in detail in Chapter 2.)

Your program may compile or assemble correctly—with no errors reported—and still not work as you intended. If so, it is usually a programming error—a bug in your programming logic. Programming errors are harder to track down than syntax errors. Borland's Debugger is designed to help you locate programming errors as quickly as possible. To use the Debugger, you must have an executable program, even if it doesn't execute correctly. You will learn how to write programs that integrate into the Debugger environment in Chapter 4, "Getting Started with Borland's Debugger and Profiler."

Finally, the Profiler is a tool that will help you write more efficient code. By using the Profiler, you will learn where your program is spending time during execution. This can help you write more efficient C and C++ code and may suggest an assembly language routine to speed up that operation. You will learn how to use the Profiler in Chapter 4.

INSTALLATION WITH YOUR SYSTEM

The success and ease of use of your Borland C++ compiler package depends a great deal on the computer system it is installed on and the installation options that you choose. The following sections suggest how to optimize your programming environment.

Your Computer

Borland's C++ package will operate on a wide range of IBM and IBM-compatible computers. The Borland C++ *Getting Started* manual discusses the minimum system requirements, but this book suggests the following system profile:

PC XT/AT or PS/2 computer
DOS 5.0 or later
2M RAM memory
Color monitor (graphics)
Coprocessor chip
40 MB hard disk
Mouse

If your computer doesn't currently have a hard disk, make the purchase of a hard disk your number one priority. As you develop your programming skills, switching floppy disks in and out of the computer will very quickly become boring and time-consuming. A hard disk will greatly improve your programming efficiency. If you have an older PC, consider adding a hard-disk card.

If your system contains the components suggested in the preceding profile, you will be able to move quickly and efficiently between the various components of the Borland C++ package.

Setting Up Your System

Start installation by placing the first disk in your disk drive and typing **install**. As you step through the installation process, accept the suggested defaults unless you know that another option will be required. You can change these defaults, including the path names, later if you want. When you install the C++ compiler, you will have to decide which memory models to include in your environment. Only the small memory model will be used in the programs in this book. If you install only the small memory model, you can free a large amount of disk space. You can add other memory models later if you need them.

Once you have installed each of the products, return to the subdirectory that contains the C++ compiler. You can enter the integrated environment by typing **bc**.

THE LAYOUT OF THIS BOOK

A complete description of the layout of this book is in the Preface. If your programming goals are a little more selective, here are some suggestions about chapters to read:

Fast start on each product: Chapters 2 through 4

Assembly language only: Chapters 3, 4, 17 through 19

C and C++ only: Chapters 2, 4 through 14

Microsoft Windows development: Chapters 20 through 25

If you want to start developing C and C++ programs as quickly as possible, turn to Chapter 2 now. If you're interested in assembly language, go to Chapter 3. Once you have finished one of these chapters, you can turn to the section of the book that is of immediate interest to you and continue to build your programming skills.

2

GETTING STARTED WITH THE BORLAND C++ COMPILER

The Borland C++ compiler you have just purchased is a robust software development environment. It enables you to do anything from examine the contents of a single variable or the values passed to a function on the call stack, to single-stepping through your program or just jumping to a particular subroutine.

In this chapter, you will learn how to use many of the development time-saving features incorporated in the programming environment along with some of those features unique to the C language. You will also learn about many additional compiler operating details that you can refer back to later as needed.

The chapter will use simple program segments to explain the features and utilities that are absolutely necessary for managing the majority of programming problems.

THE MAIN WINDOW

Welcome to the new world of windows. Depending on the compilers you have used in the past, just bringing up the Borland C++ compiler's integrated environment can be exciting. The compiler has windows, controls, scroll bars, function keys, and many menus (see Figure 2-1).

Across the top of the window are the Main menu options: " ≡ " (System menu), "File," "Edit," "Search," "Run," "Compile," "Debug," "Project," "Options," "Window," and "Help." The bottom of the window (when in Edit mode) highlights the uses for various function keys: F1 - Help (currently active), F2 - Save, F3 - Open, ALT-F9 - Compile, F9 - Make, and F10 - Menu.

Knowing a few basics will help this seem less overwhelming. You can access any Main menu option in one of three ways: You can click on the option with the mouse; you can press F10, and then use the left or right arrow key to highlight the option and press ENTER; or you can press the ALT key with the color-coded letter in the menu option you would like to activate. For example, you can select the "File" option by pressing ALT-F. (ALT-SPACEBAR selects the ≡ System menu.)

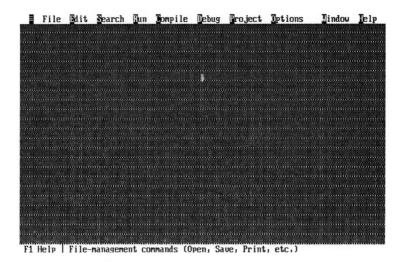

Figure 2-1.   The Main window

HELP

When all else fails, press F1. Getting context-sensitive help anywhere within the programming environment is as simple as selecting the desired menu option and then pressing the F1 key. You will see a detailed explanation of the feature. To back out of a Help window, simply press the ESC key (under most circumstances, the ESC key will undo many different operations).

Depending on the help topic invoked, you may be prompted to go to an additional Help window. To back up to the previous Help window, press ALT-F1. By the way, suppose you are using the editor and have nested yourself with several layers of Help windows and then pressed ESC to leave the Help utility. By pressing ALT-F1 instead of just F1, you will return to the last Help window that was displayed. The Help utility is so complete that you may, under many circumstances, not need to refer to Borland's C++ *User's Guide.*

Moreover, if you are in the Edit window, you can use the Help utility to get immediate assistance with key language features. Place the cursor on a C keyword and press CTRL-F1 (or position the mouse over the keyword and click the right mouse button) to get a brief explanation of the syntax and usage for the selected item.

If you find yourself totally lost, press F1 twice to see a Help screen on the Help utility. Figure 2-2 shows the second page of this Help window, which lists the help categories available.

You can also invoke help by selecting the "Help" option from the Main menu. The menu listing the various options along with their equivalent hotkeys is shown here:

```
                                  Help
         ┌─────────────────────────────┐
         │ Contents                     │
         │ Index            Shift+F1    │
         │ Topic search     Ctrl+F1     │
         │ Previous topic    Alt+F1     │
         │ Help on help                 │
         │ Active File...               │
         ├─────────────────────────────┤
         │ About...                     │
         └─────────────────────────────┘
```

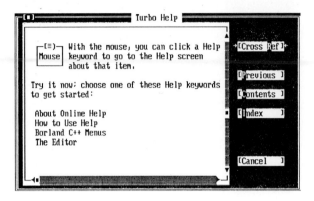

Figure 2-2.   Help window listing help topics

The "Contents" option (Figure 2-3) shows all of the major help categories, while the "Index" option (Figure 2-4) gives you access to a 204-window indexed help file. For this last option, simply highlight the desired feature or command and press ENTER, or double click the left mouse button to obtain the requested help information.

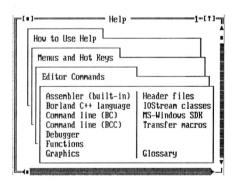

Figure 2-3.   The Help table of contents

Figure 2-4.   The Help Index

Notice that you can press ALT-F1 to bring the previously selected Help screen to the foreground. You can employ this key combination to back-track through an entire editing session's worth of help requests.

YOUR FIRST PROGRAM

This section is designed to give you the basics necessary to enter, edit, compile, run, debug, save, and reload a simple program. But before you enter your first program, you will need to make a few necessary setup decisions.

Minimal Setup

You can install Borland's C++ compiler quickly on a hard disk subdirectory. The question becomes where to put your files. If you have a hard disk, you may want to place your files on it (maybe in the same subdirectory as the compiler, maybe elsewhere). You may also want to put your program files on a floppy so that you can transport them from office to home.

An easy approach to defining output file locations is to use the ALT-O option from the Main menu and then type **D** for "Directories." Either click on the box marked "Output Directory," or tab to it and enter the location for your output files. For example, if you were developing a payroll program, you might want it saved in drive A on the PAYROLL directory (see Figure 2-5).

If, for the time being, you want all of your files to go to drive A and the PAYROLL directory, make certain that you save the definition when you press ESC to leave the Directories submenu. You accomplish this by typing **S** for "Save."

Of course, each time you create a file, you can specify where it is to be saved when you select the "Save" (F2) option. You could accomplish the same single file storage location by pressing F2 and then naming the file A:\PAYROLL\PAYROLL1.C.

Creating

If you are using the Borland compiler for the first time, you will see a screen similar to the one in Figure 2-1 when you start the compiler by typing **bc**. The largest portion of your display will show a pale blocked pattern. This is your work area and it is currently empty.

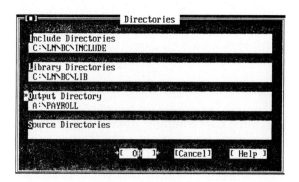

Figure 2-5.   The Directories window

Figure 2-6.   Starting a new file

Whether this is your first program or you have been experimenting with several of the supplied programs, starting a new file is as simple as clicking the mouse on the word "File," and then clicking on the word "New." Notice that the work area now changes to a solid background with a bright border (see Figure 2-6).

To gain experience with the editor, enter the following C program exactly as is, *including* any mistakes:

```
/* A simple demonstration program */

#include <stdio.h>

#define SIZE 5

void print_them(int index,char continue,int int_aray[SIZE]);

main()
{
  int index;
  int int_aray[SIZE];
  char continue=0;

  print_them(index,continue,int_aray);

  Printf("\n\nWelcome to a trace demonstration!");
  printf(\nWould you like to continue (Y/N) ");
  scanf("%c",continue);
  if(continue == 'Y')
```

```
    for(index=0; index < SIZE; index++) {
      printf("\nPlease enter an integer: ");
      scanf("%d",&int_aray[index]);
    }

  print_them(index,continue,int_aray);

  return(0);
}

void print_them(int index, char continue, int int_aray[SIZE])
{
  printf("\n\n%d",index);
  printf("\n\n%d",continue);
  for(index=0; index < SIZE, index++)
    printf("\n%d",int_aray[index]);
}
```

If you have used any of the more popular word processing packages, most of the editing keys (BACKSPACE, INS, DEL, PGUP, PGDN, and so on) work exactly the same in the Borland C and C++ editor. If you want to move to the first line in your program, press CTRL along with PGUP. To move to the last line in your program, use the CTRL key in conjunction with PGDN.

You can also use the scroll bars along the right-hand side of the window. Clicking the mouse on the up arrow symbol ▲ will move the display contents down. Clicking on the down arrow symbol ▼ will move the display contents up. The ■ symbol on the scroll bar (not [■]) indicates the relative position of the screen within the overall size of the document. Placing the mouse on either side of the ■ symbol and clicking will shift the display either up or down one whole screen, like the PGUP and PGDN keys. Placing the mouse over the ■ symbol, holding the left mouse button down, and dragging it to a new location on the scroll bar rapidly advances the display through the file.

If you want a particular window to occupy the entire screen, click the mouse on the [↑] arrow, or press F5. Repeatedly pressing F5 will toggle between original size and full-screen. Clicking the mouse on the [■] symbol closes the associated window.

The editor comes equipped with many advanced features that you can easily review by pressing F1 and then PGDN while in the editor. Two features in particular that are worth experimenting with are Find (CTRL-QF), Find & Replace (CTRL-QA), and the block commands (CTRL-KB, begin; CTRL-KK, end).

You use the block commands to highlight a section of code to be either moved (CTRL-KV), copied (CTRL-KC), deleted (CTRL-KY), or written to disk (CTRL-KW). This last option can be very useful when you are working on a large project where only a portion of a program needs to be shared with other individuals. Reading a block saved to disk is as easy as placing the cursor within your source code where you want the code inserted and pressing CTRL-KR for "read from disk." The editor will then prompt you for the name of the file to import. Don't forget the drive and subdirectory when specifying the file name for any file not in the default directory.

Saving

There is absolutely no excuse for losing a file when in the compiler. To save a file, either press F2 or click the mouse on "Save." You should *always* save after each screen's worth of data entry.

Compiling

To compile a program, press ALT-F9 or click on the Compile main menu and then the Compile command. When you pressed ALT-F9, you should have seen a compile window indicating the number of lines compiled along with any associated warning and error messages as shown here:

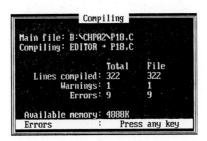

The example program has 1 warning and 9 errors. Press any key to get back to the edit process. Figure 2-7 shows a section of the program and the error messages you should have encountered if you entered and compiled the preceding program.

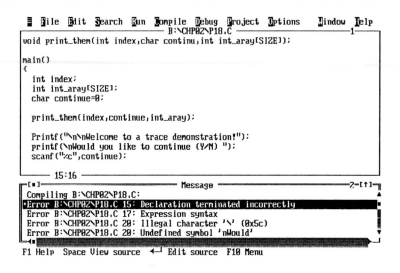

Figure 2-7.   Error messages from the example program

Syntax Errors

The Message window at the bottom of the display (press ALT-WM, if you don't see a Message window) lists the possible error conditions encountered in your program. The first error encountered is highlighted in the Message window. By pressing the F6 key, you can switch between the Message window and the Edit window. When you switch to the Edit window, the cursor will automatically be placed on the line of the error. This allows you to make any necessary corrections quickly.

The first error was caused because a C language reserved word, **continue**, was used for a variable name—something that can happen when you use a new language for the first time. Using whatever method you feel comfortable with (hopefully the Find & Replace command), change all **continue**s to *continu* and recompile the program. Notice how the number of errors went down to 5. By the way, when you changed the **continue**s, did you make sure to save the changes?

Here is the updated Message window:

```
┌[■]────────────────────── Message ──────────────────2=[↑]┐
│ Compiling B:\CHP02\P18.C:                                ▲
│•Error B:\CHP02\P18.C 20: Illegal character '\' (0x5c)    ■
│ Error B:\CHP02\P18.C 20: Undefined symbol 'nWould'
│ Error B:\CHP02\P18.C 20: Function call missing )
│ Error B:\CHP02\P18.C 20: Unterminated string or character constant ▼
└◄■─────────────────────────────────────────────────────┘
```

Notice that the error says there is an illegal character on line 20. There is a missing opening quotation mark before the \nWould. To date, there is no compiler that is entirely accurate with error messages. At best, error messages are flags indicating that a rule wasn't followed somewhere within the syntax of your source code. Sometimes the error message is right, and other times the error occurs one line above the flagged line. Worse yet, the error may be at the beginning of an entire function (this occurs most often with mismatched braces).

If you correct the quotation mark error and recompile the program, you should be down to one error. Figure 2-8 highlights the problem. The *for*

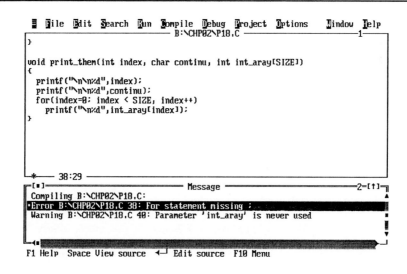

Figure 2-8.   *for* statement error message

loop repetition test hasn't been followed by a semicolon; in this case, the error message was correct. If you fix this problem, you should be able to compile your program without any errors.

Running

With an error- and warning-free compile, you are now ready to run your program. Pressing CTRL-F9 executes a program. You could also have clicked the mouse on the "Run" option and then used the Run command. Pressing CTRL-F9 will also perform a compile and then execute the program (assuming no errors) if the program has not been previously compiled.

What happened when you ran the program? You got an error message. Even though you no longer have syntax errors according to the compiler, you may still have linker or run-time errors. Figure 2-9 highlights the problem. The message says that the symbol _Printf is undefined. Pressing F6 will take you back to the Edit window but does *not* correctly position the cursor. In this case, it takes some experience with the language to realize that the error message is accurate. Since C and C++ are case sensitive, the

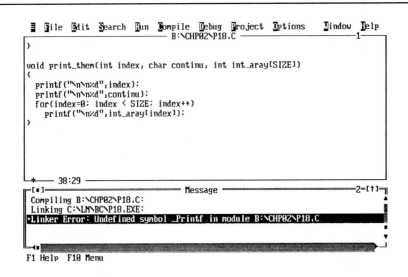

Figure 2-9.   Linker error message

printf function is not the same as the **Printf** function. Line 19 of the program has incorrectly referenced the **printf** function with an uppercase letter P. If you correct this error, you will have an executable program.

Viewing the Output Window

What happened when you ran the corrected program? First, you were asked to type a **Y** or **N** to continue (if your output statement said "continu," you used the global Find & Replace and didn't check all uses of the word). Next, you were prompted for five integer values; then, the next thing you knew, you were back in the editor. To view your output screen, simply press ALT-F5. Any key combination after this will place you back into the editor.

Debugging Made Easy

Just when you thought you had gotten rid of all of the syntax and linker errors, you encountered a run-time error. Fortunately, the Borland C and C++ environment has incorporated many powerful tracing capabilities.

Logical Errors

You can often correct logical errors by doing a single trace through your program. You accomplish this in one of several ways.

How to Single-Step Through a Program

If you press F7, you instruct the environment to run your program line by line, or in *single-step mode*. (This assumes that you have turned source debugging on. To turn source debugging on, select the Main menu "Option," and then type **B** for debugger. Click "Source Debugging" on.) However, under many circumstances this will not be enough. What good will it do you to single-step through your program if you can't see what is happening to your data? By adding *watches* in conjunction with single-step mode, you can trace each line of code as it affects selected variables.

How to Use the Watch Window

To trace a variable, put it into the Watch window by placing the cursor on the selected identifier and pressing CTRL-F7. If you press ALT-W, and then type W again, the lower portion of your screen will display the Watch window. (Depending on the options you have selected and in which order, the lower portion of your display may show the Message window. If you close the Message window, you can split the display between the Edit and the Watch windows.) Now, when you use F7 to single-step through your program, you can actually see the contents of the selected variables change.

How to Skip Debugged Subroutines

The F8 key is slightly different from F7. When you use F8 to single-step through a program and the statement about to be executed is a call to a function, F8 will execute the function completely and continue single-stepping from the line of code below the function call. In contrast, F7 would have traced into the invoked function line by line.

Add *index, array int_aray,* and *continu* to the Watch window by placing the cursor on the definition of each variable (*int index, int int_aray[SIZE],* and *char continu*) and pressing CTRL-F7 once for each variable. The Watch window should appear at the bottom of your display. If it doesn't, you have probably zoomed the Edit window. Press F5 to restore the split screen appearance. Try single-stepping through your program by using the F7 key.

How to Restart the Program

You can reset your program for another run by pressing CTRL-F2 after you have made one complete or partial pass through the source code. Try restarting the example program and single-step through it using the F8 key. Notice how this last trace option skipped over tracing into the function **print_them**.

Depending on the run options you selected, you may or may not have noticed some things going wrong as you single-stepped through the example program. For instance, did the Watch window show you that the variable *continu* ever contained a 'Y'? Did your program perform the single-step process, but execute with strange results when you ran the executable version from outside the environment? Maybe you saw an error message that said "Null pointer assignment."

The problem is small and subtle. Look closely at the following line from the source code:

```
scanf("%c",continu);
```

Here is the correction:

```
scanf("%c",&continu);
```

The difference is both subtle and disastrous. Make the correction in your program and watch what happens to *continu*'s value in the Watch window.

To move on to the next debugging example, you need to unclutter your screen. Remove the Watch window altogether by pressing ALT-D, then typing **W** and **R** to "Remove all watches."

How to Set a Breakpoint

To skip major portions of already debugged code, you can set a *breakpoint*. Place your cursor on the if(continu = = 'Y') statement in the example file you have been working with. Now press CTRL-F8. The entire line should become highlighted; you have just set a breakpoint. To run your program up to this breakpoint, press CTRL-F9. Notice how the program executes up to the *if* statement and then stops. At this point, you can go into single-step mode with either F7 or F8.

You can set multiple breakpoints throughout your program. Each time you press CTRL-F9, you will execute up to the next breakpoint. To remove a single breakpoint, simply place the cursor on the line with the breakpoint set and press CTRL-F8 again. CTRL-F8 is a toggle: The first time you press it, the breakpoint is set; the second time you press it, the breakpoint is removed. You can delete all breakpoints by pressing ALT-D, then **B** for "Breakpoints," and **D** for "Delete."

How to Evaluate and Change a Variable's Contents

The Borland C++ compiler allows you not only to view but to change the contents of variables while the program is executing. Reload the example program and set a watch on the variable *continu*. Single-step through the program with either F7 or F8 until the Watch window displays *continu*'s contents of a 'Y'.

You are now going to try the "Evaluate/Modify..." option by pressing ALT-D for "Debug," followed by E for "Evaluate/Modify...". In the Expression field, type the variable name **continu**. You should see 'Y' in the Result field. Either tab down to the New Value field, or click on the field with the mouse and enter 'N'. Notice how the New Value field now shows 'N' too (see Figure 2-10).

Press the ESC key or click on the [■] symbol to close the Evaluate and Modify window. Notice how the Watch window changes *continu*'s contents from 'Y' to 'N' also as shown here:

```
┌─────────────────────── Watch ─────────────────── 2 ───────┐
│•continu: 'N' █                                            │
│                                                          │
│                                                          │
│                                                          │
└──────────────────────────────────────────────────────────┘
```

Now when you single-step through your program, it will react as if the user had entered a No instead of a Yes.

Reloading a Program

Each time you start the editing environment, your last program is automatically loaded into memory. In addition, the last list of files you edited is

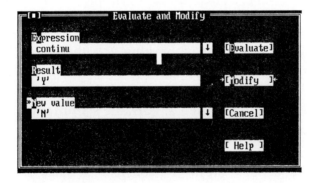

Figure 2-10.   Evaluate and Modify window

automatically saved. You can retrieve it by pressing ALT-F (for "File"), typing O (for "Open"), and using the cursor or mouse to select one of the files listed.

MANAGING WINDOWS

The new Borland programming environment allows you to simultaneously view multiple files, a Watch window, a Message window, a Project window, and more. The programming environment has a window management feature.

Here is the list of options available when you select the "Window" Main menu item:

```
                        Window

          Size/Move       Ctrl+F5
          Zoom                 F5
          Tile
          Cascade
          Next                 F6
          Close            Alt+F3
          Close all

          Message
          Output
          Watch
          User screen      Alt+F5
          Register
          Project
          Project notes

          List all...       Alt+0
```

The first option, CTRL-F5, allows you to resize or relocate the active window. By using the cursor keys after pressing CTRL-F5, you can shift the active window left or right and up or down. By holding down the SHIFT key and using the arrow keys, you can resize the active window.

The "Zoom" option forces the active window to occupy the entire display. When you select the "Tile" option, the programming environment will resize all windows and place them next to each other much like a tiled floor. By pressing F6, you can cycle through all open windows, making each one the active window. You can close any active window with the ALT-F3 hotkey.

You can also activate a window by selecting the Window menu and choosing any one of the viewable window categories ("Message," "Output," and "Watch"). As you've already seen, pressing ALT-F5 will switch you to the User Screen window.

When you must know the current contents of the microprocessor registers, just select the "Window Register" option. Here is an example CPU window:

The last two options in this menu section allow you to view the Project window and the Project Notes window. You can use the Project Notes window to save critical comments regarding the current status of a project's development.

You can use the "List" option, or the ALT-0 hotkey (the number 0, not the letter O), to display a list of open windows. You can quickly switch to any of the open windows by highlighting the desired window and pressing ENTER.

MULTIPLE SOURCE FILE MANAGEMENT

Many times a single C or C++ listing will contain multiple files. When you are ready to edit, compile, and link the individual files it will be necessary to use the editor to separate each from the composite listing.

In this section, you will use the editor's block commands as you break down the example program into separate files. You will break down the listing into the following three files. File one will be called *myinclud.h*:

```
/****************** MYINCLUD.H FILE ******************/

#include <stdio.h>
#define SIZE 5
```

File two will be called *mymain.c:*

```
/****************** MYMAIN.C FILE ********************/

void print_them(int index,char continu,int int_aray[SIZE]);
main()
{
  int index;
  int int_aray[SIZE];
  char continu=0;

  print_them(index,continu,int_aray);

  Printf("\n\nWelcome to a trace demonstration!");
  printf("\nWould you like to continue (Y/N) ");
  scanf("%c",&continue);

  if(continu == 'Y')
    for(index=0; index < SIZE; index++) {
      printf("\nPlease enter an integer: ");
      scanf("%d",&int_aray[index]);
    }
  print_them(index,continu,int_aray);

  return(0);
}
```

File three will be called *onefunc.c:*

```
/****************** ONEFUNC.C FILE ********************/
void print_them(int index, char continu, int int_aray[SIZE])
{
  printf("\n\n%d",index);
  printf("\n\n%d",continu);
  for(index=0; index < SIZE; index++)
    printf("\n%d",int_aray[index]);
}
```

Using the Editor

Reload the example program into memory if you have been experimenting with additional environment options. Marking a block of code is a simple process. Place the cursor in the row and column you wish to designate as the beginning of the code block, and then press CTRL-KB (for begin). Next, move the cursor to the row and column you wish to designate as the end of the defined block and press CTRL-KK. You can also block text by clicking and holding the left mouse button, dragging the mouse over the selected code, and then releasing the button. The entire code block will be highlighted.

Beginning at the top of your program, block off the code shown for *myinclud.h*. Once the block is highlighted, save it to the disk by pressing CTRL-KW (for write). The editor will ask you for the name of the file. Remember to include any paths if necessary. Make certain you name the file *myinclud.h*.

Repeat this process of defining the block and writing the block to disk until you have created the last two files: *mymain.c* and *onefunc.c*. If you like, you can edit each file so that it includes the file header comments:

```
/****************** MYINCLUD.H FILE ******************/

/****************** MYMAIN.C FILE ******************/

/****************** ONEFUNC.C FILE ******************/
```

Comments like these help other programmers know which file they are viewing.

Using the Project Utility

Whenever you create a C or C++ program using multiple source files, you need to tell the compiler which files are necessary for creating the executable version of the program. You do this by defining a project file. The *project file* simply contains the names of all source or object files needed to create the program.

Creating a Project File

To define a project file, press ALT-P for "Project," and type **O** for "Open." Once you have named the project file, for example, *myproj.prj*, a window will open at the bottom of the screen:

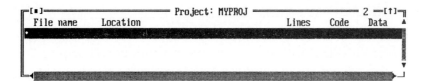

By pressing the INS key, you can enter the names of the files needed to create the program. At this time, enter the names of the files *mymain.c* and *onefunc.c*. Make certain you precede the file names with any needed paths.

Debugging with Multiple Source Files

With this accomplished, press F10 to return to the Main menu and then press F9 to compile the program. The Message window informs you that *SIZE* is undefined in *mymain.c*. Because the #include "myinclud.h" statement has not been added to *mymain.c*, *SIZE* is undefined. Edit the file so that the following statement appears at the top of *mymain.c*.

```
#include "myinclud.h"
```

You may need to precede *myinclud.h* with a path if you are using subdirectories. For example:

```
#include "a:\johnproj\myinclud.h"
```

Save the change and press F9 again. Unfortunately, you still have the same problem with *onefunc.c*. Even though the file *mymain.c* knows about *myinclud.h,* since *onefunc.c* is a separate file, it needs its own **#include** statement, exactly like the one you just entered in *mymain.c*. When you have made and saved this second change, your program should compile without any errors. Press CTRL-F9 to run it.

To ensure that you will be able to view the source code associated with each message window error automatically, perform the following check. Press ALT-O for "Options," then type **E** for "Environment," then **P** for "Preferences." If the "New Window" option is checked within the "Source Tracking" section, you're all set. If not, just click the mouse on the option or tab over to it to make the necessary switch.

The *make* Utility

You use the *make* utility to create the executable version of your program (**.exe*). When invoked with the F9 key, the *make* utility will display the name of the file it is about to create—for example, *example.exe.*

The name for the file is determined in one of two ways. If you have defined a project file, the name of the project will be used as the file name. If you have not previously defined a project file, the name used for the executable version of your program will match the name of the file that is currently in the active Edit window.

The *make* utility checks that the executable version of your program reflects all updates made to any support files. For example, suppose that *example.exe* was generated by compiling and linking four files: *a.h, a.c, b.c,* and *c.c.* Two weeks later you go back into *b.c* and rewrite the sort algorithm to make it more efficient. The problem is that *example.exe* does not include this improvement. By invoking *make,* you can update *example.exe* so that it incorporates the new sort.

OTHER MENU OPTIONS

The compiler's menu options may seem overwhelming to the novice, challenging to the moderately experienced programmer, and obvious to an expert. The beginning of this chapter tried to provide you with an overview of the most immediately needed and useful options. The rest of the chapter will highlight supplemental environment features.

Restoring a Line

Suppose you're on a deadline and you delete a line of code so complex that you could never re-create it as quickly as you would need to. Just restore it! If you deleted the entire line by pressing CTRL-QY, you can restore the entire line with CTRL-QL. You can also use the "Edit/Undo" option (ALT-BKSP) to undo any editing change made to a line as long as you have not moved the cursor off the modified line.

Find, Find and Replace

When writing an algorithm, you often need to search for every occurrence of a particular variable or constant. While you are in the Edit window, you can begin a "find" by pressing CTRL-QF. Figure 2-11 shows the Find window. You enter the text you want to find and then check off the options to be used for the search. These options include whether the search should be case sensitive, whether the search should look for whole words only, whether it should be a global or restricted search, a forward or backward search from the current cursor location, or a search of the entire file. Once you have selected the find criteria, click the mouse on the OK box, or tab over to the OK box and press ENTER. You can continue a find with the same search criteria by pressing CTRL-L.

To execute a standard search and replace operation while in the Edit window, press CTRL-QA. Figure 2-12 displays the Replace window. This window is almost identical to the Find window. After you enter the text you want to find, you need to define the replacement text in the New Text field. You also have the one additional option "Prompt on replace." If you check this box, each found occurrence of the searched for text will cause the editor to stop and ask you for permission to make the requested substitution.

Locate Function

When debugging an application, a useful feature of the Search menu is the "Locate function. . ." option. This option works very differently than Find.

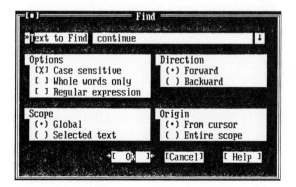

Figure 2-11.   Using the "Find" option

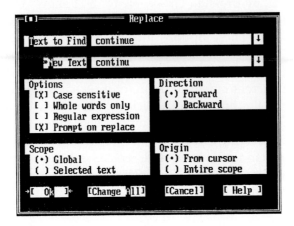

Figure 2-12.   Using the "Replace" option

If your application had a function called **calculate_payrate** that was called from four different locations in your source code, executing a Find for **calculate_payrate** would display all of the function calls, the function prototype, and the function header. "Locate function..." zips immediately to the definition of the function. In addition, when you select this option, a Locate function window opens that allows you to enter the name of the function to search for, or allows you to select any one of the functions you have searched for previously from a history list.

Cut and Paste

The Borland compiler incorporates a clipboard that you can use for cutting and pasting text. Here is the Edit menu highlighting these options:

```
Edit
┌─────────────────────────────────┐
│ Undo                    Alt+Bsp │
│ Redo                            │
├─────────────────────────────────┤
│ Cut                    Shift+Del │
│ Copy                    Ctrl+Ins │
│ Paste                  Shift+Ins │
│ Clear                   Ctrl+Del │
│ Copy example                    │
├─────────────────────────────────┤
│ Show clipboard                  │
└─────────────────────────────────┘
```

Some of the options have hotkeys. Others you need to select by pressing ALT-E (or clicking with the mouse) to select the Edit menu, and then highlighting the selected option and pressing ENTER (or clicking on the option with the mouse).

Since the editor allows you to have several files open at once, you can use the clipboard cut and paste option to make copies of, or transfer code from, one file to another. For these options to be activated, you must have previously defined a block of text (CTRL-KB to begin the block, CTRL-KK to end the block definition).

You can copy blocked text by pressing CTRL-INS. You cut blocked text by pressing SHIFT-DEL. To paste copied text from the clipboard to the selected file, first switch the Edit window emphasis to the destination file, place the cursor where you want the copied text, and press SHIFT-INS.

As a precautionary measure, you may choose to verify that the block of text you copied is correct. Do this by selecting the Edit menu and selecting the "Show clipboard" option. By selecting the "Clear" option instead, or by pressing CTRL-DEL, you can erase the contents of the clipboard.

Block Commands

At this point, you probably realize that there are many ways to perform the same editing operation. This holds true with the block commands, which in some ways resemble certain clipboard operations.

All of the block commands involve a preselected section of text. If you are using a mouse, to block the text simply click the left mouse button wherever you want the block to begin, and hold it down while you drag the cursor to where the block is to end. Notice that the selected text will be highlighted. If you don't have a mouse, pressing CTRL-KB will begin the block definition at the current cursor location. Pressing CTRL-KK will end the definition.

To cancel a block definition, either click the left mouse button, or place the cursor at the beginning of the block and press CTRL-KK. Figure 2-13 shows the Edit help window for the block commands. Some of the more frequently used block commands include CTRL-KC to copy a block, CTRL-KV to move a block, and CTRL-KY to delete a block.

In a large program, you may need to incorporate code or data created by someone else. By using the CTRL-KR command, you can instruct the editor to prompt you for the name of a file (don't forget the drive and path if necessary) to pull into the editor.

If you are creating a code segment that needs to be shared, first block the segment and then press CTRL-KW. The editor will now prompt you for a file name to be used for saving the segment. A team member could then use CTRL-KR to read the segment.

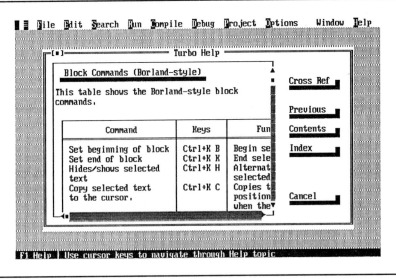

Figure 2-13.   Help for block commands

When you need a hard copy of a portion of your program or data file, just block the needed segment, turn the printer on, and press CTRL-KP. The blocked text will automatically be sent to the printer.

Change Directory

When working on several projects at once, you may forget the name of a particular file. If the file is one you haven't worked on for several days, it may no longer be in the files list. For these and similar circumstances, you may need to change the editor's default directory. Here is the File menu with the "Change dir..." option:

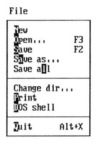

If you select this option, you will see a window that displays the current path and allows you to change it (Figure 2-14). Simply type the desired

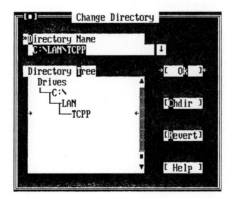

Figure 2-14.   The Change Directory window

drive and directory, (include the path when necessary). By changing the default directory, you redefine where the editor and compiler will save and look for files.

DOS Shell

The "DOS Shell" option allows you to keep the editor running while you temporarily return to the operating system. This can be extremely useful under certain circumstances. Suppose that you go to save your file and, as a result of the last editing changes, the file is now too big to fit on the disk. If you quit the editor, you lose your editing changes. This is because the editor keeps everything in memory.

With the "DOS Shell" option, you can keep your file in the editor, go back to the operating system, format your disk, and then instantly pop back into the editor by typing **EXIT**. At this point, you would just need to press F2 to complete the save.

Printing

When you want a hard copy of the text in the active Edit window, you can press ALT-F for file, and type **P** for print. This approach would be much quicker than defining and then printing a block. In contrast, you can print any portion of a file by defining a block and then using CTRL-KP.

3

GETTING STARTED WITH BORLAND'S ASSEMBLER

You probably want to try your new Assembler as soon as possible. This chapter is designed to help you get that quick start with the Assembler. For this reason, it describes how to use the Assembler, rather than how to write assembly language code.

Borland's Assembler is a fast, one-pass assembler. Assembly language programs utilize mnemonics that represent machine instructions. For example, **add** is a mnemonic that will be converted to machine code upon assembly. A *one-pass assembler* resolves all references and generates all machine code on a single pass through your source code file. Assembly language is very machine dependent. *Machine dependence* means that programs written for computers using Intel's family of microprocessors will not run on Apple computers using Motorola microprocessors. The Assembler provides support for Intel microprocessors 8088 to 80486 and math coprocessors 8087 to 80387. Assembly code, for the Intel microprocessor series, is upward compatible. *Upward compatibility* means that programs written for the 8088 microprocessor will execute correctly on an 80486 microprocessor. Each new microprocessor actually contains a superset of the previous chip's machine instruction set. During the assembly process, ASCII files containing source code (*.asm*) are converted to machine code in object files (*.obj*) and then linked to produce executable files (*.exe*).

Assembly language has two major advantages over many higher level languages. First, it enables you to program the computer at the microprocessor (hardware) level. This is an advantage because if the task can be done on a computer, it can be done at the hardware level. With compilers, you are at the mercy of the design team as to which features you can and cannot address. Second, you can write the fastest possible executable code. Ultimately, compilers must translate instructions into machine code. Thus, a **printf** function in C might translate into 30 to 60 lines (or more) of machine code. This machine code might not be optimized for fastest performance. With assembly language, you write the code directly and can thus test programs for optimum performance.

SETTING UP THE ASSEMBLER

The Assembler is installed automatically with the Borland C++ compiler. The installation program will provide default options and ask several questions during the process. You should select the default options unless you are an experienced user.

Once the installation process has been completed, your hard disk or floppies will contain numerous files. The most important files are *tasm.exe*, the Assembler; *tlink.exe*, the Linker; *make.exe*, the Command Line *make* utility; *tlib.exe*, the Librarian; and *tcref.exe*, the Cross-Reference utility. Borland includes additional utility and example programs to aid in the assembly language environment.

Borland's Assembler is highly compatible with other assemblers such as IBM's or Microsoft's MASM. In fact, the assembler you are about to use is even more powerful. Borland's TASM contains many enhancements to assembly language, including

- Extended command-line syntax

- Global directives

- Local symbols
- Extended range conditional jumps
- Ideal mode
- Union and structure nesting
- Emulated or nonemulated coprocessor operation
- Explicit segment overrides
- Constant segments
- Extended loop instructions for the 80386/80486
- Extended listing controls
- Alternate directives
- Predefined variables
- Improved operation of **shl** and **shr** mnemonics
- Enhancements to the MASM environment

You will learn about a number of these features now and in future assembly language chapters (Chapters 17, 18, and 19). Don't panic if the terms are foreign to you. They are explained in more detail later.

THE ASSEMBLY PROCESS: THE FIRST EXAMPLE

The assembly process involves three steps. First, you enter the program with an editor and save it as an ASCII file. You can use any editor that saves the file in ASCII format. For example, you could use Borland's Sprint word processor (in ASCII mode) or the Borland C++ editor. We recommend the C++ editor supplied with your package. Assembly language does not have a self-contained editing environment like other Borland products. You create all assembly language programs by issuing command-line statements. Additionally, all assembly language programs should have the *.asm* file extension. For example, you might type

```
bc myfirst.asm
```

This will take you into the Borland C++ editor and name your assembly language file *myfirst.asm*. The file *myfirst.asm* will be located on the default drive and current subdirectory. If you are using this editor to write your assembly language code, you should set the tab size to 8. You can do this by selecting "Options/Environment/Tab size." Once the program is complete, you must save the file (use the F2 function key) and exit the editor.

The second step, after you have successfully entered and saved the source code, is to run the Assembler. The syntax can be as simple as

```
tasm myfirst
```

The Assembler will look on the current drive and subdirectory for a file named *myfirst.asm* and attempt to assemble the code. If successful, the Assembler will create an additional file named *myfirst.obj*. The object file (*.obj*) contains the binary equivalents to your source code. You can combine object files for one program with object files for other programs, linking several files. If the assembly process occurs without any errors, your screen might receive a report something like this:

```
Turbo Assembler Version 3.0 Copyright (c) 1988, 1991 Borland International

Assembling file:    MYFIRST.ASM
Error messages:     None
Warning messages:   None
Passes:             1
Remaining memory:   361k
```

The third step, the linking process, is the job of the Linker. The Linker searches for a file with an *.obj* extension and converts it into an executable file with an *.exe* extension. To use the Linker, type

```
tlink myfirst
```

If the Linker is successful, you will see the following on your screen:

```
Turbo Link Version 5.0 Copyright (c) 1991 Borland International
```

The Assembler will report syntax warnings and errors to you. Sometimes you can ignore warning messages, but you can never ignore errors. If syntax errors occur in your code, you must bring the source code back into the editor and correct the mistakes.

In review, the three steps for creating an assembly language program are as follows:

1. Enter the source code with an editor, such as the Borland C++ editor.

2. Assemble the source code with TASM.

3. Link the object file with TLINK.

Entering Your First Program with the Borland C++ Editor

Assembly language programs, unlike most high-level compiler programs, require a certain amount of *overhead* in each program. This overhead tells the Assembler how to assemble your source code. You use directives to control the Assembler and specify just how the code is to be assembled. More importantly, you use them to indicate the type of microprocessor on which you expect to run the program.

What follows is a simple program, used primarily to illustrate the overhead that you will use frequently throughout the assembly language programming chapters. Later chapters will cover the details of each assembly directive. Fortunately, the overhead will remain the same for most programs and is thus a good candidate for a batch file.

Using the editor provided with Borland C++, enter the program shown in the listing. Name the program *myfirst.asm*.

```
        DOSSEG                          ;use Intel segment-ordering
        .MODEL  small                   ;set model size

        .STACK  300h                    ;set up 768 byte stack

        .DATA                           ;set up data location
SendIt  db      'Assembly Language is easy!','$'

        .CODE
Turbo   PROC    FAR                     ;main procedure declaration
        mov     ax,DGROUP               ;point ds toward .DATA
        mov     ds,ax
;**********************************************************************
```

```
        lea     dx,SendIt        ;point to the message
        mov     ah,9             ;interrupt parameter
        int     21h              ;call DOS print interrupt

;**********************************************************

        mov     ah,4Ch           ;return control to DOS
        int     21h
Turbo   ENDP                     ;end main procedure
        END                      ;end whole program
```

Once you have entered the program, save and exit the editor (by using function key F2). Figure 3-1 shows an editor screen with a partial listing of this program.

The actual program code is highlighted between the rows of asterisks (*). The other material consists of assembler directives and code for correctly entering and leaving the DOS programming environment. When it executes correctly, this program will print a text message on the screen at the current cursor position.

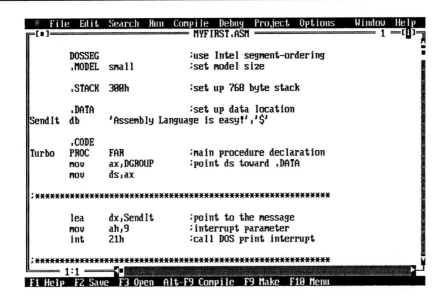

Figure 3-1.   Using the Borland C++ editor to write assembly language code

Assembling the Program with TASM

To assemble this program, type

```
tasm myfirst
```

If you receive error messages, return to the editor and make sure that your source code matches the listing.

Linking the Program with TLINK

To link this program, type

```
tlink myfirst
```

If successful, do a listing of your default directory. You should have four files starting with the name *myfirst*. The file *myfirst.asm* is the original source code. The file *myfirst.obj* is the object code produced by the Assembler. The file *myfirst.exe* is the executable code produced by the linker. TLINK will also produce a map file named *myfirst.map*. Map files are discussed later in this chapter.

To execute the program, type

```
myfirst
```

What do you see on the screen? Do you believe the message? For a large percentage of the stand-alone assembly language programs in this book, these assembly and link commands are all you need during the assembly process.

At times, however, you will need to use other link features. For example, you might want to combine several additional object modules to produce one executable file. You may also want to include the power of an external library. The Assembler and Linker provide assembly flexibility via command-line options and switches.

ASSEMBLER OPTIONS AND SWITCHES

The Borland Assembler is a powerful program with numerous command-line options. It gives you greater flexibility during assembly than the simple example shown earlier. To view a list of these options, type

```
tasm
```

You should see a list similar to Table 3-1. For example, a useful command-line syntax might look like this:

```
tasm /zi myfirst,,,myfirst
```

If executed, the command-line syntax would assemble *myfirst.asm* to an object file named *myfirst.obj* (default name). Additionally, it would generate a listing file named *myfirst.lst* (default name) and a cross-reference file named *myfirst.xrf* (discussed later in this chapter). The *.obj* file would contain additional information for the Debugger as a result of the /zi option.

The Assembler also lets you include a configuration file. This configuration file, named *tasm.cfg*, allows a number of frequently used command-line syntax statements to be included each time *tasm* is executed. For example, you could use the Borland C++ editor to create a file named *tasm.cfg*. The contents of that file might be

```
/c /la /zi
```

If you then assembled the previous assembly language example, by typing

```
tasm myfirst
```

the Assembler would read *tasm.cfg* and insert the command-line syntax in the assembly statement immediately after the letters "tasm." In effect, the Assembler would behave as if you had typed

```
tasm /c /la /zi myfirst
```

This syntax would produce *myfirst.obj* and *myfirst.lst*. The listing file would contain cross-reference information at the end of the file. The *.obj* file would contain full debug information. The next example shows what several of these options provide.

Table 3-1.   TASM's Command-Line Options

Option	Function
/a, /s	Alphabetic or source-code segment ordering
/c	Generate cross-reference in listing
/dSYM[= VAL]	Define symbol SYM = 0, or = value VAL
/e, /r	Emulated or real floating-point instructions
/h, /?	Display this help screen
/iPATH	Search PATH for include files
/jCMD	Jam in an assembler directive CMD (for example, /jIDEAL)
/kh#	Hash table capacity #
/l, /la	Generate listing: l = normal listing, la = expanded listing
/ml, /mx, /mu	Case sensitivity on symbols: ml = all, mx = globals, mu = none
/mv#	Set maximum valid length for symbols
/m#	Allow # multiple passes to resolve forward references
/n	Suppress symbol tables in listing
/o, /op	Generate overlay code, Pharlap 32-bit fixups
/p	Check for code segment overrides in protected mode
/q	Suppress OBJ records not needed for linking
/t	Suppress messages if successful assembly
/w0, /w1, /w2	Set warning level: w0 = none, w1 = w2 = warnings on
/w −xxx, /w + xxx	Disable (−) or enable (+) warning xxx
/x	Include false conditionals in listing
/z	Display source line with error message
/zi, /zd, /zn	Debug info: zi = full, zd = line numbers only, zn = none

LINKER OPTIONS AND SWITCHES

The Linker is fast and compact. As mentioned, linkers are responsible for linking one or more object modules to form final executable code. The Linker reads one or more *.obj* files and produces a final executable file with an *.exe* extension.

The Linker also provides for several command-line options. To view the current options, type

```
tlink
```

TLINK will then list the current options on the screen, as shown in Table 3-2. If you are using linker options, you might use the following syntax:

```
tlink /m /s /l /v myfirst,,,
```

Table 3-2.   TLINK's Command-Line Options

Turbo Link   Version 5.0 Copyright © 1991 Borland International

Syntax:
TLINK objfiles, exefile, mapfile, libfiles, deffile
@---- indicates use response file ----

Option	Function
/m	Map file with publics
/x	No map file at all
/i	Initialize all segments
/l	Include source line numbers
/L	Specify library search paths
/s	Detailed map of segments
/n	No default libraries
/d	Warn if duplicate symbols in libraries
/c	Case significant in symbols
/3	Enable 32-bit processing
/o	Overlay switch
/v	Full symbolic debug information
/P [=NNNNN]	Pack code segment
/A=NNNN	Set NewExe segment alignment
/e	Ignore Extended Dictionary
/t	Create COM file (same as /Tdc)
/C	Case sensitive exports and imports
/Txx	Specify output file type
/Tdx	DOS image (default)
/Twx	Windows image

(x can be c=COM, e=EXE, d=DLL)

In this situation, TLINK will produce a map file with public symbols and will include source code line numbers along with a detailed map of program segments. (Map files are discussed later in this chapter.) The executable file will be named *myfirst.exe* (by default). The map file will be named *myfirst.map* (by default). No library files are used in this link. You will see what these options provide in the next example.

IMPORTANT UTILITY PROGRAMS AND FILES

You will combine several command-line options when you assemble and link the first example again and explore the results.

For this case, assemble the program *myfirst.asm* by typing

```
tasm /zi myfirst,,,
```

Then link the resulting *.obj* file by typing

```
tlink /m /s /l /v myfirst,,,
```

When the process has been completed without errors, do a directory listing to view the files that start with *myfirst*. Type

```
dir myfirst.*
```

You should see a list of files on the screen, somewhat like this:

```
Volume in drive C is DOS
Directory of  C:\TASM

MYFIRST  OBJ      474    1-04-91   9:30a
MYFIRST  ASM      616    1-03-91   5:06a
MYFIRST  LST     2904    1-04-91   9:30a
MYFIRST  MAP      486    1-04-91   9:30a
MYFIRST  XRF      375    1-04-91   9:30a
MYFIRST  EXE      557    1-04-91   9:30a
         6 File(s)  15699968 bytes free
```

The next two sections explore the importance of the *.map* and *.lst* files and an important utility program named *make*. Later examples will illustrate further the power and usefulness of these tools. As you develop your assembly language programming skills, you can pick and choose which tools to use.

The Map File (*.map*)

Map files are created, by default, by the Linker TLINK. The default map is a bare-bones map that lists the program's segments, starting address, and error messages generated upon link. You can gain additional detail by adding the /m and /s options to the linker command line. The /m option adds a list of sorted public symbols (if your program uses them). The /s option adds a detailed segment map.

To view the *.map* file created in the previous section, type

```
type myfirst.map
```

The *.map* file should include a listing somewhat like the following:

```
Start  Stop   Length Name            Class

00000H 0001FH 00020H _TEXT           CODE
00020H 0003AH 0001BH _DATA           DATA
00040H 0033FH 00300H STACK           STACK

Detailed map of segments

0000:0000 0010 C=CODE   S=_TEXT       G=(none)  M=MYFIRST.ASM ACBP=48
0000:0010 0010 C=CODE   S=_TEXT       G=(none)  M=MYFIRST.ASM ACBP=48
0002:0000 001B C=DATA   S=_DATA       G=DGROUP  M=MYFIRST.ASM ACBP=48
0002:0020 0300 C=STACK  S=STACK       G=DGROUP  M=MYFIRST.ASM ACBP=74

  Address         Publics by Name

  Address         Publics by Value

Line numbers for myfirst.obj(MYFIRST.ASM) segment _TEXT

    12 0000:0010    13 0000:0013    17 0000:0015    18 0000:0018
    19 0000:001A    23 0000:001C    24 0000:001E
Program entry point at 0000:0000
```

This *.map* file, for the first example, does not contain any public symbols. You will learn more about map files in future assembly language chapters. This section just teaches you how to use the various tools to obtain the information.

The Listing File (.*lst*)

Listing (.*lst*) files are generated at assembly time by TASM. Listing files are not created by default; you must specifically request them. In the TASM command-line sequence, you make the request with the following syntax:

```
tasm [options]source[,object][,listing][,xref]
```

Typing

```
tasm myfirst,,,
```

creates a listing with the default name *myfirst.lst*. The first example creates a listing file. When you enter

```
type myfirst.lst
```

you can view the listing file:

```
Turbo Assembler                         01/04/91 09:30:04
Page 1
MYFIRST.ASM

 1                                      DOSSEG
 2 0000                                 .MODEL  small
 3
 4 0000                                 .STACK  300h
 5
 6 0000                                 .DATA
 7 0000   41 73 73 65 6D 62 6C + SendIt db  'Assembly Language
                                              is easy!','$'
 8        79 20 4C 61 6E 67 75 +
 9        61 67 65 20 69 73 20 +
10        65 61 73 79 21 24
11
12 001B                                 .CODE
13 0000                          Turbo  PROC    FAR
14 0000   B8 0000s                      mov     ax,DGROUP
15 0003   8E D8                         mov     ds,ax
16
17 0005   8D 16 0000r                   lea     dx,SendIt
18 0009   B4 09                         mov     ah,9
19 000B   CD 21                         int     21h
20
21 000D   B4 4C                         mov     ah,4Ch
22 000F   CD 21                         int     21h
23 0011                          Turbo  ENDP
```

```
24                                          END
Turbo Assembler                  01/04/91 09:30:04
Page 2
Symbol Table


Symbol Name              Type   Value            Cref defined at #

??DATE                   Text   "01/04/91"
??FILENAME               Text   "MYFIRST "
??TIME                   Text   "09:30:04"
??VERSION                Number 0101
@CODE                    Text   _TEXT                   #2   #12
@CODESIZE                Text   0                       #2
@CPU                     Text   0101H
@CURSEG                  Text   _TEXT                   #6   #12
@DATA                    Text   DGROUP                  #2
@DATASIZE                Text   0                       #2
@FILENAME                Text   MYFIRST
@WORDSIZE                Text   2                       #6   #12
SENDIT                   Byte   DGROUP:0000             #7   17
TURBO                    Far    _TEXT:0000              #13
Groups & Segments        Bit Size Align  Combine Class
                                            Cref defined at #

DGROUP                   Group                          #2   2   14
   STACK                 16  0300 Para  Stack    STACK  #4
   _DATA                 16  001B Word  Public   DATA   #2   #6
   _TEXT                 16  0011 Word  Public   CODE   #2   2   #12
                                                        12
```

Notice that the comments in this file have been omitted. This is a very wide listing. If you had shrunk the text size so the listing fit on a book page, you wouldn't have been able to read it. All *.lst* files normally contain the full comments originally placed in the program. Also notice that this file replicates your source code along with the equivalent machine code for each mnemonic. For example, line 18 contains the sequence:

```
mov    ah,9
```

To the left of this statement is the machine code equivalent

```
B4  09
```

The B4 value is the machine code equivalent of moving a piece of immediate data into the **ah** register. These values are always specified in hexadecimal notation.

You might have noticed some additional symbols in this listing (+, r, and s). Table 3-3 contains the special listing file symbols. Most of these symbols are necessary in listings because the assembly process (TASM) that generates the listing file has no idea where the Linker (TLINK) will place such things as code segments.

Listing files also contain symbol table information. The type and value of symbols are listed. Types include text, number, byte, far, and so on. Values can be numbers, variable names, and so on. While you now know names and types, you need a cross-reference table to know where these values are defined and used. For example, *SendIt* is defined on line 7 and used on line 17. This information can help you debug programs.

The *make* Utility

make is a Borland utility program that can facilitate your assembly and compiling process. The *make* utility is extremely powerful; only the features that fit your immediate needs are explained here.

You can use the *make* utility in large programs that require the assembly or compilation of a number of files to produce a final executable version. As you alter code, your only choice to this point has been to recompile or assemble everything each time you make a change. This is confusing and inefficient.

Table 3-3.   Special Listing File Symbols

Symbol	Function
r	Offset fixup type for symbols in the current module
s	Segment fixup type for symbols in the current module
sr	Both r and s
e	Offset fixup type for external symbol
se	Pointer fixup on an external symbol
so	Segment-only fixup
+	Object code truncated to next line

The *make* utility can free you from this routine for even the simplest programs. Here is a typical file that the *make* utility can use in the assembly process:

```
myfirst.exe: myfirst.obj
   tlink /m /l myfirst,,,

myfirst.obj: myfirst.asm
   tasm /zi myfirst,,,
```

The *make* utility works on the basis of dates and times. When you run *make*, it checks and compares the dates and times when, in this case, the *.exe, .obj,* and *.asm* files were created. If the *myfirst.asm* file has a later date and/or time than the *myfirst.obj* or *myfirst.exe* file, the *make* utility performs the specified assembly and link process to update that file. If no change has occurred in the *.obj* or *.exe* file, *make* skips the assembly and link steps.

In this fashion, a program's *make* file serves as an intelligent batch file, capable of providing all necessary information for assembly and linking. This book uses *make* files and the *make* utility frequently for C++ and assembly language programs.

To run the *make* utility, you have to create a file similar to the one in the previous listing. You can do this with the Borland C++ editor. Name the file *myfirst*, without an extension. Once the file is created and saved, simply type

```
make -fmyfirst
```

Notice the *-f* immediately in front of the file name; not even a single space is permitted. You need this option to tell *make* not to search for the default *make* file, named *makefile*. It is best to give the *make* file the same name as the program. The *-f* is a command-line option for the *make* utility. Table 3-4 shows other command-line options for *make*.

THE ASSEMBLY PROCESS: THE SECOND EXAMPLE

One of the major advantages of assembly language is its ability to control the hardware of the computer. The second example involves an assembly

Table 3-4.   Command-Line Options for *make*

Option	Function
-a	Creates an autodependency check
-D*identifier*	Defines an identifier
-D*iden* = *string*	Defines the identifier to the string
-I*directory*	*make* will search directory names for include files
-s	No commands are printed before execution
-n	Prints but doesn't execute commands (useful in debugging the *make* file)
-f*filename*	Uses the *make* file identified by *filename*
-? or -h	Prints the help message

language program that produces a chirping sound from the speaker. Sound can enhance your work on the computer by serving as a warning signal or an emphasis for a particular action.

The discussion concentrates on how to use the various assembler tools rather than on the actual assembly language program. You will learn how to control other hardware items in Chapter 19, "Binding C and Assembly Language Code."

Entering Your Second Program

Use the Borland C++ editor to enter the following assembly language program. Remember to name the program *mysecond.asm*. On the command line, type

```
bc mysecond.asm
```

The command-line argument you have just typed will open a new file. Enter the following program:

```
;TURBO Assembly Language Programming Application
;Copyright (c) Chris H. Pappas and William H. Murray, 1990

;Program will generate a sound from the computer's speaker
```

```
        DOSSEG                    ;use Intel segment-ordering
        .MODEL   small            ;set model size
        .8086                     ;8086 instructions

        .STACK   300h             ;set up 768-byte stack

        .DATA                     ;set up data location
temp    dw       0                ;storage

        .CODE
Turbo   PROC     FAR              ;main procedure declaration
        mov      ax,DGROUP        ;point ds toward .DATA
        mov      ds,ax
        mov      dx,0             ;initialize dx to zero
        in       al,61h           ;get port info from speaker to al

        and      al,0FCh          ;mask info.  Keep lower two bits
more:   mov      temp,00h         ;initialize variable to zero
        inc      dx               ;increment dx register
        cmp      dx,15            ;have we done it 15 times?
        je       finish           ;if yes, end the program
go:     xor      al,02h           ;xor two bits of al register
        mov      cx,temp          ;get current frequency
        cmp      cx,258           ;has it reached 600 hertz?
        je       more             ;if yes, repeat sequence
        inc      temp             ;if no, increase frequency
        out      61h,al           ;send it to the speaker port
delay:  loop     delay            ;a small time delay
        jmp      go               ;continue
finish:

        mov      ah,4Ch           ;return control to DOS
        int      21h
Turbo   ENDP                      ;end main procedure
        END                       ;end whole program
```

This program uses **in** and **out** mnemonics to receive and send information to the specified hardware device.

Creating the *make* File

For this example, a *make* file will handle the assembly and linking process. You can also write the *make* file in the Borland C++ editor by typing

```
bc mysecond
```

Recall that the *make* file itself doesn't use an extension.

```
mysecond.exe: mysecond.obj
  tlink /m /s /l mysecond,,,

mysecond.obj: mysecond.asm
  tasm /zi mysecond,,,
```

Assembling and Linking the Program

With the two previous files (*mysecond* and *mysecond.asm*) residing in the default directory, you are now ready to use the *make* utility. Type

```
make -fmysecond
```

If no errors are encountered, your directory should now contain the following *mysecond* files:

```
Volume in drive C is DOS
Directory of  C:\TMASM

MYSECOND ASM     1417    1-06-91    8:45p
MYSECOND          112    1-06-91    8:44p
MYSECOND OBJ      598    1-08-91    9:11a
MYSECOND LST     4704    1-08-91    9:11a
MYSECOND MAP      906    1-08-91    9:11a
MYSECOND XRF      493    1-08-91    9:11a
MYSECOND EXE      564    1-08-91    9:11a
         7 File(s)   15656960 bytes free
```

If the *make* utility encountered an error in your source code or *make* file, you will have to go back to the editor to correct the problem. You can then run the *make* utility again.

Considering All the Pieces

In the directory of *mysecond* files there are four ASCII files. The first two are the source code and *make* files that you originally created. The second two were created during the assembly and link process. Those files have the *.map* and *.lst* extensions.

The .map File (*mysecond.map*)

The *.map* file is created by the Linker and contains information on public symbols, source code line numbers, and a detailed map of program segments. You can view the *.map* file with the Borland C++ editor, or you can just type

```
type mysecond.map
```

You will then see

```
Start  Stop    Length Name            Class

00000H 00041H 00042H _TEXT            CODE
00050H 00051H 00002H _DATA            DATA
00060H 0035FH 00300H STACK            STACK

Detailed map of segments

0000:0000 0010 C=CODE    S=_TEXT       G=(none)  M=MYSECOND.ASM ACBP=48
0000:0010 0032 C=CODE    S=_TEXT       G=(none)  M=MYSECOND.ASM ACBP=48
0005:0000 0002 C=DATA    S=_DATA       G=DGROUP  M=MYSECOND.ASM ACBP=48
0005:0010 0300 C=STACK   S=STACK       G=DGROUP  M=MYSECOND.ASM ACBP=74

  Address          Publics by Name

  Address          Publics by Value

Line numbers for mysecond.obj(MYSECOND.ASM) segment _TEXT

    18 0000:0010    19 0000:0013    21 0000:0015    22 0000:0018
    24 0000:001A    25 0000:001C    26 0000:0022    27 0000:0023
    28 0000:0026    29 0000:0028    30 0000:002A    31 0000:002E
    32 0000:0032    33 0000:0034    34 0000:0038    35 0000:003A
    36 0000:003C    39 0000:003E    40 0000:0040
Program entry point at 0000:0000
```

The .lst File (*mysecond.lst*)

This is your second look at a listing file. What can you tell about the machine code values next to the mnemonics? You can also view this file with the editor or by typing

```
type mysecond.lst
```

which will generate the following output:

```
Turbo Assembler          01/06/91 20:45:23        Page 1
MYSECOND.ASM
1                                    ;TURBO Assembly Language
                                      Programming Application
2                                    ;Copyright (c) Chris H. Pappas and
                                      William H. Murray, 1990
3
4                                    ;Program will generate a sound
                                      from the computer's speaker
5
6                                              DOSSEG
7 0000                                         .MODEL  small
8                                              .8086
9
10 0000                                        .STACK  300h
11
12 0000                                        .DATA
13 0000   0000                  temp   dw      0
14
15
16 0002                                        .CODE
17 0000                          Turbo  PROC    FAR
18 0000   B8 0000s                       mov    ax,DGROUP
19 0003   8E D8                          mov    ds,ax
20
21 0005   BA 0000                        mov    dx,0
22 0008   E4 61                          in     al,61h
23 000A   24 FC                          and    al,0FCh
24 000C   C7 06 0000r 0000   more:       mov    temp,00h
25 0012   42                             inc    dx
26 0013   83 FA 0F                       cmp    dx,15
27 0016   74 16                          je     finish
28 0018   34 02              go:         xor    al,02h
29 001A   8B 0E 0000r                    mov    cx,temp
30 001E   81 F9 0102                     cmp    cx,258
31 0022   74 E8                          je     more
32 0024   FF 06 0000r                    inc    temp
33 0028   E6 61                          out    61h,al
34 002A   E2 FE              delay:      loop   delay
35 002C   EB EA                          jmp    go
36 002E                      finish:
37
38 002E   B4 4C                          mov    ah,4Ch
39 0030   CD 21                          int    21h
40 0032                      Turbo       ENDP
41                                       END


Turbo Assembler          01/06/91 20:45:23        Page 2
Symbol Table


Symbol Name          Type  Value         Cref  defined at #
??DATE               Text  "09/06/90"
??FILENAME           Text  "MYSECOND"
??TIME               Text  "20:45:22"
??VERSION            Number 0101
```

@CODE	Text	_TEXT	#7	#16		
@CODESIZE	Text	0	#7			
@CPU	Text	0101H	#8			
@CURSEG	Text	_TEXT	#12	#16		
@DATA	Text	DGROUP	#7			
@DATASIZE	Text	0	#7			
@FILENAME	Text	MYSECOND				
@WORDSIZE	Text	2	#8	#12	#16	
DELAY	Near	_TEXT:002A	#34	34		
FINISH	Near	_TEXT:002E	27	#36		
GO	Near	_TEXT:0018	#28	35		
MORE	Near	_TEXT:000C	#24	31		
TEMP	Word	DGROUP:000	#13	24	29	32
TURBO	Far	_TEXT:0000	#17			

Groups & Segments	Bit	Size	Align	Combine	Class	Cref	defined at #
DGROUP		Group				#7	7 18
STACK	16	0300	Para	Stack	STACK	#10	
_DATA	16	0002	Word	Public	DATA	#7	#12
_TEXT	16	0032	Word	Public	CODE	#7	7 #16 16

ASSEMBLER MODES: MASM AND IDEAL

If you have worked with Intel assembly language code, you are probably familiar with IBM's or Microsoft's Macro Assembler. Borland's Assembler perfectly emulates both the IBM and Microsoft assemblers by using the same directives and syntax. Thus, a program written for MASM will assemble correctly with TASM and vice versa.

Borland's Assembler actually contains a superset of MASM directives and abilities. In plain language, this means that TASM is a more powerful product that offers extended capabilities.

For example, normal assembly language programming syntax is handled the same way by all three assemblers. TASM also offers an *ideal* mode of operation. TASM's ideal mode allows you to write clear, concise code whose operation you can easily understand. Ideal mode uses MASM's keywords, operators, and statement syntax in a reorganized and easy to understand structure. You enter ideal mode in a program by using the directive **ideal**. You can return to the default *masm* mode by using the *masm* directive. One advantage to ideal mode directives, in addition to clarity, is that ideal mode programs assemble faster than conventional code.

Let's compare one line of code written in the default *masm* syntax and another written in ideal mode.

```
masm mode:        mov bx,es:[bp+10][si+4]
ideal mode:       mov bx,[es:bp+si+14]
```

This piece of code loads the value at offset **bp** + **si** + 14 in segment **es** into the **bx** register. Which is easier to understand?

```
masm mode:        mov cx,10[bx]
ideal mode:       mov cx,[bx+10]
```

This piece of code loads the value given by the address **bx** with an offset of 10 bytes, not ten times the address at **bx**. Ideal mode can help you avoid confusion.

MIXED MODES: THE THIRD AND FOURTH EXAMPLES

The Borland C++ package gives you great programming flexibility. From this environment, you can develop stand-alone C++ programs, stand-alone assembly language programs, or mixed mode programs. *Mixed mode* programs are programs that combine the best features of C++ and assembly language in one executable file. Mixed mode programs can take advantage of the speed and hardware control abilities of assembly language and combine them with the high-level programming power of C. The mixed mode environment is also used in Chapter 19.

The C Code for the Third Example

This section describes a small C program that will be combined with assembly code at link time. The C program will send two integers to the assembly code module. The assembly code module will add the numbers and return the sum to the C program. The C program will then print the

sum to the screen. You could accomplish this whole program with one line
of C code; however, the program shows you how you can splice two pieces
of code in the Borland C++ environment. Study the following listing,
named *mythird.c.*

```
/*
 *    A simple C program that is combined with assembly
 *    language code.
 *    Copyright (c) Chris H. Pappas and William H. Murray, 1990
 */

#include <stdio.h>

int Summer(int,int);

int Num1,Num2;

main()
{
    Num1=792;
    Num2=564;
    printf("The sum of the two numbers is: %d\n", Summer(Num1,Num2));
    return(0);
}
```

This C program uses an external function called **Summer**. Actually,
Summer is the name of the assembly language module. This function will
pass two variables, *Num1* and *Num2,* to the assembly language program.
The assembly language program will in turn return the sum to the **printf**
function.

The Assembly Code for the Third Example

The assembly language program is named *summer.asm.* It looks similar to
the previous examples. The first difference is in the data declaration. Most
C compilers, including Borland C++, expect all external labels to begin with
an underscore character. This fixup is handled automatically by the new
assembly language directives.

```
;TURBO Assembly Language & C Programming Application
;Copyright (c) Chris H. Pappas and William H. Murray, 1990

;This program will be interfaced to a C program named MYTHIRD.C
;It will not run in stand-alone mode.

        DOSSEG                      ;use Intel segment-ordering
```

```
        .MODEL  small               ;set model size
        .8086                       ;8086 instructions

        .CODE
        PUBLIC  C Summer
Summer  PROC    C NEAR Num1:WORD,Num2:WORD    ;main procedure declaration
        mov     ax,Num1             ;get first number
        add     ax,Num2             ;add second number

        ret                         ;return
Summer  ENDP                        ;end main procedure
        END                         ;end whole program
```

You might have noticed that the code for returning the operator to the DOS environment is missing. Only a **ret** mnemonic is used. This is because this code is not a stand-alone program, but a function called from a C program. Thus, when the assembly language program has completed its task, it must return to the calling program, not to DOS.

Splicing the C and Assembly Code for the Third Example

Before you can combine the two pieces of code, you have to enter each one with the editor. Again, name the C code *mythird.c* and the assembly language code *summer.asm.* From the command line, type

```
bcc mythird.c summer.asm
```

In one step, the C code is compiled into an *.obj* file named *mythird.obj,* the assembly language code is assembled into an *.obj* file named *summer.obj,* and the two *.obj* files are linked to form an *.exe* file named *mythird.exe.*

To execute the resulting code, type

```
mythird
```

The following message should be returned to your screen:

```
The sum of the two numbers is: 1356
```

The C Code for the Fourth Example

In the fourth example, you learn how to use a C program to report the contents of an assembly language program's **ax** registers. In assembly language, all numeric screen I/O (input and output) is done by routines that you must write yourself. By using mixed mode programming, you can tap C's powerful **printf** function and get the job done with much less effort. If used wisely, this program lets you experiment with assembly language code, investigate various mnemonic operations, and report the result to the screen without using a debugger.

The C program named *myfourth.c* is not much longer than the one in the previous example, as you can see from the listing.

```
/*
 *    A C program that is combined with assembly language
 *    code.  Reports ax register contents to screen.
 *    Copyright (c) Chris H. Pappas and William H. Murray, 1990
 */

#include <stdio.h>

int Report(void);

main()
{
  printf("The register contains: %X (hexadecimal)\n", Report());
  return(0);
}
```

The power in this program module is in the **printf** function. The **printf** function allows you to print numeric information to the screen. The last example printed the sum of two decimal numbers. This example will print the contents of the **ax** register, in hexadecimal. You'll learn more about **printf** in Chapter 5, "C and C++ Foundations." An external assembly module named **Report** is used to pass the integer from the assembly language module to the C program.

The Assembly Code for the Fourth Example

This program uses an assembly module named *report.asm*. This module does not receive any values from the C program and only returns one—the contents of the **ax** register.

```
;TURBO Assembly Language & C Programming Application
;Copyright (c) Chris H. Pappas and William H. Murray, 1990

;This program will be interfaced to a C program named MYFOURTH.C

;It will not run in stand-alone mode.
        DOSSEG                      ;use Intel segment-ordering
        .MODEL   small              ;set model size
        .8086                       ;8086 instructions

        .CODE
        PUBLIC   C Report
Report  PROC                        ;main procedure declaration

        mov      ax,0AAh            ;move value into ax
        mov      cl,2               ;get multiplier
        shl      ax,cl              ;multiply by 4

        ret                         ;return
Report  ENDP                        ;end main procedure
        END                         ;end whole program
```

Splicing the C and Assembly Code for the Fourth Example

Before you can combine the two pieces of code, you have to enter each one with the Borland C++ editor. Name the C code *myfourth.c* and the assembly language code *report.asm*. From the command line, type

```
bcc myfourth.c report.asm
```

The C code is compiled into an *.obj* file named *myfourth.obj*, the assembly language code is assembled into an *.obj* file named *report.obj* and the two *.obj* files are combined by the Linker to form an *.exe* file named *myfourth.exe*.

In this program, a hexadecimal number, AAh, is moved into the **ax** register. Then a 2 is moved into the **cl** register. Finally, the shift-left mnemonic, **shl**, is called. This will shift the information in the **ax** register two places to the left, which has the effect of multiplying the number in **ax** by 4.

In binary, 0AAh would be   0000 0000 1010 1010.

One shift to the left   0000 0001 0101 0100 (154h).

One additional shift   0000 0010 1010 1000 (2A8h).

It should therefore be no surprise that when the program is executed, this result is reported to the screen:

```
The register contains 2A8 (hexadecimal)
```

To see the results for yourself, once you have obtained an *.exe* file, type

```
myfourth
```

TRACKING DOWN ASSEMBLY LANGUAGE ERRORS: THE FIFTH EXAMPLE

Some people believe that they never make mistakes. These people don't make good programmers. Whether you program in a high-level language or in assembly language, you will make a mistake sooner or later.

In assembly language, syntax errors and bugs are bound to creep into the best of code. Catching syntax errors is the job of the Assembler, and finding bugs is the job of the Debugger. This section concentrates on what the Assembler can and can't do in terms of eliminating syntax errors. In Chapter 4, "Getting Started with Borland's Debugger and Profiler," you will learn how to operate the Debugger for C, C++, and assembly language programs.

Catching Hidden Errors

To illustrate what the Assembler can and cannot do, errors have been added to the first example in this chapter. However, if you look at the code, it seems innocent enough. This program is named *myerrors.asm*.

```
        DOSSEG                  ;use Intel segment-ordering
        .MODEL  small           ;set model size

        .STACK  300h            ;set up 768-byte stack

        .DATA                   ;set up data location
SendIt  db      'Assembly Language is easy!','$'

        .CODE
```

```
Turbo    PROC    FAR                 ;main procedure declaration
         mov     ax,DGROUP           ;point ds toward .DATA
         mov     ds,ax

         lea     dl,SendIt           ;point to the message
         mov     ah,901              ;interrupt parameter
         int     bx,cx               ;call DOS print interrupt

         mov     ah,4Dh              ;return control to DOS
         int     25h
Turbo    ENDP                        ;end main procedure
         END                         ;end whole program
```

This program can be assembled and linked with the following *make* file.

```
myerrors.exe: myerrors.obj
  tlink /m /s /l myerrors,,,

myerrors.obj: myerrors.asm
  tasm /zi myerrors,,,
```

The Assembler's Error Report

The *make* utility reports the assembly and link process of *myerrors.asm* to the screen as follows:

```
MAKE Version 3.6  Copyright (c) 1991 Borland International

Available memory 452272 bytes

       tasm /zi myerrors,,,
Turbo Assembler  Version 3.0ae  Copyright (c) 1988, 1991 Borland International
Serial No:    Tester:

Assembling file:   myerrors.ASM
**Error** myerrors.ASM(14) Argument to operation or instruction has illegal size
**Error** myerrors.ASM(15) Constant too large
**Error** myerrors.ASM(16) Illegal use of register
Error messages:    3
Warning messages:  None
Passes:            1
Remaining memory:  281k

** error 1 ** deleting myerrors.obj
```

First, notice that there are two classes of errors: error messages and warning messages. Of the two, error messages are worse. Error messages will block the completion of the assembly process. You will not get an executable file (*.exe*) if one error is detected. In contrast, warning messages let you know that something unexpected happened during assembly or that the Assembler had to make an assumption about something you were doing. Warning messages will allow the assembly process to complete. Be careful, however; the executable file might not execute.

The Assembler has detected three major errors in the *myerrors* source code. You should make note of the three line numbers and the associated error messages before returning to the editor.

The first error reported is associated with line 14:

```
**Error** MYERRORS.ASM(14) Argument to operation or instruction
                           has illegal size
```

If you look up the **lea** mnemonic, you will see that the address of *SendIt* must be returned to a 16-bit register. The **dl** register is an 8-bit register.

```
lea     dl,SendIt      ;point to the message
```

The second error occurs on line 15:

```
**Error** MYERRORS.ASM(15) Constant too large
```

The **ah** register is an 8-bit register capable of holding integers up to 0FFh (hexadecimal) or 255 (decimal). Obviously, 901 (decimal) is too large for this register. The **ax** register might be the proper choice.

```
mov     ah,901         ;interrupt parameter
```

Finally, the last error reported occurs on line 16:

```
**Error** MYERRORS.ASM(16) Illegal use of register
```

The **int** instruction uses an immediate piece of data. In this case, the line should have contained a 21h, instead of the two registers.

```
int     bx,cx          ;call DOS print interrupt
```

If you are using illegal syntax, the Assembler will catch the error. Until you become more familiar with assembly language, the error and warning messages will seem curt and not too helpful. However, as your programming experience increases, these brief messages will be all you need to get the program up and running as fast as possible.

You might not have noticed that two errors went completely undetected. Look at the following two lines of code, which are wrong:

```
mov     ah,4Dh          ;return control to DOS
int     25h
```

The value to be moved into the **ah** register should be 4Ch and the interrupt number for a return to DOS should be 21h. Why did the Assembler catch the first three errors and bypass the last two? The Assembler missed the last two errors because they are bugs, not syntax mistakes. The two lines of code are syntactically correct.

In other words, to master assembly language programming, you must learn the proper use of assembly language syntax and the various mnemonics. The Assembler will help you with syntax, and the Debugger will help you with proper use of the various instructions.

Remember, a program that does not report any error or warning messages can still crash the system.

THERE'S MORE TO COME

If you have made it this far, congratulations. If you are new to assembly language, don't be discouraged if you still don't understand how all of the pieces interlock. Remember, this chapter introduced you to the various tools for the assembly language environment. Later assembly language chapters (Chapters 17, 18, and 19) will concentrate on language features and less on the tools. If you forget how to use the Assembler, how to link a program, or how to create a *.map* or *.lst* file, return to this chapter.

4

GETTING STARTED WITH BORLAND'S DEBUGGER AND PROFILER

A carpenter goes to work with a toolbox containing saws, hammers, screwdrivers, tape measures, and so on. Carpenters even carry claw hammers to remove incorrectly placed nails. Programmers also go to work with a toolbox. Typically, programmers use editors, compilers, linkers, and assemblers. However, just as the carpenter carries a claw hammer to fix mistakes, the programmer also has a variety of tools for correcting programming errors and streamlining code. Borland provides two such tools: the Debugger and the Profiler. The Debugger will help you correct logical errors in program development, while the Profiler will help make your finished routines run as fast as possible.

This chapter will get you started quickly with the Debugger and Profiler. It does not contain detailed discussions of either product or their options. Instead, it includes several short examples that illustrate important properties and choices for each product. You can always obtain help via the F1 key in either the Debugger or Profiler. For additional information, consult the user's guides.

THE DEBUGGER – SEARCHING OUT

Programming errors can be divided into two major groups: syntax errors and logical errors. *Syntax errors* are errors in language implementation. For example, missing semicolons, brackets, or undeclared variables are syntax errors. *Logical errors* are generated when the programmer makes an incorrect assumption in implementing code. For example, not extending the range of a control loop to include the correct boundary conditions and testing the wrong variable in a decision-making process are logical errors.

Both types of errors are common in programming – no programmer writes error-free code for a program of any consequence. Syntax errors are flagged by the compiler or Assembler and must be corrected before an executable file (*.exe*) can be created. A program with no syntax errors still might not run correctly due to logical errors. You can locate logical errors with the Debugger, but you must first have an executable program to use the Debugger. In other words, you must correct all syntax errors before you can fix logical errors.

THE PROFILER – AN EFFICIENCY EXPERT

When developing professional programs, speed is a primary factor in program execution. The Profiler shows where your programs are spending time. Control loops, for example, use lots of execution time. The Profiler can indicate these areas and allow you to redesign portions of your code. The Profiler is usually used after syntax and logical errors have been removed from your program.

GETTING STARTED WITH THE DEBUGGER

The job of the Debugger is to search out and help you eliminate logical errors. For example, consider this simple program, which the developer thought would print the numbers from 1 to 5 on the screen:

```
/*
 *      C program to print the numbers 1 to 5 to
 *      the screen.
 *      Copyright (c) Chris H. Pappas and William H. Murray, 1990
 */

#include <stdio.h>

main()
{
  int i;

  for (i=0;i<5;i++)
    printf("%d\n",i);

  return(0);
}
```

Perhaps you already recognize the logical error. The *for* loop should be initialized to start at 1 and end at a value less than 6. As it appears above, the program prints the numbers 0, 1, 2, 3, and 4 to the screen. The Debugger will help find this type of error.

A Look at the Debugger

You can enter the Debugger by typing one of the following from the Debugger's subdirectory:

```
TD
TD386              (if you have an 80386/80486 computer)
TD MYFILE
TD386 MYFILE
TDW                (if operating under Microsoft Windows)
```

If the TD or TD386 command is followed by an executable file name, that file will automatically be loaded when the Debugger starts. Figure 4-1 is a Debugger screen obtained by using the program shown earlier in this chapter (compiled as: bcc /v TEST.C) and by typing

```
TD TEST.EXE
```

As you can see, the Debugger screen contains a menu bar at the top and a function-key bar at the bottom. This is Borland's typical user interface. The menu bar at the top lists *global menus,* menus that are always available and always visible at the top of the screen. They are accessible from the

```
  ≡  File  Edit  View  Run  Breakpoints  Data  Options  Window  Help      READY
┌─[■]─Module: TEST File: TEST.C 10───────────────────────────────1──[↕]─┐
│                                                                        ▓│
│  /*                                                                    ▒│
│  *      C program to print the numbers 1 to 5 to                       ▒│
│  *      the screen.                                                    ▒│
│  *      Copyright (c) Chris H. Pappas and William H. Murray, 1990      ▒│
│  */                                                                    ▒│
│                                                                        ▒│
│  #include <stdio.h>                                                    ▒│
│► main()                                                                ▒│
│  {                                                                     ▒│
│    int i;                                                              ▒│
│                                                                        ▒│
│    for (i=0;i<5;i++)                                                   ▒│
│      printf("%d\n",i);                                                 ▒│
│                                                                        ▒│
│    return(0);                                                          ▒│
│  }                                                                     ▒│
│                                                                        ▓│
│ ◄█                                                                   ►▼│
└ F1-Help F2-Bkpt F3-Mod F4-Here F5-Zoom F6-Next F7-Trace F8-Step F9-Run F10-Menu
```

Figure 4-1.   The initial Debugger screen

keyboard or the mouse. You can access global menu features by pressing F10 and using the arrow keys or by pressing the highlighted letter of the global menu name. Options chosen from a global menu often produce a local menu with additional user choices. You select options in a local menu by pressing ALT-F10, followed by the highlighted option letter or by clicking the right mouse button on the desired option.

What follows is a quick overview of the important global menu items on the Debugger screen. You can get additional information for each option from Borland's online help or the Debugger user's guide. The various function keys are also covered later in this section.

The Desktop Manager Menu   The Desktop Manager menu is shown in the following illustration. The "Repaint desktop" option allows you to clean up your screen if it has been overwritten. The "Restore standard" option restores your screen to the layout it had when you started the Debugger.

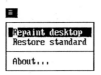

The File Menu   The most important File menu selections allow you to open a file for debugging, change the directory, return to the DOS shell, and quit the Debugger:

When you select a File menu item, a brief explanation of this item will appear at the bottom of your screen.

The Edit Menu   The Edit menu contains the expected "Copy" and "Paste" options along with two log commands ("Copy to log" and "Dump pane to log"):

These last two commands are used to make temporary copies of highlighted items ("Copy to log"), or entire windows ("Dump pane to log"). The "Log" option in the View menu allows you to view the window and compare its contents with the current state of your debugging trace.

The View Menu   The View menu contains options for some of the Debugger's most important features:

You use the "Breakpoints" option to set breakpoints in your program. The program can then operate at full speed until it encounters the breakpoint. This is useful for examining memory locations without having to single-step through the entire program. The "Watches" option allows you to track values in specified variables as your program executes. The "Variables" option shows you the currently accessible variable names for your program. The "CPU," "Dump," "Registers," and "Numeric processor" options are most useful for assembly language debugging and allow you to examine the contents of the CPU, memory, register values, and stack values on the numeric coprocessor if one is installed in your computer.

The Run Menu   The following illustration shows the Run menu options. "Run" executes your program at full CPU speed. "Go to cursor" executes your program down to the cursor. "Trace into" executes a single line of source code and stops. Procedures and function calls are not skipped. "Step over" executes a single line of source code and stops. It will skip procedure and function calls. "Execute to..." executes the program until the address specified in the dialog box is reached. "Program reset" reloads the specified file from disk for debugging.

```
Run
┌──────────────────────────────────┐
│ Run                          F9  │
│ Go to cursor                 F4  │
│ Trace into                   F7  │
│ Step over                    F8  │
│ Execute to...            Alt-F9  │
│ Until return             Alt-F8  │
│ Animate...                       │
│ Back trace               Alt-F4  │
│ Instruction trace        Alt-F7  │
│                                  │
│ Arguments...                     │
│ Program reset            Ctrl-F2 │
└──────────────────────────────────┘
```

The Breakpoints Menu   The next illustration shows the Breakpoints menu. "Toggle" sets or clears breakpoints at the specified address in the module or CPU window. "Delete all" allows you to remove all breakpoints.

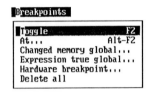

```
Breakpoints
┌──────────────────────────────┐
│ Toggle                    F2 │
│ At...                 Alt-F2 │
│ Changed memory global...     │
│ Expression true global...    │
│ Hardware breakpoint...       │
│ Delete all                   │
└──────────────────────────────┘
```

The Data Menu   The Data menu allows you to examine and change program data. "Inspect..." is a dialog box that prompts for a variable name that contains the data you want to inspect. "Evaluate/modify..." opens another dialog box that prompts for an expression to evaluate. The Data menu looks like this:

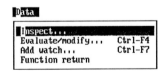

```
Data
┌──────────────────────────────┐
│ Inspect...                   │
│ Evaluate/modify...   Ctrl-F4 │
│ Add watch...         Ctrl-F7 │
│ Function return              │
└──────────────────────────────┘
```

The Options Menu   The Options menu, shown in the following illustration, enables you to set values that affect the overall operation and appearance of the Debugger. Most of the choices in this menu produce dialog boxes for changing the stated options. If you alter default settings for the Debugger, use the "Save options..." dialog box to save your new configuration. Remember, help is as close as the F1 key.

The Window Menu   The Window menu allows you to alter the window currently in the Debugger. For example, "Zoom" allows you to enlarge or shrink the current window. "Next" lets you switch or activate alternate windows on the screen. "Size/move" enables you to size the window. "User screen" permits you to view any output from your program that is sent to the screen. You can also implement many of these options with various function-key combinations, as you can see in the following illustration.

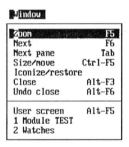

The Help Menu   The Help menu, shown in the next illustration, allows you to examine an index of items or specify a previous topic. If you select the "Index" option, the Debugger will list a group of items for which help is available. You can select these items with the arrow keys or with the mouse. Press PGDN for additional lists of items.

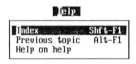

Function Keys

The function-key options listed at the bottom of your Debugger screen offer shortcuts to many of the global menu options. The function-key options will change as you switch from menu to menu. Usually, they represent a shortcut to the menu items of the currently selected global menu. Remember, you can obtain help by pressing F1. F8 will single-step you through program code while F9 will run your whole program at full CPU speed. F5 is always a quick means of zooming windows.

Debugging a Simple C Program

This next example uses the Debugger to find the error in the example program shown earlier. First, use the Debugger to enter and compile the program. The Debugger requires an *.exe* file for operation, so all syntax errors will have to be eliminated. Now, switch to the Debugger's subdirectory and start the Debugger by typing **TD TEST.EXE**.

You should now see a screen similar to Figure 4-2. Notice that two

```
≡  File  Edit  View  Run  Breakpoints  Data  Options  Window  Help       READY
┌[■]=Module: TEST File: TEST.C 10════════════════════════════1=[↑][↓]═┐
│                                                                       ▲
│   /*                                                                  ║
│    *      C program to print the numbers 1 to 5 to                    ║
│    *      the screen.                                                 ║
│    *      Copyright (c) Chris H. Pappas and William H. Murray, 1990   ║
│    */                                                                 ║
│                                                                       ║
│   #include <stdio.h>                                                  ║
│                                                                       ║
│►  main()                                                              ║
│   {                                                                   ║
│     int i;                                                            ║
│                                                                       ║
│     for (i=0;i<5;i++)                                                 ║
│       printf("%d\n",i);                                               ║
│                                                                       ║
│     return(0);                                                        ▼
│   }                                                                   
└◄█═══════════════════════════════════════════════════════════════════►┘
┌─Watches──────────────────────────────────────────────────2──────────┐
│                                                                       │
└──────────────────────────────────────────────────────────────────────┘
F1-Help F2-Bkpt F3-Mod F4-Here F5-Zoom F6-Next F7-Trace F8-Step F9-Run F10-Menu
```

Figure 4-2.   Initial Module and Watch windows for C debugging example

windows are displayed by default—the Module window and the Watch window. The double border around the Module window indicates that it is the active window. Also notice that a small arrow on the extreme left of the screen points to **main( )**. This arrow indicates the starting point for program execution.

Recall that this program is expected to print the numbers from 1 to 5 on the screen, but actually prints the digits 0, 1, 2, 3, and 4. Since there is only one variable, *i*, set that in a Watch window to keep an eye on it during program execution.

Select the Data menu and then the "Add watch. . ." dialog box, shown here:

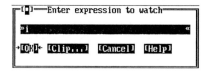

Figure 4-3 shows that *i* has been added to the Watch window. The figure shows a screen after the first pass through the *for* loop. If you use the F8 function key, you can execute the program one line at a time. Alternatively, you can set breakpoints at important locations. The 0 value of *i* is the first indication of a logical error. Since the value in *i* is printed to the screen, *i* will have to be initialized to 1 instead of 0 if the first number is to be a 1.

Figure 4-4 shows the program after the control loop has been exited. Notice that the arrow is now pointing to **return (0)**. The last value for *i* is 5. Recall that the numbers printed to the screen were 0, 1, 2, 3, and 4. What happened to the 5? The increment operator incremented *i* to 5 after the print statement, but the last value printed was 4.

To repair this program, alter the *for* loop to read (you will have to return to the editor to make this change):

```
for (i=1;i<6;i++)
```

You can exit the Debugger by using ALT-X or selecting the "Quit" option from the File menu.

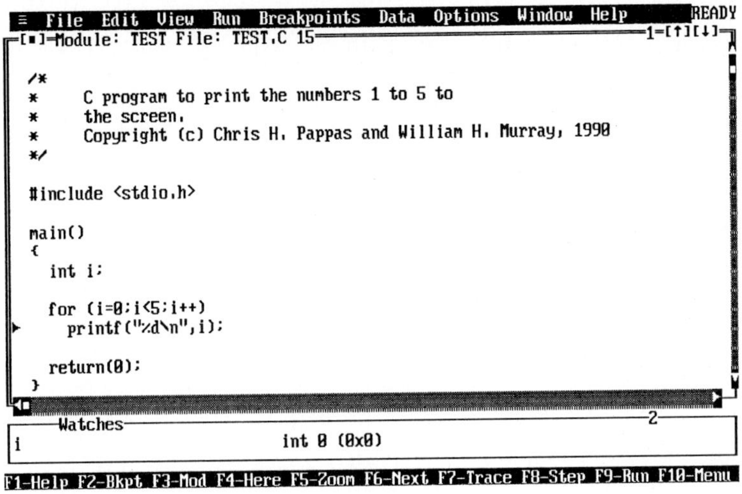

```
≡ File Edit View Run Breakpoints Data Options Window Help        READY
┌[■]═Module: TEST File: TEST.C 15══════════════════════════════1═[↑][↓]┐

    /*
    *      C program to print the numbers 1 to 5 to
    *      the screen.
    *      Copyright (c) Chris H. Pappas and William H. Murray, 1990
    */

    #include <stdio.h>

    main()
    {
      int i;

      for (i=0;i<5;i++)
►       printf("%d\n",i);

      return(0);
    }
├────Watches───────────────────────────────────────────────2─────┤
  i                            int 0 (0x0)
F1-Help F2-Bkpt F3-Mod F4-Here F5-Zoom F6-Next F7-Trace F8-Step F9-Run F10-Menu
```

Figure 4-3.   Observe the variable after one pass through the *for* loop

```
≡ File Edit View Run Breakpoints Data Options Window Help        READY
┌[■]═Module: TEST File: TEST.C 17══════════════════════════════1═[↑][↓]┐

    /*
    *      C program to print the numbers 1 to 5 to
    *      the screen.
    *      Copyright (c) Chris H. Pappas and William H. Murray, 1990
    */

    #include <stdio.h>

    main()
    {
      int i;

      for (i=0;i<5;i++)
        printf("%d\n",i);

►     return(0);
    }
├────Watches───────────────────────────────────────────────2─────┤
  i                            int 5 (0x5)
F1-Help F2-Bkpt F3-Mod F4-Here F5-Zoom F6-Next F7-Trace F8-Step F9-Run F10-Menu
```

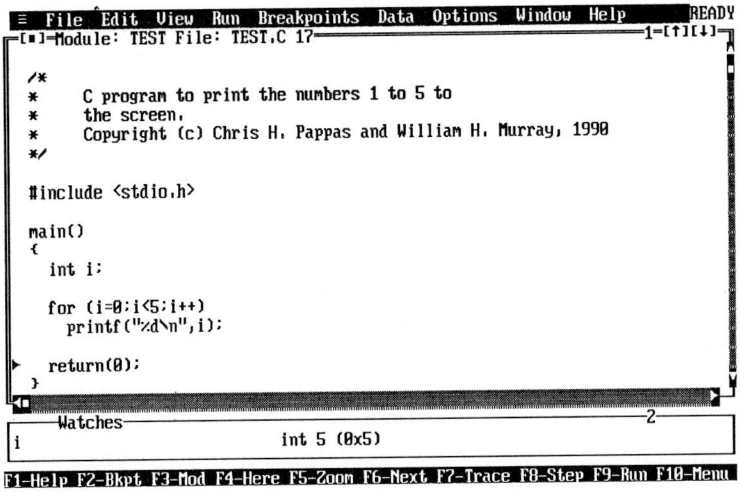

Figure 4-4.   Observe the variable after the final pass through the *for* loop

Debugging a Simple Assembly Language Program

The assembly language debugging example uses the *mysecond.asm* program from the previous chapter.

```
;TURBO Assembly Language Programming Application
;Copyright (c) Chris H. Pappas and William H. Murray, 1990

;Program will generate a sound from the computer's speaker

            DOSSEG                      ;use Intel segment-ordering
            .MODEL  small               ;set model size
            .8086                       ;8086 instructions

            .STACK  300h                ;set up 768-byte stack

            .DATA                       ;set up data location
temp        dw      0                   ;storage

            .CODE
Turbo       PROC    FAR                 ;main procedure declaration
            mov     ax,DGROUP           ;point ds toward .DATA
            mov     ds,ax

            mov     dx,0                ;initialize dx to zero
            in      al,61h              ;get port info from speaker to al

            and     al,0FCh             ;mask info.  Keep lower two bits
more:       mov     temp,00h            ;initialize variable to zero
            inc     dx                  ;increment dx register
            cmp     dx,15               ;have we done it 15 times?
            je      finish              ;if yes, end the program
go:         xor     al,02h              ;xor two bits of al register
            mov     cx,temp             ;get current frequency
            cmp     cx,258              ;has it reached 600 hertz?
            je      more                ;if yes, repeat sequence
            inc     temp                ;if no, increase frequency
            out     61h,al              ;send it to the speaker port
delay:      loop    delay               ;a small time delay
            jmp     go                  ;continue
finish:

            mov     ah,4Ch              ;return control to DOS
            int     21h
Turbo       ENDP                        ;end main procedure
            END                         ;end whole program
```

There are no logical errors in the preceding program, but you will use the Debugger to examine variables and registers during program execution. This alone makes the Debugger a very useful tool for assembly language programmers.

Recall that you must enter the assembly language program with an editor, such as the one supplied with Borland's C++, and then assemble and link it. The following *make* file will prepare this program for the Debugger:

```
mysecond.exe: mysecond.obj
  tlink /v mysecond;
mysecond.obj: mysecond.asm
  tasm /zi mysecond;
```

You might want to review Chapter 3, "Getting Started with Borland's Assembler," to understand the Assembler and Linker options shown in the *make* file. You enter the Debugger with the line of code TD MYSECOND .EXE. Figure 4-5 shows the initial Debugger screen. Notice that the arrow is pointing to the first executable line of code.

Figure 4-6 shows a breakpoint set at the **out** mnemonic. The program can be executed at full speed until this point is reached. Also notice that the

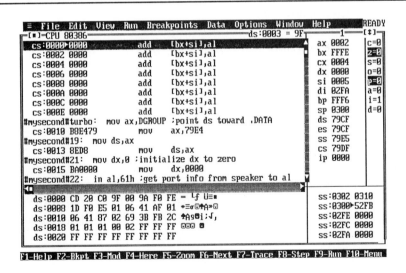

Figure 4-5.   Initial Module and Watch windows for assembly language debugging example

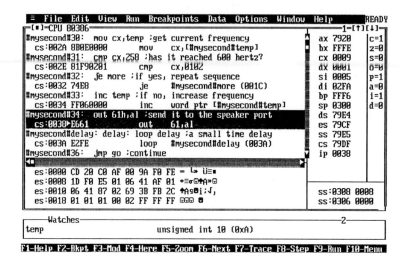

Figure 4-6.   A breakpoint set at the **out** mnemonic

temp variable was placed in the Watch window (window 2) and that the Register window (window 1) has been opened.

With the Debugger, you can now debug assembly language programs at the source code level while watching variables, registers, and so on.

Debugging a Simple C++ Program

You have already seen how the Debugger can help locate errors in C source code and display important register information for assembly language programs. The next Debugger example examines a C++ program that uses operator overloading. (Operator overloading is covered in more detail in Chapters 13, "Classes," and 15, "Power Programming: Tapping Important C and C++ Libraries.") In this example, operator overloading allows the program to add, subtract, multiply, and divide complex numbers.

This program is also free of logical errors and shows the use of the Watch window, the CPU window, the Variable window, and the Class Hierarchy window. The program, named *complex.cpp,* is shown in the following listing, compiled using the /v option:

```
//
//    A C++ program that demonstrates how to use complex
//    arithmetic with overloaded operators.  Here complex
//    numbers are directly added, subtracted, multiplied, and
//    divided.
//    Copyright (c) Chris H. Pappas and William H. Murray, 1990
//

#include <iostream.h>
#include <complex.h>

main()
{
  double x1=5.6, y1=7.2;
  double x2=-3.1, y2=4.8;

  complex z1=complex(x1,y1);
  complex z2=complex(x2,y2);

  cout << "The value of z1 + z2 is: " << z1+z2 << "\n";
  cout << "The value of z1 * z2 is: " << z1*z2 << "\n";
  cout << "The value of z1 - z2 is: " << z1-z2 << "\n";
  cout << "The value of z1 / z2 is: " << z1/z2 << "\n";
  return (0);
}
```

Details of this program's operation will not be explained until Chapters 13 and 15 but let's look at the information the Debugger can provide. First, here is a typical Watch window with two variables, z1 and z2:

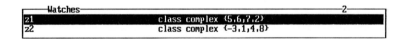

The variables belong to the **complex** class. Notice that this is the only place you actually see the values for these variables—the program does not print them to the screen. These could also be observed in the Variable window.

If you are interested in how the CPU is processing this information, you can view the CPU window. Figure 4-7 shows the CPU window when the program is about to execute the first **cout** command. The figure shows the C++ code converted to equivalent assembly language code in the upper-left corner. Register values and a small portion of the program's data dump are also shown. Previous examples have shown you how to place program variables in a Watch window for observation. As mentioned, you can also examine variable values in the Variable window. Figure 4-8 is a Variable window for this example. Can you find all of the values used in this example? Finally, here is an example of a Class Hierarchy window.

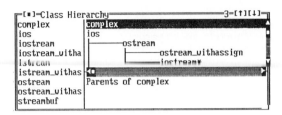

The program uses two other classes in addition to the **complex** class: **ostream** and **streambuf**. The Class Hierarchy window will help you as you study C++ classes in Chapter 13.

From now on, each programming chapter in this book will contain at least two programs that use the Debugger to help you view program parameters.

GETTING STARTED WITH THE PROFILER

The Profiler, or performance analyzer, is similar to an efficiency expert: It analyzes your program's performance in terms of hot spots and bottlenecks.

```
┌[■]═CPU 80386══════════════════════════════════════════════3═[↑][↓]═┐
│#COMPLEX#21:  cout << "The value of z1 + z2 is: " << z1+z2 <<│  ax FFB6  │c=0│
│  cs:02F4▶B8E400    mov    ax,00E4                           │  bx 0A52  │z=0│
│  cs:02F7 50        push   ax                                │  cx 0000  │s=1│
│  cs:02F8 8D46C0    lea    ax,[bp-40]                        │  dx 0A52  │o=0│
│  cs:02FB 50        push   ax                                │  si 0A34  │p=0│
│  cs:02FC 8D46D0    lea    ax,[bp-30]                        │  di 0A52  │a=0│
│  cs:02FF 50        push   ax                                │  bp FFF6  │i=1│
│  cs:0300 16        push   ss                                │  sp FF76  │d=0│
│  cs:0301 8D46B0    lea    ax,[bp-50]                        │  ds 08C6  │
│  cs:0304 50        push   ax                                │  es 08C6  │
│  cs:0305 E81001    call   operator +                        │  ss 08C6  │
│  cs:0308 83C408    add    sp,0008                           │  cs 805F  │
│  cs:030B 8D46B0    lea    ax,[bp-50]                        │  ip 02F4  │
│◄■                                                          ►│
│  ds:0000 00 00 00 00 42 6F 72 6C      Borl                 │
│  ds:0008 61 6E 64 20 43 2B 2B 20 and C++                   │  ss:FF78 33E8 │
│  ds:0010 2D 20 43 6F 70 79 72 69 - Copyri                  │  ss:FF76▶F974 │
│  ds:0018 67 68 74 20 31 39 39 31 ght 1991                  │
└─────────────────────────────────────────────────────────────────┘
```

Figure 4-7.   Viewing the CPU window

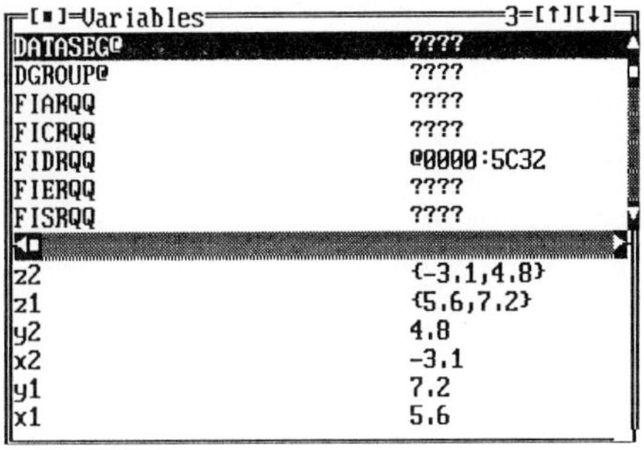

```
┌─[■]═Variables════════════════════════════3═[↑][↓]═┐
│DATASEG@                          ????              ▲│
│DGROUP@                           ????              █│
│FIARQQ                            ????               │
│FICRQQ                            ????               │
│FIDRQQ                            0000:5C32          │
│FIERQQ                            ????               │
│FISRQQ                            ????               │
│◄█                                                 ►│
│z2                                {-3,1,4,8}          │
│z1                                {5,6,7,2}           │
│y2                                4,8                 │
│x2                                -3,1                │
│y1                                7,2                 │
│x1                                5,6                 │
└────────────────────────────────────────────────────┘
```

Figure 4-8.   The Variable window

Hot spots are places where your program spends a lot of time, while bottlenecks are places where program execution slows due to poorly developed algorithms, and so on. By pointing out these problem areas, the Profiler helps you develop code that operates faster and more efficiently.

The Profiler operates with almost any programming language that also produces a *.map* file. This includes Assembler, BASIC, C, Pascal, and even programs compiled with Microsoft products.

To get you started with the Profiler, this section uses a program that is developed and explained in Chapter 16, "System Resources and Graphics." This program is an interactive graphics program that draws a presentation-quality pie chart on the EGA or VGA screen. Again, details of the program's operation are not necessary for our purposes.

```
/*
 *    A C++ program that demonstrates how to produce a
 *    presentation quality pie chart for EGAHI or VGAHI screens.
 *    Copyright (c) Chris H. Pappas and William H. Murray, 1990
 */

#include <graphics.h>
#include <conio.h>
#include <stdlib.h>

#define MAXWEDGE 10
```

```
main()
{
  char sl[10];
  char leg[10][50];
  char label1[50],label2[50];
  int gdriver=DETECT,gmode,errorcode;
  int nwedges,midx,midy,i;
  double totalwedge,temp;
  double startangle,endangle;
  double wedgesize[MAXWEDGE],wedgeangle[MAXWEDGE];

  printf("THIS PROGRAM WILL DRAW A PIE CHART.\n\n");
  printf("Chart titles are optional.\n");
  printf("Enter top of chart label.\n");
  gets(label1);
  printf("Enter bottom of chart label.\n");
  gets(label2);
  printf("\n\n");

  printf("Enter up to 10 values for the pie wedges.\n");
  printf("Value are followed by a carriage return.\n");
  printf("No value and carriage return ends input.\n");

  nwedges=0;
  for (i=0;i<MAXWEDGE;i++) {
    printf("wedge value #%d ",i+1);
    gets(sl);
    if (strlen(sl) == 0) break;
    wedgesize[i]=atof(sl);
    nwedges++;
    printf("legion label: ");
    gets(leg[i]);
  }

  totalwedge=0.0;
  for (i=0;i<nwedges;i++)
    totalwedge+=wedgesize[i];

  for (i=0;i<nwedges;i++)
    wedgeangle[i]=(wedgesize[i]*360.0)/totalwedge;

  initgraph(&gdriver,&gmode,"");

  errorcode=graphresult();
  if (errorcode != grOk) {
    printf("Graphics Function Error: %s\n",
            grapherrormsg(errorcode));
    printf("Hit key to stop:");
    getch();
    exit(1);
  }

  /* get maximum x & y coordinate values for mode */
  midx=getmaxx()/2;
  midy=getmaxy()/2;
```

```
startangle=0.0;
endangle=wedgeangle[0];
for (i=0;i<nwedges;i++) {
  setcolor(BLACK);
  setfillstyle(SOLID_FILL,BLUE+i);
  pieslice(midx/2,midy,(int)startangle,(int)endangle,midy/2);

  startangle+=wedgeangle[i];
  endangle+=wedgeangle[i+1];
}

/* print legend names and colors */
setcolor(WHITE);
moveto(midx+100,midy-80);
outtext("Legend");
for (i=0;i<nwedges;i++) {
  setfillstyle(SOLID_FILL,BLUE+i);
  bar(midx+100,(midy-50)+10*i,midx+110,(midy-40)+10*i);
  moveto(midx+120,(midy-48)+10*i);
  outtext(leg[i]);
}

/* print optional pie chart labels */
setcolor(WHITE);
settextjustify(CENTER_TEXT,CENTER_TEXT);
moveto(midx/2,midy+150);
outtext(label2);
settextstyle(0,0,2);
moveto(midx,midy-150);
outtext(label1);
getch();
closegraph();
return (0);
}
```

A Look at the Profiler

You must enter, compile, and link the preceding program with the Borland C++ compiler. You can then enter the Profiler by typing either of the following two lines from the Profiler subdirectory:

TPROF
TPROF *program _ name*

For this example, enter **TPROF PIE.**

Figure 4-9 shows the initial Profiler screen with the source code in the Module window. Notice that the Profiler also has a global menu bar at the

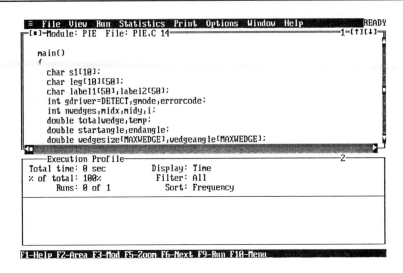

```
 ≡  File  View  Run  Statistics  Print  Options  Window  Help          READY
┌[■]─Module: PIE   File: PIE.C 14─────────────────────────────1=[↑][↓]─┐
│                                                                       ▓
│   main()                                                              ▓
│   {                                                                   ▓
│     char s1[10];                                                      ▓
│     char leg[10][50];                                                 ▓
│     char label1[50],label2[50];                                       ▓
│     int gdriver=DETECT,gmode,errorcode;                               ▓
│     int nwedges,midx,midy,i;                                          ▓
│     double totalwedge,temp;                                           ▓
│     double startangle,endangle;                                       ▓
│     double wedgesize[MAXWEDGE],wedgeangle[MAXWEDGE];                   ▓
│◄■                                                                    ►▼
├─Execution Profile──────────────────────────────────────2───────────┐
│ Total time: 0 sec        Display: Time                               │
│ % of total: 100%         Filter: All                                 │
│          Runs: 0 of 1       Sort: Frequency                          │
│                                                                      │
│                                                                      │
│                                                                      │
│                                                                      │
└──────────────────────────────────────────────────────────────────────┘
 F1-Help F2-Area F3-Mod F5-Zoom F6-Next F9-Run F10-Menu
```

Figure 4-9.   Initial Module window for the Profiler

top of the screen and a function-key bar at the bottom—like the Debugger. The View, Run, and Statistics global menus are the most important for getting started.

View   The View menu is shown here:.

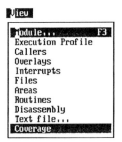

```
View
┌────────────────────┐
│ Module...       F3 │
│ Execution Profile  │
│ Callers            │
│ Overlays           │
│ Interrupts         │
│ Files              │
│ Areas              │
│ Routines           │
│ Disassembly        │
│ Text file...       │
│ Coverage           │
└────────────────────┘
```

The "Module . . ." option shows the source code for the program. The "Execution Profile" option provides the statistical information for the program after execution. The "Callers" option provides information on how many times a routine is called. "Overlays" gives information on language overlays used. "Interrupts" provides information on system interrupts used by the program. "Files" shows file activity during program execution. The "Areas" option gives information concerning data collection in your program, at marked locations. "Routines" lists routines that can be used by area markers. "Disassembly" converts the current profile area into assembly language code.

Run   The Run menu is shown in the following illustration. The most important option in this menu is the "Run" option, which will execute your program code and collect the statistical information for the Profiler. You can also execute the program with the F9 function key.

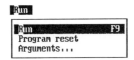

Statistics   The Statistics menu, shown next, allows you to specify which statistical information will be gathered. You can enable the following options: "Callers," "Files," "Interrupts," and "Overlays." You can obtain additional information from the Help menu or by selecting help with the F1 function key.

Profiling a Program

You can execute *pie,* the graphics program shown earlier in this section, by selecting the Run menu and then the "Run" option (make certain you have access to EGAVGA.BGI). The information retrieved is returned to the Execution Profile window, which has been sized to full screen, as shown in Figure 4-10.

```
 ≡ File  View  Run  Statistics  Print  Options  Window  Help        READY
┌[■]═Execution Profile══════════════════════════════2═══[↕]┐
│ Total time: 13.160 sec    Display: Time                   │
│ % of total: 99 %          Filter: All                     │
│      Runs: 1 of 1          Sort: Frequency                │
│                                                            │
│#PIE#40        4.5838 sec  34% ════════════════════════════▲│
│#PIE#45        3.2784 sec  24% ══════════════════════════   │
│#PIE#28        2.3523 sec  17% ══════════════════           │
│#PIE#101       1.0788 sec   8% ══════════                   │
│#PIE#75        0.6485 sec   4% ══════                       │
│#PIE#30        0.5076 sec   3% ════                         │
│#PIE#55        0.2731 sec   2% ══                           │
│#PIE#102       0.1259 sec  <1% ═                            │
│#PIE#39        0.0380 sec  <1%                              │
│#PIE#25        0.0354 sec  <1%                              │
│#PIE#44        0.0350 sec  <1%                              │
│#PIE#31        0.0278 sec  <1%                              │
│#PIE#35        0.0228 sec  <1%                              │
│#PIE#33        0.0226 sec  <1%                              │
│#PIE#34        0.0225 sec  <1%                              │
│#PIE#29        0.0198 sec  <1%                              │
│#PIE#26        0.0195 sec  <1%                             ▼│
└ F1-Help F2-Area F3-Mod F5-Zoom F6-Next F9-Run F10-Menu ────┘
```

Figure 4-10.   An Execution Profile window for the sample program

The execution times for various lines of program code are listed from greatest to least. If you examine the original listings, note that, for this example, the greatest time is spent gathering information from the user.

Figure 4-11 is a composite collection of the Routine, Areas, and Interrupts windows. The Routines window shows which C routines are called. The Areas window shows locations marked in the source code for data collection. Finally, the Interrupts window shows which system interrupts are called and how often.

PLANNING PROGRAM DEVELOPMENT

As you can see, writing the original C, C++, or assembly language program is only the first step in producing the best, fastest, and perhaps smallest executable program. For a C program, for example, you would usually use the Borland C++ tools in the following manner:

- Use the Borland C++ integrated programming environment to write, compile, and link your C program. The compiler identifies any syntax errors that occur.

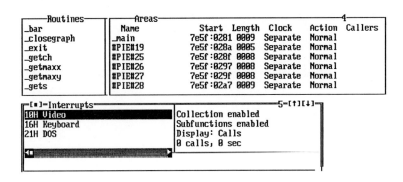

Figure 4-11.   A composite Profiler window of Routines, Areas, and Interrupts
windows

- Use the Debugger to eliminate stubborn bugs in programming logic. To use the Debugger, you must eliminate all syntax errors for the compiler and Linker to produce an executable file.

- Use the Profiler to streamline program operation. The Profiler shows you where your program is spending time and suggests where you might try another programming approach. While you can use the Profiler any time an executable file is available, it is usually the last step in the program design process.

II

C AND C++ FUNDAMENTALS

5

C AND C++ FOUNDATIONS

By now, you should be thoroughly familiar with the Borland C++ environment. You have installed the package, configured it to your personal requirements, and practiced using the C compiler, the Assembler, and the Debugger.

Starting with this chapter, you will explore the origins, syntax, and usage of the C and C++ languages. A study of C's history is a worthy endeavor. For example, you may fully appreciate the architectural beauty of a brand new house that you have just seen completed. However, it is the underlying structure of the edifice that will determine whether or not the building will still be standing in fifty years. Likewise, to recognize the valid popularity of the C language you need to understand its fundamental strengths.

HISTORY OF C

A history of the C language begins with a discussion of the UNIX operating system, since both the system and most of the programs that run on it are written in C. However, C is not tied to UNIX or any other operating system or machine. This codevelopment environment has given C a reputation for being a *system programming language* because it is useful for writing compilers and operating systems. It can also write major programs in many different domains.

UNIX was originally developed in 1969, on what would now be considered a small DEC PDP-7 at Bell Laboratories in New Jersey. UNIX was written entirely in PDP-7 assembly language. By design, this operating system was intended to be "programmer-friendly," providing useful development tools, lean commands, and a relatively open environment. Soon after the development of UNIX, Ken Thompson implemented a compiler for a new language called B.

At this point we need to digress to the origins and history behind Ken Thompson's B language. A true C ancestry would look like this:

Algol 60	Designed by an international committee in early 1960
CPL	(Combined Programming Language) developed at both Cambridge and the University of London in 1963
BCPL	(Basic Combined Programming Language) developed at Cambridge, by Martin Richards, in 1967
B	Developed by Ken Thompson, Bell Labs, in 1970
C	Developed by Dennis Ritchie, Bell Labs, in 1972
ANSI C	The American National Standards Institute committee is formed for the purpose of standardizing the C language, in 1983

Algol appeared only a few years after FORTRAN was introduced. This new language was more sophisticated and greatly influenced the design of future programming languages. Its authors paid careful attention to the regularity of syntax, modular structure, and other features associated with high-level structured languages. Unfortunately, Algol never really caught on in the United States, perhaps because of its abstractness and generality.

The inventors of CPL intended to bring Algol's lofty intent down to the realities of an actual computer. But like Algol, CPL was big. This made the language hard to learn and difficult to implement and explains its eventual downfall. Still clinging to the best of what CPL had to offer, BCPL's creators wanted to boil CPL down to its basic good features.

Bringing the discussion back to the origins of B, when Ken Thompson designed the B language for an early implementation of UNIX, he was trying to further simplify CPL. He succeeded in creating a very sparse language that was well suited for use on the hardware available to him. However, both BCPL and B may have carried their streamlining attempts a bit too far. They became limited languages, useful only for certain kinds of problems.

For example, shortly after Ken Thompson implemented the B language, a new machine was introduced, the PDP-11. UNIX and the B compiler were immediately transferred to this machine. While the PDP-11 was larger than its PDP-7 predecessor, it was still quite small by today's standards. It had only 24K of memory, of which the system used 16K, and one 512K fixed disk. Some considered rewriting UNIX in B, but the B language was slow due to its interpretive design. There was another problem: B was word-oriented while the PDP-11 was byte-oriented. For these reasons, work began in 1971 on a successor to B, appropriately named C.

Dennis Ritchie is credited with creating C, which restored some of the generality lost in BCPL and B. He accomplished this with his shrewd use of data types, while maintaining the simplicity and computer contact that were the original design goals of CPL.

Many languages that have been developed by a single individual (C, Pascal, LISP, and APL) have a cohesiveness missing from languages developed by large programming teams (Ada, PL/I, and Algol 68). In addition, a language written by one person typically reflects the author's field of expertise. Dennis Ritchie was noted for his work in systems software— computer languages, operating systems, and program generators. With C having a genetic link to its creator, one can quickly understand why C is a language of choice for systems software design. C is a relatively low-level language that lets you specify every detail in an algorithm's logic to achieve maximum computer efficiency. But C is also a high-level language that can hide the details of the computer's architecture, thereby increasing programming efficiency.

Relationship to Other Languages

You may be wondering about C's relationship to other languages. Here is a possible continuum:

Direct Neural Path Communication

.

.

.

Artificial Intelligence
Operating System Command Languages
Problem-Oriented Languages
Machine-Oriented Languages
Assembly Language

.

.

.

Actual Hardware

Starting at the bottom of the continuum and moving upward, the languages go from the tangible and empirical to the elusive and theoretical. The dots represent major advancements, with many steps left out. Early ancestors of the computer, like the Jacquard loom (1805) or Charles Babbage's "analytical engine" (1834), were programmed in hardware. The day may well come when you will program a machine by plugging a neural path communicator into a socket implanted into the temporal lobe (language memory) or Broca's area (language motor area) of the brain's cortex.

Assembly languages provide a fairly painless way for programmers to work directly with a computer's built-in instruction set and go back to the first days of electronic computers. Assembly languages forced you to think in terms of the hardware; you had to specify every operation in the machine's terms. You were always moving bits in or out of registers, adding them, shifting register contents from one register to another, and finally storing the results in memory. This was a tedious and error-prone endeavor.

The first high-level languages, such as FORTRAN, were created as alternatives to assembly languages. High-level languages were by design much more general and abstract, and they allowed the programmer to think in terms of the problem at hand rather than in terms of the computer's hardware.

Unfortunately, the creators of high-level languages made the fallacious assumption that everyone who had been driving a standard would always prefer driving an automatic! Excited about providing ease in programming, they left out some necessary options. FORTRAN and Algol are too abstract for systems-level work; they are *problem-oriented languages,* the kind used for solving problems in engineering, science, or business. Programmers who wanted to write systems software still had to rely on their machine's assembler.

Out of this frustration, a few systems software developers took a step backwards or lower in terms of the continuum and created the category of *machine-oriented languages.* As you saw in C's genealogy, BCPL and B fit into this class of very low-level software tools. These languages were excellent for a specific machine, but not much use for anything else—they were too closely related to a particular architecture. The C language is one step above machine-oriented languages yet is still a step below most problem-oriented languages. It is close enough to the computer to give you great control over the details of an application's implementation, yet far enough away to ignore the details of the hardware. This is why the C language is both a high- and low-level language.

Strengths of C

All computer languages have a particular look. APL has its hieroglyphic appearance, assembly language has its columns of mnemonics, Pascal has its easily read syntax, and then there's C. Many programmers new to C will find its syntax cryptic and perhaps intimidating. C contains few of the familiar and friendly English-like syntax structures found in many other programming languages. Instead, C has unusual-looking operators and a plethora of pointers. You will quickly grow used to C's syntax. New C programmers will soon discover a variety of language characteristics whose roots stem back to its original hardware/software progenitor. The following sections highlight the strengths of the C language.

Small Size

There are fewer syntax rules in C than in many other languages, and you can write a top-quality C compiler that will operate in only 256K of total memory. There are actually more operators and combinations of operators in C than there are keywords.

Language Command Set

As you would therefore expect, C is an extremely small language. In fact, the original C language contained a mere 27 keywords. The ANSI C standard (discussed later in the chapter) has an additional 5 reserved words. Borland C++ added 45 more keywords. This brings the total keyword count to 77.

C does not include many of the functions commonly defined as part of other programming languages. For example, C does not contain any built-in input and output capabilities, nor does it contain any arithmetic operations (beyond those of basic addition or subtraction) or string-handling functions. Since any language lacking these capabilities is of little use, C provides a rich set of library functions for input/output, arithmetic operations, and string manipulation. This agreed-upon library set is so common that it is practically part of the language. One of the strengths of C, however, is its loose structure, which enables you to recode these functions easily.

Speed

The C code produced by most compilers tends to be very efficient. The combination of a small language, a small run-time system, and a language close to the hardware makes many C programs run at speeds close to their assembly language equivalents.

Not Strongly Typed

Unlike Pascal, which is a strongly typed language, C treats data types somewhat more loosely. This is a carryover from B, which was also an untyped language. This flexibility allows you to view data in different ways. For example, at one point in a program the application may need to see a variable as a character and yet for purposes of upcasing (by subtracting 32) may want to see the same memory cell as the ASCII equivalent of the character.

A Structured Language

C includes all of the control structures you would expect of a modern language. This is impressive when considering that C predated formal structured programming. C incorporates *for* loops, *if* and *if-else* constructs, *case* (switch) statements, and *while* loops. C also enables you to compartmentalize code and data by managing their scope. For example, C provides local variables for this purpose and call-by-value for subroutine data privacy.

Support of Modular Programming

C supports the concept of separate compilation and linking, which allows you to recompile only the parts of a program that have been changed during development. This feature can be extremely important when you are developing large programs, or even medium-sized programs on slow systems. Without support for modular programming, the amount of time required to compile a complete program can make the change, compile, test, and modify cycle prohibitively slow.

Easy Interface to Assembly Language Routines

There is a well-defined method of calling assembly language routines from most C compilers. Combined with the separation of compilation and linking, this makes C a strong contender in applications that require a mix of high-level and assembler routines. You can also integrate C routines into assembly language programs on most systems.

Bit Manipulation

In systems programming, you often need to manipulate objects at the bit level. Because C's origins are so closely tied to the UNIX operating system, the language provides a rich set of bit manipulation operators.

Pointer Variables

An operating system must be able to address specific areas of memory. This capability also enhances the execution speed of a program. The C language meets these design requirements by using pointers. While other languages implement pointers, C is noted for its ability to perform pointer arithmetic. For example, if the variable *index* points to the first element of an array *student _ records[index + 1]* will be the address of the second element of *student _ records.*

Flexible Structures

In C all arrays are one-dimensional. Multidimensional arrangements are built from combinations of these one-dimensional arrays. You can join arrays and structures (records) in any manner, creating database organizations that are limited only by your ability.

Memory Efficiency

C programs tend to be very memory efficient for many of the reasons that they tend to be fast. The lack of built-in functions saves programs from having to include support for functions that are not needed by a particular application.

Portability

Portability is a measure of how easy it is to convert a program that runs on one computer or operating system to run on another computer or operating system. Programs written in C are currently among the most portable in the computer world. This is especially true for mini- and microcomputers.

Special Function Libraries

There are many commercial function libraries available for all popular C compilers. There are libraries for graphics, file handling, database support, screen windowing, data entry, communications, and general support functions. By using these libraries, you can save a great deal of development time.

Weaknesses of C

There are no perfect programming languages. Different programming problems require different solutions. It is the software engineer's task to choose the best language for a project. On any project, this is one of the first decisions that you need to make, and it is nearly irrevocable once you start coding. The choice of a programming language can also make the difference between a project's success or failure. This section covers some of the weaknesses of the C language so that you will have a better idea of when and when *not* to use C for a particular application.

Not Strongly Typed

The fact that it is not strongly typed is one of C's strengths but is also one of its weaknesses. Technically, typing is a measure of how closely a language enforces the use of variable types (for example, integer and floating point are two different types of numbers). In some languages, you cannot assign one data type to another without invoking a conversion function. This protects the data from being compromised by unexpected roundoffs.

As mentioned, C will allow an integer to be assigned to a character variable or vice versa. This means that you have to manage your variables properly. For experienced programmers, this task presents no problem. However, novice program developers may want to remind themselves that mismatched data type assignments can be the source of side effects.

A side effect in a language is an unexpected change to a variable or other item. Because C is a weakly typed language, it gives you great flexibility to manipulate data. For example, the assignment operator, =, can appear more than once in the same expression. This feature, which you can use to your advantage, means that you can write expressions that have no definite value. If C had restricted the use of the assignment and similar operators, or had eliminated all side effects and unpredictable results, C would have lost much of its power and appeal as a high-level assembly language.

Lack of Run-Time Checking

C's lack of checking in the run-time system can cause many mysterious and transient problems to go undetected. For example, the run-time system would not warn you if your application exceeded an array's bounds. This is one of the costs of streamlining a compiler for the sake of speed and efficiency.

Why C?

C's tremendous range of features—from bit-manipulation to high-level formatted I/O—and its relative consistency from machine to machine have led to its acceptance in science, engineering, and business applications. It has directly contributed to the wide availability of the UNIX operating system on computers of all types and sizes.

Like any other powerful tool, however, C imposes a heavy responsibility on its users. C programmers quickly adopt various rules and conventions in order to make their programs understandable both to themselves and to others. In C, programming discipline is essential. The good news is that it comes almost automatically with practice.

THE ANSI C STANDARD

The ANSI (American National Standards Institute) committee has developed standards for the C language. This section describes some of the significant changes suggested by the committee. A number of these changes are intended to increase the flexibility of the language while others attempt to standardize features previously left to the discretion of the compiler implementor.

Previously, the only standard was *The C Programming Language* by Brian Kernighan and Dennis Ritchie. This book was not specific on some language details, which led to a divergence among compilers. The ANSI standard strives to remove these ambiguities. Although a few of the proposed changes could cause problems for some previously written programs, they should not affect most existing code.

The ANSI C standard provides an even better opportunity to write portable C code. The standard has not corrected all areas of confusion in the language, however, and because C interfaces efficiently with machine hardware, many programs will always require some revision when you move them to a different environment. The ANSI committee adopted as guidelines several phrases that collectively have been called the "spirit of C." Some of those phrases are

- Trust the programmer.

- Don't prevent the programmer from doing what needs to be done.

- Keep the language small and simple.

Additionally, the international community was consulted to ensure that ANSI (American) standard C would be identical to the ISO (International Standards Organization) standard version. Because of these efforts, C is the only language that effectively deals with alternate collating sequences, enormous character sets, and multiuser cultures.

The following list highlights just some of the areas that the ANSI committee addressed:

Feature	Standardized
Data types	Character, integer, floating point, and enumeration.
Comments	/* means opening, */ means closing, // means that anything to symbol's right is ignored by the compiler.
Identifier length	31 characters to distinguish uniqueness.
Standard identifiers and header files	An agreed-upon minimum set of identifiers and header files necessary to perform basic operations such as I/O.
Preprocessor statements	The **#** in preprocessor directives can have leading whitespace (any combination of spaces and tabs), permitting indented preprocessor directives for clarity. Some earlier compilers insisted that all preprocessor directives begin in column one.

New preprocessor directives	Two new preprocessor directives have been added:
	    #if defined (*expression*)
	    #elif (*expression*).

Adjacent strings	Adjacent literal strings should be concatenated. For example, this would allow a **#define** directive to extend beyond a single line.
Standard libraries	The ANSI standard specifies a basic set of system-level and external routines, such as **read** and **write**.
Output control	An agreed-upon set of escape codes representing formatting control codes such as newline, new page, and tabs.
Keywords	An agreed-upon minimum set of verbs used to construct valid C statements.
sizeof	The committee agreed that the **sizeof** function should return the type *size_t*, instead of a variable of size integer, which would possibly be system limiting.
Prototyping	All C compilers should handle programs that do/don't employ prototyping.

Command-line arguments	For the C compiler to handle command-line arguments properly, an agreed-upon syntax was defined.
void pointer type	The *void* keyword can be applied to functions that do not return a value. A function that does return a value can have its return value cast to *void* to indicate to the compiler that the value is being deliberately ignored.
Structure handling	Structure handling has been greatly improved. The member names in structure and union definitions need not be unique. Structures can be passed as arguments to functions, returned by functions, and assigned to structures of the same type.
Function declarations	Function declarations can include argument-type lists (function prototyping) to notify the compiler of the number and types of arguments.
Hexadecimal character constants	Hexadecimal character constants can be expressed by using an introductory \x followed by from one to three hexadecimal digits (0-9, a-f, A-F). For example, 16 decimal = \x10, which can be written as 0x10 using the current notation.
Trigraphs	Trigraphs define standard symbol sequences that represent characters that may not be readily available on all keyboards. For example, you can substitute ??< for the more elaborate { } symbol.

EVOLUTION OF C++ AND OBJECT-ORIENTED PROGRAMMING

Simply stated, C++ is a superset of the C language. C++ retains C's power and flexibility in dealing with the hardware/software interface, its low-level system programming, and its efficiency, economy, and powerful expressions. More exciting, C++ brings the C language into the dynamic world of object-oriented programming and makes it a platform for high-level problem abstraction, going beyond even Ada in this respect. C++ accomplishes all this with a simplicity and support for modularity similar to Modula-2, while maintaining the compactness and execution efficiency of C.

This new hybrid language combines the standard procedural language constructs, familiar to so many programmers, and the object-oriented model, which you can exploit fully to produce a purely object-oriented solution to a problem. In practice, a C++ application can incorporate both the procedural programming model and the newer object-oriented model. For the beginning C++ programmer, not only is there a new language to learn but there is also a new way of thinking and problem solving.

HISTORY OF C++

Not surprisingly, C++ has an origin similar to C. While C++ is somewhat like BCPL and Algol 68, it also contains components of Simula67. C++ can overload operators and include declarations close to their first point of application, features that are found in Algol 68. The concept of subclasses (or derived classes) and virtual functions is taken from Simula67. Like so many other popular programming languages, C++ represents an evolution and refinement of some of the best features of previous languages. Of course, it is closest to C.

Bjarne Stroustrup of Bell Labs is credited with developing the C++ language in the early 1980s. C++ was originally developed to solve some very rigorous event-driven simulations for which considerations of efficiency precluded the use of other languages. C++ was first used outside Dr. Stroustrup's language development group in 1983, and by the summer of 1987, the language was still going through a natural refinement and evolution. To date, there is no equivalent ANSI C++ organization involved in standardizing the language. However, the ANSI C standard does contain some of the key features of C++, such as function prototyping.

One key design goal of C++ was to maintain compatibility with C. The idea was to preserve the integrity of millions of lines of previously written and debugged C code, the integrity of many existing C libraries, and the usefulness of previously developed C tools. Because of the high degree of success in achieving this goal, many programmers find the transition to C++ much simpler than the transition from some other language (Pascal, for example) to C.

C++ supports large-scale software development. Because it includes increased type checking, many of the side effects experienced with loosely typed C applications are no longer possible.

The most significant enhancement of the C++ language is its support for object-oriented programming (abbreviated OOP). You will have to modify your approach to problem solving to derive all of the benefits of C++. For example, objects and their associated operations must be identified and all necessary classes and subclasses must be constructed.

What follows is an example of how an abstract data object in C++ can improve upon an older language's limited built-in constructs and features. For example, a FORTRAN software engineer may want to keep records on employees. You could accomplish this with multiple arrays of scalar data that represent each set of data. All of the arrays are necessarily tied together by a common index. Should there be ten fields of information on each employee, ten array accesses would have to be made using the same index location in order to represent the array of records.

In C++, the solution involves the declaration of a simple object, *employee_records*, that can receive messages to insert, delete, access, or display information contained within the object. The manipulation of the *employee_records* object can then be performed in a natural manner. Inserting a new record into the *employee_records* object becomes as simple as

```
employee_records.insert(new_employee)
```

The *employee_records* object has been appropriately declared, the **insert** function is a method suitably defined in the class that supports *employee_records* objects, and the *new_employee* parameter is the specific information that is to be added. Note that the class of objects called *employee_records* is not a part of the underlying language itself. Instead, you extend the language to suit the problem. By defining a new class of objects or by modifying existing classes (creating a subclass), you achieve a more natural mapping from the problem space to the program space (or solution space). The biggest challenge is mastering this powerful enhancement.

Small Enhancements to C

The following sections detail minor (non-object-oriented) enhancements to the C language.

Comments   C++ introduces the comment to end-of-line delimiter, //. However, you can still use the comment brackets, /* and */.

Enumeration Names   The name of an enumeration is a type name. This feature streamlines the notation by not requiring you to place the qualifier **enum** in front of the enumeration type name.

struct or class Names   The name of a **struct** or **class** is a type name. This class construct does not exist in C. In C++, you don't need to use the qualifier **struct** or **class** in front of a **struct** or **class** name.

Block Declarations   C++ permits declarations within blocks and after code statements. This feature allows you to declare an identifier closer to its first point of application. It even permits you to declare the index for a loop within the loop.

```
for(int index=0;index<10;index++)
```

Scope Qualifier Operator   The scope qualifier operator :: is a new operator used to resolve name conflicts. For example, if a function has a local declaration for a variable *vector_location* and there exists a global variable *vector_location,* the qualifier ::*vector_location* allows the global variable to be accessed within the scope of the local function. The reverse is not possible.

The const Specifier   You can use the **const** specifier to lock the value of an entity within its scope. You can also use it to lock the data pointed to by a pointer variable, the value of the pointer address, or the values of both the pointer address and the data pointed to.

Anonymous Unions   You can define unions without a name anywhere that you can define a variable or field. You can use this feature for the economy of memory storage by allowing two or more fields of a structure to share memory.

Explicit Type Conversions   You can use the name of a predefined type or programmer-defined type as a function to convert data from one type to another. Under certain circumstances, you can use such an explicit type conversion as an alternative to a cast conversion.

Function Prototyping   C++ will make many Pascal, Modula-2, and Ada programmers happy, since it permits the specification by name and type for each function parameter inside the parentheses next to the function name. For example,

```
float income_average(float incomes[], int size)
{
    .
    .
    .
```

The equivalent C interface, under the ANSI standard, would look exactly the same. In this case, C++ influenced the ANSI standards committee.

The C++ translator will perform type checking to ensure that the number and type of values sent into a function when it is invoked match the number and type of the formal arguments defined for the function. The translator also checks that the function's return type matches the variable used in the expression invoking the function. This type of parameter checking is missing in most C systems.

Function Overloading   In C++, functions can use the same function names and each of the overloaded functions can be distinguished on the basis of the number and type of its parameters.

Default Function Parameter Values   You can assign default values to trailing sets of C++ function parameters. In this case, you can invoke the function using fewer than the total number of parameters. Any missing trailing parameters assume their default values.

Functions with an Unspecified Number of Parameters   You can define C++ functions with an unknown number and type of parameters by employing the ellipsis (. . .). When you use this feature, parameter type checking is suppressed to allow flexibility in the interface to the function.

Reference Parameters in a Function   By using the ampersand operator, &, you can declare a formal function parameter as a reference parameter. For example:

```
void increment(int& value)
{
  value++;
}

int i;
increment(i);
    .
    .
    .
```

Because &*value* is defined as a reference parameter, its address is assigned to the address of *i* when **increment** is invoked. The value of *i* that is sent in is incremented within function **increment** and returned to variable *i* outside of function **increment**. The address of *i* need not be explicitly passed into function **increment**, as in C.

inline Specifier   You can use the **inline** specifier to instruct the compiler to perform inline substitution of a given function at the location where the function is invoked.

The new and delete Operators   The **new** and **delete** operators that are introduced in C++ allow for programmer-controlled allocation and deallocation of heap storage.

Void Pointers and Functions that Return Void   In C++, the type *void* is used to indicate that a function returns nothing. You can declare pointer variables to point to *void*. You can then assign such pointers to any other pointer that points to an arbitrary base type.

Major Enhancements to C

The major enhancement to C involves the concept of object-oriented programming. The following sections briefly explain the C++ enhancements that make object-oriented programming possible.

Class Constructs and Data Encapsulation   The class construct is the fundamental vehicle for object-oriented programming. A class definition can encapsulate all of the data declarations, the initial values, and the set of operations (called methods) for data abstraction. Objects can be declared to be of a given class and messages can be sent to objects. Additionally, each object of a specified class can contain its own private and public set of data representative of that class.

Struct Class   A struct in C++ is a subset of a class definition and has no private or protected sections. This subclass can contain both data (as is expected in ANSI C) and functions.

Constructors and Destructors   Constructor and destructor methods are used to guarantee the initialization of the data defined within an object of a specified class. When you declare an object, the specified initialization constructor is activated. Destructors automatically deallocate storage for the associated object when the scope in which the object is declared is exited.

Messages   As you have seen, the object is the basic fabric of object-oriented programming. You manipulate objects by sending them messages. You send messages to objects (variables declared to be of a given class) by using a mechanism similar to invoking a function. The set of possible messages that you can send to an object is specified in the class description for the object. Each object responds to a message by determining an appropriate action to take based on the nature of the message. For example, if *my_obj* represents an object, and *my_method* represents a method with a single integer parameter, you could send a message to the object by using the following statement:

```
my_obj.my_method(5);
```

Friends   The concept of data hiding and data encapsulation implies a denied access to the inner structures that make up an object. The private section of a class is normally off limits to any function outside of the class.

C++ allows you to declare other functions outside functions or classes to be a *friend* to a specified class. Friendship breaks down this normally impenetrable wall and permits access to the private data and functions of the class.

Operator Overloading   With C++, you can give multiple meanings to the set of predefined or user-defined operators and functions supplied with the compiler. For example, different functions typically have different names. However, when functions perform similar tasks on different types of objects, it is sometimes better to let these functions have the same name. When their argument types are different, the compiler can distinguish them anyway and choose the right function to call. What follows is a coded example; you could have one power function for integers and another for floating point variables:

```
int my_power(int,int);
double my_power(double,double);
        .
        .
        .
```

Having declared the two different functions by the same name, the compiler can look at the invoking statement and automatically decide which function is appropriate for the formal parameter list's arguments:

```
x=my_power(3,12);
y=my_power(3.0,12.0);
```

Derived Classes   A *derived class* is like a subclass of a specified class. Derived class objects typically inherit all or some of the methods of the parent class. It is also common for a derived class to incorporate these inherited methods with new methods specific to the subclass. All subclass objects contain the fields of protected and public data from the parent class but not of private data members.

Polymorphism Using Virtual Functions   *Polymorphism* involves a tree structure of parent classes and their subclasses. Each subclass within this tree can receive one or more messages with the same name. When an object of a class within this tree receives a message, the object determines the particular application of the message that is appropriate for an object of the specified subclass.

Stream Libraries   An additional library stream is included with the C++ language. The three classes **cin, cout,** and **cerr** are provided for terminal and file input and output. All of the operators within these three classes can be overloaded within a programmer-defined class. This capability allows the input and output operations to be tailored easily to an application's needs.

THE BASIC ELEMENTS OF A C PROGRAM

You may have heard that C is difficult to learn and to master. This is not true. While a brief encounter with C code may leave you scratching your head, this is only due to C's foreign syntax, structure, and indentation schemes. By the time you finish this chapter, you will have a working knowledge of the C language and will be able to write short but meaningful code. But first you will learn about the nine fundamental components of a program.

The Nine Basic Components of a Program

In one of your introductory programming courses, you may have learned a problem-solution format called an IPO diagram. IPO diagrams were a stylized approach to the input/process/output programming problem. The following list elaborates on these three fundamentals and encapsulates the entire application development cycle. All programs must address the following nine components:

- Programs must obtain information from some input source.

- Programs must decide how this input is to be arranged and stored.

- Programs must use a set of instructions to manipulate the input. These instructions can be divided into four major categories:

Single statements
Conditional statements
Loops
Subroutines

- Programs must report the results of the data manipulation.

- A well-written application incorporates all of the fundamentals just listed, expressed using good modular design, self-documenting code (for instance, meaningful variable names), and a good indentation scheme.

Your First C Program

The following C program will illustrate the basic components of a C application. You should enter each example as you read about it.

```
/*
*    Your first example C program.
*    Copyright (c) Chris H. Pappas and William H. Murray, 1990
*/

#include <stdio.h>

main()
{
  printf(" HELLO World! ");
  return(0);
}
```

There is a lot happening in this short piece of code. First is the comment block:

```
/*
*    Your first example C program.
*    Copyright (c) Chris H. Pappas and William H. Murray, 1990
*/
```

All well-written source code includes meaningful comments. A *meaning-ful* comment respects the intelligence of the programmer while not assuming too much. In C or C++, comments begin with the /* symbols and end with */. The compiler ignores anything between these unique symbol pairs. The next statement

```
#include <stdio.h>
```

represents one of C's unique features known as a preprocessor statement. A *preprocessor statement* is like a precompile instruction. In this case, the statement instructs the compiler to retrieve the code stored in the predefined *stdio.h* file into the source code on the line requested. *stdio.h* is called a header file. *Header files* can include symbolic constants, identifiers, and function prototypes and have these declarations pulled out of the main program for purposes of modularity.

Following the **#include** statement is the **main** function declaration:

```
main()
{
  .
  .
  .
return(0);
}
```

All C programs are made up of function calls. Every C program must have one called **main**. The **main** function is usually where program execution begins and ends with a **return(0)** from **main**. A 0 return value indicates that the program terminated without any errors.

Following the **main** function header is the body of the function itself. Notice the { and } symbol pairs. These are called braces. Technically, braces are used to encapsulate multiple statements. These statements may define the body for a function, or they may bundle statements that are dependent on the same logic control statement, as is the case when several statements are executed based on the validity of an *if* statement. In this example, the braces define the body of the main program.

The line

```
printf(" HELLO World! ");
```

is the only statement in the body of the main program and is the simplest example of an output statement. The **printf** function has been previously prototyped in *stdio.h*. Because no other parameters are specified, the sentence will be printed to the display monitor.

Your First C++ Program

The next example performs the same function as the previous one, but it takes advantage of the features that are unique to C++.

```
//
//    Your first C++ example program.
//    Copyright (c) Chris H. Pappas and William H. Murray, 1990
//

#include <iostream.h>

main()
{
  cout << " HELLO World! ";

  return(0);
}
```

There are three major differences. First, the comment designator has been changed from the /* and */ pair to a //. Second, the **#include** file name has been changed to *iostream.h,* with the third change involving a different output call, **cout**. Many of the examples in the book will highlight the sometimes subtle and sometimes dazzling differences between C and C++.

Your Second C Program

At this point, you are probably waiting for a slightly more meaningful example. The following program not only outputs information but also prompts the user for input.

```
/*
 *    This C program prompts the user for a specified length,
 *    in yards, and then outputs the value converted to
 *    feet and inches.
 *    Copyright (c) Chris H. Pappas and William H. Murray, 1990
 */

#include <stdio.h>

main()
{
  int yard,feet,inch;

  printf("Please enter the length to be converted: ");
  scanf("%d",&yard);
  while(yard > 0 ) {
```

```
    inch=36*yard;
    feet=3*yard;
    printf("%d yard(s) = \n",yard);
    printf("%d feet \n",feet);
    printf("%d inches \n",inch);
    printf("Please enter another length to be \n");
    printf("converted (0 stops program): ");
    scanf("%d",&yard);
  }
  printf(">>> End of Program <<<");
  return(0);
}
```

Data Declarations   The first new thing in the program is the declaration
of three variables:

```
int yard,feet,inch;
```

All C variables must be declared before they are used. The syntax for
declaring variables in C requires the definition of the variable's type before
the name of the variable. One of the standard data types supplied by the C
language is integer. In this example, the integer type is represented by the
keyword *int*, and the three variables *yard*, *feet*, and *inch* are defined.

User Input   The next unconventional statement is used to input information from the keyboard:

```
printf("Please enter the length to be converted: ");
scanf("%d",&yard);
```

The **scanf** function has a requirement that is called a format string. *Format
strings* define how the input data is to be interpreted and represented
internally. The *"%d"* function parameter instructs the compiler to interpret
the input as integer data (in BorlandC++ an integer occupies 2 bytes).
(Chapter 6, "Data," contains a detailed explanation of all of the C and C++
language data types.)

Address Operator   In the previous listing, the integer variable *yard* was preceded by an ampersand symbol, **&**. The **&** is known as an *address operator*. Whenever a variable is preceded by this symbol, the compiler uses the address of the specified variable instead of the value stored in the variable. The **scanf** function has been written to expect the address of the variable to be filled.

Loop Structure   One of the simplest loop structures to code in C is the *while* loop:

```
while(yard > 0) {
   .
   .
   .
}
```

This pretest loop starts with the reserved word *while* followed by a Boolean expression that evaluates to either TRUE or FALSE. The opening brace, {, and closing brace, }, are optional and are only needed when more than one executable statement is to be associated with the loop repetition. Braced statements are sometimes referred to as compound statements, compound blocks, or code blocks.

If you are using compound blocks, make certain that you use the agreed-upon brace style. While the compiler doesn't care where you place the braces (skipped spaces/lines), programmers reading your code will certainly appreciate the style and effort. You place opening loop braces at the end of the test condition, and the closing brace in the same column as the first character in the test condition.

Formatted Output   The second program contains more complex **printf** function calls:

```
printf("%d yard(s) = \n", yard);
printf("%d feet \n",feet);
printf("%d inches \n",inch);
printf("Please enter another length to be \n");
printf("converted (0 stops program): ");
```

If you are familiar with the PL/I language developed by IBM, you will be at home with the concept of a control string. Whenever a **printf** function is invoked to print not only literal strings (any set of characters between double quotation marks) but also values, a format string is required. The format string represents two things: a picture of how the output string is to look, and the format interpretation for each of the values printed. Format strings are always between double quotation marks.

The following table breaks down the first **printf** format string

("%d yard(s) = \n", yard)

into its separate components:

Control	Action
%d	Takes the value of *yard*, interprets it as an integer, and prints it
yard(s)	After printing the integer *yard*, skips one blank space and then prints the literal 'yard(s) ='
\n	Once the line is complete, executes a newline feed
,	In this example, the comma separates the format string from the variable name(s) used to satisfy all format descriptors (in this case, only one %d)

The next two **printf** statements are similar in execution. Each statement prints a formatted integer value, followed by a literal string, and ending with a newline feed. If you ran the program, your output would look much like this:

```
Please enter the length to be converted: 4
4 yard(s) =
12 feet
144 inches
Please enter another length to be
converted (0 stops program): 0
```

Table 5-1 lists all of the output control symbols and describes how they can be used in format strings. Table 5-2 lists all of the C language value formatting controls. As you learn more about the various C data types, you can refer back to these two tables for a reminder of how the various controls affect input and output.

Using the Debugger   To examine the actual operation of this C code, you can use the Debugger. From the Integrated Environment, go to the

Table 5-1.   C Output Controls

Borland C++ Escape Sequences	Sequences	Value	Char	What It Does
	\a	0 × 07	BEL	Audible bell
The \\ must be used to	\b	0 × 08	BS	Backspace
represent a real ASCII	\f	0 × 0C	FF	Formfeed
backslash, as used in	\n	0 × 0A	LF	Newline (linefeed)
DOS paths.	\r	0 × 0D	CR	Carriage return
	\t	0 × 09	HT	Tab (horizontal)
	\v	0 × 0B	VT	Vertical tab
	\\	0 × Sc	\	Backslash
	\'	0 × 27	'	Single quote (apostrophe)
	\"	0 × 22	"	Double quote
	\?	0 × 3F	?	Question mark
	\O		Any	O = a string of up to three octal digits
	\xH		Any	H = a string of hex digits
	\XH (uppercase)		Any	H = a string of hex digits

Options menu, select the Debugger submenu, and change "Source Debugging" to ON. Now, start the Debugger and single-step through the program. Use the Watch window to keep an eye on the variables *yard*, *feet*, and *inch*. Figure 5-1 shows a Debugger window.

Your Second C++ Program

The following C++ example is identical in function to the previous C example. However, there are some minor variations in the syntax.

```
//
//    This C++ program prompts the user for a specified length,
//    in yards, and then outputs the value converted to
//    feet and inches.
//    Copyright (c) Chris H. Pappas and William H. Murray, 1990
//

#include <iostream.h>

main()
{
```

```
int yard,feet,inch;

cout << "Please enter the length to be converted:  \n";
cin >> yard;
while(yard > 0 ) {
   inch=36*yard;
   feet=3*yard;
   cout << "yard(s) = " << yard << "\n";
   cout << "feet = " << feet << "\n";
   cout << "inches = " << inch << "\n";
   cout << "Please enter another length to be \n";
   cout << "converted (0 stops program): ";
   cin >> yard;
}
cout << ">>> End of Program <<<";
return(0);
}
```

Table 5-2.   C Value Formatting Controls

Function	scanf	printf
Size of value (modifies data type):		
Specify short integer	%hd	
Specify long integer	%ld	%ld
Specify double	%lf	%lf
Use with float to indicate a long double	%Lf	%Lf
Type of data to be read or displayed:		
Single character	%c	%c
Signed integer	%d	%d
Signed double or float in exponential format	%e	%e
Signed double or float in decimal format	%f	%f
Octal (letter "O" not 0)	%O	%O
Character string	%s	%s
Unsigned decimal integer	%u	%u
Hexadecimal (%X for uppercase letters)	%x	%x
Prints percent symbol		%%
Decimal integer, six digits wide		%6d
Floating point, six digits wide		%6f
Floating point, two digits after decimal point		%.2f
Floating point, six digits wide, two after decimal		%6.2f

The **cout** and **cin** statements are the only major difference between the C++ example and its C counterpart. These statements use the << (put to) and >> (get from) stream operators. These two operators have been overloaded to handle the output/input of all the predefined types. They can also be overloaded to handle the output/input of user-defined types such as rational numbers.

C++ programmers who like the power and flexibility of the C output function **printf** can use **printf** directly from library *stdio.h.* You can also use the **cout** form. The next two statements show the C and C++ function form equivalents:

```
printf("%d yard(s) = \n", yard);
cout << "yard(s) = " << yard << "\n";
```

Files

Of course, there will be times when an application wants either its input or output to deal directly with files rather than the keyboard and display

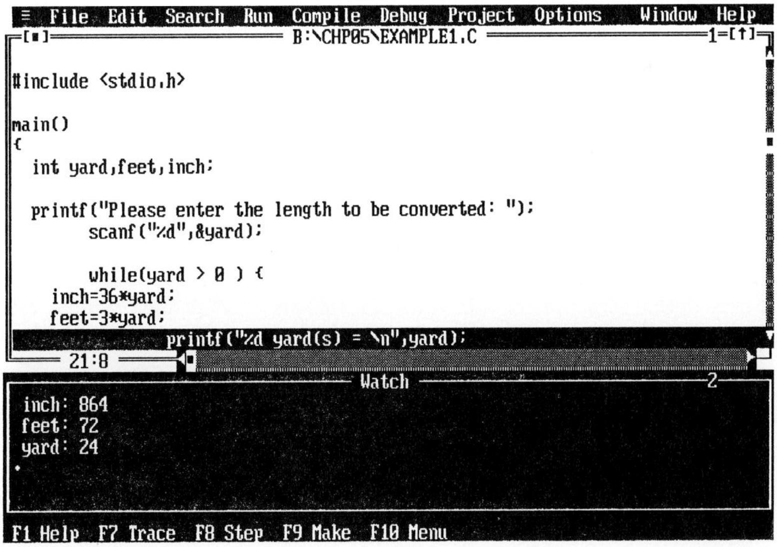

Figure 5-1.   Integrated Debugger converting 24 yards

monitor. This brief introduction is an example of how to declare and use simple data files:

```
/*
 *    This C program demonstrates how to declare and use both
 *    input and output files.  The input file earnings.dat
 *    contains integer values that are taxed at a rate of
 *    20% for earnings less than $5000, and at 50% if greater
 *    than or equal to $5000.  The calculated tax value
 *    is written to the taxrate.dat file in integer form.
 *    Copyright (c) Chris H. Pappas and William H. Murray, 1990
 */

#include <stdio.h>

main()
{
  int earnings,tax;
  FILE *fin,*fout;

  fin=fopen("a:\\earnings.dat","r");
  fout=fopen("a:\\taxrate.dat","w");
  while (!feof(fin)) {
    fscanf(fin,"%d",&earnings);
    fprintf(fout,"Earnings = %d greenbacks\n",earnings);
    if (earnings < 5000)
      tax=0.2*earnings;
      else
         tax=0.5*earnings;
    fprintf(fout,"Tax = %d greenbacks\n",tax);
  }

  return(0);
}
```

Each file in a C program must be associated with a *file pointer*. The file pointer points to information that defines various things about a file, including the path to the file, its name, and its status. A file pointer is a pointer variable of type **FILE** and is defined in *stdio.h*. The following statement from the example program declares two files *fin* and *fout*:

```
FILE *fin,*fout;
```

The next two statements in the program

```
fin=fopen("a:\\earnings.dat","r");
fout=fopen("a:\\taxrate.dat","w");
```

Table 5-3.   C Valid File Modes

Mode	Usage
"r"	Opens a text file for reading
"w"	Opens a text file for writing
"r+"	Opens a text file for update reading or writing
"w+"	Creates a new file for update (if file exists it is overwritten)
"a"	Opens a file in append mode or creates a file for writing if the file does not exist
"a+"	Opens a file in append mode for updating at the end of the file or creates a file for writing if the file does not exist
"rb"	Opens a binary file for reading
"wb"	Opens a binary file for writing

open two separate streams and associate each file with its respective stream. The statements also return the file pointer for each file. Since these are pointers to files, your application should never alter their values.

The second parameter to the **fopen** function is the file mode. Files may be opened in either text or binary mode. When in text mode, most C compilers translate carriage return-linefeed sequences into newline characters on input. During output, the opposite occurs. However, binary files do not go through such translations. Table 5-3 lists several valid file modes.

C performs its own file closing automatically whenever the application closes. However, at times you may want direct control over when a file is closed. The following listing shows the same program modified to include the necessary closing function calls:

```
/*
*    This C program demonstrates how to declare and use both
*    input and output files.  The input file earnings.dat
*    contains integer values that are taxed at a rate of
*    20% for earnings less than $5000, and at 50% if greater
*    than or equal to $5000.  The calculated tax value
*    is written to the taxrate.dat file in integer form.
*    Copyright (c) Chris H. Pappas and William H. Murray, 1990
*/

#include <stdio.h>
```

```
main()
{
  int earnings,tax;
  FILE *fin,*fout;

  fin=fopen("a:\\earnings.dat","r");
  fout=fopen("a:\\taxrate.dat","w");
  while (!feof(fin)) {
    fscanf(fin,"%d",&earnings);
    fprintf(fout,"Earnings = %d dollars\n",earnings);
    if (earnings < 5000)
      tax=0.2*earnings;
      else
        tax=0.5*earnings;
    fprintf(fout,"Tax = %d dollars\n",tax);
    }
  fclose(fin);
  fclose(fout);

  return(0);
}
```

The following program performs the same function as the previous one, but is coded in C++:

```
//
//    This C++ program demonstrates how to declare and use both
//    input and output files.  The input file earnings.dat
//    contains integer values that are taxed at a rate of
//    20% for earnings less than $5000, and at 50% if greater
//    than or equal to $5000.  The calculated tax value
//    is written to the taxrate.dat file in integer form.
//    Copyright (c) Chris H. Pappas and William H. Murray, 1990
//

#include <fstream.h>

main()
{
  int earnings,tax;
  ifstream f_in("a:\\earnings.dat");
  ofstream f_out("a:\\taxrate.dat");

  f_in >> earnings;
  while (!f_in.eof()) {
    f_out << "Earnings = " << earnings << " dollars\n";
    if (earnings < 5000)
      tax=0.2*earnings;
      else
        tax=0.5*earnings;
    f_out << "Tax = " << tax << " dollars\n";
    f_in >> earnings;
  }
```

```
    f_in.close();
    f_out.close();
    return(0);
}
```

Disk file input and output are slightly different in C++ than with C. Input and output facilities are not defined within the C++ language, but rather are implemented in C++ and provided as a component of a C++ standard library. This library is referred to as the **iostream** library. To perform file I/O the derived classes **ifstream** and **ofstream** must be used.

The short sample program above demonstrates how to declare an input file f_in and an output file f_out which are both opened in the default text mode. The program reads in integer values from *earnings.dat*, performs a simple calculation, and writes the results to *taxrate.dat*.

Some of you looking at the code may think that the file structure used looks slightly different from what you are normally used to. If so, you have probably been using the file structure for a C++ compiler using Release 1.2 specifications. The sample program was written using the new Release 2.0 standard. Chapter 11, "Input and Output in C and C++," will explain the new Release 2.0 file structure and discuss those changes necessary to upgrade a Release 1.2 program to the improved format.

6

DATA

What you have learned so far of C and the C++ enhancements is only the tip of the iceberg. Starting with this chapter, you will explore the underlying structures of the C and C++ language. The great stability of C++ comes from the standard C and C++ data types and the modifiers and operations that you can perform on them.

WHAT ARE IDENTIFIERS?

Identifiers are the names that you use to represent variables, constants, types, functions, and labels in your program. You create an identifier by specifying it in the declaration of a variable, type, or function. You can then use the identifier in later program statements to refer to the associated item.

An identifier is a sequence of one or more letters, digits, or underscores that begins with a letter or underscore. Identifiers can contain any number of characters, but only the first 32 characters are significant to the compiler. (Other programs that read the compiler output, such as the Linker, may recognize even fewer characters.)

C and C++ are case sensitive. This means that the compiler considers uppercase and lowercase letters to be distinct characters. For example, the

compiler sees the variables *MAX* and *max* as two unique identifiers representing different memory cells. This feature enables you to create distinct
identifiers that have the same spelling but different cases for one or more of
the letters.

The selection of case can also help a programmer understand your code.
For example, identifiers declared in *include* header files are often created
with only uppercase letters. Because of this, whenever you encounter an
uppercase identifier in the source file, you can assume that that identifier's
definition is in an *include* header file.

Although it is syntactically legal, you should not use leading underscores in identifiers that you create. Often, identifiers beginning with an
underscore can cause conflicts with the names of system routines or variables, and produce errors. As a result, programs that contain names beginning with leading underscores are not guaranteed to be portable.

Here are some sample identifiers:

```
k
count
temp1
reservations_plane1
fathom_6_ft
```

See if you can determine why the following identifiers are illegal:

```
1st_place
#lbs
action_taken!
```

The first identifier is illegal because it begins with a decimal number. The
second identifier begins with a # symbol, and the last identifier ends with
an illegal character.

Guess whether the following identifiers are legal or not:

```
0
00
000
```

_____

Actually, all four identifiers are legal. The first three use a different number of the uppercase letter "O." The fourth identifier consists of five underscore characters. These identifiers are not meaningful, but they are legal. However, while these identifiers meet the letter of the law, they greatly miss the spirit of the law, since all identifiers, function names, constants, and variables should use meaningful names.

Since uppercase and lowercase letters are considered distinct characters, each of the following identifiers is unique:

```
SIZE
size
Size
siZe
```

The C compiler's case sensitivity can create tremendous headaches for the novice C programmer. For example, trying to reference the **printf** function, when it was typed **PRINTF**, will invoke unknown identifier complaints from the compiler. In Pascal, however, a **writeln** is a **WRITELN** is a **WriteLn**.

With experience, you would probably detect the preceding **printf** error, but can you see what's wrong with this next statement?

```
printf("%C",one_character);
```

Assuming that *one_character* was defined properly, you might think that nothing was wrong. Remember, however, that C is case sensitive—the "%C" print format has never been defined; only "%c" has.

For more advanced applications, some linkers may further restrict the number and type of characters for globally visible symbols. Also, the Linker, unlike the compiler, may not distinguish between uppercase and lowercase letters. By default, the Borland C++ TLINK sees all public and external symbols, such as *MYVARIABLE, MyVariable,* and *myvariable,* as the same. However, you can make TLINK case sensitive by using the /c option. This would force TLINK to see the three example variables above as being unique. See your Borland C++ *Programmer's Guide* for additional information on how to use this switch.

Finally, an identifier cannot have the same spelling and case as a keyword. The next section lists C and C++ keywords.

KEYWORDS

Keywords are predefined identifiers that have special meanings to the C compiler. You can use them only as defined. Remember, the name of a program identifier cannot have the same spelling and case as a C keyword. The C language keywords are listed in Table 6-1.

You cannot redefine keywords. However, you can specify text that can be substituted for keywords before compilation by using C preprocessor directives.

STANDARD C AND C++ DATA TYPES

When you write a program, you are working with some kind of information that you can usually represent by using one of the seven basic C and C++ types: text or **char**, integer values or **int**, floating-point values or **float**, double floating-point values or **double**, enumerated or **enum**, valueless or **void**, and pointers.

- Text (data type **char**) is made up of single characters (a, Z, ?, 3) and strings ("He who has an ear to hear, let him hear"), usually, 8 bits, or 1 byte, with the range of 0 to 255.

- Integer values are those numbers you learned to count with (1, 2, 7, −45, and 1345), usually, 16 bits wide, 2 bytes, or 1 word, with the range of −32,768 to 32,767.

- Floating-point values are numbers that have a fractional portion such as π (3.14159), and exponents (7.563 × 1021). These are also known as real numbers (usually, 32 bits, 4 bytes, or 2 words, with the range of 3.4E −38 to 3.4E + 38).

- Double floating-point values have an extended range (usually, 64 bits, 8 bytes, or 4 words, with the range of 1.7E −308 to 1.7E + 308).

- Enumerated data types allow for user-defined types.

- The type **void** signifies values that occupy 0 bits and have no value. You can also use this type to create generic pointers (see Chapter 10, "Pointers").

- The pointer data type doesn't hold information as do the other data types. Instead, each pointer contains the address of the memory location holding the actual data (see Chapter 10).

Table 6-1.   Borland C and C++ Keywords

Borland C++ Keywords

asm	else	long	_ss
auto	enum	_near	static
break	_es	near	struct
case	_export	new	switch
catch	extern	operator	template
_cdecl	_far	_pascal	this
cdecl	far	pascal	typedef
char	float	private	union
class	for	protected	unsigned
const	friend	public	virtual
continue	goto	register	void
_cs	huge	return	volatile
default	if	_saveregs	while
delete	inline	_seg	
do	int	short	
double	interrupt	signed	
_ds	_loadds	sizeof	

Borland C++ ANSI C Extensions

_cdcel	_export	_loadds	_regparam
cdecl	_far	_near	_saveregs
_cs	far	near	_seg
_ds	huge	_pascal	_ss
_es	interrupt	pascal	

C++-Specific Keywords

catch	inline	protected	virtual
class	new	public	
delete	operator	template	
friend	private	this	

Pseudovariables for Borland C++

_AH	_BP	_CX	_DX
_AL	_BX	_DH	_ES
_AX	_CH	_DI	_FLAGS
_BH	_CL	_DL	_SI
_BL	_CS	_DS	_SP
			_SS

Characters

Every language uses a set of characters to construct meaningful statements. For instance, all books written in English use combinations of 26 letters of the alphabet, the 10 digits, and the punctuation marks. Similarly, C and C++ programs are written with a set of characters consisting of the 26 lowercase letters of the alphabet,

```
abcdefghijklmnopqrstuvwxyz
```

the 26 uppercase letters of the alphabet,

```
ABCDEFGHIJKLMNOPQRSTUVWXYZ
```

the 10 digits,

```
0 1 2 3 4 5 6 7 8 9
```

and the following symbols:

```
+ - * / =, . _ : ; ? \ " ' ~ | ! # % $ & ( ) [ ] { } ^ @
```

C and C++ also use the blank space, sometimes referred to as white-space. Combinations of symbols, with no intervening blank space, are also valid C and C++ characters. In fact, the following code is a mixture of valid C and C++ symbols:

```
++ -- == && || << >> >= <= += -= *= /= ?: :: /* */ //
```

The following C program illustrates how to declare and use **char** data types:

```
/*
 *    A C program demonstrating the char data type and showing
 *    how a char variable can be interpreted as an integer.
 *    Copyright (c) Chris H. Pappas and William H. Murray, 1990
 *
 */
```

```
#include <stdio.h>

main()
{
  char uppercase_A='A', lowercase_a='a';

  printf("The character \'%c\' has a decimal ASCII"  \
         " value of %d\n",uppercase_A,uppercase_A);
  printf("The ASCII value represented in hexadecimal"\
         " is %X\n",uppercase_A);
  printf("If you add sixteen will you get \'%c\'\n",
         uppercase_A+16);
  printf("The calculated ASCII value in hexadecimal" \
         " is %X\n",(uppercase_A+16));
  printf("The character \'%c\' has a decimal ASCII"  \
         " value of %d\n",lowercase_a,lowercase_a);

  return(0);
}
```

The output from the program looks like this:

```
The character 'A' has a decimal ASCII value of 65
The ASCII value represented in hexadecimal is 41
If you add sixteen will you get 'Q'
The calculated ASCII value in hexadecimal is 51
The character 'a' has a decimal ASCII value of 97
```

The %X format control instructs the compiler to interpret the value as a hexadecimal number.

Three Integers

Borland C++ actually supports three types of integers. Along with the standard type **int**, the compiler supports **short int** and **long int**. These are most often abbreviated to **short** and **long**. Since the C language is so tied to the hardware, the actual sizes of **short**, **int**, and **long** depend upon the implementation. However, a variable of type **short** will not be larger than one of type **long**. Borland C++ allocates 2 bytes for both types **short** and **int**. The type **long** occupies 4 bytes of storage.

Unsigned Modifier

Many C and C++ compilers also allow you to declare certain types as **unsigned**. Currently, you can apply the **unsigned** modifier to four types: **char**, **short int**, **int**, and **long int**. When one of these data types is modified to be **unsigned**, you can think of the range of values it holds as representing the numbers displayed on a car odometer. An automobile odometer starts at 000. . ., increases to a maximum of 999. . ., and then recycles back to 000. . ., it also only displays positive whole numbers. In a similar way, an unsigned data type can hold only positive values from 0 to the maximum number that can be represented.

For example, suppose that you are designing a new data type called **tiny**, and decide that **tiny** variables can hold only 3 bits. You also decide that the data type **tiny** is signed by default. Since a variable of type **tiny** can only contain the bit patterns 000 through 111 (or 0 to 7 decimal), and you want to represent both positive and negative values, you have a problem. You can't have both positive and negative numbers in the range 0 to 7 because you need one of the 3 bits to represent the sign of the number. Therefore, **tiny**'s range is a subset. When the most significant bit is 0, the value is positive. When the most significant bit is 1, the value is negative. This gives a **tiny** variable the range of −4 to +3, as shown in Table 6-2.

However, applying the unsigned data type modifier to a **tiny** variable would yield a range of 0 to 7, since the most significant bit can be combined

Table 6-2.   The Hypothetical Signed **tiny** Data Type

Unique Combinations of 0's and 1's	Decimal Equivalent
000	+0
001	+1
010	+2
011	+3
100	−1
101	−2
110	−3
111	−4

with the lower 2 bits to represent a broader range of positive values instead of identifying the sign of the number (see Table 6-3).

This simple analogy holds true for any of the valid C data types defined to be of type **unsigned**. The storage and range for the fundamental C data types are summarized in Table 6-4. Table 6-5 lists the valid data type modifiers in all of the various legal and abbreviated combinations.

Floating Point

Borland C++ uses the three floating-point types: **float, double,** and **long double**. While the ANSI C standard does not specifically define the values and storage to be allocated for each of these types, the standard does require each type to hold a minimum of any value in the range 1E−37 to 1E+37. As you see in Table 6-4, the Borland C++ environment has greatly expanded upon this minimum requirement. Most C compilers have always had the types **float** and **double**. The ANSI C committee added the third type **long double**. Here are some examples of floating-point numbers:

```
float body_temp = 98.6;
double my_balance;
long double IRS_balance;
```

Table 6-3.   The Hypothetical Unsigned **tiny** Data Type

Unique Combinations of 0's and 1's	Decimal Equivalent
000	+0
001	+1
010	+2
011	+3
100	+4
101	+5
110	+6
111	+7

Table 6-4.   Fundamental Type Storage and Range of Values

Type	Storage	Range of Values (Internal)
char	1 byte	−128 to 127
int	2 bytes	−32,768 to 32,767
short	2 bytes	−32,768 to 32,767
long	4 bytes	−2,147,483,648 to 2,147,483,647
unsigned char	1 byte	0 to 255
unsigned int	2 bytes	0 to 65,535
unsigned short	2 bytes	0 to 65,535
unsigned long	4 bytes	0 to 4,294,967,295
float	4 bytes	3.4E −38 to 3.4E + 38
double	8 bytes	1.7E −308 to 1.7E + 308
long double	10 bytes	3.4E −4932 to 1.1E + 4932
pointer	2 bytes	(near, _ cs, _ ds, _ es, _ ss pointers)
pointer	4 bytes	(far,huge pointers)

Table 6-5.   Valid Data Type Modifier Abbreviations

Type Modifier	Abbreviations
signed char	char
signed int	signed, int
signed short int	short, signed short
signed long int	long, signed long
unsigned char	no abbrv.
unsigned int	unsigned
unsigned short int	unsigned short
unsigned long int	unsigned long

You can use **long double** on any computer, even one that has only two types of floating-point numbers. However, if the computer does not have a **long double** data type, the data item will have the same size and storage capacity as a **double**.

The following C++ program illustrates how to declare and use **float** variables:

```
//
//      A C++ program demonstrating use of the float data type.
//      Copyright (c) Chris H. Pappas and William H. Murray, 1990
//

#include <iostream.h>

main()
{

  long original_flags = cin.flags();
  float float1 = 3601.234, float2 = 0.0028, float3 = -142.1;

  cout << "\t\t" << float1 << "\t";
  cout.setf(ios::scientific);
  cout << float1 << "\n\n";

  cout.setf(ios::fixed);
  cout << "\t\t" << float2 << "\t\t";
  cout.flags(original_flags);
  cout.setf(ios::scientific);
  cout << float2 << "\n\n";

  cout.setf(ios::fixed);
  cout << "\t\t" << float3 << "\t";
  cout.flags(original_flags);
  cout.setf(ios::scientific);
  cout << float3 << "\n\n";

  cout.flags(original_flags);

  return(0);
}
```

The output looks like this:

```
3601.233887      3.601234e+03

0.00028          2.8e-03

-142.100006      -1.421e+02
```

Notice the different value printed depending on the print format specification **fixed** (default) or **scientific**.

Enumerated

When an enumerated variable is defined, it is associated with a set of named integer constants called the *enumeration set* (also see Chapter 12, "Structures, Unions, and Miscellaneous Items"). The variable can contain any one of the constants at any time, and you can refer to the constants by name. For example, the definition

```
enum tank_pressure { OK,
                     LOW,
                     GULP=5 }  bills_tank;
```

creates the **enum** type of *tank_pressure,* the **enum** constants of *OK, LOW,* and *GULP,* and the **enum** variable of *bills_tank.* All the constants and variables are of type **int,** and each constant is automatically provided a default initial value unless another value is specified. In the preceding example, the constant name *OK* has the **int** value 0 by default since it is the first in the list and was not specifically overridden. The value of *LOW* is 1 since it occurs immediately after a constant with the value 0. The constant *GULP* was specifically initialized to the value 5. If another constant were included after *GULP,* it would have the **int** value of 6.

Having created *tank_pressure,* you can later define another variable, *chriss_tank,* as follows:

```
enum tank_pressure chriss_tank;
```

After this statement, it is legal to say

```
bills_tank  = OK;
chriss_tank = GULP;
```

which will place the value 0 into the variable *bills_tank,* and the value 5 into the variable *chriss_tank.*

One common mistake is to think that *tank_pressure* is a variable. It is a "type" of data that you can use later to create additional **enum** variables, such as *chriss_tank.*

Since the name *bills_tank* is an enumeration variable of type *tank_pressure,* you can use *bills_tank* on the left of an assignment operator and it can receive a value. This occurred when the **enum** constant *OK* was explicitly assigned to it. The names *OK, LOW,* and *GULP* are names of constants; they are not variables and you cannot change their values.

You can perform tests on the variables in conjunction with the constants. The following C program shows a complete program that uses the preceding definitions:

```
/*
 *      A C program demonstrating the use of enumeration variables
 *      Copyright (c) Chris H. Pappas and William H. Murray, 1990
 */

#include <stdio.h>

main()
{
  enum tank_pressure { OK,
                       LOW,
                       GULP=5 }  bills_tank;
  enum tank_pressure chriss_tank;

  bills_tank = OK;
  chriss_tank = GULP;

  printf("The value of bills_tank is %d\n",bills_tank);

  if (chriss_tank == GULP)
    printf("The value of chriss_tank is %d\n",chriss_tank);

  if (bills_tank == chriss_tank)
    printf("bills_tank equals chriss_tank");
  else
    printf("bills_tank does not equal chriss_tank");

  return(0);
}
```

ACCESS MODIFIERS

The **const** and **volatile** modifiers are new to C and C++. They were added by the ANSI C standard to help identify variables that will never change (**const**) and variables that can change unexpectedly (**volatile**).

const Modifier

At times, you may need to use a value that does not change throughout the program. Such a quantity is called a *constant*. For example, if a program deals with the area and circumference of a circle, it will frequently use the constant value *pi=3.14159*. In a financial program, an interest rate might be a constant. In such cases, you can improve the readability of the program by giving the constant a descriptive name.

Using descriptive names can also help prevent errors. Suppose that you use a constant value (not a constant variable) at many points throughout the program. Suppose also that you type the wrong value at one or more of these points. If the constant has a name, a typographical error would then be detected by the compiler because you probably didn't declare the incorrect name.

Suppose that you are writing a program that repeatedly uses the value π. You might think that you should declare a variable called *pi* with an initial value of 3.14159. However, the program should not be able to change the value of a constant. For instance, if you inadvertently wrote *pi* to the left of an equal sign, the value of *pi* would be changed, causing all subsequent calculations to be in error. C and C++ provide mechanisms that prevent such errors from occurring—that is, you can establish constants whose values cannot be changed.

In C and C++, you declare a constant by writing **const** before the keyword (for instance, **int, float, double**) in the declaration. For example:

```
const int MAX=9,INTERVAL=15;
const float rate=0.7;
int index=0,count=10,object;
double distance=0.0,velocity;
```

Because a constant cannot be changed, it must be initialized in its declaration. The **int** constants *MAX* and *INTERVAL* are declared with values 9 and 15, respectively. The constant *rate* is of type **float** and has been initialized to 0.7. In addition, the **int** (nonconstant) variables *index, count,* and *object* have been declared. Initial values of 0 and 10 have been established for *index* and *count,* respectively. Finally, *distance* and *velocity* have been declared to be (nonconstant) variables of type **double.** An initial value of 0.0 has been established for *distance.*

You use constants and variables in the same way in a program. The only difference is that you cannot change the initial values assigned to the constants—that is, the constants are not *lvalues;* they cannot appear to the left of an equal sign.

Normally, the assignment operation assigns the value of the right-hand operand to the storage location named by the left-hand operand. Therefore, the left-hand operand of an assignment operation (or the single operand of a unary assignment expression) must be an expression that refers to a modifiable memory location.

Expressions that refer to memory locations are called *lvalue expressions.* Expressions referring to modifiable locations are modifiable *lvalues.* One example of a modifiable *lvalue* expression is a variable name declared without **const.**

#define Constants

C and C++ provide another method for establishing constants—the **#define** compiler directive. Suppose that you have the following statement at the beginning of a program:

```
#define VOLUME 10
```

The form of this statement is **#define** followed by two strings of characters separated by spaces. When the program is compiled, several passes are made through it. First, the compiler preprocessor carries out the **#include** and **#define** directives. When the preprocessor encounters the **#define** directive, it replaces every occurrence of *VOLUME* in the source files with the number 10.

In general, when the preprocessor encounters a **#define** directive, it replaces every occurrence of the first string of characters (*VOLUME*) in the program with the second string of characters (10). Additionally, no value can be assigned to *VOLUME* because it has never been declared as a variable. As a result of the syntax, *VOLUME* has all the attributes of a constant. Note that the **#define** statement is not terminated by a semicolon. If a semicolon followed the value 10, every occurrence of *VOLUME* would be replaced with 10;. The directive replaces the first string with *everything* in the second string.

The short programs that have been discussed so far would usually be stored in a single file. If a statement such as the **#define** for *VOLUME* appeared at the beginning of the file, the substitution of 10 for *VOLUME* would take place throughout the program. In Chapter 10, you will learn how to divide a program into many subprograms, with each subprogram being divided into separate files. Under these circumstances, the **#define** compiler directive would be effective only for the single file in which it is written.

You have just learned two methods for defining constants: the keyword **const** and the **#define** compiler directive. In many programs, the action of each of these two methods is essentially the same. On the other hand, the use of the modifier keyword **const** results in a "variable" whose value cannot be changed. Later you will see how you can declare variables in such a way that they exist only over certain regions of a program. The same can be said for constants declared with the keyword **const**. Thus, the **const** declaration is somewhat more versatile than the **#define** directive. Also, the **#define** directive is found in standard C and is therefore already familiar to C programmers.

volatile Modifier

The **volatile** keyword signifies that a variable can unexpectedly change because of events outside the control of the program. For example, the following definition indicates that the variable *timer* can have its value changed without the knowledge of the program:

```
volatile int timer;
```

You need a definition like this, for example, if *timer* is updated by hardware that maintains the current clock time. The program that contains the variable *timer* could be interrupted by the time-keeping hardware and the variable *timer* changed.

You should declare a data object **volatile** if it is a memory-mapped device register or a data object shared by separate processes, as would be the case with a multitasking operating environment.

const and volatile

You can use the two modifiers **const** and **volatile** with any other data types—for example, **char** and **float**—as well as with each other. The following definition

```
const volatile constant_timer;
```

specifies that the program does not intend to change the value in the variable *constant_timer*. However, the compiler is also instructed, because of the **volatile** modifier, to make no assumptions about the variable's value from one moment to the next. Therefore, the compiler first issues an error message for any line of source code that attempts to change the value of the variable *constant_timer*. Second, the compiler will not remove the variable *constant_timer* from inside loops, since an external process can also be updating the variable while the program is executing.

pascal, cdecl, near, far, AND huge MODIFIERS

The modifiers **pascal** and **cdecl** are used most frequently in advanced applications. Borland C++ allows you to write programs that can easily call other routines written in different languages. The opposite of this also holds true. For example, you can write a Pascal program that calls a C++ routine. When you mix languages in this way, you have to consider two very important issues: identifier names, and the way that parameters are passed.

When Borland C++ compiles your program, it places all of the program's global identifiers (functions and variables) into the resulting object code file for linking purposes. By default, the compiler saves those identifiers using the case in which they were defined (upper, lower, or mixed). Additionally, the compiler appends an underscore to the front of the identifier (you can turn this feature off with the -u option). Since Borland's C++ integrated linking is case sensitive by default, any external identifiers that you declare in your program are also assumed to be in the same form, with a preceding underscore and the same spelling and case as defined.

pascal

The Pascal language uses a different calling sequence than C and C++. Pascal (along with FORTRAN) passes function arguments from left to right and does not allow variable-length argument lists. In Pascal, the called function removes the arguments from the stack. (In C and C++, the invoking function does so when control returns from the invoked function.)

A C or C++ program can generate this calling sequence in one of two ways: It can use the compile-time switch -p, which makes the Pascal calling sequence the default for all enclosed calls and function definitions; it can also override the default C calling sequence explicitly by using the **pascal** keyword in the function definition.

As mentioned, when C generates a function call, by default it precedes the function name with an underscore and declares the function as external. It also preserves the case of the name. However, with the **pascal** keyword, the underscore is not used and the identifier (function or variable) is converted to all uppercase.

The following code segment demonstrates how to use the **pascal** keyword on a function (you can use the same keyword to ensure FORTRAN code compatibility):

```
int pascal myfunction(int value1, long value2, double value3)
{
      .
      .
      .
}
```

Of course, you can also give variables a Pascal convention, as shown here:

```
#define MAXELEMENTS 100

int pascal myfunction(int value1, long value2, double value3)
{
      .
      .
      .
}

int pascal mytable[MAXELEMENTS];

main()
{
   int a=5,result;
   long b=2.345;
   double c=7832.89901;

   result=myfunction(a,b,c);

   return(0);
}
```

In this example, **mytable** has been globally defined with the **pascal** modifier. Function **main** also shows how to make an external reference to a Pascal function type. Since both functions **main** and **myfunction** are in the same source file, the function **myfunction** is global to **main**.

cdecl

If the -p compile-time switch was used to compile your C or C++ program, all function and variable references were generated matching the Pascal calling convention. However, you will sometimes want to guarantee that certain identifiers in your program remain case sensitive and retain the initial underscore. This is most often the case for identifiers being used in another C file.

To maintain this C compatibility (preserving the case and the leading underscore), you can use the **cdecl** keyword. When you use the **cdecl** keyword in front of a function, it also affects how the parameters are passed.

Note: All C and C++ functions defined in the header files of Borland C++, for example *stdio.h,* are of type **cdecl**. This ensures that you can link with the library routines, even when you are compiling by using the -p option. The following example was compiled by using the -p option and shows how you would rewrite the previous example to maintain C compatibility:

```
#define MAXELEMENTS 100

int cdecl myfunction(int value1, long value2, double value3)
{
    .
    .
    .
}

int cdecl mytable[MAXELEMENTS];

main()
{
  int a=5,result;
  long b=2.345;
  double c=7832.89901;
  extern int cdecl myfunction();

  result=myfunction(a,b,c);
```

```
   return(0);
}
```

near, far, and huge

The three modifiers **near**, **far**, and **huge** affect the action of the indirection operator *. In other words, they modify pointer sizes to data objects. A **near** pointer is only 2 bytes long, a **far** pointer is 4 bytes long, and a **huge** pointer is also 4 bytes long. The difference between **far** and **huge** pointers deals with the form of the address (see Chapter 10, "Pointers").

DATA TYPE CONVERSIONS

In the programs so far, the variables and numbers used in any particular statement were all of the same type—for example, **int** or **float**. You can write statements that perform operations involving variables of different types. These operations are called *mixed mode* operations. Unlike some other programming languages, C and C++ perform automatic conversions from one type to another.

Data of different types are stored differently in memory. Suppose that the number 10 is being stored. Its representation will depend upon its type; that is, the pattern of 0's and 1's in memory will be different when 10 is stored as an **int** or when it is stored as a **float**.

Suppose that the following operation is executed,

```
float_result = float_value2 * int_value;
```

where both *float_result* and *float_value2* are of type **float**, and the variable *int_value* is of type **int**. The statement is therefore a mixed mode operation. When the statement is executed, the value of *int_value* will be converted into a floating-point number before the multiplication takes place. The compiler recognizes that a mixed mode operation is taking place. Therefore, it generates code to perform the following operations. The integer value assigned to *int_value* is read from memory. This value is then converted to the corresponding **float** value, which is then multiplied by the real value assigned to *float_value2*, and the resulting **float** value is assigned to *float_result*. In other words, the compiler performs the conversion automatically. Note that the value assigned to *int_value* is unchanged by this process and remains of type **int**.

There is a *hierarchy of conversions*, in that the object of lower priority is temporarily converted to the type of higher priority for the performance of the calculation. Here is the hierarchy of conversions, from highest to lowest priority:

double
float
long
int
short

For example, the type **double** has a higher priority than type **int**. When a type is converted to one that has more significant digits, the value of the number and its accuracy are unchanged.

Look at what happens when a conversion from type **float** to type **int** takes place. Suppose that the variables *int_value1* and *int_value2* have been defined to be of type **int**, while *float_value* and *float_result* have been defined to be of type **float**. Consider the following sequence of statements:

```
int_value1 = 3;
int_value2 = 4;
float_value = 7.0;
float_result = float_value + int_value1/int_value2;
```

The division of *int_value1/int_value2* is not a mixed mode operation; instead, it represents the division of two integers, and its result is zero since the fractional part, 0.75 in this case, is discarded when integer division is performed. Therefore, the value stored in *float_result* is 7.0.

What if *int_value2* had been defined to be of type **float**? In this case, *float_result* would have been assigned the floating-point value 7.75, since the division of *int_value1/int_value2* was a mixed mode operation. Under these circumstances, the value of *int_value1* is temporarily converted to the floating-point value 3.0, and the result of the division is 0.75. When added to *float_value*, the result is 7.75.

The type of the value to the left of the equal sign determines the type of the result of the operation. For example, suppose that *float_x* and *float_y* were declared to be of type **float** and *int_result* was declared to be of type **int**. Consider the following statements:

```
float_x = 7.0;
float_y = 2.0;
int_result = 4.0 + float_x/float_y
```

The result of the division *float_x/float_y* is 3.5; when this is added to 4.0, the floating-point value generated is 7.5. However, this value cannot be assigned to *int_result* because *int_result* is of type **int**. The number 7.5 is therefore converted into an integer. When this is done, the fractional part is truncated. The resulting whole number is converted from a floating-point representation to an integer representation, and the value assigned to *int_result* is the integer number 7.

Explicit Type Conversions Using the Cast Operator

You have seen that the C and C++ compilers automatically change the format of a variable in mixed mode operations using different types. However, under certain circumstances, type conversions would be desirable although automatic conversion is not performed. For those occasions, you must specifically designate that a change of type is to be made. These explicit specifications also clarify to other programmers the statements involved. The C language provides several procedures that allow you to indicate that type conversion must occur.

One of these procedures is called the *cast operator*. Whenever you want to change the format of a variable temporarily, you simply precede the variable's identifier with the type (in parentheses) that you want it converted to. For example, if *int_value1* and *int_value2* were defined as type **int**, and *float_value* and *float_result* were defined as type **float**, the following three statements would perform the same operation:

```
float_result = float_value + (float)int_value1/int_value2;
float_result = float_value + int_value1/(float)int_value2;
float_result = float_value + (float)int_value1/(float)int_value2;
```

All three statements would perform a **float** conversion and division of the variables *int_value1* and *int_value2*. Due to the usual rules of mixed mode arithmetic, if either variable is cast to type **float**, a **float** division occurs. The third statement explicitly highlights the operation to be performed.

STORAGE CLASSES

Borland C++ supports four storage class specifiers:

- **auto**

- **register**

- **static**

- **extern**

The storage class precedes the variable's declaration and instructs the compiler how the variable should be stored. Items declared with the **auto** or **register** specifier have local lifetimes. Items declared with the **static** or **extern** specifier have global lifetimes.

The four storage class specifiers affect the visibility of a variable or function, as well as its storage class. *Visibility* (sometimes defined as *scope*) refers to that portion of the source program in which the variable or function can be referenced by name. An item with a global lifetime exists throughout the execution of the source program.

The placement of a variable or a function declaration within a source file also affects storage class and visibility. Declarations outside all function definitions are said to appear at the *external* level. Declarations within function definitions appear at the *internal* level.

The exact meaning of each storage class specifier depends on whether the declaration appears at the external or internal level, and whether the item being declared is a variable or a function.

Variable Declarations at the External Level

Variable declarations at the external level may only use the **static** or **extern** storage classes. They are either definitions of variables or references to variables defined elsewhere. An external variable declaration that also initializes the variable (implicitly or explicitly) is a defining declaration:

```
static int int_value1 = 16; // explicit

static int int_value1;      // implicit 0 by default

int int_value2 = 20;
```

Once a variable is defined at the external level, it is visible throughout the rest of the source file in which it appears. The variable is not visible prior to its definition in the same source file. Also, the variable is not visible in other source files of the program, unless a referencing declaration makes it visible.

You can define a variable at the external level only once within a source file. If you give the **static** storage class specifier, you can define another variable with the same name and the **static** storage class specifier in a different source file. Since each **static** definition is visible only within its own source file, no conflict occurs.

The **extern** storage class specifier declares a reference to a variable defined elsewhere. You can use an **extern** declaration to make visible a definition in another source file, or to make a variable visible above its definition in the same source file. The variable is visible throughout the remainder of the source file in which the declared reference occurs.

For an **extern** reference to be valid, the variable it refers to must be defined once, and only once, at the external level. The definition can be in any of the source files that form the program. The following C++ program demonstrates the use of the **extern** keyword:

```
//
//      Source File A
//

#include <iostream.h>

void function_a(void);
void function_b(void);

extern int int_value;               // makes int_value visible
                                    // above its declaration
```

```
main()
{
  int_value++;                     // uses the above extern
                                   // reference
  cout << "\n" << int_value;       // prints 11
  function_a();

  return(0);
}

int int_value = 10;               // actual definition of
                                  // int_value

void function_a(void)
{
  int_value++;                    // references int_value
  cout << "\n" << int_value;      // prints 12
  function_b();
}

//
//      Source File B
//

#include <iostream.h>

extern int int_value;             // references int_value
                                  // declared in Source A

void function_b(void)
{
  int_value++;
  cout << "\n" << int_value;      // prints 13
}
```

Variable Declarations at the Internal Level

You can use any of the four storage class specifiers for variable declarations at the internal level (the default is **auto**). The **auto** storage class specifier declares a variable with a local lifetime. It is visible only in the block in which it is declared and can include initializers.

The **register** storage-class specifier tells the compiler to give the variable storage in a **register**, if possible. It speeds access time and reduces code size. It has the same visibility as the **auto** variable. If no registers are available when the compiler encounters a **register** declaration, the variable is given **auto** storage class and stored in memory.

A variable declared at the internal level with the **static** storage class specifier has a global lifetime but is visible only within the block in which it is declared. Unlike **auto** variables, **static** variables keep their values when the block is exited. You can initialize a **static** variable with a constant expression. It is initialized to 0 by default.

A variable declared with the **extern** storage class specifier is a reference to a variable with the same name defined at the external level in any of the source files of the program. The internal **extern** declaration is used to make the external level variable definition visible within the block. The next program segment demonstrates these concepts:

```
//
//      A simple C++ program illustrating the differences
//      between variables declared at the internal and
//      external levels.
//      Copyright (c) Chris H. Pappas and William H. Murray, 1990
//

#include <iostream.h>

void function_a(void);

int int_value1=1;

main()
{
  // references the int_value1 defined above
  extern int int_value1;

  // default initialization of 0, int_value2 only visible
  // in main()
  static int int_value2;

  // stored in a register (if available), initialized
  // to 0
  register int register_value = 0;

  // default auto storage class, int_value3 initialized
  // to 0
  int int_value3 = 0;

  // values printed are 1, 0, 0, 0:
  cout << int_value1 << "\n" << register_value << "\n";
  cout << int_value2 << "\n" << int_value3 << "\n";
  function_a();

  return(0);
}

void function_a(void)
{
```

```
// stores the address of the global variable int_value1
static int *pointer_to_int_value1= &int_value1;

// creates a new local variable int_value1 making the
// global int_value1 unreachable
int int_value1 = 32;

// new local variable int_value2
// only visible within function_a
static int int_value2 = 2;

int_value2 += 2;

// the values printed are 32, 4, and 1:
cout << int_value1 << "\n" << int_value2 << "\n";
cout << *pointer_to_int_value1;
}
```

Since *int_value1* is redefined in **function_a**, access to the global *int_value1* is denied. However, using a data pointer (see Chapter 10), the address of the global *int_value1* was used to print the value stored there.

Variable Scope Review

To review, there are four rules for variable visibility, also called *scope rules*. The four scopes for a variable are block, function, file, and program. A variable declared within a block or function is known only within the block or function. A variable declared external to a function is known within the file in which it appears, from the point of its appearance to the end of the file. A variable declared as **extern** in one source file and declared as **extern** in other files has program scope.

Function Declarations at the External and Internal Levels

When declaring a function at the external or internal level, you can use either the **static** or the **extern** storage class specifier. Unlike variables, functions always have a global lifetime. The visibility rules for functions are slightly different from the rules for variables.

Functions declared to be **static** are visible only within the source file in which they are defined. Functions in the same source file can call the **static** function, but functions in other source files cannot. Also, you can declare another **static** function with the same name in a different source file without conflict.

Functions declared as **extern** are visible throughout all source files that make up the program (unless you later redeclare such a function as **static**). Any function can call an **extern** function. Function declarations that omit the storage class specifier are **extern** by default.

OPERATORS

C has many operators not found in other languages. These include bitwise operators, increment and decrement operators, conditional operators, the comma operator, and assignment and compound assignment operators.

Bitwise Operators

Bitwise operators treat variables as combinations of bits rather than as numbers. They are useful for accessing the individual bits in memory, such as the screen memory for a graphics display. Bitwise operators can only operate on integral data types, not on floating-point numbers. Three bitwise operators act just like the logical operators, but they act on each bit in an integer. These are the AND &, OR |, and XOR ^. An additional operator is the one's complement ~, which simply inverts each bit.

AND

The logical AND operation compares two bits. If both bits are a 1, the result is a 1. Note that this is different from binary addition, where the comparison of two 1 bits results in a sum flag set to 0 and the carry flag set to 1.

	Logical AND	
Bit 0	Bit 1	Result
0	0	0
0	1	0
1	0	0
1	1	1

Very often, the AND operation is used to select out, or *mask*, certain bit positions.

OR

The logical OR operation compares two bits and generates a 1 result if either or both bits are a 1. The OR operation is useful for setting specified bit positions.

Logical OR

Bit 0	Bit 1	Result
0	0	0
0	1	1
1	0	1
1	1	1

XOR

The exclusive OR operation (XOR) compares two bits and returns a result of 1 only when the two bits are complementary. This logical operation can be useful when you need to complement specified bit positions, as with computer graphics applications.

Exclusive OR (XOR)

Bit 0	Bit 1	Result
0	0	0
0	1	1
1	0	1
1	1	0

The following example uses these operators with the hexadecimal and octal representation of constants. The bit values are shown for comparison.

```
0xF1       &   0x35        yields 0x31        (hexadecimal)
0361       &   0065        yields 061         (octal)
11110011   &   00110101    yields 00110001    (bitwise)

0xF1       |   0x35        yields 0xF5        (hexadecimal)
0361       |   0065        yields 0365        (octal)
11110011   |   00110101    yields 11110111    (bitwise)
```

```
0xF1      ^   0x35         yields 0xC4       (hexadecimal)
0361      ^   0065         yields 0304       (octal)
11110011  ^   00110101     yields 00000000 11000110 (bitwise)

~0xF1                      yields 0xFF0E     (hexadecimal)
~0361                      yields 7777416    (octal)
~11110011                 yields 11111111 00001100 (bitwise)
```

Left Shift and Right Shift

C incorporates two shift operators: the left shift, <<, and the right shift, >>. The left shift moves the bits to the left and sets the rightmost bit (least significant bit) to 0. The leftmost bit (most significant bit) shifted out is discarded.

With unsigned **int** numbers, shifting the number one position to the left and filling the LSB with a 0 will double the number's value. The following C++ code demonstrates how you would code this:

```
unsigned int value1 = 65;
value1 <<= 1;
cout << value1;
```

In memory, examining the lower byte, you would see the following bit changes performed:

```
<< 0100 0001 (65 decimal)
_____

   1000 0010 (130 decimal)
```

The right shift operator, >>, moves bits to the right. The lower order bits shifted out are discarded. Halving an unsigned **int** number is as simple as shifting the bits one position to the right, filling the MSB position with a 0. A C-coded example would look similar to the preceding example, except for the compound operator assignment statement (discussed later in the chapter) and the output statement:

```
unsigned int value1 = 10;
value1 >>= 1;
printf("%d",value1);
```

Examining just the lower byte of the variable *value1* would reveal the following bit changes:

>> 0000 1010 (10 decimal)
_____

0000 0101 (5 decimal)

Increment and Decrement

Adding one to or subtracting one from a number is so common in programs that C has a special set of operators to do this. They are the *increment* **++** and *decrement* − − operators. You must place the two characters next to each other without any whitespace. You can only apply them to variables, not to constants. Instead of coding

```
value1 = value1 + 1;
```

you can write

```
value1++;
```

or

```
++value1;
```

When these two operators are the sole operators in an expression, you don't have to worry about the different syntax. A *for* loop very often uses this type of increment for the loop control variable:

```
total = 0;
for(i = 1; i <= 10; i++)
  total = total + i;
```

A decrement loop would be coded as:

```
total = 0;
for(i = 10; i >= 1; i--)
  total = sum + i;
```

If you use these operators in complex expressions, you have to consider when the increment or decrement actually takes place. The postfix increment, for example i++, uses the value of the variable in the expression first, and then increments its value. However, the prefix increment, for example ++i, increments the value of the variable first, and then uses the value in the expression. Assume the following data declarations:

```
int i=3,j,k=0;
```

See if you can determine what happens in each of the following statements. For simplicity, assume the original initialized values of the variables for each statement:

```
k = ++i;            // i = 4, k = 4
k = i++;            // i = 4, k = 3
k = --i;            // i = 2, k = 2
k = i--;            // i = 2, k = 3
i = j = k--;        // i = 0, j = 0, k = -1
```

While the subtleties of these two operations may currently elude you, they are included in the C language because of definite situations that could not be eloquently handled in any other way. In Chapter 10 you will look at a program that uses array indices that need to be manipulated using the initially confusing prefix syntax.

Arithmetic Operators

The C language incorporates the standard set of arithmetic operators for addition +, subtraction −, multiplication *, division /, and modulus %. The first four operators need no explanation. However, the following example will help you understand the modulus operator:

```
int a=3,b=8,c=0,d;

d = b % a;          // returns 2
d = a % b;          // returns 3

d = b % c;          // returns an error message
```

The modulus operator returns the remainder of integer division. The last assignment statement attempts to divide 8 by 0, resulting in an error message.

Assignment Operator

The assignment operator in C is unlike the assignment statement in other languages. It is performed by an assignment operator, rather than an assignment statement. As with other C operators, the result of an assignment operator is a value that is assigned. An expression with an assignment operator can be used in a large expression such as:

```
value1 = 8 * (value2 = 5);
```

Here, *value2* is first assigned the value 5. This is multiplied by 8, with *value1* receiving a final value of 40.

If you overuse this feature, you can wind up with unmanageable expressions. There are two places in which this feature is normally applied. First, you can use it to set several variables to a particular value, as in:

```
value1 = value2 = value3 = 0;
```

The second use is most often seen in the condition of a *while* loop, for example:

```
while ((c = getchar()) != EOF) {
    .
    .
    .
}
```

This assigns the value that **getchar** returned to *c* and then tests the value against **EOF**. If it is **EOF**, the loop is not executed. The parentheses are necessary because the assignment operator has a lower precedence than the nonequality operator. Otherwise, the line would be interpreted as:

```
c = (getchar() != EOF)
```

The variable *c* would be assigned a value of 1 (TRUE) each time **getchar** returned **EOF**.

Compound Assignment Operators

The C language also incorporates an enhancement to the assignment state-ment used by other languages. This additional set of assignment operators allows for a more concise way of expressing certain computations. The following code segment shows the standard assignment syntax applicable in many high-level languages:

```
result = result + increment;
depth = depth - one_fathom;
cost = cost * 1.07;
square_feet = square_feet / 9;
```

The C language compound assignment statements would look like this:

```
result += increment;
depth -= one_fathom;
cost *= 1.07;
square_feet /= 9;
```

Looking closely at these two code segments, you will quickly see the required syntax. If you use a C compound assignment operator, you must remove the redundant variable reference from the right-hand side of the assignment operator and place the operation to be performed immediately before the =.

Relational and Logical Operators

All relational operators are used to establish a relationship between the values of the operands. They always produce a value of 1 if the relationship evaluates to TRUE or a value of 0 if the relationship evaluates to FALSE. Table 6-6 lists the C and C++ relational operators.

The logical operators AND &&, OR ||, and NOT ! produce a TRUE (1) or FALSE (0) based on the logical relationship of their arguments. The simplest way to remember how the logical AND && works is to say that an ANDed expression will only return a TRUE (1) when both arguments are TRUE (1). The logical OR || operation in turn will only return a FALSE (0) when both arguments are FALSE (0). The logical NOT ! simply inverts the value. Table 6-7 lists the C and C++ logical operators.

Table 6-6.   C and C++ Relational Operators

Operator	Meaning
= =	Equal (not assignment)
!=	Not equal
>	Greater than
<	Less than
>=	Greater than or equal
<=	Less than or equal

Have some fun with the following C program as you test the various combinations of relational and logical operators. See if you can predict the results.

```
/*
 *    A C program demonstrating some of the subtleties of logical
 *    and relational operators.
 *    Copyright (c) Chris H. Pappas and William H. Murray, 1990
 */

#include <stdio.h>

main()
{
  float value1, value2;

  printf("\nPlease enter a value1: " );
  scanf("%f",&value1);
  printf("Please enter a value2: ");
  scanf("%f",&value2);
  printf("\n");
  printf("  value1  > value2 is %d\n", (value1 > value2));
  printf("  value1  < value2 is %d\n", (value1 < value2));
  printf("  value1 >= value2 is %d\n",(value1 >= value2));
  printf("  value1 <= value2 is %d\n",(value1 <= value2));
  printf("  value1 == value2 is %d\n",(value1 == value2));
  printf("  value1 != value2 is %d\n",(value1 != value2));
  printf("  value1 && value2 is %d\n",(value1 && value2));
  printf("  value1 || value2 is %d\n",(value1 || value2));

  return(0);
}
```

Table 6-7.   C and C++ Logical Operators

&&	AND
||	OR
!	NOT

You may be surprised at the results obtained for some of the logical comparisons. Remember, however, a strict comparison occurs for both data types **float** and **double** when values of these types are compared with zero—a number that is very slightly different from another number is still not equal. Also, a number that is just slightly above or below zero is still TRUE (1).

Here is the C++ equivalent of the preceding program:

```
//
//    A C++ program demonstrating some of the subtleties of logical
//    and relational operators.
//    Copyright (c) Chris H. Pappas and William H. Murray, 1990
//

#include <iostream.h>

main()
{
  float value1, value2;

  cout << "\nPlease enter a value1: ";
  cin >> value1;
  cout << "Please enter a value2: ";
  cin >> value2;
  cout << "\n";
  cout << "  value1  > value2 is " << (value1  > value2) << "\n";
  cout << "  value1  < value2 is " << (value1  < value2) << "\n";
  cout << "  value1 >= value2 is " << (value1 >= value2) << "\n";
  cout << "  value1 <= value2 is " << (value1 <= value2) << "\n";
  cout << "  value1 == value2 is " << (value1 == value2) << "\n";
  cout << "  value1 != value2 is " << (value1 != value2) << "\n";
  cout << "  value1 && value2 is " << (value1 && value2) << "\n";
  cout << "  value1 || value2 is " << (value1 || value2) << "\n";

  return(0);
}
```

Conditional Operator

You can use the *conditional operator* in normal coding, but its main use is creating macros (see Chapter 15, "Power Programming: Tapping Important C and C++ Libraries"). The operator has the syntax:

condition ? *true-expression* : *false-expression*

If the condition is TRUE, the value of the conditional expression is *true-expression*. Otherwise, it is the value of *false-expression*. For example, you could rewrite the following statement

```
if('A' <= c && c <= 'Z')
  printf("%c",'a' + c - 'A');
else
  printf("%c",c);
```

using the conditional operator:

```
printf("%c",('A' <= c && c <= 'Z') ? ('a' + c - 'A') : c );
```

Both statements will make certain that the character printed, *c*, is always lowercase.

Comma Operator

The *comma operator* evaluates two expressions where the syntax allows only one. The value of the comma operator is the value of the right-hand expression. The format for the expression is

left-expression, right-expression

The comma operator commonly appears in a *for* loop, where more than one variable is being iterated. For example:

```
for(min=0,max=length-1; min < max; min++,max--) {
    .
    .
    .
}
```

UNDERSTANDING OPERATOR PRECEDENCE LEVELS

The order of evaluation of an expression in C is determined by the compiler. This normally does not alter the value of the expression, unless you have written one with side effects. *Side effects* are those operations that change the value of a variable while yielding a value that is used in the expression, as seen with the increment and decrement operators. The other operators that have side effects are the assignment and compound assignment. Calls to functions that change values of external variables also are subject to side effects. For example:

```
value1 = 3;
result = (value1 = 4) + value1;
```

This could be evaluated in one of two ways: *value1* is assigned 4, and *result* is assigned 8 (4+4); value of 3 is retrieved from *value1*, and 4 is then assigned to *value1*, with *result* being assigned a 7.

There are, however, four operators for which the order of evaluation is guaranteed to be left-to-right: logical AND (&&), logical OR (||), the comma operator, and the conditional operator. Because of this default order of evaluation, you can specify a typical test as

```
while((c=getchar() != EOF) && (c!='\n'))
```

and know that the second part of the logical AND (&&) is performed after the character value is assigned to *c*.

Table 6-8 lists all of the C and C++ operators from highest to lowest precedence and describes how each operator is associated (left-to-right or right-to-left). All operators between lines have the same precedence level.

Table 6-8.   Operator Precedence Levels

Description	Operator	Associates from	Precedence
Function expr	( )	left	Highest
Array expr	[]	left	
Struct indirection	->	left	
Struct member	.	left	
Incr/decr	++ −−	right	
One's complement	~	right	
Unary NOT	!	right	
Address	&	right	
Dereference	*	right	
Cast	(type)	right	
Unary minus	−	right	
Size in bytes	sizeof	right	
Multiplication	*	left	
Division	/	left	
Remainder	%	left	
Addition	+	left	
Subtraction	−	left	
Shift left	<<	left	
Shift right	>>	left	
Less than	<	left	
Less than or equal	<=	left	
Greater than	>	left	
Greater than or equal	>=	left	
Equal	==	left	
Not equal	!=	left	
Bitwise AND	&	left	
Bitwise XOR	^	left	
Bitwise OR	|	left	
Logical AND	&&	left	
Logical OR	||	left	
Conditional	? :	right	
Assignment	= %= += −= *= /= >>= <<= &= ^= |=	right	
Comma	,	left	Lowest

STANDARD C AND C++ LIBRARIES

Certain calculations are routinely performed in many programs and are written by almost all programmers. Taking the square root of a number is such a calculation. Mathematical procedures for calculating square roots use combinations of the basic arithmetic operations of addition, subtraction, multiplication, and division.

It would be a waste of effort if every programmer had to design and code a routine to calculate the square root and then to incorporate that routine into the program. C and C++ resolve these difficulties by providing the programmer with *libraries of functions* that perform particular common calculations. With the libraries, you need only a single statement to invoke such a function.

This section will discuss functions that are commonly provided with the C and C++ compiler. These library functions are usually not provided in source form but in compiled form. When linking is performed, the code for the library functions is combined with the compiled programmer's code to form the complete program.

Library functions not only perform mathematical operations, but also handle many other common operations. For example, there are library functions that deal with reading and writing disk files, managing memory, input/output, and a variety of other operations. Library functions are not part of standard C or C++, but virtually every system provides certain library functions.

Most library functions are designed to use information contained in particular files that are supplied with the system. These files, therefore, must be included when the library functions are used. These files are also provided with the C++ compiler. They usually have the extension *.h* and are called header files. Table 6-9 lists the header files supplied with your compiler.

Table 6-9.   Borland C++ Include Files

Language	Header File Name	Brief Description
	alloc.h	Defines memory management functions (allocation, deallocation, and so on).
ANSI C	assert.h	Declares the **assert** debugging macro.

Table 6-9.   Borland C++ Include Files (*continued*)

Language	Header File Name	Brief Description
C++	bcd.h	Defines the C++ class **bcd** and the overloaded operators for **bcd** and **bcd** math functions.
	bios.h	Defines various functions used in calling IBM-PC ROM BIOS routines.
C++	complex.h	Defines the C++ complex math functions.
	conio.h	Defines various functions used in calling the DOS console I/O routines.
ANSI C	ctype.h	Contains information used by the character classification and character conversion macros (such as **isalpha** and **toascll**).
	dir.h	Contains structures, macros, and functions for working with directories and path names.
	dos.h	Declares various constants and gives declarations needed for DOS and 8086-specific calls.
ANSI C	errno.h	Declares constant mnemonics for the error codes.
	fcntl.h	Declares symbolic constants used in connection with the library routine **open**.
ANSI C	float.h	Contains parameters for floating-point routines.
C++	fstream.h	Defines the C++ stream classes that support file input and output.
C++	generic.h	Contains macros for generic class declarations.
C++	graphics.h	Defines prototypes for the graphics functions.
	io.h	Contains structures and declarations for low-level input/output routines.
C++	iomanip.h	Defines the C++ streams I/O manipulators and contains macros for creating parameterized manipulators.
C++	iostream.h	Defines the basic C++ (version 2.0) streams (I/O) routines.
ANSI C	limits.h	Contains environmental parameters, information about compile-time limitations, and ranges of integral quantities.
ANSI C	locale.h	Defines functions that provide country- and language-specific information.
ANSI C	math.h	Defines prototypes for the math functions; also defines the macro HUGEVAL and declares the exception structure used by the **matherr** routine.

Table 6-9.   Borland C++ Include Files *(continued)*

Language	Header File Name	Brief Description
	mem.h	Defines the memory-manipulation functions. (Many are defined in string.h.)
	process.h	Contains structures and declarations for the **spawn...** and **exec...** functions.
ANSI C	setjmp.h	Declares a type **jmp_buf** used by the **longjmp** and **setjmp** functions and declares the routines longjmp and **setjmp**.
	share.h	Declares parameters used in functions that make use of file-sharing.
ANSI C	signal.h	Declares constants and declarations for use by the **signal** and **raise** functions.
ANSI C	stdarg.h	Declares macros used for reading the argument list in functions declared to accept a variable number of arguments (such as **vscanf**, **vprintf**, and so on).
ANSI C	stddef.h	Declares several common data types and macros.
ANSI C	stdio.h	Declares types and macros needed for the Standard I/O Package defined in Kernighan and Ritchie and extended under UNIX System V. Declares the standard I/O predefined streams **stdin, stdout, stdprn,** and **stderr,** and declares stream-level I/O routines.
C++	stdiostr.h	Defines the C++ stream classes for use with **stdio** file structures.
ANSI C	stdlib.h	Defines several commonly used routines: conversion routines, search/sort routines, and many others.
C++	stream.h	Defines the C++ (version 1.2) streams (I/O) routines.
ANSI C	string.h	Defines several string-manipulation and memory-manipulation routines.
C++	strstrea.h	Defines the C++ stream classes for use with byte arrays in memory.
	sys\stat.h	Declares symbolic constants used for opening and creating files.
	sys\timeb.h	Defines the function **ftime** and the structure *timeb* that **ftime** returns.
	sys\types.h	Defines the type **time_t** used with time functions.

Table 6-9.   Borland C++ Include Files (*continued*)

Language	Header File Name	Brief Description
ANSI C	time.h	Declares a structure filled in by the time-conversion routines **asctime**, **localtime**, and **gmtime**, and a type used by the routines **ctime**, **difftime**, **gmtime**, **localtime**, and **stime**; also provides prototypes for these routines.
	values.h	Declares important constants, including machine dependencies; provided for UNIX System V compatibility.

In general, different header files are required by different library functions. The required header files for a function will be listed in the description for that function. For example, the **sqrt** function needs the declarations found in the *math.h* header file. Your Borland C++ reference manual lists all of the library functions and their associated header files.

The following list highlights the library categories provided with your compiler.

- Classification routines

- Conversion routines

- Directory control routines

- Diagnostic routines

- Graphics routines

- Input/output routines

- Interface routines (DOS, 8086, BIOS)

- Manipulation routines

- Math routines

- Memory allocation routines

- Process control routines

- Standard routines

- Text window display routines

- Time and date routines

Check your reference manual for a detailed explanation of the individual functions provided by each library.

7

CONTROL

To begin writing simple C programs, you need a few more tools. This chapter will discuss C's control statements. Many of these control statements are similar to other high-level language controls, such as *if, if-else,* and *switch* statements and *for, while,* and *do-while* loops. However, there are several new control statements unique to C, such as the **?** conditional, **break**, and **continue** statements.

CONDITIONAL STATEMENTS

The C language supports four basic conditional statements: the *if*, the *if-else*, the conditional *?*, and the *switch*. Most of the conditional statements can be used to selectively execute either a single line of code or multiple lines of related code (called a *block*). Whenever a conditional statement is associated with only one line of executable code, braces **{ }** are *not* required around the executable statement. However, if the conditional statement is associated with multiple executable statements, braces are required to connect the block of executable statements with the conditional test.

if Statements

The *if* statement is used to execute a segment of code conditionally. The simplest form of the *if* statement is

if (*expression*)

   action;

Notice that the expression must be enclosed in parentheses. To execute an *if* statement, the expression must be evaluated to either TRUE (any non-zero value) or FALSE (0). If *expression* is TRUE, the *action* will be performed and execution will continue on to the next statement following the *action*. However, if *expression* evaluates to FALSE, the *action* will *not* be executed, and the statement following *action* will be executed. For example, the following code segment will print the message "Enjoy your health!" whenever the variable *body_temp* equals 98.6:

```
if(body_temp == 98.6)
  printf("Enjoy your health!");
```

The syntax for an *if* statement associated with a block of executable statements looks like this:

if (*expression*) {

   action;

   action;

   action;

   action;

}

The syntax requires that all of the associated statements be enclosed in a pair of braces { } and that each statement within the block end with a semicolon ;. Here is an example compound *if* statement:

```
/*
*     A C program demonstrating a compound if statement.
*     Copyright (c) Chris H. Pappas and William H. Murray, 1990
*/

#include <stdio.h>
```

```
main()
{
  float trade_in_worth,new_car_cost,bank_loan,
        grandma_good_for,sons_motor_bike_worth,
        wifes_wedding_ring;

  printf("Ok, enter your dream car's cost: ");
  scanf("%f",&new_car_cost);

  trade_in_worth = 3000;
  bank_loan = new_car_cost - trade_in_worth;
  if(new_car_cost > 15000) {
    grandma_good_for = 2000;
    sons_motor_bike_worth = 1500;
    wifes_wedding_ring = 2500;
    bank_loan = new_car_cost - (trade_in_worth +
                                grandma_good_for +
                                sons_motor_bike_worth +
                                wifes_wedding_ring);
  }

  printf("Help, I need $%8.2f dollars!",bank_loan);

  return(0);
}
```

In this example, if the *new_car_cost* is more than $15,000, the new car buyer will have to beg, borrow, and hock everything that he or she can to purchase that new vehicle. Regardless of whether the *if* block was entered, the loan amount needed is printed.

if-else Statements

The *if-else* statement allows a program to take two separate actions based on the validity of a particular expression. The simplest syntax for an *if-else* statement looks like this:

if (*expression*)

   action1;

else

   action2;

In this case, if *expression* evaluates to TRUE, *action1* will be taken. Otherwise, when *expression* evaluates to FALSE, *action2* will be executed. A coded example looks like this:

```
if(mouse_move == LEFT)
  xposition = xposition - a_pixel;
else
  xposition = xposition + a_pixel;
```

This example increments or decrements the mouse's horizontal coordinate location based on the current contents of the variable *mouse_move*.

Of course, either *action1, action2,* or both could be compound statements, or blocks, requiring braces. The syntax for these three combinations is straightforward:

if (*expression*) {	if (*expression*)	if (*expression*) {
action1a;	*action1;*	*action1a;*
action1b;	else {	*action1b;*
action1c;	*action2a;*	*action1c;*
}	*action2b;*	}
else	*action2c;*	else {
action2;	}	*action2a;*
		action2b;
		action2c;
		}

Remember, whenever a block *action* is being taken, you don't follow the closing brace with a semicolon.

The following C program uses an *if-else* statement; the *if* part is a compound block:

```
/*
 *    A C program demonstrating the use of an if-else statement.
 *    Copyright (c) Chris H. Pappas and William H. Murray, 1990
 */

#include <stdio.h>

main()
{
```

```
char c;
int how_many,i,more_input;

more_input=1;

while(more_input == 1) {
  printf("Please enter the product name: ");
  if(scanf("%c",&c) != EOF) {
    while(c != '\n') {
      printf("%c",c);
      scanf("%c",&c);
    }
    printf("s purchased? ");
    scanf("%d",&how_many);
    scanf("%c",&c);
    for(i = 1;i <= how_many; i++)
      printf("*");
    printf("\n");
  }
  else
    more_input=0;
}
return(0);
}
```

The program prompts the user for a product name. While the user hasn't entered a ^Z (EOF), the program inputs the product name character by character, echoing the information to the next line. The "s purchased" string is appended to the product, requesting the number of items sold. Finally, a *for* loop prints the appropriate number of *s. Had the user entered a ^Z, the *if* portion of the *if-else* statement would have been ignored and program execution would have picked up with the *else* setting the *more_input* flag to 0, thereby terminating the program.

Nested *if-else*s

When nesting *if* statements, make sure that you know which *else action* will be matched up with which *if*. See if you can determine what will happen in this example:

```
if(out_side_temp < 50)
if(out_side_temp < 30) printf("Wear the down jacket!");
else printf("Parka will do.");
```

The listing is purposely misaligned so you have no visual clues about which statement goes with which *if*. If *out_side_temp* is 55, does the

"Parka will do." message get printed? The answer is no. In this example, the *else action* is associated with the second *if expression*.

To simplify debugging under such circumstances, the C++ compiler has been written to associate each *else* with the closest *if* that does not already have an associated *else*.

Of course, proper indentation will always help clarify the situation:

```
if(out_side_temp < 50)
  if(out_side_temp < 30) printf("Wear the down jacket!");
  else printf("Parka will do.");
```

The same logic can also be represented by this listing:

```
if(out_side_temp < 50)
  if(out_side_temp < 30)
    printf("Wear the down jacket!");
  else
    printf("Parka will do.");
```

Each application you write will benefit most by one of the preceding two styles, as long as you are consistent throughout the source code.

See if you can figure out this example:

```
if(test1_expression)
  if(test2_expression)
    test2_action;
else
  test1_false_action;
```

This looks like just another example of what has been discussed. However, what if you wanted *test1_false_action* to be associated with *test1* rather than *test2*? The examples so far have all associated the *else action* with the second or closest *if*. They're indented to work the way you are logically thinking (as was the previous example); unfortunately, the compiler disregards indentation.

To correct this situation, you need to use braces:

```
if(test1_expression) {
  if(test2_expression)
    test2_action;
  }
else
  test1_false_action;
```

You solve the problem by making *test2_expression* and its associated *test2_action* a block associated with a TRUE evaluation of the *test1_expression*. This makes it clear that *test1_false_action* will be associated with the *else* clause of *test1_expression*.

if-else-if Statements

The *if-else-if* statement is often used to perform multiple successive comparisons. Its general form looks like this:

if(*expression1*)

   action1;

else if(*expression2*)

   action2;

else if(*expression3*)

   action3;

Of course, each *action* could be a compound block requiring its own set of braces (with the closing brace not followed by a semicolon). This type of logical control flow evaluates each expression until it finds one that is TRUE. When this occurs, all remaining test conditions are bypassed. In the previous example, no action would be taken if none of the expressions evaluated to TRUE.

See if you can guess the result of this next example.

if (*expression1*)

   action1;

else if(*expression2*)

   action2;

else if(*expression3*)

   action3;

else

   default_action;

Unlike the previous example, this *if-else-if* statement will always perform some *action*. If none of the *if(expression)*s evaluates to TRUE, the *else default_action* will be executed. For example, the following program checks the value assigned to *conversion* to decide which type of conversion to perform. If the requested conversion is not one of the ones provided, the code segment prints an appropriate message.

```
if(conversion == YARDS)
   measurement = length / 3;
else if(conversion == INCHES)
   measurement = length * 12;
else if(conversion == CENTIMETERS)
   measurement = length * 12 * 2.54;
else if(conversion == METERS)
   measurement = (length * 12 * 2.54)/100;
else
   printf("No conversion required");
```

The ? Conditional Statement

The conditional statement ? provides a quick way to write a test condition. Associated *actions* are performed depending on whether the *expression* evaluates to TRUE or FALSE. You can use the ? operator to replace an equivalent *if-else* statement. The syntax for a conditional statement looks like this:

expression ? action1 : action2;

The ? operator is also sometimes referred to as the *ternary operator* because it requires three operands. The next two listings demonstrate how to rewrite an *if-else* statement using the conditional operator:

```
if(test)
   x = y;
else
   x = y * y;
```

Here is the same statement rewritten with the conditional operator:

```
x = test ? y : y * y;
```

The following C++ program uses the ? operator to calculate the sum or the difference of two integer values:

```
//
//     A C++ program demonstrating the use of the conditional?.
//     Copyright (c) Chris H. Pappas and William H. Murray, 1990
//

#include <iostream.h>

main()
{
  char ch;
  int answer,value1,value2;

  cout << "Please enter two integer values.\n";
  cin >> value1 >> value2;
  cout << "\nEnter '+' to get the sum, anything else " \
    "for subtraction: ";
  cin >> ch;
  answer = (ch == '+') ? value1 + value2 : value1 - value2;
  cout << "\n\nThe result is: " << answer;

  return(0);
}
```

The program uses the conditional assignment. The user enters two integers and a character. If the character is a +, the *answer* is assigned the sum of *value1* and *value2*. However, if the character is not a +, *value2* is subtracted from *value1*.

switch Statements

You will often want to test a variable or an expression against several values. You could use nested *if-else-if* statements to do this, or you could use a *switch* statement. Be very careful. Unlike many other high-level language selection statements, the C *switch* statement has a few peculiarities. The syntax for a *switch* statement looks like this:

switch (*integral expression*) {

    case *constant1*:

        statements1;

        break;

    case *constant2*:

        statements2;

        break;

        .

        .

        .

case *constantn*:

statementsn;

break;

default: *statements;*

}

Pay particular attention to the **break** statement. If this example had been coded in Pascal and *constant1* equaled the *integral expression, statements1* would have been executed, with program execution picking up with the next statement at the end of the *switch* statement (below the closing brace).

In C, the situation is quite different. If the **break** statement had been removed from *constant1's* code segment, a similar match used in the previous paragraph would have left *statements2* the next statement to be executed. The **break** statement causes the remaining portion of the *switch* statement to be skipped.

The following *if-else-if* code segment

```
if(x == 4)
  y = 7;
else if(x == 5)
  y = 9;
else if(x == 9)
  y = 14;
else
  y = 22;
```

can be rewritten using a *switch* statement:

```
switch(x) {
  case   4:
    y = 7;
    break;
  case   5:
    y = 9;
    break;
  case   9:
    y = 14;
    break;
  default:
    y = 22;
}
```

In this example, the value of *x* is consecutively compared to each *case* value looking for a match. When one is found, *y* is assigned the appropriate value and then the **break** statement is executed, skipping over the remainder of the *switch* statements. However, if no match is found, the *default* assignment is performed (y = 22). Since this is the last option in the *switch* statement, there is no need to include a **break**. A *switch default* is optional.

Proper placement of the **break** statement within a *switch* statement can be very useful. Look at the following example:

```
/*
 *    A C program demonstrating the drop-through capabilities
 *    of the switch statement.
 *    Copyright (c) Chris H. Pappas and William H. Murray, 1990
 */

main()
{
  char letter='z';
  int vowel_count=0,constant_count=0;

  switch(letter) {
    case 'a':
    case 'A':
    case 'e':
    case 'E':
    case 'i':
    case 'I':
    case 'o':
    case 'O':
    case 'u':
    case 'U': vowel_count++;
              break;
    default : constant_count++;
  }
  return(0);
}
```

The preceding program illustrates two characteristics of the *switch* statement: how to enumerate several test values that all execute the same code section, and the drop-through characteristic.

Some other high-level languages have their own form of selection that allows for several test values, all producing the same result, to be included on the same selection line. In contrast, C requires a separate *case* for each. In the preceding example, the same effect has been created by not inserting a **break** statement until all possible vowels have been checked. Should *letter* contain a consonant, all of the vowel *case* tests will be checked and skipped until the *default* statement is reached.

The next C program uses a *switch* statement to invoke the appropriate function:

```
/*
 *      A C program demonstrating the switch statement
 *      Copyright (c) Chris H. Pappas and William H. Murray, 1990
 */

#include <stdio.h>

#define QUIT 0
#define BLANK ' '

double fadd(float x,float y);
double fsub(float x,float y);
double fmul(float x,float y);
double fdiv(float x,float y);

main()
{
  float x,y;
  char blank,operator = BLANK;

  while (operator != QUIT) {
    printf("\nPlease enter an expression (a (operator) b): ");
    scanf("%f%c%c%f", &x, &blank, &operator, &y);

    switch (operator) {
      case '+': printf("answer = %4.2f\n", fadd(x,y));
                break;
      case '-': printf("answer = %4.2f\n", fsub(x,y));
                break;
      case '*': printf("answer = %4.2f\n", fmul(x,y));
                break;
      case '/': printf("answer = %4.2f\n", fdiv(x,y));
                break;
      case 'x': operator = QUIT;
                break;
      default : printf("\nOperator not implemented");
    }
  }
  return(0);
}

double fadd(float x,float y)
{
  return(x + y);
}

double fsub(float x,float y)
{
  return(x - y);
}

double fmul(float x,float y)
{
  return(x * y);
}

double fdiv(float x,float y)
```

```
{
  return(x / y);
}
```

While the use of functions in this example is a bit advanced (functions are discussed in the next chapter), the use of the *switch* statement is very effective. After the user has entered an expression such as 10 + 10, or 23 * 15, the *operator* is compared in the body of the *switch* statement to determine which function to invoke. Of particular interest are the last set of statements, where the *operator* equals **x**, and the *default* statement.

If the user enters an expression with an **x** operator, the *operator* variable is assigned a QUITing value and the **break** statement is executed, skipping over the *default* **printf** statement. However, if the user enters an unrecognized operator, for example **%**, only the *default* statement is executed, printing the message that the *operator* has not been implemented.

The following C++ program illustrates the similarity in syntax between a C *switch* statement and its C++ counterpart:

```
//
//    A C++ program using a switch statement to print a yearly
//    calendar.
//    Copyright (c) Chris H. Pappas and William H. Murray, 1990
//

#include <iostream.h>

main()
{
  int jan_1_start_day,num_days_per_month,
      month,date,leap_year_flag;

  cout << "Please enter January 1's starting day;\n";
  cout << "\nA 0 indicates January 1 is on a Monday,";
  cout << "\nA 1 indicates January 1 is on a Tuesday, etc: ";
  cin >> jan_1_start_day;
  cout << "\nEnter the year you want the calendar generated: ";
  cin >> leap_year_flag;
  cout << "\n\n The calendar for the year " << leap_year_flag;

  leap_year_flag=leap_year_flag % 4;
  cout.width(20);

  for (month = 1;month <= 12;month++) {
    switch(month) {
    case 1:
      cout << "\n\n\n" << " January" << "\n";
      num_days_per_month = 31;
      break;
    case 2:
      cout << "\n\n\n" << " February" "\n";
```

```
      num_days_per_month = leap_year_flag ? 28 : 29;
      break;
   case 3:
      cout << "\n\n\n" << "  March " << "\n";
      num_days_per_month = 31;
      break;
   case 4:
      cout << "\n\n\n" << "  April " << "\n";
      num_days_per_month = 30;
      break;
   case 5:
      cout << "\n\n\n" << "   May   " << "\n";
      num_days_per_month = 31;
      break;
   case 6:
      cout << "\n\n\n" << "  June   " << "\n";
      num_days_per_month = 30;
      break;
   case 7:
      cout << "\n\n\n" << "  July   " << "\n";
      num_days_per_month = 31;
      break;
   case 8:
      cout << "\n\n\n" << " August " << "\n";
      num_days_per_month = 31;
      break;
   case 9:
      cout << "\n\n\n" << "September" << "\n";
      num_days_per_month = 30;
      break;
   case 10:
      cout << "\n\n\n" << " October " << "\n";
      num_days_per_month = 31;
      break;
   case 11:
      cout << "\n\n\n" << "November " << "\n";
      num_days_per_month = 30;
      break;
   case 12:
      cout << "\n\n\n" << "December " << "\n";
      num_days_per_month = 31;
      break;
   }

cout.width(0);

cout << "\nSun  Mon  Tue  Wed  Thu  Fri  Sat\n";
cout << "---  ---  ---  ---  ---  ---  ---\n";

for ( date = 1; date <= 1 + jan_1_start_day * 5; date++ )
   cout << "  ";

for ( date = 1; date <= num_days_per_month; date++ ) {
   cout.width(2);
   cout << date;
   cout.width(0);
   if ( ( date + jan_1_start_day ) % 7 > 0 )
```

```
      cout << "    ";
    else
      cout << "\n ";
  }
  jan_1_start_day=(jan_1_start_day + num_days_per_month) % 7;
  }
  return(0);
}
```

The program first asks the user to enter an integer code representing the day of the week that January begins on (0 for Monday, 1 for Tuesday, and so on). The second prompt asks for the year for the calendar, and then prints the year entered. The year entered is also used to generate a *leap_year_flag*. Using the modulus operator (**%**) with a value of 4 generates a remainder of 0 whenever it is leap year, and a nonzero value whenever it is not leap year.

Next, a 12 iteration loop is entered, printing the current month's name, and assigning *num_days_per_month* the correct number of days for that particular month. You accomplish all of this by using a *switch* statement to test the current *month* integer value.

Outside the *switch* statement, after the month's name has been printed, day-of-the-week headings are printed, and an appropriate number of blank columns are skipped depending on when the first day of the month was.

The last *for* loop actually generates and prints the dates for each month. The last statement in the program prepares the *day_code* for the next month to be printed.

if-else-if and *switch* Statements Combined

The following example program uses an enumerated type (**enum**) to perform the specified length conversions:

```
/*
*      A C program demonstrating the if-else-if statement
*      used in a meaningful way with several switch statements.
*      Copyright (c) Chris H. Pappas and William H. Murray, 1990
*/

typedef enum conversion_type {YARDS, INCHES, CENTIMETERS, \
                              METERS} C_TYPE;
#include <stdio.h>

main()
{
  int user_response;
```

```
C_TYPE conversion;
int length=30;
float measurement;

printf("\nPlease enter the measurement to be converted : ");
scanf("%f",&measurement);
printf("\nPlease enter :                \
        \n\t\t 0 for YARDS         \
        \n\t\t 1 for INCHES        \
        \n\t\t 2 for CENTIMETERS \
        \n\t\t 3 for METERS        \
        \n\n\t\tYour response -->> ");

scanf("%d",&user_response);

switch(user_response) {
  case 0  :  conversion=YARDS;
             break;
  case 1  :  conversion=INCHES;
             break;
  case 2  :  conversion=CENTIMETERS;
             break;
  default :  conversion=METERS;
}

if(conversion == YARDS)
  measurement = length / 3;
else if(conversion == INCHES)
  measurement = length * 12;
else if(conversion == CENTIMETERS)
  measurement = length * 12 * 2.54;
else if(conversion == METERS)
  measurement = (length * 12 * 2.54)/100;
else
  printf("No conversion required");

switch(conversion) {
  case YARDS       : printf("\n\t\t  %4.2f yards",measurement);
                     break;
  case INCHES      : printf("\n\t\t  %4.2f inches",measurement);
                     break;
  case CENTIMETERS : printf("\n\t\t  %4.2f centimeters",
                               measurement);
                     break;
  default          : printf("\n\t\t  %4.2f meters",measurement);
}

return(0);
}
```

In standard C, enumerated types only exist within the code itself, and cannot be input or output directly except as integers. The program uses the first *switch* statement to convert the input code to its appropriate conversion type. The nested *if-else-if* statements perform the proper conversion.

The last *switch* statement prints the converted value with its appropriate literal type. Of course, the nested *if-else-if* statements could have been implemented by using a *switch* statement. (See Chapter 12, "Structures, Unions, and Miscellaneous Items," for more on enumerated types.)

LOOP STATEMENTS

The C language includes the standard set of repetition control statements: *for* loops, *while* loops, and *do-while* loops (called *repeat-until* loops in several other high-level languages). However, C provides four methods for altering the repetitions in a loop. All repetition loops can naturally terminate based on the expressed Boolean test condition. In C, however, a repetition loop can also terminate because of an anticipated error condition using either a **break** or **exit** statement. Repetition loops can also have their logic control flow altered by **break** or **continue** statements.

The basic difference between a *for* loop and a *while* or *do-while* loop has to do with the known number of repetitions. Typically, *for* loops are used whenever there is a definite predefined required number of repetitions. In contrast, *while* and *do-while* loops are reserved for an unknown number of repetitions.

for Loops

The syntax for a *for* loop looks like this:

for(*initialization_exp; test_exp; increment_exp*)

   statement;

When the *for* loop statement is encountered, the *initialization_exp* is executed first, at the start of the loop, and is never executed again. Usually, this statement involves the initialization of the loop control variable. Following this, the *test_exp*, which is called the loop terminating condition, is tested. Whenever the *test_exp* evaluates to TRUE, the statement or statements within the loop are executed. If the loop was entered, the *increment_exp* is executed after all of the statements within the loop are executed. However, if *test_exp* evaluates to FALSE, the statements within the loop are ignored, along with the *increment_exp*, and execution continues with the statement following the end of the loop. The indentation scheme for *for* loops with several statements to be repeated looks like this:

for(*initialization_exp; test_exp; increment_exp*) {

    statement_a;

    statement_b;

    statement_c;

    statement_n;

}

When several statements need to be executed, a pair of braces, **{ }**, is required to tie their execution to the loop control structure.

The following example sums up the first ten integers. It assumes that *int_sum* and *int_value* have been predefined as integers.

```
int_sum = 0;
for(int_value=1; int_value <= 10; int_value++)
    int_sum += int_value;
```

After *int_sum* has been initialized to 0, the *for* loop is encountered. First, *int_value* is initialized to 1 (this is done only once). Then *int_value*'s value is checked against the loop terminating condition, <= 10. Since this is TRUE, a 1 is added to *int_sum*. Once the statement is executed, the loop control variable (*int_value*) is incremented by 1. This process continues nine more times until *int_value* is incremented to 11 and the loop terminates.

In C++, the same code segment could be written as follows (see if you can detect the subtle difference):

```
int_sum = 0;
for(int int_value=1; int_value <= 10; int_value++)
    int_sum += int_value;
```

C++ allows the loop control variable to be declared and initialized within the *for* loop. This brings up the issue of the proper placement of variable declarations. In C++, you can declare variables right before the statement that actually uses them. In the previous example, the local declaration for *int_value* is harmless, since *int_value* is only used to generate an *int_sum*, with *int_sum* having a larger scope than *int_value*. However, the following code segment

```
int int_sum = 0;
for(int int_value=1; int_value <= 10; int_value++)
  int_sum += int_value;
```

would obscure the visual "desk check" of the variable *int_sum*, because it was not declared below the function head. For the sake of structured design and debugging, it is best to localize all variable declarations. You can rarely justify moving a variable declaration to a nonstandard place, sacrificing easily read, easily checked, and easily modified code.

The value used to increment *for* loop control variables does not have to be 1 or ++. The following example sums the even numbers up to 20:

```
even_sum = 0;
for(even_value=2; even_value <= 20; even_value+=2);
  even_sum += even_value;
```

In this example, the loop control variable *even_value* is initialized to 2 and is incremented by 2. Of course, *for* loops don't always have to go from a smaller value to a larger one. The next example uses a *for* loop to read into an array of characters and then print the character string backwards:

```
//
//   A C++ program that accesses a for loop to read
//   characters into an array and then to print it backwards.
//   Copyright (c) Chris H. Pappas and William H. Murray, 1990
//

#include <stdio.h>

#define MAXLETTERS 10

main()
{
  char char_array[MAXLETTERS];
  int index;

  for(index = 0; index < MAXLETTERS; index++)
    char_array[index]=getchar();
  for(index = MAXLETTERS-1; index >= 0; index--)
    putchar(char_array[index]);

  return(0);
}
```

In this example, the first *for* loop initializes *index* to 0 (necessary since all array indexes are offsets from the starting address of the first array element) and reads characters in one at a time while there is room in the *char_array*.

The second *for* loop initializes the loop control variable *index* to the offset of the last element in the array, and prints the characters in reverse order while *index* contains a valid offset. You could use this process to parse an infix expression that was being converted to prefix notation.

When you combine *for* loops, as in this next example, take care to include the appropriate braces { }, to make certain the statements execute properly:

```
/*
 *      A C program demonstrating the need for caution when
 *      nesting for loops.
 *      Copyright (c) Chris H. Pappas and William H. Murray, 1990
 */

#include <stdio.h>

main()
{
  int outer_value, inner_value;

  for(outer_value = 1; outer_value <= 4; outer_value++) {
    printf("\n%3d  --",outer_value);
    for(inner_value = 1; inner_value <= 5; inner_value++ )
      printf("%3d",outer_value * inner_value);
  }

  return(0);
}
```

The output produced by this program looks like this:

```
1  --  1  2  3  4   5
2  --  2  4  6  8  10
3  --  3  6  9 12  15
4  --  4  8 12 16  20
```

Had the outer *for* loop been written without the braces, like this

```
/*
 *      A C program demonstrating what happens when you nest
 *      for loops without the logically required braces { }.
 *      Copyright (c) Chris H. Pappas and William H. Murray, 1990
 */

#include <stdio.h>

main()
{
  int outer_value, inner_value;
```

```
  for(outer_value = 1; outer_value <= 4; outer_value++)
    printf("\n%3d   --",outer_value);
    for(inner_value = 1; inner_value <= 5; inner_value++ )
      printf("%3d",outer_value * inner_value);

  return(0);
}
```

the output would have looked quite different:

```
1  --
2  --
3  --
4  --   5 10 15 20 25
```

Without the braces enclosing the first *for* loop, only the first **printf** statement is associated with the loop. Once the **printf** statement is executed four times, the second *for* loop is entered. The inner loop uses the last value stored in *outer_value,* or 5, to generate the values printed by its **printf** statement.

The use of braces is a tricky matter that needs to be approached with some thought to readability. See whether you can determine if these next two examples would produce the same output:

```
/*
 *      Another C program demonstrating the need for caution when
 *      nesting for loops.
 *      Copyright (c) Chris H. Pappas and William H. Murray, 1990
 */

#include <stdio.h>

main()
{
  int outer_value, inner_value;

  for(outer_value = 1; outer_value <= 4; outer_value++) {
    for(inner_value = 1; inner_value <= 5; inner_value++ )
      printf("%d ",outer_value * inner_value);
  }

  return(0);
}
```

Compare the last program with the following example:

```
/*
 *      A comparison C program demonstrating the need for
 *      caution when nesting for loops.
```

```
*       Copyright (c) Chris H. Pappas and William H. Murray, 1990
*/

#include <stdio.h>

main()
{
  int outer_value, inner_value;

  for(outer_value = 1; outer_value <= 4; outer_value++)
    for(inner_value = 1; inner_value <= 5; inner_value++ )
      printf("%d ",outer_value * inner_value);

  return(0);
}
```

Both programs produce identical output:

```
1 2 3 4 5 2 4 6 8 10 3 6 9 12 15 4 8 12 16 20
```

In these two examples, the only statement associated with the outer *for* loop is the inner *for* loop, which is considered a single statement. This would be the case even if the inner *for* loop had multiple statements to execute. Since braces are only needed around code blocks, or multiple statements, the outer *for* loop does not need braces to execute the program properly.

while Loops

Just like the *for* loop, the C *while* loop is a *pretest* loop. This means that *test_exp* is evaluated before the statements within the body of the loop are entered. Because of this, pretest loops may be executed from zero to many times. The syntax for a C *while* loop looks like this:

while(*test_exp*)

   statement;

   For *while* loops with several statements, braces are needed:

while(*test_exp*) {

   statement_a;

   statement_b;

   statement_c;

   statement_n;

}

Usually *while* loop control structures are used whenever an indefinite number of repetitions is expected. The following C program uses a *while* loop to average a user-defined list of numbers:

```
/*
 *      A C program using a simple while loop with a BOOLEAN flag.
 *      Copyright (c) Chris H. Pappas and William H. Murray, 1990
 */

#include <stdio.h>

#define TRUE 1
#define FALSE 0

main()
{
  int how_many=0, done=FALSE;
  float sum=0.0,input_value=0.0;
  double average=0.0;

  while(!done) {
    printf("\n Input a number to average (0 to quit): ");
    scanf("%d",&input_value);
    if(input_value != 0.0) {
      sum += input_value;
      how_many++;
    }
    else
      done = TRUE;
  }

  how_many > 0 ? (average = sum/how_many) : (average = 0);

  printf("\n The sum of %d numbers is %d",how_many,sum);
  printf("\n The average of these numbers is %f",average);

  return(0);
}
```

The program begins by defining two **int** constants TRUE and FALSE that will be used as a flag to determine when the *while* loop will terminate. The *done* flag is initialized to FALSE, with the *while* loop repeating until the user enters a 0 value, which sets the *done* flag to TRUE. Since *while* loops only repeat while the test condition evaluates to TRUE, *!done* or *!TRUE* stops the repetitions.

The next C program prompts the user for input and output file names. The program then uses a *while* loop to read in and echo the input file of unknown size.

```
/*
 *      A C program demonstrating how a while loop can be used
 *      to process an input file of undetermined length.
 *      Copyright (c) Chris H. Pappas and William H. Murray, 1990
 */

#include <stdio.h>
#include <process.h>

#define NAMELENGTH 30
#define NULLCHAR 1

main()
{
  FILE *in_file;
  FILE *out_file;
  char in_file_name[NAMELENGTH+NULLCHAR],
  out_file_name[NAMELENGTH+NULLCHAR];
  int c,file_name_length;

  fputs("Please enter input file name: ",stdout);
  gets(in_file_name);

  fputs("Please enter output file name: ",stdout);
  gets(out_file_name);
  if(( in_file=fopen(in_file_name,"r")) == NULL){
    printf("Input file cannot be opened");
   exit(1);
   }
  if(( out_file=fopen(out_file_name,"w")) == NULL){
    printf("Output file cannot be opened");
    exit(2);
    }

  while(!feof(in_file)) {
    c=fgetc(in_file);
    fputc(c,out_file);
  }

  fclose(in_file);
  fclose(out_file);

  return(0);
}
```

In this example, the *while* loop contains two executable statements, so the brace pair is required. The program also illustrates the use of several file I/O statements such as **fgets, fgetc, fputc,** and **feof** (discussed in Chapter 11, "Input and Output in C and C++").

do-while Loops

The *do-while* loop differs from both the *for* and *while* loops in that it is a *post-test* loop. In other words, the loop is always entered at least once, and the loop condition is tested at the end of the first iteration. In contrast, *for* and *while* loops may execute from zero to many times, depending on the loop control variable. Since *do-while* loops always execute at least one time, they are best used whenever you are certain that you want the particular loop entered. For example, your program may need to present a menu to the users even if they just want to immediately quit the program. They will need to see the menu to know which key terminates the application.

The syntax for a *do-while* loop looks like this:

do

    action;

while(*test_condition*);

Braces are required for *do-while* statements that have compound actions:

do {

    action1;

    action2;

    action3;

    actionn;

} while(*test_condition*);

The following C++ program uses a *do-while* loop to print a menu and obtain a valid user response:

```
//
//    A C++ program using a do-while loop to print a menu
//    and obtain a valid user response.
//    Copyright (c) Chris H. Pappas and William H. Murray, 1990
//

#include <iostream.h>
#include <conio.h>
```

```
main()
{
  int user_response,X,Y;

  clrscr();
  do {
    cout << "\t\t\t>>> Welcome to MenuIt <<<\n\n";

    cout << "\t\t\t    Instructions:    1\n";
    cout << "\t\t\t    Amortization:    2\n";
    cout << "\t\t\t    Loan Payoff:     3\n";
    cout << "\t\t\t    Principle:       4\n";
    cout << "\t\t\t    Interest Rate:   5\n";
    cout << "\t\t\t    Quit:            6\n";
    cout << "\n\t\t\tPlease enter your selection: ";

    X=wherex();
    Y=wherey();

    do {
      gotoxy(X,Y);
      cout << "     ";
      gotoxy(X,Y);
      cin >> user_response;
    } while ((user_response < 1) || (user_response > 6));

  } while(user_response != 6 );

  return(0);
}
```

To add interest to the program, the Turbo C++ *conio.h* header file has been included. The header file contains many useful function prototypes for controlling the monitor. The program uses three of these functions: **wherex**, **wherey**, and **gotoxy**. The two functions **wherex** and **wherey** return the current screen coordinates of the cursor. The **gotoxy** function moves the cursor to any preselected screen coordinate. All three functions either return or expect **int** arguments.

The program uses an outer *do-while* loop to print menu items, and continues to reprint the menu items until the user selects option 6 to quit.

Notice that the program also has a nested inner *do-while* loop. This loop makes certain that the user has entered an acceptable response (a number from 1 through 6). Since you don't want the user's incorrect guesses to be newlined all the way down the display screen, the inner loop uses the **gotoxy** statements to keep the cursor on the same line as the first response. This is accomplished by obtaining the cursor's original position after the input prompt "Please enter your selection: " is printed. Functions **wherex** and **wherey** were designed for this purpose.

Once the user has typed a response, the cursor's x and y coordinates change, which requires their original values to be stored in the variables *x* and *y* for repeated reference. Once inside the inner *do-while* loop, the first **gotoxy** statement blanks out any previously entered values (superfluous for the first user response entered), and then obtains the next number entered. This process continues until an acceptable *user_response* is obtained. When the inner *do-while* loop is exited, control returns to the outer *do-while* loop, which repeats the menu until the user enters a **6** to quit. See if you can rewrite the program using **gotoxy** so that the entire menu doesn't need to be reprinted with each valid *user_response*.

break Statement

The C **break** statement can be used to exit a loop before the test condition becomes FALSE. The **break** statement is similar in many ways to a **goto** statement, only the point jumped to is not known directly. When breaking out of a loop, program execution continues with the next statement following the loop itself.

```
/*
 *      A C program demonstrating the use of the break statement.
 *      Copyright (c) Chris H. Pappas and William H. Murray, 1990
 */

main()
{
  int i=1,sum=0;

  while(i < 10){
    sum += i;
    if(sum > 20)
      break;
    i++;
  }

  return(0);
}
```

Use the Debugger to trace through the program. Trace the variables *sum* and *i*. Pay particular attention to which statements are executed after *sum* reaches the value 21.

Notice that when *sum* reaches the value 21, the **break** statement is executed. This causes the increment of *i* to be jumped over, *i++*, with program execution continuing on the line of code below the loop. In this example, the next statement executed was the **return**.

continue Statement

There is a subtle difference between the C **break** statement and the C **continue** statement. As you have seen, **break** causes the loop to terminate execution altogether. In contrast, **continue** causes all of the statements following it to be ignored but does not circumvent incrementing the loop control variable or the loop control test condition. In other words, if the loop control variable still satisfies the loop test condition, the loop will continue to iterate.

The following program demonstrates this concept using a number guessing game:

```
/*
 *    A C program demonstrating the use of the continue statement.
 *    Copyright (c) Chris H. Pappas and William H. Murray, 1990
 */

#include <stdio.h>

#define TRUE 1
#define FALSE 0
main()
{
  int lucky_number=77,
      input_value,
      number_of_tries=0,
      lucky=FALSE;

  while(!lucky){
    printf("Please enter your lucky guess: ");
    scanf("%d",&input_value);
    number_of_tries++;
    if(input_value == lucky_number)
      lucky=TRUE;
    else
      continue;
    printf("It only took you %d tries to get lucky!",
      number_of_tries);
  }

  return(0);
}
```

Enter the preceding program and trace the variables *input_value*, *number_of_tries*, and *lucky*. Pay particular attention to which statements are executed after *input_value* is compared to the *lucky_number*.

The program uses a *while* loop to prompt the user for a value, increments the *number_of_tries* for each guess entered, and then determines the appropriate action to take based on the success of the match. If no match was found, the *else* statement is executed. This is the **continue** statement. Whenever the **continue** statement is executed, the **printf** statement is ignored. Note, however, that the loop continues to execute. When the *input_value* matches the *lucky_number*, the *lucky* flag is set to TRUE and the **continue** statement is ignored, allowing the **printf** statement to execute.

Using break and continue Together

Both the **break** and **continue** statements can be combined to solve some interesting program problems. Consider the following C++ example:

```
//
//     A C++ program demonstrating the usefulness of combining
//     the break and continue statements.
//     Copyright (c) Chris H. Pappas and William H. Murray, 1990
//

#include <stdio.h>
#include <ctype.h>

#define NEWLINE '\n'

main()
{
  int c;

  while((c=getchar()) != EOF)
  {
    if(isascii(c) == 0) {
      cout << "Not an ASCII character; ";
      cout << "not going to continue/n";
      break;
    }

    if(ispunct(c) || isspace(c)) {
      putchar(NEWLINE);
      continue;
```

```
    }

    if(isprint(c) == 0) {
      c = getchar();
      continue;
    }

    putchar(c);
  }

  return(0);
}
```

If the program receives the input

```
word control ^B exclamation! apostrophe' period. ^Z
```

it produces this output:

```
word
control
exclamation

apostrophe

period
```

The program continues to read character input until the EOF character ^Z is typed. It then examines the input, removing any nonprintable characters, and places each "word" on its own line. It accomplishes this via some interesting macros defined in the *ctype.h*, including **isascii, ispunct, isspace,** and **isprint**. Each function is passed a character parameter and returns either a 0 or some other value indicating the result of the comparison.

The function **isascii** indicates whether the character passed falls into the acceptable ASCII value range; **ispunct** indicates whether the character is a punctuation mark; **isspace** indicates if the character is a space; and **isprint** reports whether the character parameter is a printable character.

Using these functions, the program determines whether to continue the program and what to do with the characters input if it continues.

The first test within the *while* loop evaluates whether the file is in readable form. For example, the input data could have been saved in binary format, rendering the program useless. If so, the associated *if* statements execute, printing a warning message and breaking out of the *while* loop permanently.

If all is well, the second *if* statement checks whether the character input is a punctuation mark or a blank space. If either of these conditions is TRUE, the associated *if* statements are executed, causing a blank line to be skipped in the output and executing the **continue** statement. The **continue** statement efficiently jumps over the remaining test condition and output statement but does not terminate the loop. It merely indicates that the character's form has been diagnosed properly and that it is time to obtain a new character.

If the file format is acceptable and the character input is not punctuation or a blank, the third *if* statement asks whether the character is printable. This test takes care of any control codes. Notice that the example input to the program included a ^B. Since ^B is not printable, this *if* statement immediately obtains a new character and then executes a **continue** statement. Similarly, this **continue** statement indicates that the character in question has been diagnosed, the proper action has been taken, and it is time to get another character. The **continue** statement also causes the **putchar** statement to be ignored while not terminating the *while* loop.

Finally, if all other tests have proved invalid, the input character is printed by the **putchar** statement and the loop is iterated again until a ^Z is entered. As you can see, the combination of the **break** and **continue** statements can lead to some interesting problem solutions.

exit Statement

Under certain circumstances, it is proper for a program to terminate long before all of its statements have been examined and/or executed. For these circumstances, C incorporates the **exit** library function. The **exit** function expects one integer argument called a *status value*. The UNIX and MS-DOS operating systems interpret a status value of 0 as a normal program termination and any nonzero status values as different kinds of errors.

The process that invoked the program can use the particular status value passed to **exit** to take some action. For example, if the program were invoked from the command line and the status value indicated some type of error, the operating system might display a message. In addition to terminating the program, **exit** writes all output waiting to be written and closes all open files.

The following C++ program averages a list of up to 30 grades. The program will exit if the user requests to average more than *SIZE* number of integers:

```
//
//     A C++ program demonstrating the use of the exit function
//     Copyright (c) Chris H. Pappas and William H. Murray, 1990
//

#include <iostream.h>
#include <process.h>

#define SIZE 30

main()
{
  int index,how_many,grades[SIZE];
  float sum=0,max_grade=0,min_grade=100,average;

  cout << "\nEnter the number of grades to be averaged: ";
  cin >>  how_many;
  if(how_many > SIZE) {
    cout << "\nYou can only enter up to " << SIZE << " grades" \
            << " to be averaged.\n";
    cout << "\n         >>> Program was exited. <<<\n";
    exit(1);
  }

  for(index = 0; index < how_many; index++) {
    cout << "\nPlease enter a grade " << index++ << ":   ";
    cin >> grades[index];
  }

  for(index = 0; index < how_many; index++)
    sum = sum + grades[index];

  average = sum/(float)how_many;

  for(index = 0; index < how_many; index++) {
    if(grades[index] > max_grade)
      max_grade = grades[index];
    if(grades[index] < min_grade)
      min_grade = grades[index];
  }

  cout << "\nThe maximum grade is " << max_grade;
  cout << "\nThe minimum grade is " << min_grade;
  cout << "\nThe average grade is " << average;

  return(0);
}
```

The program begins by including the *process.h* header file. Either *process.h* or *stdlib.h* can be included to prototype the function **exit**. The constant *SIZE* is declared to be 30 and is used to dimension the array of **ints**, *grades*. After the remaining variables are declared, the program prompts the user for the number of grades to be entered. For this program, the user's response is to be typed next to the prompt.

The program inputs the requested value into the variable *how__many* and uses this for the *if* comparison. When the user wants to average more numbers than will fit in *grades,* the two warning messages are printed and then the **exit** statement is executed, terminating the program.

See if you can detect the two subtle differences between this program and the previous listing:

```
//
//      A C++ program demonstrating the use of the exit function
//      in relation to the difference between the process.h
//      and stdlib.h header files.
//      Copyright (c) Chris H. Pappas and William H. Murray, 1990
//

#include <iostream.h>
#include <stdlib.h>
#define SIZE 30

main()
{
  int index,how_many,grades[SIZE];
  float sum=0,max_grade=0,min_grade=100,average;

  cout << "\nEnter the number of grades to be averaged: ";
  cin >> how_many;
  if(how_many > SIZE) {
    cout << "\nYou can only enter up to " << SIZE << " grades" \
            << " to be averaged.\n";
    cout << "\n         >>> Program was exited. <<<\n";
    exit(EXIT_FAILURE);
  }

  for(index = 0; index < how_many; index++) {
    cout << "\nPlease enter a grade " << index+1 << ":   ";
    cin >> grades[index];
  }

  for(index = 0; index < how_many; index++)
    sum = sum + grades[index];

  average = sum/(float)how_many;

  for(index = 0; index < how_many; index++) {
    if(grades[index] > max_grade)
      max_grade = grades[index];
    if(grades[index] < min_grade)
      min_grade = grades[index];
  }

  cout << "\nThe maximum grade is " << max_grade;
  cout << "\nThe minimum grade is " << min_grade;
  cout << "\nThe average grade is " << average;

  return(0);
}
```

Including the *stdlib.h* header file instead of *process.h* makes visible two additional definitions: **EXIT_SUCCESS** (returns a value of 0) and **EXIT_FAILURE** (returns an unsuccessful value). This program used **EXIT_FAILURE** for a more readable parameter to the **exit** function.

atexit Statement

Whenever a program invokes the **exit** function or performs a normal program termination, it can also call any registered **exit** functions posted with **atexit**, as shown in the following C program:

```
/*
 *      A C program demonstrating the relationship between the
 *      function atexit and the order in which the functions
 *      declared are executed.
 *      Copyright (c) Chris H. Pappas and William H. Murray, 1990
 */

#include <stdio.h>
#include <stdlib.h>

void atexit_function1(void);
void atexit_function2(void);
void atexit_function3(void);

main()
{

  atexit(atexit_function1);
  atexit(atexit_function2);
  atexit(atexit_function3);

  printf("Atexit program entered.\n");
  printf("Atexit program exited.\n\n");
  printf(">>>>>>>>>> <<<<<<<<<<\n\n");

  return(0);
}

void atexit_function1(void)
{
  printf("atexit_function1 entered.\n");
}

void atexit_function2(void)
{
  printf("atexit_function2 entered.\n");
}

void atexit_function3(void)
{
  printf("atexit_function3 entered.\n");
}
```

The program output looks like this:

```
Atexit program entered.
Atexit program exited.

>>>>>>>>>>> <<<<<<<<<<<

atexit_function3 entered.
atexit_function2 entered.
atexit_function1 entered.
```

The **atexit** function uses the name of a function as its only parameter and registers the specified function as an **exit** function. Whenever the program terminates normally (as in the previous example) or invokes the **exit** function, all **atexit** declared functions are executed.

Technically, each time the **atexit** statement is encountered in the source code, the specified function is added to a list of functions that execute when the program terminates. When the program terminates, any functions that have been passed to **atexit** are executed, and the last function added is the first one executed. This explains why the *atexit_function3* output statement was printed before the similar output statement in *atexit_function1*.

8

FUNCTIONS

Functions form the cornerstone of C and C++ programming. As you expand your programming skills, your programs will take on a modular appearance when you begin programming with functions. You do all C and C++ programming within a function. This is because all programs must include **main**, which is itself a function. If you have programmed in other languages, you will find C functions similar to modules in other languages. Pascal uses procedures and functions, FORTRAN uses just functions, and assembly language uses just procedures. How functions work determines to a large degree the efficiency, readability, and portability of C program code.

This chapter includes numerous C and C++ examples that illustrate how to write simple functions to perform specific tasks. The functions are short to make the concepts easier to understand and to prevent you from being lost in reams of code. Many of these examples use functions contained in the standard C and C++ libraries. Some C++ examples also show features unique to the C++ language. If you learn to write good functions, you are well on your way to becoming a power C programmer.

FUNCTION STYLE AND PROTOTYPING

C functions changed greatly during the ANSI standardization process. This new C standard is largely based on the function prototype used in C++. As you read various articles, books, and magazines dealing with C, you will see many variations used to describe C functions, as programmers attempt (or don't attempt) to conform to the ANSI C standard. Borland C++ recognizes the ANSI standard and also earlier forms of C. The programs in this book conform to the ANSI standard whenever possible. This book also applies ANSI C standards to C++ code where appropriate.

Function Prototyping

Function declarations begin with the C and C++ function prototype. The function prototype is simple and is included at the start of program code to notify the compiler of the type and number of arguments that a function will use. It also enforces a stronger type checking than was possible when C was not standardized.

Although other variations are legal, whenever possible you should use the function prototype form that is a replication of the function's declaration line. For example,

```
return_type function_name(argument_type(s) argument_name(s));
```

The function can be of type **void, int, float,** and so on. The *return_type* gives this specification. The *function_name* is any meaningful name you choose to describe the function. If any information is passed to the function, you should give an *argument_type* followed by an *argument_name*. Argument types may also be of type **void, int, float,** and so on. You can pass many values to a function by repeating the argument type and name separated by a comma. It is also correct to list just the argument type, but that prototype form is not used as frequently.

The function itself is an encapsulated piece of code that usually follows the **main** function definition. The function can take on the following form:

```
return_type function_name(argument_types and names)
{
    .
    .
```

```
(data declarations and body of function)
    .
    .
    .
    return();
}
```

Notice that the first line of the function is identical (except for the missing ;) to the prototype that is listed at the beginning of a program. An actual function prototype and function, used in a program, is shown in the following C example:

```
/*
*    C program to illustrate function prototyping.
*    Function subtracts two integers and returns an integer
*    result.
*    Copyright (c) Chris H. Pappas and William H. Murray, 1990
*/

#include <stdio.h>

int subtractor(int x,int y);        /* function prototype */

main()
{
   int a=5;
   int b=93;
   int c;

   c=subtractor(a,b);
   printf("The difference is: %d\n", c);
   return (0);
}

int subtractor(int x,int y)          /* function declaration */
{
   int z;

   z=y-x;
   return(z);                         /* function return type */
}
```

The function is called **subtractor**. The prototype states that the function will accept two **int** arguments and return an **int** type. Actually, the ANSI standard suggests that every function be prototyped in a separate header file. As you might guess, this is how header files are associated with their appropriate C libraries. For simple programs, you can include the function prototype within the body of the program.

The equivalent function written for C++ looks almost identical:

```
//
//     C++ program to illustrate function prototyping.
//     Function subtracts two integers and returns an integer
//     result.
//     Copyright (c) Chris H. Pappas and William H. Murray, 1990
//

#include <iostream.h>

int subtractor(int x,int y);        // function prototype

main()
{
  int a=5;
  int b=93;
  int c;

  c=subtractor(a,b);
  cout << "The difference is: " << c << "\n";
  return (0);
}

int subtractor(int x,int y)         // function declaration
{
  int z;

  z=y-x;
  return(z);                        // function return type
}
```

Call-By-Value and Call-By-Reference

In the previous two examples, arguments were passed by value to the functions. When variables are passed in this manner, a copy of the variable's value is actually passed to the function. Since a copy is passed, the variable in the calling program is not altered. Calling a function by *value* is a popular means of passing information to a function and is the default method in C and C++. The major limitation to the call-by-value technique is that typically only one value is returned by the function.

In a call-by-*reference*, the address of the argument, rather than its value, is passed to the function. This approach requires less program memory than a call-by-value. When you use a call-by-reference, the variables in the calling program can be altered. Additionally, more than one value can be returned by the function; but more on that later.

The next example uses the **subtractor** function from the previous section. The arguments are now passed as a call-by-reference. In C, you achieve a call-by-reference by using a pointer as an argument. You can use this same technique with C++.

```
/*
 *    C program to illustrate a call-by-reference.
 *    Copyright (c) Chris H. Pappas and William H. Murray, 1990
 */

#include <stdio.h>

int subtractor(int *x,int *y);

main()
{
  int a=5;
  int b=93;
  int c;

  c=subtractor(&a,&b);
  printf("The difference is: %d\n", c);
  return (0);
}

int subtractor(int *x, int *y)
{
  int z;

  z=*y-*x;
  return(z);
}
```

In C, you can use variables and pointers as arguments in function declarations. C++ accepts these and adds a third argument type called a **reference** type. The **reference** type refers to a location, but does not require a dereferencing operator. Examine the following syntax carefully:

```
//
//    C++ program to illustrate an equivalent
//    call-by-reference.  Using the C++ reference type.
//    Copyright (c) Chris H. Pappas and William H. Murray, 1990
//

#include <iostream.h>

int subtractor(int& x,int& y);

main()
{
  int a=5;
  int b=93;
  int c;

  c=subtractor(a,b);
  cout << "The difference is:"
       << c << endl;
  return (0);
}
```

```
int subtractor(int& x,int& y)
{
  int z;

  z=y-x;
  return(z);
}
```

Notice the lack of pointers in the C++ program. The **reference** types are *x* and *y*. References to references, references to bit fields, arrays of references, and pointers to references are not allowed. Regardless of the method, a call-by-reference or **reference** type always uses the address of the argument. A call-by-reference is a favorite method of passing array information to a function. More about this technique in the next chapter.

Storage Classes and Functions

Data types can have storage classes affixed to their declarations, as you saw in Chapter 6, "Data." For example, a variable might be declared as:

```
static   int   myvariable;
```

Functions can also use **extern** and **static** storage class types. A function is declared with an **extern** storage class when it has been defined in another file, external to the present program. In a somewhat related manner, a function can be declared **static** when external access, apart from the present program, is not permitted.

Scope

The scope rules for variables used with functions are similar in C and C++. Variables can have a *local, file,* or *class* scope. Class scopes are discussed in Chapter 6.

A local variable may be used completely within a function definition. Its scope is then limited to the function. The variable is said to be accessible or visible within the function and has a local scope.

Variables with a file scope are declared outside of individual functions or classes. They have visibility or accessibility throughout the whole file. Variables of this type are global in range.

The same variable may be used with a file scope and later within a function definition with a local scope. In this case, the local scope takes precedence. C++ offers a new feature called the *scope resolution operator, : :.* When you use the resolution operator, a variable with local scope is changed to one with file scope. In this situation, the variable would possess the value of the global variable. The syntax is

: :*myvariable*

There are programming problems involving scope rules near the end of this chapter.

Recursion

Recursion occurs when a function calls itself. Recursion is permitted in both C and C++. You can generate the factorial of a number with recursion. (The factorial of a number is defined as the number multiplied by all successively lower integers.) For example,

$$6! = 6 * 5 * 4 * 3 * 2 * 1$$
$$= 720$$

Take care when choosing data types, since the product increases very rapidly. As an example, the factorial of 14 is 87178291200.

```
/*
 *      C program illustrates recursive function calls.
 *      Calculation of the factorial of a number.
 *      Example:  5! = 5 x 4 x 3 x 2 x 1 = 120
 *      Copyright (c) Chris H. Pappas and William H. Murray, 1990
 */

#include <stdio.h>

double factorial(double answer);

main()
{
  double number=20.0;
  double fact;

  fact=factorial(number);
```

```
   printf("The factorial is: %15.01f \n",fact);
   return (0);
}

double factorial(double answer)
{
  if (answer <= 1.0)
    return(1.0);
  else
    return(answer*factorial(answer-1.0));
}
```

Notice that the function includes a call to itself. Also notice that the **printf** function uses a new format code for printing a **double** value, %...lf. Here, the l is a modifier to the **f** and specifies a **double** instead of a **float**.

FUNCTION ARGUMENTS

The following sections cover function arguments, which are arguments or parameters that are passed to the function. Function arguments are optional; some functions may receive no arguments while others may receive many. Function arguments can be mixed—that is, you can use any of the standard data types. Many of the following examples use functions from various C or C++ libraries. For additional details on these functions and their prototypes, consult your Borland C++ reference manuals.

Formal and Actual Function Arguments

The function definition contains an argument (or parameter) list called the *formal* argument list. The list may be empty or may contain any combination of types, such as integer, float, or character. When the function is actually called from within the body of the program, an argument list is also passed to the function. This list is called the *actual* argument list. When you write ANSI C code, there is usually a one-to-one match between the formal and actual argument lists, although in reality no strong enforcement is used. In many cases, the first argument supplied will provide information for any missing arguments in the list. In C, for example,

```
printf("This is decimal %d and octal %o",num);
```

passes only one argument to **printf**, although two are expected. The **printf** function replicates the *num* variable for the missing argument. In other cases, when fewer arguments are supplied, the missing arguments are initialized to meaningless values. C++ overcomes this problem, to a degree, by permitting a default value to be supplied with the argument. When an argument is missing in a call to the function, the default argument is automatically substituted. In C++, for example, consider

```
void myfunction(int x, int y=4, float z=4.78)
```

Here, if either *y* or *z* is not specified in the call to the function **myfunction**, the values shown (4 or 4.78) will be used.

Using void as an Argument

In ANSI C, you must use **void** to state explicitly the absence of function arguments. In C++, using **void** is wise but is not yet required. The following program has a simple function named **printer** that receives no arguments and does not return a value. The **main** function calls the function **printer**. When **printer** has completed its task, control is returned to the **main** function.

```
/*
 *    C program will print a message with a function.
 *    Function uses a type void argument and sqrt function
 *    from the standard C library.
 *    Copyright (c) Chris H. Pappas and William H. Murray, 1990
 */

#include <stdio.h>
#include <math.h>

void printer(void);

main()
{
  printf("This program will extract a square root. \n\n");
  printer();
  return (0);
}

void printer(void)
{
  double z=5678.0;
  double x;
```

```
   x=sqrt(z);
   printf("The square root of %lf is %lf  \n",z,x);
}
```

Notice that the **printer** function calls a C library function named **sqrt**. The prototype for this library function, contained in *math.h*, accepts a **double** and returns the square root as a **double** value.

Characters as Arguments

Characters can also be passed to a function. In the next example, a single character is intercepted from the keyboard in the function **main** and passed to the function **printer**. The **getch** function intercepts the character. In the standard C library, these other character functions are closely related to **getch: getc, getchar,** and **getche.** You can also use these functions in C++, but in many cases **cin** is probably a better choice. For more on **getch**, consult your Borland reference manuals. The function intercepts a character from the standard input device (keyboard) and returns a character value, without echo to the screen.

```
/*
 *     C program will accept a character from keyboard,
 *     pass it to a function and print a message using
 *     the character.
 *     Copyright (c) Chris H. Pappas and William H. Murray, 1990
 */

#include <stdio.h>

void printer(char ch);

main()
{
  char mychar;

  printf("Enter a single character from the keyboard. \n");
  mychar=getch();
  printer(mychar);
  return (0);
}

void printer(char ch)
{
  int i;
  for(i=0;i<10;i++)
    printf("The character is %c  \n",ch);
}
```

Note that a single character is passed to the function. The function then prints a message and the character ten times. The %c in the **printf** function specifies that a single character is to be printed.

Integers as Arguments

In the next example, a single **int** will be read from the keyboard with C's **scanf** function. That **int** will be passed to the function **radius**. The **radius** function uses the supplied radius to calculate and print the area of a circle, the volume of a sphere, and the surface area of a sphere.

```
/*
*     C program will calculate values given a radius.
*     Function uses a type int argument, accepts radius
*     from keyboard with scanf function.
*     Copyright (c) Chris H. Pappas and William H. Murray, 1990
*/

#include <stdio.h>

const float PI=3.14159;

void radius(int r);

main()
{
  int myradius;
  printf("Enter the radius, as an integer,\n");
  printf("from the keyboard. \n");
  scanf("%d",&myradius);
  radius(myradius);
  return (0);
}

void radius(int r)
{
  float area,volume,sarea;

  area=PI*(float) (r*r);
  volume=PI*4.0/3.0*(float) (r*r*r);
  sarea=PI*4.0*(float) (r*r);

  printf("The radius is %d  \n\n",r);
  printf("A circle would have an area of %f \n",area);
  printf("A sphere would have a volume of %f \n",volume);
  printf("The surface area of the sphere is %f \n",sarea);
}
```

While the value of **radius** is an **int** type, the calculations are cast to **float**. Notice that *PI* was defined as a **const**.

Floats as Arguments

Floats are just as easy to pass as arguments as are integers. In the following C example, two **float** values are passed to a function called **hypotenuse**. **Scanf** intercepts both **float** values from the keyboard.

```
/*
 *    C program will find hypotenuse of a right triangle.
 *    Function uses a type float argument and accepts
 *    input from the keyboard with the scanf function.
 *    Copyright (c) Chris H. Pappas and William H. Murray, 1990
 */

#include <stdio.h>
#include <math.h>

void hypotenuse(float x,float y);

main()
{
  float ylength,xlength;

  printf("Enter the height of a right triangle. \n");
  scanf("%f",&ylength);
  printf("Enter the base of a right triangle. \n");
  scanf("%f",&xlength);
  hypotenuse(ylength,xlength);
  return (0);
}

void hypotenuse(float x,float y)
{
  double myhyp;

  myhyp=hypot((double) x,(double) y);
  printf("The hypotenuse of the triangle is %g \n",myhyp);
}
```

Notice that both arguments received by the **hypotenuse** are cast to **doubles** when used by the **hypot** function from *math.h*. All *math.h* functions accept and return **double** types. Table 8-1 shows other mathematical functions that your programs can use.

Table 8-1.   Mathematical Functions Described in *math.h*

Function Name	Description
abs	Absolute value of a number
acos	Arc cosine
asin	Arc sine
atan	Arc tangent
atan2	Arc tangent of two numbers
atof	ASCII string to type **float**
cabs	Absolute value of complex number
ceil	Largest integer in list
cos	Cosine
cosh	Hyperbolic cosine
exp	Exponential value
fabs	Absolute value of float
floor	Smallest integer in list
fmod	Floating-point mod
hypot	Hypotenuse of right triangle
log	Natural logarithm
log10	Common logarithm
modf	Return mantissa and exponent
poly	Create polynomial
pow	Raise n to power x
pow10	Raise 10 to power x
sin	Sine
sinh	Hyperbolic sine
sqrt	Square root
srand	Random number initializer
tan	Tangent
tanh	Hyperbolic tangent

Doubles as Arguments

The **double** type is a very precise **float** value. As you have learned, all *math.h* functions accept and return **double** types. The following program will accept two **double** values from the keyboard. The function will raise the first number to the power specified by the second number. Now you can find out that $146.6^{3.2}$ is really equal to 8358270.07182.

```
/*
 *    C program will raise a number to a power.
 *    Function uses a type double argument and the pow function.
 *    Copyright (c) Chris H. Pappas and William H. Murray, 1990
 */

#include <stdio.h>
#include <math.h>

void power(double x,double y);

main()
{
  double xnum,ynum;

  printf("Enter the number to be raised to a power. \n");
  scanf("%lf",&xnum);
  printf("Enter the power. \n");
  scanf("%lf",&ynum);
  power(xnum,ynum);
  return (0);
}
void power(double x,double y)
{
  double result;

  result=pow(x,y);
  printf("The result is %lf \n",result);
}
```

This function uses the **pow** function prototyped in *math.h.*

Arrays as Arguments

In the following example, the contents of an array are passed to a function as a call-by-reference. Actually, the address of the first array element is passed via a pointer.

```
/*
 *    C program will call a function with an array.
 *    Function uses a pointer to pass array information.
 *    Copyright (c) Chris H. Pappas and William H. Murray, 1990
 */

#include <stdio.h>

void printer(int *data);

main()
{
  int myarray[5]={5,8,20,21,78};
```

```
    printf("Send information to function. \n");
    printer(myarray);
    return (0);
}

void printer(int *data)
{
    int i;

    for(i=0;i<5;i++)
        printf("The result is %d \n",data[i]);
}
```

Notice that when the function is called, only the name *myarray* is specified. In Chapter 9, "Arrays," you will learn more about arrays. In this case, by specifying the name of the array, you are providing the address of the first element in the array. Since *myarray* is an array of integers, you can pass an array by specifying a pointer of the element type.

You can also pass the address information by using an unsized array, as you can see in the C++ example. The information in *myarray* is transferred by passing the address of the first element.

```
//
//      C++ program will call a function with an array.
//      Function passes array information, and calculates
//      the average of the numbers.
//      Copyright (c) Chris H. Pappas and William H. Murray, 1990
//

#include <iostream.h>

void average(float data[]);

main()
{
    float myarray[10]={70.0,23.5,67.2,4.1,0.0,
                       1.25,8.0,3.14,1.0,78.234};
    cout << "Send information to averaging function. \n";
    average(myarray);
    return (0);
}

void average(float data[])
{
    int i;
    float total=0.0;
    float avg;

    for(i=0;i<10;i++) {
        total+=data[i];
        cout << "number " << i+1 << " is " << data[i] << "\n";
```

```
   }
   avg=total/i;
   cout << "\nThe average is " << avg << "\n";
}
```

The average is determined by summing each of the terms together and dividing by the total number of terms. The **cout** stream is used to format the output to the screen.

FUNCTION TYPES

This section will illustrate numerous function types. A *function type* is the type of value returned by the function. None of the previous examples have returned information from the function and thus were of type **void**.

Function Type void

You have already learned about **void** function types so the next example will be dressed up a bit. C and C++ permit numeric information to be formatted in hexadecimal, decimal, and octal, but not binary. Specifying data in a binary format is useful when you are doing binary arithmetic or developing bit masks. The function **binary** will convert a decimal number entered from the keyboard to a binary representation. The binary digits are not packed together as a single binary number but are stored individually in an array. To view the binary number, you must print the contents of the array.

```
/*
 *     C program illustrates the void function type.
 *     Program will print the binary equivalent of a number.
 *     Copyright (c) Chris H. Pappas and William H. Murray, 1990
 */

#include <stdio.h>

void binary(int number);

main()
{
   int number;
```

```
    printf("Enter a decimal number for conversion to binary.\n");
    scanf("%d",&number);
    binary(number);
    return (0);
}

void binary(int number)
{
    int i=0;
    int myarray[40];

    while (number !=0) {
        myarray[i]=(number % 2);
        number/=2;
        i++;
    }

    i--;
    for(;i>=0;i--)
        printf("%ld",myarray[i]);
    printf("\n");
}
```

You can convert base ten numbers to another base by dividing the number by the new base a successive number of times. In the case of conversion to a binary number, a two is repeatedly divided into a base ten number. The base ten number becomes the quotient from the previous division. The remainder, after each division, is either a one or a zero. The remainder becomes the binary digit. For example, to convert 10 to binary:

```
        quotient  remainder        --->1  0  1  0 (binary)
10/2    5           0  (lsb)       |   (msb)    (lsb)
5/2     2           1              |
2/2     1           0              |
1/2     0           1  (msb)       |
```

In the function, a *while* loop performs the arithmetic as long as *number* has not reached zero. The modulo operator determines the remainder and saves the bit in the array. Division is then performed on *number*, saving only the integer result. This process is repeated until the quotient (also *number* in this case) is reduced to zero.

The individual array bits, which form the binary result, must be unloaded from the array in reverse order, as you can see from the preceding numeric example. Study the *for* loop used in the function. Can you think of a way to perform this conversion and save the binary representation in a variable instead of an array?

Function Type char

Here is a minor expansion to an earlier example. The C function **uppercase** accepts a **char** argument and returns the same. For this example, a lowercase letter received from the keyboard is passed to the function. The function uses the **toupper** function (which is from the standard library and is prototyped in *ctype.h*) to convert the character to uppercase. Functions related to **toupper** include **toascii** and **tolower**.

```
/*
*     C program illustrates the character function type.
*     Function receives lowercase character and
*     converts it to uppercase.
*     Copyright (c) Chris H. Pappas and William H. Murray, 1990
*/

#include <stdio.h>
#include <ctype.h>

char uppercase(char letter);

main()
{
  char lowchar,hichar;
  printf("Enter a lowercase character.\n");
  lowchar=getchar();
  hichar=uppercase(lowchar);
  printf("%c\n",hichar);
  return (0);
}

char uppercase(char letter)
{
  return(toupper(letter));
}
```

Function Type int

The following function accepts and returns **int** types. The function **cube-number** accepts a number generated in **main** (0,2,4,6,8,10...), cubes the number, and returns the **int** value to **main**. The original number and the cube are printed to the screen.

```
/*
*     C program illustrates the integer function type.
*     Function receives integers, one at a time, and
*     returns the cube of each, one at a time.
```

```
*      Copyright (c) Chris H. Pappas and William H. Murray, 1990
*/

#include <stdio.h>

int cubenumber(int number);

main()
{
  int i,cube;

  for (i=0;i<20;i+=2) {
    cube=cubenumber(i);
    printf("The cube of %d is %d \n",i,cube);
  }
  return (0);
}

int cubenumber(int number)
{
  return (number*number*number);
}
```

Function Type long

The following C++ program accepts an **int** value as an argument and returns a **long**. The **long** type, used by Borland C++ and other compilers, is not recognized as a standard ANSI type. The function will raise the number 2 to an integer power.

```
//
//       C++ program illustrates the long integer function type.
//       Function receives integers, one at a time, and
//       returns 2 raised to that integer power.
//       Copyright (c) Chris H. Pappas and William H. Murray, 1990
//

#include <iostream.h>
long twopower(int number);

main()
{
  int i;
  long weight;

  for (i=0;i<31;i++) {
    weight=twopower(i);
    cout << "2 raised to the " << i << " power is "
         << weight << endl;
  }
  return (0);
}
```

```
long twopower(int number)
{
  int t;
  long value=1;

  for (t=0;t<number;t++)
    value*=2;
  return (value);
}
```

The function simply multiplies the original number by the number of times it is to be raised to the power. For example, if you want to raise 2 to the fourth power (2^4), the program will perform the following multiplication equation:

$$2 * 2 * 2 * 2 = 16$$

Can you think of a function described in *math.h* that could achieve the same results?

Function Type float

The next C++ example will find the product of all the elements in an array. The array contains **float**s and will return a **float** product.

```
//
//      C++ program illustrates the float function type.
//      Function receives an array of floats and returns
//      their product as a float.
//      Copyright (c) Chris H. Pappas and William H. Murray, 1990
//

#include <iostream.h>
float times(float floatarray[]);

main()
{
  float myarray[5]={1.2,4.5,7.05,6.14,0.09876};
  float product;

  product=times(myarray);
  cout << "The product of the array's numbers is: "
       << product << "\n";
  return (0);
}
```

```
float times(float floatarray[])
{
  int t;
  float temp;

  temp=floatarray[0];
  for (t=1;t<5;t++)
    temp*=floatarray[t];
  return (temp);
}
```

Since the elements are multiplied together, the first element of the array must be loaded into *temp* before the *for* loop is entered.

Function Type double

The following C example accepts and returns a **double** type. The function **trigsine** will convert an angle, expressed in degrees, to its sine value.

```
/*
 *     C program illustrates the double function type.
 *     Function receives integers from 0 to 90, one at a
 *     time, and returns the sine of each, one at a time.
 *     Copyright (c) Chris H. Pappas and William H. Murray, 1990
 */

#include <stdio.h>
#include <math.h>

const double PI=3.14159265359;

double trigsine(double angle);

main()
{
  int i;
  double sine;

  for (i=0;i<91;i++) {
    sine=trigsine((double) i);
    printf("The sine of %d degrees is %20.18lf \n",i,sine);
  }
  return (0);
}

double trigsine(double angle)
{
  double temp;
  temp=sin((PI/180.0)*angle);
  return (temp);
}
```

Notice that the **sin** function described in *math.h* is utilized by **trigsine** to obtain the answer. Angles must be converted from degrees to radians for all trigonometric functions. Recall that PI radians equal 180 degrees.

FUNCTION ARGUMENTS FOR MAIN

C and C++ can both accept command-line arguments. Command-line arguments are passed when the program is called from DOS. For example,

```
C>MYPROGRAM  Bill Chris Jeff Cindy Herb 10 20 30
```

In this example, eight values are passed from the command line to *myprogram*. Actually, it is **main** that is given specific information. One argument received by **main**, *argc,* is an **int** giving the number of command-line terms plus one. The program title is counted as the first term. The second argument is a pointer to the strings called *argv*. All arguments are strings of characters, so *argv* is of type **char** *[argc]. Since all programs have a name, *argc* is always one or greater. The following examples explain various techniques for retrieving information from the command line. The argument names *argc* and *argv* are required by the compiler and cannot be changed.

Strings

Since the arguments are passed as strings of characters, they are the easiest to work with. In the following example, the program anticipates that the user will enter several names on the command line. In fact, if *argc* isn't greater than two, the user will be returned to the command line with a reminder to try again and enter several names.

```
/*
 *    C program illustrates how to read string data
 *    into the program with a command-line argument.
 *    Copyright (c) Chris H. Pappas and William H. Murray, 1990
 */

#include <stdio.h>
```

```
main(int argc, char *argv[])
{
  int i;
  double sine;

  if(argc<2) {
    printf("You must enter several names on the command\n");
    printf("line when executing this program!  Try again.\n");
    exit(1);
  }

  for (i=1; i<argc; i++)
    printf("Name #%d is %s\n",i,argv[i]);
  return (0);
}
```

The program is completely contained in **main**, with no additional functions. The names are received on the command line and printed to the screen in the same order. If numbers are entered on the command line, they will be interpreted as ASCII strings and must be printed as character data.

Integers

This C++ example will accept a single **int** number on the command line. Since the number is actually a character string, it must be converted to an integer via the **atoi** function. Then *number* is passed to the **binary** function. The function will convert the value in *number* to a string of binary digits and print them to the screen. When control is returned to **main**, *number* will be printed in octal and hexadecimal formats.

```
//
//     C++ program illustrates how to read an integer
//     into the program with a command-line argument.
//     Copyright (c) Chris H. Pappas and William H. Murray, 1990
//

#include <iostream.h>
#include <stdlib.h>

void binary(int digits);
main(int argc, char *argv[])
{

  int number;
```

```
if(argc!=2) {
  cout << "Enter a decimal number on the command line.\n";
  cout << "It will be converted to binary, octal and\n";
  cout << "hexadecimal.\n";
  exit(1);
}

number=atoi(argv[1]);
binary(number);
cout << "The octal equivalent is: "
     << oct << number << endl;
cout.setf(ios::uppercase);
cout << "The hexadecimal equivalent is: "
     << hex << number << endl;
return (0);
}

void binary(int digits)
{
  int i=0;
  int myarray[40];

  while (digits != 0) {
    myarray[i]=(digits % 2);
    digits/=2;
    i++;
  }

  i--;
  cout << "The binary equivalent is: ";
  for(;i>=0;i--)
    cout << dec << myarray[i];
    cout << "\n";
}
```

Of particular interest is the formatting of the various numbers. You learned earlier that the binary number is printed one digit at a time by unloading the array, *myarray,* in reverse order.

```
cout <<  dec << myarray[i]
```

When printing in octal format, the statement is

```
cout << "The octal equivalent is: "
     << oct << number
```

You could also print the hexadecimal equivalent by substituting *hex* for *oct.* The problem is that the hexadecimal values a, b, c, d, e, and f are printed in lowercase. To print these values in uppercase, you need to use a different strategy:

```
cout.setf(ios::uppercase);
```

The formatter in **cout** permits formatting much like that permitted in C's **printf** function. See Chapter 11, "Input and Output in C and C++," for more details.

Figures 8-1 and 8-2 show a Debugger screen for this program. Examine the variables in each Watch window.

Floats

As you can imagine, floats will not be any more difficult to intercept than integers. The following C example allows several angles to be entered on the command line. The sine of the angles will be extracted and printed to

```
≡  File  View  Run  Breakpoints  Data  Options  Window  Help        READY
┌[■]=Module: READ  File: READ.CPP (modified) 12══════════════1=[↑][↓]┐
  //
  //      C++ program illustrates how to read an integer
  //      into the program with a command-line argument.
  //      Copyright (c) Chris H. Pappas and William H. Murray, 1990
  //

  #include <iostream.h>
  #include <stdlib.h>

  void binary(int digits);

► main(int argc, char *argv[])
  {
      void exit(char *c);

      int number;
┌─────Watches────────────────────────────────────2─┐
myarray                     ????
argv[0]                     char * ds:FFE6 "C:\\LAN\\TD\\READ.EXE"
argv[1]                     char * ds:FFF9 "18"
F1-Help F2-Bkpt F3-Mod F4-Here F5-Zoom F6-Next F7-Trace F8-Step F9-Run F10-Menu
```

Figure 8-1.   Using the Debugger to examine a C++ numeric base converting program. argv[0] shows the title of the program while argv[1] is the number entered on the command line

```
≡  File  View  Run  Breakpoints  Data  Options  Window  Help        READY
┌[■]─Module: READ   File: READ.CPP 42════════════════════════════1=[↑][↓]┐
    return (0);                                                          │
  }                                                                      │
                                                                         │
  void binary(int digits)                                               │
  {                                                                      │
    int i=0;                                                            │
    int myarray[40];                                                    │
                                                                         │
    while (digits != 0) {                                               │
      myarray[i]=(digits % 2);                                          │
      digits/=2;                                                        │
►     i++;                                                              │
    }                                                                   │
                                                                         │
    i--;                                                                │
    cout << "The binary equivalent is: ";                              │
    for(;i>=0;i--)                                                      │
│◄                                                                     ►│
└─────────────────────────────────────────────────────────────────────┘
┌──Watches────────────────────────────────────────────────────2─┐
│myarray[i]              int 1 (0x1)                             │
│i                       int 4 (0x4)                             │
└────────────────────────────────────────────────────────────────┘
 F1-Help F2-Bkpt F3-Mod F4-Here F5-Zoom F6-Next F7-Trace F8-Step F9-Run F10-Menu
```

Figure 8-2.   The **binary** function of the base converting program is inspected

the screen. Since the angles are of type **float**, they can take on values such as 45.0, 76.32, or 0.02345.

```
/*
 *      C program illustrates how to read float data types
 *      into the program with a command-line argument.
 *      Copyright (c) Chris H. Pappas and William H. Murray, 1990
 */

#include <stdio.h>
#include <math.h>

const double PI=3.14159265359;

main(int argc, char *argv[])
{
  int i;
  double angle;

  if(argc<2) {
    printf("Enter several angles on the command line.\n");
    printf("Program will return the sine of the angles.\n");
    exit(1);
  }
```

```
  for (i=1; i<argc; i++) {
    angle=(double) atof(argv[i]);
    printf("The sine of %f is %15.141f\n",
           angle,sin((PI/180.0)*angle));
  }
  return (0);
}
```

The **atof** function converts the command-line string argument to a **float** type. The program uses the **sin** function within the **printf** function to retrieve the sine information.

SPECIAL C++ FEATURES

C++ offers several special features for functions. The code for an *inline* function is replicated where the function is called in the program. By actually placing the code at the point of the function call, you save execution time in frequently called short functions. Inline functions are similar to assembly language macros, which are covered in Chapter 18, "Power Programming: Macros and Procedures. " C++ also permits function *overloading.* Overloading permits you to give several function prototypes the same function name. Individual prototypes are then recognized by their type and argument list, not just by name. Overloading is useful where a function might have to work with different data types. C++ also lets you enter a variable number of arguments in the function's argument list. You can use ellipses where it is not possible, for whatever reason, to list all of a function's arguments. Since ellipses sidestep type checking, use them with caution.

The *inline* Keyword

The *inline* keyword is a directive, or rather a suggestion, to the C++ compiler to insert the function in a line. The compiler may ignore this suggestion for any of several reasons. For example, the function cannot contain a *for* loop or it might bc too long. The *inline* keyword is used primarily to save time when short functions are called many times within a program.

```
//
//       C++ program illustrates the use of an inline function.
//       Inline functions work best on short functions that are
//       used repeatedly.  This example just prints a message
//       several times to the screen.
//       Copyright (c) Chris H. Pappas and William H. Murray, 1990
//

#include <iostream.h>

inline void printit(void) {cout << "This is treated ";
                cout << "as an inline function!";
                cout << endl;}

main()
{
  int i;

  cout << "PRINT A MESSAGE SEVERAL TIMES: \n";

  for (i=0;i<11;i++)
    printit();
  return (0);
}
```

Overloading

The following example illustrates function overloading. Notice that two functions with the same name are prototyped within the same scope. The correct function will be selected based on the arguments provided. A function call to **times** will process **int** or **float** data correctly.

```
//
//       C++ program illustrates the function overloading.
//       Overloaded function receives an array of integers or
//       floats and returns either an integer or float product.
//       Copyright (c) Chris H. Pappas and William H. Murray, 1990
//

#include <iostream.h>

int times(int dataarray[]);
float times(float dataarray[]);

main()
{
  int firstarray[5]={1,2,3,4,5};
  float secondarray[5]={1.2,4.5,7.05,6.14,0.09876};
  int product1;
  float product2;
```

```
   product1=times(firstarray);
   product2=times(secondarray);
   cout << "The product of the integer numbers is: "
        << product1 << "\n";
   cout << "The product of the float numbers is: "
        << product2 << "\n";
   return (0);
}

int times(int dataarray[])
{
  int t;
  int temp;

  temp=dataarray[0];
  for (t=1;t<5;t++)
    temp*=dataarray[t];
  return (temp);
}

float times(float dataarray[])
{
  int t;
  float temp;
  temp=dataarray[0];
  for (t=1;t<5;t++)
    temp*=dataarray[t];
  return (temp);
}
```

There are a few things to avoid when overloading a function. For example, if a function only differs in the function type (and not arguments), it cannot be overloaded. Also, a function cannot have the following argument list:

```
float  myfunction(int value)
float  myfunction(int &data)    //not allowed
```

This argument list is not allowed because each function would accept the same type of arguments. Overloading will also be discussed in Chapter 13, "Classes."

Using a Variable Number of Arguments

You can use *ellipses* within the function's argument statement to indicate a variable number of arguments. For example,

```
void  myfunction(int x, float y, ...);
```

This syntax tells the C++ compiler that other arguments may follow. Naturally, type checking is suspended with ellipses.

PROGRAMMING PROBLEMS INVOLVING SCOPE

You may experience unexpected program results when using variables with different scope levels. For example, you can use a variable of the same name with both file and local scopes. The scope rules state that the variable with local scope (called a local variable) will take precedence over the variable with file scope (called a global variable). However, there are some problem areas that you might encounter in programming.

An Undefined Symbol in a C Program

In the following example, four variables are given a local scope within the function **main**. Copies of the variables *a* and *b* are passed to the function **multiplier**. This does not violate scope rules. However, when the **multiplier** function attempts to use the variable *c*, it cannot find the variable because the scope of the variable was to **main** only.

```
/*
*     C program to illustrate problems with scope rules.
*     Function is supposed to form a product of three numbers.
*     Compiler signals problems since variable c isn't known
*     to the function multiplier.
*     Copyright (c) Chris H. Pappas and William H. Murray, 1990
*/

#include <stdio.h>

int multiplier(int x,int y);

main()
{
  int a=5;
  int b=9;
  int c=4;
  int d;

  d=multiplier(a,b);
  printf("The product is: %d\n", d);
  return (0);
}
```

```
int multiplier(int x,int y)
{
   int z;

   z=x*y*c;
   return(z);
}
```

The compiler issues a warning and an error message. It first warns you that the *c* variable is never used within the function and then issues the error message that *c* has never been declared in the function **multiplier**. One way around this problem is to give *c* a file scope.

Use a Variable with File Scope

In this example, the variable *c* is given a file scope. If you make *c* global to the whole file, both **main** and **multiplier** can use it. Also note that both **main** and **multiplier** can change the value of the variable. If you want functions to be truly portable, you should not allow them to change program variables.

```
/*
 *      C program to illustrate problems with scope rules.
 *      Function is supposed to form a product of three numbers.
 *      Previous problem is solved, c variable is given file scope.
 *      Copyright (c) Chris H. Pappas and William H. Murray, 1990
 */

#include <stdio.h>

int multiplier(int x,int y);

int c=4;

main()
{
   int a=5;
   int b=9;
   int d;

   d=multiplier(a,b);
   printf("The product is: %d\n", d);
   return (0);
}

int multiplier(int x,int y)
{
   int z;
```

```
  z=x*y*c;
  return(z);
}
```

This program will compile correctly and print the product 180 to the screen.

Overriding a Variable with File Scope by a Variable with Local Scope

The scope rules state that variables with both file and local scope will use the local variable value over the global value.

```
/*
 *    C program to illustrate problems with scope rules.
 *    Function forms a product of three numbers, but which
 *    three?  Two are passed as function arguments.  The
 *    variable c has both a file and local scope.
 *    Copyright (c) Chris H. Pappas and William H. Murray, 1990
*/

#include <stdio.h>

int multiplier(int x,int y);

int c=4;

main()
{
  int a=5;
  int b=9;
  int d;

  d=multiplier(a,b);
  printf("The product is: %d\n", d);
  return (0);
}

int multiplier(int x,int y)
{
  int z;
  int c=2;

  z=x*y*c;
  return(z);
}
```

In this example, the variable *c* has both file and local scope. When *c* is used within the function **multiplier,** the local scope takes precedence and the product of 5 * 9 * 2 = 90 is returned.

A Scope Problem in C++

In the C++ example, everything proceeds smoothly until you print the information to the screen. The **cout** function prints the values for *a* and *b* correctly. When selecting the *c* value, it chooses the global variable with file scope. The program reports that the product of 5 * 9 * 4 = 90, clearly a mistake. You know that in this case, the **multiplier** function used the local value of *c*.

```
//
//    C++ program to illustrate problems with scope rules.
//    Function forms a product of three numbers.  The c
//    variable is of local scope and used by the function
//    multiplier.  However, main function reports that
//    the c value used is 4.   What's wrong here?
//    Copyright (c) Chris H. Pappas and William H. Murray, 1990
//

#include <iostream.h>

int multiplier(int x,int y);

int c=4;

main()
{
   int a=5;
   int b=9;
   int d;

   d=multiplier(a,b);
   cout << "The product of " << a << " * " << b
        << " * " << c << " is: " << d;
   return (0);
}

int multiplier(int x,int y)
{
   int z;
   int c=2;
   z=x*y*c;
   return(z);
}
```

If you actually want to form the product with a global value of *c*, how could you resolve this conflict? C++ would permit you to use the scope resolution operator mentioned earlier in the chapter.

Using the C++ Scope Resolution Operator

In this example, the scope resolution operator is used to avoid conflicts between a variable with both file and local scope. The last program reported an incorrect product since the local value was used in the calculation. Notice in the **multiplier** function the use of the scope resolution operator, ::.

```
//
//    C++ program to illustrate problems with scope rules,
//    and how to use the scope resolution operator.
//    Function multiplier uses resolution operator to
//    "override" local and utilize variable with file scope.
//    Copyright (c) Chris H. Pappas and William H. Murray, 1990
//

#include <iostream.h>
int multiplier(int x,int y);

int c=4;

main()
{
  int a=5;
  int b=9;
  int d;

  d=multiplier(a,b);
  cout << "The product of " << a << "  *  " << b
       << " * " << c << " is: " << d;
  return (0);
}

int multiplier(int x,int y)
{
  int z;
  int c=2;

  z=x*y*(::c);
  return(z);
}
```

The scope resolution operator, ::, need not be enclosed in parentheses—they are for emphasis. Now, the value of the global variable, with file scope, will be used in the calculation. When the results are printed to the screen, you will now see that 5 * 9 * 4 = 180.

9

ARRAYS

Arrays, pointers, and strings are related topics in C. However, this chapter just covers arrays. In C and in C++, there are many uses for arrays that don't depend on a detailed understanding of pointers. In addition, since arrays are a large topic in themselves, it is best not to confuse the issue with a discussion of pointers. Pointers, however, allow you to understand how an array is processed. Chapter 10, "Pointers," will examine the topic of pointers and will complete this chapter's discussion of arrays.

WHAT ARE ARRAYS?

Arrays are indexed variables that contain many data items of the same type. Each array has one name, and you refer to the individual elements of the array by associating a subscript, or index, with the array name. In the C language, an array is not a basic type of data; instead, it is an aggregate type made up of other data types. In C, you can have an array of anything: characters, integers, floats, doubles, arrays, pointers, structures, and so on. The concept of arrays is more or less the same in both C and C++.

THE BASIC PROPERTIES OF AN ARRAY

An array has four basic properties:

- The individual data items in the array are called *elements.*

- All elements must be of the same data type.

- All elements are stored contiguously in the computer's memory, and the subscript (or index) of the first element is zero.

- The name of the array is a constant value that represents the address of the first element in the array.

Because all elements are assumed to be of the same size, you cannot define arrays using mixed data types. If you did, it would be very difficult to determine where any given element was stored. The fact that all elements in an array are of the same size helps determine how to locate a given element. The elements are stored contiguously in the computer's memory (with the lowest address corresponding to the first element, and the highest address to the last element). In other words, there is no filler space between elements, and they are physically adjacent in the computer.

It is possible to have arrays within arrays—that is, multidimensional arrays. Actually, if an array element is a structure (covered in Chapter 12, "Structures, Unions, and Miscellaneous Items"), other data types can exist in the array by existing inside the structure member.

Finally, the name of an array represents a constant value that cannot change during the execution of the program. For this reason, some forms of expressions that might appear to be valid are not allowed. You will eventually learn these subtleties.

DEFINING AN ARRAY

Here are two example array definitions:

```
char array_one[10];   /* an array of ten characters  */
int  array_two[12];   /* an array of twelve integers */
```

To define an array, write the array type, followed by a valid array name and a pair of square brackets enclosing a constant expression. The constant expression defines the size of the array. You cannot use a variable name inside the square brackets—in other words, you can't avoid specifying the array size until the program actually runs. The expression must reduce to a constant value, because the compiler has to know exactly how much storage space to reserve for the array. It is best to use defined constants to specify the size of the array, as in:

```
#define ARRAY_ONE_SIZE 10
#define ARRAY_TWO_SIZE 12

char array1[ARRAY_ONE_SIZE];
char array2[ARRAY_TWO_SIZE];
```

By using defined constants, you can ensure that subsequent references to the array will not exceed the defined array size. For instance, it is very common to use a defined constant as a terminating condition in a *for* loop that accesses array elements, as in this example:

```
#include <stdio.h>
#define ARRAY_ONE_SIZE 10
#define ARRAY_TWO_SIZE 12

char array1[ARRAY_ONE_SIZE];
char array2[ARRAY_TWO_SIZE];

main()
{
  int i;
  for(i = 0;i < ARRAY_ONE_SIZE; i++) {
  .
  .
  .
  }
  return(0);
}
```

INITIALIZING AN ARRAY

There are three methods for initializing arrays:

- By default when they are created. This only applies to global and static automatic arrays.

- Explicitly when they are created by supplying constant initializing data.

- During program execution by assigning or copying data into the array.

Only constant data can be used to initialize an array when it is created. If the array elements must receive their values from variables, you must initialize the array by writing explicit statements as part of the program code.

Initializing by Default

The ANSI C standard specifies that arrays are either *global* (defined outside of **main** and any other function) or *static automatic* (static, but defined after any opening brace) and will always be initialized to binary zero if no other initialization data is supplied. You can run the following program to make certain that your compiler meets this standard:

```
/*
*    A C program to test default data initializations
*    Copyright (c) Chris H. Pappas and William H. Murray, 1990
*/

#include <stdio.h>

#define ARRAY_ONE_SIZE 5
#define ARRAY_TWO_SIZE 5

int array_one[ARRAY_ONE_SIZE];          /* a global array */

main()
{
  static int array_two[ARRAY_TWO_SIZE]; /* a static array */
  printf("array_one[0]: %d\n",array_one[0]);
  printf("array_two[0]: %d\n",array_two[0]);
  return(0);
}
```

When you run the program, zeroes should verify that both array types are indeed automatically initialized. This program also shows that the first subscript for all arrays in C is zero. Unlike programs in other languages, a C program cannot think that the first subscript is 1. Remember, one of C's strengths was its close link to assembly language. In assembly language, the first element in a table is always at the zeroth offset.

Explicitly Initializing an Array

Just as you can define and initialize variables of type *int, char, float, double,* and so on, you can also initialize arrays. The ANSI C standard lets you supply initialization values for any array, global or otherwise, defined anywhere in a program. The following code segment illustrates how to define and initialize four arrays:

```
int numbers[3] = {1,2,3};
static float cost[5] =  {5.45,6.78,3.88,9.12,0.0};
static int more_numbers[3] = {1,2,3,4,5,6,7};
char vowels[] = {'a','e','i','o','u'};
```

The first example declares the *numbers* array to be 3 integers and provides the values of the elements in curly braces, separated by commas. As usual, a semicolon ends the statement. After the compiled program loads into the computer's memory, the reserved space for the *numbers* array will now contain the initial values, so they won't need assignments when the program executes. This is more than just a convenience—the actual initialization happens at a different time. If the program goes on to change the values of the *numbers* array, they stay changed. Many compilers permit you to initialize arrays only if they are global or static, as in the second example, where the initialization happens when the entire program loads.

The third example shows what happens if you put the wrong count in the array declaration. Many compilers consider this an error, while others reserve enough space to hold either the number of values you ask for or the number of values you provide, whichever is greater. This example will result in an error message indicating too many initializers. In contrast, when you ask for more space than you provide values for, the values go into the beginning of the array and the extra elements become zeroes. This also means that you don't need to count the values when you provide all of them. If the count is empty, as in the fourth example, the number of values determines the size of the array.

Unsized Array Initializations

Most compilers require either the size of the array or the list of actual values, but not both. For example, a program will frequently want to define its own set of error messages. You can do this in one of two ways. Here is one method:

```
char error1[31] = "File I/O ERROR - Notify SYSOP\n";
char error2[16] = "Disk not ready\n";
char error3[16] = "File not found\n";
```

This approach can become tedious—straining your eyes as you count the number of characters—and is very error prone. Here is an example of the second method:

```
char error1[] = "File I/O ERROR - Notify SYSOP\n";
char error2[] = "Disk not ready\n";
char error3[] = "File not found\n";
```

This method allows C to dimension the arrays automatically with unsized arrays. Whenever C encounters an array initialization statement and the array size is not specified, the compiler automatically creates an array large enough to hold all of the specified data.

An array with an empty size declaration and no list of values has a **NULL** length. If any declaration follows, the name of the **NULL** array refers to the same address, and storing values in the **NULL** array puts them in addresses allocated to *other* variables.

Also, unsized array initializations are not restricted to one-dimensional arrays. For multidimensional arrays, you must specify all but the leftmost dimension for C to index the array properly. With this approach, you can build tables of varying length and the compiler will automatically allocate enough storage.

USING ARRAY SUBSCRIPTS

A variable declaration usually reserves one or more cells in internal memory and through a lookup table associates a name with the cell or cells that you can use to access the cells. For example, the definition

```
int book;
```

reserves only one integer-sized cell in internal memory and associates the name *book* with that cell (see Figure 9-1). On the other hand, the definition

```
int books_in_stock[5];
```

reserves five contiguous cells in internal memory and associates the name *books_in_stock* with the five cells (see Figure 9-1). Since all array elements must be of the same data type, each of the five cells in the array *books_in_stock* can hold one *int*.

Consider the difference between accessing the single cell associated with the variable *book* and the five cells associated with the array *books_in_stock*. To access the cell associated with the variable *book*, you simply use the name *book*. For the array *books_in_stock*, you must specify an index to indicate exactly which cell among the five you wish to access. The statements

```
books_in_stock[0];
books_in_stock[1];
books_in_stock[2];
```

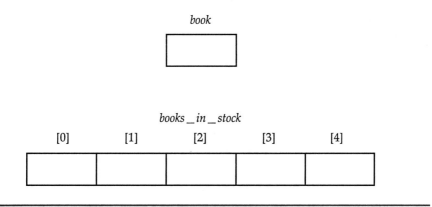

Figure 9-1.   How variables and arrays are stored in memory

designate the first cell, the second cell, and the third cell of the array. When you access an array element, the integer enclosed in square brackets is the index, which indicates the *offset,* or the distance between the cell to be accessed and the first cell. Beginning programmers often make mistakes in the index value used to reference an array's first element. The first element is at index position [0] (not at index position [1]) since there is 0 distance between the first element and itself. As you can see, the third cell has an index value of 2 because its distance from the first cell is 2.

When dealing with arrays, you can use the square brackets in two quite different ways. When you are *defining* an array, you specify the number of cells in square brackets:

```
int books_in_stock[10];
```

But when you are *accessing* a specific array element, you use the array's name with an index enclosed in square brackets:

```
books_in_stock[5];
```

Assuming the previous declaration for the array *books_in_stock,* the following statement is illegal:

```
books_in_stock[10];
```

This statement attempts to reference a cell that is a distance of 10 from the first cell—that is, the eleventh cell. Because there are only 10 cells in *books_in_stock,* the reference is an error. It is up to you to make sure that index expressions remain within the array's bounds.

Assume the following declarations:

```
#define NUMBER_OF_TITLES 10

int books_in_stock[NUMBER_OF_TITLES];
int index1 = 1;
int index2 = 2;
```

Now look what happens with the following set of executable statements:

```
books_in_stock[2];
books_in_stock[index2];
books_in_stock[index1 + index2];
books_in_stock[index2 - index1];
books_in_stock[index1 - index2];
```

The first two statements reference the third element of the array. The first statement uses a constant value expression, while the second statement uses a variable. The last three statements show that you can use expressions as subscripts as long as they evaluate to a valid integer index. Statement three has an index value of 3 and references the fourth element of the array. The fourth statement, with an index value of 1, accesses the second element of the array. The last statement is illegal because the index value −1 is invalid.

You can access any element in an array without knowing its size. For example, suppose that you want to access the third element in *books_in_stock,* an array of *ints.* Remember from Chapter 6, "Data," that different systems allocate different cell sizes to the same data type. On one computer system, an *int* might occupy 2 bytes of storage, whereas on another system, an *int* might occupy 4 bytes of storage. However, you can access the third element as *books_in_stock[2]* on *either* system. The index value indicates the number of elements to move, regardless of the number of bits allocated.

This offset addressing holds true for other array types. On one system, *int* variables might require twice as many bits of storage as *char* variables; on another system, *int* variables might require four times as many bits as *char* variables. Yet to access the fourth element in either an array of *ints* or an array of *chars,* you would use an index value of 3.

USING sizeof WITH ARRAYS

As you have learned, the **sizeof** operator returns the physical size, in bytes, of the data item to which it is applied. You can use it with any type of data item except bit fields. Programmers frequently use **sizeof** to determine the physical size of a variable when the size of the variable's data type can vary from machine to machine. You have seen how an integer can be either 2 or 4 bytes depending on the machine being used. If the operating system will request additional memory to hold ten integers, you need some way to determine whether you require 20 bytes (10 × 2 bytes/integer) or 40 bytes (10 × 4 bytes/integer). The following program will automatically take this size requirement into consideration (and print a value of 20 for systems allocating 2 bytes per *int* cell):

```
/*
 *    A C program using sizeof to verify an array's size
 *    Copyright (c) Chris H. Pappas and William H. Murray, 1990
 */

#include <stdio.h>

#define NUMBER_OF_TITLES 10

main()
{
  int books_in_stock[NUMBER_OF_TITLES];

  printf("There are %d number of bytes in the array",
    " books_in_stock.\n",(int)sizeof(books_in_stock));
  return(0);
}
```

The concept of using **sizeof** becomes essential when the program must be portable and independent of any particular hardware. If you are wondering why the *int* type cast on the result returned by **sizeof** was necessary, in the ANSI C standard **sizeof** does not return an *int* type. Instead, **sizeof** returns a data type *size_t*, which is large enough to hold the return value. This was added to C by the ANSI standard because an *int* is not large enough to represent the size of all data items on certain computers. In our example, casting the return value to an *int* allows it to match the **%d** conversion character of the **printf** function. Otherwise, if the returned value were larger than an integer, the **printf** function would not have worked properly.

With only a few modifications to the following C program, you can explore how various data types are stored internally:

```
/*
 *    A C program to illustrate internal data storage.
 *    Copyright (c) Chris H. Pappas and William H. Murray, 1990
 */

#include <stdio.h>

#define SIZE 10
```

```
main()
{
  int array_index, int_array[SIZE];

  printf("sizeof(int) is %d\n\n", (int) sizeof(int));

  for(array_index = 0; array_index < SIZE; array_index++)
    printf("&array[%d] = %X\n", array_index,
             &int_array[array_index]);
  return(0);
}
```

If you run the program on a machine with a word length of 2 bytes, the output will look much like this:

```
sizeof(int) is 2

&array[0] = FF32
&array[1] = FF34
&array[2] = FF36
&array[3] = FF38
&array[4] = FF3A
&array[5] = FF3C
&array[6] = FF3E
&array[7] = FF40
&array[8] = FF42
&array[9] = FF44
```

Notice how the & (address) operator can be applied to any variable, including an array element. An array element can be treated like any other variable; its value can form an expression, it can be assigned a value, and it can be passed as an argument (or parameter) to a library function. In this example, notice that the array elements' addresses are exactly 2 bytes apart. You will see the importance of this contiguous storage when you use arrays with pointer variables.

The following listing is the C++ equivalent of the program just discussed:

```
//
//    A C++ program to illustrate internal data storage.
//    Copyright (c) Chris H. Pappas and William H. Murray, 1990
//

#include <iostream.h>

#define SIZE 10
```

```
main()
{
  int array_index, int_array[SIZE];

  cout << "sizeof(int) is %d" << (int) sizeof(int) << "\n\n";
  cout.setf(ios::uppercase);

  for(array_index = 0; array_index < SIZE; array_index++) {
    cout << "&array[" << array_index << "] ";
    cout << hex << &int_array[array_index] << "\n";
  }

  return(0);
}
```

ARRAY BOUNDARY CHECKING

C array types offer faster executing code at the expense of zero boundary checking. Remember, since C was designed to replace assembly language code, error checking was left out of the compiler to keep the code concise. Without any compiler error checking, you must be very careful when dealing with array boundaries. For example, the following program incites no complaints from the compiler, and yet it can change the contents of other variables or even crash the program:

```
/*
 *    A C program you shouldn't run
 *    Copyright (c) Chris H. Pappas and William H. Murray, 1990
 */

#include <stdio.h>

#define LIMIT 10
#define TROUBLE 50

main()
{
  int collide[LIMIT], index;

  for(index=0; index < TROUBLE; index++)
    collide[index]=index;
  return(0);
}
```

ARRAYS AND STRINGS

While C supplies the data type *char*, it does not have a data type for character strings. Instead, you must represent a string as an array of characters. The array uses one cell for each character in the string, with the final cell holding the null character '\0';

The following program shows how you can represent the three states of water as a character string. The array *water_state1* is initialized character by character with the assignment operator; the array *water_state2* is initialized by using the function **scanf**; and the array *water_state3* is initialized in the definition:

```
/*
 *     This C program will illustrate character strings
 *     Copyright (c) Chris H. Pappas and William H. Murray, 1990
 */

#include <stdio.h>

main()
{
  char         water_state1[4],            /* gas    */
               water_state2[6];            /* solid  */
  static char water_state3[7] = "liquid";  /* liquid */

  water_state1[0] = 'g';
  water_state1[1] = 'a';
  water_state1[2] = 's';
  water_state1[3] = '\0';
  printf("\n\n\tPlease enter the water state --> solid ");
  scanf("%s",water_state2);

  printf("%s\n",water_state1);
  printf("%s\n",water_state2);
  printf("%s\n",water_state3);
  return(0);
}
```

The definitions

```
char         water_state1[4],            /* gas    */
             water_state2[6];            /* solid  */
static char water_state3[7] = "liquid";  /* liquid */
```

show how C treats character strings as arrays of characters. Even though the state "gas" has three characters, the array *water_state1* has four cells— one cell for each letter in the state "gas" and one for the null character. Remember, '\0' counts as one character. Similarly, the state "solid" has five characters ("liquid" has six) but requires six storage cells (seven for *water_state3*), including the null character. Remember, you could also have initialized the *water_state3[7]* array of characters with braces:

```
static char water_state3[7] = {'l','i','q','u','i','d','\0'};
```

When you use double quotes to list the initial values of the character array, the system will automatically add the null terminator '\0'. You could also have written the same line as follows,

```
static char water_state3[] = "liquid";
```

using an unsized array. Of course, you could choose the tedious approach to initializing an array of characters, as was done with *water_state1*. A more common approach is to use the **scanf** function to read the string directly into the array, as was done with *water_state2*. The **scanf** function uses a '%s' conversion specification. This causes the function to skip whitespace (blanks, tabs, and carriage returns) and then to read into the character array *water_state2* all characters up to the next whitespace. The system will then automatically add a null terminator. Remember, the array's dimension must be large enough to hold the string along with a null terminator. Look at this statement one more time:

```
scanf("%s",water_state2);
```

Did you notice that *water_state2* was not preceded by the address operator &? While **scanf** was written to expect the address of a variable, an array's name, unlike simple variable names, is an *address expression*—the address of the first element in the array.

When you use the **printf** function with a '%s', the function is expecting the corresponding argument to be the address of some character string. The string is printed up to but not including the null character.

The following listing illustrates these principles using an equivalent C++ algorithm:

```
//
//   This C++ program will illustrate the use of character strings
//   Copyright (c) Chris H. Pappas and William H. Murray, 1990
//

#include <iostream.h>

main()
{
   char         water_state1[4],            // gas
                water_state2[6];            // solid
   static char water_state3[7] = "liquid";  // liquid
```

```
water_state1[0] = 'g';
water_state1[1] = 'a';
water_state1[2] = 's';
water_state1[3] = '\0';

cout << "\n\n\tPlease enter the water state --> solid ";
cin >> water_state2;

cout << water_state1 << "\n";
cout << water_state2 << "\n";
cout << water_state3 << "\n";
return(0);
}
```

The output from the program looks like this:

```
gas
solid
liquid
```

MULTIDIMENSIONAL ARRAYS

The term *dimension* represents the number of indexes used to reference a particular element in an array. All of the arrays discussed so far have been one-dimensional and require only one index to access an element. You can tell how many dimensions an array has by looking at its declaration. If there is only one set of brackets, the array is one-dimensional. Two sets of brackets indicate a two-dimensional array, and so on. Arrays of more than one dimension are called *multidimensional arrays*. The working maximum number of dimensions is usually three.

The following declarations set up a status array for disk sectors (although for a very small disk). The array is initialized while the program executes.

```
/*
*    A C program using a two-dimensional array
*    Copyright (c) Chris H. Pappas and William H. Murray, 1990
*/

#include <stdio.h>

#define TRACKS 5
#define SECTORS 4
```

```
main()
{
  int track;
  int sector;
  int status[TRACKS][SECTORS];
  int add;
  int multiple;

  for(track=0; track<TRACKS; track++)
    for(sector=0; sector<SECTORS; sector++) {
      add = SECTORS - sector;
      multiple = track;
      status[track][sector] = (track+1) *
      sector + add * multiple;
    }

  for(track=0; track<TRACKS; track++) {
    printf("ROW NUMBER: %d\n",track);
    printf("CELL OFFSETS\n");
    for(sector=0; sector<SECTORS; sector++)
      printf(" %d ",status[track][sector]);
    printf("\n\n");
  }
  return(0);
}
```

The program uses two *for* loops to calculate and initialize each of the array elements to their respective offset from the first element. The created array has five rows (TRACKS) and four columns (SECTORS) per row, for a total of 20 integer elements. Multidimensional arrays are stored in a linear fashion in the computer's memory. Elements in multidimensional arrays are grouped from the rightmost index inward. In the preceding example, *track* 1 *sector* 1 would be element five of the storage array. While the calculation of the offset appears to be a little tricky, note how easily each array element itself is referenced:

```
status[track][sector] = . . .
```

The output from the program looks like this:

```
ROW NUMBER: 0
CELL OFFSETS
  0   1   2   3

ROW NUMBER: 1
CELL OFFSETS
  4   5   6   7
```

```
ROW NUMBER: 2
CELL OFFSETS
  8   9   10   11

ROW NUMBER: 3
CELL OFFSETS
 12   13   14   15

ROW NUMBER: 4
CELL OFFSETS
 16   17   18   19
```

Multidimensional arrays can also be initialized in the same way as one-dimensional arrays. For example, the following program defines a two-dimensional array *powers* and initializes the array when it is defined. The function **pow** returns the value of *x* raised to the *y* power.

```c
/*
 *    A C program that demonstrates how to initialize and access
 *    a two-dimensional array of double
 *    Copyright (c) Chris H. Pappas and William H. Murray, 1990
 */

#include <stdio.h>
#include <math.h>

#define ROWS 5
#define COLUMNS 3
#define BASE 0
#define RAISED_TO 1
#define RESULT 2
main()
{
  double powers[ROWS][COLUMNS]={
    2.3, 1, 0,
    2.9, 2, 0,
    2.1, 3, 0,
    2.2, 4, 0,
    2.4, 5, 0
  };

  int row_index, column_index;

  for(row_index=0; row_index < ROWS; row_index++)
    powers[row_index][RESULT] =
      pow(powers[row_index][BASE],powers[row_index][RAISED_TO]);

  for(row_index=0; row_index < ROWS; row_index++) {
    printf("     %d\n",(int)powers[row_index][RAISED_TO]);
    printf(" %2.1f = %.2f\n\n",powers[row_index][BASE],
      powers[row_index][RESULT]);
  }
```

```
  return(0);
}
```

The array *powers* was declared to be of type *double* because the function **pow** expects two *double* variables and returns a *double*. Of course, you must be careful when initializing two-dimensional arrays. Make certain that you know which dimension is increasing the fastest (always the rightmost dimension). The output from the program looks like this:

```
    1
2.3 = 2.30

    2
2.9 = 8.41

    3
2.1 = 9.26

    4
2.2 = 23.43

    5
2.4 = 79.63
```

ARRAYS AND FUNCTIONS

Just like other C variables, arrays can be passed from one function to another. Because you must understand pointers to understand arrays as function arguments, the topic is covered in more detail in Chapter 10, "Pointers."

Array Arguments in C

Consider a function **total** that computes the sum of the array elements *array_value[0]*, *array_value[1]*,..., *array_value[n]*. Two parameters are required: an array parameter *array_value_received* to catch the array passed, and a parameter *current_index* to catch the index of the last item in the array to be totaled. Assuming that the array is an array of *ints* and that the index is also of type *int*, the parameters in **total** can be described as

```
int total(int array_value_received[], int current_index)
```

The parameter declaration for the array includes square brackets to tell the function **total** that *array_value_received* is an array name and not the name of an ordinary parameter. Note that the number of cells is *not* enclosed within the square brackets. Of course, the simple parameter *current_index* is declared as previously described. Invoking the function is as easy as

```
result = total(array_value,actual_index);
```

Passing the array *array_value* just involves entering its name as the argument. When passing an array's name to a function, you are actually passing the address of the array's first element. The expression

```
array_value
```

is really shorthand for

```
&array_value[0]
```

Technically, you can invoke the function **total** with either of the two following valid statements:

```
result = total(array_value,actual_index);
result = total(&array_value[0],actual_index);
```

In either case, within the function **total** you can access every cell in the array.

When a function is going to process an array, the calling function includes the name of the array in the function's argument list. This means that the function receives and carries out its processing on the actual elements of the array, not on a local copy as in single-value variables where functions pass only their values.

When a function is to receive an array name as an argument, there are two ways to declare the argument locally: as an array or as a pointer. Which method you use depends on how the function processes the set of values. If the function steps through the elements with an index, the declaration must be an array with square brackets following the name. The size can be empty since the declaration does not reserve space for the entire array, just for the address where it begins. Having seen the array declaration at the beginning of the function, the compiler permits brackets with an index to appear after the array name anywhere in the function.

The following program declares an array of five elements and, after printing its values, calls in a function to determine the largest value in the array. To do this, it passes the array name and size to the function **find_biggest**, which declares them as an array called *array[]*, and an integer called *size*. The function then passes through the array, comparing each element against the largest value it has seen so far. Every time it encounters a bigger value, it stores that new value in the variable *so_far_biggest*. At the end, it returns the largest value that it has detected for **main** to print.

```
/*
 *    A C program that demonstrates the passing of arrays
 *    Copyright (c) Chris H. Pappas and William H. Murray, 1990
 */

#include <stdio.h>

#define SIZE 5
int find_biggest(int array[],int size);

main()
{
  int numbers[SIZE] = {2,5,1,9,7};
  int i, is_big;
  printf("Here is the initial set of numbers -- ");
  for(i = 0; i < SIZE; i++)
    printf("%d ",numbers[i]);
  is_big = find_biggest(numbers,SIZE);
  printf("\nThe biggest number is %d: \n",is_big);
  return(0);
}

int find_biggest(int array[], int size)
{
  int k, so_far_biggest;

  so_far_biggest = 0;
  for(k = 0; k < size; k++)
    if (array[k] > so_far_biggest)
      so_far_biggest = array[k];
  return(so_far_biggest);
}
```

Array Arguments in C++

The following program has a format similar to the C programs examined so far. It demonstrates how to declare and pass an array argument.

```
//
//    A C++ program to demonstrate how to declare and pass arrays
//    Copyright (c) Chris H. Pappas and William H. Murray, 1990
//

#include <iostream.h>

#define MAXVALUES 10
void increment(int array[]);

main()
{
  int value_array[MAXVALUES]={1,2,3,4,5,6,7,8,9,10};
  int index;

  cout << "value_array before calling increment\n";
  for(index=0; index < MAXVALUES; index++)
    cout << "  " << value_array[index];

  increment(value_array);

  cout << "\n\nvalue_array after calling increment\n";
  for(index=0; index < MAXVALUES; index++)
    cout << "  " << value_array[index];
  return(0);
}

void increment(int array[])
{
  int local_index;

  for(local_index=0; local_index < MAXVALUES; local_index++)
    array[local_index] = array[local_index] + 1;
}
```

The output from the program looks like this:

```
value_array before calling increment
  1   2   3   4   5   6   7   8   9   10

value_array after calling increment
  2   3   4   5   6   7   8   9   10   11
```

What do the values in the output tell you about the array argument? Is the array passed call-by-value or call-by-reference? The function **increment** simply adds one to each array element. Since this incremented change is reflected back in **main**'s *value_array,* it seems that the parameter was passed call-by-reference. Remember, you know that this is true because you know that array names are addresses to the first array cell.

The following C++ program incorporates many of the array features discussed so far, including multidimensional array initialization, referencing, and arguments:

```
//
//    A C++ program that demonstrates how to define, pass,
//    and walk through the different dimensions of an array
//    Copyright (c) Chris H. Pappas and William H. Murray, 1990
//

#include <iostream.h>

void print_it(char char_array[][3][4]);

char array1[3][4][5]= {
                {
                  {'T','h','i','s',' '},
                  {'t','e','x','t',' '},
                  {'i','s',' ','1','a'},
                  {'y','e','r',' ','0'},
                },
                {
                  {'A','B','C','D','E'}
                },
                };

int array2[4][3]={ {5},{6},{7},{8} };

main()
{
  int index_d1, index_d2, index_d3;
  static char array3[2][3][4];

  cout << "sizeof array3          = " << sizeof(array3) << "\n";
  cout << "sizeof array3[0]       = " << sizeof(array3[0]) << "\n";
  cout << "sizeof array3[0][0]    = " << sizeof(array3[0][0])
                                      << "\n";
  cout << "sizeof array3[0][0][0] = " << sizeof(array3[0][0][0])
                                      << "\n";

  print_it(array3);

  cout << "array1[0][1][2] is     = " << array1[0][1][2] << "\n";
  cout << "array1[1][0][2] is     = " << array1[1][0][2] << "\n";

  cout << "print part of array1\n";
  for(index_d2=0; index_d2 < 4; index_d2++)
    for(index_d3=0; index_d3 < 5; index_d3++)
      cout << array1[0][index_d2][index_d3];

  cout << "\nprint all of array2\n";
  for(index_d1=0; index_d1 < 4; index_d1++) {
    for(index_d2=0; index_d2 < 3; index_d2++)
      cout << array2[index_d1][index_d2];
```

```
        cout << "\n";
    }
}

void print_it(char array[][3][4])
{
    cout << "sizeof array          = " << sizeof(array) << "\n";
    cout << "sizeof array[0]       = " << sizeof(array[0]) << "\n";
    cout << "sizeof array1         = " << sizeof(array1) << "\n";
    cout << "sizeof array1[0]      = " << sizeof(array1[0]) << "\n";
}
```

Note how *array1* is defined and initialized. Braces group the characters so that they have a form similar to the dimensions of the array. This helps you to visualize the form of the array. The braces are not required in this case since you are not leaving any gaps in the array with the initializing data. If you were initializing just a portion of any dimension, various sets of the inner braces would be required to designate which initializing values should apply to which part of the array. The easiest way to visualize the three-dimensional array is to imagine three layers, each having a two-dimensional four-row-by-five-column array (see Figure 9-2).

The first four lines of the program output show the size of the array, various dimensions, and an individual element. The output illustrates how the total size of the multidimensional array is the product of all the dimensions times the size of the array data type—in this case, 2 * 3 * 4 * **sizeof**(*char*) or 24.

Notice how the array element *array1[0]* is in itself an array containing a two-dimensional array of [3][4], which gives *array1[0]* the size of 12. The size of *array1[0][0]* is 4, which is the number of elements in the final dimension since each element has a size of 1, as **sizeof**(*array1[0][0][0]*) shows.

To understand multidimensional arrays, you must realize that *array1[0]* is both an array name and a pointer constant. Because the program did not subscript the last dimension, the expression does not have the same type as the data type of each fundamental array element. Because *array1[0]* does not refer to an individual element, but rather to another array, it does not have the type of *char*! Since *array1[0]* has the type of pointer constant, it also cannot appear on the left of an assignment operator in an assignment expression.

Something very interesting happens when you use an array name in a function argument list, as was done when the function **print_it** was invoked with *array3*. While inside the function, if you perform a **sizeof**

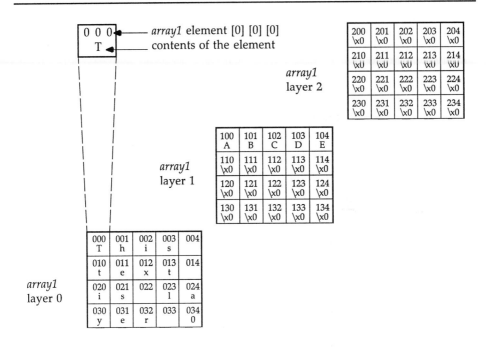

Figure 9-2.   A visual representation of *array1*

operation against the formal parameter that represents the array name, you do not correctly compute the actual size of the array. What the function sees is only a copy of the address of the first element in the array. Therefore, the function **sizeof** will return the size of the address, not the item to which it refers.

The **sizeof** *array[0]* in function **print_it** is 12 because it was declared in the function that the formal parameter was an array whose last two dimensions were [3] and [4]. You could not have used any other values when you declared the size of these last two dimensions, because the function prototype defined them to be [3] and [4]. Without a prototype, the compiler would not be able to detect the difference in the way the array was dimensioned. This would let you redefine the way you viewed the array's organization. The function **print_it** also outputs the **sizeof** of the global *array1*. Interestingly, this shows that while a function may have access to global data directly, it only has access to the address of an array that is passed to a function as an argument.

Returning to the **main** function, the next two statements executed demonstrate how to reference specific elements in the *array1*. *array1[0][1][2]* references the zeroth layer, second row, third column, or 'x'. *array1[1][0][2]* references the second layer, row 0, third column, or 'C'.

The next block of code in **main** contains two nested *for* loops demonstrating that the arrays are stored in *row major order*. As you've already seen, the rightmost subscript (column) of the array varies the fastest when you view the array in a linear fashion. The first *for* loop pair hardwires the output to the zeroth layer and selects a row, with the inner loop traversing each column in *array1*.

The last nested *for* loop pair displays the elements of *array2* in the form of a rectangle, similar to the way that many people visualize a two-dimensional array. Look at the initialization of *array2*. Because each inner set of braces corresponds to one row of the array, and enough values were not supplied inside the inner braces, the system padded the remaining elements with zeroes!

The output from the program looks like this:

```
sizeof array3          = 24
sizeof array3[0]       = 12
sizeof array3[0][0]    = 4
sizeof array3[0][0][0] = 1
sizeof array          = 2
sizeof array[0]        = 12
sizeof array1         = 60
sizeof array1[0]      = 20
array1[0][1][2] is    = x
array1[1][0][2] is    = C
print part of array1
This text is layer 0
print all of array2
500
600
700
800
```

STRING FUNCTIONS THAT USE ARRAYS

When standard input and output were discussed, functions that use character arrays as function arguments were not covered. Specifically, these functions are **gets**, **puts**, **fgets**, **fputs**, and **sprintf** (which are string I/O functions), and **stpcpy**, **strcat**, **strcmp**, and **strlen** (which are string manipulation functions).

gets, puts, fgets, fputs, and sprintf

```
/*
 *    A C program demonstrating string I/O functions
 *    Copyright (c) Chris H. Pappas and William H. Murray, 1990
 */

#include <stdio.h>

#define SIZE 20

main()
{
  char test_array[SIZE];

  fputs("Please enter the first string  : ",stdout);
  gets(test_array);
  fputs("The first string entered is     : ",stdout);
  puts(test_array);

  fputs("Please enter the second string : ",stdout);
  fgets(test_array,SIZE,stdin);
  fputs("The second string entered is    : ",stdout);
  fputs(test_array,stdout);
  sprintf(test_array,"This was %s a test","just");
  fputs("sprintf() created               : ",stdout);
  fputs(test_array,stdout);
  return(0);
}
```

Here is the output from the first run of the program:

```
Please enter the first string  : string one
The first string entered is    : string one
Please enter the second string : string two
The second string entered is   : string two
sprintf() created              : This was just a test
```

Because the strings that were entered were less than the size of *test_array*, the program works fine. However, when you enter a string that is longer than *test_array*, something like the following can occur when the program is run a second time:

```
Please enter the first string  : one two three four five
The first string entered is    : one two three four five
Please enter the second string : six seven eight nine ten
The second string entered is   : six seven eight ninsprintf() created
 : This was just a testPlease enter the first string : The first string entered
is    :e ten
The second string entered is   :
```

Take care when running the program. The **gets** function receives characters from standard input (**stdin**, the keyboard by default for most computers) and places them into the array whose name is passed to the function. When you press ENTER to terminate the string, a newline character is transmitted. When the **gets** function receives this newline character, it changes it into a null character, ensuring that the character array contains a string. No checking occurs to ensure that the array is large enough to hold all the characters entered.

The **puts** function echoes to the terminal just what was entered with **gets**. It also appends a newline character to the string where the null character appeared. Remember, the null character was automatically inserted into the string by the **gets** function. Therefore, strings that are properly entered with **gets** can be displayed with **puts**.

When you use the **fgets** function, you can guarantee a maximum number of input characters. This function stops reading the designated file stream when one fewer characters are read than the second argument specifies. Since the *test_array size* is 20, only 19 characters will be read by **fgets** from **stdin**. A null character is automatically placed into the string in the twentieth position, and if you entered a newline character from the keyboard it would be retained in the string (it would appear before the null). The **fgets** function does not eliminate the newline character, as **gets** did, but merely appends the null character so that a valid string is stored. Much like **gets** and **puts**, **fgets** and **fputs** are symmetrical. **fgets** does not eliminate the newline character, nor does **fputs** add one.

To see how important the newline character is to these functions, look closely at the preceding output from the second run. Notice the phrase "sprintf( ) created" that follows immediately after the characters "six seven eight nin" that had just been entered. The second input string actually had five more characters than the **fgets** function read in (one less than SIZE of 19 characters). The others were left in the input buffer. The newline character that terminated the input from the keyboard was also dropped (it is left in the input stream because it occurs after the nineteenth character). Therefore, no newline character was stored in the string. Since **fputs** does not add one back, the next **fputs** output begins on the line where the previous output ended. You were relying on the newline character read by **fgets** and printed by **fputs** to help control the display formatting.

The function **sprintf**, which stands for "string **printf**," uses a control string with conversion characters, just like **printf**. However, **sprintf** places the resulting formatted data in a string rather than immediately sending the result to standard output. This can be beneficial if the exact same output must be created twice—for example, when the same string must be output to both the display monitor and the printer.

To review these functions:

- **gets** converts newline to a null.

- **puts** converts null to a newline.

- **fgets** retains newline and appends a null.

- **fputs** drops the null and does not add a newline; instead it uses the retained newline (if one was entered).

strcpy, strcat, strcmp, and strlen

All of the functions discussed in this section are predefined in the *string.h* header file. Whenever you wish to use one of these functions, make certain that you include the header file in your program. The following program shows how to use the **strcpy** function:

```
/*
*    A C program demonstrating how to use the strcpy function
*    Copyright (c) Chris H. Pappas and William H. Murray, 1990
*/

#include <stdio.h>
#include <string.h>

#define LENGTH 17

main()
{
  char origin_string[LENGTH]="Here I go again!",
       destination_string[LENGTH];

  strcpy(destination_string,"String Constant");
  printf("%s\n",destination_string);

  strcpy(destination_string,origin_string);
  printf("%s\n",destination_string);
  return(0);
}
```

The **strcpy** function is used to copy the contents of one string, *origin_string,* into a second string, *destination_string.* The preceding program initializes *origin_string* with the message, "Here I go again!" The first **strcpy** function call actually copies the "String Constant" into *destination_string.* The second call to the **strcpy** function copies *origin_string* into the *destination_string* variable. The program outputs the following message:

```
String Constant
Here I go again!
```

The equivalent C++ program follows.

```
//
//    A C++ program demonstrating how to use the strcpy function
//    Copyright (c) Chris H. Pappas and William H. Murray, 1990
//

#include <iostream.h>
#include <string.h>

#define LENGTH 17

main()
{
   char origin_string[LENGTH]="Here I go again!",
        destination_string[LENGTH];

   strcpy(destination_string,"String Constant");
   cout << "\n" << destination_string;

   strcpy(destination_string,origin_string);
   cout << "\n" << destination_string;
   return(0);
}
```

You can use the **strcat** function to append two separate strings. Both strings must be null terminated and the result itself is null terminated. The following program builds on your understanding of the **strcpy** function and introduces **strcat**:

```
/*
*    A C program demonstrating how to use the strcat function
*    Copyright (c) Chris H. Pappas and William H. Murray, 1990
*/

#include <stdio.h>
#include <string.h>
```

```
#define WORD_LENGTH 6
#define STRING_LENGTH 20

main()
{
  char part1[WORD_LENGTH]="In",
       part2[WORD_LENGTH]=" the ",
       prologue[STRING_LENGTH];

  strcpy(prologue,part1);
  strcat(prologue,part2);
  strcat(prologue,"beginning...");
  printf("%s\n",prologue);
  return(0);
}
```

In this example, both *part1* and *part2* are initialized, while *prologue* is not. First, the program **strcpy**s *part1* into *prologue*. Next, the **strcat** function is used to concatenate *part2* (" the ") to "In", which is stored in *prologue*. The last **strcat** function call demonstrates how a string constant can be concatenated to a string. Here, "beginning. . ." is concatenated to the now current contents of *prologue* ("In the "). The program outputs

```
In the beginning...
```

The following C program demonstrates how to use the **strcmp** function:

```
/*
 *    A C program that compares two strings using strcmp with
 *    the aid of the strlen function
 *    Copyright (c) Chris H. Pappas and William H. Murray, 1990
 */

#include <stdio.h>
#include <string.h>

main()
{
  char string1[]="one", string2[]="one";
  int shorter_one,result=0;

  shorter_one=strlen(string1);
  if (strlen(string2) >= strlen(string1))
    result = strncmp(string1,string2,shorter_one);
  printf("The string %s found", result == 0 ? "was" : "wasn't");
  return(0);
}
```

The **strlen** function returns the integer length of the string pointed to. In the preceding program, it is used in two different forms just to show what it can do. The first call to the function assigns the length of *string1* to the variable *shorter_one*. The second invocation of the function is actually encountered within the if condition. Remember, all test conditions must evaluate to a TRUE (!0) or FALSE (0). The if test takes the results returned from the two calls to **strcmp** and then asks the relational question greater than or equal to (> =). If the length of *string2* is greater than or equal to that of *string1*, the **strcmp** function is invoked.

You might wonder why you use the greater than or equal to test instead of an equal to test. This method illustrates further how **strcmp** works. The **strcmp** function begins comparing two strings starting with the first character in each string. If both strings are identical, the function returns a value of 0. However, if the two strings aren't identical, **strcmp** returns a value less than 0 if *string1* is less than *string2*, or a value greater than 0 if *string1* is greater than *string2*. The relational test (> =) was used in case you would want to modify the code to include a report of equality, greater than, or less than for the compared strings.

The program terminates by using the value returned by *result*, along with the conditional operator (?:) to determine which message is printed. For this example, the program output is as follows:

```
The string was found
```

10

POINTERS

Most introductory programming courses use only static variables. *Static* variables, in this sense, are variables declared in the variable declaration block of the source code. While the program is executing, the application can neither obtain more of these variables nor deallocate storage for a variable. In addition, you have no way of knowing the address in memory for each individual variable or constant. To access an actual cell, you simply use the variable's name. For example, in C if you want to increment the **int** variable *century* by 100, you access *century* by name:

```
century += 100;
```

WHAT IS A POINTER VARIABLE?

An often more convenient and efficient way to access a variable is through a second variable that holds the address of the variable to be accessed. Chapter 8, "Functions," introduced the concept of pointer variables, which are covered in more detail in this chapter. For example, suppose that you have an **int** variable called *contents_of_house* and another variable called *address_of_house* that can hold the address of a variable of type **int**. In C,

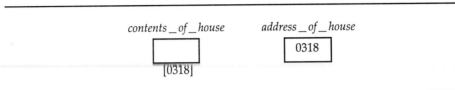

Figure 10-1.   A pointer variable

preceding a variable with the address operator **&** returns the address of the variable instead of its contents. The syntax for assigning the address of a variable to a variable that holds addresses should look familiar:

```
address_of_house = &contents_of_house;
```

A variable that holds an address, such as *address_of_house,* is called a *pointer variable,* or simply a *pointer.* Figure 10-1 illustrates this relationship. The variable *contents_of_house* has been placed in memory at address 0318. After executing the preceding statement, the address of *contents_of_house* will be assigned to the pointer variable *address_of_house.* You express this relationship in English by saying that *address_of_house* points to *contents_of_house.* Figure 10-2 shows how this situation is often represented. The arrow is drawn from the cell that stores the address to the cell whose address is stored.

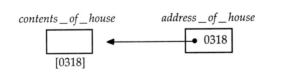

Figure 10-2.   The pointer variable *address_of_house* pointing to
contents_of_house

To access the contents of the cell whose address is stored in *address_of_house*, just precede the pointer variable with an *, as in *address_of_house*. You have *dereferenced* the pointer *address_of_house*. For example, if you execute the following two statements,

```
address_of_house = &contents_of_house;
*address_of_house = 10;
```

the value of the cell named *contents_of_house* will be 10 (see Figure 10-3). You can think of the * as a directive to follow the arrow (Figure 10-3) to find the cell referenced. Notice that if *address_of_house* holds the address of *contents_of_house*, both statements that follow will have the same effect; that is, both will store the value of 10 in *contents_of_house:*

```
contents_of_house = 10;
*address_of_house = 10;
```

Declaring Pointer Variables

As with any other language, C requires a definition for each variable. The following statement defines a pointer variable *address_of_house* that can hold the address of an **int** variable:

```
int *address_of_house;
```

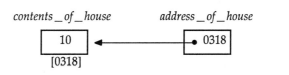

Figure 10-3.   Assignment using a pointer variable

Actually, there are two separate parts to this declaration. The data type of *address _ of _ house* is

```
int *
```

and the identifier for the variable is

```
address_of_house
```

The asterisk following **int** means "pointer to"; that is, the data type

```
int *
```

is a pointer variable that can hold an address to an **int**.

This is a very important concept to remember. In C, unlike many other languages, a pointer variable holds the address of a particular data type. Here's an example:

```
char *address_to_a_char;
int *address_to_an_int;
```

The data type of *address _ to _ a _ char* is different from the type of *address _ to _ an _ int*. Run-time errors and compile-time warnings may occur in a program that defines a pointer to one data type and then uses it to point to some other data type. It is also poor programming practice to define a pointer in one way and then use it in another way. For example, look at the following code segment:

```
int *int_ptr;
float real_value = 23.45;
int_ptr = &real_value;
```

Here, *int _ ptr* has been defined to be of type **int ***, meaning that it can hold the address of a memory cell of type **int**. The third statement attempts to assign *int _ ptr* the address *&real _ value* of a declared **float** variable.

Using Pointer Variables

The following code segment will exchange the contents of the variables *value1* and *value2* by using the address and dereferencing operators:

```
int value1 = 10, value2 = 20, temp;
int *int_ptr;

int_ptr = &value1;
temp = *int_ptr;
*int_ptr = value2;
value2 = temp;
```

The first line of the program contains standard definitions and initializations. The statement allocates three cells to hold a single **int**, gives each cell a name, and initializes two of them (Figure 10-4). It is assumed that the cell named *value1* is located at address 1395, that the cell named *value2* is located at address 3321, and that the cell named *temp* is located at address 0579.

The second statement in the program defines *int_ptr* as a pointer to an **int** data type. The statement allocates the cell and gives it a name (placed at address 1925). Remember, when the asterisk is combined with the data type (in this case **int**), the variable contains the address of a cell of the same data type. Because *int_ptr* has not been initialized, it does not point to any particular **int** variable. The fourth statement assigns *int_ptr* the address of *value1* (see Figure 10-5). The next statement in the program

```
temp = *int_ptr;
```

Figure 10-4.   Allocation and initialization of memory cells

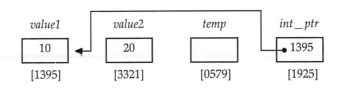

Figure 10-5.   Assignment to a pointer variable

uses the expression *int_ptr* to access the contents of the cell to which *int_ptr* points: *value1*. Therefore, the integer value 10 is stored in the variable *temp* (see Figure 10-6). If you had omitted the asterisk in front of *int_ptr*, the assignment statement would illegally store the contents of *int_ptr*, the address 1395, in the cell named *temp*, but *temp* is supposed to hold an **int**, not an address. The fifth statement in the program

```
*int_ptr = value2;
```

copies the contents of the variable *value2* into the cell pointed to by the address stored in *int_ptr* (see Figure 10-7). The last statement in the program simply copies the contents of one integer variable, *temp*, into another integer variable, *value2* (see Figure 10-8). Make certain that you understand the difference between what is being referenced when a pointer variable is preceded (*int_ptr*) and is not preceded (*int_ptr*) by an

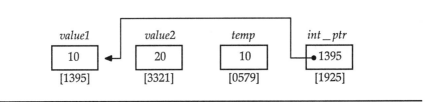

Figure 10-6.   Assignment using a pointer

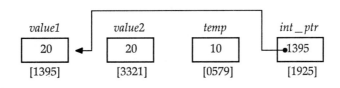

Figure 10-7.   Another assignment using a pointer

asterisk. For this example, the first syntax is a pointer to a cell that can contain an **int** value. The second syntax references the cell that holds the address to another cell that can hold an **int**.

The following short program illustrates how you can manipulate the addresses in pointer variables:

```
char code1 = 'A', code2 = 'B';
char *char_ptr1, *char_ptr2, *temp;

char_ptr1 = &code1;
char_ptr2 = &code2;
temp = char_ptr1;
char_ptr1 = char_ptr2;
char_ptr2 = temp;
printf( "%c%c", *char_ptr1, *char_ptr2);
```

Figure 10-9 shows the cell configuration and values after the first four statements of the program have executed. When the fifth statement is

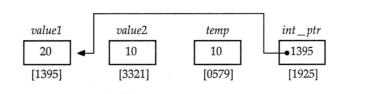

Figure 10-8.   An ordinary assignment

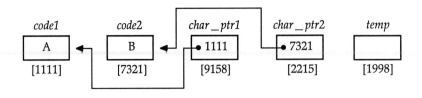

Figure 10-9.   Initial status of the program

executed, the contents of *char_ptr1* are copied into *temp* so that both *char_ptr1* and *temp* point to *code1* (see Figure 10-10). Executing the next statement

```
char_ptr1 = char_ptr2;
```

copies the contents of *char_ptr2* into *char_ptr1*, so that both pointers point to *code2* (see Figure 10-11). The next to last statement copies the address stored in *temp* into *char_ptr2* (see Figure 10-12). When the **printf** statement is executed, you will see

BA

since the value of *char_ptr1* is "B", and the value of *char_ptr2* is "A". Notice how the actual values stored in the variables *code1* and *code2* haven't changed from their original initializations. However, since you have swapped the contents of their respective pointers, *char_ptr1* and

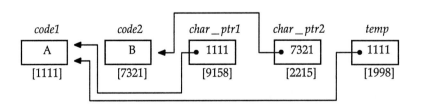

Figure 10-10.   After *temp = char_ptr1;*

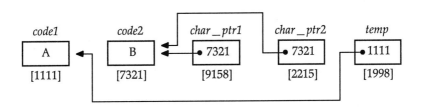

Figure 10-11.   After *char__ptr1* = *char__ptr2;*

char__ptr2, it appears that their order has been reversed. This is an important concept to grasp. Depending on the size of the data object, moving a pointer to the object can be much more efficient than copying the entire contents of the object.

Initializing Pointer Variables

Pointer variables, like many other variables in C, can be initialized in their definition. For example, the following two statements

```
int value1;
int *int_ptr = &value1;
```

allocate storage for the two cells *value1* and *int__ptr*. The variable *value1* is an ordinary **int** variable and *int__ptr* is a pointer to an **int**. Additionally, the

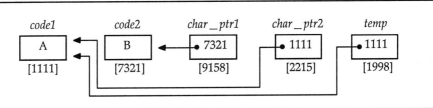

Figure 10-12.   After *char__ptr2* = *temp;*

code initializes the pointer variable *int_ptr* to the address of *value1*. Be careful, however; the syntax is somewhat misleading. You are not initializing *int_ptr* (which would have to be an **int** value) but *int_ptr* (which must be an address to an **int**). The second statement in the previous listing can be translated into the equivalent two statements:

```
int *int_ptr;
int_ptr = &value1;
```

The following code segment shows how to declare and then initialize a string pointer:

```
/*
 *    A C program that initializes a string pointer and
 *    then prints out the string backwards then forwards
 *    Copyright (c) Chris H. Pappas and William H. Murray, 1990
 */

#include <stdio.h>
#include <string.h>

main()
{
  char *palindrome_ptr="Poor Dan is in a droop";
  int index;

  for (index=strlen(palindrome_ptr)-1; index >= 0; index--)
    printf("%c",palindrome_ptr[index]);
    printf(palindrome_ptr);

  return(0);
}
```

Technically, the compiler stores the address of the first character of the string "Poor Dan is in a droop" in the variable *palindrome_ptr*. While the program is running, it can use *palindrome_ptr* like any other string. This is because all C compilers create what is called a *string table*, which is used internally by the compiler to store the string constants a program is using.

Limitations on the Address Operator

You cannot use the address operator on every C expression. The following examples demonstrate those situations in which you cannot apply the **&** address operator:

```
/* not with CONSTANTS */

variable_address = &23;

/* not with expressions involving operators such as + and /
   given the definition int value1 = 8; */

variable_address = &(value1 + 10);

/* not preceding register variables
   given the definition register reg1;   */

variable_address = &reg1;
```

The first statement tries to obtain the address of a hard-wired constant value illegally. Since the 23 has no memory cell associated with it, the statement is meaningless.

The second assignment statement attempts to return the address of the expression (*value1* + *10*). Since the expression itself is actually a stack manipulation process, there is no address associated with the expression.

The last example honors the programmer's request to define *reg1* as a register rather than as a storage cell in internal memory. Therefore, no memory cell address can be returned and stored.

Pointers to Arrays

As mentioned in Chapter 9, "Arrays," pointers and arrays are closely related. Remember that an array's name is a constant whose value represents the address of the array's first element. For this reason, an assignment statement or any other statement cannot change the value of an array's name. Given the data declarations

```
#define MAXSTUDENTS 30

float grades[MAXSTUDENTS];
float *float_ptr;
```

the array's name, *grades,* is a constant whose value is the address of the first element of the array of 10 **float**s. The following statement assigns the address of the first element of the array to the pointer variable *float_ptr:*

```
float_ptr = grades;
```

An equivalent statement looks like this:

```
float_ptr = &grades[0];
```

However, if *float_ptr* holds the address of a **float**, the following statements are illegal:

```
grades = float_ptr;
&grades[0] = float_ptr;
```

These statements attempt to assign a value to the constant *grades* or its equivalent *&grades[0]*, which makes about as much sense as:

```
5 = float_ptr;
```

Pointers to Pointers

In C, you can define pointer variables that point to other pointer variables, which, in turn, point to the data, such as a **char**. Figure 10-13 represents this relationship visually; *char_ptr* is a pointer variable that points to another pointer variable whose contents can be used to point to 'A'.

   You may wonder why this is necessary. The advent of OS/2 and the Windows programming environment signals the development of multitasking operating environments designed to maximize the use of memory. In order to compact the use of memory, the operating system has to be able to move objects in memory whenever necessary. If your program points directly to the physical memory cell where the object is stored, and the operating system moves it, disaster will strike. Instead, your application points to a memory cell address that will not change while your program is running (a *virtual_address*), and the *virtual_address* memory cell holds the *current_physical_address* of the data object. Now, whenever the operating

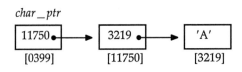

Figure 10-13.   A pointer to a pointer of type **char**

environment wants to move the data object, the operating system just has to update the *current_physical_address* stored at the *virtual_address*. As far as your application is concerned, it still uses the unchanged address of the *virtual_address* to point to the updated address of the *current_physical_address*.

To define a pointer to a pointer in C, you simply increase the number of asterisks preceding the identifier:

```
char **char_ptr;
```

In this example, the variable *char_ptr* is defined to be a pointer to a pointer that points to a **char** data type. *char_ptr*'s data type is

```
char **
```

Each asterisk is read "pointer to." The number of pointers that must be followed to access the data item, or the number of asterisks that must be attached to the variable to reference the value to which it points, is called the *level of indirection* of the pointer variable. A pointer's level of indirection determines how much dereferencing must be done to access the data type given in the definition. Figure 10-14 illustrates several variables with different levels of indirection.

```
int int_data=5;
int *int_ptr1;
int **int_ptr2;
int ***int_ptr3;
int_ptr1=&int_data;
int_ptr2=&int_ptr1;
int_ptr3=&int_ptr2;
```

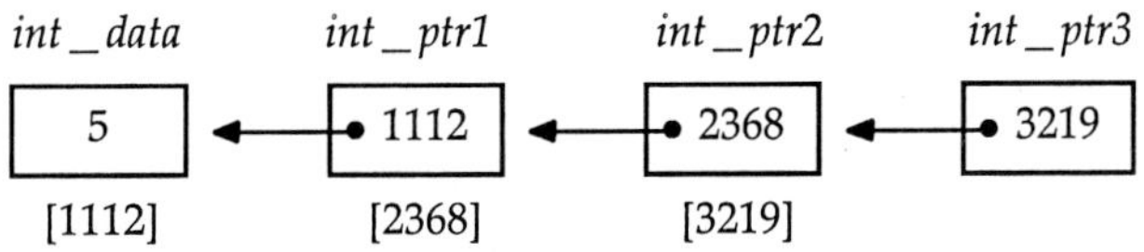

int_data	*int_ptr1*	*int_ptr2*	*int_ptr3*
5 ←	1112 ←	2368 ←	3219
[1112]	[2368]	[3219]	

Figure 10-14.   Three variables using different levels of indirection: *int_ptr1*, *int_ptr2*, and *int_ptr3*

The first four lines of code in Figure 10-14 define three variables; the **int** variable *int_data*, the *int_ptr1* pointer variable that points to an **int** (one level of indirection), the *int_ptr2* variable that points to a pointer that points to an **int** (two levels of indirection), and *int_ptr3*, which illustrates that this process can be extended beyond two levels of indirection. The fifth line of code

```
int_ptr1 = &int_data;
```

is an assignment statement that uses the address operator. The expression assigns the address of *&int_data* to *int_ptr1*. Therefore, *int_ptr1*'s contents include 1112. Notice that there is only one arrow from *int_ptr1* to *int_data*. This indicates that *int_data*, or 5, can be accessed by dereferencing *int_ptr1* just once. The next statement,

```
int_ptr2 = &int_ptr1;
```

along with its accompanying picture, illustrates double indirection. Because *int_ptr2*'s data type is **int ****, to access an **int** you need to dereference the variable twice. After the preceding assignment statement, *int_ptr2* holds the address of *int_ptr1* (not the contents of *int_ptr1*); so *int_ptr2* points to *int_ptr1*, which in turn points to *int_data*. Notice that you must follow two arrows to get from *int_ptr2* to *int_data*.

The last statement demonstrates three levels of indirection

```
int_ptr3 = &int_ptr2;
```

and assigns the address of *int_ptr2* to *int_ptr3* (not the contents of *int_ptr2*). Note that the accompanying illustration shows that three arrows are now necessary to reference *int_data*.

To review, *int_ptr3* is assigned the address of a pointer variable that indirectly points to an **int**, as in the previous statement. However, ***int_ptr3* (the cell pointed to) can only be assigned an **int** value, not an address

```
***int_ptr3 = 10;
```

since ***int_ptr3* is an **int**.

C allows you to initialize pointers like any other variable. For example, you could have defined and initialized *int_ptr3* with the following single statement:

```
int ***int_ptr3=&int_ptr2;
```

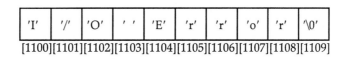

Figure 10-15.   String constant stored as an array of characters

Pointers to char and Arrays of Type char

A string constant such as "I/O Error" is actually stored as an array of characters with a null terminator added as the last character (see Figure 10-15). Because a **char** pointer can hold the address of a **char**, you can define and initialize it. For example,

```
char *char_ptr = "I/O Error";
```

defines the **char** pointer *char_ptr* and initializes it to the address of the first character in the string (see Figure 10-16). Additionally, the storage is allocated for the string itself. You could have written the same statement as:

```
char *char_ptr;
char_ptr = "I/O Error";
```

Once again, you must realize that *char_ptr* was assigned the address, not *char_ptr*, which points to the 'I'. The second example clarifies this by using two separate statements to define and initialize the pointer variable.

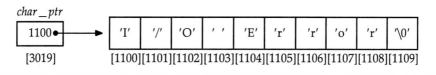

Figure 10-16.   Initializing the pointer *char_ptr*

The following example highlights a common misconception about pointers to strings and pointers to arrays of characters:

```
char *string_ptr = "I/O Error";
static char char_array[0] = "Drive not ready";
```

The main difference between these two statements is that the value of *string_ptr* can be changed (since it is a pointer variable), but the value of *char_array* cannot be changed (since it is a pointer constant). Similarly, the following assignment statement is illegal:

```
/* NOT LEGAL */
char char_array[16];
char_array = "Drive not ready";
```

While the syntax looks similar to the correct code in the previous example, the assignment statement attempts to copy the address of the first cell of the storage for the string "Drive not ready" into *char_array*. Because *char_array* is a pointer constant, an error results.

The following input statement is incorrect because the pointer *string_ptr* has not been initialized:

```
/* NOT LEGAL */
char *string_ptr;
cin >> s;
```

To correct the problem, simply reserve storage for and initialize the pointer variable *string_ptr:*

```
char string[10];
char *string_ptr = string;
cin.get(string_ptr,10);
```

Since the value of *string* is the address of the first cell of the array, the second statement in the code not only allocates storage for the pointer variable, but initializes it to the address of the first cell of the array *string*. At this point, the **cin.get** statement is satisfied since it is passed the valid address of the character array storage.

Pointer Arithmetic

If you are familiar with assembly language programming, you have undoubtedly used actual physical addresses to reference information stored in tables. If you have only used subscript indexing into arrays, you have been effectively using the same assembly language equivalent. The only difference is that in the latter case, you allowed the compiler to manipulate the addresses for you.

Remember, one of C's strengths is its closeness to the hardware. In C, you can actually manipulate pointer variables. Many of the example programs have demonstrated how you can assign one pointer variable's address, or address contents, to another pointer variable of the same data type. C allows you to perform only two arithmetic operations on a pointer address—addition and subtraction. What follows are two different pointer variable types and some simple pointer arithmetic:

```
//
//   A C++ program demonstrating pointer arithmetic
//   Copyright (c) Chris H. Pappas and William H. Murray, 1990
//

#include <iostream.h>

void main()
{
  int *int_ptr;
  float *float_ptr;

  int an_integer;
  float a_real;

  int_ptr = &an_integer;
  float_ptr = &a_real;

  int_ptr++;
  float_ptr++;

  return(0);
}
```

Assume that an **int** is 2 bytes and a **float** is 4 bytes. Also, *an_integer* is stored at memory cell address 2000, and *a_real* is stored at memory cell address 4000. When the last two lines of the program are executed, *int_ptr* will contain the address 2002 and *float_ptr* will contain the address 4004. You may have assumed that the increment operator **++** incremented by 1. However, this is not always true for pointer variables. Chapter 6, "Data," introduced the concept of operator overloading. Increment, **++**, and decrement, **−−**, are examples of this C++ construct. For the immediate example, *int_ptr* was defined to point to **int**s (which for your system are 2 bytes).

For this reason, when the increment operation is invoked, it checks the variable's type and then chooses an appropriate increment value. For **int**s this value is 2 and for **float**s the value is 4 (on your system). This same principle holds true for whatever data type the pointer is pointing to. If the pointer variable pointed to a structure of 20 bytes, the increment or decrement operators would add or subtract 20 from the current pointer's address.

You can also modify a pointer's address by using integer addition and subtraction, not just the **++** and **−−** operators. For example, you can move four **float** values over from the one currently pointed to with the following statement:

```
float_ptr = float_ptr + 4;
```

Using the Debugger

Think about what this program does:

```
//
//    A C++ program to test your understanding of sizeof and
//    pointer arithmetic
//    Copyright (c) Chris H. Pappas and William H. Murray, 1990
//

#include <iostream.h>

main()
{
  float float_value = 23.45;
  float *float_ptr;
  size_t float_width;

  float_ptr = &float_value;

  float_width = sizeof(float);

  float_ptr = float_ptr + float_width;

  return(0);
}
```

From the Integrated Environment, go to the Options menu, select the Debugger submenu, and change "Source Debugging" to ON. Now start the

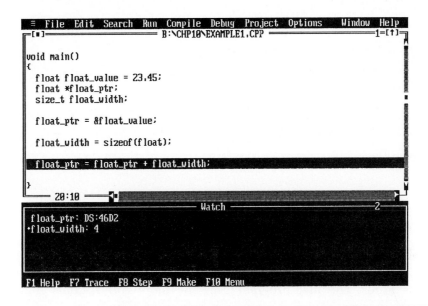

Figure 10-17.   Integrated Debugger showing current values for *float_ptr* and
float_width

Debugger and single-step through the program. Use the Watch window to
keep an eye on the variables *float_ptr* and *float_width*. Figure 10-17 shows
a Debugger window.

The Debugger has assigned *float_ptr* the address of *float_value*, so
float_ptr contains 46D2. The variable *float_width* is assigned the
sizeof(float), which returns a 4. What happened when you executed the
final statement in the program? The variable *float_ptr* changed to 46E2
rather than 46D6. You forgot that pointer arithmetic considers the size of
the object pointed to (4 × 4 byte **floats** = 16).

Actually, you were intentionally misled by the name of the one variable
float_width. To make logical sense, the program should have been written
in this way:

```
//
//     A C++ program using pointer arithmetic and variable
//     names not meant to trick the reader!
//     Copyright (c) Chris H. Pappas and William H. Murray, 1990
//
```

```
#include <iostream.h>

main()
{
  float float_value = 23.45;
  float *float_ptr;
  int number_of_elements_to_skip;
  float_ptr = &float_value;

  number_of_elements_to_skip = 4;

  float_ptr = float_ptr + number_of_elements_to_skip;

  return(0);
}
```

Pointer Arithmetic and Arrays

The following two programs index into a five-character array. Both programs read in five characters and then print the same five characters in reverse order. The first program uses the more conventional high-level language approach of indexing with subscripts. The second program is identical except that the array elements are referenced by address using pointer arithmetic.

Here is the first example:

```
//
//    A C++ program that accesses array elements using array syntax
//    Copyright (c) Chris H. Pappas and William H. Murray, 1990
//

#include <iostream.h>

#define MAXLETTERS 5

main()
{
  char char_array[MAXLETTERS];
  int index;

  for(index = 0; index < MAXLETTERS; index++)
    char_array[index]=getchar();

  for(index = MAXLETTERS-1; index >= 0; index--)
    putchar(char_array[index]);

  return(0);
}
```

Here is the second example:

```
//
//    A C++ program that accesses array elements using pointer syntax
//    Copyright (c) Chris H. Pappas and William H. Murray, 1990
//

#include <iostream.h>

#define MAXLETTERS 5

main()
{
  char char_array[MAXLETTERS];
  char *char_ptr;

  int count;

  char_ptr=char_array;

  for(count = 0; count < MAXLETTERS; count++) {
    *char_ptr=getchar();
    char_ptr++;
}

  char_ptr=char_array + (MAXLETTERS - 1);

  for(count = 0; count < MAXLETTERS; count++) {
    putchar(*char_ptr);
    char_ptr--;
  }

  return(0);
}
```

Since the first example is straightforward, the discussion focuses on the second program. *char_ptr* has been defined to be of type **char ***, which means that it is a pointer to a **char**. Because each cell in the array *char_array* holds a **char**, *char_ptr* is suitable for pointing to each. The following statement

```
char_ptr=char_array;
```

stores the address of the first cell of *char_array* in the variable *char_ptr*.

The *for* loop reads MAXLETTERS and stores them in the array *char_array*. The statement

```
*char_ptr=getchar();
```

uses the dereference operator * to ensure that the target (that is, the left-hand side) of this assignment will be the cell to which *char_ptr* points, rather than *char_ptr* (which itself contains just an address). The idea is to store a character in each cell of *char_array*, not in *char_ptr*.

To start printing the array backwards, the program first initializes *char_ptr* to the last element in the array:

```
char_ptr = char_array + (MAXLETTERS - 1);
```

By adding 4 (MAXLETTERS − 1) to the initial address of *char_array*, *char_ptr* points to the fifth element. (Remember, these are offsets; the first element in the array is at offset 0.) Within the *for* loop, *char_ptr* is decremented to move backwards through the array elements. Make certain that you use the Debugger to trace through this example if you are unsure how *char_ptr* is modified.

Trouble with Increment and Decrement Operators

Just as a reminder, the following two statements do not perform the same cell reference:

```
*char_ptr++ = getchar();
*++char_ptr = getchar();
```

The first statement assigns the character returned by **getchar** to the current cell pointed to by *char_ptr* and then increments *char_ptr*. The second statement increments the address in *char_ptr* first and then assigns the character returned by the function to the cell pointed to by the updated address. Later in this chapter, you will use these two different types of pointer assignments to reference the elements of *argv*.

Pointer Comparisons

You have already seen the effect of incrementing and decrementing pointers using the ++ and −− operators, and the effect of adding an integer to a pointer. Other operations may be performed on pointers. Some of these include

- Subtracting an integer from a pointer
- Subtracting two pointers (usually pointing to the same object)
- Comparing pointers using a relational operator such as <=, =, or >=

Since (pointer − integer) subtraction is so similar to (pointer + integer) addition, it should be no surprise that the resultant pointer value points to a storage location integer element before the original pointer.

Subtracting two pointers yields a constant value that is the number of array elements between the two pointers. This assumes that both pointers are of the same type and initially point into the same array. Subtracting pointers that are not of the same type or that initially point to different arrays will yield unpredictable results. No matter which pointer arithmetic operation you choose, however, there is no check to see if the pointer value calculated is outside the defined boundaries of the array.

Pointers of like type (that is, pointers that reference the same kind of data, like **int** and **float**) can also be compared to each other; the resulting TRUE (**int** 1) or FALSE (**int** 0) can either be tested or assigned to an integer, just like the result of any logical expression. Comparing two pointers tests whether they are equal, not equal, greater than, or less than each other. One pointer is less than another pointer if the first pointer refers to an array element with a lower number subscript (remember that pointers and subscripts are virtually identical). This operation also assumes that the pointers reference the same array.

Last of all, pointers can be compared to zero, the null value. In this case, only the test for equal or not equal is valid since testing for negative pointers makes no sense. The null value in a pointer means that the pointer has no value, or does not point to anything. Null, or zero, is the only numeric value that can be directly assigned into a pointer without a type cast.

Note that pointer conversions are performed on pointer operands. This means that any pointer may be compared to a constant expression evaluating to zero and any pointer can be compared to a pointer of type **void *** (in this last case, the pointer is first converted to **void ***).

Pointer Do's and Don'ts

The examples in this section have represented addresses as integers. This may suggest that a C pointer is of type **int**. However, a pointer holds the address of a particular type of variable but is not itself one of the primitive data types **int**, **float**, and so on. A particular system may allow a pointer to be copied into an **int** variable and an **int** variable to be copied into a pointer. However, C does not guarantee that pointers can be stored in **int** variables. To guarantee code portability, you should avoid the practice.

Also, not all arithmetic operations on pointers are allowed. For example, it is illegal to add two pointers, to multiply two pointers, or to divide one pointer by another.

sizeof Pointers

The actual size of a pointer variable depends on one of two things; the size of the memory model you have chosen for the application, or the use of the nonportable, implementation-specific *near, far,* and *huge* keywords.

The 80486 to 8088 microprocessors use a *segmented addressing* scheme that breaks an address into two pieces: a *segment* and an *offset.* Many local post offices have several walls of post office boxes, each with its own unique number. Segment:offset addressing is similar. To get to your post office box, you first need to know which bank of boxes, or wall, yours is on (the segment). You also need to know the actual box number (the offset).

When you know that all of your application's code and data will fit within one single 64K block of memory, you choose the small memory model. Applying this to the post office box metaphor, this means that all of your code and data will be in the same location (segment) or "wall," with the application's code and data having a unique box number (offset).

For applications that would occupy more than 64K, you would choose a large memory model. This could mean that all of your application's code would be located on one "wall," while all of the data would be on a completely separate "wall."

When an application shares the same memory segment for code and data, calculating an object's memory location simply involves finding out the object's offset within the segment—a simple calculation.

When an application has separate segments for code and data, calculating an object's location is a bit more complicated. First, you must calculate the code or data's segment, and then its offset within the respective segment. Naturally, this requires more processor time.

C++ also allows you to override the default pointer size for a specific variable by using the keywords **near, far,** and **huge.** Note however, that by including these in your application, you make your code less portable, since the keywords produce different results on different compilers. The **near** keyword forces an offset-only pointer when the pointers would normally default to segment:offset. The **far** keyword forces a segment:offset pointer when the pointers would normally default to offset-only. The **huge** keyword also forces a segment:offset pointer that has been normalized (check your user's guide for additional information on normalized pointers). The

near keyword is generally used to increase execution speed, while the **far** keyword forces a pointer to do the right thing regardless of the memory model chosen.

For many applications, you can simply ignore this problem and allow the compiler to choose a default memory model. Eventually, however, you will run into problems with this approach, such as when you try to address an absolute location (some piece of hardware, perhaps, or a special area in memory) outside your program's segment area.

You may wonder why you can't just use the largest available memory model for your application. You can, but there is an efficiency price to pay. If all of your data is in one segment, the pointer is the size of the offset. However, if your data and code range all over memory, your pointer is the size of the segment and the offset, and both must be calculated every time you change the pointer. The next program uses the **sizeof** function to print the smallest pointer size and largest pointer size available.

The following C program prints the default pointer sizes, their **far** sizes, and their **near** sizes. The program also uses the *stringize* preprocessor directive, #, with the CURRENT_POINTER argument, so the name as well as the size of the pointer will be printed.

```
/*
 *   A C program illustrating the sizeof(pointers)
 *   Copyright (c) Chris H. Pappas and William H. Murray, 1990
 */

#include <stdio.h>

#define PRINT_SIZEOF(CURRENT_POINTER) \
  printf("sizeof\t("#CURRENT_POINTER")\t= %d\n", \
  sizeof(CURRENT_POINTER))

void main()
{
  char *reg_char_ptr;
  long double *reg_ldbl_ptr;
  char far *far_char_ptr;
  long double far *far_ldbl_ptr;
  char near *near_char_ptr;
  long double near *near_ldbl_ptr;

  PRINT_SIZEOF(reg_char_ptr);
  PRINT_SIZEOF(reg_ldbl_ptr);
  PRINT_SIZEOF(far_char_ptr);
  PRINT_SIZEOF(far_ldbl_ptr);
  PRINT_SIZEOF(near_char_ptr);
  PRINT_SIZEOF(near_ldbl_ptr);

  return(0);
}
```

The output from the program looks like this:

```
sizeof  (reg_char_ptr)   = 2
sizeof  (reg_ldbl_ptr)   = 2
sizeof  (far_char_ptr)   = 4
sizeof  (far_ldbl_ptr)   = 4
sizeof  (near_char_ptr)  = 2
sizeof  (near_ldbl_ptr)  = 2
```

FUNCTION POINTERS

So far, you have seen how various data items can be referenced by a pointer. As it turns out, you can also use pointers to access portions of code by using a pointer to a function. Pointers to functions serve the same purpose as pointers to data—they allow the function to be referenced indirectly, just as a pointer to a data item allows the data item to be referenced indirectly.

Pointers to functions have a number of important uses. For example, consider the **qsort** function, which has as one of its parameters a pointer to a function. The referenced function contains the necessary comparison that is to be performed between the array elements being sorted. **qsort** has been written to require a function pointer because the comparison process between two elements can be a complex process beyond the scope of a single control flag. You cannot pass a function by value—that is, pass the code itself. However, C does support passing a pointer to the code, or a pointer to the function.

Many C and C++ books use the **qsort** function supplied with the compiler to illustrate function pointers. Unfortunately, they usually declare the function pointer to be of a type that points to other built-in functions. The following C and C++ programs demonstrate how to define a pointer to a function and how to create your own function to be passed to the *stdlib.h* function **qsort**:

```
/*
 *    A C program showing how to declare and use a
 *    function pointer with qsort()
 *    Copyright (c) Chris H. Pappas and William H. Murray, 1990
 */

#include <stdio.h>
#include <stdlib.h>

#define MAX 10
```

```
int my_compare(const void *value1, const void *value2);
int (*function_ptr)(const void *, const void *);

main()
{
  int index;
  int int_array[MAX]={2,5,9,3,1,7,4,6,0,8};

  function_ptr=my_compare;
  qsort(int_array,MAX,sizeof(int),function_ptr);
  for(index = 0; index < MAX; index++)
    printf("%d ",int_array[index]);

  return(0);
}

int my_compare(const void *value1, const void *value2)
{
  return((*(int *)value1) - (*(int *) value2));
}
```

The function *my_compare* (the reference function) was prototyped to match the requirements for the fourth parameter to the function **qsort** (the invoking function).

The fourth parameter to the function **qsort** must be a function pointer. This reference function must be passed two **const void** * parameters and must return a type **int**. This is because **qsort** uses the reference function for the sort comparison algorithm. Now that you understand the reference function **my_compare**'s prototype, take a minute to study the body of the reference function.

If the reference function returns a value less than zero, the reference function's first parameter value is less than the second parameter's value. A return value of zero indicates parameter value equality, and a return value greater than zero indicates that the value of the first parameter was greater than that of the second. All of this is accomplished by the single statement in **my_compare**:

```
return((*(int *)value1) - (*(int *) value2));
```

Since both of the pointers were passed as type **void** *, they were cast to their appropriate pointer type **int** * and were then dereferenced, *. The subtraction of the two values pointed to returns an appropriate value to satisfy **qsort**'s comparison criterion.

While the prototype requirements for **my_compare** were interesting, the heart of the program begins with the pointer function declaration below the **my_compare** function prototype:

```
int my_compare(const void *value1, const void *value2);
int (*function_ptr)(const void *, const void *);
```

A function's type is determined by its return value and argument list signature. A pointer to **my_compare** must specify the same signature and return type. You might think that the following statement would accomplish this:

```
int *function_ptr(const void *, const void *);
```

Unfortunately, the compiler interprets the statement as the definition of a function *function_ptr* taking two arguments and returning a pointer of type **int ***. The dereference operator is associated with the type specifier, and not *function_ptr*. Parentheses are necessary to associate the dereference operator with *function_ptr*.

The corrected statement declares *function_ptr* to be a pointer to a function taking two arguments and with a return type **int**—that is, a pointer of the same type required by the fourth parameter to **qsort**.

In the body of **main**, the only thing left to do is to initialize *function_ptr* to the address of the function **my_compare**. The parameters to **qsort** are the address to the base or zeroth element of the table to be sorted (*int_array*), the number of entries in the table (*MAX*), the size of each table element (*sizeof(int)*), and a function pointer to the comparison function (*function_ptr*). The C++ equivalent follows:

```
//
//    A C++ program showing how to declare and use a
//    function pointer with qsort()
//    Copyright (c) Chris H. Pappas and William H. Murray, 1990
//

#include <iostream.h>
#include <stdlib.h>

#define MAX 10

int my_compare(const void *value1, const void *value2);
int (*function_ptr)(const void *,const void *);
```

```
main()
{
  int index;
  int int_array[MAX]={2,5,9,3,1,7,4,6,0,8};
  function_ptr=my_compare;
  qsort(int_array,MAX,sizeof(int),function_ptr);
  for(index = 0; index < MAX; index++)
    cout << " " << int_array[index];

  return(0);
}

int my_compare(const void *value1, const void *value2)
{
  return((*(int *)value1) - (*(int *)value2));
}
```

Learning the syntax of a function pointer can be challenging. Here are a few examples:

```
int *(*(*ifunction_ptr)(int))[5];
float (*(*ffunction_ptr)(int,int))(float);
typedef double (*(*(*dfunction_ptr)())[5])();
  dfunction_ptr A_dfunction_ptr;
(*(*function_ary_ptrs())[5])();
```

The first statement defines *ifunction_ptr* as a function pointer to a function that is passed an **int** argument and returns a pointer to an array of five **int** pointers.

The second statement defines *ffunction_ptr* as a function pointer to a function that takes two **int** arguments and returns a pointer to a function taking a **float** argument and returning a **float.**

By using the **typedef** declaration, you can avoid the unnecessary repetition of complicated declarations. The **typedef** declaration (see Chapter 12, "Structures, Unions, and Miscellaneous Items") is read as "*dfunction_ptr* is defined as a pointer to a function that is passed nothing and returns a pointer to an array of five pointers that point to functions that are passed nothing and return a **double.**"

The last statement is a function declaration, not a variable declaration. The statement defines **function_ary_ptrs** to be a function taking no arguments and returning a pointer to an array of five pointers that point to functions taking no arguments and returning **int**s. The outer functions return the default C and C++ type **int**.

Luckily, you will rarely encounter complicated declarations and definitions like these. However, if you understand these declarations, you will be able to confidently parse the everyday variety.

DYNAMIC MEMORY ALLOCATION

When a C program is compiled, the computer's memory is broken down into four zones that contain the program's code, all global data, the stack, and the heap. The *heap* is an area of free memory (sometimes referred to as the *free store*) that is manipulated with the dynamic allocation functions **malloc** and **free**.

When **malloc** is invoked, it allocates a contiguous block of storage for the object specified and then returns a pointer to the start of the block. The function **free** returns previously allocated memory to the heap, permitting that portion of memory to be reallocated.

The argument passed to **malloc** is an unsigned integer that represents the needed number of bytes of storage. If the storage is available, **malloc** will return a **void** * that can be cast into the desired type pointer. The concept of **void** pointers was introduced in the ANSI C standard and means a pointer of unknown type, or a generic pointer. A **void** pointer cannot itself be used to reference anything (since it doesn't point to any specific type of data), but it can contain a pointer of any other type. Therefore, you can convert any pointer into a **void** pointer and back without any loss of information.

The following code segment allocates enough storage for 200 **float** values:

```
float *float_ptr;
int num_floats = 200;

float_ptr = malloc(num_floats * sizeof(float));
```

The **malloc** function has been instructed to obtain enough storage for 200 *, the current size of a float. Each block of storage requested is entirely separate and distinct from all other blocks of storage. You can make no assumptions about where the blocks are located. Blocks are typically "tagged" with some sort of information that allows the operating system to manage their location and size. When the block is no longer needed, you can return it to the operating system by using the following statement:

```
free(float_ptr);
```

Like C, C++ allocates available memory in two ways. When variables are declared, C++ creates them on the stack by pushing down the stack pointer. When these variables go out of scope automatically (for instance, when a local variable is no longer needed), C++ frees the space for that variable by moving up the stack pointer. The size of stack-allocated memory must always be known at compilation.

Your application may also have to use variables with an unknown size at compilation. Under these circumstances, you must allocate the memory yourself, on the heap. You can think of the heap as occupying the bottom of the program's memory space and growing upward, while the stack occupies the top and grows downward.

Your C and C++ programs can allocate and release heap memory at any point. Unlike other variables, heap-allocated memory variables are not subject to scoping rules. These variables never go out of scope, so once you allocate memory on the heap, you are responsible for freeing it. If you continue to allocate heap space without freeing it, your program could eventually crash.

Most C compilers use the library functions **malloc** and **free** to provide dynamic memory allocation. In C++, however, these capabilities were considered so important that they were made a part of the core language. C++ uses **new** and **delete** to allocate and free heap memory. The argument to **new** is an expression that returns the number of bytes allocated; the value returned is a pointer to the beginning of this memory block. The argument to **delete** is the starting address of the memory block to be freed. The following two programs illustrate the similarities and differences between C and C++ applications that use dynamic memory allocation. Here is the C example:

```
/*
 *    A simple C program demonstrating the functions:
 *    malloc(), free()
 *    Copyright (c) Chris H. Pappas and William H. Murray, 1990
 */

#include <stdio.h>
#include <stdlib.h>

#define MAX 256

main()
{
  int *memory_block;
  memory_block=malloc(MAX * sizeof(int));
  if(memory_block == NULL)
    printf("Insufficient memory\n");
  else {
    printf("Memory allocated\n");
    free(memory_block);
  }
  return(0);
}
```

Note the second **#include** statement that brings in the *stdlib.h* header file, containing the definitions for both functions **malloc** and **free**. After the program defines the **int** * pointer variable *memory_block,* the **malloc** function is invoked to return the address to a memory block that is *MAX* * *sizeof(int) big.* A robust algorithm will always check for the success or failure of the memory allocation and explains the purpose behind the *if-else* statement. The function **malloc** returns a null whenever there is not enough memory to allocate the block. This simple program ends by returning the allocated memory back to the heap with the function **free** and passing it the beginning address of the allocated block.

The C++ program does not look very different:

```
//
//    A simple C++ program demonstrating the functions:
//    new and delete
//    Copyright (c) Chris H. Pappas and William H. Murray, 1990
//

#include <iostream.h>
// #include <stdlib.h> not needed for malloc(), free()

#define MAX 256
main()
{
  int *memory_block;

  memory_block=new int[MAX];
  if(memory_block == NULL)
    cout << "Insufficient memory\n";
    else {
    cout << "Memory allocated\n";
  delete(memory_block);
  }
  return(0);
}
```

The only major difference between the two programs is the syntax used with the functions **new** and **delete**. Whereas the function **malloc** requires the **sizeof** function to ensure proper memory allocation, the function **new** has been written to perform the **sizeof** function automatically on the declared data type it is passed. Both programs will allocate 256 2-byte blocks of consecutive memory (on systems that allocate 2 bytes per **int**).

Why void Pointers Are So Powerful

Now that you have a detailed understanding of pointer variables, you may begin to appreciate the need for the pointer type **void**. To review, a pointer is a variable that contains the address of another variable. If you always knew how big the object pointed to was, you wouldn't have to determine the pointer type at compile time. You would, therefore, also be able to pass an address of any type to a function. The function could then cast the address to a pointer of the proper type (based on some other piece of information) and perform operations on the result. This process would enable you to create functions that operate on a number of different data types.

That is precisely why C++ invented the **void** pointer type. The term **void** applied to a pointer means something different from **void** applied to function argument lists and return values (meaning "nothing"). A **void** pointer means a pointer to any type of data. The following C++ program demonstrates this use of **void** pointers:

```
//
//    A C++ program demonstrating the use of void pointers
//    Copyright (c) Chris H. Pappas and William H. Murray, 1990
//

#include <iostream.h>

#define LENGTH 40

void print_it(void *object, char flag);

main()
{
  char *string_ptr;
  int *int_ptr;
  float *float_ptr;
  char user_response,newline;

  cout << "Please enter the dynamic data type\n";
  cout << "    you would like to create.\n\n";
  cout << " Use (s)tring, (i)nt, or (f)loat ";
  cin >> user_response;
  cin.get(newline);

  switch(user_response) {
    case 's':
      string_ptr=new char[LENGTH];
      cout << "\nPlease enter a string: ";
      cin.get(string_ptr,LENGTH);
      print_it(string_ptr,user_response);
      break;
    case 'i':
      int_ptr=new int;
      cout << "\nPlease enter an integer: ";
      cin >> *int_ptr;
      print_it(int_ptr,user_response);
      break;
```

```
   case 'f':
     float_ptr=new float;
     cout << "\nPlease enter a float: ";
     cin >> *float_ptr;
     print_it(float_ptr,user_response);
     break;
   default:
     cout << "\n\n  Object type not implemented!";
 }

 return(0);
}

void print_it(void *object, char flag)
{
 switch(flag) {
   case 's':
     cout << "\nThe string read in:   " << ((char *) object);
     delete object;
     break;
   case 'i':
     cout << "\nThe integer read in: " << *((int *) object);
     delete object;
     break;
   case 'f':
     cout << "\nThe float value read in: ";
     cout <<  *((float *) object);
     delete object;
     break;
 }
}
```

The first statement of interest in the program is the **print_it** function prototype. Notice that the function's first formal parameter *object* is of type **void ***, or a generic pointer. Moving down to the data declarations notice three pointer variable types: **char ***, **int ***, and **float ***. These will eventually be assigned valid pointer addresses to their respective memory cell types.

The action in the program begins with a prompt that asks you to enter the data type you would like to create dynamically. Two separate input statements are used to handle your response. The first **cin** statement reads in the single character response but leaves the \n linefeed. The second input statement, **cin.get**(newline), remedies this situation.

The switch statement takes the user's response and invokes the appropriate prompt and pointer initialization. The pointer initialization takes one of three forms:

```
string_ptr=new char[LENGTH];

int_ptr=new int;

float_ptr=new float;
```

The statement

```
cin.get(string_ptr,LENGTH);
```

is used to input the character string and in this example limits the length of the string to LENGTH (40) characters. Since the **cin.get** input statement expects a string pointer first parameter, there is no need to dereference the variable when the **print_it** function is invoked:

```
print_it(string_ptr,user_response);
```

Things get quieter if you want to input an **int** or **float**. The last two **case** options are the same except for the prompt and the reference variable's type.

Notice how the three invocations of the function **print_it** have different pointer types:

```
print_it(string_ptr,user_response);

print_it(int_ptr,user_response);

print_it(float_ptr,user_response);
```

Function **print_it** only accepts these parameters because the matching formal parameter's type is **void** *. Remember, to use these pointers you must first cast them to their appropriate pointer type. When using a string pointer with **cout**, you must cast the pointer to type **char** *. When passing a string to **cout** in this form, you do not dereference the cast pointer.

Creating **int** and **float** dynamic variables was similar; printing their values is also similar. The only difference between the last two **case** statements is the output string and the cast operator used.

While all dynamic variables disappear whenever a program terminates, each of the **case** options explicitly deletes the pointer variable. When and where your program creates and deletes dynamic storage is application dependent.

POINTERS AND ARRAYS

The following section includes many example programs that illustrate arrays and how they relate to pointers.

Character Arrays

Many string operations in C are performed by using pointers and pointer arithmetic to reference character array elements. This is because character arrays or strings tend to be accessed in a strictly sequential manner. Remember, all strings in C are terminated by a null, \0. The following C++ program is a modification of a program used earlier to print palindromes. It illustrates the use of pointers with character arrays:

```
//
//    A C++ program that initializes a char pointer and
//    then prints out the array of chars backwards using pointers
//    Copyright (c) Chris H. Pappas and William H. Murray, 1990
//

#include <iostream.h>
#include <string.h>

main()
{
  char char_aray[]="Madam I'm Adam";
  char *char_ptr;
  int count;

  char_ptr=char_aray+(strlen(char_aray)-1);
  do {
    cout << *char_ptr;
    char_ptr--;
  } while (char_ptr >= &char_aray[0]);

  return(0);
}
```

After the program declares and initializes the *char_aray* palindrome, it creates a *char_ptr* of type **char ***. Remember that the name of an array is in itself an address variable. The body of the program begins by setting the *char_ptr* to the address of the last character in the array. This requires a call to the function **strlen**, which calculates the length of the character array. (The **strlen** function counts just the number of characters; it does not include in the count the null terminator, \0.)

You probably thought that was the reason for subtracting 1 from the function's returned value. Actually, the program has to consider that the first array character's address is at offset 0. Therefore, you want to increment the pointer variable's offset address to one less than the number of valid characters.

Once the pointer for the last valid array character has been calculated, the *do-while* loop is entered. The loop uses the pointer variable to point to the memory location of the character to be printed and then prints it. It subsequently calculates the next character's memory location and compares this value with the starting address of *char_aray*. As long as the calculated value is greater than or equal to the starting address, the loop iterates.

Arrays of Pointers

In C and C++, you are not restricted to making simple arrays and simple pointers. You can combine the two into arrays of pointers. An array of pointers is an array whose elements are pointers to other objects. Those objects can themselves be pointers. This means that you can have an array of pointers that point to other pointers.

The concept of an array of pointers to pointers is used extensively in the *argc* and *argv* command-line arguments for **main** (see Chapter 8, "Functions"). The following program finds the largest or smallest value entered on the command line. Command-line arguments can include numbers only, or they may be prefaced by a command selecting a choice for the smallest value entered (-s,-S), or the largest value entered (-l,-L).

```
//
//    A C++ program that uses an array of pointers to process
//    the command-line arguments argc, argv
//    Copyright (c) Chris H. Pappas and William H. Murray, 1990
//

#include <iostream.h>
#include <process.h>      // exit()
#include <stdlib.h>       // atoi()

#define BIGGEST 1
#define SMALLEST 0

int main(int argc,char *argv[])
{
  char *string_ptr;
  int num_values;
  int size_flag=0;
  int chosen_extreme=32767;
```

```
   if(argc < 2) {
     cout << "\nYou need to enter an -S,-s,-L,-l"
       " and at least one integer value";
     exit(1);
   }

  while(--argc > 0 && (*++argv)[0] == '-') {
     for(string_ptr=argv[0]+1; *string_ptr != '\0'; string_ptr++)
{
       switch(*string_ptr) {
         case 's':
         case 'S':
           size_flag=SMALLEST;
           chosen_extreme=32767;
           break;
         case 'l':
         case 'L':
           size_flag=BIGGEST;
           chosen_extreme=0;
           break;
         default:
         cout << "unknown argument " << *string_ptr << "\n";
           exit(1);
       }
     }
   }

   if(argc==0) {
     cout << "Please enter at least one number\n";
     exit(1);
   }

   num_values=argc;

   while(argc--) {
     int present_value;
     present_value=atoi(*(argv++));
     if(size_flag==BIGGEST && present_value > chosen_extreme)
       chosen_extreme=present_value;
     if(size_flag==SMALLEST && present_value < chosen_extreme)
       chosen_extreme=present_value;
   }

   cout << "The " << (size_flag ? "largest" : "smallest");
   cout << " of the " << num_values;
   cout << " value(s) input is " << chosen_extreme<< "\n";

   return(0);
}
```

Before looking at the source code, familiarize yourself with the following possible command combinations for invoking the program:

```
analyze
analyze 87
analyze 87 34
analyze -s 87
```

```
analyze -S 87 34
analyze -l 23
analyze -L 23 52
```

Looking at the **main** program, you will see the formal parameters *argc* and *argv* (see Chapter 8). To review, *argc* is an integer value containing the number of separate items, or arguments, that appeared on the command line. The variable *argv* refers to an array of pointers to character strings. Note that *argv* is not a constant; it is a variable whose value can be altered. The first element of the array, *argv[0]*, is a pointer to a string of characters that contains the program name.

At the first *if* statement, you find a test to determine if the value of *argc* is less than 2. If this test evaluates to TRUE, the user has typed just the name of the program *analyze* without any switches. Since this action would indicate that the user does not know the switch and value options, the program will prompt the user at this point with the valid options and then **exit**.

The *while* loop test condition evaluates from left to right, beginning with the decrement of *argc*. If *argc* is still greater than 0, the right side of the logical expression will be examined.

The right side of the logical expression first increments the array pointer *argv* past the first pointer entry (++*argv*), skipping the program's name, so that it now points to the second array entry. Once the pointer has been incremented, it is used to point (*++*argv*) to the zeroth offset ((*++*argv*)[0]) of the first character of the string pointed to. Obtaining this character, if it is a "-" symbol, the program concludes that the second program command was a possible switch, for example -*s or -L*.

The *for* loop initialization begins by taking the current pointer address of *argv*, which was just incremented in the line above to point to the second pointer in the array. Since *argv*'s second element is a pointer to a character string, the pointer can be subscripted, *argv[0]*. The complete expression argv[0]+1 points to the second character of the second string pointed to by the current address stored in *argv*. This second character is the one past the command switch symbol '-'. Once the program calculates this character's address, it stores it in the variable *string_ptr*. The *for* loop repeats as long as the character pointed to, *string_ptr, is not the null terminator, \0.

The program continues by analyzing the switch to see if the user wants to obtain the smallest or largest of the values entered. Based on the switch, the appropriate constant is assigned to the *size_flag*. Each *case* statement also initializes the variable *chosen＿extreme* to an appropriate value for the comparisons that follow. Should the user enter an unrecognized switch, for example, -d, the default *case* will take care of printing an appropriate message.

The second *if* statement now checks to see if *argc* has been decremented to 0. An appropriate message is printed if the switches have been examined on the command line and there are no values left to process. If so, the program terminates with an exit code of decimal 1.

A successful skipping of this *if* test means that there are now values from the command line that need to be examined. Since the program will now decrement *argc,* the variable *num＿values* is assigned *argc's* current value.

The *while* loop continues while there are at least two values to compare. The *while* loop only needs to be entered if there is more than one value to be compared, since the **cout** statement following the *while* loop can handle the command line with a single value.

The function **atoi** converts each of the remaining arguments into an integer and stores the result in the variable *present＿value.* Remember, *argv++* needs to be incremented first, so that it points to the first value to be compared. Also, the *while* loop test condition has already decremented the pointer to make certain that the loop wasn't entered with only a single command value.

The last two *if* statements update the variable *chosen＿extreme* based on the user's desire to find either the smallest or largest of all values entered. Finally, the results of the program are printed using an interesting combination of string literals and the conditional operator. The parentheses are needed around the conditional statement to prevent **cout** from printing a 0 or 1 based on the validity of the expression.

Pointers to Pointers

This next program demonstrates the use of pointer variables that point to other pointers. It is included here because it uses dynamic memory allocation. You may want to refer back to the general discussion of pointers to pointers before looking at the following program:

```
/*
 *    A C program demonstrating the use of double indirection
 *    Copyright (c) Chris H. Pappas and William H. Murray, 1990
 */
#include <stdlib.h>
```

```c
#include <stdio.h>

#define MAXELEMENTS 3

void print_values(int **value1, int **value2, int **value3);

void assign(int *vir_mem_ptr_aray[],int *dyn_blk_ptr);

main()
{
  int **value1, **value2, **value3;
  int *vir_mem_ptr_aray[MAXELEMENTS];
  int *dyn_mem_blk_ptr, *old_mem_blk_ptr;

  value1=&vir_mem_ptr_aray[0];
  value2=&vir_mem_ptr_aray[1];
  value3=&vir_mem_ptr_aray[2];

  dyn_mem_blk_ptr=(int *)malloc(MAXELEMENTS * sizeof(int));
  old_mem_blk_ptr=dyn_mem_blk_ptr;

  assign(vir_mem_ptr_aray,dyn_mem_blk_ptr);

  **value1=1;
  **value2=2;
  **value3=3;

  print_values(value1,value2,value3);

  dyn_mem_blk_ptr=(int *)malloc(MAXELEMENTS * sizeof(int));

  *dyn_mem_blk_ptr=**value1;
  *(dyn_mem_blk_ptr+1)=**value2;
  *(dyn_mem_blk_ptr+2)=**value3;

  free(old_mem_blk_ptr);

  assign(vir_mem_ptr_aray,dyn_mem_blk_ptr);

  print_values(value1,value2,value3);

  return(0);
}

void assign(int *vir_mem_ptr_aray[],int *dyn_mem_blk_ptr)
{
  vir_mem_ptr_aray[0]=dyn_mem_blk_ptr;
  vir_mem_ptr_aray[1]=dyn_mem_blk_ptr+1;
  vir_mem_ptr_aray[2]=dyn_mem_blk_ptr+2;
}

void print_values(int **value1, int **value2, int **value3)

{
  printf("%d\n",**value1);
  printf("%d\n",**value2);
  printf("%d\n",**value3);
}
```

The program highlights the concept of a pointer variable *value1, value2,* and *value3* pointing to a constant address, *&vir_mem_ptr_aray[0]*, *&vir_mem_ptr_aray[1]*, and *&vir_mem_ptr_aray[2]*, whose pointer address contents can dynamically change.

Look at the data declarations in **main**. *value1, value2,* and *value3* have been defined as pointers to pointers that point to integers. Look at the various syntax combinations:

```
value1
*value1
**value1
```

The first syntax references the address stored in the pointer variable *value1*. The second syntax references the pointer address pointed to by the address in *value1*. The last syntax references the integer that is pointed to by the pointer address pointed to by *value1*. Make certain that you do not proceed until you understand these three different references.

The three variables *value1, value2,* and *value3* have all been defined as pointers to pointers that point to integers (**int ****). The variable *vir_mem_ptr_aray* has been defined as an array of integer pointers (**int ***) of the size MAXELEMENTS. The last two variables, *dyn_mem_blk_ptr* and *old_mem_blk_ptr*, are also pointers to integers (**int ***). Figure 10-18 shows what these six variables look like after their storage has been allocated, and in particular, after *value1, value2,* and *value3* have been assigned the address of their respective elements in the *vir_mem_ptr_aray*.

This array will hold the addresses of the dynamically changing memory cell addresses. Something similar actually happens in a true multitasking environment. Your program thinks that it has the actual physical address of a variable stored in memory, when it really has a fixed address to an array of pointers that in turn points to the current physical address of the data item in memory. When the multitasking environment needs to conserve memory by moving your data objects, it simply moves their storage locations and updates the array of pointers. However, the variables in your program are still pointing to the same physical address, albeit not the physical address of the data, but of the array of pointers.

To understand how this operates, pay particular attention to the fact that the physical addresses stored in the pointer variables *value1, value2,* and *value3* never change once they are assigned.

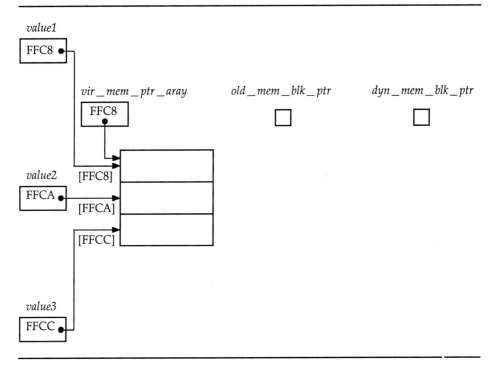

Figure 10-18.   How *value1*, *value2*, and *value3* get their initial addresses

Figure 10-19 illustrates what happens to the variables after the dynamic array *dyn_mem_blk_ptr* has been allocated, *old_mem_blk_ptr* has been initialized to the same address of the new array, and most importantly, how the physical addresses of *dyn_mem_blk_ptr*'s individual elements have been assigned to their respective counterparts in *vir_mem_ptr_aray*.

The pointer assignments were all accomplished by the **assign** function. **assign** was passed *vir_mem_ptr_aray* (call-by-value) and the address of the recently allocated dynamic memory block in the variable *dyn_mem_blk_ptr*. The function assigns the addresses of the dynamically allocated memory cells to each individual element of *vir_mem_ptr_aray*. Since the array was passed call-by-value, the changes are effective in the **main**.

If you used the Debugger to print *value1* at this point, you would see FFC8 (the address of *vir_mem_ptr_aray*'s first element), and *value1*

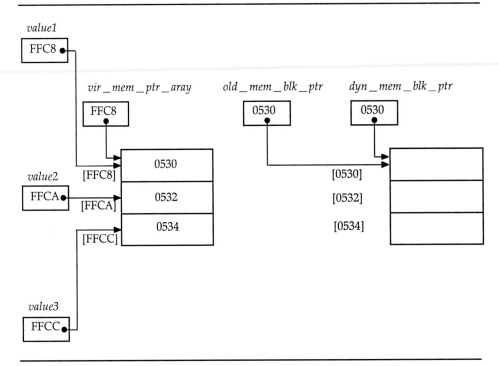

Figure 10-19.   The creation of the dynamic memory block

would print 0530 (or the contents of the address pointed to). You would encounter a similar dump for the other two pointer variables, *value2* and *value3*.

Figure 10-20 shows the assignment of three **int** values to the physical memory locations. Notice the syntax for accomplishing this:

```
**value1=1;
**value2=2;
**value3=3;
```

At this point, the program prints the values 1, 2, and 3, by calling the function **print_values**. Notice that the function has been defined as receiving three **int** ** variables. Note also that the actual parameter list does not need to precede the variables with the double indirection operator, **, since that is their type by declaration.

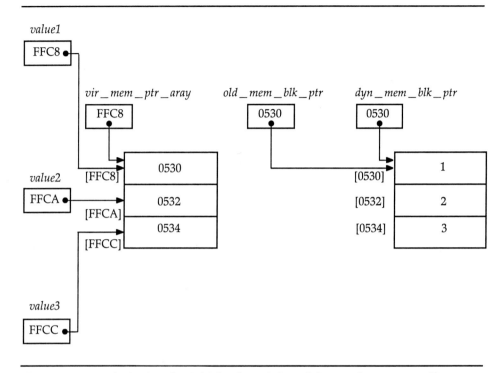

Figure 10-20.   Assigning the initial values 1, 2, and 3 to each memory cell

In Figure 10-21, the situation has become very interesting. A new block of dynamic memory has been allocated with the **malloc** function, with its new physical memory address stored in the pointer variable *dyn_mem_blk_ptr*. *old_mem_blk_ptr* still points to the previously allocated block of dynamic memory. Using the incomplete analogy to a multi-tasking environment, the figure would illustrate the operating system's desire to move the data objects' memory locations physically. Figure 10-21 also shows that the data objects themselves were copied into the new memory locations. The program accomplished this with the following three lines of code:

```
*dyn_mem_blk_ptr=**value1;
*(dyn_mem_blk_ptr+1)=**value2;
*(dyn_mem_blk_ptr+2)=**value3;
```

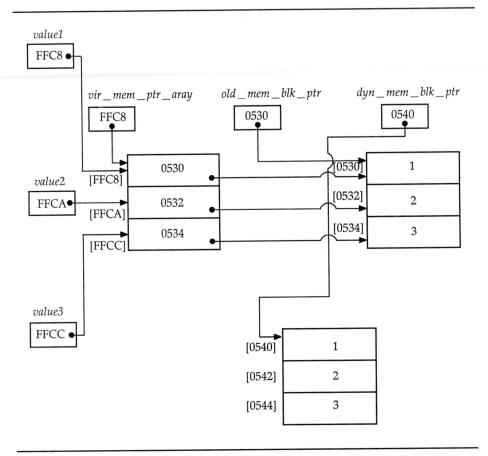

Figure 10-21.   Creation and assignments of the second dynamic memory block

Since the pointer variable *dyn_mem_blk_ptr* holds the address to the first element of the dynamic block, its address is dereferenced, pointing to the memory cell itself, and the 1 is stored there. Using a little pointer arithmetic, the other two memory cells are accessed by incrementing the pointer. The parentheses were necessary so that the pointer address was incremented before the dereference operator was applied.

Figure 10-22 shows what happens when the function **free** and the function **assign** are called to link the new physical address of the dynamically allocated memory block to the *vir_mem_ptr_aray* pointer address elements.

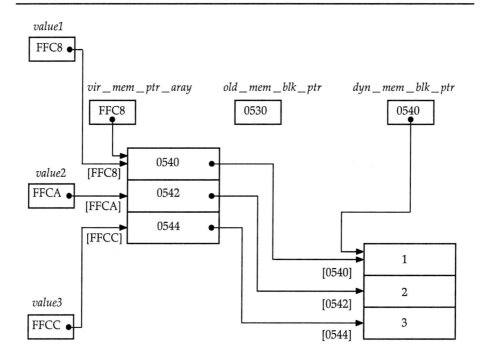

Figure 10-22.   Shows *vir_mem_ptr_aray* with its new physical memory addresses

The most important fact to notice in this last figure is that the actual physical address of the three pointer variables *value1*, *value2*, and *value3* has not changed. When the program prints the values pointed to, **value1*, and so on, you still see the values 1, 2, and 3, even though their physical location in memory has changed.

C++ REFERENCE TYPE

C++ provides a form of call-by-reference that is even easier to use than pointers. First, let's examine the use of reference variables in C++. Like C, C++ enables you to declare regular variables or pointer variables. In the first case, memory is actually allocated for the data object; in the second case, a memory location is set aside to hold an address for an object that will be allocated at another time. C++ has a third kind of declaration — the *reference* type. Like a pointer variable, it refers to another variable location, but like a regular variable, it requires no special dereferencing operators. The syntax for a reference variable is

```
int value1=5;
int& ref_value1=value1;  // valid
int& value2;             // invalid: uninitialized
```

This example sets up the reference variable *ref_value1* and assigns it to the existing variable *value1*. The referenced location now has two names associated with it: *value1* and *ref_value1*. Because both variables point to the same location in memory, they are in fact the same variable. Any assignment made to *ref_value1* is reflected through *value1*; the inverse is also true, and changes to *value1* occur through any access to *ref_value1*. Therefore, with the reference data type, you can create what is sometimes referred to as an *alias* for a variable.

The reference type has a restriction that distinguishes it from pointer variables. You must set the value of the reference type at declaration, and you cannot change it during the run of the program. After you initialize this type in the declaration, it always refers to the same memory location. Therefore, any assignments that you make to a reference variable change only the data in memory, not the address of the variable itself. In other words, you can think of a reference variable as a pointer to a constant location. For example, using the preceding declarations, the following statement

```
ref_value1 *= 2;
```

doubles the contents of *value1* by multiplying 5 * 2. The next statement assigns *copy_value* (assuming that it is of type **int**) a copy of the value associated with *ref_value1*:

```
copy_value = ref_value1;
```

The next statement is also legal when you are using reference types:

```
int *value1_ptr = &ref_value1;
```

This statement assigns the address of *value1* to the **int** * variable *value1_ptr*.

The primary use of a reference type is as an argument (see Chapter 8, "Functions") or as a return type of a function, especially when applied to user-defined class types (see Chapter 13, "Classes").

Returning Addresses

When you return an address from a function using either a pointer variable or a reference type, you are giving the user a memory address. The user can read the value at the address, and if you haven't declared the pointer type to be **const**, the user can always write the value. By returning an address, you are giving the user permission to read and, for non-**const** pointer types, write to private data. This is a significant design decision. See if you can anticipate what will happen in this next program.

```
//
//    A C++ program demonstrating what NOT to do with
//    C++ reference variables
//    Copyright (c) Chris H. Pappas and William H. Murray, 1990
//

#include <iostream.h>

int *function_a(void);
int *function_b(void);

main()
{
  int *int_ptr=function_a();
  function_b();
  cout << "Correct value? " << *int_ptr;

  return(0);
}

int *function_a(void)
{
  int local_a=10;
  return &local_a;
}

int *function_b(void)
{
  int local_b=20;
  return &local_b;
}
```

Using the Debugger

To examine the actual operation of this code, you can use the Debugger. From the Integrated Environment, go to the Options menu, select the Debugger submenu, and change "Source Debugging" to ON. Now start the Debugger and single-step through the program. Use the Watch window to keep an eye on the variable *int_ptr*.

When **function_a** is called, local space is allocated on the stack for the variable *local_a*, and the value 10 is stored in it. At this point, **function_a** returns the address of this local variable (bad news). The second statement in the main program invokes **function_b**. **function_b** in turn allocates local space for *local_b* and assigns it a value of 20. So how does the **printf** statement print a value of 20 when it was passed the address of *local_a* when **function_a** was invoked?

Actually, when the address of the temporary local variable *local_a* was assigned to *int_ptr* by **function_a**, the address to the temporary location was retained even after *local_a* went out of scope. When **function_b** was invoked, it also needed local storage. Since *local_a* was gone, *local_b* was given the same storage location as its predecessor. With *int_ptr* hanging on to this same busy memory cell, you can see why printing the value it now points to yields a 20. Take extreme care not to return the addresses of local variables.

When to Use Reference Types

To review, there are three main reasons for using C++ reference types (also see Chapter 13):

- Reference types lend themselves to more readable code by allowing you to ignore the details of how a parameter is passed.

- Reference types put the responsibility for argument passing on the programmer who writes the functions and not on the individual who uses them.

- Reference types are a necessary counterpart to operator overloading.

11

INPUT AND OUTPUT IN C AND C++

Programmers are often frustrated by the inadequate input and output (I/O) facilities provided by many high-level languages. This is not the case with C, which has a very complete I/O function library. This chapter discusses the more than 20 different ways to perform I/O in C and C++.

INPUT AND OUTPUT IN C

The standard C library I/O routines allow you to read and write data to and from files and devices. The C language does not include any pre-defined file structures. Instead, all data is treated as a sequence of bytes. There are three basic types of I/O functions: stream, console and port, and low-level.

All of the stream I/O functions treat data files or data items as a stream of individual characters. If you select the appropriate stream function, your application can process data in any size or format required, from single characters to large, complicated data structures.

Technically, when a program uses the stream function to open a file for I/O, the opened file is associated with a structure of type **FILE** (predefined in *stdio.h*) that contains basic information about the file. Once the stream is opened, a pointer to the **FILE** structure is returned. This **FILE** pointer—sometimes called the *stream pointer* or *stream*—is used to refer to the file for all subsequent I/O.

All stream I/O functions provide buffered, formatted, or unformatted input and output. A buffered stream provides an intermediate storage location for all information that is input from the stream and output that is being sent to the stream. Disk I/O is time consuming, but stream buffering will streamline your application. Instead of inputting stream data one character or one structure at a time, stream I/O functions access data a block at a time. As the application needs to process the input, it merely accesses the buffer, a much faster process. When the buffer is empty, another disk block access is made.

The reverse is true for stream output. Instead of physically outputting all data as the output statement is executed, stream I/O functions place all output data into the buffer. When the buffer is full, the data is written to the disk.

Depending on the high-level language you use, there may be a problem with buffered I/O. For example, if your program has executed several output statements that do not fill the output buffer, causing it to dump to the disk, that information is lost when your program terminates. The solution usually involves making a call to an appropriate function to "flush" the buffer. Unlike other high-level languages, C solves this problem by automatically flushing the buffer's contents whenever the program terminates. Of course, a well written application should not rely on these automatic features but should always explicitly detail every action the program is to take. One additional note: If the application terminates abnormally when you are using stream I/O, the output buffers may not be flushed, resulting in loss of data.

The console and port I/O routines are similar in function and can be seen as an extension of the stream routines. They allow you to read or write to a terminal (console) or an input/output port (such as a printer port). The port I/O functions simply read and write data in bytes. Console I/O functions provide several additional options. For example, they enable you to detect whether a character has been typed at the console and whether the characters entered are echoed to the screen as they are read.

The last type of input and output is called low-level I/O. None of the low-level I/O functions perform buffering and formatting; instead, they invoke the operating system's I/O capabilities directly. These routines let you access files and peripheral devices at a more basic level than the stream functions. Files opened in this mode return a *file handle,* an integer value that is used to refer to the file in subsequent operations.

In general, it is bad programming practice to mix stream I/O functions with low-level routines. Since stream functions are buffered and low-level functions are not, attempting to access the same file or device by two different methods leads to confusion and eventual loss of data in the buffers. Therefore, you should use either stream or low-level functions exclusively on a given file. Table 11-1 lists the most commonly used C stream I/O functions.

Streams

To use the stream functions, your application must include the file *stdio.h.* This file contains definitions for constants, types, and structures used in the stream functions, as well as function declarations and macro definitions for the stream routines.

Many of the constants predefined in *stdio.h* can be useful in your application. For example, **EOF** is defined to be the value returned at end of file and **NULL** is the null pointer. Also, **FILE** defines the structure used to maintain information about a stream and **BUFSIZ** defines the default size, in bytes, of the stream buffers.

Opening Streams

You can use one of three functions to open a stream before input and output can be performed on it: **fopen, fdopen,** or **freopen.** The file mode and form are set at the time the stream is opened. The stream file may be opened for reading, writing, or both, and can be opened either in text or in binary mode.

All three functions—**fopen, fdopen,** and **freopen**—return a **FILE** pointer, which is used to refer to the stream. For example, if your program contains the line

```
infile = fopen("sample.dat","r");
```

you can use the **FILE** pointer variable *infile* to refer to the stream. (Table 5-3 in Chapter 5, "C and C++ Foundations" listed the possible file modes.)

Table 11-1.   Common C Stream I/O Functions

Function	Definition
clearerr	Clears the error indicator for a stream and resets the end-of-file indicator to 0
fclose	Closes a stream
fcloseall	Closes all open streams
fdopen	Opens a stream using its handle obtained from **creat, dup, dup2,** or **open**
feof	Tests for end of file on a stream
ferror	Tests the stream for a read or write error
fflush	Flushes a stream
fgetc	Reads a character from a stream
fgetchar	Reads a character from **stdin**
fgetpos	Gets the current file pointer
fgets	Gets a string from a stream
filelength	Gets the stream size in bytes
fileno	Gets the file handle associated with a stream
flushall	Flushes all stream buffers
fopen	Opens a stream
fprintf	Writes formatted output to a stream
fputc	Writes a character to a stream
fputchar	Writes a character to **stdout**
fputs	Outputs a string to a stream
fread	Reads unformatted data from a stream
freopen	Reassigns a **FILE** pointer
fscanf	Reads formatted data from a stream
fseek	Repositions the **FILE** pointer to a given location
fsetpos	Positions the **FILE** pointer of a stream
fstat	Gets open file information
ftell	Returns current **FILE** pointer position
fwrite	Writes unformatted data items to a stream
getc	Reads a character from a stream (macro)
getchar	Reads a character from **stdin** (macro)
gets	Gets a string from **stdin**
getw	Reads an **int** item from the stream
perror	Prints a system error to **stderr**
printf	Writes formatted output to **stdout**
putc	Writes a character to a stream (macro)

Table 11-1.   Common C Stream I/O Functions *(continued)*

Function	Definition
putchar	Writes a character to **stdout** (macro)
puts	Writes a string to **stdout**
putw	Writes an **int** to a stream
remove	Removes a file
rename	Renames a file
rewind	Repositions the **FILE** pointer to the beginning of a stream
scanf	Scans and inputs formatted data from **stdin**
setbuf	Overrides automatic buffering, allowing the application to define its own stream buffer
setvbuf	Same as **setbuf** but also allows the size of the buffer to be defined
sprintf	Writes formatted data to a string
sscanf	Scans and inputs formatted data from a string
tmpnam	Generates a unique temporary file name in a given directory
ungetch	Pushes a character back to the keyboard buffer
vfprintf	Writes formatted output to a stream using a pointer to the format string
vfscanf	Scans and formats input from a stream using a pointer to the format string
vprintf	Writes formatted output to **stdout** using a pointer to the format string
vscanf	Scans and formats input from **stdin** using a pointer to the format string
vsprintf	Writes formatted output to a string using a pointer to the format string
vsscanf	Scans and formats input from a stream using a pointer to the format string

When your application begins execution, five streams are automatically opened. These streams are the standard input (**stdin**), standard output (**stdout**), standard error (**stderr**), standard printer (**stdprn**), and standard auxiliary (**stdaux**). By default, the standard input, standard output, and standard error refer to the user's console. This means that whenever a program expects input from the standard input, it receives that input from the console. Likewise, a program that writes to the standard output prints its data to the console. Any error messages generated by the library routines are sent to the standard error stream—that is, they appear on the user's console. The standard auxiliary and standard print streams usually refer to an auxiliary port and a printer.

You can use the five **FILE** pointers in any function that requires a stream pointer as an argument. Some functions, such as **getchar** and **putchar**, are designed to use **stdin** or **stdout** automatically. Since the pointers **stdin**, **stdout**, **stderr**, **stdprn**, and **stdaux** are constants rather than variables, don't try to reassign them to a new stream pointer value.

Redirecting Streams

Modern operating systems consider the keyboard and video display as files. This is reasonable, since the system can read from the keyboard as well as from a disk or tape file. Similarly, the system can write to the video display as well as to a disk or tape file. Suppose that your application reads from the keyboard and outputs to the video display. Now suppose that you want the input to come from a file called *test.dat*. You can use the same application if you tell the system to replace input from the keyboard, considered now as a file, with input from another file, namely *test.dat*. Changing the standard input or standard output is called *input redirection* or *output redirection*.

In MS-DOS, input or output redirection is effortless. You use < to redirect the input and > to redirect the output. Suppose that the executable version of your application is called *redirect*. The following system-level command will run the program *redirect* and use the file *test.dat* instead of the video display as input:

```
redirect < test.dat
```

The next statement will redirect both the input (*test.dat*) and the output (*out.dat*):

```
redirect < test.dat > out.dat
```

The last example will redirect the output (*out.dat*) only:

```
redirect > out.dat
```

Note, however, that you cannot redirect the standard error file **stderr**.

There are two techniques for managing the association between a standard file name and its connection to a physical file or device: redirection and piping. *Piping* involves directly connecting the standard output of one program to the standard input of another. Redirection and piping are normally controlled and invoked outside the program. In this way, the program need not concern itself with where the data is coming from or going to.

To connect the standard output from one program to the standard input of another program, you pipe them together by using the vertical bar symbol, I. Therefore, to connect the standard output of the program *stage1* to the standard input of the program *stage2*, you would type

```
stage1 | stage2
```

The operating system handles all the details of getting the output from *stage1* to the input of *stage2*.

Changing the Stream Buffer

All functions opened using the stream functions are buffered by default, except for the preopened streams **stdin**, **stdout**, **stderr**, **stdprn**, and **stdaux**. The two streams **stderr** and **stdaux** are unbuffered by default, unless they are used in one of the **printf** or **scanf** family of functions, in which case they are assigned a temporary buffer. These two streams can also be buffered with **setbuf** or **setvbuf**. The **stdin**, **stdout**, and **stdprn** streams are buffered; each buffer is flushed whenever it is full.

You can use the two functions **setbuf** and **setvbuf** to make a stream unbuffered, or you can use them to associate a buffer with an unbuffered stream. Note that buffers allocated by the system are not accessible to the user, but buffers allocated with the function **setbuf** or **setvbuf** are named by the user and can be manipulated as if they were variables. You can define a buffer to be of any size; if you use the function **setbuf**, the size is set by the constant **BUFSIZ** defined in *stdio.h*. If the application uses the function **setvbuf**, the program determines the size of the buffer.

Closing a Stream

The two functions **fclose** and **fcloseall** close a stream or streams. The **fclose** function closes a single file, while **fcloseall** closes all open streams except **stdin, stdout, stderr, stdprn,** and **stdaux.** However, if your program does not explicitly close a stream, the stream is automatically closed when the application terminates. Since the number of open streams is limited, it is good practice to close a stream when you finish with it.

Low-Level I/O

Table 11-2 lists the most commonly used low-level I/O functions. Low-level input and output calls do not buffer or format data. Files opened by low-level calls are referenced by a file handle. You use the **open** function to open files. You can use the **sopen** function to open a file with file-sharing attributes.

Low-level functions are different from their stream counterparts because they do not require the inclusion of the *stdio.h* header file. However, some common constants that are predefined in *stdio.h,* such as **EOF** and **NULL,** may be useful. Declarations for the low-level functions are given in the *io.h* header file.

The low-level disk-file I/O system was originally created under the UNIX operating system. Because the ANSI standard committee has not standardized this low-level UNIX-like unbuffered I/O system, you should use the standardized buffered I/O system (described throughout this chapter) for all new projects.

Table 11-2.   Low-Level Input and Output Functions

Function	Definition
close	Closes a disk file
lseek	Seeks to the specified byte in a file
open	Opens a disk file
read	Reads a buffer of data
unlink	Removes a file from the directory
write	Writes a buffer of data

Character Functions

Certain character input and output functions are defined in the ANSI standard and supplied by all C compilers. These functions access standard input and output and are considered high-level routines (as opposed to low-level routines, which access the machine hardware more directly). I/O in C is implemented through vendor-supplied functions rather than keywords defined as part of the language.

getc, putc, fgetc, and fputc

The most basic of all I/O functions are those that receive and send one character. The **getc** function receives one character from a specified file stream, like this:

```
int input_char;
input_char = getc(stdin);
```

The received character is passed back in the name of the function **getc** and then assigns the returned value to *input_char*. By the way, *input_char* isn't of type **char** because **getc** has been written to return an **int** type. Since the end-of-file marker size is system dependent, the marker might not fit in a single **char** byte size.

Function **getc** converts the integer into an unsigned character, guaranteeing that the ASCII values above 127 are not represented as negative values. Therefore, negative values can be used to represent unusual situations such as errors and the end of the input file. For example, the end of file has traditionally been represented by −1, although the ANSI standard states that the constant **EOF** represents some negative value.

Because **getc** returns an integer value, the data item that receives the value from **getc** must also be defined as an integer. While it may seem odd to use an integer in a character function, C actually makes little distinction between characters and integers. If a character is provided when an integer is needed, the character will be converted to an integer.

The complement to the **getc** function is **putc**. The **putc** function outputs one character to the file stream represented by the specified **FILE** pointer. To send the character that was just input to the standard output, use the following statement:

```
putc(input_char,stdout);
```

The **getc** function is normally buffered. In other words, when the application requests a character, control is not returned to the program until a carriage return is entered into the standard input file stream. All characters entered before the carriage return are held in a buffer and delivered to the program one at a time. The application invokes the **getc** function repeatedly until the buffer has been exhausted. After **getc** has sent the carriage return to the program, the next request for a character results in more characters accumulating in the buffer until a carriage return is entered again. This means that you cannot use the **getc** function for one-key input techniques that don't require pressing the carriage return.

Note that **getc** and **putc** are actually implemented as macros rather than as "true" functions. The functions **fgetc** and **fputc** are identical to their macro **getc** and **putc** counterparts.

getchar, putchar, fgetchar, and fputchar

The two macros **getchar** and **putchar** are actually specific implementations of the **getc** and **putc** macros. They are always associated with standard input (**stdin**) and standard output (**stdout**). The only way to use them on other file streams is to redirect either standard input or standard output from within the program.

The two examples used before could be rewritten using these two functions:

```
int input_char;
input_char = getchar();
```

and

```
putchar(input_char);
```

Like **getc** and **putc**, **getchar** and **putchar** are implemented as macros. The function **putchar** has been written to return an **EOF** value whenever an error condition occurs. You can use the following code to check for an output error condition. It's a bit confusing due to the check for **EOF** on output.

```
if(putchar(input_char) == EOF)
  printf("An error has occurred writing to stdout");
```

Both **fgetchar** and **fputchar** are the function equivalents of their macro **getchar** and **putchar** counterparts.

getch and putch

Both **getch** and **putch** are true functions. However, they do not fall under the ANSI C standard because they are low-level functions that interface closely with the hardware. For the IBM PC and compatible systems, these functions do not use buffering, which means that they immediately receive a character typed into the keyboard. They can be redirected, however, so they are not associated exclusively with the keyboard.

You can use the functions **getch** and **putch** exactly like **getchar** and **putchar**. Usually, a program running on the IBM PC will use **getch** to trap keystrokes ignored by **getchar**—for example, PGUP, PGDN, HOME, and END. The function **getch** sees a character entered from the keyboard as soon as the key is pressed; a carriage return is not needed to send the character to the program. This ability allows the **getch** function to provide a one-key technique that is not available with **getc** or **getchar**.

On an IBM PC or true compatibles, the function **getch** operates very differently from **getc** and **getchar**. This is partly because the IBM PC family can easily determine when an individual key on the keyboard has been pressed. Other systems, such as the DEC and VAX C, do not allow the hardware to trap individual keystrokes. These systems typically echo the input character and require that you press a carriage return (the carriage return character is not seen by the program unless no other characters have been entered). Under such circumstances, the carriage return returns a null character or a decimal zero. Additionally, the function keys are not available and produce unreliable results if they are pressed.

String Functions

In many applications, it is more natural to handle input and output in larger parcels than one character. For example, a file of car salespeople may contain one record per line, with each record consisting of four fields: salesperson's name, base pay, commission, and number of cars sold, with whitespace separating the fields. It would be tedious to use character I/O under these circumstances.

gets, puts, fgets, and fputs

Because of the organization of the file of salespeople, it's better to treat each record as a single character string and read or write it as a unit. The **fgets** function, which reads whole strings rather than single characters, is well suited to this task. In addition to the function **fgets** and its inverse **fputs**, there are the macro counterparts **gets** and **puts**.

The function **fgets** expects three arguments: the address of an array in which to store the character string, the maximum number of characters to store, and a pointer to a file to read. The function will read characters into the array until either the number of characters read in is one less than the size specified, all of the characters up to and including the next newline character have been read, or the end of file is reached, whichever comes first.

If **fgets** reads in a newline, the newline will be stored in the array. If at least one character was read, the function will automatically append the null string terminator \0. Suppose that the file *saleteam.dat* looks like this:

```
Harry Wilson 28000 0.10 10
Jane McMurphy 28000 0.10 10
Bob Anderson 35000 0.15 12
```

Assuming a maximum record length of 40 characters, including the newline, the following program will read the records from the file and write them to the standard output:

```
/*
 *      A C program that demonstrates how to read in whole records
 *      using fgets and print them out to stdio using fputs.
 *      Copyright (c) Chris H. Pappas and William H. Murray, 1990
 */

#include <stdio.h>

#define MAX_REC_SIZE 40
#define NULL_CHAR 1
```

```
main()
{
  FILE *in_file;
  char record[MAX_REC_SIZE + NULL_CHAR];

  in_file=fopen("a:\\sales\\june\\saleteam.dat", "r");
  while(fgets(record,MAX_REC_SIZE + NULL_CHAR,in_file) != NULL)
    fputs(record,stdout);
  fclose(in_file);

  return(0);
}
```

Because the maximum record size is 40, you must reserve 41 cells in the array; the extra cell holds the null terminator \0. The program does not generate its own newline when it prints each record to the terminal; instead, it relies on the newline read into the array by **fgets**. The **fputs** function writes the contents of the array *record* to the file specified by the file pointer **stdout**.

If your program is accessing a file on a disk drive other than the one the compiler resides on, you may need to include a path in your file name. Notice this description in the preceding program; the double backslashes \\ are necessary to indicate a subdirectory. Remember that a single backslash \ usually indicates that a control or line continuation follows.

While the **gets** and **fgets** functions are similar in usage, the **puts** and **fputs** functions operate differently. The **fputs** function writes to a file and expects two arguments: the address of a null-terminated character string and a pointer to a file. **fputs** simply copies the string to the specified file; it does not add a newline to the end of the string.

The macro **puts**, however, does not require a pointer to a file, since the output automatically goes to **stdout**, and the function **puts** automatically adds a newline character to the end of the output string. See "String Functions That Use Arrays" in Chapter 9, "Arrays," for an excellent example of how these functions differ.

Integer Functions

For certain applications, you may need to read and write *stream* (or buffered) integer information. The C language incorporates two functions for this purpose: **getw** and **putw**.

getw and putw

The **getw** and **putw** functions are similar to **getc** and **putc**, but they input and output integer data instead of character data. You should use both **getw** and **putw** only on files that are opened in binary mode. The following program opens a binary file, writes ten integers to it, closes the file, and then reopens the file for input and echo:

```
/*
 *      A C program that uses the functions getw and putw on
 *      a file created in binary mode.
 *      Copyright (c) Chris H. Pappas and William H. Murray, 1990
 */

#include <stdio.h>

#define SIZE 10

main()
{
  FILE *integer_file;
  int a_value,values[SIZE],index;

  integer_file=fopen("a:\\integer.dat", "wb");
  if(integer_file == NULL) {
    printf("File could not be opened");
    exit(1);
  }

  for(index = 0;index < SIZE;index++) {
    values[index]=index+1;
    putw(values[index],integer_file);
  }

  fclose(integer_file);

  integer_file=fopen("a:\\integer.dat", "rb");
  if(integer_file == NULL) {
    printf("File could not be re-opened");
    exit(1);
  }

  while(!feof(integer_file)) {
    a_value=getw(integer_file);
    printf("%3d",a_value);
  }

    return(0);
}
```

Review the output from this program and see if you can discover what went wrong:

```
1  2  3  4  5  6  7  8  9 10 -1
```

Because the integer value read in by the last loop may have a value equal to **EOF**, the program uses the function **feof** to check for the end-of-file marker. However, the function does not perform a look-ahead operation, as do some other high-level language end-of-file functions. In C, an actual read of the end-of-file value must be performed in order to flag the condition.

To correct this situation, you need to rewrite the program using a *priming read* statement:

```c
/*
 *    A C program that uses the functions getw and putw on
 *    a file created in binary mode, correcting the EOF test.
 *    Copyright (c) Chris H. Pappas and William H. Murray, 1990
 */

#include <stdio.h>
#include <process.h>

#define SIZE 10

main()
{
  FILE *integer_file;
  int a_value,values[SIZE],index;

  integer_file=fopen("a:\\integer.dat", "wb");
  if(integer_file == NULL) {
    printf("File could not be opened");
    exit(1);
  }

  for(index = 0;index < SIZE;index++) {
    values[index]=index+1;
    putw(values[index],integer_file);
  }

  fclose(integer_file);

  integer_file=fopen("a:\\integer.dat", "rb");
  if(integer_file == NULL) {
    printf("File could not be opened");
    exit(1);
  }

  a_value=getw(integer_file);
  while(!feof(integer_file)) {
    printf("%3d",a_value);
    a_value=getw(integer_file);
```

```
    }

    return(0);
}
```

Before entering the final *while* loop, the priming read checks whether the file is empty. If it is not, a valid integer value is stored in *a_value*. If the file is empty, however, the function **feof** will prevent the *while* loop from executing.

Notice that the priming read necessitated a rearrangement of the statements within the *while* loop. If the loop is entered, *a_value* contains a valid integer. If the statements within the loop were the same as the original program, an immediate second **getw** function call would be performed, overwriting the first integer value. Because of the priming read, the first statement within the *while* loop must be an output statement. This is next followed by a call to **getw** to obtain another value.

Suppose that the *while* loop has been entered nine times. At the end of the ninth iteration, the integer numbers 1 through 8 have been echoed and *a_value* has been assigned a 9. The next iteration of the loop prints the 9 and inputs the 10. Since 10 is not **EOF**, the loop iterates, echoing the 10 and reading **EOF**. At this point, the *while* loop terminates because the **feof** function sees the end-of-file condition.

These two simple example programs highlight the need to proceed carefully when writing code based on the **feof** function. This programming task is peculiarly frustrating, since each high-level language tends to treat the end-of-file condition differently. Some languages read a piece of data and look ahead at the same time to see the end of file. Others, like C, do not.

Formatted Output

C's rich assortment of output formatting controls makes it easy to create a neatly printed graph, report, or table. The two main functions that produce this formatted output are **printf** and the file equivalent form **fprintf**.

printf and fprintf

The following example program defines four variable types—character, array-of-characters, integer, and real—and then demonstrates how to use the appropriate format controls on each variable. The source code contains many comments, and includes output line numbering to simplify associating the output generated with the statement that created it.

```c
/*
*       A C program demonstrating advanced conversions and formatting
*       Copyright (c) Chris H. Pappas and William H. Murray, 1990
*/

#include <stdio.h>

main()
{
  char letter='A';
  static char string1[]="he who has an ear, ",
              string2[]="let him hear.";
  int int_value=4444;
  double pi=3.14159265;
  int ln=0;


  /*              conversions                */

  /*print the letter                         */
    printf("\n[%2d] %c",++ln,letter);

  /*print the ASCII code for letter */
    printf("\n[%2d] %d",++ln,letter);

  /*print character with ASCII 90     */
    printf("\n[%2d] %c",++ln,90);

  /* print int_value as octal value */
  printf("\n[%2d] %o",++ln,int_value);

  /* print lower-case hexadecimal     */
  printf("\n[%2d] %x",++ln,int_value);

  /* print upper-case hexadecimal     */
  printf("\n[%2d] %X",++ln,int_value);


  /* conversions and format options   */

  /* minimum width 1                         */
  printf("\n[%2d] %c",++ln,letter);

  /* minimum width 5, right-justify */
  printf("\n[%2d] %5c",++ln,letter);

  /* minimum width 5, left-justify   */
  printf("\n[%2d] %-5c",++ln,letter);

  /* 19 non-null, automatically         */
  printf("\n[%d] %s",++ln,string1);
```

```
/* 13 non-null, automatically    */
printf("\n[%d] %s",++ln,string2);

/* minimum 5 overridden, auto 19   */
printf("\n[%d] %5s",++ln,string1);

/* minimum width 25, right-justify */
printf("\n[%d] %25s",++ln,string1);

/* minimum width 25, left-justify  */
printf("\n[%d] %-25s",++ln,string2);

/* default int_value width, 4     */
printf("\n[%d] %d",++ln,int_value);

/* printf int_value with + sign    */
printf("\n[%d] %+d",++ln,int_value);

/* minimum 3 overridden, auto 4    */
printf("\n[%d] %3d",++ln,int_value);

/* minimum width 10, right-justify */
printf("\n[%d] %10d",++ln,int_value);

/* minimum width 10, left-justify  */
printf("\n[%d] %-d",++ln,int_value);

/* right-justify with leading 0's  */
printf("\n[%d] %010d",++ln,int_value);

/* using default number of digits  */
printf("\n[%d] %f",++ln,pi);

/* minimum width 20, right-justify */
printf("\n[%d] %20f",++ln,pi);

/* right-justify with leading 0's  */
printf("\n[%d] %020f",++ln,pi);

/* minimum width 20, left-justify  */
printf("\n[%d] %-20f",++ln,pi);

/* left-justify with trailing 0's  */
printf("\n[%d] %-020f",++ln,pi);


/* additional formatting precision */

/* minimum width 19, print all 17  */
printf("\n[%d] %19.19s",++ln,string1);

/* prints first 2 chars           */
printf("\n[%d] %.2s",++ln,string1);

/* prints 2 chars, right-justify   */
```

```
    printf("\n[%d] %19.2s",++ln,string1);

    /* prints 2 chars, left-justify    */
    printf("\n[%d] %-19.2s",++ln,string1);

    /* using printf arguments          */
    printf("\n[%d] %*.*s",++ln,19,6,string1);

    /* width 10, 8 to right of '.'     */
    printf("\n[%d] %10.8f",++ln,pi);

    /* width 20, 2 to right-justify    */
    printf("\n[%d] %20.2f",++ln,pi);

    /* 4 decimal places, left-justify  */
    printf("\n[%d] %-20.4f",++ln,pi);

    /* 4 decimal places, right-justify */
    printf("\n[%d] %20.4f",++ln,pi);

    /* width 20, scientific notation   */
    printf("\n[%d] %20.2e",++ln,pi);

    return(0);
}
```

The output generated by the program looks like this:

```
[ 1] A
[ 2] 65
[ 3] Z
[ 4] 10534
[ 5] 115c
[ 6] 115C
[ 7] A
[ 8]         A
[ 9] A
[10] he who has an ear,
[11] let him hear.
[12] he who has an ear,
[13]         he who has an ear,
[14] let him hear.
[15] 4444
[16] +4444
[17] 4444
[18]         4444
[19] 4444
[20] 0000004444
[21] 3.141593
[22]             3.141593
[23] 0000000000003.141593
[24] 3.141593
[25] 3.141593
[26] he who has an ear,
```

```
[27] he
[28]                      he
[29] he
[30]                he who
[31] 3.14159265
[32]               3.14
[33] 3.1416
[34]            3.1416
[35]            3.14e+00
```

You can neatly format your application's output by studying the previous example and selecting the combinations that apply to your program's data types.

fseek, ftell, and rewind

You can use the **fseek**, **ftell**, and **rewind** functions to determine or change the location of the file position marker. The function **fseek** resets the file position marker in the file pointed to by *file_pointer* to the number of *offset_bytes* from the beginning of the file (*from_where* = 0), from the current location of the file position marker (*from_where* = 1), or from the end of the file (*from_where* = 2). Borland C++ has predefined three constants that you can also use in place of the variable *from_where*: **SEEK_SET** (offset from the beginning of the file), **SEEK_CUR** (current file marker position), and **SEEK_END** (offset from end of file). The function **fseek** will return 0 if the seek is successful, and **EOF** otherwise. The general syntax for the function **fseek** looks like this:

fseek(*file_pointer,offset_bytes,from_where*);

The **ftell** function returns the current location of the file position marker in the file pointed to by *file_pointer*. This location is indicated by an offset, measured in bytes, from the beginning of the file. The syntax for the function **ftell** looks like this:

long_variable = ftell(*file_pointer*);

The value returned by **ftell** can be used in a subsequent call to **fseek**.

The function **rewind** simply resets to the beginning of the file the file-position marker in the file pointed to by *file_pointer*. The syntax for the function **rewind** looks like this:

rewind(*file_pointer*);

The following C program illustrates the functions **fseek, ftell,** and **rewind**:

```
/*
 *      A C program demonstrating the use of fseek, ftell, and rewind.
 *      Copyright (c) Chris H. Pappas and William H. Murray, 1990
 */

#include <stdio.h>

main()
{
  FILE *in_file;
  long location;
  char a_char;

  in_file=fopen("sample.dat","rt+");
  a_char=fgetc(in_file);
  putchar(a_char);
  a_char=fgetc(in_file);
  putchar(a_char);
  location=ftell(in_file);
  a_char=fgetc(in_file);
  putchar(a_char);
  fseek(in_file,location,0);
  a_char=fgetc(in_file);
  putchar(a_char);
  fseek(in_file,location,0);
  fputc('E',in_file);
  fseek(in_file,location,0);
  a_char=fgetc(in_file);
  putchar(a_char);
  rewind(in_file);
  a_char=fgetc(in_file);
  putchar(a_char);

  return(0);
}
```

The variable *location* has been defined to be of type **long**. This is because Borland C++ supports files larger than 64K. The input file *sample.dat* contains the string ABCD. After opening the file, the first call to **fgetc** gets the letter "A" and then prints it to the video display. The next statement pair inputs and prints the letter "B."

When the function **ftell** is invoked, *location* is set equal to the file-position marker's current location. This is measured as an offset, in bytes, from the beginning of the file. Since the letter "B" has already been processed, *location* contains a 2. This means that the file-position marker is pointing to the third character, which is 2 bytes over from the first letter "A."

Another I/O pair of statements now reads the letter "C" and prints it to the video display. After having executed this last statement pair, the file-position marker is 3 offset bytes from the beginning of the file, pointing to the fourth character "D."

At this point, the function **fseek** is invoked. It is instructed to move *location* offset bytes (or 2 offset bytes) from the beginning of the file (since the third parameter to the function **fseek** is a 0, as defined previously). This repositions the file-position marker to the third character in the file. The variable *a_char* is again assigned the letter "C" and is printed a second time.

The second time the **fseek** function is invoked, it uses the same parameters. The function **fseek** moves the pointer to the third character "C" (2 offset bytes into the file). However, the statement that follows doesn't input the "C" a third time, instead overwriting it with a new letter, "E." Since the file-position marker has now moved past this new "E," to verify that the letter was indeed placed in the file, the **fseek** function is invoked still another time.

The next statement pair inputs the new "E" and prints it to the video display. With this accomplished, the program invokes the **rewind** function, which moves the *file_pointer* back to the beginning of the file. When the **fgetc** function is then invoked, it returns the letter "A" and prints it to the file. The output from the program looks like this:

```
ABCCEA
```

You can use the same principles illustrated in this simple character example to create a random access file of records. Suppose that you have the following information for a file of individuals: social security number, name, and address. Suppose also that you are allowing 11 characters for the social security number, in the form *ddd-dd-dddd,* and that the name and address have an additional 60 characters (or bytes). So far, each record would be 11 + 60 bytes long, or 71 bytes.

All of the possible contiguous record locations on a random access disk file may not be full. The personnel record needs to contain a flag indicating whether or not that disk record location has been used or not, which will require adding 1 more byte to the personnel record. You'll also need 2 additional bytes to represent the record number, bringing the total for one person's record to 74 bytes. One record could look like this:

1 U123-45-6789Tina Tomassetti, 435 Main Street, Anywhere, USA

Record 1 in the file would occupy bytes 0 through 73, record 2 would occupy bytes 74 through 147, record 3 would occupy bytes 148 through 221, and so on. Using the record number in conjunction with the **fseek** function, you can locate any record location on the disk. For example, to find the beginning of record 2, you use the following statements:

```
offset_in_bytes=(record_number-1) * sizeof(ONE_PERSON)
fseek(in_file,offset_in_bytes,0);
```

Once the file-position marker has been moved to the beginning of the selected record, the information at that location can either be read or written using various I/O functions such as **fread** and **fwrite**.

With the exception of the comment block delimiter symbols, **/*** and ***/**, and the header file *stdio.h,* many C programs can be modified to work the same as C++. The program just discussed would work the same in C++. Just substitute the symbol **//** for both **/*** and ***/** (optional) and change *stdio.h* to *iostream.h.*

Using the Debugger

Try entering the next program and printing the value stored in the variable *current_person.record_number* after you have asked to search for record 25:

```
/*
*     A C random access file program using fseek, fread, and fwrite.
*     Copyright (c) Chris H. Pappas and William H. Murray, 1990
*/

#include <stdio.h>

#define START 1
#define FINISH 50
#define SS_LENGTH 11
#define DATA_LENGTH 60
#define VACANT 'V'
#define USED 'U'

typedef struct a_record {
  int record_number;
  char occupied;                /* V free, U used */
```

```
    char social_security[SS_LENGTH];
    char data[DATA_LENGTH];
}   ONE_PERSON;

main()
{
    FILE *in_file;
    ONE_PERSON current_person;
    int index,record_choice;
    long int offset;

    in_file=fopen("A:\\random.dat","r+");

    for(index = START;index <= FINISH; index++) {
      current_person.occupied=VACANT;
      current_person.record_number=index;
      fwrite(&current_person,sizeof(ONE_PERSON),1,in_file);
    }

    printf("Please enter the record you would like to find.");
    printf("\nYour response must be between 1 and 50: ");
    scanf("%d",&record_choice);

    offset=(record_choice - 1) * sizeof(ONE_PERSON);
      fseek(in_file,offset,0);
      fread(&current_person,sizeof(ONE_PERSON),1,in_file);

    fclose(in_file);

    return(0);
}
```

The **typedef** has defined *ONE_PERSON* as a structure that has a 2-byte record number, a 1-byte occupied character code, an 11-byte character array to hold a social security number, and a 60-byte data field. This brings the total structure size to 2 + 1 + 11 + 60, or 74 bytes.

Once the program has opened the file in read-and-update text mode, it creates and stores 50 records, each with its own unique record number and all initialized to *VACANT*. The **fwrite** statement wants the address of the structure to output, the size in bytes of what it is outputting, how many objects to output, and which file to send it to. With this accomplished, the program asks the user which record they want to search for.

The program finds the record in two steps. First, an offset address from the beginning of the file must be calculated. For example, record 1 is stored in bytes 0 to 73, record 2 is stored in bytes 74 to 148, and so on. After subtracting 1 from the record number entered by the user, the program multiplies this value by the number of bytes occupied by each structure and calculates the offset. For example, record 2 is found with the following calculation: $(2 - 1) \times 74$. This gives the second record a starting byte offset of 74. Using this calculated value, the **fseek** function is then invoked and moves the file-position marker *offset* bytes into the file.

If you ask to view records 1 through 10, all seems fine. However, when you ask to view record 11, you get garbage because the program opened the file in text mode. Records 1 through 9 are all exactly 74 bytes. Records 10 and up occupy 75 bytes. Therefore, the tenth record starts at the appropriate offset calculation but goes 1 byte further into the file. Record 11 is at the address calculated via the following modified calculation:

```
offset=((record_choice - 1) * sizeof(ONE_PERSON)) + 1;
```

This calculation won't work with the first nine records, however. The solution is to open the file in binary mode:

```
in_file=fopen("A:\\random.dat","r+b");
```

In text mode, the program tries to interpret any two-digit number as two single characters, increasing records with two-digit record numbers by 1 byte. In binary mode, the integer *record_number* is interpreted properly. Exercise care when deciding how to open a file for I/O.

Formatted Input

You can obtain formatted input for a C program by using the versatile **scanf** and **fscanf** functions. The **fscanf** function requires that you specifically designate the input file from which the data is to be obtained, while **scanf** does not. Table 11-3 lists all possible control string codes that you can use with **scanf**, **fscanf**, and **sscanf**.

scanf, fscanf, and sscanf

You can use all three input functions—**scanf**, **fscanf**, and **sscanf**—for extremely sophisticated data input. For example, consider the statement:

```
scanf("%2d%5s%4f",&int_value,a_string,&real_value);
```

Table 11-3.   Control Codes for **scanf**, **fscanf**, and **sscanf**

Code	Interpretation	Example Input	Receiving Address Parameter Type
c	a character	W	char
s	a string	William	char
d	**int**	23	int
hd	**short**	−99	short
ld	**long**	123456	long
o	octal	1727	int
ho	short octal	1727	short
lo	long octal	1727	long
x	hexadecimal	2b5	int
hx	short hexadecimal	2b5	short
lx	long hexadecimal	2b5	long
e	float as **float**	3.14159e + 03	float
f	same as e		
le	float as **double**	3.14159e + 03	double
lf	same as le		
[A-Za-z]	string with only chars	Test String	char
[0-9]	string with only digits	098231345	char

The statement inputs only a two-digit integer, a five-character string, and a real number that occupies a maximum of four spaces (2.97, 12.5, and so on). See if you can begin to imagine what this next statement does:

```
scanf("%*[ \t\n]\"%[^A-Za-z]%[^\"]\"",s1,s2);
```

The statement begins by reading and not storing any whitespace. This is accomplished with the following format specification: "%*[\t\n]". The * symbol instructs the function to obtain the specified data but not to save it in any variable. As long as only a space, tab, or newline are on the input line, **scanf** will keep reading until it encounters a double quote, ". This is accomplished by the \" format specification, which says that the input must match the designated symbol. However, the double quote is not input.

Once **scanf** has found the double quote, it is instructed to input all characters that are digits into *s1*. The %[^A-Za-z] format specification accomplishes this with the caret modifier, ^, which says to input anything not an uppercase letter "A" through "Z" or lowercase letter "a" through "z." Had the caret been omitted, the string would have contained only alphabetic characters. The hyphen between *A* and *Z* and *a* and *z* indicates that the entire range is to be considered.

The next format specification, %[^\"], instructs the input function to read into *s2* all remaining characters up to but not including a double quote. The last format specification, \", indicates that the string must match and end with a double quote. You can use the same types of input conversion control with the functions **fscanf** and **sscanf**. The only difference between these two functions is that **fscanf** requires that an input file be specified. The **sscanf** function is identical to **scanf** except that it reads the data from an array rather than a file.

This next example shows how you can use **sscanf** to convert a string (of digits) to an **int**. If *int_value* is of type **int** and *a_string* is an array of **chars** that holds a string of digits, the following statement

```
sscanf(a_string,"%d",&int_value);
```

will convert the string *a_string* into type **int** and store it in the variable *int_value*. Often the **gets** and **sscanf** functions are used in combination since **gets** reads in an entire line of input and **sscanf** interprets a string according to the specified format specifications.

A frequent problem with **scanf** occurs when students try to use it in conjunction with various other character input functions such as **getc**, **getch, getchar, gets,** and so on. For example, suppose **scanf** is used to input various data types that would otherwise require conversion from characters to something else. If the programmer tries to use a character input function such as **getch**, the function will not work as expected. The problem occurs because **scanf** sometimes doesn't read all of the data that is waiting to be read, and the waiting data can fool other functions (including **scanf**) into thinking that input has already been entered. To be safe, don't use other input functions in a program in which you use **scanf**.

INPUT AND OUTPUT IN C++

This section describes input and output in C++. Your Borland C++ compiler has been shipped with the latest C++ I/O Library. Starting with Release 2.0, certain I/O Library functions operate differently from their earlier Release 1.2 ancestor. This portion of the chapter begins by explaining those I/O operations that are most similar in the two releases. The last part of the chapter highlights the more dramatic library function changes.

The standard I/O library for C, described by the header file *stdio.h* is still available in C++. However, C++ introduces its own header files; for example, *iostream.h, fstream.h,* and *strstream.h,* which implement their own collection of I/O functions.

The stream I/O is described as a set of classes in *iostream.h.* These classes overload the "put to" and "get from" operators << and >>. To understand better why C++'s stream library is more convenient than its C counterpart, first review how C handles input and output. Recall that C has no built-in input or output statements; functions such as **printf** are part of the standard library, but not part of the language itself. Similarly, C++ has no built-in I/O facilities, giving you greater flexibility to produce the most efficient user interface.

In C, there is unfortunately little consistency among the I/O functions in terms of return values and parameter sequences. Because of this, programmers tend to rely on the formatted I/O functions **printf, scanf,** and so on—especially when the objects being manipulated are numbers or other noncharacter values. These formatted I/O functions are convenient and for the most part share a consistent interface. However, they are large and unwieldy because they must manipulate many kinds of values.

In C++, the class provides modular solutions to your data manipulation needs. The standard C++ library provides three I/O classes as an alternative to C's general-purpose I/O functions. These classes contain definitions for the same pair of operators, >> for input and << for output, that are optimized for all kinds of data (see Chapter 13, "Classes," for further discussion).

cin, cout, and cerr

The C++ stream counterparts to **stdin, stdout,** and **stderr** are **cin, cout,** and **cerr.** These three streams are opened automatically when your program begins execution and becomes the interface between the program and the user. The **cin** stream is associated with the terminal keyboard. The **cout** and **cerr** streams are associated with the video display.

The >> and << Operators

Input and output in C++ has been significantly enhanced and streamlined by the stream library operators >> ("get from" or *extraction*) and << ("put to" or *insertion*). One of the major enhancements that C++ added to C was operator overloading. Operator overloading allows the compiler to determine which like-named function or operator is to be executed based on the associated variables' data types. The extraction and insertion operators are good examples of this new C++ capability. Each operator has been overloaded so that it can handle all of the standard C++ data types, including classes.

The following example illustrates the greater ease of use for basic I/O operations in C++. First a quick look at a C output statement using **printf**:

```
printf("An integer %d, a float %f",my_integer,my_float);
```

Now the C++ equivalent:

```
cout << "An integer " << my_integer << ", a float " << my_float;
```

A careful examination of the C++ equivalent will reveal how the insertion operator has been overloaded to handle the three separate data types: string, integer, and float. If you are like many C programmers you are not going to miss having to hunt down the % symbol needed for your **printf** and **scanf** format specifications. As a result of operator overloading the insertion operator will examine the data type you have passed to it and determine an appropriate format.

An identical situation exists with the extraction operator, which performs data input. Look at the following C example and its equivalent C++ counterpart:

```
/* input in C */
scanf("%d%f%c",&my_integer,&my_float,&my_char);

// input in C++
cin >> my_integer >> my_float >> my_char;
```

No longer is it necessary to precede your input variables with the & address operator. In C++ the extraction operator takes care of calculating the storage variable's address, storage requirements, and formatting.

Having looked at two examples of the C++ operators << and >> you might be slightly confused as to why they are named the way they are. The simplest way to remember which operator performs output and which performs input is to think of these two operators as they relate to the stream I/O files. When you want to input information, you extract (>>) it from the input stream (**cin**) and put the information into a variable, for example, *my_integer*. To output information you take a copy of the information from the variable (*my_float*) and insert (<<) it into the output stream (**cout**).

As a direct result of operator overloading, C++ will allow a program to expand upon the insertion and extraction operators. The following code segment illustrates how the insertion operator can be overloaded to print the new type **employee**:

```
ostream& operator<< (ostream& out_file, employee one_employee)
{
  out_file << " " << one_employee.name;
  out_file << " " << one_employee.address;
  out_file << " " << one_employee.phone;
  return out_file;
}
```

Assuming the structure variable *one_employee* has been initialized, printing the information becomes a simple one line statement:

```
cout << one_employee;
```

Last but not least, the insertion and extraction operators have an additional advantage — their final code size. The general purpose I/O functions **printf** and **scanf** carry along code segments into the final executable version of a program that are often unused. In C, even if you are only dealing with integer data, you still pull along all of the conversion code for the additional standard data types. In contrast, the C++ compiler only incorporates those routines actually needed.

A Demonstration Program

The following program demonstrates how to use the input operator >> to read different types of data:

```
//
//    A C++ program demonstrating how to use the >> operator
//    to input a char, integer, float, double, and string.
//    Copyright (c) Chris H. Pappas and William H. Murray, 1990
//

#include <iostream.h>

#define LENGTH 30
#define NULL_CHAR 1

main()
```

```
{
  char response;
  int int_value;
  float float_value;
  double double_value;
  char your_name[LENGTH + NULL_CHAR];

  cout << "Would you like to enter some information?" << "\n";
  cout << "Please type a Y for yes and an N for no: ";

  cin  >> response;

  if(response == 'Y') {

    cout << "\n" << "Please enter an integer value: ";

    cin >> int_value;
    cout << "\n\n";

    cout << "Please enter a float value: ";
    cin >> float_value;
    cout << "\n\n";

    cout << "Please enter a double value: ";
    cin >> double_value;
    cout << "\n\n";

    cout << "Please enter your first name: ";
    cin >> your_name

    cout << "\n\n";
  }
  return(0);

}
```

In this example, the output operator **<<** is used in its simplest form to output literal string prompts. Notice that although the program uses four different data types, each input statement looks identical except for the variable's name.

If you ran the preceding program using Release 1.2, you would have noticed a formatting inconsistency. When the program started, you would have seen something like this:

```
Would you like to enter some information?
Please type a Y for yes and an N for no: Y

Please enter an integer value:
                  5
```

This is because the Release 1.2 input stream is processing the carriage return you entered after typing the letter **Y**. The input operator **>>** reads up to but does not get rid of the carriage return. The following program demonstrates how to correct the problem. Fortunately, starting with Release 2.0, none of this is necessary.

```
//
//      A C++ program demonstrating how to use the >> operator
//      to input a char, integer, float, double, and string.
//      Copyright (c) Chris H. Pappas and William H. Murray, 1990
//

#include <iostream.h>

#define LENGTH 30
#define NULL_CHAR 1

main()
{
   char response,carriage_return;
   int int_value;
   float float_value;
   double double_value;
   char your_name[LENGTH + NULL_CHAR];

   cout << "Would you like to enter some information?" << "\n";
   cout << "Please type a Y for yes and an N for no: ";
   cin  >> response;
   cin.get(carriage_return);

   if(response == 'Y') {

      cout << "\n" << "Please enter an integer value: ";
      cin >> int_value;
      cout << "\n\n";

      cout << "Please enter a float value: ";
      cin >> float_value;
      cout << "\n\n";

      cout << "Please enter a double value: ";
      cin >> double_value;
      cout << "\n\n";

      cout << "Please enter your first name: ";
      cin >> your_name;
      cout << "\n\n";
   }

   return(0);
}
```

When the program runs now, it looks like this:

```
Would you like to enter some information?
Please type a Y for yes and an N for no: Y

Please enter an integer value: 5
```

The following example demonstrates how to use the output operator << in its various forms:

```
//
//      A C++ program demonstrating how to use the << operator
//      to output a char, integer, float, double, and string.
//      Copyright (c) Chris H. Pappas and William H. Murray, 1990
//

#include <iostream.h>

main()
{
  char c='A';
  int int_value=10;
  float float_value=45.67;
  double double_value=2.3e32;
  char fact[]="For all have...";

  cout << "Once upon a time there were ";
  cout << int_value << " people. \n";
  cout << "Some of them earned " << float_value;
  cout << " dollars per hour." << "\n";
  cout << "While others earned " << double_value << " per year!";
  cout << "\n\n" << "But you know what they say: \"";
  cout << fact << "\"" << "\n\n";
  cout << "So, none of them get an ";
  cout.put(c);
  cout << "!";

  return(0);
}
```

The output from the program looks like this:

```
Once upon a time there were 10 people.
Some of them earned 45.669998 dollars per hour.
While others earned 2.3e+32 per year!

But you know what they say: "For all have..."

So, none of them get an A!
```

Compare the C++ source code with the output from the program. Notice that the output operator << does not automatically generate a newline character. You can still completely control when this occurs by including the newline symbol \n or **endl** when necessary. **endl** is very useful for outputting data in an interactive program because it not only inserts a newline into the stream but also flushes the output buffer. You can also use **flush**; however this does not insert a newline. Notice too that the newline symbol can be included after its own << output operator, or as part of a literal string (look at the second and fourth << statements in the program). In addition, note that the output operator isn't very helpful with **doubles**.

Had the following line of code,

```
cout.put(c);
```

been written using Release 1.2

```
cout << c;
```

the last line of the program would have output:

```
So, none of them get an 65!
```

Under Release 1.2 the character is translated into its ASCII equivalent. This would have required you to use the **put** function to output character data.

Try running this next example:

```
//
//     A C++ program demonstrating what happens when you use
//     the input operator >> with string data.
//     Copyright (c) Chris H. Pappas and William H. Murray, 1990
//

#include <iostream.h>

#define LENGTH 30
#define NULL_CHARACTER 1

main()
{
  char name[LENGTH + NULL_CHARACTER];

  cout << "Please enter your first and last name: ";
  cin >> name;
  cout << "\n\nThank you, " << name;

  return(0);
}
```

A sample execution of the program looks like this:

```
Please enter your first and last name: Dave Deehan

Thank you, Dave
```

The input operator, **>>**, stops reading in information as soon as it encounters whitespace. Whitespace can be a blank, tab, or newline. Therefore, when *name* is printed, only the first name entered is output.

You can solve this problem by rewriting the program and using the **cin.get** function:

```
//
//     A C++ program demonstrating what happens when you use
//     the input operator >> with cin.get to process an
//     entire string.
//     Copyright (c) Chris H. Pappas and William H. Murray, 1990
//

#include <iostream.h>

#define LENGTH 30
#define NULL_CHARACTER 1

main()
{
  char name[LENGTH + NULL_CHARACTER];

  cout << "Please enter your first and last name: ";
  cin.get(name,LENGTH);
  cout << "\n\nThank you, " << name;

  return(0);
}
```

The output from the program now looks like this:

```
Please enter your first and last name: Dave Deehan

Thank you, Dave Deehan
```

The **cin.get** function has two additional parameters. Only one of these, the number of characters to input, was used in the previous example. The function **cin.get** will read everything, including whitespace, until the maximum number of characters specified has been read in, up to the next newline. The optional third parameter, not shown, identifies a terminating symbol. For example,

```
cin.get(name,LENGTH,'*');
```

would read *LENGTH* characters into *name*, or all of the characters up to but not including a * symbol, or a newline, whichever comes first.

Formatted C++ Output (Release 1.2)

This section provides an explanation and example program demonstrating how to perform formatted output using the I/O Library Release 1.2. If you have no need to perform any program conversions from Release 1.2, continue your reading with "Advanced C++ Input and Output" later in this section.

You can view the output operator, <<, as a quick and dirty means for outputting many common types of information. However, when you need more precision, C++ provides the **form** function. The **form** function has two properties that allow flexible use at a high level. First, you can print a list of arguments of arbitrary length. Second, the printing is controlled by simple formats. This is analogous to the **printf** function in *stdio.h*. For this reason, the previous example program written with **printf** can be rewritten with **cout << form**:

```
//
// A C++ program demonstrating advanced conversions and
// formatting using the form function with <<.
// Copyright (c) Chris H. Pappas and William H. Murray, 1990
//

#include <stream.h>

main()
{
  char letter='A';
  static char string1[]="he who has an ear, ",
  string2[]="let him hear.";
  int int_value=4444;
  double pi=3.14159265;
  int ln=0;


  //conversions                        //

  // print the letter                  //
  cout << form("\n[%2d] %c",++ln,letter);

  // print the ASCII code for letter //
  cout << form("\n[%2d] %d",++ln,letter);

  // print character with ASCII 132  //
  cout << form("\n[%2d] %c",++ln,90);

  // print int_value as octal value  //
  cout << form("\n[%2d] %o",++ln,int_value);

  // print lower-case hexadecimal     //
```

```
cout << form("\n[%2d] %x",++ln,int_value);

// print upper-case hexadecimal    //
cout << form("\n[%2d] %X",++ln,int_value);


// conversions and format options   //

// minimum width 1                  //
cout << form("\n[%2d] %c",++ln,letter);

// minimum width 5, right-justify   //
cout << form("\n[%2d] %5c",++ln,letter);

// minimum width 5, left-justify    //
cout << form("\n[%2d] %-5c",++ln,letter);

// 19 non-null, automatically       //
cout << form("\n[%d] %s",++ln,string1);

// 13 non-null, automatically       //
cout << form("\n[%d] %s",++ln,string2);

// minimum 5 overridden, auto 19    //
cout << form("\n[%d] %5s",++ln,string1);

// minimum width 25, right-justify //
cout << form("\n[%d] %25s",++ln,string1);

// minimum width 25, left-justify  //
cout << form("\n[%d] %-25s",++ln,string2);

// default int_value width, 4       //
cout << form("\n[%d] %d",++ln,int_value);

// printf int_value with + sign     //
cout << form("\n[%d] %+d",++ln,int_value);

// minimum 3 overridden, auto 4     //
cout << form("\n[%d] %3d",++ln,int_value);

// minimum width 10, right-justify //
cout << form("\n[%d] %10d",++ln,int_value);

// minimum width 10, left-justify  //
cout << form("\n[%d] %-d",++ln,int_value);

// right-justify with leading 0's  //
cout << form("\n[%d] %010d",++ln,int_value);

// using default number of digits  //
cout << form("\n[%d] %f",++ln,pi);

// minimum width 20, right-justify //
cout << form("\n[%d] %20f",++ln,pi);
```

```
// right-justify with leading 0's  //
cout << form("\n[%d] %020f",++ln,pi);

// minimum width 20, left-justify  //
cout << form("\n[%d] %-20f",++ln,pi);

// left-justify with trailing 0's  //
cout << form("\n[%d] %-020f",++ln,pi);

// additional formatting precision //

// minimum width 19, print all 17  //
cout << form("\n[%d] %19.19s",++ln,string1);

// prints first 2 chars            //
cout << form("\n[%d] %.2s",++ln,string1);

// prints 2 chars, right-justify   //
cout << form("\n[%d] %19.2s",++ln,string1);

// prints 2 chars, left-justify    //
cout << form("\n[%d] %-19.2s",++ln,string1);

// using printf arguments          //
cout << form("\n[%d] %*.*s",++ln,19,6,string1);

// width 10, 8 to right of '.'     //
cout << form("\n[%d] %10.8f",++ln,pi);

// width 20, 2 to right-justify    //
cout << form("\n[%d] %20.2f",++ln,pi);

// 4 decimal places, left-justify  //
cout << form("\n[%d] %-20.4f",++ln,pi);

// 4 decimal places, right-justify //
cout << form("\n[%d] %20.4f",++ln,pi);

// width 20, scientific notation   //
cout << form("\n[%d] %20.2e",++ln,pi);

return(0);
}
```

You will find that the output from this program is identical to the output from its C counterpart.

ADVANCED C++ INPUT AND OUTPUT

One of the most exciting enhancements to the compiler is the new C++ I/O library, referred to as the *iostream* library. By not including input/output facilities within the C++ language itself, but rather implementing them in C++ and providing them as a component of a C++ standard library, I/O can evolve as needed. This new library replaces the earlier version of the I/O library referred to as the *stream* library (described in Stroustrup's *The C++ Programming Language*) discussed in the previous section.

Undoubtedly, many of you will have encountered the earlier Release 1.2 *stream* library. This portion of the chapter is designed to both familiarize you with the newer release *iostream* library and to highlight the most frequently needed changes to upgrade to the new format.

At its lowest level, C++ interprets a file as a sequence, or *stream*, of bytes. At this level, the concept of a data type is missing. One component of the I/O library is involved in the transfer of these bytes. From the user's perspective, however, a file is comprised of a series of intermixed alphanumerics, numeric values, or possibly, class objects. A second component to the I/O library takes care of the interface between these two viewpoints. The *iostream* library predefines a set of operations for handling reading and writing of the built-in data types. The library also provides for user-definable extensions to handle class types.

Basic input operations are supported by the **istream** class and basic output via the **ostream** class. Bi-directional I/O is supported via the **iostream** class, which is derived from both **istream** and **ostream**. There are four stream objects predefined for the user:

- **cin**   An **istream** class object linked to standard input

- **cout**   An **ostream** class object linked to standard output

- **cerr**   An unbuffered output **ostream** class object linked to standard error

- **clog**   A buffered output **ostream** class object linked to standard error.

Any program using the *iostream* library must include the header file *iostream.h*. Since *iostream.h* treats *stream.h* as an alias, programs written using *stream.h* may or may not need alterations depending on the particular structure used.

The new I/O library can also be used to perform input and output operations on files. A file can be tied to your program by defining an instance of one of the following three class types:

- **fstream**   Derived from **iostream** and links a file to your application for both input and output

- **ifstream**   Derived from **istream** and links a file to your application for input only

- **ofstream**   Derived from **ostream** and links a file to your application for output only

Operators and Member Functions

The **>>** *extraction* operator and the **<<** *insertion* operator have been modified to accept arguments of any of the built-in data types including **char** *. They can also be extended to accept class argument types.

Probably the first upgrade incompatibility you will experience when converting a C++ program using the older I/O library will be the demised **cout << form** extension. Under the new release each *iostream* library class object maintains a *format state* that controls the details of formatting operations, such as the conversion base for integral numeric notation or the precision of a floating-point value. A programmer can manipulate the format state flags using the **setf** and **unsetf** functions.

The **setf** member function sets a specified format state flag. There are two overloaded instances:

```
setf(long);
setf(long,long);
```

Table 11-4.   Format Flags

Flag	Meaning
ios::showbase	Display numeric base
ios::showpoint	Display decimal point
ios::dec	Decimal numeric base
ios::hex	Hexadecimal numeric base
ios::oct	Octal numeric base
ios::fixed	Decimal notation
ios::scientific	Scientific notation

Table 11-5.   Format Bit Fields

Bit Field	Meaning	Flags
ios::basefield	Integral base	ios::hex, ios::oct, ios::dec
ios::floatfield	Floating point	ios::fixed ios::scientific

The first argument can be either a format bit *flag* or a format bit *field*. Table 11-4 lists the format flags you can use with the **setf(long)** instance (using just the format flag). Table 11-5 lists the format bit fields you can use with the **setf(long,long)** instance (using a format flag and format bit field).

There are certain predefined defaults. For example, integers are written and read in decimal notation. The programmer can change the base to octal, hexadecimal, or back to decimal. By default, a floating-point value is output with six digits of precision. This can be modified by using the **precision** member function. The following C++ program uses these new member functions to rewrite an earlier program that was written using I/O library Release 1.2. Each code section takes the original Release 1.2 statement and demonstrates how to convert to an equivalent for the new I/O library.

Undoubtedly, as you study other example C++ programs from magazine articles, trade journals, and the like, you will encounter the older Release 1.2 formatting. This program can be an invaluable reference tool for making the necessary conversions.

```
//
//      A C++ program demonstrating advanced conversions and
//      formatting member functions of Release 2.0.  The program
//      will illustrate how to convert each of the older
//      Release 1.2 form statements.
//      Copyright (c) Chris H. Pappas and William H. Murray, 1990
//

#include <string.h>
#include <strstream.h>

#define NULL_TERMINATOR 1
```

```
void row (void);

main()
{
  char letter = 'A';
  static char string1[] = "he who has an ear, ",
    string2[] = "let him hear.";
  int int_value = 4444;
  double pi = 3.14159265;

  // new declarations needed for Release 2.0

  char padstring5[5+NULL_TERMINATOR],
    padstring25[25+NULL_TERMINATOR];

  // conversions

  // print the letter
  // R1.2 cout << form("\n[%2d] %c",++ln,letter);
  // Notice that << has been overloaded to output char
  row(); // [ 1]
  cout << letter;

  // print the ASCII code for letter
  // R1.2  form("\n[%2d] %d",++ln,letter);
  row(); // [ 2]
  cout << (int)letter;

  // print character with ASCII 90
  // R1.2  form("\n[%2d] %c",++ln,90);
  row(); // [ 3]
  cout << (char)90;

  // print int_value as octal value
  // R1.2  form("\n[%2d] %o",++ln,int_value);
  row(); // [ 4]
  cout << oct << int_value;

  // print lowercase hexadecimal
  // R1.2  form("\n[%2d] %x",++ln,int_value);
  row(); // [ 5]
  cout << hex << int_value;

  // print uppercase hexadecimal
  // R1.2  form("\n[%2d] %X",++ln,int_value);
  row(); // [ 6]
  cout.setf(ios::uppercase);
  cout << hex << int_value;
  cout.unsetf(ios::uppercase);      // turn uppercase off
  cout << dec;                      // return to decimal base

  // conversions and format options

  // minimum width 1
  // R1.2  form("\n[%2d] %c",++ln,letter);
  row(); // [ 7]
```

```
cout << letter;
// minimum width 5, right-justify
// R1.2  form("\n[%2d] %5c",++ln,letter);
row(); // [ 8]
ostrstream(padstring5,sizeof(padstring5)) << "    "
  << letter << ends;
cout << padstring5;

// minimum width 5, left-justify
// R1.2  form("\n[%2d] %-5c",++ln,letter);
row(); // [ 9]
ostrstream(padstring5,sizeof(padstring5)) << letter << "    "
  << ends;
cout << padstring5;

// 19 automatically
// R1.2  form("\n[%d] %s",++ln,string1);
row(); // [10]
cout << string1;

// 13 automatically
// R1.2  form("\n[%d] %s",++ln,string2);
row(); // [11]
cout << string2;

// minimum 5 overridden, auto 19
// R1.2  form("\n[%d] %5s",++ln,string1);
// notice that the width of 5 cannot be overridden!
row(); // [12]
cout.write(string1,5);

// minimum width 25, right-justify
// R1.2  form("\n[%d] %25s",++ln,string1);
// notice how the width of 25 appended the second string!
row(); // [13]
cout.write(string1,25);
// the following is the correct approach
cout << "\n\nCorrected approach:\n";
ostrstream(padstring25,sizeof(padstring25)) << "        "
  << string1 << ends;
row(); // [14]
cout << padstring25;

// minimum width 25, left-justify
// R1.2  form("\n[%d] %-25s",++ln,string2);
ostrstream(padstring25,sizeof(padstring25))
  << string2 << "               " << ends;
row(); // [15]
cout << padstring25;

// default int_value width, 4
// R1.2  form("\n[%d] %d",++ln,int_value);
row(); // [16]
cout << int_value;

// printf int_value with + sign
```

```
// R1.2  form("\n[%d] %+d",++ln,int_value);
row(); // [17]
cout.setf(ios::showpos);         // don't want row number with +
cout << int_value;
cout.unsetf(ios::showpos);

// minimum 3 overridden, auto 4
// R1.2  form("\n[%d] %3d",++ln,int_value);
row(); // [18]
cout.width(3); // don't want row number padded to width of 3
cout << int_value;

// minimum width 10, right-justify
// R1.2  form("\n[%d] %10d",++ln,int_value);
row(); // [19]
cout.width(10); // only in effect for first value printed
cout << int_value;

// minimum width 10, left-justify
// R1.2  form("\n[%d] %-d",++ln,int_value);
row(); // [20]
cout.width(10);
cout.setf(ios::left);
cout << int_value;
cout.unsetf(ios::left);

// right-justify with leading 0's
// R1.2  form("\n[%d] %010d",++ln,int_value);
row(); // [21]
cout.width(10);
cout.fill('0');
cout << int_value;
cout.fill(' ');

// using default number of digits
// R1.2  form("\n[%d] %f",++ln,pi);
row(); // [22]
cout << pi;

// minimum width 20, right-justify
// R1.2  form("\n[%d] %20f",++ln,pi);
row(); // [23]
cout.width(20);
cout << pi;

// right-justify with leading 0's
// R1.2  form("\n[%d] %020f",++ln,pi);
row(); // [24]
cout.width(20);
cout.fill('0');
cout << pi;
cout.fill(' ');

// minimum width 20, left-justify
// R1.2  form("\n[%d] %-20f",++ln,pi);
row(); // [25]
```

```
cout.width(20);
cout.setf(ios::left);
cout << pi;

// left-justify with trailing 0's
// R1.2  form("\n[%d] %-020f",++ln,pi);
row(); // [26]
cout.width(20);
cout.fill('0');
cout << pi;
cout.unsetf(ios::left);
cout.fill(' ');

// additional formatting precision

// minimum width 19, print all 17
// R1.2  form("\n[%d] %19.19s",++ln,string1);
row(); // [27]
cout << string1;

// prints first 2 chars
// R1.2  form("\n[%d] %.2s",++ln,string1);
row(); // [28]
cout.write(string1,2);

// prints 2 chars, right-justify
// R1.2  form("\n[%d] %19.2s",++ln,string1);
row(); // [29]
cout << "                  ";
cout.write(string1,2);

// prints 2 chars, left-justify
// R1.2  form("\n[%d] %-19.2s",++ln,string1);
row(); // [30]
cout.write(string1,2);

// using printf arguments
// R1.2  form("\n[%d] %*.*s",++ln,19,6,string1);
row(); // [31]
cout << "              ";
cout.write(string1,6);

// width 10, 8 to right of '.'
// R1.2  form("\n[%d] %10.8f",++ln,pi);
row(); // [32]
cout.precision(9);
cout << pi;

// width 20, 2 to right-justify
// R1.2  form("\n[%d] %20.2f",++ln,pi);
row(); // [33]
cout.width(20);
cout.precision(2);
cout << pi;

// 4 decimal places, left-justify
```

```
   // R1.2  form("\n[%d] %-20.4f",++ln,pi);
   row(); // [34]
   cout.precision(4);
   cout << pi;

   // 4 decimal places, right-justify
   // R1.2  form("\n[%d] %20.4f",++ln,pi);
   row(); // [35]
   cout.width(20);
   cout << pi;

   // width 20, scientific notation
   // R1.2  form("\n[%d] %20.2e",++ln,pi);
   row(); // [36]
   cout.setf(ios::scientific);
   cout.width(20);
   cout << pi;
   cout.unsetf(ios::scientific);

   return(0);
}

void row (void)
{
   static int ln=0;
   cout << "\n[";
   cout.width(2);
   cout << ++ln << "] ";

}
```

The output from the program follows:

```
[ 1] A
[ 2] 65
[ 3] Z
[ 4] 10534
[ 5] 115c
[ 6] 115C
[ 7] A
[ 8]      A
[ 9] A
[10] he who has an ear,
[11] let him hear.
[12] he wh
[13] he who has an ear, let h

Corrected approach:

[14]        he who has an ear,
[15] let him hear.
[16] 4444
[17] +4444
[18] 4444
```

```
[19]          4444
[20] 4444
[21] 0000004444
[22] 3.141593
[23]                  3.141593
[24] 0000000000003.141593
[25] 3.141593
[26] 3.141593000000000000
[27] he who has an ear,
[28] he
[29]                       he
[30] he
[31]                  he who
[32] 3.14159265
[33]                     3.14
[34] 3.1416
[35]                   3.1416
[36]               3.1416e+00
```

The following section highlights those output statements used in the program above that need special clarification. One point needs to be made: *iostream.h* is automatically included by *strstream.h*. The latter file is needed to perform string output formatting. If your application needs to output numeric data or simple character and string output you will only need to include *iostream.h*.

Character Output

In the new I/O library the insertion operator << has been overloaded to handle character data. With the earlier release the following statement,

```
cout << letter;
```

would have output the ASCII value of *letter*. In the current I/O Library the letter itself is output. For those programs needing the ASCII value a cast is required:

```
cout << (int)letter;
```

Base Conversions

There are two approaches to outputting a value using a different base:

```
cout << hex << int_value;

// or
cout.setf(ios::hex,ios::basefield);
cout << int_value;
```

Both approaches cause the base to be *permanently* changed from the statement forward (not always the effect you want). Each value output will now be formatted as a hexadecimal value. Returning to some other base is accomplished with the **unsetf( )** function:

```
cout.unsetf(ios::hex,ios::basefield);
```

If you are interested in uppercase hexadecimal output use the following statement:

```
cout.setf(ios::uppercase);
```

When no longer needed you will have to turn this option off:

```
cout.unsetf(ios::uppercase);
```

String Formatting

Printing an entire string using the current I/O library is the same as with Release 1.2. However, string formatting has changed because the *cout <<* *form* method is no longer available. One approach to string formatting is to declare an array of characters and then select the desired output format, printing the string buffer:

```
padstring25[25+NULL_TERMINATOR];
   .
   .
   .
ostrstream(padstring25,sizeof(padstring25)) << "         "
   << string1;
```

The **ostrstream** member function is part of *strstream.h* and has three parameters; a pointer to an array of characters, the size of the array, and the information to be inserted. This statement appends leading blanks to right justify *string1*.

Portions of a string can be output using the **write** form of **cout**:

```
cout.write(string1,5);
```

This statement will output the first five characters of *string1*.

Numeric Formatting

Numeric data can be easily formatted with right or left justification, varying precisions, varying formats (floating point or scientific), leading or trailing fill patterns, and signs. There are certain defaults. For example, justification defaults to right, and to floating-point precision of six. The following code segment outputs *pi* left justified in a field width of 20, with trailing 0's:

```
cout.width(20);
cout.setf(ios::left);
cout.fill('0');
cout << pi;
```

Had the following statement been included, *pi* would have been printed with a precision of two:

```
cout.precision(2);
```

With many of the output flags such as left justify, selecting uppercase hexadecimal output, base changes, and many others, it is necessary to unset these flags when no longer needed. The following statement turns left justification off:

```
cout.unsetf(ios::left);
```

Selecting scientific format is a matter of flipping the correct bit flag:

```
cout.setf(ios::scientific);
```

Values can be printed with a leading **+** sign by setting the **showpos** flag:

```
cout.setf(ios::showpos);
```

There are many minor details to the current I/O library functions that will initially cause some confusion. This has to do with the fact that certain operations once executed make a permanent change until turned off, while others only take effect for the next output statement. For example, an output width change, as in *cout.width(20);*, only affects the next value printed. That is why function **row** has to repeatedly change the width to get the output row numbers formatted within two spaces as in [1]. However, other formatting operations like base changes, uppercase, precision, and floating-point/scientific, remain active until specifically turned off.

File Input and Output

All of the examples so far have used the predefined streams **cin** and **cout**. It is possible that your program will need to create its own streams for I/O. If an application needs to create a file for input or output it must include the *fstream.h* header file (*fstream.h* **#includes** *iostream.h*). The classes **ifstream** and **ofstream** are derived from **istream** and **ostream** and inherit the extraction and insertion operations respectively. The following C++ program demonstrates how to declare a file for reading and writing using **ifstream** and **ofstream** respectively:

```
//
//      A C++ program demonstrating how to declare an
//      ifstream and ofstream for file input and output.
//      Copyright (c) Chris H. Pappas and William H. Murray, 1990
//

#include <fstream.h>

main()
{
  char ch;

  ifstream my_input("a:\my_input.in");
  if( !my_input )
    cerr << " Unable to open 'my_input' for input.";

  ofstream my_output("a:\myoutput.out");
  if( !my_output )
    cerr << " Unable to open 'my_output' for output.";

  while( my_output && my_input.get(ch) )
    my_output.put(ch);
```

```
    my_input.close();
    my_output.close();

    return(0);
}
```

The program declares *my_input* to be of class **ifstream** and is associated with the file *my_input.in* stored on the A: drive. It is always a good idea for any program dealing with files to verify the existence or creation of the specified file in the designated mode. By using the handle to the file *my_input*, a simple *if* test can be generated to check the condition of the file. A similar process is applied to *my_output* with the exception that the file is derived from the **ostream** class.

The *while* loop continues inputting and outputting single characters while the *my_input* exists and the character read in is not **EOF**. The program terminates by closing the two files. Closing an output file can be essential to dumping all internally buffered data.

There may be circumstances when a program will want to delay a file specification or when an application may want to associate several file streams with the same file descriptor. The following code segment demonstrates this concept:

```
ifstream an_in_file;
       .
       .
       .
an_in_file.open("bobsales");
       .
       .
       .
an_in_file.close();
an_in_file.open("joesales");
       .
       .
       .
an_in_file.close();
```

Whenever an application wishes to modify the way in which a file is opened or used it can apply a second argument to the file stream constructors. For example:

```
ofstream my_output("my_output.out",ios::app|ios::noreplace);
```

Table 11-6.   Stream Operation Modes

Mode Bit	Action
ios::in	Open for reading
ios::out	Open for writing
ios::ate	Seek to EOF after file is created
ios::app	All writes added to end of file
ios::trunc	If file already exists truncate
ios::nocreate	Unsuccessful open if file does not exist
ios::noreplace	Unsuccessful open if file does exist
ios::binary	Opens file in binary mode (default text)

declares *my_output* and attempts to append it to the file named *my_output.out*. Because **ios::noreplace** is specified, the file will not be created if *my_output.out* doesn't already exist. The **ios::app** parameter appends all writes to an existing file. Table 11-6 lists the second argument flags to the file stream constructors that can be logically ORed together.

An **fstream** class object can also be used to open a file for *both* input and output. For example, the following definition opens file *update.dat* in both input and append mode:

```
fstream io("update.dat", ios::in|ios::app);
```

All **iostream** class types can be repositioned by using either the **seekg** or **seekp** member functions, which can move to an absolute address within the file or move a byte offset from a particular position. Both **seekg** (sets or reads the *get* pointer's position) and **seekp** (sets or reads the *put* pointer's position) can take one or two arguments. When used with one parameter, the **iostream** is repositioned to the specified pointer position. When used with two parameters, a relative position is calculated. The following listing highlights these differences assuming the declaration for *io* above:

```
streampos current_position = io.tellp();

io << my_object1 << my_object2 << my_object3;

io.seekp(current_position);
io.seekp( sizeof(MY_OBJECT), ios::cur );

io << new_object2;
```

Table 11-7.   iostream Library Member Stream State Functions

Member Function	Action
eof	Returns a nonzero value on end of file
fail	Returns a nonzero value if an operation failed
bad	Returns a nonzero value if an error occurred
good	Returns a nonzero value if no state bits are set
rdstate	Returns the current stream state
clear	Sets the stream state (int=0)
operator	Returns a zero if the state failed

The pointer *current_position* is first derived from **streampos** and initialized to the current position of the *put-file* pointer by the function **tellp**. With this information stored, three objects are written to *io*. Using **seekp**, the *put-file* pointer is repositioned to the beginning of the file. The second **seekp** statement uses the **sizeof** function to calculate the number of bytes necessary to move one object's width into the file. This effectively skips over *my_object1*'s position permitting a *new_object2* to be written.

If a second argument is passed to **seekg** or **seekp**, it defines the direction to move: **ios::beg** (from the beginning), **ios::cur** (from the current position), and **ios::end** (from the end of file). For example,

```
io.seekg(5,ios::cur);
```

will move into the *get_file* pointer file five bytes from the current position, while

```
io.seekg(-7,ios::end);
```

will move the *get_file* pointer seven bytes backward from the end of the file.

File Condition States

Associated with every stream is an error state. When an error occurs, bits are set in the state according to the general category of the error. By convention, inserters ignore attempts to insert things into an **ostream** with error bits set, and such attempts do not change the stream's state. The **iostream** library object contains a set of predefined condition flags, which monitor the ongoing state of the stream. Table 11-7 lists the seven member functions that can be invoked.

These member functions can be used in various algorithms to solve unique I/O conditions and to make the code more readable:

```
ifstream in_file("my_file,ios::in);

if(my_file.eof())
  my_file.clear();  // sets the state of my_file to 0

if(my_file.fail())
  cerr << ">>> my_file create error <<<";

if(my_file.good())
  cin >> my_object;

if(!my_file)        // shortcut
  cout << ">>> my_file create error <<<";
```

12

STRUCTURES, UNIONS, AND MISCELLANEOUS ITEMS

This chapter focuses on two important C and C++ features, the structure and union, along with other miscellaneous topics. You can think of the C or C++ structure as an array or vector of closely related items. However, unlike an array or vector, a structure permits the items to be of different data types. Unions allow you to store different data types at the same place in memory. These two data structures are the foundation of most database and spreadsheet programs. Structures are also the precursor to a more advanced C++ type, called the *class*, covered in Chapter 13, "Classes."

This chapter explains how to build simple structures, create arrays of structures, pass structures and arrays of structures to functions, access structure elements with pointers, and create simple linked lists.

STRUCTURES

The concept of a data structure is common in everyday life. A card file of client information is a structure of related items. A file of favorite recipes is a structure. A computer's directory listing is a structure. You can think of a structure as a group of variables, which can be of different types, held together in a single unit.

The Syntax and Rules for Structures

You create a structure by using the keyword *struct* and the following syntax:

```
struct type {
   type var1;
   type var2;
      .
      .
      .
   type varn;
};
```

You must use a semicolon to terminate the statement because the structure definition is actually a C and C++ statement.

Several of the following examples will use the next structure:

```
struct car {
   char make[15];
   char model[15];
   char title[20];
   int year;
   long int mileage;
   float price_new;
};
```

The structure is defined with the keyword *struct* followed by a tag, which specifies the type for the structure. In this example, **car** is the tag for the structure. This structure contains several members: The *make, model,* and *title* are character arrays of the specified length. These character arrays are followed by an integer, *year,* a long integer, *mileage,* and a float, *price_new.* This structure will be used to save information on an automobile.

However, no variable has been associated with the structure at this point. In your program code, you can associate a variable with a structure by using the following statement:

```
struct   car   mycar;
```

If this statement is contained in a function, the structure is local in scope to that function. If the statement is contained outside of all functions, the structure will be global in scope. You can also use this form:

```
struct car {
  char make[15];
  char model[15];
  char title[20];
  int year;
  long int mileage;
  float price_new;
} mycar;
```

In both cases, *mycar* is declared as structure type **car**. Actually, you can omit the tag name when only one variable is associated with a structure type. So you could also write

```
struct {
  char make[15];
  char model[15];
  char title[20];
  int year;
  long int mileage;
  float price_new;
} mycar;
```

You can also associate several variables with the same structure type, as shown here:

```
struct car {
  char make[15];
  char model[15];
  char title[20];
  int year;
  long int mileage;
  float price_new;
} hiscar,hercar,bankscar;
```

As with normal variable types, C and C++ allocate all necessary memory for the structure members.

You reference members of a structure by using the dot (.) operator. The syntax is

```
struct_name.member_name
```

where *struct_name* is the variable associated with the structure type and *member_name* is the name of any member of the structure.

In C, for example, you can place information in the *model* variable with a statement such as

```
gets(mycar.model);
```

Here, *mycar* is the name associated with the structure and *model* is a member of the structure. Likewise, you can use a **printf** function to print information for a structure member:

```
printf("%ld",mycar.mileage);
```

In C++, the syntax for accessing structure members is essentially the same:

```
cin >> mycar.make;
```

This statement will read the make of the car into the character array while

```
cout << mycar.price_new;
```

will display the purchase price of the car on the screen.

Structure members are treated like any other C or C++ variable, but you must always use the dot operator with them.

Creating a Simple Structure

The programming example in this section will use a structure similar to the **car** structure shown earlier. Study the listing that follows and see if you understand how the various structure elements are accessed.

```
/*
 *      C program illustrates how to create a structure.
 *      This example stores data about your car in
 *      the C structure.
 *      Copyright (c) Chris H. Pappas and William H. Murray, 1990
 */

#include <stdio.h>
```

```
struct car {
  char make[15];
  char model[15];
  char title[20];
  int year;
  long int mileage;
  float price_new;
} myauto;

main()
{
  printf("Enter the make of the car.\n");
  gets(myauto.make);
  printf("Enter the model of the car.\n");
  gets(myauto.model);
  printf("Enter the title number for the car.\n");
  gets(myauto.title);
  printf("Enter the model year for the car.\n");
  scanf("%d",&myauto.year);
  printf("Enter the current mileage for the car.\n");
  scanf("%ld",&myauto.mileage);
  printf("Enter the purchase price of the car.\n");
  scanf("%f",&myauto.price_new);
  getchar();      /* flush keyboard buffer */

  printf("\n\n\n");
  printf("A %d %s %s with title number #%s\n",myauto.year,
      myauto.make,myauto.model,myauto.title);
  printf("currently has %ld miles",myauto.mileage);
  printf(" and was purchased for $%5.2f\n",
      myauto.price_new);
  return (0);
}
```

The single **getchar** function call flushes the carriage return from the keyboard buffer. You may or may not need this function call in your program, depending on the type of computer you are using. A typical output from the preceding example illustrates how information can be manipulated with a structure:

```
A 1987 Ford LTD with title number #A143LFG3489FD
currently has 56732 miles and was purchased for $14879.54
```

Note that *myauto* has a global scope since it was declared outside of any function.

Passing a Structure to a Function

You will have many occasions to pass structure information to functions. When a structure is passed to a function, structure information is passed by value, thus the function will not alter the original structure. You can pass a structure to a function by using the following syntax:

```
function_name(variable associated with structure);
```

If *myauto* were local in scope to the **main** function, it could be passed to a function named **dataout** with the statement

```
dataout(myauto);
```

Naturally, the **dataout** prototype must declare the structure type it is about to receive.

```
void dataout(struct car autocompany);
```

Passing entire structures to functions is not always the most efficient way to reduce time and memory requirements. Where time is a factor, the use of pointers might be a better choice. The **malloc** function is often used for dynamically allocating structure memory when using linked lists. The last example in this chapter shows how that's done.

The following example shows how to pass a structure to a function. It is a simple modification of the last example. Observe how the *myauto* structure is passed to the **dataout** function.

```
/*
 *      C program illustrates how to pass a structure
 *      to a function.
 *      Copyright (c) Chris H. Pappas and William H. Murray, 1990
 */

#include <stdio.h>

struct car {
  char make[15];
  char model[15];
  char title[20];
  int year;
  long int mileage;
  float price_new;
};

void dataout(struct car autocompany);

main()
{
  struct car myauto;
```

```
      printf("Enter the make of the car.\n");
      gets(myauto.make);
      printf("Enter the model of the car.\n");
      gets(myauto.model);
      printf("Enter the title number for the car.\n");
      gets(myauto.title);
      printf("Enter the model year for the car.\n");
      scanf("%d",&myauto.year);
      printf("Enter the current mileage for the car.\n");
      scanf("%ld",&myauto.mileage);
      printf("Enter the purchase price of the car.\n");
      scanf("%f",&myauto.price_new);
      getchar();       /* flush keyboard buffer */
      dataout(myauto);
      return (0);
}

void dataout(struct car autocompany)
{
   printf("\n\n\n");
   printf("A %d %s %s with title number #%s\n",autocompany.year,
         autocompany.make,autocompany.model,autocompany.title);
   printf("currently has %ld miles",autocompany.mileage);
   printf(" and was purchased for $%5.2f\n",
         autocompany.price_new);
}
```

In this example, a whole structure was passed by value to the function. As you will see later in this chapter, you can also pass individual structure members to a function by value. The output from this program is similar to the output from the previous example.

Creating an Array of Structures

As you have seen, a structure is similar to a single card from a card file. You exploit the real power of structures when you use a collection of structures, called an *array of structures*. An array of structures is similar to the whole card file containing a great number of individual cards. By maintaining an array of structures, you can manipulate a database of information for a wide range of items. This array of structures might include information on all of the cars on a used car lot. This could enable a car dealer to use the database to determine, for example, all cars less than $3000 or all cars with automatic transmissions. (Note that the function __linkfloats is a temporary floating Point fix to the compiler that may not be required in future compiler releases.) Notice how the following code has been changed from earlier listings:

```
/*
 *      C program illustrates the use of an array of structures.
 *      This example creates a "used car inventory" for
 *      P and M Car Sales.
 *      Copyright (c) Chris H. Pappas and William H. Murray, 1990
 */

#include <stdio.h>

#define MAX_CARS 50

void __linkfloats (void);

struct car {
  char make[15];
  char model[15];
  char title[20];
  char comment[80];
  int year;
  long int mileage;
  float retail;
  float wholesale;
};

main()
{
  int i,inven;
  struct car P_and_M[MAX_CARS];

  __linkfloats();
  printf("How many cars in inventory?\n");
  scanf("%d",&inven);
  flushall();      /* flush keyboard buffer */
  for (i=0; i<inven; i++) {
    printf("Enter the make of the car.\n");
    gets(P_and_M[i].make);
    printf("Enter the model of the car.\n");
    gets(P_and_M[i].model);
    printf("Enter the title number for the car.\n");
    gets(P_and_M[i].title);
    printf("Enter a one line comment about the car.\n");
    gets(P_and_M[i].comment);
    printf("Enter the model year for the car.\n");
    scanf("%d",&P_and_M[i].year);
    printf("Enter the current mileage for the car.\n");
    scanf("%ld",&P_and_M[i].mileage);
    flushall();
    printf("Enter the retail price of the car.\n");
    scanf("%f",&P_and_M[i].retail);
    printf("Enter the wholesale price of the car.\n");
    scanf("%f",&P_and_M[i].wholesale);
    flushall();      /* flush keyboard buffer */
  }

  printf("\n\n\n");
  for (i=0; i<inven; i++) {
```

```
    printf("A %d %s %s cream-puff with %ld low miles.\n",
           P_and_M[i].year,P_and_M[i].make,P_and_M[i].model,
           P_and_M[i].mileage);
    printf("%s\n",P_and_M[i].comment);
    printf("Ask your P and M salesperson for bargain");
    printf(" #%s ONLY! $%5.2f.\n",P_and_M[i].title,
           P_and_M[i].retail);
    printf("\n\n");
  }
  return (0);
}

void __linkfloats(void)
{
  /* __linkfloats is a fix that loads in the floating point
                   routines needed for the following statements
                   to execute properly:
                   scanf("%f",&P_and_M[i].retail/wholesale);
  */
  float f,*fp;
  fp=&f;
  f=*fp;
}
```

Here, P and M Auto Sales (not affiliated with Pappas and Murray) has an array of structures for holding information about the cars on their lot.

The variable, *P_and_M[MAX_CARS]*, associated with the structure is actually an array. In this case, *MAX_CARS* sets the maximum array size to 25. This means that data on 25 cars can be maintained in the array of structures. Now, however, you need to indicate which of the cars in the file you wish to view. The first array element is 0. Thus, you can access information on the first car in the array of structures with statements such as the following:

```
gets(P_and_M[0].title);
```

Notice that the array elements in the previous listing are actually accessed in a loop. Thus, element members are obtained with code such as

```
gets(P_and_M[i].title);
```

The following program output illustrates the small stock of cars on hand at P and M Auto Sales. It also shows how structure information can be rearranged in output statements.

```
A 1987 Lincoln Mark VII cream-puff with 89476 low miles.
A great riding car owned by a poor school teacher.
Ask your P and M salesperson for bargain #DS1543267BGDF ONLY!
$21567.00.
```

A 1967 Honda motorcycle cream-puff with 4564 low miles.
An economical means of transportation. Owned by grandmother.
Ask your P and M salesperson for bargain #AG1543RED219 ONLY!
$1237.99.

A 1985 Buick Park Avenue cream-puff with 43500 low miles.
Runs great. Owned by former dean of college.
Ask your P and M salesperson for bargain #156YUBA12ERR56 ONLY!
$10599.99.

When you work with arrays of structures, be aware of the memory limitations of the memory model you are programming with—arrays of structures require large amounts of memory.

Examine the Debugger screen shown in Figure 12-1. What does it tell you about the memory locations of structure items?

Using Pointers with Structures

The following example establishes an array of structures similar to the last example. However, this example uses the arrow operator to access structure

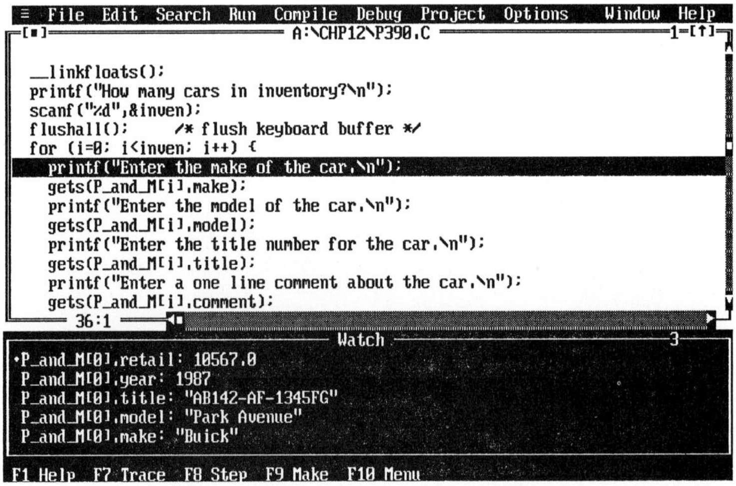

Figure 12-1.   The Debugger is used to examine selected items in the program's **car** structure. Notice all six items that were added to the Watch window.

members. You can only use the arrow operator when a pointer to a structure has been established.

```
/*
 *     C program illustrates the use of pointers to an
 *     array of structures. P and M used car inventory
 *     example is used again.
 *     Copyright (c) Chris H. Pappas and William H. Murray, 1990
 */

#include <stdio.h>

#define MAX_CARS 50

void __linkfloats(void);

struct car {
  char make[15];
  char model[15];
  char title[20];
  char comment[80];
  int year;
  long int mileage;
  float retail;
  float wholesale;
};

main()
{
  int i,inven;
  struct car P_and_M[MAX_CARS],*P_and_Mptr;
  P_and_Mptr=&P_and_M[0];

  __linkfloats();
  printf("How many cars in inventory?\n");
  scanf("%d",&inven);
  flushall();      /* flush keyboard buffer */
  for (i=0; i<inven; i++) {
    printf("Enter the make of the car.\n");
    gets(P_and_Mptr->make);
    printf("Enter the model of the car.\n");
    gets(P_and_Mptr->model);
    printf("Enter the title number for the car.\n");
    gets(P_and_Mptr->title);
    printf("Enter a one line comment about the car.\n");
    gets(P_and_Mptr->comment);
    printf("Enter the model year for the car.\n");
    scanf("%d",&P_and_Mptr->year);
    printf("Enter the current mileage for the car.\n");
    scanf("%ld",&P_and_Mptr->mileage);
    printf("Enter the retail price of the car.\n");
    scanf("%f",&P_and_Mptr->retail);
    printf("Enter the wholesale price of the car.\n");
    scanf("%f",&P_and_Mptr->wholesale);
    flushall();    /* flush keyboard buffer */
    P_and_Mptr++;
  }
```

```
    P_and_Mptr=&P_and_M[0];
    printf("\n\n\n");
    for (i=0; i<inven; i++) {
      printf("A %d %s %s cream-puff with %ld low miles.\n",
             P_and_Mptr->year,P_and_Mptr->make,P_and_Mptr->model,
             P_and_Mptr->mileage);
      printf("%s\n",P_and_Mptr->comment);
      printf("Ask your P and M salesperson for bargain");
      printf(" #%s ONLY! $%5.2f.\n",P_and_Mptr->title,
             P_and_Mptr->retail);
      printf("\n\n");
      P_and_Mptr++;
    }
    return (0);
}

void __linkfloats(void)
{
  /* __linkfloats is a fix that loads in the floating point
                   routines needed for the following statements
                   to execute properly:
                   scanf("%f",&P_and_Mptr->retail/wholesale); */
  */
  float f,*fp;
  fp=&f;
  f=*fp;
}
```

The array variable *P_and_M[MAX_CARS]* and the **P_and_Mptr* pointer are associated with the structure via the following statement:

```
struct car P_and_M[MAX_CARS],*P_and_Mptr;
```

The address of the array is then passed to the pointer with

```
P_and_Mptr=&P_and_M[0];
```

It is syntactically correct to refer to array members with this syntax:

```
gets((*P_and_Mptr).make);
```

However, the arrow operator makes the operation much cleaner:

```
gets(P_and_Mptr->make);
```

Passing an Array of Structures to a Function

Remember, using a pointer to a structure is faster than simply passing the whole structure to a function. This becomes evident when a program makes heavy use of structures. The following example shows how an array of structures can be accessed by a function with the use of a pointer:

```c
/*
 *      C program illustrates how a function can access an array
 *      of structures with the use of a pointer.
 *      The P and M used car inventory is used again.
 *      Copyright (c) Chris H. Pappas and William H. Murray, 1990
 */

#include <stdio.h>

#define MAX_CARS 50

void __linkfloats(void);

int inven;

struct car {
  char make[15];
  char model[15];
  char title[20];
  char comment[80];
  int year;
  long int mileage;
  float retail;
  float wholesale;
};

void dataout(struct car *autocompanyptr);

main()
{
  int i;
  struct car  P_and_M[MAX_CARS],*P_and_Mptr;
  P_and_Mptr=&P_and_M[0];

  __linkfloats();
  printf("How many cars in inventory?\n");
  scanf("%d",&inven);
  flushall();      /*  flush keyboard buffer */
  for (i=0; i<inven; i++) {
    printf("Enter the make of the car.\n");
    gets(P_and_Mptr->make);
    printf("Enter the model of the car.\n");
    gets(P_and_Mptr->model);
    printf("Enter the title number for the car.\n");
    gets(P_and_Mptr->title);
    printf("Enter a one line comment about the car.\n");
    gets(P_and_Mptr->comment);
```

```
        printf("Enter the model year for the car.\n");
        scanf("%d",&P_and_Mptr->year);
        printf("Enter the current mileage for the car.\n");
        scanf("%ld",&P_and_Mptr->mileage);
        printf("Enter the retail price of the car.\n");
        scanf("%f",&P_and_Mptr->retail);
        printf("Enter the wholesale price of the car.\n");
        scanf("%f",&P_and_Mptr->wholesale);
        flushall();   /* flush keyboard buffer */
        P_and_Mptr++;
    }
    P_and_Mptr=&P_and_M[0];
    dataout(P_and_Mptr);
    return (0);
}

void dataout(struct car *autocompanyptr)
{
   int i;
   printf("\n\n\n");
   for (i=0; i<inven; i++) {
      printf("A %d %s %s cream-puff with %ld low miles.\n",
             autocompanyptr->year,autocompanyptr->make,
             autocompanyptr->model,autocompanyptr->mileage);
      printf("%s\n",autocompanyptr->comment);
      printf("Ask your P and M salesperson for bargain");
      printf(" #%s ONLY! $%5.2f.\n",autocompanyptr->title,
             autocompanyptr->retail);
      printf("\n\n");
      autocompanyptr++;
   }
}

void __linkfloats(void)
{
   /* __linkfloats is a fix that loads in the floating point
                    routines needed for the following statements
                    to execute properly:
                    scanf("%f",&P_and_Mptr->retail/wholesale);
   */
   float f,*fp;
   fp=&f;
   f=*fp;
}
```

The first clue that this program will operate a little differently from the previous example comes from the **dataout** function prototype:

```
void dataout(struct car *autocompanyptr);
```

The function will expect to receive a pointer to the structure mentioned. In the **main** function, the array *P_and_M[MAX_CARS]* and the pointer *P_and_Mptr* are associated with the structure by

```
struct car  P_and_M[MAX_CARS],*P_and_Mptr;
```

After the information has been gathered for P and M Auto Sales, it is passed to **dataout** by passing the pointer.

```
dataout(P_and_Mptr);
```

The output from this example is similar to the output from the previous examples.

Using Structures in C++

The C++ example that follows is a modification of the previous C program. Syntactically, both of these languages handle structures in an identical manner.

```
//
//    C++ program illustrates the use of pointers when
//    accessing structure information from a function.
//    Note:  Comment line terminates with a period (.)
//    Copyright (c) Chris H. Pappas and William H. Murray, 1990
//

#include <iostream.h>

#define MAX_CARS 50

int inven;

struct car {
  char make[15];
  char model[15];
  char title[20];
  char comment[80];
  int year;
  long int mileage;
  float retail;
  float wholesale;
};

void dataout(struct car *autocompanyptr);

main()
{
  int i;
  char newline;
  struct car P_and_M[MAX_CARS],*P_and_Mptr;
  P_and_Mptr=&P_and_M[0];
```

```
  cout << "How many cars in inventory?" << endl;
  cin >> inven;
  for (i=0; i<inven; i++) {
    cout << "Enter the make of the car." << endl;
    cin >> P_and_Mptr->make;
    cout << "Enter the model of the car." << endl;
    cin >> P_and_Mptr->model;
    cout << "Enter the title number for the car." << endl;
    cin >> P_and_Mptr->title;
    cout << "Enter the model year for the car." << endl;
    cin >> P_and_Mptr->year;
    cout << "Enter the current mileage for the car." << endl;
    cin >> P_and_Mptr->mileage;
    cout << "Enter the retail price of the car." << endl;
    cin >> P_and_Mptr->retail;
    cout << "Enter the wholesale price of the car." << endl;
    cin >> P_and_Mptr->wholesale;
    cout << "Enter a one line comment about the car." << endl;
    cin.get(newline);    // process carriage return
    cin.get(P_and_Mptr->comment,80,'.');
    cin.get(newline);    // process carriage return
    cout << flush;
    P_and_Mptr++;
  }
  P_and_Mptr=&P_and_M[0];
  dataout(P_and_Mptr);
  return (0);
}

void dataout(struct car *autocompanyptr)
{
  int i;
  cout.setf(ios::fixed);   //format output for dollars and cents
  cout.precision(2);
  cout << "\n\n\n";
  for (i=0; i<inven; i++) {
    cout << "A " << autocompanyptr->year << " "
         << autocompanyptr->make  << " "
         << autocompanyptr->model << " with "
         << autocompanyptr->mileage << " low miles.\n";
    cout << autocompanyptr->comment << endl;
    cout << "Ask your P and M salesperson for bargain ";
    cout << "#" << autocompanyptr->title << " ONLY! $"
         << autocompanyptr->retail;
    cout << "\n\n";
    autocompanyptr++;
  }
}
```

The real difference between the two programs lies in how stream I/O is handled. Usually, you can use simple C++ **cout** and **cin** streams to replace the standard C **gets** and **printf** functions. For example:

```
cout << "Enter the wholesale price of the car.\n";
cin >> P_and_Mptr->wholesale;
```

However, when it comes to accepting a comment line, you use a different approach. Remember that **cin** will read character information until the first whitespace. In this case, a space between words in a line of comments serves as a whitespace. If **cin** were used, only the first word would be saved in the comment member of the structure. Instead, a variation of **cin** is used so that a whole line of text can be entered:

```
cout << "Enter a one line comment about the car.\n";
cin.get(newline);    // process carriage return
cin.get(P_and_Mptr->comment,length,'.');
cin.get(newline);    // process carriage return
```

First, **cin.get(**_newline_**)** is used much like the **getchar** function of earlier C programs. In a buffered keyboard system, you often need to strip the carriage return from the buffer. There are other ways to accomplish this, but they are less eloquent. The statement **cin.get(**_newline_**)** receives the carriage return character and saves it in _newline_. The variable _newline_ is just a receptacle for the information, and is not actually used by the program. The comment line is accepted by

```
cin.get(P_and_Mptr->comment,length,'.');
```

Here, **cin.get** uses a pointer to the structure member, followed by the maximum length of the comment, _length,_ followed by a termination character (.). In this case, the comment line will be terminated when 79 (_length_ −1) characters are entered or a period is typed. The period is not saved as part of the comment, so the period is added back when the comment is printed. Can you find where this is done?

More on Structures

There are a few things about structures that the previous examples have not touched upon. For example, you can pass individual structure members to a function. Furthermore, you can nest structures.

Passing Individual Members of a Structure to a Function

Passing individual structure members is an easy and efficient means of accessing limited structure information with a function. For example, you might use a function to print a list of wholesale prices of the cars available on the lot. In that case, just the wholesale price, which is a member of the structure, would be passed to the function. The call to the function might look like this

```
print_price(P_and_M.wholesale);
```

where **print_price** is the function name and *P_and_M.wholesale* is the structure name and member.

Nesting Structures Within Structures

You can nest structures—that is, make one structure a part of a second structure. For example, you could include the following structure in another structure:

```
struct maintenance {
  long int oilchange;
  long int plugs;
  long int airfilter;
  long int tirerotation;
} carmain;
```

In the main structure, you could include the *carmain* structure as follows:

```
struct car {
  char make[15];
  char model[15];
  char title[20];
  char comment[80];
  struct maintenance carmain;
  int year;
  long int mileage;
  float retail;
  float wholesale;
} P_and_M[MAX_CARS];
```

If you want a particular member from *carmain*, you can reach it like this:

```
printf("%ld\n",P_and_M[0].carmain.oilchange);
```

Structures and Bit Fields

C, C++, and assembly language enable you to access individual bits within a larger data type, such as a byte. This feature is useful when you want to alter data masks used for system information and graphics. The ability to access individual data bits is built around the C and C++ structure.

For example, you may want to alter the keyboard status register in the computer. The register contains the following information:

register bits

keyboard status: 7 6 5 4 3 2 1 0
port (417h)

where bit 0 = Right SHIFT depressed (1)

bit 1 = Left SHIFT depressed (1)

bit 2 = CTRL depressed (1)

bit 3 = ALT depressed (1)

bit 4 = SCROLL LOCK active (1)

bit 5 = NUMLOCK active (1)

bit 6 = CAPS LOCK active (1)

bit 7 = INS active (1)

To access and manipulate this information, you could create this structure:

```
struct keybits {
  unsigned char
              rshift  : 1,        /* lsb */
              lshift  : 1,
              ctrl    : 1,
              alt     : 1,
              scroll  : 1,
              numlock : 1,
              caplock : 1,
              insert  : 1;        /* msb */
} mykeys;
```

The bits are specified in the structure starting with the least significant bit (LSB) and progressing down to the most significant bit (MSB). You can specify more than one bit by typing the quantity (in place of the 1). Naturally, you can only use integer data types for bit fields.

The members of the bit field structure are accessed in the normal fashion.

UNIONS

A *union* is a data type that can be used in many different ways. For example, a particular union could be interpreted as an integer in one operation and a float or double in another. Although unions take on the appearance of a structure, they are quite different. A union can contain a group of many data types, all sharing the same location in memory. Nevertheless, a union can only contain information on one data type at a time.

The Syntax and Rules for Unions

You create a union by using the following syntax:

```
union type {
   type var1;
   type var2;
      .
      .
      .
   type varn;
};
```

Use a semicolon for termination because the structure definition is actually a C and C++ statement.

The next example will use the following union:

```
union all_types {
   char c;
   int i;
   float f;
   double d;
} tdata;
```

The union is defined with the keyword *union* followed by the type or tag for the structure. In this example, **all_types** is the tag for the union. This union contains several members: a character, integer, float, and double. This union will allow **all_types** to save information on any one data type at a time.

The variable associated with the union is *tdata*. If this statement is contained in a function, the union is local in scope to that function. If the statement is contained outside of all functions, the structure will be global in scope. As with structures, you can associate several variables with the same union. In addition, you reference members of a union by using the dot operator with the following syntax

```
union_name.member_name
```

where *union_name* is the variable associated with the union type and *member_name* is the name of any member of the union.

Union members are treated like any other C or C++ variable, but you must always use the dot operator with them. However, unlike a structure, you cannot pass a union to a function. One way around this is to pass the value of the data type currently stored in the union. Almost all other operations that were valid for structures are also valid for unions.

Creating a Simple Union

The following C++ program creates a union of the type just discussed. This example shows that a union can contain the definitions for many types, but can only hold the value for one data type at a time.

```
//
//     C++ program illustrates the use of a union.
//     Creates a union containing several data types.
//     Copyright (c) Chris H. Pappas and William H. Murray, 1990
//

#include <iostream.h>

union all_types {
   char c;
   int i;
   float f;
   double d;
} tdata;

main()
{
   // valid I/O
   tdata.c='b';
   cout << tdata.c << "\n";
   tdata.i=1234;
   cout << tdata.i << "\n";
   tdata.f=12.34;
   cout << tdata.f << "\n";
   tdata.d=123456.78E+12;
   cout << tdata.d << "\n";
```

```
// invalid I/O
cout << tdata.c << "\n";
cout << tdata.i << "\n";
cout << tdata.f << "\n";
cout << tdata.d << "\n";

// union size
cout << "The size of this union is: "
    << sizeof(all_types) << " bytes." << "\n";
return (0);
}
```

The first part of this program simply loads and unloads information from the union. Everything works fine because the union is only called upon to store one type at a time. However, the second part of the program attempts to output each data type from the union. The only valid value is the double, since it was the last value loaded in the previous section of code.

```
98 1234
12.34
1.234568e+17
-128
14208
-5.382278e-24
1.234568e+17
The size of this union is: 8 bytes.
```

Unions set aside storage for the largest data type contained within the union. All other data types within the union share this memory.

You can use the Debugger to get an idea of what is happening with storage within a union. Examine Figure 12-2 and the Watch window.

MISCELLANEOUS ITEMS

There are two additional topics worth mentioning at this point: **typedef** and **enum**. Both **typedef** and **enum** can help clarify program code when used correctly.

Typedef

You can associate new data types with existing data types by using **typedef**. For example, in a mathematically intensive program, you might want to use the data types **fixed, whole, real,** or **complex.** These new types can be associated with standard C types. The following example creates two new data types:

```
/*
 *      C program illustrates typedef.
 *      Creates two new types, "whole" and "real",
 *      which can be used in place of "int" and "float".
 *      Copyright (c) Chris H. Pappas and William H. Murray, 1990
 */

#include <stdio.h>

typedef int whole;
typedef float real;

main()
{
  whole i=567;
  real  myreal=3.14159;

  printf("The whole number is %d.\n",i);
  printf("The real number is %f.\n",myreal);
  return (0);
}
```

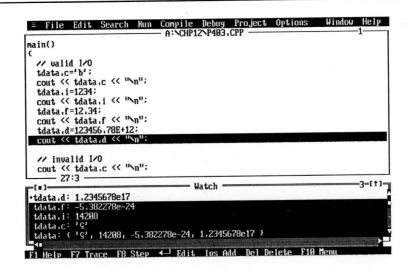

Figure 12-2.   The Watch window of the Debugger is used to examine various sized values being placed in the union

Employ **typedef** with care, since using too many newly created types can decrease program readability.

Enum

An **enum** data type allows you to create a data type with your choice in items. **enum** is useful when information can be best represented by a list of integer values such as the number of months in a year or the number of days in a week.

The following example contains a list of the number of months in a year. These are in an enumeration list with a tag name **months**. The variable associated with the list is *finish*. Enumerated lists will always start with 0 unless forced to a different integer value. In this case, January is the first month of the year.

```
/*
 *      C program illustrates enum types.
 *      Example calculates elapsed months in year, and
 *      remaining months using enum type.
 *      Copyright (c) Chris H. Pappas and William H. Murray, 1990
 */

#include <stdio.h>

enum months {
   January=1,
   February,
   March,
   April,
   May,
   June,
   July,
   August,
   September,
   October,
   November,
   December
} finish;

main()
{
   int current_month;
   int sum,diff;

   printf("Enter the current month (1 to 12).\n");
   scanf("%d",&current_month);
   getchar();
   finish=December;
```

```
sum=(int)current_month;
diff=(int)finish - (int)current_month;

printf("\n%d month(s) down, %d to go this year.\n",sum,diff);
return (0);
}
```

The enumerated list is actually a list of integer values, from 1 to 12 in this example. Since the names are equivalent to consecutive integer values, you can perform integer arithmetic with them. Thus, the integer variable *finish* is actually set to 12 when set equal to *December*.

This short program will perform some simple arithmetic and report the result to the screen:

```
Enter the current month (1 to 12).
3
3 month(s) down, 9 to go this year.
```

LINKED LISTS

Linked lists form the gateway to advanced data structure techniques, and offer the advantage of dynamic allocation of structures. So far, every example program involving an array of structures has also included a definition for the total number of such structures. For example, MAX_CARS has been set to 25. This simply means that the program will accept data on 25 automobiles. If 60 or 70 cars are brought onto the car lot, the program itself will have to be altered to accommodate the increased number. This is because the structure allocation is *static*. You can immediately see the disadvantage of static allocation. One way around the problem is to set the number of structures higher than needed. If MAX_CARS is set to 5000, not even P and M Auto Sales could have an inventory that large. However, 5000 means that you are requiring the computer to set aside 100 times more memory than before. This is not a wise or efficient way to program. A better approach is to set aside memory *dynamically* as it is needed. With this approach, memory allocation for structures is requested as the inventory grows. Linked lists allow the use of dynamic memory allocation.

A *linked list* is a collection of structures. Each structure in the list contains an element or pointer that points to another structure in the list. This pointer serves as the link between structures. The concept is similar to an array but enables the list to grow dynamically. Figure 12-3 shows a simple linked list for the P and M Auto Sales program.

The linked list for this example includes a pointer to the next car in the inventory:

```
struct car {
  char make[15];
  char model[15];
  char title[20];
  char comment[80];
  int year;
  long int mileage;
  float retail;
  float wholesale;
  struct car *nextcar;
} P_and_M, *firstcar,*currentcar;
```

The pointer, *nextcar*, points to the address of the next related structure. Thus, the pointer in the first structure points to the address of the second structure, and so on. This is the concept of a linked list of structures.

Components and Concerns in a Linked List

To make the linked list dynamic, you need a means for allocating memory as each new item is added to the list. In C, memory allocation is accom-

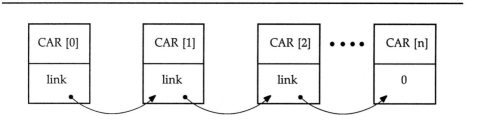

Figure 12-3.   The implementation of a traditional linked list

plished with the **malloc** function; in C++, **new** is used. In the complete program, in the section "A Simple Linked List," memory is allocated to the first structure with the code:

```
firstcar=(struct car *) new (struct car);
```

You can achieve subsequent memory allocation for each additional structure by placing a similar piece of code in a *while* loop:

```
while (datain(&P_and_M)==0) {
currentcar->nextcar=
  (struct car *) new (struct car);
if (currentcar->nextcar==NULL) exit(1);
currentcar=currentcar->nextcar;
*currentcar=P_and_M;
}
```

Thus, memory is allocated as needed. Note that the value returned by **new** was cast to an appropriate pointer type, using the structure's tag name **car**. The last structure in the list will have its pointer location set to **NULL**. Using **NULL** marks the end of a linked list. Can you see how that's done in the program code?

A Simple Linked List

The following program converts the P and M Auto Sales example to a linked list. Study the listing and see which items seem similar and which items have changed.

```
//
//     C++ program demonstrates a simple linked list.
//     P and M used car inventory example is used.
//     Copyright (c) Chris H. Pappas and William H. Murray, 1990
//

#include <stdlib.h>
#include <iostream.h>

struct car {
  char make[15];
  char model[15];
  char title[20];
  char comment[80];
  int year;
  long int mileage;
```

```
  float retail;
  float wholesale;
  struct car *nextcar;
} P_and_M, *firstcar,*currentcar;

void carlocation(struct car *node);
void dataout(struct car *carptr);
int datain(struct car *P_and_Mptr);

main()
{
  firstcar=(struct car *) new (struct car);
  if (firstcar==NULL) exit(1);
  if (datain(&P_and_M) != 0) exit(1);
  *firstcar=P_and_M;
  currentcar=firstcar;

  while (datain(&P_and_M)==0) {
  currentcar->nextcar=
    (struct car *) new (struct car);
  if (currentcar->nextcar==NULL) exit(1);
  currentcar=currentcar->nextcar;
  *currentcar=P_and_M;
  }
  currentcar->nextcar=NULL;
  carlocation(firstcar);
  return (0);
}

void carlocation(struct car *node)
{
  do {
    dataout(node);
  } while ((node=node->nextcar) != NULL);
}

void dataout(struct car *carptr)
{
  cout.setf(ios::fixed);    //set format for dollars and cents
  cout.precision(2);
  cout << "\n\n\n";
  cout << "A " << carptr->year << " " << carptr->make
       << " " << carptr->model << " cream-puff with "
       << carptr->mileage << " low miles." << endl;
  cout << carptr->comment << "." << endl;
  cout << "Ask your P and M salesperson for bargain ";
  cout << "#" << carptr->title << ", " << "ONLY! $"
       << carptr->retail << endl;
}
int datain(struct car *P_and_Mptr)
{
  char newline;

  cout << "\n(Enter new car information - a Q quits)\n\n";
  cout << "Enter the make of the car." << endl;
  cin >> P_and_Mptr->make;
```

```
if (*(P_and_Mptr->make) == 'Q') return(1);
cout << "Enter the model of the car." << endl;
cin >> P_and_Mptr->model;
cout << "Enter the title number for the car." << endl;
cin >> P_and_Mptr->title;
cout << "Enter the model year for the car." << endl;
cin >> P_and_Mptr->year;
cout << "Enter the current mileage for the car." << endl;
cin >> P_and_Mptr->mileage;
cout << "Enter the retail price of the car." << endl;
cin >> P_and_Mptr->retail;
cout << "Enter the wholesale price of the car." << endl;
cin >> P_and_Mptr->wholesale;
cout << "Enter a one line comment about the car." << endl;
cin.get(newline);      // process carriage return
cin.get(P_and_Mptr->comment,80,'.');
cin.get(newline);      // process carriage return
return(0);
}
```

First notice the three function prototypes:

```
void carlocation(struct car *node);
void dataout(struct car *carptr);
int datain(struct car *P_and_Mptr);
```

Note that all three functions are passed pointers. The first function, **carloca-tion**, checks the linked list for entries before calling the **dataout** function. The **dataout** function formats the output to each linked list structure, and is basically the same as in previous examples. For this program, input is done in a function called **datain**. This function returns an integer, 0 or 1. A 0 indicates successful data input, while a 1 indicates the user's wish to terminate input. The value returned by **datain** tells the code in the **main** function whether to allocate more memory and whether to set the *nextcar* pointer to a new linked item or **NULL**. If the user enters a **Q** when the make of the car is requested, the program will end data entry. With just those exceptions, the **datain** function is the same as in earlier examples.

Can you explain where the *nextcar* pointer will be pointing with each trip around the *while* loop? If you can, you have captured the essence of the linked list.

Linked lists in C++ are best implemented with object-oriented program-ming. The advantages of OOP will be shown in Chapter 14, "Introduction to Object-Oriented Programming."

13

CLASSES

The various data types, discussed in earlier chapters, give C and C++ the flexibility needed by programmers today. The *class* is a new C++ user-defined data type that gives you the advantages of a structure and the ability to limit access to specific data to functions that are also members of the class. As such, classes are one of C++'s greatest contributions to programming. The advanced features of the class include the ability to initialize and protect sensitive functions and data.

Think about this progression of power: One-dimensional arrays or vectors permit a collection of like data types to be held together. Next, structures permit related items of different data types to be combined in a group. Finally, C++ classes permit you to implement a data type and associate operators and member functions with it. Thus, you have the storage concept associated with a structure along with the member functions to operate on the storage variables. The *class* object forms the foundation for object-oriented programming in C and is discussed in more detail in Chapter 14, "Introduction to Object-Oriented Programming."

FUNDAMENTAL CLASS CONCEPTS

In the following sections, you will learn how to create and manipulate the fundamental components of a C++ class. A class can have data and function members. Moreover, a class can include public, private, and protected parts. This concept allows parts, typically class variables, to be hidden from all functions except those that are members of the class.

The Syntax and Rules for Classes

The definition of a class begins with the keyword *class*. The class name or tag type immediately follows the keyword. The framework of the class is very similar to other type definitions that you have seen.

```
class type {
  type var1
  type var2
       .
       .
       .
public:
  member function1
  member function2
  member function3
       .
       .
       .
} name associated with class type;
```

Member variables immediately follow the class declaration. These variables are by default *private* to the class and can only be accessed by the member functions that follow. Member functions usually follow a *public* declaration that allows access from functions external to the class. All class member functions have access to both public and private parts of a class.

What follows is a class definition that will be used in the second programming example in this chapter:

```
class angle {
  double value;

public:
  void set_value(double);
  double get_sine(void);
  double get_cosine(void);
```

```
    double get_tangent(void);
} deg;
```

This class has a type or tag name **angle**. A private variable, *value*, will share degree values among the various member functions. Four functions make up the function members of the class: **set_value**, **get_sine**, **get_cosine**, and **get_tangent**. The name that is associated with this class type is *deg*. Unlike this example, the association of a variable name with the class name or tag is most frequently made in the **main( )** function.

Structures as a Class

The last chapter developed numerous programs with the *struct* type, using the same format for both C and C++ structures. However, the keyword *struct* in C++ is more powerful than the equivalent keyword in C. In many respects, the structure in C++ is an elementary form of class. Examine the following code:

```
//
//      C++ program illustrates the simplest form of a class,
//      built on the C++ keyword "struct".  This program uses a
//      structure class to obtain the sine, cosine and tangent
//      of an angle.
//      Copyright (c) Chris H. Pappas and William H. Murray, 1990
//

#include <iostream.h>
#include <math.h>

const double ANG_TO_RAD=0.0174532925;

struct angle {
  double value;

  void set_value(double);
  double get_sine(void);
  double get_cosine(void);
  double get_tangent(void);
} deg;

void angle::set_value(double a)
{
  value=a;
}

double angle::get_sine(void)
{
  double temp;
```

```
    temp=sin(ANG_TO_RAD*value);
    return (temp);
}

double angle::get_cosine(void)
{
    double temp;

    temp=cos(ANG_TO_RAD*value);
    return (temp);
}

double angle::get_tangent(void)
{
    double temp;

    temp=tan(ANG_TO_RAD*value);
    return (temp);
}

main()
{
    // set angle to 60.0 degrees
    deg.set_value(60.0);

    cout << "The sine of the angle is: "
         << deg.get_sine() << "\n";
    cout << "The cosine of the angle is: "
         << deg.get_cosine() << "\n";
    cout << "The tangent of the angle is: "
         << deg.get_tangent() << "\n";
    return (0);
}
```

Notice that the structure definition contains member functions. These member functions can act upon the data contained in the class itself.

```
struct angle {
    double value;

    void set_value(double);
    double get_sine(void);
    double get_cosine(void);
    double get_tangent(void);
} deg;
```

Immediately under the *struct* definition, the various member functions are defined. The member functions are associated with the class via the scoping operator (::) and are usually defined immediately after the class or structure definition to which they belong. Other than that, they look like normal functions. The variable name associated with the *struct* (or *class*) definition is *deg*.

Examine the first part of the **main** function:

```
// set angle to 60 degrees
deg.set_value(60);
```

Here, the value 60 is being passed as an argument to the **set_value** function. Observe the syntax for this operation; **set_value** itself is very simple.

```
void angle::set_value(double a)
{
  value=a;
}
```

The function accepts the argument and assigns the value to the class variable *value*. This is one way of initializing class variables. From this point on in the class, each of the three remaining functions can access *value*. Their job is to calculate the sine, cosine, and tangent of the given angle. The respective values are printed to the screen from the **main** function with statements similar to this:

```
cout << "The sine of the angle is: "
     << deg.get_sine() << "\n";
```

You access the class member functions with the dot notation also used for structures. You can also assign pointer variables to a class, in which case you use the arrow operator. (You will see an example of this shortly.)

Structures in C++ can also contain a specification of public, private, or protected. Structure members are public by default. In this example, they are global in visibility with respect to the program. A private specification limits the visibility of the specified items to the members of the structure. You will learn more about the privacy specification in the next section.

A Simple Class

In a C++ class, the visibility of class members is private by default; that is, variables and functions are accessible only to members of the class. If the functions are to be visible beyond the class, you must specify this explicitly.

The conversion of the last example's structure to a true C++ class is straightforward. First, the *struct* keyword is replaced by the *class* keyword. Second, the members that are to have public visibility are separated from the private members of the class with the public declaration. Examine the complete program:

```
//
//      C++ program illustrates a simple but true class and
//      introduces the concept of private and public.
//      This program uses a class to obtain the sine,
//      cosine and tangent of an angle.
//      Copyright (c) Chris H. Pappas and William H. Murray, 1990
//

#include <iostream.h>
#include <math.h>

const double ANG_TO_RAD=0.0174532925;
class angle {
  double value;

public:
  void set_value(double);
  double get_sine(void);
  double get_cosine(void);
  double get_tangent(void);
} deg;

void angle::set_value(double a)
{
  value=a;
}

double angle::get_sine(void)
{
  double temp;

  temp=sin(ANG_TO_RAD*value);
  return (temp);
}

double angle::get_cosine(void)
{
  double temp;

  temp=cos(ANG_TO_RAD*value);
  return (temp);
}
```

```
double angle::get_tangent(void)
{
  double temp;

  temp=tan(ANG_TO_RAD*value);
  return (temp);
}

main()
{
  // set angle to 60.0 degrees
  deg.set_value(60.0);

  cout << "The sine of the angle is: "
      << deg.get_sine() << "\n";
  cout << "The cosine of the angle is: "
      << deg.get_cosine() << "\n";
  cout << "The tangent of the angle is: "
      << deg.get_tangent() << "\n";
  return (0);
}
```

In this simple example, the body of the program remains the same. The structure definition has been converted to a true class definition with private and public parts.

```
class angle {
  double value;

public:
  void set_value(double);
  double get_sine(void);
  double get_cosine(void);
  double get_tangent(void);
} deg;
```

The *value* variable is private to the class and is only accessible by the members of the class. The member functions have been declared public and are accessible from outside of the class. However, each class member, whether public or private, has access to all other class members, public or private.

Again, notice that class member functions are usually defined immediately after the class has been defined and before the **main( )** function.

Nonmember class functions are still defined after the function **main( )** and are prototyped in the normal fashion.

Nesting Structures and Classes

Recall from the previous chapter that you can nest structures in both C and C++. You can also nest C++ classes; however, be sure not to make the resulting declaration more confusing than necessary. The following example illustrates the concept of nesting:

```
//
//      C++ program illustrates the use of nesting classes.
//      This program calculates the wages for the employee named.
//      Copyright (c) Chris H. Pappas and William H. Murray, 1990
//

#include <iostream.h>

char newline;

class emp_class {
  struct emp_name {
    char first[20];
    char middle[20];
    char last[20];
  } name;
  struct emp_wage {
    double hours;
    double reg_sal;
    double ot_sal;
  } wage;

public:
  void info_in(void);
  void info_out(void);
};

void emp_class::info_in(void)
{
  cout << "Enter first name: ";
  cin >> name.first;
  cin.get(newline);      // flush carriage return
  cout << "Enter middle name or initial: ";
  cin >> name.middle;
  cin.get(newline);
  cout << "Enter last name:   ";
  cin >> name.last;
  cin.get(newline);

  cout << "Enter hours worked:   ";
  cin >> wage.hours;
  cout << "Enter hourly wage:    ";
```

```
    cin >> wage.reg_sal;
    cout << "Enter overtime wage: ";
    cin >> wage.ot_sal;
    cout << "\n\n";
}

void emp_class::info_out(void)
{
  cout.setf(ios::fixed);
  cout.precision(2);
  cout << name.first << " " << name.middle
       << " " << name.last << "\n";
  if (wage.hours <= 40)
    cout << "Regular Pay:  $"
         << wage.hours * wage.reg_sal << endl;
    else {
      cout << "Regular Pay:  $"
           <<  40 * wage.reg_sal << endl;
      cout << "Overtime Pay: $"
           << (wage.hours-40) * wage.ot_sal << endl;
      }

}

main()
{
  emp_class widget;     // associate widget with class

  widget.info_in();
  widget.info_out();
  return (0);
}
```

In this example, two structures (simple classes) are nested within a class definition. The definition of a nested class can be quite straightforward.

```
class emp_class {
  struct emp_name {
    char first[20];
    char middle[20];
    char last[20];
  } name;
  struct emp_wage {
    double hours;
    double reg_sal;
    double ot_sal;
  } wage;

public:
  void info_in(void);
  void info_out(void);
};
```

The **emp _ class** class includes two nested class structs; **emp _ name** and **emp _ wage**. The nested classes, while part of the private section of the class, are actually available outside of the class. In other words, the visibility of the nested classes is the same as if they were defined outside of the **emp _ class** class. The individual member variables, for this example, are accessed through the public member functions: **info _ in** and **info _ out**.

These two member functions do not accept arguments and are of type **void**. The **info _ in** function prompts the user for data that will be passed to the nested structures. The information collected here includes the person's full name, the total hours worked during the week, the regular pay rate, and the overtime pay rate. When **info _ out** is called, the person's name, regular pay, and overtime pay will be printed to the screen.

```
Enter first name: John
Enter middle name or initial: James
Enter last name: Jones
Enter hours worked: 45
Enter hourly wage: 5.62
Enter overtime wage: 8.23

John James Jones
Regular Pay:   $224.80
Overtime Pay: $41.15
```

Examine the **main** function. The contents of this function are fairly short since most of the work is being done by the member functions of the class.

```
emp_class widget;      // associate widget with class
widget.info_in();
widget.info_out();
```

The variable *widget,* representing the Widget Manufacturing Company, is associated with **emp _ class**. To request a member function, the dot operator is used. Next, *widget.info _ in* is called to collect the employee information and then *widget.info _ out* is called to calculate and print the payroll results.

Constructors and Destructors

A *constructor* is a class member function whose chief goal is to initialize class variables or allocate memory storage. The constructor has the same name as the class in which it is defined. Constructors can accept arguments and can be overloaded. The constructor is automatically executed when an object of the *class* type is created. Free store objects are allocated with the **new** operator and serve to allocate memory for the objects created. Constructors are generated by C++ if they are not explicitly defined.

A *destructor* is a class member function that is usually used to return memory allocated from free store memory. The destructor has the same name as the class in which it is defined, preceded by the tilde character ∼. Destructors are typically the opposite of their constructor counterparts. The destructor is called automatically when a program passes beyond the scope of a class object or when the **delete** operator is applied to a class pointer. Unlike a constructor, a destructor cannot accept an argument and cannot be overloaded. Destructors can also be generated by C++ if not explicitly defined.

Creating a Simple Constructor and Destructor

The following program uses a constructor and destructor in the simplest form:

```
//
//      C++ program illustrates the use of constructors and
//      destructors in a simple program.
//      This program converts cents into appropriate coinage
//      (quarters, dimes, nickels and pennies).
//      Copyright (c) Chris H. Pappas and William H. Murray, 1990
//

#include <iostream.h>

const int QUARTER=25;
const int DIME=10;
const int NICKEL=5;
class coinage {                       // class name
   int i;

public:
   coinage() {cout << "Start!\n";}  // constructor
   ~coinage() {cout << "\nDone!";}  // destructor
   void get_pennies(int);
   int conv_to_quarters();
   int conv_to_dimes(int);
   int conv_to_nickels(int);
};
```

```
void coinage::get_pennies(int pen)
{
  i=pen;
  cout << i << " cents, converts to:\n";
}

int coinage::conv_to_quarters()
{
  cout << i/QUARTER << " quarter(s), ";
  return(i%QUARTER);
}

int coinage::conv_to_dimes(int d)
{
  cout << d/DIME << " dime(s), ";
  return(d%DIME);
}

int coinage::conv_to_nickels(int n)
{
  cout << n/NICKEL << " nickel(s), and ";
  return(n%NICKEL);
}

main()
{
  int c,d,n,p;

  cout << "Enter your cash in cents: ";
  cin >> c;

  // associate cash_in_cents with coinage class.
  coinage cash_in_cents;

  cash_in_cents.get_pennies(c);
  d=cash_in_cents.conv_to_quarters();
  n=cash_in_cents.conv_to_dimes(d);
  p=cash_in_cents.conv_to_nickels(n);
  cout << p << " penny(ies).";
  return (0);
}
```

This program uses four member functions. The first function passes the number of pennies to the private class variable i. The remaining three functions convert a quantity of pennies to the equivalent cash in quarters, dimes, and nickels. Examine the class and observe the placement of the constructor and destructor. The constructor and destructor function descriptions contain a simple message that will be displayed to prove that they were used automatically by the program.

```
class coinage {                          // class name
  int i;

public:
  coinage() {cout << "Start!\n";}  // constructor
  ~coinage() {cout << "\nDone!";}  // destructor
  void get_pennies(int);
  int conv_to_quarters();
  int conv_to_dimes(int);
  int conv_to_nickels(int);
};
```

The output from this program takes the form:

```
Enter your cash in cents: 69
Start!
69 cents, converts to:
2 quarter(s), 1 dime(s), 1 nickel(s), and 4 penny(ies).
Done!
```

When the function definition is included with member functions, it is said to be implicitly defined. Otherwise, member functions can be defined in the usual manner or declared inline explicitly.

Using a Constructor to Initialize a Member Variable

You can use constructors to initialize private class variables. In this case, the original class was modified slightly to eliminate the need for user input. However, with or without user input, the variable i will be initialized to 511 pennies.

```
class coinage {                          // class name
  int i;

public:
  coinage() {i=511;}               // constructor
  ~coinage() {cout << "\nDone!";}  // destructor
  int conv_to_quarters();
  int conv_to_dimes(int);
  int conv_to_nickels(int);
};
```

Creating and Deleting Free Store Memory

The following example illustrates one of the most frequent uses for a constructor. A constructor is used to allocate memory for the *str* pointer with the **new** operator. The destructor is used to release the allocated memory back to the system when the object is destroyed, with the **delete** operator.

```
class string_data {
  char *str;
  int  max_len;

public:
  string_data(char *) {str=new char[max_len];}
  ~string_data() {delete str;}
  void get_info(char *);
  void send_info(char *);
};
```

The memory allocated by **new** to the pointer *str* can only be deallocated with a subsequent call to **delete**. For this reason, you will usually see memory allocated to pointers in constructors and deallocated in destructors. This also ensures that the allocated memory will be returned to the system if the variable assigned to the class passes out of its scope.

The memory used by ordinary data types, such as **integer** and **float**, is automatically restored to the system.

Overloading Class Member Functions

Class member functions, like ordinary functions, can be overloaded. The first example in this section illustrates the overloading of a class function named **ab**. This overloaded function will return the absolute value of an integer or double with the use of the math functions **abs**, which accepts and returns integer values, and **fabs**, which accepts and returns double values. With an overloaded function, the argument types determine which member function will actually be used.

```
//
//      C++ program illustrates overloading member functions
//      with a very simple class definition
//      Copyright (c) Chris H. Pappas and William H. Murray, 1990
//
```

```
#include <iostream.h>
#include <math.h>
#include <stdlib.h>

class absolute {
public:
   int ab(int);
   double ab(double);
};

int absolute::ab(int val1)
{
   int temp;

   temp=abs(val1);
   return (temp);
}

double absolute::ab(double val2)
{
   double temp;

   temp=fabs(val2);
   return (temp);
}

main()
{
   absolute number;

   cout << "the absolute value is "
        << number.ab(-123) << endl;
   cout << "the absolute value is "
        << number.ab(-123.45678) << endl;
   return (0);
}
```

Notice that the dot operator is used in conjunction with the member function name to pass a negative integer and negative double value. The value returned by each function is printed to the screen.

```
the absolute value is 123
the absolute value is 123.45678
```

Examine Figures 13-1 to 13-4 and notice the functions chosen as the various values are passed to the class.

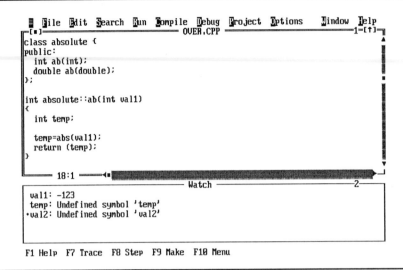

Figure 13-1.   Here, *absolute* can accept an **integer** or **double**

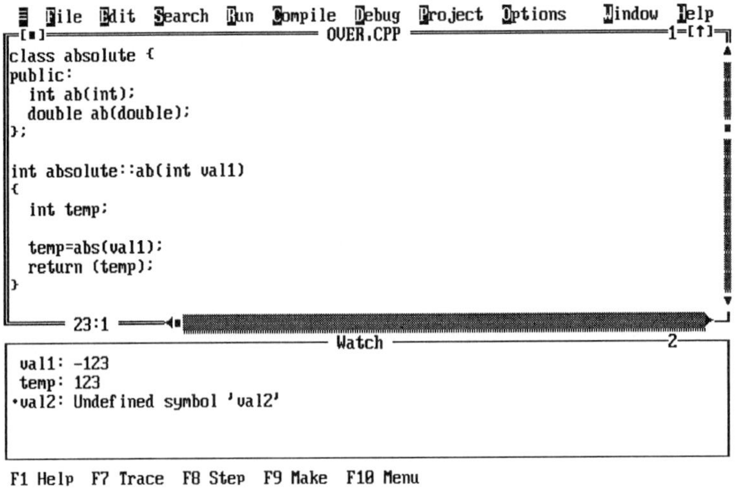

Figure 13-2.   The value of *val1* and *temp* after the absolute value has been determined

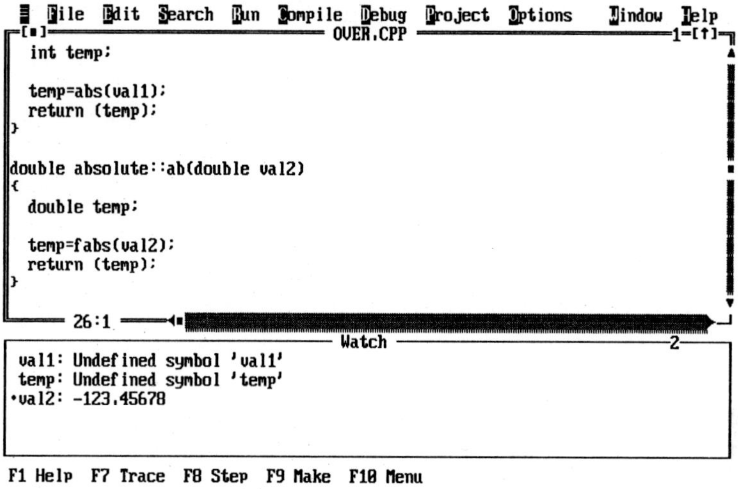

```
  ≣  File  Edit  Search  Run  Compile  Debug  Project  Options    Window  Help
┌─[■]───────────────────── OVER.CPP ─────────────────────1─[↑]─┐
│   int temp;                                                  ▲│
│                                                              ║│
│   temp=abs(val1);                                            ║│
│   return (temp);                                             ║│
│}                                                             ║│
│                                                              ║│
│double absolute::ab(double val2)                              ║│
│{                                                             ║│
│   double temp;                                               ║│
│                                                              ║│
│   temp=fabs(val2);                                           ║│
│   return (temp);                                             ║│
│}                                                             ║│
│                                                              ▼│
├── 26:1 ──◄■■■■■■■■■■■■■■■■■■■■■■■■■■■■■■■■■■■■■■■■■■■■■■■■■►─┘
├──────────────────────── Watch ────────────────────────2─┐
│ val1: Undefined symbol 'val1'                            │
│ temp: Undefined symbol 'temp'                            │
│•val2: -123.45678                                         │
│                                                          │
└──────────────────────────────────────────────────────────┘
  F1 Help  F7 Trace  F8 Step  F9 Make  F10 Menu
```

Figure 13-3.   The Trace (F7) has been moved to a new position in this Debugger screen. The absolute value of *val2* has not been determined, so *temp* does not contain valid data

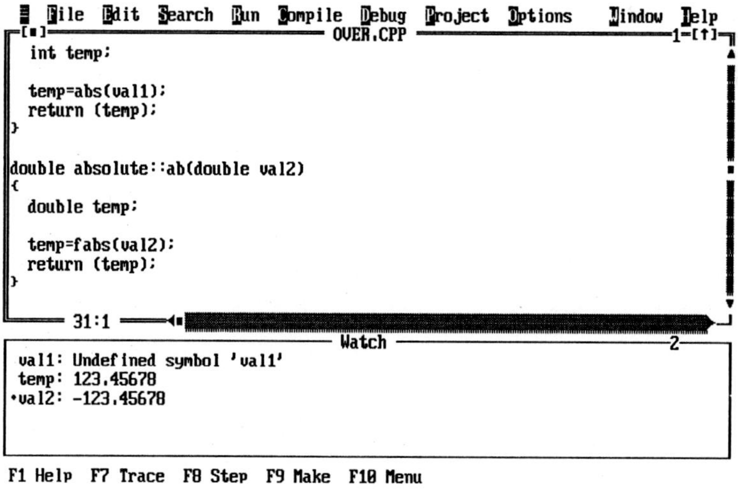

```
  ≣  File  Edit  Search  Run  Compile  Debug  Project  Options    Window  Help
┌─[■]───────────────────── OVER.CPP ─────────────────────1─[↑]─┐
│   int temp;                                                  ▲│
│                                                              ▓│
│   temp=abs(val1);                                            ▓│
│   return (temp);                                             ▓│
│}                                                             ║│
│                                                              ║│
│double absolute::ab(double val2)                              ■│
│{                                                             ║│
│   double temp;                                               ║│
│                                                              ║│
│   temp=fabs(val2);                                           ║│
│   return (temp);                                             ▓│
│}                                                             ▼│
├── 31:1 ──◄■■■■■■■■■■■■■■■■■■■■■■■■■■■■■■■■■■■■■■■■■■■■■■■►─┘
├──────────────────────── Watch ────────────────────────2─┐
│ val1: Undefined symbol 'val1'                            │
│ temp: 123.45678                                          │
│•val2: -123.45678                                         │
│                                                          │
└──────────────────────────────────────────────────────────┘
  F1 Help  F7 Trace  F8 Step  F9 Make  F10 Menu
```

Figure 13-4.   The value of *val2* and *temp* after the absolute value has been determined

In another example, angle information is passed to member functions in one of two formats—a double or a string. With member function overloading, you can process both types.

```
//
//        C++ program illustrates overloading member functions.
//        Allows angle to be entered in decimal or deg min sec
//        formats.
//        Copyright (c) Chris H. Pappas and William H. Murray, 1990
//

#include <iostream.h>
#include <math.h>
#include <string.h>

const double ANG_TO_RAD=0.0174532925;

class trig_angle {
  double angle;
  double ang_sine;

public:
  void mysine(double);
  void mysine(char *);
};

void trig_angle::mysine(double degrees)
{
  angle=degrees;
  ang_sine=sin(angle * ANG_TO_RAD);
  cout << "For an angle of " << angle << "\n";
  cout << "The sine is " << ang_sine << "\n";
}

void trig_angle::mysine(char *dat)
{
  char *deg,*min,*sec;

  deg=strtok(dat,"° ");
  min=strtok(0,"' ");
  sec=strtok(0,"\"");
  angle=atof(deg)+((atof(min))/60.0)+((atof(sec))/360.0);
  ang_sine=sin(angle * ANG_TO_RAD);
  cout << "For an angle of " << angle << "\n";
  cout << "The sine is " << ang_sine << "\n\n";
}

main()
{
  trig_angle value;

  value.mysine(45.0);
  value.mysine("45° 30' 15\"");   //make ° with alt-248
  value.mysine(60.45);
  value.mysine("30° 10' 00\"");
  return (0);
}
```

The **strtok** function prototyped in *string.h* is used three times in this program. Here is the syntax for **strtok**:

```
char *strtok(strl, str2);   //Finds token in strl
char *strl;                 //String that has token(s)
const char *str2;           //String with delimiter chars
```

The **strtok** function will scan *str1*, looking for a series of character tokens. In this case, the tokens represent the angle reading in degrees, minutes, and seconds. The length of the tokens can vary. The string *str2* contains a set of delimiters, such as spaces, commas, or other special characters. The tokens in *str1* are separated by the delimiters in *str2*. Thus, all of the tokens in *str1* can be retrieved with a series of calls to the function. Function calls to **strtok** alter *str1* by inserting a null character after each token retrieved. With the first call to the function, the function returns a pointer to the first token. Subsequent calls return a pointer to the next token, and so on. When no more tokens exist, a null pointer is returned.

Since angle readings can include degrees, minutes, and seconds, **strtok** uses a degree symbol ° to find the first token. Next, a minute symbol ' will pull out the token containing the number of minutes. Finally, a \" is used for seconds (recall that the double quote, used by itself, is for terminating strings). Examine Figures 13-5 to 13-7, and see how the **strtok** function separates the string tokens.

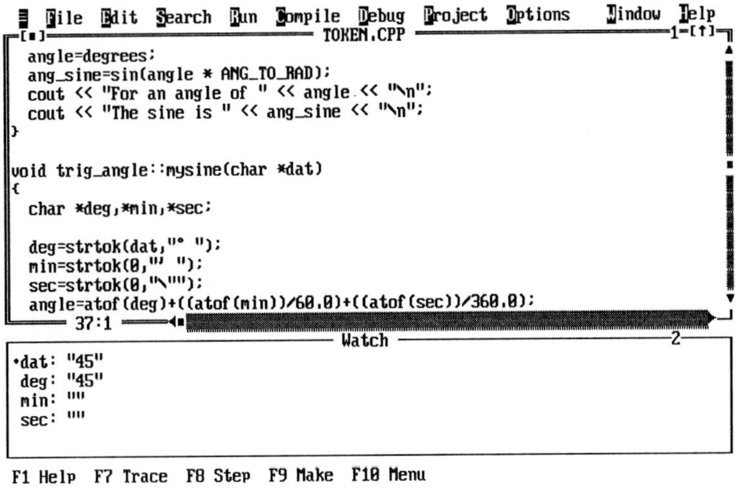

```
File  Edit  Search  Run  Compile  Debug  Project  Options    Window  Help
[•]════════════════════ TOKEN.CPP ═══════════════════1=[↑]═╗
   angle=degrees;
   ang_sine=sin(angle * ANG_TO_RAD);
   cout << "For an angle of " << angle << "\n";
   cout << "The sine is " << ang_sine << "\n";
}

void trig_angle::mysine(char *dat)
{
   char *deg,*min,*sec;

   deg=strtok(dat,"° ");
   min=strtok(0,"' ");
   sec=strtok(0,"\"");
   angle=atof(deg)+((atof(min))/60.0)+((atof(sec))/360.0);
═ 37:1 ══◄■▓▓▓▓▓▓▓▓▓▓▓▓▓▓▓▓▓▓▓▓▓▓▓▓▓▓▓▓▓▓▓▓▓▓▓▓▓▓▓▓
══════════════════════ Watch ════════════════2═╗
•dat: "45"
 deg: "45"
 min: ""
 sec: ""

F1 Help  F7 Trace  F8 Step  F9 Make  F10 Menu
```

Figure 13-5.   The Debugger's Watch window will help show how the function **strtok** separates the angle information

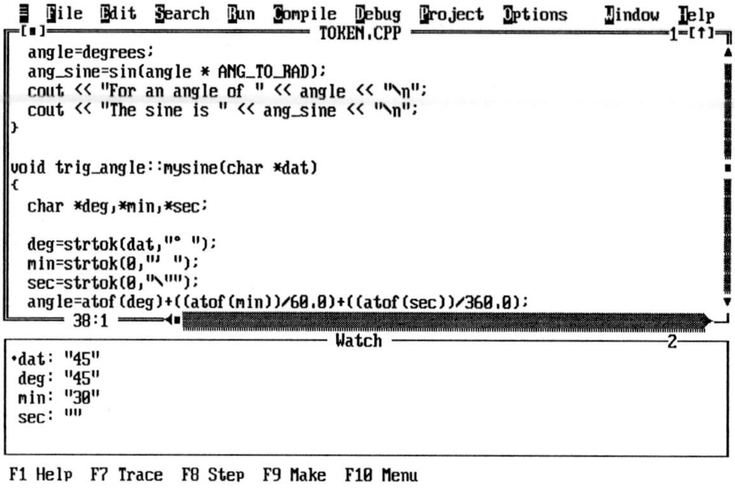

```
 ▌ File  Edit  Search  Run  Compile  Debug  Project  Options    Window  Help
┌[■]────────────────────────── TOKEN.CPP ──────────────────────1=[↑]─┐
│  angle=degrees;                                                     ▲
│  ang_sine=sin(angle * ANG_TO_RAD);                                  ▒
│  cout << "For an angle of " << angle << "\n";                       ▒
│  cout << "The sine is " << ang_sine << "\n";                        ▒
│ }                                                                   ▒
│                                                                     ▒
│ void trig_angle::mysine(char *dat)                                  ■
│ {                                                                   ▒
│   char *deg,*min,*sec;                                              ▒
│                                                                     ▒
│   deg=strtok(dat,"° ");                                             ▒
│   min=strtok(0,"' ");                                               ▒
│   sec=strtok(0,"\"");                                               ▒
│   angle=atof(deg)+((atof(min))/60.0)+((atof(sec))/360.0);           ▼
│═══ 38:1 ═══◄■▒▒▒▒▒▒▒▒▒▒▒▒▒▒▒▒▒▒▒▒▒▒▒▒▒▒▒▒▒▒▒▒▒▒▒▒▒▒▒▒▒▒▒▒▒▒▒▒▒▒►│
├─────────────────────────────── Watch ──────────────────────────2─┤
│ •dat: "45"                                                         │
│  deg: "45"                                                         │
│  min: "30"                                                         │
│  sec: ""                                                           │
└───────────────────────────────────────────────────────────────────┘
  F1 Help  F7 Trace  F8 Step  F9 Make  F10 Menu
```

Figure 13-6. The Watch window shows readings for *dat, deg,* and *min*

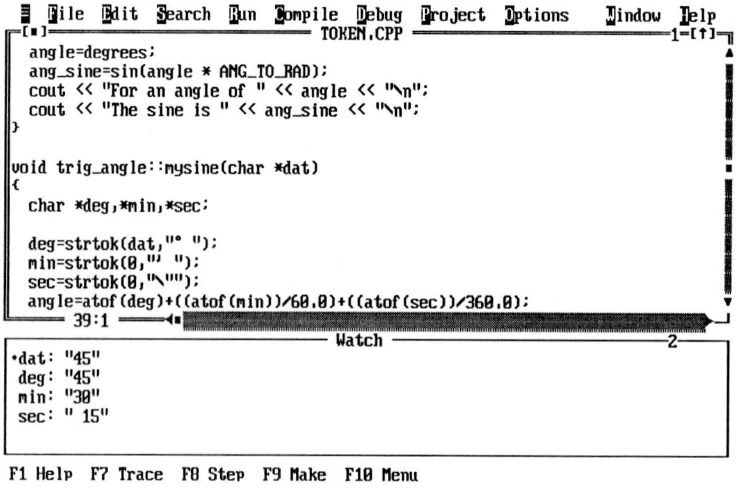

```
 ▌ File  Edit  Search  Run  Compile  Debug  Project  Options    Window  Help
┌[■]────────────────────────── TOKEN.CPP ──────────────────────1=[↑]─┐
│  angle=degrees;                                                     ▲
│  ang_sine=sin(angle * ANG_TO_RAD);                                  ▒
│  cout << "For an angle of " << angle << "\n";                       ▒
│  cout << "The sine is " << ang_sine << "\n";                        ▒
│ }                                                                   ▒
│                                                                     ▒
│ void trig_angle::mysine(char *dat)                                  ■
│ {                                                                   ▒
│   char *deg,*min,*sec;                                              ▒
│                                                                     ▒
│   deg=strtok(dat,"° ");                                             ▒
│   min=strtok(0,"' ");                                               ▒
│   sec=strtok(0,"\"");                                               ▒
│   angle=atof(deg)+((atof(min))/60.0)+((atof(sec))/360.0);           ▼
│═══ 39:1 ═══◄■▒▒▒▒▒▒▒▒▒▒▒▒▒▒▒▒▒▒▒▒▒▒▒▒▒▒▒▒▒▒▒▒▒▒▒▒▒▒▒▒▒▒▒▒▒▒▒▒▒▒►│
├─────────────────────────────── Watch ──────────────────────────2─┤
│ •dat: "45"                                                         │
│  deg: "45"                                                         │
│  min: "30"                                                         │
│  sec: " 15"                                                        │
└───────────────────────────────────────────────────────────────────┘
  F1 Help  F7 Trace  F8 Step  F9 Make  F10 Menu
```

Figure 13-7. The Watch window now contains four valid values

You can see from the previous two examples that class member overloading gives you flexibility when dealing with different data formats.

Friend Functions

One of the advantages of classes is their ability to hide data. However, a class of functions called *friend functions* allows the sharing of private class information with nonmember functions. Friend functions, which are not defined in the class itself, can share the same class resources as member functions while remaining external to the class definition.

```
//
//      C++ program illustrates friend functions.
//      Program will collect a string of date and time
//      information from system.  Time information will
//      be processed and converted into seconds.
//      Copyright (c) Chris H. Pappas and William H. Murray, 1990
//

#include <iostream.h>
#include <string.h>   // for strtok function prototype

#include <stdlib.h>   // for atol & ltoa function prototype
#include <time.h>     // for time_t & tm structure

class main_time {
  long seconds;
  friend char * current_time(main_time);
public:
  main_time(char *);
};
main_time::main_time(char *tm)
{
  char *hrs,*mins,*secs;

  // info returned in string in format:
  // (day month date hours:minutes:seconds year)
  // move over three tokens, ie.
  // skip day, month and date!
  hrs=strtok(tm," ");
  hrs=strtok(0," ");
  hrs=strtok(0," ");

  // now begin to collect time info from string
  hrs=strtok(0,":");
  mins=strtok(0,":");
  secs=strtok(0," ");
  // convert to longs and accumulate total secs.
  seconds=atol(hrs)*3600;
  seconds+=atol(mins)*60;
  seconds+=atol(secs);
}
```

```
char * current_time(main_time);   // prototype

main()
{
    // get string of time & date information
    struct tm *ptr;
    time_t ltime;
    ltime=time(NULL);
    ptr=localtime(&ltime);

    main_time tz(asctime(ptr));

    cout << "Time string information: " << asctime(ptr)
         << "\n";
    cout << "Time in seconds: " << current_time(tz)
         << "\n";
    return (0);
}

char * current_time(main_time tz)
{
    char *ctbuf;
    ctbuf=new char[30];
    long int total_seconds;

    total_seconds=tz.seconds;
    ltoa(total_seconds,ctbuf,10);
         return (ctbuf);
}
```

In the class definition, notice the use of the keyword *friend* along with a description of the **current_time** function itself. Examine the listing and note that this function definition occurs after the **main( )** function.

In addition to illustrating the use of friend functions, this program has a number of other interesting features. In the function **main( )**, the system's time is retrieved with the use of *time_t* and its associated structure *tm*. In this program, *ltime* is the name of the variable associated with *time_t*. Local time is initialized and retrieved into the pointer, *ptr*, with the next two lines of code. By using *asctime(ptr)*, the pointer will point to an ASCII string of date and time information.

```
struct tm *ptr;
time_t ltime;
ltime=time(NULL);
ptr=localtime(&ltime);

main_time tz(asctime(ptr));
```

The date and time string is formatted in this manner:

day month date hours:minutes:seconds year \n \0

For example:

```
Wed Jan 24 15:26:35 1990
```

Chapter 15, "Power Programming: Tapping Important C and C++ Libraries," contains a more detailed discussion of built-in functions, including those prototyped in *time.h*. For now, you need to follow these steps to retrieve the string information.

The string information is sent to the class by associating *tz* with the class **main_time**.

```
main_time tz(asctime(ptr));
```

The constructor **main_time(char ∗)** executes the code necessary to convert the string information to integer values. This is achieved with the **strtok** function.

Since we have a strange date/time format, **strtok** uses a space as the delimiter to skip over the day, month, and date. At this point, *hrs* collects unwanted tokens. The next delimiter is a colon, which will aid in collecting both hour and minute tokens from the string. Finally, the number of seconds can be found by reading the string until another space is encountered. The string information is then converted to a long and converted to the appropriate number of seconds. The *seconds* variable is private to the class, but accessible to the friend function.

When the function is called from **main( )**, it takes the number of accumulated seconds, *tz.seconds*, and converts it back to a character string with a call to the **ltoa** function. The memory for the string is allocated with the **new** operator. This newly created string is just an excuse for using the friend function.

Two pieces of information are printed to the screen. First, **cout** prints the string produced by **asctime**. This information is obtainable from the **time_t** function and is available to the **main( )** function. Next, the present system time is printed by simply passing **current_time** to the **cout** stream.

What uses can you think of for friend functions? What kind of trouble could C++ programmers get themselves into by using friend functions?

Using the *this* Pointer

The keyword *this* indicates a self-referential pointer that is implicitly declared by the language. For example:

```
myclass *this;    //myclass is class type.
```

The *this* pointer points to the object for which the member function is invoked.

Examine the following class definition:

```
class myclass {
  char ch;

public:
  void start_up(char pz) {ch=pz;}
  char conv_ch() {return (this -> ch);}
};
```

In this example, the pointer *this* accesses the class variable *ch*.

Other uses for *this* include a link on a doubly linked list or writing constructors and destructors involving memory allocations. For example:

```
class myclass {
  int x,y,x;
  char ch;

public:
  myclass(size) {this=new(size);}
  ~myclass() {delete(this);}
};
```

OPERATOR OVERLOADING

This section explains C++ techniques for overloading operators. In C++, new definitions can be applied to operators such as **+**, **−**, *****, and **/** in a specific class.

The concept of operator overloading is familiar, if not implemented specifically in numerous languages. For example, you can add two integers, two floats, two doubles, and so on with the **+** operator in any compiled language—including C and C++. Typically, however, you can't take two complex types, such as a complex number, matrix, or character string, and add them with the **+** operator. For example, these operations are usually valid:

  2 + 4

2.3 + 4.1

These operations are not valid:

  (2 + j4) + (−5 −j10)

(20° 15′ 30″) + (45° 27′ 10″)

  "paste" + "together"

Obviously, if these last operations were permitted, your job would be greatly simplified. In C++, the operators can be overloaded and these operations can be made valid. Operator overloading is used extensively for the functions prototyped in the C++ *complex.h* header file, described in Chapter 15.

Operators and Function Calls Available for Overloading

In C++, operators can be overloaded. The main restrictions are that the syntax and precedence of the operator remain unchanged from its originally defined meaning. Also, the overloading is only valid within the context of the class in which overloading occurs. Table 13-1 shows the operators and functions that can be overloaded.

Table 13-1.   Operators and Function Calls that Can Be Overloaded

+	−	*	/	=	<	>	+ =	− =	* =	/ =
<<	>>	>>=	<<=	==	!=	<=	>=	+ +	− −	%
&	^	!	|	~	& =	^=	|=	&&	||	% =
[ ]	( )	new	delete							

The Syntax of Overloading

To overload an operator, you follow the keyword *operator* by the operator itself.

type operator opr(param list)

For example:

angle_sum operator + (time_sum);

Here, **angle_sum** is the name of the class type, followed by the *operator* keyword, the operator itself, and a parameter to be passed to the overloaded operator.

Assuming that the class is properly defined, the sum of several angle values could be achieved with:

```
angle_sum al("60° 45' 30\"");
angle_sum a2("20° 50' 40\"");
angle_sum a3("10° 20' 30\"");
angle_sum angle;

angle=al+a2+a3;
```

Again, it is unfortunate that the symbol for seconds is the double quote mark, since this also signals the beginning and end of a character string. Since the quote symbol can be printed to the screen by preceding it with a backslash, the input shown in the previous listing uses this format.

In addition to adding three columns of numbers, the seconds and minutes columns can produce a carry when their total exceeds 59. That will have to be taken into account.

```
//
//       C++ program illustrates operator overloading.
//       Program will overload the "+" operator so that
//       several angles, in the format degrees minutes seconds
//       can be added directly.
//       Copyright (c) Chris H. Pappas and William H. Murray, 1990
//

#include <strstream.h>
#include <stdlib.h>
#include <string.h>

class angle_sum {
  int deg,mins,secs;

  public:
  angle_sum() {deg=0,mins=0,secs=0;}  // constructor
  angle_sum(char *);
  angle_sum operator +(angle_sum);
  char * display(void);
};

angle_sum::angle_sum(char *addangle)
{
  deg=atoi(strtok(addangle,"° "));
  mins=atoi(strtok(0,"' "));
  secs=atoi(strtok(0,"\""));
}

angle_sum angle_sum::operator+(angle_sum addangle)
{
  angle_sum temp;
  temp.secs=(secs+addangle.secs)%60;
  temp.mins=((secs+addangle.secs)/60+mins+addangle.mins)%60;
  temp.deg=((secs+addangle.secs)/60+mins+addangle.mins)/60;
  temp.deg+=deg+addangle.deg;
  return temp;
}

char * angle_sum::display()
{
  char *temp[15];
  // strstream.h required for incore formatting
  ostrstream(*temp,sizeof(temp)) << deg << "° "
                                 << mins << "' "
                                 << secs << "\""
                                 << ends;
  return *temp;
}
```

```
main()
{
  angle_sum a1("60° 45' 30\"");     //make ° with alt-248
  angle_sum a2("20° 50' 40\"");
  angle_sum a3("10° 20' 30\"");
  angle_sum sum;

  sum=a1+a2+a3;
  cout << "sum = " << sum.display() << "\n";
  return (0);
}
```

When overloading operators, make sure to maintain proper operator syntax and precedence. The output from the previous program takes this form:

```
sum = 91° 56' 40"
```

DERIVED CLASSES

You can think of a derived class as an extension to an existing class, known as a base class. A derived class provides a simple means for expanding the capabilities of a base class, without re-creating the base class itself. With a base class in place, a common interface to one or more derived classes is also possible. Any class can serve as a base class, and any derived class reflects the description of the base class. The derived class can also modify access privileges, add new members, or overload existing ones. When a derived class overloads a function declared in the base class, it is said to be a *virtual* member function.

The Syntax of a Derived Class

A derived class is described with the following syntax:

class derived-class-type:(public/private/protected) . . .
　　base-class-type { . . . .};

For example, you might actually write

class savings:public customer { . . . .};

In this case, the derived class tag is **savings**. The base class has public
visibility and its tag is **customer**.

As you know, members of a class are private by default. With derived
classes, the protected visibility specifier is often used. A *protected* specifier is
the same as a private specifier, but member functions and friends of derived
classes are given access to the class.

Creating Derived Classes

The following program illustrates the concept of a derived class. The base
class collects and reports information on a customer's name, address, city,
state, and zip code. Two similar derived classes are created. One derived
class maintains information on a customer's savings activities, while the
other maintains information on a different customer's loan activities. Both
derived classes *attach* or *inherit* information from the base class.

```
//
//      C++ program illustrates derived classes.
//      The base class contains name, street, city, state
//      and zip information.  Derived classes add either
//      loan or savings information to base class info.
//      Copyright (c) Chris H. Pappas and William H. Murray, 1990
//

#include <iostream.h>
#include <string.h>

char newline;

class customer {
  char name[60],
       street[60],
       city[20],
       state[15],
       zip[10];
public:
  void info_out(void);
  void info_in(void);
};
```

```
void customer::info_out(void)
{
  cout << "Name: " << name << "\n";
  cout << "Street: " << street << "\n";
  cout << "City: " << city << "\n";
  cout << "State: " << state << "\n";
  cout << "Zip: " << zip << "\n";
}

void customer::info_in(void)
{
  cout << "Enter Customer Name: ";
  cin.get(name,59,'\n');
  cin.get(newline);        //flush carriage return
  cout << "Enter Street Address: ";
  cin.get(street,59,'\n');
  cin.get(newline);
  cout << "Enter City: ";
  cin.get(city,19,'\n');
  cin.get(newline);
  cout << "Enter State: ";
  cin.get(state,14,'\n');
  cin.get(newline);
  cout << "Enter Zip Code: ";
  cin.get(zip,9,'\n');
  cin.get(newline);
}

class loan::public customer {
  char loan_type[20];
  float l_bal;
public:
  void loan_customer();
  void l_disp();
};

void loan::loan_customer()
{
  info_in();
  cout << "Enter Loan Type: ";
  cin.get(loan_type,19,'\n');
  cin.get(newline);
  cout << "Enter Loan Balance: ";
  cin >> l_bal;
  cin.get(newline);        //flush carriage return
}

void loan::l_disp()
{
  info_out();

  cout << "Loan Type: " << loan_type << "\n";
  cout << "Loan Balance: $ " << l_bal << "\n";
}
```

```
class savings:public customer {
  char savings_type[20];
  float s_bal;
public:
  void savings_customer();
  void s_disp();
};
void savings::savings_customer()
{
  info_in();
  cout << "Enter Savings Account Type: ";
  cin.get(savings_type,19,'\n');
  cin.get(newline);       //flush carriage return
  cout << "Enter Account Balance: ";
  cin >> s_bal;
  cin.get(newline);
}

void savings::s_disp()
{
  info_out();

  cout << "Savings Type: " << savings_type << "\n";
  cout << "Savings Balance: $ " << s_bal << "\n";
}

main()
{
  loan borrow;                    //get loan information
  cout << "\n--Loan Customers--\n";
  borrow.loan_customer();

  savings save;                   //get savings information
  cout << "\n--Savings Customers--\n";
  save.savings_customer();

                                  //display all information
  cout << "\n--Loan Customers--\n";
  borrow.l_disp();

  cout << "\n--Savings Customers--\n";
  save.s_disp();

  return (0);
}
```

In the example, the base class is type **customer**. The private part of this class accepts customer information for name, address, city, state, and zip code. The public part describes two functions: **info_out** and **info_in**. Just beyond the function descriptions is the first derived class, **loan**.

```
class loan::public customer {
  char loan_type[20];
```

```
    float l_bal;
public:
  void loan_customer();
  void l_disp();
};
```

This derived class contains two functions: **loan_customer** and **l_disp**. The first function, **loan_customer**, uses the base class to obtain name, address, city, state, and zip code, and attaches the loan type and amount.

```
void loan::loan_customer()
{
  info_in();
  cout << "Enter Loan Type: ";
  cin.get(loan_type,19,'\n');
  cin.get(newline);
  cout << "Enter Loan Balance: ";
  cin >> l_bal;
  cin.get(newline);        //flush carriage return
}
```

The call to the **info_in** function is a call to a function that is part of the base class. The remainder of the preceding function obtains the loan type and amount.

The loan information is displayed in a similar manner. The base class function, **info_out**, prints the information gathered by the base class, while **l_disp** attaches the information from the derived class to the display. The process is repeated for the savings account customer. Thus, one base class serves as the data gathering base for two derived classes, each obtaining its own specific information.

The output from the program can take the form:

```
--Loan Customers--
Name: Iam Broke
Street: 401 Poor House Lane
City: Philadelphia
State: Pennsylvania
Zip: 19804
Loan Type: Auto Loan
Loan Balance: $ 9878.56

--Savings Customers--
Name: Igot Money
Street: 678 Snob Hill Parkway
City: Seattle
State: Washington
Zip: 23987
Savings Type: Money Market Saving
Savings Balance: $ 5643.11
```

14

INTRODUCTION TO OBJECT-ORIENTED PROGRAMMING

This book has introduced you to C and C++ concepts in a traditional *procedural* programming environment. In a procedural environment, there is typically a main function and many additional functions (subroutines) that are called from the main one. In this top-down approach, the main function is usually short, farming the work out to the remaining functions. Program execution generally flows from the top of the main function and terminates at the bottom of the same function. This technique is common among all structured languages, including C, C++, FORTRAN, Pascal, and PL/I. The procedural approach suffers from several disadvantages, the chief of which is program maintenance. When you have to make additions or deletions to the program, you must often rework the entire program to include the new routines.

Object-oriented programming (OOP), on the other hand, is different from the traditional procedural approach. If you have written program code for Microsoft's Windows or the OS/2 Presentation Manager, you have gotten a taste of object-oriented programming techniques. In object-oriented programming, your program consists of a group of often related *objects*. C++ classes form the foundation of object-oriented programming, since classes provide a set of values and the operations that act on those values. Objects are manipulated with *messages*. It is the message-based system that is common to Windows and the Presentation Manager. Object-oriented programs offer many advantages over procedural ones, the chief of which is less program maintenance. You can often make additions and deletions to object-oriented programs by simply adding or deleting objects.

Earlier chapters explained that many C programs can be converted to C++ programs by simple program alterations. This is because the conversion was from and to a procedural programming structure. However, you can work with object-oriented programs only in C++, as C does not provide the class structure.

C++ AND OBJECT-ORIENTED PROGRAMMING

Classes are what make C++ suitable for developing object-oriented programs. The class structure meets the requirements for creating objects. However, object-oriented programming is also supported by C++'s strong typing, operator overloading, and less reliance on the preprocessor.

You already learned a good deal about classes in Chapter 13. The next section formulates object-oriented programming terms more clearly, and shows how C++ classes fit in with this new programming style.

OBJECT-ORIENTED PROGRAMMING DEFINITIONS AND TERMINOLOGY

Object-oriented programming allows you to view concepts as a variety of objects. You can represent the interaction, the tasks that are to be performed, and any given conditions that must be observed among the stated objects. The C++ class can contain closely related objects that share attributes, and is thus the prototype for objects in C++. In a more formal definition, a class defines the properties and attributes that depict the actions of an object that is an instance of that class.

Encapsulation

Encapsulation refers to how each object is defined. Typically, this definition is part of a C++ class and includes a description of the object's internal structure, a description of how the object relates to other objects, and some form of protection that isolates the functional details of the object outside of the class. The C++ class structure does all of this.

Recall from Chapter 13, "Classes," that a class can have private, public, and/or protected sections. In object-oriented programming, the public section is used for the interface information that makes the class reusable across applications. The private section is used to define the data structure for the data type. Thus, the class meets the object-oriented requirements for encapsulation.

Class Hierarchy

In C++, classes actually serve as a pattern for creating objects. The objects created are *instances* of the class. You can develop a *class hierarchy* where there is a *root* or *parent* class and several *subclasses* or *child classes*. In C++, the basis for class hierarchies is *derived classes*. Parent classes represent more generalized tasks while derived child classes are given specific tasks.

Inheritance

Inheritance refers to deriving a new class from an existing parent class. The parent class serves as a pattern for the derived class and can be altered in several ways. For example, you can overload member functions, add new members, and change access privileges. Inheritance is an important concept since it allows you to reuse a class definition, for simple changes, without requiring major code changes.

Polymorphism

Common messages can be sent to the root class objects and all derived subclass objects. In formal terms, this is called *polymorphism*. Polymorphism allows each subclass object to respond to the message format in a manner appropriate to its definition. Imagine a class hierarchy for gathering data. The root class might be responsible for gathering the name, social security number, occupation, and number of years of employment for an individual. Subclasses could then be used to decide what additional information would be added based on occupation. In one case, a supervisory position might include yearly salary while in another case a sales position might include an hourly rate and commission information. Thus, the root class gathers general information common to all subclasses while the subclasses gather additional information relating to specific job descriptions. Polymorphism allows a common data gathering message to be sent to each class. Both the root and subclasses respond in an appropriate manner to the message.

Virtual Functions

Virtual functions, first introduced in Chapter 13, are closely associated with the concept of polymorphism. Virtual functions are defined in the root class when subsequent derived classes will overload the function by redefining its implementation. When you use virtual functions, messages are passed to a pointer that points to the object instead of being passed directly to the object itself.

   As you follow the example program for this chapter, many of these definitions will become more clear and will fit in with what you have already learned.

DEVELOPING AN OBJECT-ORIENTED LINKED-LIST PROGRAM

Chapter 12, "Structures, Unions, and Miscellaneous Items," included a linked-list program that was developed in C++ using the traditional procedural programming approach. This program created a linked list for the P and M used car inventory. With the traditional procedural approach, this linked-list program is difficult to alter or maintain. This chapter develops a linked-list C++ program using objects that let you establish a list of employee information and then add and delete items from that list. To limit the size of the program, the user interface for gathering data has not been included in this program. Input information for the linked list has been "hard wired" in the **main** function. If you want to continue developing this program, Chapter 13 shows how to gather input information in an interactive way.

The Root or Parent Class

The parent class that will be used for this linked-list example is **P_and_M_auto_dealership**. The linked-list program will keep pertinent information on a variety of company employees. The job of the parent class, **P_and_M_auto_dealership**, is to gather information that is common to all subsequent derived subclasses. In this case, that information includes an employee's last name, first name, occupation title, social security number, and years employed at the dealership. The protected section of this class indicates the structure for gathering the data common to each derived class. The public section shows how that information will be intercepted from the function **main**.

```
// ROOT OR PARENT CLASS
class P_and_M_auto_dealership {

friend class employee_list;

protected:
  char lastname[20];
  char firstname[20];
  char occupation[20];
  char social_security[12];
  int years_employed;
  P_and_M_auto_dealership *pointer;
  P_and_M_auto_dealership *next_link;

public:
  P_and_M_auto_dealership(char *lname,char *fname,char *ssnum,
                          char *occup,int c_years_employed)
  {
    strcpy(lastname,lname);
    strcpy(firstname,fname);
    strcpy(social_security,ssnum);
    strcpy(occupation,occup);
    years_employed=c_years_employed;
    next_link=0;
  }
    .
    .
    .
    .
```

Notice that this class and all subsequently derived subclasses will use a friend class named **employee_list**.

A Sample Derived Subclass

The following sample program uses four child classes derived from the parent class in the last section. This section looks at one representative example, the **salespersons** class. A portion of this derived class is shown next. The C++ derived class satisfies the concept of inheritance.

```
//SUB OR CHILD DERIVED CLASS
class salespersons:public P_and_M_auto_dealership {

friend class employee_list;

private:
  float unit_sales_average;
  int comm_rate;

public:
  salespersons(char *lname,char *fname,char *ssnum,
               char *occup,int c_years_employed,
               float w_avg,int c_rate):
               P_and_M_auto_dealership(lname,fname,ssnum,
               occup,c_years_employed)
  {
    unit_sales_average=w_avg;
    comm_rate=c_rate;
  }
      .
      .
      .
```

In this case, the **salespersons** child class gathers information and adds it to the information gathered by the parent class. This then forms a structure of last name, first name, social security number, years employed, weekly average of total monthly sales, and appropriate commission rate.

Here is the remainder of the child class description:

```
void fill_average(float w_avg)
{
  unit_sales_average=w_avg;
}

void fill_comm_rate(int c_rate)
{
  comm_rate=c_rate;
}

void add_data()
{
  pointer=new salespersons(lastname,
                           firstname,
                           social_security,
                           occupation,
                           years_employed,
                           unit_sales_average,
                           comm_rate);
```

```
  }

  void send_info()
  {
    P_and_M_auto_dealership::send_info();
    cout << "\n Weekly Sales Average (units): "
         << unit_sales_average;
    cout << "\n Commission Rate: "
         << comm_rate << "%";
  }

};
```

Add _ data sets aside memory for an additional linked-list node with the use of the **new** free store operator. Remember that this node is being assigned a pointer to a variable, *pointer,* that in turn points to a **P _ and _ M _ auto _ dealership** node.

When you examine the full program listing, note that the **delete** free store operator is used in the **employee _ list** class for deleting items from the linked list.

Of particular interest here is the technique for printing the salesperson's information. Notice that **salespersons'** *send _ info* makes a call to the root class's **send _ info** function. This function prints the information common to all derived classes. Then **salespersons'** *send _ info* prints the information unique to the child class. That information includes the weekly sales average and the commission rate.

By altering the objects, you could have printed all of the information about the salesperson from this subclass. However, this example illustrated another advantage of using C++ in object-oriented programming: the successful use of virtual functions.

The Friend Class

The friend class, **employee _ list**, is how the linked list is printed, and how items are inserted and deleted from the list. This class is divided to make the explanation more clear.

```
//FRIEND CLASS
class employee_list {

private:
  P_and_M_auto_dealership *location;
```

```
public:
  employee_list()
  {
    location=0;
  }

  void print_employee_list();

  void insert_employee(P_and_M_auto_dealership *node);

  void remove_employee_id(char *social_security);

};
     .
     .
     .
     .
```

Messages which are sent to **print_employee_list**, **insert_employee**, and **remove_employee_id** form the functional part of the linked-list program.

Consider the function **print_employee_list**, which begins by assigning the pointer (to the list) to the pointer variable *present*. As long as the pointer, *present*, is not 0, it will continue to point to items in the linked list, send them to **send_info**, and update the pointer until all items have been printed. Observe how this is achieved here:

```
       .
       .
       .
void employee_list: :print_employee_list()
{
  P_and_M_auto_dealership *present=location;

  while(present!=0) {
    present->send_info();
    present=present->next_link;
  }
}
       .
       .
       .
```

Remember that *pointer* contains the memory address of nodes inserted via **add_data**. This value is used by **insert_employee** to form the link with the linked list. Since the technique inserts alphabetically by an employee's last name, the linked list is always ordered alphabetically by the last name.

Correct insertion is achieved by comparing the last name with those already in the list. When it finds a name (*node—>lastname*) already in the list that is greater than *current_node—>lastname,* the first *while* loop terminates. This standard linked-list insert procedure leaves the pointer variable *previous_node* pointing to the node behind where the new node is to be inserted and leaves *current_node* pointing to the node that will follow the insertion point for the new node.

When the insertion point is determined, a new link or node is created by a calling *node—>add_data.* The *current_node* is linked to the new node's *next_link.* The last decision to make is whether the new node is to be placed as the front node in the list or between existing nodes. The program accomplishes this by examining the contents of the pointer variable *previous_node.* If the pointer variable is 0, it cannot be pointing to a valid previous node so *location* is updated to the address of the new node. If *previous_node* contains a nonzero value, it is assumed to be pointing to a valid previous node. In this case, *previous_node—>next_link* is assigned the address of the new node's address or *node—>pointer.*

```
            .
            .
            .
void employee_list::insert_employee(P_and_M_auto_dealership
                            *node)
{
  P_and_M_auto_dealership *current_node=location;
  P_and_M_auto_dealership *previous_node=0;

  while (current_node != 0 &&
         strcmp(current_node->lastname,node->lastname) < 0) {

    previous_node=current_node;
    current_node=current_node->next_link;
  }
  node->add_data();
  node->pointer->next_link=current_node;
  if (previous_node==0)
    location=node->pointer;
  else
    previous_node->next_link=node->pointer;
}
            .
            .
            .
```

You can only remove items from the linked list if you know the employee's social security number. This adds a small level of protection against accidental deletion of an employee. As you examine *remove_employee_id,* shown in the next listing, note that the structure for examining the nodes in the linked list is almost identical to that of *insert_employee.* However, the first *while* loop leaves the *current_node* pointing to the node to be deleted, not the node after the one to be deleted.

The first compound *if* statement deletes a node in the front of the list. It accomplishes this by examining the contents of *previous_node* to see if it contains a 0. If so, the front of the list, *location,* needs to be updated to the node following the one to be deleted or *current_node->next_link.* The second *if* statement deletes a node between two existing nodes. This requires the node behind to be assigned the address of the node after the one being deleted, or *previous_node->next_link=current_node->next_link.*

```
        .
        .
        .
        .
void employee_list::remove_employee_id(char *social_security)
{
  P_and_M_auto_dealership *current_node=location;
  P_and_M_auto_dealership *previous_node=0;

  while(current_node != 0 &&
      strcmp(current_node->social_security,
      social_security) != 0) {
    previous_node=current_node;
    current_node=current_node->next_link;
  }

  if(current_node != 0 && previous_node == 0) {
    location=current_node->next_link;
    delete current_node;
  }
  else if(current_node != 0 && previous_node != 0) {
    previous_node->next_link=current_node->next_link;
    delete current_node;
  }
}
```

The Whole Linked List

The next listing is a completely operational C++ object-oriented program. Again, the only thing it lacks is an interactive user interface. When executed, this program will add eight employees, with different occupations, to the linked list and then print the list. The program will next delete several employees from the list by giving their social security numbers. Finally, the altered list will be printed.

```
//
//      C++ program illustrates object-oriented programming
//      with a linked list.  This program keeps track of
//      employee data at the P & M automobile dealership.
//      Copyright (c) Chris H. Pappas and William H. Murray, 1990
//

#include <iostream.h>
#include <string.h>

// ROOT OR PARENT CLASS
class P_and_M_auto_dealership {

friend class employee_list;

protected:
  char lastname[20];
  char firstname[20];
  char occupation[20];
  char social_security[12];
  int years_employed;
  P_and_M_auto_dealership *pointer;
  P_and_M_auto_dealership *next_link;

public:
  P_and_M_auto_dealership(char *lname,char *fname,char *ssnum,
                          char *occup,int c_years_employed)
  {
    strcpy(lastname,lname);
    strcpy(firstname,fname);
    strcpy(social_security,ssnum);
    strcpy(occupation,occup);
    years_employed=c_years_employed;
    next_link=0;
  }

  P_and_M_auto_dealership()
  {
    lastname[0]=NULL;
    firstname[0]=NULL;
    social_security[0]=NULL;
    occupation[0]=NULL;
    years_employed=0;
    next_link=0;
  }

  void fill_lastname(char *l_name)
  {
    strcpy(lastname,l_name);
  }
```

```
  void fill_firstname(char *f_name)
  {
    strcpy(firstname,f_name);
  }

  void fill_social_security(char *soc_sec)
  {
    strcpy(social_security,soc_sec);
  }

  void fill_occupation(char *o_name)
  {
    strcpy(occupation,o_name);
  }

  void fill_years_employed(int c_years_employed)
  {
    years_employed=c_years_employed;
  }

  virtual void add_data() {
  }

  virtual void send_info()
  {
    cout << "\n\n" << lastname << ", " << firstname
         << "\n Social Security: #" << social_security;
    cout << "\n Job Title: " << occupation;
    cout << "\n Years With Company: " << years_employed;
  }

};

//SUB OR CHILD DERIVED CLASS
class deal_closer:public P_and_M_auto_dealership {

friend class employee_list;

private:
  float yearly_salary;

public:
  deal_closer(char *lname,char *fname,char *ssnum,
              char *occup,int c_years_employed,
              float y_salary):
              P_and_M_auto_dealership(lname,fname,ssnum,
              occup,c_years_employed)
  {
    yearly_salary=y_salary;
  }

  deal_closer():P_and_M_auto_dealership()
  {
    yearly_salary=0.0;
  }
```

```
  void fill_yearly_salary(float salary)
  {
    yearly_salary=salary;
  }

  void add_data()
  {
    pointer=new deal_closer(lastname,
                            firstname,
                            social_security,
                            occupation,
                            years_employed,
                            yearly_salary);
   }

  void send_info()
  {
    P_and_M_auto_dealership::send_info();
    cout << "\n Yearly Salary: $" << yearly_salary;
  }

};

//SUB OR CHILD DERIVED CLASS
class salespersons:public P_and_M_auto_dealership {

friend class employee_list;

private:
  float unit_sales_average;
  int comm_rate;

public:
  salespersons(char *lname,char *fname,char *ssnum,
               char *occup,int c_years_employed,
               float w_avg,int c_rate):
               P_and_M_auto_dealership(lname,fname,ssnum,
               occup,c_years_employed)
  {
    unit_sales_average=w_avg;
    comm_rate=c_rate;
  }

  salespersons():P_and_M_auto_dealership()
  {
    unit_sales_average=0.0;
    comm_rate=0;
  }

  void fill_average(float w_avg)
  {
    unit_sales_average=w_avg;
  }

  void fill_comm_rate(int c_rate)
```

```
   {
     comm_rate=c_rate;
   }

   void add_data()
   {
     pointer=new salespersons(lastname,
                              firstname,
                              social_security,
                              occupation,
                              years_employed,
                              unit_sales_average,
                              comm_rate);
   }

   void send_info()
   {
     P_and_M_auto_dealership: :send_info();
     cout << "\n Weekly Sales Average (units): "
          << unit_sales_average;
     cout << "\n Commission Rate: "
          << comm_rate << "%";
   }

};

//SUB OR CHILD DERIVED CLASS
class mechanics:public P_and_M_auto_dealership {

friend class employee_list;

private:
  float hourly_salary;

public:
  mechanics(char *lname,char *fname,char *ssnum,char *occup,
            int c_years_employed,float h_salary):
            P_and_M_auto_dealership(lname,fname,ssnum,
            occup,c_years_employed)
  {
    hourly_salary=h_salary;
  }

  mechanics():P_and_M_auto_dealership()
  {
    hourly_salary=0.0;
  }

  void fill_hourly_salary(float h_salary)
  {
    hourly_salary=h_salary;
  }

  void add_data()
  {
```

```
      pointer=new mechanics(lastname,
                            firstname,
                            social_security,
                            occupation,
                            years_employed,
                            hourly_salary);
    }

    void send_info()
    {
      P_and_M_auto_dealership: :send_info();
      cout << "\n Hourly Salary: $" << hourly_salary;
    }

};

//SUB OR CHILD DERIVED CLASS
class parts:public P_and_M_auto_dealership {

friend class employee_list;

private:
  float hourly_salary;

public:
  parts(char *lname,char *fname,char *ssnum,char *occup,
        int c_years_employed,float h_salary):
        P_and_M_auto_dealership(lname,fname,ssnum,
        occup,c_years_employed)
  {
    hourly_salary=h_salary;
  }

  parts():P_and_M_auto_dealership()
  {
    hourly_salary=0.0;
  }

  void fill_hourly_salary(float h_salary)
  {
    hourly_salary=h_salary;
  }

  void add_data()
  {
    pointer=new parts(lastname,
                      firstname,
                      social_security,
                      occupation,
                      years_employed,
                      hourly_salary);
  }

  void send_info()
  {
```

```
      P_and_M_auto_dealership: :send_info();
      cout << "\n Hourly Salary: $" << hourly_salary;
   }

};

//FRIEND CLASS
class employee_list {

private:
  P_and_M_auto_dealership *location;

public:
  employee_list()
  {
    location=0;
  }

  void print_employee_list();

  void insert_employee(P_and_M_auto_dealership *node);

  void remove_employee_id(char *social_security);

};

void employee_list::print_employee_list()
{
  P_and_M_auto_dealership *present=location;

  while(present!=0) {
    present->send_info();
    present=present->next_link;
  }
}

void employee_list::insert_employee(P_and_M_auto_dealership
                                 *node)
{
  P_and_M_auto_dealership *current_node=location;
  P_and_M_auto_dealership *previous_node=0;

  while (current_node != 0 &&
         strcmp(current_node->lastname,node->lastname) < 0) {
    previous_node=current_node;
    current_node=current_node->next_link;
  }
  node->add_data();
  node->pointer->next_link=current_node;
  if (previous_node==0)
    location=node->pointer;
  else
    previous_node->next_link=node->pointer;
}

void employee_list::remove_employee_id(char *social_security)
```

```
{
  P_and_M_auto_dealership *current_node=location;
  P_and_M_auto_dealership *previous_node=0;

  while(current_node != 0 &&
     strcmp(current_node->social_security,
     social_security) != 0) {
    previous_node=current_node;
    current_node=current_node->next_link;
  }

  if(current_node != 0 && previous_node == 0) {
    location=current_node->next_link;
    delete current_node;
  }
  else if(current_node != 0 && previous_node != 0) {
    previous_node->next_link=current_node->next_link;
    delete current_node;
  }
}

main()
{
  employee_list workers;

  cout.setf(ios::fixed);
  cout.precision(d2);

  // static data to add to linked list
  salespersons salesperson1("Friendly","Fran","212-98-7654",
                            "Salesperson",1,7.5,4.00);
  salespersons salesperson2("Pest","Perry","567-45-3412",
                            "Salesperson",2,2.0,2.20);
  salespersons salesperson3("Yourfriend","Yancy","213-44-9873",
                            "Salesperson",1,10.6,5.70);
  mechanics mechanicperson1("Hardwork","Harriet","076-45-3121",
                            "Mechanic",7,10.34);
  mechanics mechanicperson2("Lugwrench","Larry","886-43-1518",
                            "Mechanic",1,8.98);
  deal_closer closerperson("Slick","Sally","111-22-4444",
                            "Closer",10,40000.00);
  parts partperson1("Muffler","Mike","555-66-7891",
                    "Parts",4,7.34);
  parts partperson2("Horn","Hazel","345-77-7654",
                    "Parts",5,9.50);

  // add the eight workers to the linked list
  workers.insert_employee(&mechanicperson1);
  workers.insert_employee(&closerperson);
  workers.insert_employee(&salesperson1);
  workers.insert_employee(&partperson1);
  workers.insert_employee(&partperson2);
  workers.insert_employee(&salesperson2);
  workers.insert_employee(&mechanicperson2);
  workers.insert_employee(&salesperson3);
```

```
// print the linked list
workers.print_employee_list();

// remove three workers from the linked list
workers.remove_employee_id("555-66-7891");
workers.remove_employee_id("111-22-4444");
workers.remove_employee_id("213-44-3412");

cout << "\n\n*********************************";

// print the revised linked list
workers.print_employee_list();
}
```

Study this listing and see if you understand how workers are inserted into and deleted from the list.

A Sample Output

The next listing is a composite listing that shows the output of the linked-list example. The first part of the listing contains the eight names that were originally used to create the list. The remaining part of the listing shows the list after an attempt to remove three workers.

```
Friendly, Fran
 Social Security: #212-98-7654
 Job Title: Salesperson
 Years With Company: 1
 Weekly Sales Average (units): 7.50
 Commission Rate: 4%

Hardwork, Harriet
 Social Security: #076-45-3121
 Job Title: Mechanic
 Years With Company: 7
 Hourly Salary: $10.34

Horn, Hazel
 Social Security: #345-77-7654
 Job Title: Parts
 Years With Company: 5
 Hourly Salary: $9.50

Lugwrench, Larry
 Social Security: #886-43-1518
 Job Title: Mechanic
```

```
    Years With Company: 1
    Hourly Salary: $8.98

Muffler, Mike
  Social Security: #555-66-7891
  Job Title: Parts
  Years With Company: 4
  Hourly Salary: $7.34

Pest, Perry
  Social Security: #567-45-3412
  Job Title: Salesperson
  Years With Company: 2
  Weekly Sales Average (units): 2.00
  Commission Rate: 2%

Slick, Sally
  Social Security: #111-22-4444
  Job Title: Closer
  Years With Company: 10
  Yearly Salary: $40000.00

Yourfriend, Yancy
  Social Security: #213-44-9873
  Job Title: Salesperson
  Years With Company: 1
  Weekly Sales Average (units): 10.60
  Commission Rate: 5%

***********************************

Friendly, Fran
  Social Security: #212-98-7654
  Job Title: Salesperson
  Years With Company: 1
  Weekly Sales Average (units): 7.50
  Commission Rate: 4%

Hardwork, Harriet
  Social Security: #076-45-3121
  Job Title: Mechanic
  Years With Company: 7
  Hourly Salary: $10.34

Horn, Hazel
  Social Security: #345-77-7654
  Job Title: Parts
  Years With Company: 5
  Hourly Salary: $9.50

Lugwrench, Larry
  Social Security: #886-43-1518
  Job Title: Mechanic
  Years With Company: 1
  Hourly Salary: $8.98
```

```
Pest, Perry
  Social Security: #567-45-3412
  Job Title: Salesperson
  Years With Company: 2
  Weekly Sales Average (units): 2.00
  Commission Rate: 2%

Yourfriend, Yancy
  Social Security: #213-44-9873
  Job Title: Salesperson
  Years With Company: 1
  Weekly Sales Average (units): 10.60
  Commission Rate: 5%
```

Notice that only two workers have been removed from the original list. What happened? The social security number for the third worker did not match anyone on the list!

Debugger Information

The Debugger will allow you to view this program's class hierarchy. Enter the Debugger after compiling and linking the linked-list program and select the View menu. One of the menu options is "Hierarchy." Select this option to open the Class Hierarchy window, shown in Figure 14-1.

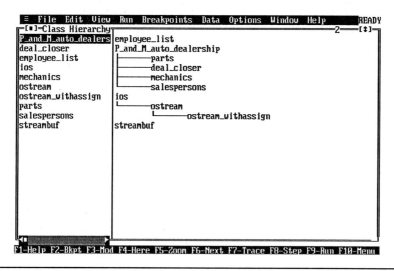

Figure 14-1. "Debugger Hierarchy" menu option

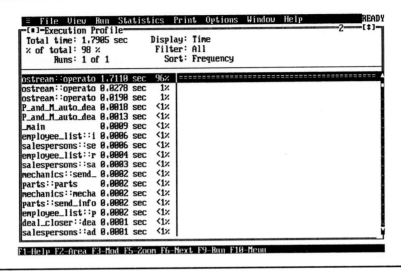

Figure 14-2.   Execution profile for the linked-list program

Profiler Information

The Profiler can also yield some interesting results for overall program performance. Figure 14-2 shows a snapshot of the execution profile for the linked-list program.

III

POWER PROGRAMMING

POWER PROGRAMMING: TAPPING IMPORTANT C AND C++ LIBRARIES

In C and C++ programming, you rely heavily on functions built into compiler libraries. By using built-in functions, you are saved from having to "reinvent the wheel" each time you need a special routine. C and C++ offer extensive support for character, string, and math work. Most of these standard library functions are portable from one computer to another and from one operating system to another. Still, other functions are system or compiler dependent. Many of these special functions will be explained in the next chapter. Knowing where to locate the routines you need and how to call them properly will help you become a better programmer.

Many of the C and C++ functions have already been used heavily in earlier chapters. These include, for example, functions in *stdio.h* and *iostream.h*. Indeed, it is hard to do serious programming without these functions. However, this chapter will not review these routines. Instead, it focuses on the powerful built-in functions for character, string, and math work.

C AND C++ HEADER FILES

If you do a directory listing of your Borland C++ *include* subdirectory, the following frequently used header files should be present. There will be others, but these are the header files that you will use most often. Since these files are in ASCII format, you should print a copy of their contents for a reference. These header files contain macros or function prototypes for the C library functions that you may wish to use in your programs.

bios.h	BIOS interrupts
complex.h∗	Complex numbers for C++
conio.h	Console and port I/O
ctype.h∗	Character functions
dos.h	DOS interrupts
graphics.h	Borland graphics routines
io.h	File handling and low-level I/O
iostream.h	Stream routines for C++
math.h∗	Math functions
stdio.h	Stream routines for C
stdlib.h∗	Standard library routines
string.h∗	String functions
time.h∗	Date and time utilities

Some header files are short while others are quite long. All contain function prototypes and many contain built-in macros.

This chapter will examine popular functions contained in the header files (marked with asterisks in the previous list). These files include *stdlib.h, complex.h, ctype.h, math.h, string.h,* and *time.h.* Additional system-dependent functions and functions unique to Borland C++, contained in *bios.h, dos.h,* and *graphics.h,* will be discussed in the next chapter. Note that other functions, contained in *stdio.h, iostream.h,* and so on, have been covered throughout the book.

STANDARD LIBRARY FUNCTIONS

You can use the standard library functions (*stdlib.h*), listed next, for data conversion, memory allocation, and other miscellaneous operations:

_ exit	Terminates program
_ lrotl	Rotates an unsigned long to the left

_ lrotr	Rotates an unsigned long to the right
_ rotl	Rotates an unsigned integer to the left
_ rotr	Rotates an unsigned integer to the right
abort	Aborts program—terminates abnormally
abs	Derives absolute value of an integer
atexit	Registers termination function
atof	Converts a string to a float
atoi	Converts a string to an integer
atol	Converts a string to a long
bsearch	Performs binary search of an array
calloc	Allocates main memory
div	Divides integers
ecvt	Converts a float to a string
exit	Terminates program
fcvt	Converts a float to a string
free	Frees memory
gcvt	Converts a float to a string
getenv	Gets a string from the environment
itoa	Converts an integer to a string
labs	Derives absolute value of a long
ldiv	Divides two long integers
lfind	Performs a linear search
lsearch	Performs a linear search
ltoa	Converts a long to a string
malloc	Allocates memory
putenv	Puts a string in the environment
qsort	Performs a quick sort
rand	Generates random numbers
realloc	Reallocates main memory
srand	Initializes random number generator
strtod	Converts a string to a double
strtol	Converts a string to a long
strtoul	Converts a string to an unsigned long
swap	Swaps bytes from *s1* to *s2*
system	Invokes DOS *command.com* file
ultoa	Converts an unsigned long to a string

Notice that almost half of the functions detailed in this header file perform data conversion from one format to another. Since the memory operations have already been used in several chapters, their operations will not be repeated in the following sections.

Data Conversions

The first important group of functions described in *stdlib.h* is the data converting functions. The principal job of these functions is to convert data from one format to another. For example, the **atof** function converts string information to a float.

The syntax of each function is shown in the following prototypes:

```
double atof(const char *s)
int atoi(const char *s)
long atol(const char *s)
char *ecvt(double value,int n,int *dec,int *sign)
char *fcvt(double value,int n,int *dec,int *sign)
char *gcvt(double value,int n,char *buf)
char *itoa(int value,char *s,int radix)
char *ltoa(long value,char *s,int radix)
double strtod(const char *s,char **endptr)
long strtol(const char *s,char **endptr,int radix)
unsigned long strtoul(const char *s,char **endptr,int radix)
char *ultoa(unsigned long value,char *s,int radix)
```

In these functions, *s* points to a string, *value* is the number to be converted, *n* represents the number of digits in the string, and *dec* locates the decimal point relative to the start of the string. *sign* represents the sign of the number, *buf* is a character buffer, *radix* represents the number base for the converted value, and *endptr* is usually null. If not, the function sets it to the character that stops the scan.

Several of these functions will be illustrated in the following programs.

Converting a Float to a String

The **fcvt** function converts a float to a string. Information regarding the sign and location of the decimal point is also returned.

```
/*
*    A C program that demonstrates how to use the fcvt
*    function.
*    Copyright (c) Chris H. Pappas and William H. Murray, 1990
*/

#include <stdlib.h>

main()
{
  int dec_pt,sign;
  char *ch_buffer;
```

```
    int num_char=7;

    ch_buffer = fcvt(-10.567845,num_char,&dec_pt,&sign);
    printf("The buffer holds: %s\n",ch_buffer);
    printf("The sign (+=0, -=1) is stored as a: %d\n",sign);
    printf("The decimal place is %d characters from left\n",
      dec_pt);
    return (0);
}
```

The output from this program is shown in the following listing. What potential uses might this function have?

```
The buffer holds: 105678450
The sign (+=0, -=1) is stored as a: 1
The decimal place is 2 characters from left
```

Converting a String to a Long Integer

The **strtol** function converts the supplied string, in the specified base, to its decimal equivalent. For example:

```
/*
 *    A C program that demonstrates how to use the strtol
 *    function.
 *    Copyright (c) Chris H. Pappas and William H. Murray, 1990
 */

#include <stdlib.h>
#include <stdio.h>

main()
{
  char *s="110011",*endptr;
  long long_number;

  long_number=strtol(s,&endptr,2);
  printf("The binary value %s is equal to %ld decimal.\n",
    s,long_number);
  return (0);
}
```

In this case, 110011 is contained in a string in binary format. The program produces the following results:

```
The binary value 110011 is equal to 51 decimal.
```

This is an interesting function since it allows a string of digits to be specified in one base and converted to another. You could use this function in a general base change program.

Searches and Sorts

The **bsearch** function performs a binary search of an array. The **qsort** function performs a quick sort. The **lfind** function performs a linear search for a key in an array of sequential records while the **lsearch** function performs a linear search on a sorted or unsorted table.

```
void *bsearch(const void *key,const void *base,
    size_t nelem,size_t width,int(*fcmp)(const void *,
    const void *)),

void qsort(void *base,size_t nelem,size_t width,
    int(*fcmp)(const void *,const void *)),

void *lfind(const void *key,const void *base,
    size_t *num,size_t width,int(*fcmp)
    (const void *,const void *)),

void *lsearch(const void *key, void *base,
    size_t *num,size_t width,int(*fcmp)
    (const void *,const void *)),
```

Note: Here, *key* represents the search key. *base* is the array to search. *nelem* contains the number of elements in the array. *width* is the number of bytes for each table entry. *fcmp* is the comparison routine used. *num* reports the number of records.

The next two programs illustrate the sort functions just described.

Sorting Integers with Quick Sort

Sorting data is important in any language. C and C++ provide the **qsort** function for sorting data, illustrated in the following example:

```
/*
 *    A C program that demonstrates how to use qsort.
 *    Copyright (c) Chris H. Pappas and William H. Murray, 1990
 */
```

```
#include <stdlib.h>

int int_comp(const void *i,const void *j);

int list[12]={96,54,72,87,12,29,35,54,11,12,75,-45};

main()
{
  int i;

  qsort(list,12,sizeof(int),int_comp);

  printf("The array after qsort:\n");
  for(i=0;i<12;i++)
    printf("%d ",list[i]);
    return (0);
}

int int_comp(const void *i,const void *j)
{
  return ((*(int *)i)-(*(int *)j));
}
```

The original list contains signed integers. The **qsort** function will arrange the original list in ascending order.

```
The array after qsort:
-45 11 12 12 29 35 54 54 72 75 87 96
```

Can you use **qsort** with floats? Why not alter the preceding program to see if you can.

Searching for an Integer in an Array

You can use the **bsearch** function to perform a search of an integer array. The value to be searched for, in the following example, is contained in *search_number*.

```
/*
 *    A C program that demonstrates how to use the bsearch
 *    function.
 *    Copyright (c) Chris H. Pappas and William H. Murray, 1990
 */

#include <stdlib.h>
#include <stdio.h>

int int_comp(const void *i,const void *j);
int data_array[]={111,222,333,444,555,
```

```
                   666,777,888,999};
main()
{
  int *search_result;
  int search_number=444;

  printf("Is 444 in the data_array? ");
  search_result=bsearch(&search_number,data_array,9,
                      sizeof(int),int_comp);
  if (search_result) printf("Yes!\n");
    else printf("No!\n");
  return (0);
}

int int_comp(const void *i,const void *j)
{
  return ((*(int *)i)-(*(int *)j));
}
```

This program will print a simple message to the screen if the number is found in the array.

```
Is 444 in the data_array? Yes!
```

You can also use this function to search for a string of characters in an array.

Miscellaneous Operations

The functions described in this section perform a variety of operations, from calculating the absolute value of an integer to bit rotations. The bit rotation functions enable C to perform operations that were once exclusively in the realm of assembly language programs.

Abort or End

void abort(void)	Returns an exit code of 3
int atexit(atexit_t func)	Calls function prior to exit
void exit(int status)	Returns 0 for normal exit
int system(const char *command)	Command is a DOS command
void _exit(int status)	Terminates without action

Math

div _ t div(int numer,int denom)	Divides and returns quotient and re mainder in *div _ t*
int abs(int x)	Determines absolute value of x
long labs(long x)	Determines absolute value of x
ldiv _ t ldiv(long numer,long denom)	Similar to **div** with longs
int rand(void)	Calls random number generator
void srand(unsigned seed)	Seeds the random number generator

Rotate

unsigned long _ lrotl(unsigned long val,int count)	Rotates the long *val* to the left
unsigned long _ lrotr(unsigned long val,int count)	Rotates the long *val* to the right
unsigned _ rotl(unsigned val, int count)	Rotates the integer *val* to the left
unsigned _ rotr(unsigned val, int count)	Rotates the integer *val* to the right

Miscellaneous

char *getenv(const char *name)	Gets environment string
int putenv(const char *name)	Puts environment string
void swap(char *from,char *to,int nbytes)	Swaps the number of characters specified

Using the Random Number Function

C and C++ provide a random number generator. The generator can be initialized or seeded with a call to **srand**. The seed function accepts an integer argument and starts the random number generator.

```
/*
 *    A C program that demonstrates how to use the srand and
 *    rand, random number functions.
```

```
*      Copyright (c) Chris H. Pappas and William H. Murray, 1990
*/

#include <stdlib.h>
#include <stdio.h>

main()
{
  int x;

  srand(3);

  for (x=0;x<10;x++)
    printf("Trial #%d, random number=%d\n",
            x,rand());
  return (0);
}
```

The following listing shows a sample of random numbers generated by
rand:

```
Trial #0, random number=1038
Trial #1, random number=32467
Trial #2, random number=32686
Trial #3, random number=14075
Trial #4, random number=20
Trial #5, random number=30807
Trial #6, random number=5783
Trial #7, random number=16822
Trial #8, random number=23247
Trial #9, random number=14713
```

Random number generators are important in programming for statistical
work and for applications that rely on generating random patterns.

Performing Bit Rotations on Data

C and C++ enable you to rotate the individual bits of integers and longs to
the right and left. The next example performs two rotations in each direction:

```
/*
*      A C program that demonstrates how to use the _rotl and
*      _rotr bit rotate functions.
*      Copyright (c) Chris H. Pappas and William H. Murray, 1990
*/
```

```
#include <stdlib.h>

main()
{
 unsigned int val = 0x1234;

 printf("rotate bits of %X to the left 2 bits and get %X\n",
        val,_rotl(val,2));
 printf("rotate bits of %X to the right 2 bits and get %X\n",
        val,_rotr(val,2));
}
```

The results of the rotations are shown next:

```
rotate bits of 1234 to the left 2 bits and get 48D0
rotate bits of 1234 to the right 2 bits and get 48D
```

With the bit rotation functions and the use of logical operators such as **and** and **or,** C enables you to manipulate data bit by bit.

CHARACTER FUNCTIONS

Characters are defined in most languages as single-byte values. The character macros and functions in C and C++, prototyped or contained in *ctype.h,* take integer arguments but only utilize the lower byte of the integer value. Automatic type conversion usually permits character arguments to be passed to the macros or functions. The following macros and functions are available:

isalnum	Checks for alphanumeric character
isalpha	Checks for alpha character
isascii	Checks for ASCII character
iscntrl	Checks for control character
isdigit	Checks for decimal digit (0-9)
isgraph	Checks for printable character (no space)
islower	Checks for lowercase character
isprint	Checks for printable character
ispunct	Checks for punctuation character
isspace	Checks for whitespace character

isupper	Checks for uppercase character
isxdigit	Checks for hexadecimal digit
toascii	Translates character to ASCII equivalent
tolower	Translates character to lowercase if uppercase
toupper	Translates character to uppercase if lowercase

The character macros and functions allow characters to be tested for various conditions or to be converted between uppercase and lowercase characters.

Checking for Letters, Numbers, and ASCII Values

The following three macros allow ASCII-coded integer values to be checked via a lookup table. A zero is returned for false and a nonzero for true. A valid ASCII character set is assumed.

int isalnum(ch)	Checks for alphanumeric values A-Z, a-z, and 0-9. *ch* is integer.
int isalpha(ch)	Checks for alpha values A-Z and a-z. *ch* is integer.
int isascii(ch)	Checks for ASCII values 0-127 (0-7Fh). *ch* is integer.

The following program checks the ASCII integer values from 0 to 127 and reports which of the preceding three functions produce a true condition for each case.

```
/*
 *    A C program that demonstrates how to use isalnum,
 *    isalpha, and isascii library functions.
 *    Copyright (c) Chris H. Pappas and William H. Murray, 1990
 */

#include <ctype.h>

main()
{
  int ch;
  for (ch=0;ch<=127;ch++) {
    printf("The ASCII digit %d is an:\n",ch);
    printf("%s",isalnum(ch) ? "  alpha-numeric char\n" : "");
    printf("%s",isalpha(ch) ? "  alpha char\n" : "");
    printf("%s",isascii(ch) ? "  ascii char\n" : "");
    printf("\n");
  }
  return (0);
}
```

A portion of the screen display is shown in the following listing:

```
The ASCII digit 56 is an:
  alpha-numeric char
  ascii char

The ASCII digit 64 is an:
  ascii char

The ASCII digit 65 is an:
  alpha-numeric char
  alpha char
  ascii char

The ASCII digit 90 is an:
  alpha-numeric char
  alpha char
  ascii char

The ASCII digit 127 is an:
  ascii char
```

These functions are useful in checking string data for correct data.

Checking for Control, Whitespace, Punctuation, and So On

The following nine macros allow ASCII-coded integer values to be checked via a lookup table. A zero is returned for false and a nonzero for true. A valid ASCII character set is assumed. The value *ch* is an integer.

int iscntrl(ch)	Checks for control character
int isdigit(ch)	Checks for digit 0-9
int isgraph(ch)	Checks for printable characters (no space)
int islower(ch)	Checks for lowercase a-z
int isprint(ch)	Checks for printable character
int ispunct(ch)	Checks for punctuation
int isspace(ch)	Checks for whitespace
int isupper(ch)	Checks for uppercase A-Z
int isxdigit(ch)	Checks for hexadecimal value 0-9, a-f, or A-F

The following program checks the ASCII integer values from 0 to 127 and reports which of the preceding nine functions give a true condition for each value:

```
/*
 *    A C program that demonstrates several character
 *    functions such as isprint, isupper, iscntrl, etc.
 *    Copyright (c) Chris H. Pappas and William H. Murray, 1990
 */

#include <ctype.h>

main()
{
  int ch;
  for (ch=0;ch<=127;ch++) {
    printf("The ASCII digit %d is a(n):\n",ch);
    printf("%s",isprint(ch)  ? "  printable char\n" : "");
    printf("%s",islower(ch)  ? "  lower case char\n" : "");
    printf("%s",isupper(ch)  ? "  upper case char\n" : "");
    printf("%s",ispunct(ch)  ? "  punctuation char\n" : "");
    printf("%s",isspace(ch)  ? "  space char\n" : "");
    printf("%s",isdigit(ch)  ? "  char digit\n" : "");
    printf("%s",isgraph(ch)  ? "  graphics char\n" : "");
    printf("%s",iscntrl(ch)  ? "  control char\n" : "");
    printf("%s",isxdigit(ch) ? "  hexadecimal char\n" : "");
    printf("\n");
  }
  return (0);
}
```

A portion of the screen output is shown in the following listing:

```
The ASCII digit 29 is a(n):
  control char

The ASCII digit 38 is a(n):
  printable char
  punctuation char
  graphics char

The ASCII digit 52 is a(n):
  printable char
  char digit
  graphics char
  hexadecimal char

The ASCII digit 80 is a(n):
  printable char
  upper case char
  graphics char

The ASCII digit 96 is a(n):
  printable char
  punctuation char
  graphics char
```

```
The ASCII digit 127 is a(n):
  control char
```

Converting to ASCII, Lowercase, and Uppercase

The following three macros or functions allow ASCII-coded integer values to be translated. The macro **toascii** converts *ch* to ASCII by retaining only the lower 7 bits. The functions **tolower** and **toupper** convert the character value to the format specified. The macros **_tolower** and **_toupper** return identical results when supplied proper ASCII values. A valid ASCII character set is assumed. The value *ch* is an integer.

int toascii(ch)	Translates to ASCII character
int tolower(ch)	Translates *ch* to lowercase if uppercase
int _tolower(ch)	Translates *ch* to lowercase
int toupper(ch)	Translates *ch* to uppercase if lowercase
int _toupper(ch)	Translates *ch* to uppercase

The next example illustrates how the macro **toascii** translates integer information to correct ASCII values:

```
/*
 *     A C program that demonstrates how to use the
 *     toascii library function.
 *     Copyright (c) Chris H. Pappas and William H. Murray, 1990
 */

#include <ctype.h>

int ch;

main()
{
  for(ch=0;ch<=1024;ch++) {
    printf("The ASCII value for %d is %d\n",
           ch,toascii(ch));
  }
  return (0);
}
```

The following listing shows a portion of the output from this program:

```
The ASCII value for 0 is 0
The ASCII value for 1 is 1
The ASCII value for 2 is 2
The ASCII value for 3 is 3
```

```
The ASCII value for 4 is 4
The ASCII value for 5 is 5
                .
                .
                .
The ASCII value for 128 is 0
The ASCII value for 129 is 1
The ASCII value for 130 is 2
The ASCII value for 131 is 3
The ASCII value for 132 is 4
The ASCII value for 133 is 5
                .
                .
                .
The ASCII value for 256 is 0
The ASCII value for 257 is 1
The ASCII value for 258 is 2
The ASCII value for 259 is 3
The ASCII value for 260 is 4
The ASCII value for 261 is 5
                .
                .
                .
The ASCII value for 384 is 0
The ASCII value for 385 is 1
The ASCII value for 386 is 2
The ASCII value for 387 is 3
The ASCII value for 388 is 4
The ASCII value for 389 is 5
```

MEMORY AND STRING FUNCTIONS

Strings in C and C++ are usually considered one-dimensional character arrays terminated with a null character. The string functions, prototyped in *string.h*, typically use pointer arguments and return pointer or integer values. You can study the syntax of each command in the next section, or in more detail in your Borland C++ library reference. Buffer-manipulation functions such as **memccpy** through **memset** are also prototyped in *string.h*. The following functions are available:

memccpy	Copies from source to destination
memchr	Searches buffer for first *ch*
memcmp	Compares *n* characters in *buf1* and *buf2*
memcpy	Copies *n* characters from source to destination

memicmp	Same as **memcmp**, except case-insensitive
memset	Copies *ch* into *n* character positions in *buf*
strcat	Appends a string to another string
strchr	Locates first occurrence of a character in a string
strcmp	Compares two strings
strcmpi	Compares two strings (case-insensitive)
strcpy	Copies string to another string
strcspn	Locates first occurrence of a character in string from given character set
strdup	Replicates the string
strerror	System-error message saved
stricmp	Same as **strcmpi**
strlen	Length of string
strlwr	String converted to lowercase
strncat	Characters of string appended
strncmp	Characters of separate strings compared
strncpy	Characters of one string copied to another
strnicmp	Characters of two strings compared (case-insensitive)
strnset	Sets string characters to given character
strpbrk	First occurrence of character from one string in another string
strrchr	Last occurrence of character in string
strrev	Reverses characters in a string
strset	Sets all characters in string to given character
strspn	Locates first sub-string from given character set in string
strstr	Locates one string in another string
strtok	Locates tokens within a string
strupr	Converts string to uppercase

The memory and string functions provide C and C++ programmers with flexibility.

Experimenting with Memory Functions

Here are the syntax statements for the memory operations described in the previous section:

```
void *memccpy(void *dest,void *source,int ch,unsigned count)
void *memchr(void *buf,int ch,unsigned count)
int memcmp (void *buf1,void *buf2,unsigned count)
void *memcpy(void *dest,void *source,unsigned count)
```

```
int memicmp (void *buf1,void *buf2,unsigned count)
void *memmove(void *dest,void *source,unsigned count)
void *memset(void *dest,int ch,unsigned count)
```

*buf, *buf1, *buf2, *dest,* and *source* are pointers to the appropriate string
buffer. The integer *ch* points to a character value. The unsigned *count* holds
the character count for the function.

The examples in the next sections illustrate several of these functions.

Finding the Occurrence of a Character in a String

The following example uses the **memchr** function to search the buffer for
the uppercase character "E":

```
/*
 *   A C program that demonstrates how to use the memchr
 *   library function to locate a character in a buffer.
 *   Copyright (c) Chris H. Pappas and William H. Murray, 1990
 */

#include <string.h>
#include <stdio.h>

char buf[50];
char *ptr;

main()
{
  strcpy(buf,"The results of this test are perfectly clear." );
  ptr = (char *)memchr(buf, 'E',50);
  if (ptr != NULL)
    printf("character found at location: %d\n",ptr-buf);
  else
    printf("character not found.\n");
  return (0);
}
```

Since an uppercase "E" is not in the string, the **memchr** function will report
that the "character was not found."

Comparing Characters in Two Strings

The next example will highlight the **memicmp** function. This function will
compare two strings contained in *buf1* and *buf2*. Recall that this function is
not sensitive to the case of the string characters.

```
/*
 *    A C program that demonstrates how to use the memicmp
 *    library function to compare two string buffers.
 *    Copyright (c) Chris H. Pappas and William H. Murray, 1990
 */

#include <string.h>

char buf1[40],
     buf2[40];

main()
{
  strcpy(buf1,"Well, are they similar or not?");
  strcpy(buf2,"Well, are they similiar or not?");
  /* 0 - identical strings except for case */
  /* x - any integer, means not identical */
  printf("%d\n",memicmp(buf1,buf2,40));
  /* returns a non-zero value */
  return (0);
}
```

If "similar" had not been spelled incorrectly in the second string, both strings would have been identical. A nonzero value is returned by **memi-cmp**.

Using memset to Load a Buffer

It is often necessary to load or clear a buffer with a predefined character. In those cases, you might consider using the **memset** function.

```
/*
 *    A C program that demonstrates how to use the memset
 *    library function to set the contents of a string buffer.
 *    Copyright (c) Chris H. Pappas and William H. Murray, 1990
 */

#include <string.h>

char buf[20];

main()
{
  buf[15] = '\0';
  printf("The contents of buf: %s",memset(buf,'%',15));
  return (0);
}
```

In this example, the buffer is loaded with 15 percent characters and a null character. The program will print 15 percent characters to the screen.

String Functions

Here are the syntax statements for the various string manipulating functions contained in *string.h*:

char *strerror(int errnum)	ANSI-supplied number
char *_strerror(char *s)	User-supplied message
size_t strlen(const char *s)	Null-terminated string
char *strlwr(char *s)	String to lowercase
char *strncat(char *s1, const char *s2,size_t n)	Append *n* char *s2* to *s1*
int strncmp(const char *s1, const char *s2,size_t n)	Compares first *n* characters of two strings
int strnicmp(const char *s1, const char *s2,size_t n)	Compares first *n* characters of two strings (case insensitive)
char *strncpy(char *s1, const char *s2,size_t n)	Copy *n* characters of *s2* to *s1*
char *strnset(char *s, int ch,size_t n)	Set first *n* characters of string to char setting
char *strpbrk(const char *s1, const char *s2)	Locate character from *s2* in *s1*
char *strrchr(const char *s, int ch)	Locate last occurrence of *ch* in string
char *strrev(char *s)	String to reverse
char *strset(char *s,int ch)	String to be set with *ch*
size_t strspn(const char *s1, const char *s2)	Search *s1* with char set in *s2*
char *strstr(const char *s1, const char *s2)	Search *s1* with *s2*
char *strtok(char *s1, const char *s2)	Finds token in *s1*. *s1* contains token(s), *s2* contains the delimiters
char *strupr(char *s)	String to uppercase

*s is a pointer to a string. *s1 and *s2 are pointers to two strings. Usually, *s1 points to the string to be manipulated and *s2 points to the string doing the manipulation. *ch* is a character value.

Comparing Two Strings

The following program uses the **strcmp** function and reports how one string compares to another:

```
/*
 *    A C program that demonstrates how to use the strcmp
 *    library function to compare two strings.
 *    Copyright (c) Chris H. Pappas and William H. Murray, 1990
 */

#include <string.h>
char s1[40] = "What makes a good string great.";
char s2[40] = "What makes a good string great?";
int answer;

main()
{
  answer = strcmp(s1,s2);
  if (answer>0) printf("s1 is greater than s2");
    else if (answer==0) printf("s1 is equal to s2");
      else printf("s1 is less than s2");
  return (0);
}
```

Can you predict which string will be greater?

Searching a String for Several Characters

The next program will search a string for the first occurrence of one or more characters:

```
/*
 *    A C program that demonstrates how to use the strcspn
 *    library function to find the occurrence of one of a group
 *    of characters.
 *    Copyright (c) Chris H. Pappas and William H. Murray, 1990
 */

#include <string.h>

char s1[40];
int answer;
```

```
main()
{
  strcpy(sl,"Numerical examples are instructive." );
  answer=strcspn(sl,"xyz");
  printf("The first x,y,z appeared at position %d\n",
         answer+1);
  return (0);
}
```

This program will report the position of the first occurrence of either an x, y, or z. A 1 is added to the answer since the first character is at index position 0.

Finding the First Occurrence of a Single Character in a String

You can use the **strchr** function to check a sentence for the occurrence of a particular character.

```
/*
 *    A C program that demonstrates how to use the strchr
 *    library function to locate the first occurrence of a
 *    character in a string.
 *    Copyright (c) Chris H. Pappas and William H. Murray, 1990
 */

#include <string.h>

char sl[40] = "Purple people eater.";
char *answer;

main()
{
  answer=strchr(sl,' ');
  printf("After the first blank: %s\n",answer);
  return (0);
}
```

Run the program to see what's left of a string when the purple people eater gets done with it.

Determining the Length of a String

You can use the **strlen** function to report on the length of any given string. Here is a simple example:

```
/*
 *     A C program that demonstrates how to use the strlen
 *     library function to determine the length of a string.
 *     Copyright (c) Chris H. Pappas and William H. Murray, 1990
 */

#include <string.h>

char *sl="The length of a string is a character measure!";

main()
{
  printf("The length of this string is %d",strlen(sl));
  return (0);
}
```

The **strlen** function reports the total number of characters in the string. In this example, there are 46 characters.

Finding One String in Another String

The **strstr** function will search a given string with a group (a string) of characters.

```
/*
 *     A C program that demonstrates how to use the strstr
 *     library function to locate a string within a string.
 *     Copyright (c) Chris H. Pappas and William H. Murray, 1990
 */

#include <string.h>

main()
{
  char *sl="If you can not find a character try a word.";
  char *s2="act";

  printf("%s\n",strstr(sl,s2));
  return (0);
}
```

This program sends the remainder of the string to the **printf** function after the first occurrence of "act." The string printed is "acter try a word."

Converting a String to Uppercase

In a case-sensitive language, it is handy to have a function that can convert the characters in a string to another case. The **strupr** function converts lowercase characters to uppercase.

```
/*
*    A C program that demonstrates how to use the strupr
*    library function to convert lowercase letters to
*    uppercase.
*    Copyright (c) Chris H. Pappas and William H. Murray, 1990
*/

#include <string.h>

char *s1="The Roller Coaster went UP and down.";
char *s2;

main()
{
  s2=strupr(s1);
  printf("The results: %s",s2);
  return (0);
}
```

This program converts each lowercase character to uppercase. Only lowercase letters are affected.

Compare the contents of *s1* and *s2* shown in the Debugger window of Figure 15-1.

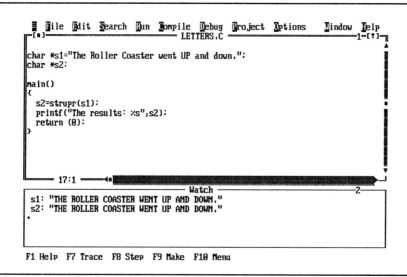

Figure 15-1.   Using the Debugger to keep a Watch window on *s1* and *s2*

MATH FUNCTIONS

The functions prototyped in the *math.h* header file permit a great variety of mathematical, algebraic, and trigonometric operations. In addition to the functions contained in *math.h*, C++ adds the complex functions described in *complex.h*. The *math.h* header file also contains the definitions for several popular constants:

```
M_E            2.71828182845904523536
M_LOG2E        1.44269504088896340736
M_LOG10E       0.434294481903251827651
M_LN2          0.693147180559945309417
M_LN10         2.30258509299404568402
M_PI           3.14159265358979323846
M_PI_2         1.57079632679489661923
M_PI_4         0.785398163397448309616
M_1_PI         0.318309886183790671538
M_2_PI         0.636619772367581343076
M_1_SQRTPI     0.564189583547756286948
M_2_SQRTPI     1.12837916709551257390
M_SQRT2        1.41421356237309504880
M_SQRT_2       0.707106781186547524401
```

You might find that access to these constant values is handy, even if you don't utilize the functions described.

Mathematical Operations in C and C++

The math functions are relatively easy to use and understand if you are familiar with algebraic and trigonometric concepts. Many of these functions have been demonstrated in earlier chapters. Remember that all angle arguments are specified in radians.

double acos(double x)	Arc cosine
double asin(double x)	Arc sine
double atan(double x)	Arc tangent
double atan2(double y,double x)	Arc tan
double ceil(double x)	Greatest integer
double cos(double x)	Cosine
double cosh(double x)	Hyperbolic cosine
double exp(double x)	Exponential value
double fabs(double x)	Absolute value

double floor(double x)	Smallest integer
double fmod(double x,double y)	Modula operator
double frexp(double x,int *exponent)	Split to mantissa & exp
double hypot(double x,double y)	Hypotenuse
double ldexp(double x,int exponent)	x times 2 to exp power
double log(double x)	Natural log
double log10(double x)	Common log
double modf(double x,double *ipart)	Mantissa and exponent
double poly(double x,int degree, double coeffs[])	Polynomial
double pow(double x,double y)	x to y power
double pow10(int p)	10 raised to p
double sin(double x)	Sine
double sinh(double x)	Hyperbolic sine
double sqrt(double x)	Square root
double tan(double x)	Tangent
double tanh(double x)	Hyperbolic tangent

If you program in C and need to use complex number arithmetic, you must resort to using **struct complex** and the **cabs** function described in *math.h*. This is the only function available for complex arithmetic in C.

```
struct complex {double x,double y}
```

This structure is used by the **cabs** function. The **cabs** function returns the absolute value of a complex number.

Complex Arithmetic In C++

C++ programmers should use the C++ class **complex** described in *complex.h* for complex arithmetic. Operator overloading is provided for +, −, *, /, +=, −=, *=, /=, =, ==, and !=. The stream operators, << and >>, are also overloaded.

The following *math.h* functions, described in the previous section, are also overloaded:

```
friend double abs(complex&)
friend complex acos(complex&)
friend complex asin(complex&)
```

```
friend complex atan(complex&)
friend complex cos(complex&)
friend complex cosh(complex&)
friend complex exp(complex&)
friend complex log(complex&)
friend complex log10(complex&)
friend complex pow(complex& base,double expon)
friend complex pow(double base,complex& expon)
friend complex pow(complex& base,complex& expon)
friend complex sin(complex&)
friend complex sinh(complex&)
friend complex sqrt(complex&)
friend complex tan(complex&)
friend complex tanh(complex&)
friend complex acos(complex&)
friend complex asin(complex&)
friend complex atan(complex&)
friend complex log10(complex&)
friend complex tan(complex&)
friend complex tanh(complex&)
```

Here are some additional complex mathematical operations described in *complex.h:*

friend double real(complex&)	Real part of a complex number
friend double imag(complex&)	Imaginary part of a complex number
friend complex conj(complex&)	Complex conjugate
friend double norm(complex&)	Square of the magnitude
friend double arg(complex&)	Angle in the plane
friend complex polar(double mag, double angle=0)	Create a complex object given polar co-ordinates as arguments

Since the standard functions prototyped in *math.h* have been used extensively in earlier chapters, the next several examples are devoted to the new functions in *complex.h*.

Real and Imaginary Parts of a Complex Result

The following program shows how to use the complex functions **real** and **imaginary** to break apart a complex number:

```
//
//    A C++ program that demonstrates how to use the complex
//    function real and imaginary to break apart a complex number.
```

```
//    This program utilizes operator and function overloading.
//    Copyright (c) Chris H. Pappas and William H. Murray, 1990
//

#include <iostream.h>
#include <complex.h>

main()
{
  double x1=5.6, y1=7.2;
  double x2=-3.1, y2=4.8;

  complex z1=complex(x1,y1);
  complex z2=complex(x2,y2);
  complex zt;

  zt=z1+z2;

  cout << "The value of zt is: " << zt << "\n";
  cout << "The real part of the sum is: "
       << real(zt) << "\n";
  cout << "The imaginary part of the sum is: "
       << imag(zt) << "\n";
  return (0);
}
```

In this example, two complex numbers are added to form the complex sum, *zt*. Adding numbers in rectangular coordinates is fairly easy for humans, but look at the simplicity of the program and appreciate what C++ is accomplishing. Here are the results for this example:

```
The value of zt is: (2.5, 12)
The real part of the sum is: 2.5
The imaginary part of the sum is: 12
```

Overloaded Operators with Complex Numbers

The fundamental mathematical operators +, −, *, and / are overloaded. This means that you can use them to perform complex arithmetic directly. Examine the following program code:

```
//
//    A C++ program that demonstrates how to use complex
//    arithmetic with overloaded operators.  Here complex
//    numbers are directly added, subtracted, multiplied and
//    divided.
//    Copyright (c) Chris H. Pappas and William H. Murray, 1990
//

#include <iostream.h>
```

```
#include <complex.h>

main()
{
  double x1=5.6, y1=7.2;
  double x2=-3.1, y2=4.8;
  complex z1=complex(x1,y1);
  complex z2=complex(x2,y2);

  cout << "The value of z1 + z2 is: " << z1+z2 << "\n";
  cout << "The value of z1 * z2 is: " << z1*z2 << "\n";
  cout << "The value of z1 - z2 is: " << z1-z2 << "\n";
  cout << "The value of z1 / z2 is: " << z1/z2 << "\n";
  return (0);
}
```

This example shows how various operators can be overloaded. The program prints the sum, product, difference, and division of two complex numbers.

```
The value of z1 + z2 is: (2.5, 12)
The value of z1 * z2 is: (-51.92, 4.56)
The value of z1 - z2 is: (8.7, 2.4)
The value of z1 / z2 is: (0.5267994, -1.506891)
```

This opens new vistas for those inclined toward mathematics and engineering. Since **cout** can print the complex rectangular result, it must also be overloaded.

Rectangular to Polar Transformations

Complex numbers are often expressed in polar or rectangular forms. The following program adds two complex numbers, in polar format, and prints the result.

```
//
//    A C++ program that demonstrates how to use complex
//    arithmetic with overloaded operators.  Here rectangular
//    numbers are directly converted to their polar
//    equivalents.  Arithmetic is also done directly on polar
//    numbers.
//    Copyright (c) Chris H. Pappas and William H. Murray, 1990
//

#include <iostream.h>
#include <complex.h>

main()
```

```
{
  double m1=10.0,ang1=M_PI/6;      // 60 deg in radians
  double m2=20.0,ang2=M_PI_4;      // 45 deg in radians

  cout << "m1 and ang1 from polar to rectangular: "
       << polar(m1,ang1) << "\n";
  cout << "m2 and ang2 from polar to rectangular: "
       << polar(m2,ang2) << "\n";
  cout << "Add polar values then convert: "
       << polar(m1,ang1)+polar(m2,ang2) << "\n";
  return (0);
}
```

Use your calculator to check the results of these complex operations.

```
m1 and ang1 from polar to rectangular: (8.660254, 5)
m2 and ang2 from polar to rectangular: (14.14214, 14.14214)
Add polar values then convert: (22.80239, 19.14214)
```

If you work with complex numbers in mathematics or electrical engineering, these new features will be a big help. Don't forget that the functions require all angles to be radians.

Overloaded Functions and Complex Arithmetic

Many of the *math.h* functions are overloaded to let you use them with complex numbers. The following program illustrates several of these functions:

```
//
//    A C++ program that demonstrates how to use complex
//    arithmetic with overloaded math.h functions.  Here
//    the square root, cube, and absolute value of a number
//    in polar form is obtained.
//    Copyright (c) Chris H. Pappas and William H. Murray, 1990
//

#include <iostream.h>
#include <complex.h>

main()
{
  double m1=-10.4,ang1=M_PI/6;  // 30 deg in radians

  cout << "square root of polar m1 @ ang1: "
       << sqrt(polar(m1,ang1)) << "\n";
  cout << "cube of polar m1 @ ang1: "
       << pow(polar(m1,ang1),3) << "\n";
```

```
    cout << "absolute value of polar ml @ angl: "
        << abs(polar(ml,angl)) << "\n";
    return (0);
}
```

Imagine being able to take the square root of a complex number with nothing more than a call to **sqrt**.

```
square root of polar ml @ angl: (0.8346663, -3.115017)
cube of polar ml @ angl: (3.443789e-13, -1124.864)
absolute value of polar ml @ angl: 10.4
```

TIME FUNCTIONS

The following section covers several time and date functions described in *time.h*. These functions offer a variety of ways to obtain different time and/or date formats for your program code.

asctime	Converts date and time to an ASCII string and uses the *tm* structure
clock	Determines the microprocessor's clock time for the current session
ctime	Converts date and time to a string
difftime	Calculates the difference between two times
gmtime	Converts date and time to GMT using *tm* structure
localtime	Converts date and time to *tm* structure
mktime	Converts time to calendar format. Uses *tm* structure
stime	Sets date and time for system
strftime	Allows formatting of date and time data for output
time	Obtains current time (system)
tzset	Sets time variables for environment variable *TZ*

For details of each function's syntax, see the next section.

Date and Time Variations

Many of the date and time functions described in the previous section use the *tm* structure defined in *time.h.*

```
struct tm  {
  int      tm_sec;
  int      tm_min;
  int      tm_hour;
  int      tm_mday;
  int      tm_mon;
  int      tm_year;
  int      tm_wday;
  int      tm_yday;
  int      tm_isdst;
};
```

The syntax for calling each date and time function differs according to the function's ability. The next listing shows the syntax for each:

char *asctime(const struct tm *tblock)	Converts the structure information to a 26-char string.
clock_t clock(void)	Determines the time in seconds. The returned value should be divided by the macro *CLK_TCK.*
char *ctime(const time_t *time)	Converts a time value, pointed to by *time,* into a 26-char string.
double di(time_t time2, time_t time1)	Calculates the difference between *time2* and *time1* and returns a double.
struct tm *gmtime(const time_t *timer)	Accepts address of a value returned by the function **time** and returns a pointer to the structure with GMT information.
struct tm *localtime(const time_t *timer)	Accepts address of a value returned by the function **time** and returns a pointer to the structure with local time information.
time_t mktime(struct tm *tptr)	Converts time pointed to *tptr* to a calendar time of same format as used by **time** function.

int stime(time_t *tp)	Sets the system time. *tp* points to the time in seconds as measured from GMT, January 1, 1970.
size_t strftime(char *s, size_t maxsize, const char *fmt, const struct tm *t)	Formats date and time information for output.
time_t time(time_t *timer)	Returns the time in seconds since 00:00:00 GMT, January 1, 1970.
void tzset(void)	Sets the global variables *daylight*, *timezone*, and *tzname* based on the environment string.

For **size** and **strftime**, *s* points to the string information, *maxsize* is maximum string length, *fmt* represents the format, and *t* points to a structure of type *tm*. The formatting options include

%a	Abbreviate weekday name
%A	Full weekday name
%b	Abbreviate month name
%B	Full month name
%c	Date and time information
%d	Day of month (01 to 31)
%H	Hour (00 to 23)
%I	Hour (00 to 12)
%j	Day of year (001 to 366)
%m	Month (01 to 12)
%M	Minutes (00 to 59)
%p	AM or PM
%S	Seconds (0 to 59)
%U	Week number (00 to 52), Sunday 1st day
%w	Weekday (0 to 6)
%W	Week number (00 to 52), Monday 1st day
%x	Date
%X	Time
%y	Year, without century (00 to 99)
%Y	Year, with century
%Z	Time zone name
%%	Character %a

For **tzset**, the *TZ* environment string uses the following syntax:

TZ = zzz[+/−]d[d]{lll}

Here, zzz represents a three-character string with the local time zone – for example, "EST" for Eastern Standard Time. The *[+/−]d[d]* argument contains an adjustment for the difference between the local time zone and the GMT (Greenwich Mean Time). Positive numbers are a westward adjustment while negative numbers are an eastward adjustment. For example, a five (5) would be used for EST. The last argument, *{lll}*, represents the local time zone daylight saving time – for example, EDT, for Eastern daylight saving time.

Several of these functions will be used in example programs in the next section.

Using the localtime and asctime Functions

The following program will return date and time information by using the **localtime** and **asctime** functions:

```
/*
 *    A C program that demonstrates how to call the localtime and
 *    asctime functions.
 *    Copyright (c) Chris H. Pappas and William H. Murray, 1990
 */

#include <time.h>
#include <stdio.h>

struct tm *date_time;
time_t timer;

main()
{
  time(&timer);
  date_time=localtime(&timer);

  printf("The present date and time is: %s\n",
         asctime(date_time));
  return (0);
}
```

This program produces output similar to the following sample:

```
The present date and time is: Mon Jan 29 13:16:20 1990
```

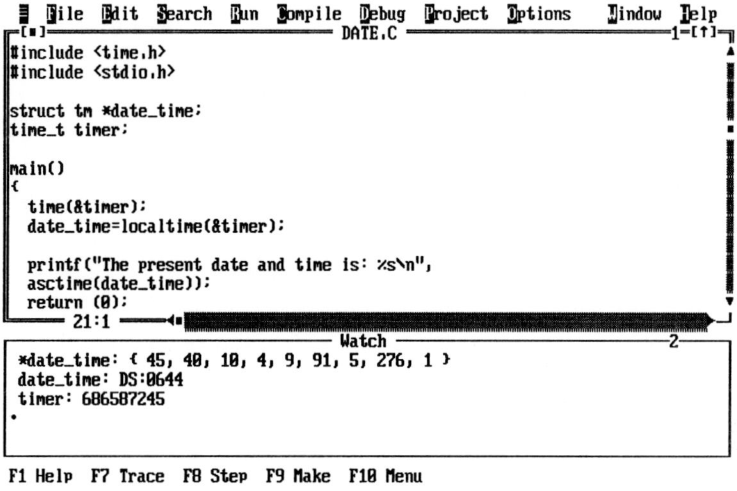

```
 █ File Edit Search Run Compile Debug Project Options    Window Help
┌[■]──────────────────── DATE.C ────────────────────1═[↑]─┐
│#include <time.h>                                        ▲
│#include <stdio.h>                                       ▓
│                                                         ▓
│struct tm *date_time;                                    ▓
│time_t timer;                                            ■
│                                                         
│main()                                                   
│{                                                        
│  time(&timer);                                          
│  date_time=localtime(&timer);                           
│                                                         
│  printf("The present date and time is: %s\n",           
│  asctime(date_time));                                   
│  return (0);                                            ▼
└── 21:1 ──◄■▓▓▓▓▓▓▓▓▓▓▓▓▓▓▓▓▓▓▓▓▓▓▓▓▓▓▓▓▓▓▓▓▓▓▓▓▓▓►──┘
┌──────────────────────── Watch ────────────────────2─┐
│ *date_time: { 45, 40, 10, 4, 9, 91, 5, 276, 1 }      │
│ date_time: DS:0644                                   │
│ timer: 686587245                                     │
│ ■                                                    │
└──────────────────────────────────────────────────────┘
 F1 Help  F7 Trace  F8 Step  F9 Make  F10 Menu
```

Figure 15-2.   The Debugger's Watch window reports information on several items

Watch the *date_time* variable, shown in Figure 15-2, from the Debugger screen. The Debugger helps you get a feel for how data is being returned.

Using the gmtime and asctime Functions

This program is similar to the last example. Instead of using the **localtime** function, it uses the **gmtime** function. Do you notice what's different about the output?

```
/*
 *    A C program that demonstrates how to call the gmtime and
 *    asctime functions.
 *    Copyright (c) Chris H. Pappas and William H. Murray, 1990
 */

#include <time.h>
#include <stdio.h>
```

```
main()
{
  struct tm *date_time;
  time_t timer;
  time(&timer);
  date_time=gmtime(&timer);

  printf("%.19s\n",asctime(date_time));
  return (0);
}
```

The following date and time information was returned by this program:

```
Mon Jan 29 18:16:28
```

Using the strftime Function

The **strftime** function is the most flexible date and time function. The following program illustrates several formatting options:

```
/*
 *    A C program that demonstrates how to call the strftime
 *    function.
 *    Copyright (c) Chris H. Pappas and William H. Murray, 1990
 */

#include <time.h>
#include <stdio.h>

main()
{
  struct tm *date_time;
  time_t timer;
  char str[80];

  time(&timer);
  date_time=localtime(&timer);
  strftime(str,80,"It is %X on %A, %x",
           date_time);
  printf("%s\n",str);
  return (0);
}
```

The sample output for this program is

```
It is 13:16:35 on Monday, 01/29/90
```

The **strftime** function might not be portable from one system to another, so use it with caution if portability is a consideration.

Using the ctime Function

The following C++ program illustrates how to make a call to the **ctime** function. It shows how easy it is to obtain date and time information from the system.

```
//
//    A C++ program that demonstrates how to call the
//    ctime function.
//    Copyright (c) Chris H. Pappas and William H. Murray, 1990
//

#include <time.h>
#include <iostream.h>

time_t longtime;

main()
{
  time(&longtime);
  cout << "The time is " << ctime(&longtime) << "\n";

  return (0);
}
```

A typical output would appear in the following form:

```
The time is Mon Jan 29 13:16:42 1990
```

16

SYSTEM RESOURCES AND GRAPHICS

In the previous chapter, you learned about powerful C and C++ library functions that allow you to work with characters, strings, math functions, and so on. For the most part, these functions meet the ANSI standard and are portable from one C compiler to another and from one system to another. In other words, they are as close to a standard C as you can get.

Most compiler manufacturers also provide functions in their C libraries that are not as standardized. The standardization problem develops because of different operating systems and computer equipment. Borland's C and C++ provide functions that allow you to tap the software and hardware features of the system you are working on. Unfortunately, these system features usually make programs nonportable from one system to another and from one C compiler to another. They are obviously not part of the ANSI standard. However, since many programmers and users work on IBM-compatible computers under DOS with Borland C++, compatibility doesn't become a major problem. Why use functions like this at all? These functions allow you to tap the power of the computer's hardware and provide sound, control of printers, plotters, CD ROM drives, mice, and graphics capabilities.

Without the BIOS and DOS capabilities provided with C and C++, hardware control would be exclusively in the realm of assembly language programmers. With these built-in C and C++ functions, you can now write many programs without assembly language patches. In Chapters 17 and 18, you will see how assembly language can provide many of the same features for controlling system hardware. In Chapter 19, you will learn how to combine C code and assembly code to solve programming problems that you cannot handle with the simple functions described in this chapter.

The *bios.h, dos.h,* and *graphics.h* header files prototype several hundred functions. This section attempts to list each of these functions with a short description and the prototype information. However, it is beyond the scope of this book to illustrate each function; that task alone could fill another book. Instead, this chapter illustrates frequently used functions and functions that will give your programs the professional touch. You should print the three header files just mentioned to view the available definitions, macros, and function prototypes. Keep your library reference handy for a detailed description of each function.

THE BIOS HEADER FILE

The following seven functions allow immediate access to powerful BIOS (basic input and output services) built into IBM-compatible computers. These functions are very hardware dependent and may not operate on systems that are not 100 percent compatible with IBM equipment.

bioscom	Performs RS-232 serial communications
biosdisk	Issues disk operations through BIOS
biosequip	Checks system hardware
bioskey	Keyboard interface via BIOS
biosmemory	Returns RAM (640K max) size
biosprint	Performs printer I/O with BIOS
biostime	Sets or reads the BIOS timer

With the BIOS functions, disk control, RS-232 communications, memory size, and even timer control are possible. As you saw in the last chapter, other standard C and C++ functions also permit many of these operations. You should use ANSI functions when possible and avoid the problem of incompatibility with systems that don't permit you to use BIOS functions. At other times, the use of BIOS functions will be your only solution to the problem at hand.

BIOS Function Call Syntax

The syntax for each BIOS function is relatively simple, as you can see from the function prototypes included here. Again, for detailed information on the various arguments, consult the C library reference.

```
int bioscom(int cmd,char abyte,int port);

int biosdisk(int cmd,int drive,int head,int track,int sector,
             int nsects,void *buffer);

int biosequip(void);

int bioskey(int cmd);

int biosmemory(void);

int biosprint(int cmd,int abyte,int port);

long biostime(int cmd,long newtime);
```

The seven BIOS functions accept various arguments. The next two examples demonstrate how to use several of these functions. Use the previous listing in conjunction with your reference manual as a quick reference for the BIOS routines.

Checking Base Memory

The following C++ program uses the BIOS functions to check for base memory in a system. The range of memory can be between 0 and 640K. Making the function call is straightforward.

```
//
//   A C++ program that demonstrates how to use the biosmemory
//   function for obtaining the amount of installed RAM memory.
//   This value can vary from 0 to 640K bytes and does not
//   include extended or expanded memory.
//   Copyright (c) Chris H. Pappas and William H. Murray, 1990
//

#include <iostream.h>
#include <bios.h>

main()
{
  int base_memory;

  base_memory=biosmemory();
```

```
   cout << "There is " << base_memory
        << "K of base memory installed.";
   return (0);
}
```

The **biosmemory** function is limited to reporting memory in the range 0 to 640K and will not report on display, extended, or expanded memory. Currently, no function in the *run-time* library will allow you to determine this extra memory.

Checking for a Game Adapter

The following program allows a software program to check for the presence of a game adapter card in the system. If a game adapter is present, bit 12 of the value returned by the function will be high or logic 1. Otherwise, the bit is a zero, or logic 0. Binary bit 12, alone, produces the binary number 1000000000000_2. This is equivalent to the hexadecimal value 1000_{16}. An AND mask is created with this same value. Masks will be described in more detail in Chapter 17, "Assembly Language." The purpose of the mask is to isolate that single bit, examine it, and determine if it is 1 or 0.

```
/*
 *    A C++ program that demonstrates how to use the biosequip
 *    function for obtaining current hardware information.
 *    Copyright (c) Chris H. Pappas and William H. Murray, 1990
 */

#include <iostream.h>
#include <bios.h>

#define GAMEADP 0x1000

main()
{
  int online_equip;

  online_equip=biosequip();

  if (online_equip & GAMEADP)
    cout << "There is a game adapter present.\n";
  else
    cout << "There is no game adapter present.\n";
  return (0);
}
```

If the values returned by the BIOS function call and the mask produce a true condition, a game adapter is present. Otherwise, a game adapter is not available. Programs like this can help you determine which hardware items your program can use in a given system.

THE DOS HEADER FILE

The following DOS functions allow immediate access to powerful DOS interrupt capabilities built into IBM and 100 percent compatible computers. These functions are very hardware dependent and may not function properly on noncompatible machines. The DOS functions permit a broader range of operations than the previous BIOS functions, as you can see from this list:

absread	Reads specified disk sectors
abswrite	Writes to specified disk sectors
allocmem	Allocates memory segment
bdos	DOS system call
bdosptr	DOS system call, using pointer argument
ctrlbrk	Handler for CTRL-BREAK
delay	Suspends execution (in milliseconds)
disable	Disables system interrupts
dosexterr	Provides extended DOS error information
dostounix	Converts date/time to UNIX format
emit	Inserts literal values into code
enable	Permits hardware interrupts
freemem	Frees allocated memory segment
getcbrk	Gets CTRL-BREAK setting
getdate	Gets current system date
getdfree	Gets free disk space
getfat	Obtains FAT from given drive
getfatd	Obtains FAT of default drive
getpsp	Gets program segment prefix
gettime	Gets system time
getverify	Gets state of DOS verify flag
harderr	Creates hardware error handler
hardresume	Returns from hardware error handler

hardretn	Returns to program from **harderr**
inport	Reads a word from specified port
inportb	Reads a byte from specified port
int86	General hardware interrupt
int86x	General hardware interrupt with segment
intdos	DOS interrupt
intdosx	DOS interrupt with segment
intr	Alternate software interrupt
keep	Exits and remains resident
nosound	Turns speaker off
outport	Sends a word to given port
outportb	Sends a byte to given port
parsfnm	Parses file name
peek	Returns word from memory location
peekb	Returns byte from memory location
poke	Sends word to memory location
pokeb	Sends byte to memory location
randbrd	Reads a random block from file
randbwr	Writes a random block to file
segread	Reads segment registers
setblock	Modifies size of allocated block
setcbrk	Sets CTRL-BREAK setting
setdate	Sets system date
settime	Sets system time
setvect	Sets interrupt vector entry
setverify	Sets state of DOS verify flag
sleep	Suspends program execution (in milliseconds)
sound	Turns speaker on (frequency is Hertz)
unixtodos	Converts date/time to DOS format
unlink	Deletes the given file

Many of the DOS functions permit operations similar to the BIOS routines. For example, notice that there are several time and date functions, delay functions, disk I/O functions, and so on. DOS functions tend to be more robust. However, you should use the functions included in the ANSI C standard where possible if they achieve the same results for your program.

DOS Function Call Syntax

The syntax for each DOS function is as simple as that for the BIOS function calls. Examine the DOS function prototypes and notice the wide range of

services that they provide. For detailed information on the various DOS
function arguments, consult the library reference.

```
int absread(int drive,int nsects,int lsect,void *buffer);

int abswrite(int drive,int nsects,int lsect,void *buffer);

int allocmem(unsigned size,unsigned *segp);

int bdos(int dosfun,unsigned dosdx,unsigned dosal);

int bdosptr(int dosfun,void *argument,unsigned dosal);

struct country country(int xcode, struct country *cp);

void ctrlbrk(int (*handler)(void));

void delay(unsigned milliseconds);

void disable(void);

int dosexterr(struct DOSERROR *eblkp);

long dostounix(struct date *d,struct time *t);

void __emit__();

void enable(void);

int freemem(unsigned segx);

int getcbrk(void);

void getdate(struct date *datep);

void getdfree(unsigned char drive,struct dfree *dtable);

void getfat(unsigned char drive, struct fatinfo *dtable);

void getfatd(struct fatinfo *dtable);

unsigned getpsp(void);

void gettime(struct time *timep);

int getverify(void);

void harderr(int (*handler)());

void hardresume(int axret);

void hardretn(int retn);
```

```
int inport(int portid);

unsigned char inportb(int portid);

int int86(int intno,union REGS *inregs,union REGS *outregs);

int int86x(int intno,union REGS *inregs,union REGS *outregs,
        struct SREGS *segregs);

int intdos(union REGS *inregs,union REGS *outregs);

int intdosx(union REGS *inregs,union REGS *outregs,
        struct SREGS *segregs);

void intr(int intno,struct REGPACK *preg);

void keep(unsigned char status,unsigned size);

void nosound(void);

void outport(int portid,int value);

void outportb(int portid,unsigned char value);

char *parsfnm(const char *cmdline,struct fcb *fcb,int opt);

int peek(unsigned segment,unsigned offset);

char peekb(unsigned segment,unsigned offset);

void poke(unsigned segment,unsigned offset,int value);

void pokeb(unsigned segment,unsigned offset,char value);

int randbrd(struct fcb *fcb,int rcnt);

int randbwr(struct fcb *fcb,int rcnt);

void segread(struct SREGS *segp);

int setblock(unsigned segx,unsigned newsize);

int setcbrk(int cbrkvalue);

void setdate(struct date *datep);

void settime(struct time *timep);

void setvect(int interruptno,void interrupt (far *isr) ());

void setverify(int value);

void sleep(unsigned seconds);

void sound(unsigned frequency);
```

```
void unixtodos(long time,struct date *d,struct time *t);

int unlink(const char *path);
```

The following section illustrates several of the DOS functions. When a particular function call is not available, a general DOS interrupt will be used.

Slowing Down Program Output

Usually, you want your programs to execute as quickly as possible. However, sometimes slowing down information makes it easier for the user to view and understand. The **delay** function delays program execution in milliseconds. The following C program includes a one-second delay between each line of output to the screen:

```
/*
 *    A C program that demonstrates how to use the delay
 *    function for slowing program output.
 *    Copyright (c) Chris H. Pappas and William H. Murray, 1990
 */

#include <dos.h>
#include <stdio.h>

main()
{
  int i;

  for (i=0;i<25;i++) {
    delay(1000);
    printf("The count is %d\n",i);
  }
  return (0);
}
```

What other uses might the **delay** function have? Suppose your computer is connected to an external data sensing device, such as a thermocouple or strain gauge. You could use the **delay** function to permit samples every minute, hour, or day.

Examining Free Memory on a Disk

You learned how to read and write to the disk drive in Chapter 11, "Input and Output in C and C++." It is often a good idea to know how much free disk space is available before you make a write attempt. The **getdfree** function provides that information. The following C example reports to the user the available space on drive C:

```
/*
*    A C program that demonstrates how to use the getdfree
*    function for obtaining free disk space on drive C.
*    Copyright (c) Chris H. Pappas and William H. Murray, 1990
*/

#include <dos.h>
#include <stdio.h>

main()
{
  struct dfree df;
  long f_disk;

  getdfree(3,&df);
  f_disk=(long)df.df_avail*(long)df.df_bsec*(long)df.df_sclus;
  printf("Drive C has %ld bytes of memory for use.\n",f_disk);
  return (0);
}
```

Drive C is identified with the number 3 (A is 1 and B is 2). Data concerning memory are returned to the **dfree** structure. This structure holds information on the available clusters, total clusters, bytes per sector, and sectors per cluster. The preceding program combines that information to provide the total free disk space.

Using DOS Interrupt Functions

The DOS and BIOS functions provide a "hook" to many of the interrupts on the computer. When there is not a particular function for your needs, you can call a general interrupt function and supply the necessary parameters. The next C++ example does just that, issuing an interrupt 33h and making the mouse pointer (if a mouse is installed) visible for 1 minute:

```
//
//    A C++ program that demonstrates how to use the int86
//    function to show mouse pointer for 1 minute!
//    (Appendix B lists all possible mouse interrupts).
//    Copyright (c) Chris H. Pappas and William H. Murray, 1990
//

#include <dos.h>
```

```
main()
{
  union REGS regs;

  regs.x.ax=1;
  int86(0x33,&regs,&regs);

  delay(60000);

  regs.x.ax=0;
  int86(0x33,&regs,&regs);

  return (0);
}
```

If you examine the mouse interrupts in Appendix B, you can detect mouse button clicks and coordinate positions using this function. This program simply switched the default pointer on and off. While the pointer is on, you can move the mouse around on the screen.

This program also uses the *REGS* union, described in the *dos.h* header file. Using this union, the user has access to the **ax, bx, cx, dx, bp, si, di, ds, es,** and **flag** registers of the system. Examine the prototype of this function, shown earlier in the chapter. Notice that register information can be set and passed into the microprocessor registers with *inregs*. Likewise, the function can return the contents of the system registers through the union *outregs*. For 16-bit registers, use *reg.x* and for 8-bit registers use *reg.h*. The syntax is

```
regs.x.ax = (desired value), for 16-bit registers
regs.h.bl = (desired value), for 8-bit registers
```

The Dimension of Sound

Most small computers have poor quality sound reproduction facilities. Nevertheless, sound plays an important role in communicating information to the computer user. Various pitched notes can warn the user of an error or tell them to enter data in a spreadsheet. When you combine sound with graphics, you can get into the realm of computer games.

This simple C++ program demonstrates how to create a simple sound that increases in pitch over a short period of time:

```
//
//   A C++ program that demonstrates how to use the sound
//   function to produce a unique musical sound from the
//   system's speaker.
```

```
//    Copyright (c) Chris H. Pappas and William H. Murray, 1990
//

#include <dos.h>

main()
{

  unsigned frequency=0;
  int i;

  for (i=0;i<2500;i++) {
    sound(frequency);
    delay(5);
    frequency++;
  }

  nosound();
  return (0);
}
```

This program starts with a frequency of 0 hertz and increases to 2500 hertz. A 5-millisecond delay is introduced to slow the overall action just a bit. Can you think of a way to make the tone start at a high frequency and drop to a low frequency? If you are creative, you can have a lot of fun tinkering with the sound function.

THE GRAPHICS HEADER FILE

Borland's C and C++ provide an extensive set of graphics routines. The prototypes for the graphics functions are in *graphics.h.* These graphics functions contain *primitives* for drawing pixels, lines, rectangles, arcs, circles, and ellipses. (They are called primitives because they only draw a basic shape.) More advanced graphics functions include routines for drawing two- and three-dimensional bars and pie slices. Additional graphics functions allow the user to set the graphics mode, select the viewport, size the image, fill objects with colors and patterns, and so on. The *viewport* refers to that portion of the screen that is currently active. By default, the size of the viewport and the screen are identical.

Examine this extensive list of graphics functions:

arc	Draws a circular arc
bar	Draws a two-dimensional bar

bar3d	Draws a three-dimensional bar
circle	Draws a circle
cleardevice	Clears the graphics screen
clearviewport	Clears the current viewport
closegraph	Closes the graphics system
detectgraph	Determines driver and mode from hardware
drawpoly	Draws a polygon outline
ellipse	Draws an elliptical arc
fillellipse	Draws and fills an ellipse
fillpoly	Draws and fills a polygon
floodfill	Flood-fills a bound region
getarccoords	Gets coordinates of last call to arc
getaspectratio	Gets aspect ratio for current mode
getbkcolor	Returns current background color
getcolor	Gets the current drawing color
getdefaultpalette	Gets the palette definition structure
getdrivername	Points to string with current graphics driver
getfillpattern	Copies user fill pattern to memory
getfillsettings	Gets info on current fill pattern and color
getgraphmode	Returns the current graphics mode
getimage	Saves specified image to memory
getlinesettings	Gets line style, pattern, and thickness
getmaxcolor	Returns max value that can be sent to setcolor
getmaxmode	Returns max value for mode for current driver
getmaxx	Returns max x screen coordinate (in pixels)
getmaxy	Returns max y screen coordinate (in pixels)
getmodename	Returns pointer to string with graphics mode
getmoderange	Returns range of modes for current driver
getpalette	Returns information on current palette
getpalettesize	Gets size of palette color lookup table
getpixel	Gets the color of the specified pixel
gettextsettings	Returns current graphics text font information
getviewsettings	Returns current graphics viewport settings
getx	Gives current x position on screen
gety	Returns current y position on screen
graphdefaults	Resets all graphics to default values
grapherrormsg	Returns pointer to error message string
_graphfreemem	Gives hook to graphics memory deallocation
_graphgetmem	Gives hook to graphics memory allocation
graphresult	Returns error code for last failed operation
imagesize	Returns number of bytes needed to store an image

initgraph	Initializes the graphics system
installuserdriver	Installs a vendor supplied driver
installuserfont	Installs a user supplied font
line	Draws a line
linerel	Draws a line a given distance from a point
lineto	Draws a line from current to specified point
moverel	Moves the current position a given distance
moveto	Moves the current position to a given point
outtext	Displays a string to the viewport
outtextxy	Displays a string to the given position
pieslice	Draws and fills a pie slice
putimage	Outputs a bit image to the screen
putpixel	Plots a pixel at a given point
rectangle	Draws a rectangle
registerbgidriver	Registers a user's driver code to system
registerbgifont	Registers linked stroked font code
restorecrtmode	Returns screen to pregraphics mode
sector	Draws and fills an elliptical pie slice
setactivepage	Sets active page for graphics output
setallpalette	Changes all palette colors as specified
setaspectratio	Changes default aspect ratio
setbkcolor	Changes the background color
setcolor	Changes the default drawing color
setfillpattern	Changes the fill pattern
setfillstyle	Changes the fill style
setgraphbufsize	Changes size of graphics buffer
setgraphmode	Sets the graphics mode and clears screen
setlinestyle	Sets line width and style
setpalette	Changes one palette color
setrgbpalette	Defines colors for IBM 8514 display
settextjustify	Sets text justification for graphics
settextstyle	Sets text characteristics for graphics
setusercharsize	Sets width and height of stroked fonts
setviewport	Sets the viewport size
setvisualpage	Sets the visual page number
setwritemode	Sets writing mode for line drawing
textheight	Returns the height of a string in pixels
textwidth	Returns the width of a string in pixels

With this group of functions, you can obtain professional graphics results. Indeed, you can draw and label presentation-quality bar, pie, and line charts.

Graphics Function Call Syntax

The syntax for each graphics function just involves formulating and passing the required arguments. Examine the prototypes for each of the graphics functions; notice that many arguments are self-explanatory. You can find detailed information for others in the library reference.

```
void far arc(int x,int y,int stangle,int endangle,
          int radius);

void far bar(int left,int top,int right,int bottom);

void far bar3d(int left,int top,int right,int bottom,
          int depth, int topflag);

void far circle(int x,int y,int radius);

void far cleardevice(void);

void far clearviewport(void);

void far closegraph(void);

void far detectgraph(int far *graphdriver,int far
                *graphmode);

void far drawpoly(int numpoints,int far *polypoints);

void far ellipse(int x,int y,int stangle,int endangle,
          int xradius,int yradius);

void far fillellipse(int x,int y,int xradius,int yradius);

void far fillpoly(int numpoints,int far *polypoints);

void far floodfill(int x,int y,int border);

void far getarccoords(struct arccoordstype far *arccoords);

void far getaspectratio(int far *xasp,int far *yasp);

int far getbkcolor(void);

int far getcolor(void);

struct palettetype *far getdefaultpalette(void);

char *far getdrivername(void);

void far getfillpattern(char far *pattern);

void far getfillsettings(struct fillsettingstype far
                *fillinfo);
```

```
int far getgraphmode(void);

void far getimage(int left,int top,int right,int bottom,
                  void far *bitmap);

void far getlinesettings(struct linesettingstype far
                         *lineinfo);

int far getmaxcolor(void);

int far getmaxmode(void);

int far getmaxx(void);

int far getmaxy(void);

char * far getmodename(int mode_number);

void far getmoderange(int graphdriver,int far *lomode,
                      int far *himode);

void far getpalette(struct palettetype far *palette);

int far getpalettesize(void);

unsigned far getpixel(int x,int y);

void far gettextsettings(struct textsettingstype far
                         *texttypeinfo);

void far getviewsettings(struct viewporttype far *viewport);

int far getx(void);

int far gety(void);

void far graphdefaults(void);

char * far grapherrormsg(int errorcode);

void far _graphfreemem(void far *ptr,unsigned size);

void far * far _graphgetmem(unsigned size);

int far graphresult(void);

unsigned far imagesize(int left,int top,int right,int
                       bottom);

void far initgraph(int far *graphdriver,
                   int far *graphmode,
                   char far *pathtodriver);

int far installuserdriver(char far *name,int huge
                          (*detect)(void) );
```

```
int far installuserfont(char far *name);

void far line(int xl,int yl,int x2,int y2);

void far linerel(int dx,int dy);

void far lineto(int x,int y);

void far moverel(int dx,int dy);

void far moveto(int x,int y);

void far outtext(char far *textstring);

void far outtextxy(int x,int y,char far *textstring);

void far pieslice(int x,int y,int stangle,int endangle,
                  int radius);

void far putimage(int left,int top,void far *bitmap,int
                  op);

void far putpixel(int x,int y,int color);

void far rectangle(int left,int top,int right,int bottom);

int registerbgidriver(void(*driver)(void));

int registerbgifont(void (*font)(void));

void far restorecrtmode(void);

void far sector(int X,int Y,int StAngle,int EndAngle,
                int XRadius,int YRadius);

void far setactivepage(int page);

void far setallpalette(struct palettetype far *palette);

void far setaspectratio(int xasp,int yasp);

void far setbkcolor(int color);

void far setcolor(int color);

void far setfillpattern(char far *upattern,int color);

void far setfillstyle(int pattern,int color);

unsigned far setgraphbufsize(unsigned bufsize);

void far setgraphmode(int mode);

void far setlinestyle(int linestyle, unsigned upattern,
                      int thickness);
```

```
void far setpalette(int colornum,int color);

void far setrgbpalette(int colornum,
                       int red,int green,int blue);

void far settextjustify(int horiz,int vert);

void far settextstyle(int font,int direction,int charsize);

void far setusercharsize(int multx,int divx,
                         int multy,int divy);

void far setviewport(int left,int top,int right,int
                     bottom,int clip);

void far setvisualpage(int page);

void far setwritemode(int mode);

int far textheight(char far *textstring);

int far textwidth(char far *textstring);
```

Many of these functions will be illustrated in the next sections. You can
use an almost intuitive approach when supplying argument values to the
various functions, but you should always have your library reference
handy. In most cases, you need nothing more than the preceding function
prototypes to use your system's graphics capabilities.

Getting Started with Graphics

The graphics environment is very hardware dependent. In fact, most of
Borland C++'s graphics functions will only operate on IBM or compatible
computers. Even so, you can use many different video cards and monitors
with these systems. If you are writing code for your equipment only, you
can write in a more relaxed and less portable manner. However, if your
code is to be transported between various video cards and monitors, you
must be able to detect what hardware is installed in the system. The first
example in this section reports back to you information on the adapter
card, video mode, drawing and background colors, and the 16 VGA/EGA
drawing colors. The second program was written exclusively for the VGA
environment (one with screen dimensions of 640×480 pixels). This program
demonstrates many of the graphics primitives with the simplest possible
calling sequence. You can easily adapt it to an EGA or CGA screen.

When using graphics, you first need to get the system into graphics mode. This book uses a technique employed by Borland, in many of their examples, for making the switch. While other approaches are possible, this is also the method we prefer and use in the next four examples.

You also need to attach the graphics library to your program code. If you forget, you will be bombarded with error messages stating that the various functions cannot be found. If the graphics library resides in the default directory, you can enter the following command-line statement:

```
bcc program_name.exe graphics.lib
```

Determining Installed Equipment and Modes

The following program uses 18 graphics functions to provide information concerning the graphics environment. These functions include **initgraph, graphresult, grapherrormsg, setbkcolor, setcolor, getmaxx, getmaxy, outtextxy, getaspectratio, getmodename, getbkcolor, getcolor, getpalettesize, setfillstyle, bar, moveto, outtext,** and **closegraph.**

```
/*
 *    A C program that demonstrates how to use several
 *    graphics routines for obtaining information
 *    concerning hardware parameters.
 *    Also draws sample of VGA/EGA default palette.
 *    Copyright (c) Chris H. Pappas and William H. Murray, 1990
 */

#include <graphics.h>
#include <stdio.h>
#include <stdlib.h>
#include <process.h>
#include <conio.h>

main()
{
  char s1[10],s2[10];
  char mcol[5];
  char dcolor[10],bkcolor[10];
  char *drivername;
  char colorlog[16][15]={"Black",
                         "Blue",
                         "Green",
                         "Cyan",
                         "Red",
                         "Magenta",
                         "Brown",
                         "Light Gray",
                         "Dark Gray",
```

```
                              "Light Blue",
                              "Light Green",
                              "Light Cyan",
                              "Light Red",
                              "Light Magenta",
                              "Yellow",
                              "White"};
    int gdriver=DETECT,gmode,errorcode;
    int xasp,yasp,maxx,maxy,psize,i,deltay,deltax;
    double ratio;

    initgraph(&gdriver,&gmode,"");

    errorcode=graphresult();
    if (errorcode != grOk) {
      printf("Graphics Function Error: %s\n",
             grapherrormsg(errorcode));
      printf("Hit key to stop:");
      getch();
      exit(1);
    }

    setbkcolor(BLACK);
    setcolor(WHITE);

    maxx=getmaxx();
    maxy=getmaxy();

    deltay=maxy/24;
    deltax=maxx/2;

    /* print graphics driver name */
    outtextxy(0,deltay,"Graphics Driver:");
    outtextxy(deltax,deltay,getdrivername());

    /* determine aspect ratio */
    getaspectratio(&xasp,&yasp);
    itoa(xasp,s1,10);
    itoa(yasp,s2,10);
    outtextxy(0,deltay*2,"Aspect Ratio (x:y):");
    outtextxy(deltax,deltay*2,s1);
    outtextxy(deltax+50,deltay*2,s2);

    /* get graphics mode */
    outtextxy(0,deltay*3,"The video mode is:");
    outtextxy(deltax,deltay*3,getmodename(gmode));

    /* determine current background color */
    outtextxy(0,deltay*4,"The present background color:");
    outtextxy(deltax,deltay*4,colorlog[getbkcolor()]);

    /* determine current drawing color */
    outtextxy(0,deltay*5,"The present drawing color:");
    outtextxy(deltax,deltay*5,colorlog[getcolor()]);
```

```
psize=getpalettesize();
itoa(psize,mcol,10);
outtextxy(0,deltay*6,"Max. drawing colors:");
outtextxy(deltax,deltay*6,mcol);
outtextxy(0,deltay*7,"VGA/EGA 16 color palette:");
for (i=0;i<16;i++) {
  setfillstyle(SOLID_FILL,i);
  bar(deltax,deltay*(i+7),deltax+10,deltay*(i+7)+10);
  moveto(deltax+15,deltay*(i+7));
  outtext(colorlog[i]);
}

getch();
closegraph();

return (0);
}
```

The **initgraph** function is passed arguments that will automatically detect the adapter card and set the video mode to the highest mode possible
for the hardware. This is done by passing DETECT to the graphics driver
argument. This system is automatically placed on the 640×480 VGA mode
with 16 drawing colors. If this function call fails, an error code can be
intercepted and reported to the user with the **graphresult** function. As
mentioned, Borland uses this technique in their examples and this chapter
does as well.

Now step through the remainder of the program, examining each function call along the way. When you compare the function call with the
function prototype given in the earlier graphics section, notice that the
argument values are fairly easy to understand without another reference.
Enter this program and give it a try. Don't forget to link the graphics library
to your program. Tinker with the various function calls and see what you
can learn. You will be impressed with the information that you can obtain
with simple graphics function calls in this program. A typical screen output
is shown in Figure 16-1.

Using Various Graphics Primitives

The following program uses several new graphics functions. These functions include **circle, bar3d, ellipse, pieslice, sector,** and **settextstyle.** This
program will demonstrate how to use the various graphics primitives in the

```
Graphics Driver:                    EGAUGA
Aspect Ratio (x:y):                 10000 10000
The video mode is:                  640 x 480 UGA
The present background color:       Black
The present drawing color:          White
Max. drawing colors:                16
UGA/EGA 16 color palette:              Black
                                    ■ Blue
                                    ≡ Green
                                    ╱ Cyan
                                    ╱ Red
                                    ╲ Magenta
                                    ╲ Brown
                                    ╫ Light Gray
                                    ╳ Dark Gray
                                    ▦ Light Blue
                                    ⋮ Light Green
                                    ▒ Light Cyan
                                    ▒ Light Red
                                    ▒ Light Magenta
                                    ▒ Yellow
                                    ▒ White
```

Figure 16-1.   Current system graphics parameters with VGA/EGA 16-color palette

simplest possible manner. Notice the use of enumerated types for the colors, fill modes, and text styles.

```
/*
 *    A C program that demonstrates how to use several
 *    graphics primitives on the VGA screen.
 *    Copyright (c) Chris H. Pappas and William H. Murray, 1990
 */

#include <graphics.h>
#include <stdio.h>
#include <stdlib.h>
#include <process.h>
#include <conio.h>

main()
{
  int gdriver=DETECT,gmode,errorcode;
  int midx,midy;

  initgraph(&gdriver,&gmode,"");
```

```
errorcode=graphresult();
if (errorcode != grOk) {
  printf("Graphics Function Error: %s\n",
          grapherrormsg(errorcode));
  printf("Hit key to stop:");
  getch();
  exit(1);
}

setbkcolor(BLACK);

/* draw a small circle */
setcolor(BLUE);
circle(50,50,40);

/* draw a two-dimensional bar, outline & fill */
setcolor(GREEN);
setfillstyle(SOLID_FILL,GREEN);
bar(100,10,150,90);

/* draw a three-dimensional bar, outline & fill */
setcolor(CYAN);
setfillstyle(LINE_FILL,CYAN);
bar3d(200,20,250,90,15,1);

/* draw an ellipse */
setcolor(RED);
ellipse(400,50,0,360,70,40);

/* draw an ellipse, outline & fill */
setcolor(MAGENTA);

setfillstyle(SLASH_FILL,MAGENTA);
fillellipse(50,200,40,70);

/* draw a pie slice, outline & fill */
setcolor(BROWN);
setfillstyle(HATCH_FILL,BROWN);
pieslice(150,200,0,45,100);

/* draw an elliptical pie slice, outline & fill */
setcolor(LIGHTGRAY);
setfillstyle(WIDE_DOT_FILL,LIGHTGRAY);
sector(350,200,0,135,75,50);

/* print some fancy text */
settextstyle(DEFAULT_FONT,HORIZ_DIR,3);
outtextxy(50,400,"Now this is fancy!");

getch();
closegraph();

return (0);
}
```

Your library reference contains the full list of color, fill styles, and fonts. The arguments used in this example are entered directly as numeric values. This is usually the easiest way to implement any graphics command, and also the most restrictive. The technique is restrictive because the argument values are set for one video mode only. For example, the function **outtextxy** uses the VGA screen coordinate values (50,400). If used on a CGA or EGA screen, the vertical position exceeds the maximum value for either screen. A better approach is to detect the video mode and scale the graphics to that screen. Of course, this approach also requires much more programming, as you will see in the next two examples. This example produces a VGA screen, shown in Figure 16-2.

Toward More Advanced Graphics

Graphics are a way of communicating ideas and concepts in a pictorial format. Depending on your area of interest, you may want to express information in the form of bar, pie, or line charts. If you have a scientific or

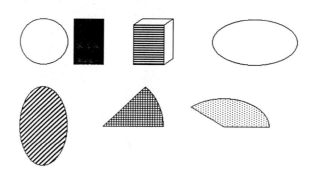

Figure 16-2.   Graphics primitives and fonts coming to life

engineering background, you might be more interested in plotting a mathematical, scientific, or engineering equation. The two examples in this section do just that. The first example will plot a damped sine wave. This is a simple mathematical equation that involves the trigonometric sine function multiplied by the natural number (e) raised to a power. The plot of this function is similar to the physical representation of an oscillating spring or auto shock absorber. The second example will show you how to create a presentation-quality pie chart. This program will allow a user to enter data on the various pie slices, scale them to size, and plot them correctly on an EGA or VGA screen.

Plotting a Damped Sine Wave

The only new graphics function in this example is **lineto**. This function connects the various points generated by the mathematical equation.

```
/*
 *    A C program that demonstrates how to correctly draw a
 *    damped sine wave on either an EGA or VGA screen.
 *    Copyright (c) Chris H. Pappas and William H. Murray, 1990
 */

#include <graphics.h>
#include <conio.h>
#include <process.h>
#include <math.h>

main()
{
   int gdriver=DETECT,gmode,errorcode;
   int midy,maxx,i,y;

   initgraph(&gdriver,&gmode,"");

   errorcode=graphresult();
   if (errorcode != grOk) {
     printf("Graphics Function Error: %s\n",
            grapherrormsg(errorcode));
     printf("Hit key to stop:");
     getch();
     exit(1);
   }

   setbkcolor(BLUE);
   setcolor(WHITE);

   /* get maximum x & y coordinate values for mode */
```

```
maxx=getmaxx();
midy=getmaxy()/2;

/* draw several cycles of a damped sine wave */
moveto(0,midy);
for (i=0;i<maxx;i++) {
  y=midy-((exp(-.007*i))*midy*sin(2*M_PI*i*5/360));
  lineto(i,y);
}

/* draw horizontal axis */
setcolor(YELLOW);
moveto(maxx,midy);
lineto(0,midy);

getch();
closegraph();
return (0);
}
```

In this example, the **getmaxx** and **getmaxy** functions find the maximum x and y coordinate values for the current screen. For this particular hardware, x is 639 and y is 479. This might be different for your equipment. Since the wave form is plotted above and below the horizontal axis, the value returned by **getmaxy** is divided by two. The mathematical equation is scaled to fit the current screen.

```
y=midy-((exp(-.007*i))*midy*sin(2*M_PI*i*5/360));
```

The variable *midy* serves as the midpoint of the graph and the maximum value that the sine wave can reach. Several complete sine wave cycles are plotted by converting the angles to radians (2*M_PI/360), multiplying them by the constant 5 and the current pixel position *i*. For each increasing value of *i*, the amplitude of the wave form decreases according to the exponential decay expressed by:

```
exp(-.007*i)
```

Even if you don't understand the mathematics, you can appreciate the graphic results, shown in Figure 16-3.

A Presentation-Quality Pie Chart Program

The next program will allow the user to specify between one and ten pie slice sizes. A complete pie chart will be scaled and plotted. The colors of

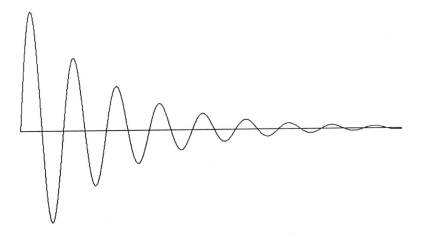

Figure 16-3.   A damped sine wave

adjacent slices will change sequentially through the list of EGA and VGA colors. A legend relating colors and pie slice labels is also available.

This example uses many of the graphics functions demonstrated earlier. In fact, only **pieslice** and **settextjustify** are new. The complete listing is as follows:

```
/*
 *    A C program that demonstrates how to produce a
 *    presentation quality pie chart for EGAHI or VGAHI screens.
 *    Copyright (c) Chris H. Pappas and William H. Murray, 1990
 */

#include <graphics.h>
#include <conio.h>
#include <process.h>
#include <stdlib.h>

#define MAXWEDGE 10

main()
{
    char s1[10];
    char leg[10][50];
    char label1[50],label2[50];
    int gdriver=DETECT,gmode,errorcode;
```

```
int nwedges,midx,midy,i;
double totalwedge,temp;
double startangle,endangle;
double wedgesize[MAXWEDGE],wedgeangle[MAXWEDGE];

printf("THIS PROGRAM WILL DRAW A PIE CHART.\n\n");
printf("Chart titles are optional.\n");
printf("Enter top of chart label.\n");
gets(label1);
printf("Enter bottom of chart label.\n");
gets(label2);
printf("\n\n");

printf("Enter up to 10 values for the pie wedges.\n");
printf("Values are followed by a carriage return.\n");
printf("No value and carriage return ends input.\n");

nwedges=0;
for (i=0;i<MAXWEDGE;i++) {
  printf("wedge value #%d ",i+1);
  gets(s1);
  if (strlen(s1) == 0) break;
  wedgesize[i]=atof(s1);
  nwedges++;
  printf("legion label: ");
  gets(leg[i]);
}

totalwedge=0.0;
for (i=0;i<nwedges;i++)
  totalwedge+=wedgesize[i];

for (i=0;i<nwedges;i++)
  wedgeangle[i]=(wedgesize[i]*360.0)/totalwedge;

initgraph(&gdriver,&gmode,"");

errorcode=graphresult();
if (errorcode != grOk) {
  printf("Graphics Function Error: %s\n",
         grapherrormsg(errorcode));
  printf("Hit key to stop:");
  getch();
  exit(1);
}

/* get maximum x & y coordinate values for mode */
midx=getmaxx()/2;
midy=getmaxy()/2;

startangle=0.0;
endangle=wedgeangle[0];
for (i=0;i<nwedges;i++) {
  setcolor(BLACK);
  setfillstyle(SOLID_FILL,BLUE+i);
  pieslice(midx/2,midy,(int)startangle,(int)endangle,midy/2);
```

```
     startangle+=wedgeangle[i];
     endangle+=wedgeangle[i+1];
  }

  /* print legend names and colors */
  setcolor(WHITE);
  moveto(midx+100,midy-80);
  outtext("Legend");
  for (i=0;i<nwedges;i++) {
     setfillstyle(SOLID_FILL,BLUE+i);
     bar(midx+100,(midy-50)+10*i,midx+110,(midy-40)+10*i);
     moveto(midx+120,(midy-48)+10*i);
     outtext(leg[i]);
  }

  /* print optional pie chart labels */
  setcolor(WHITE);
  settextjustify(CENTER_TEXT,CENTER_TEXT);
  moveto(midx/2,midy+150);
  outtext(label2);
  settextstyle(0,0,2);
  moveto(midx,midy-150);
  outtext(label1);

  getch();
  closegraph();
  return (0);
}
```

The program allows you to enter values for a number of pie slices. For example, if the pie chart is to have three slices, you might enter the numbers 30, 10, and 20. Data is entered with the following portion of code:

```
nwedges=0;
for (i=0;i<MAXWEDGE;i++) {
  printf("wedge value #%d ",i+1);
  gets(s1);
  if (strlen(s1) == 0) break;
  wedgesize[i]=atof(s1);
  nwedges++;
  printf("legion label: ");
  gets(leg[i]);
}
```

Input is terminated when you enter a carriage return without data. The number of pie slices is determined by the number of loops that are made in the previous code. Thus, *nwedges* will hold the correct count of pie slices. For the example, a 3 would be stored in *nwedges*. The numbers must be scaled, since, regardless of the number of slices or their values, the number of pic slices must fill a 360-degree pie. To do this, you must determine a total for the entered data.

```
totalwedge=0.0;
for (i=0;i<nwedges;i++)
  totalwedge+=wedgesize[i];
```

For the example, the total would be 30 + 10 + 20 = 60. Therefore, a 60.0 would be stored in *totalwedge*. Now, each wedge is scaled so that it takes a proportional amount of 360 degrees.

```
for (i=0;i<nwedges;i++)
  wedgeangle[i]=(wedgesize[i]*360.0)/totalwedge;
```

For the first slice of 30, *wedgeangle[0]* will be 180 degrees. For *wedgeangle[1]*, the angle will be 60 degrees and, finally, for *wedgeangle[2]*, the angle will be 120 degrees. Now, 180 + 60 + 120 adds up to the required 360 degrees, or one whole pie. These values will serve as the arc size for each pie slice.

In the complete listing shown earlier, notice that the initialization of the graphics mode is done in the same manner as previous examples. You can use this code as a template for your graphics work. The pie chart is plotted with the following portion of code:

```
startangle=0.0;
endangle=wedgeangle[0];
for (i=0;i<nwedges;i++) {
  setcolor(BLACK);
  setfillstyle(SOLID_FILL,BLUE+i);
  pieslice(midx/2,midy,(int)startangle,(int)endangle,midy/2);
  startangle+=wedgeangle[i];
  endangle+=wedgeangle[i+1];
}
```

The first pie slice is drawn, starting at angle 0 and plotting in the counterclockwise direction 180 degrees. The starting angle is given by *startangle* and the end of the pie arc by *endangle*. The *endangle* value for the first pie wedge is 180. The pie slices are drawn in black, but filled with an indexed color and solid pattern. The first slice is blue. After the first slice is drawn, the *startangle* value is set to the *endangle* value of the previous slice. The remaining slices are drawn in a similar manner.

The legend and chart titles are drawn last. Examine the complete program and see how these items are placed. Notice in particular that the text

Figure 16-4.   A simple pie chart

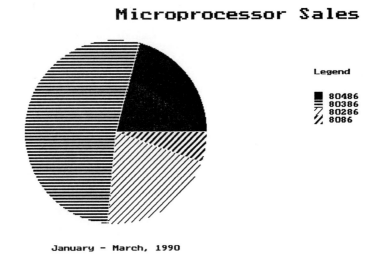

Figure 16-5.   A pie chart with title, legend, labels, and subtitle

for main labels is centered with the **settextjustify** function. Figures 16-4 and 16-5 show two variations on the pie chart that you can produce with this program.

17

ASSEMBLY LANGUAGE

This chapter concentrates on teaching assembly language program syntax by developing numerous programming examples. The examples are simple but complete programs designed to teach individual commands or special techniques. For example, the first part of the chapter focuses on computer arithmetic. All programmers must know how to add, subtract, multiply, and divide. Another section deals with lookup tables. You learn how to create and use a simple lookup table for performing mathematical operations that are not available in the Intel instruction set. The final section teaches you how to tap into the powerful system resources that your computer has built into its BIOS and DOS routines. By using interrupts, you will learn how to control the keyboard, screen, and speaker port. These interrupts are explained in the various IBM technical reference manuals for each computer.

The programs in this chapter have been designed to teach you elementary assembly language programming concepts. All of the necessary program overhead has been included with each assembly language example. Every program is complete in itself; if you enter, assemble, and link an example, it will work. Many of the programs in this chapter use the power of the Debugger. Each program is brief and uncomplicated.

ARITHMETIC PROGRAMS

This section presents several arithmetic assembly language examples. These include the basic arithmetic operators such as addition, subtraction, multiplication, and division. The programs are developed using several different programming modes. One example examines a simple algorithm for determining the square root of a hexadecimal integer. Unless otherwise mentioned, all assembly language arithmetic is done in hexadecimal format. You should buy a calculator that can convert numbers from one base (radix) to another to aid in program debugging.

Hexadecimal Addition with Immediate Addressing

Addition is one of the most basic mathematical operations. This first example illustrates hexadecimal addition using the immediate addressing mode. The program code is called *straight-line* programming since the program is executed line by line until the whole program is completed. Straight-line programming is simple but not always efficient.

```
;TURBO Assembly Language Programming Application
;Copyright (c) Chris H. Pappas and William H. Murray, 1990

;program to illustrate simple hexadecimal addition with
;immediate addressing

        DOSSEG                  ;use Intel segment-ordering
        .MODEL  small           ;set model size
        .8086                   ;8086 instructions

        .STACK  300h            ;set up 768-byte stack

        .CODE
Turbo   PROC    FAR             ;main procedure declaration

;addition of three numbers using immediate addressing
        mov     ax,01BCh        ;put hex number 1BC into ax
        add     ax,78h          ;add to ax the number 78h
        add     ax,78           ;add to ax the number 4Eh

        mov     ah,4Ch          ;return control to DOS
        int     21h
Turbo   ENDP                    ;end main procedure
        END                     ;end whole program
```

Notice that there are only three lines of actual program code in addition to the program overhead. These three lines are called the *body* of the program. Examine the overall structure of the program. It starts with four lines of comments that briefly describe the program's function. Placing comments at the start of a program not only informs other users of the program's purpose but also reminds you what the program does. Remember, you can place comments in any of the four fields as long as you start the comments with a semicolon. The pseudo-ops DOSSEG, .MODEL small, .8086, .STACK, .CODE, and PROC inform the Assembler how to assemble your program code. These commands don't appear in the operating version of your program and are only used to communicate with the Turbo Assembler (TASM). Of the four program segments commonly found in assembly language programs, this program uses only a .STACK and .CODE segment directive. This example did not use any separately stored data, so you do not need to establish a data segment. Every code segment (.CODE) must have at least one procedure. The procedure for this example is called Turbo. The following lines of code make up the heart of the hexadecimal addition program:

```
mov    ax,01BCh    ;put hex number 1BC into ax
add    ax,78h      ;add to ax the number 78h
add    ax,78       ;add to ax the number 4Eh
```

In this example, the hexadecimal number (01BCh) is moved to the **ax** register. Recall that the **ax** register is a 16-bit register. This means that **ax** can hold hexadecimal numbers from 0000h to 0FFFFh. The mov command is one of the most frequently encountered commands in 80486/8088 programming since it enables you to load or save information. The next operand adds the number 78h to the current contents of the **ax** register. The **ax** register will now contain 234h. Another **add** instruction adds a 78, specified in decimal, or 4Eh to **ax**, giving the final sum of 282h. You can observe this process by watching the **ax** register, as you single-step through the program with the Debugger. Figure 17-1 shows the Debugger screen, and the final value in the **ax** register. (If your screen appears different, use the Module option in the View menu to load the source code. Single step through your program until you see the first mov command. At this point close the CPU window and zoom the source module. You can now watch the trace while viewing the source code.)

Recall that during the assembly you must use the command-line argument, -zi, to obtain debugging information. Also, use the /v command-line argument during the link process.

This program has a number of subtle limitations. First, it does not take into account overflow if the sum in **ax** exceeds 0FFFFh. Second, the program does not allow for the addition of numbers greater than 0FFFFh.

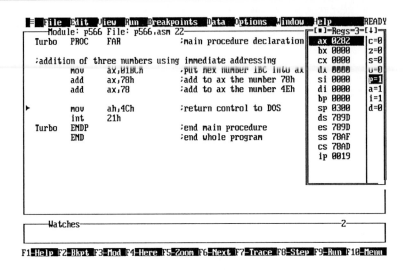

Figure 17-1.   Illustration of a simple hexadecimal addition program with the Debugger's Register window opened

Third, what would happen to the program's length if there were 2000 numbers to add? Fourth, if the numbers to be added change, you must return to the code segment and change each program line to accommodate the change. Even with these shortcomings, this program illustrates a very popular technique for adding several numbers. However, good programmers always understand the limitations of their programs.

Hexadecimal Subtraction with Direct Addressing

In assembly language, subtraction is just as easy as addition. In the last example, the immediate addressing mode dictated that the numbers to be added were immediately entered into the individual registers. In the next example, the numbers will first be assigned variable names, in a separate data segment, and then subtracted via direct addressing techniques. This program will also use 16-bit registers. The 16-bit register is the maximum register size in the 80286/8088 chip family. Recall that 80486 and 80386 machines allow 32-bit general registers.

```
;TURBO Assembly Language Programming Application
;Copyright (c) Chris H. Pappas and William H. Murray, 1990

;program to perform hexadecimal subtraction with
;direct addressing

        DOSSEG                    ;use Intel segment-ordering
        .MODEL   small            ;set model size
        .8086                     ;8086 instructions

        .STACK   300h             ;set up 768-byte stack

        .DATA                     ;set up data location
num1    dw       7823             ;1st number, 1E8Fh
num2    dw       45h              ;2nd number, 0045h
num3    dw       0BCh             ;3rd number, 00BCh
ans     dw       ?

        .CODE
Turbo   PROC     FAR              ;main procedure declaration
        mov      ax,DGROUP        ;point ds toward .DATA
        mov      ds,ax

;actual subtraction using three 16-bit numbers
        mov      ax,num1          ;place num1 in ax register
        sub      ax,num2          ;subtract num2 from ax
        sub      ax,num3          ;subtract num3 from ax
        mov      ans,ax           ;save ax in variable

        mov      ah,4Ch           ;return control to DOS
        int      21h

Turbo   ENDP                      ;end main procedure
        END                       ;end whole program
```

This program introduces a number of new features. For example, this is the first time that a program has used a separate data segment.

```
num1    dw       7823             ;1st number, 1E8Fh
num2    dw       45h              ;2nd number, 0045h
num3    dw       0BCh             ;3rd number, 00BCh
ans     dw       ?
```

This segment declares four variables. The variables *num1*, *num2*, and *num3* contain three numbers to be used in the subtraction example. Each variable is declared as a defined word (dw). The numbers 7823, 45h, and 0BCh will be padded by the Assembler to 16 bits. You can think of these numbers being stored in memory as 1E8Fh, 0045h, and 00BCh. The fourth variable, *ans,* is declared but not initialized to any value, so the entry is a ?. The ? reserves 16 bits of storage for the answer.

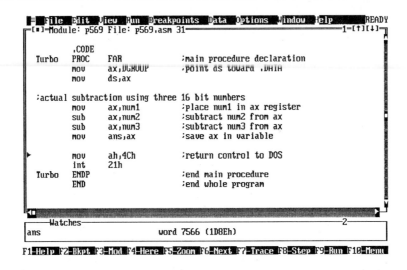

Figure 17-2.   Illustration of hexadecimal subtraction, using the Debugger's Watch window to examine the variable *ans*

The actual code for subtraction is straightforward. The first number is moved into the **ax** register. The next two lines of code subtract *num2* and *num3* from the contents of the **ax** register. Finally, the fourth line of code moves the contents of the **ax** register (1D8Eh) into the variable *ans*.

At this point, you cannot view the actual results of the subtraction except by using either a register or data-segment dump from memory, or the Debugger. No routine will place the results directly on your screen. Figure 17-2 shows the Debugger screen, immediately after the program was executed.

This program illustrates hexadecimal subtraction and also shows one technique for overcoming a programming limitation of the previous addition example. Because the program used a data segment, you could change the numbers to be subtracted without having to alter the actual program code. Data segments allow your program code to remain unchanged even when you alter numeric values.

Multiple Precision Addition with Direct Addressing

The general-purpose registers (**ax**, **bx**, **cx**, and **dx**) of the Intel family are limited to 16 bits. If there were not a technique for getting around this

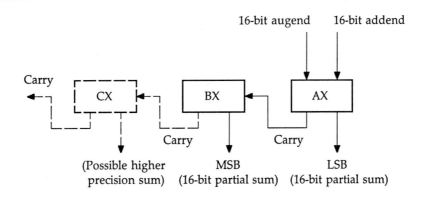

Figure 17-3. How multiple precision arithmetic is achieved with microprocessor registers

limitation, you would be restricted to working with integer numbers from 0000h to 0FFFFh (0 to 65,535 decimal). The next example illustrates a general technique for 32-bit arithmetic. When the range of the arithmetic exceeds the register size, multiple precision arithmetic is used. Thirty-two-bit arithmetic will allow numbers as large as 0FFFFFFFFh (4,294,967,295 decimal) on 80286/8088 machines. While the 80486 and 80386 allow direct 32-bit arithmetic with the use of **eax, ebx, ecx,** and **edx** registers, you would still need multiple precision programming for numbers greater than 0FFFFFFFFh. Multiple precision arithmetic is possible because all microprocessors can set/clear a carry flag or overflow flag when an arithmetic operation dictates. The first two programs have not used this feature. If a carry or borrow had occurred, it would have gone unnoticed by the program and produced an incorrect answer. The **adc** (add with carry) instruction will allow this program to take advantage of any carry information and permit multiple precision arithmetic. Figure 17-3 shows how you can carry out multiple precision arithmetic with 16-bit registers.

```
;TURBO Assembly Language Programming Application
;Copyright (c) Chris H. Pappas and William H. Murray, 1990

;program of multiple precision addition using
;direct addressing

        DOSSEG                  ;use Intel segment-ordering
        .MODEL  small           ;set model size
        .8086                   ;8086 instructions
```

```
        .STACK  300h                ;set up 768-byte stack

        .DATA                       ;set up data location
num1    dw      0FFABh
num2    dw      4CC0h
num3    dw      0C00Ah
num4    dw      0DD34h
lsbans  dw      0
msbans  dw      0

        .CODE
Turbo   PROC    FAR                 ;main procedure declaration
        mov     ax,DGROUP           ;point ds toward .DATA
        mov     ds,ax

;actual code for multiple precision addition
        mov     bx,00h              ;clear bx register
        mov     ax,num1             ;first number moved to ax
        add     ax,num2             ;add second number
        adc     bx,00h              ;accumulate carry in bx
        add     ax,num3             ;add third number
        adc     bx,00h              ;accumulate carry in bx
        add     ax,num4             ;add fourth number
        adc     bx,00h              ;accumulate carry in bx
        mov     lsbans,ax           ;put ax in lsbans storage
        mov     msbans,bx           ;put bx in msbans storage

        mov     ah,4Ch              ;return control to DOS
        int     21h
Turbo   ENDP                        ;end main procedure
        END                         ;end whole program
```

This program illustrates how easily you can accomplish multiple precision addition. Recall that the carry flag is evaluated (set or cleared) after each **add** or **adc** operation, but only utilized by the **adc** instruction. In general, the program will start with the LSBs (least significant bits) and work toward the MSBs (most significant bits). The addition of two 16-bit numbers may or may not produce a carry. For example, adding 01234h to 11h does not produce a carry, but adding 0FFDEh to 0DC6h does. If the digits being added are LSB numbers, by definition, nothing will be passing a carry to them from a previous addition. For that reason, LSB additions are usually done with the **add** command. If the LSBs produce a carry, the carry flag will be set and utilized by the **adc** instruction when doing the next higher 16-bit addition. In this program, only carry information will be accumulated in the higher 16 bits, since any given number in the data segment is limited to the lower 16 bits. Thus, you must do add with carry operations with a 00h in the immediate addressing mode. The variable

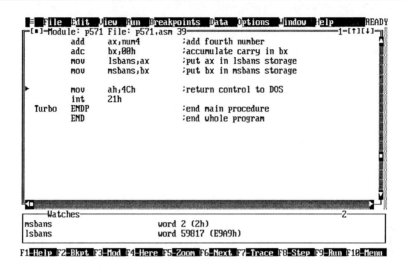

Figure 17-4. An illustration of multiprecision arithmetic with the results shown in *lsbans* and *msbans*

num1 is added to the variable *num2* with the simple **move/add** sequence of the first addition example. Since this addition set the carry flag (FFAB + 4CC0 = (1)4C6B), the next line of code will add the carry to the contents of the **bx** register. The **add/adc** sequence is repeated for each number to be added. The final sum is found in two registers. The **bx** register contains the MSBs and the **ax** register the LSBs of the 32-bit answer. The register contents are moved back to the data segment in two variables, *lsbans* and *msbans*. If these final two numbers are concatenated, the answer can be read as 0002E9A9h. Examine Figure 17-4 and find the answer.

You could extend this programming technique to add or accumulate any number, even something as large as the national debt. Multiple precision arithmetic overcomes the limitations of register size.

Performing Addition on 80486/80386 Machines

If you are using an 80486 or 80386 computer, you can perform 32-bit additions by using the **eax**, **ebx**, **ecx**, or **edx** registers. The following program performs the same addition as the previous example. However, the numbers to be added are now stored in 32-bit variables.

```
;TURBO Assembly Language Programming Application
;Copyright (c) Chris H. Pappas and William H. Murray, 1990

;program to use the 80486 or 80386 and 32-bit registers
;to add several numbers without the need for
;multiple-precision addition.

            DOSSEG                  ;use Intel segment-ordering
            .MODEL   small          ;set model size
            .386                    ;80386 instructions

            .STACK   300h           ;set up 768-byte stack

            .DATA                   ;set up data location
num1        dd       0FFABh
num2        dd       4CC0h
num3        dd       0C00Ah
num4        dd       0DD34h
ans         dd       0

            .CODE
Turbo       PROC     FAR            ;main procedure declaration
            mov      ax,DGROUP      ;point ds toward .DATA
            mov      ds,ax

;actual addition of numbers using 32-bit registers
            mov      eax,num1       ;load num1 in eax
            add      eax,num2       ;add num2 to eax
            add      eax,num3       ;add num3 to eax
            add      eax,num4       ;add num4 to eax
            mov      ans,eax        ;save eax in ans variable

            mov      ah,4Ch         ;return control to DOS
            int      21h
Turbo       ENDP                    ;end main procedure
            END                     ;end whole program
```

In this example, all additions are accomplished with the **add** mnemonic since no carry information will be passed. You can view the results of this operation in Figure 17-5, which shows the Debugger screen after program execution. Notice that you are viewing the 32-bit results.

There is still one major limitation to these programming techniques, even with the use of 32-bit registers. For each number to be added or subtracted from a register, you need at least one line (sometimes two) of program code. For one or two additions, this is not a problem. However, if the number of additions increases even to 50, the code becomes cumbersome and inefficient.

Multiplication and Division Instructions

The multiply and divide commands are easy to use, but you must use them with caution and with a firm understanding of how they operate. The next

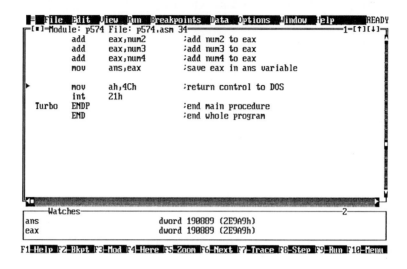

Figure 17-5.   An illustration of multiprecision arithmetic with 80386 32-bit registers

example uses the multiply (**mul**) and divide (**div**) instructions to perform a simple algebraic operation. In this example, *num1* is multiplied by *num2* and the resulting product is divided by *num3*. When performing 16-bit arithmetic, the **mul** instruction produces a 32-bit product. The LSBs are stored in the **ax** register and the MSBs in the **dx** register. In a similar manner, the **div** command divides a 32-bit dividend stored in the **ax** and **dx** registers by a 16-bit divisor. The resulting quotient is stored in the **ax** register. Any remainder will appear in the **dx** register.

Pay particular attention to the syntax for the multiply and divide commands.

```
;TURBO Assembly Language Programming Application
;Copyright (c) Chris H. Pappas and William H. Murray, 1990

;program to demonstrate the multiply & divide instructions

        DOSSEG                  ;use Intel segment-ordering
        .MODEL  small           ;set model size
        .8086                   ;8086 instructions

        .STACK  300h            ;set up 768-byte stack
```

```
         .DATA                    ;set up data location
num1     dw       3E78h
num2     dw       3Ah
num3     dw       3Eh
quo      dw       ?
rem      dw       ?

         .CODE
Turbo    PROC     FAR             ;main procedure declaration
         mov      ax,DGROUP       ;point ds toward .DATA
         mov      ds,ax

;code for performing:  (num1 x num2) / num3
         mov      ax,num1         ;place first number in ax
         mul      num2            ;x num2.  answer in dx:ax
         div      num3            ;divides dx:ax by num3
                                  ;quot in ax, remain in dx
         mov      quo,ax          ;save quotient
         mov      rem,dx          ;save remainder

         mov      ah,4Ch          ;return control to DOS
         int      21h
Turbo    ENDP                     ;end main procedure
         END                      ;end whole program
```

This is one of the first examples in which a mnemonic has used a single operand. The **mul** mnemonic expects to find one number (the multiplicand) in the **ax** register. You can specify the other number, the multiplier, with a variable name. Likewise, **div** expects to find the dividend in the **dx:ax** pair of registers; thus, only the divisor is specified with the **div** mnemonic. The actual program is straightforward. The variables *num1* and *num2* are multiplied, producing a product that is located in the **dx:ax** registers. This product is the dividend for the **div** instruction, which divides it by *num3*. The quotient is moved from **ax** to *quo* and the remainder from **dx** to *rem*. In this particular example, the quotient is 3A70h and the remainder is 10h. Can you find this information in Figure 17-6?

Raising a Number to an Integer Power

The basic arithmetic operations available with the Intel family of microprocessors include addition, subtraction, multiplication, and division. If you want additional abilities, you have to develop your own function by writing the program code or developing an algorithm. Raising a number to an integer power is one such useful function. In mathematical or scientific

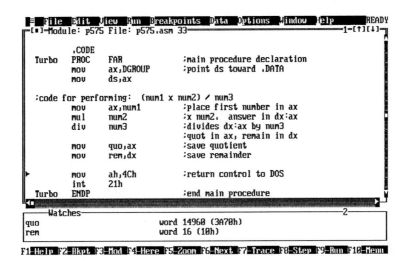

Figure 17-6.   The Debugger allows us to examine the results of a division program. The Watch window contains the quotient and the remainder with results given in both decimal and hexadecimal

work, you will frequently need to square or cube a number. To square a number, a program can merely multiply the number by itself. You can accomplish cubing in a similar manner. Perhaps there is a way to write a general algorithm for raising a number to an integer power.

If a program will loop through code, performing one multiplication for each higher power needed, you will have the algorithm.

```
;TURBO Assembly Language Programming Application
;Copyright (c) Chris H. Pappas and William H. Murray, 1990

;program to raise a small number to an integer power

        DOSSEG                    ;use Intel segment-ordering
        .MODEL  small             ;set model size
        .8086                     ;8086 instructions

        .STACK  300h              ;set up 768-byte stack

        .DATA                     ;set up data location
pow     dw      05h               ;raise 4 to the 5th power
num     dw      04h
```

```
ans      dw       ?

         .CODE
Turbo    PROC     FAR                  ;main procedure declaration
         mov      ax,DGROUP            ;point ds toward .DATA
         mov      ds,ax

         mov      ax,num               ;place number in ax register
         mov      cx,pow               ;place power in cx
         dec      cx                   ;decrease by one
more:    mul      num                  ;obtain another power of number
         loop     more                 ;is cx decremented to zero?
         mov      ans,ax               ;save result in ans variable

         mov      ah,4Ch               ;return control to DOS
         int      21h
Turbo    ENDP                          ;end main procedure
         END                           ;end whole program
```

For this example, the number (*num*) 04h is raised to the power (*pow*) 05h. This produces the hexadecimal result (*ans*) of 400h. Since the multiply instruction expects to find the first number in the **ax** register, *num* is loaded into **ax** before entering the loop. The number of multiplies is set in the loop counter, **cx**. Since *num* has already been loaded into **ax**, the program only need multiply it by itself three more times. Thus, **cx** is decremented (**dec**) before actually entering the loop. Each time around the loop, the contents in **ax** are multiplied by *num*, raising it to a successively higher power. When **cx** is decremented to zero, the loop is exited and the results are stored in *ans*. Figure 17-7 shows the Debugger results for this application.

Determining the Square Root of a Number with a Simple Algorithm

The last example used an algorithm to raise a number to an integer power by repeated multiplication. This example creates another algorithm for extracting the square root of a number.

What follows is an interesting mathematical approach for extracting a square root of a hexadecimal number. The algorithm is as follows: You can approximate the square root of a number by subtracting successively higher odd numbers from the original number until that original number is reduced to zero. The number of subtractions is equal to the approximate square root of the original number. For example, to find the square root of 110 decimal:

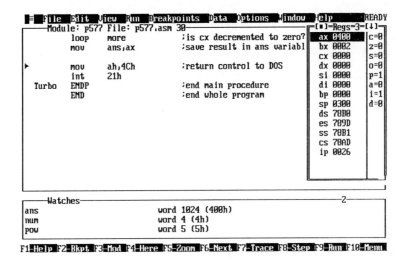

Figure 17-7. The number 4h is raised to the 5h power

$$110 - 1 = 109$$
$$109 - 3 = 106$$
$$106 - 5 = 101$$
$$101 - 7 = 94$$
$$94 - 9 = 85$$
$$85 - 11 = 74$$
$$74 - 13 = 61$$
$$61 - 15 = 46$$
$$46 - 17 = 29$$
$$29 - 19 = 10 \leftarrow \text{subtraction \#10}$$
$$10 - 21 = -11$$

Thus, the approximate square root of 110 is 10. The same mathematical procedure works in hexadecimal. The following listing is a square root algorithm used with the 32-bit registers of the 80486 or 80386:

```
;TURBO Assembly Language Programming Application
;Copyright (c) Chris H. Pappas and William H. Murray, 1990
;program for finding the square root of a number
;using repeated subtraction technique
;program utilizes 80486 or 80386 32-bit registers
```

```
            DOSSEG                        ;use Intel segment-ordering
            .MODEL   small                ;set model size
            .386                          ;80386 instructions

            .STACK   300h                 ;set up 768-byte stack

            .DATA                         ;set up data location
num         dd       0ACDEA452h
sqrt        dd       ?

            .CODE
Turbo       PROC     FAR                  ;main procedure declaration
            mov      ax,DGROUP            ;point ds toward .DATA
            mov      ds,ax

;program to find the square root of number
            mov      edx,0h               ;zero temp. storage locat.
            mov      ecx,1h               ;seed number for subtraction
            mov      eax,num              ;get original number
cont:       sub      eax,ecx              ;perform subtraction
            jb       done                 ;if less than zero, done
            inc      edx                  ;increment sq root value
            add      ecx,02h              ;increase ecx to next odd number
            jmp      cont                 ;continue loop
done:       mov      sqrt,edx             ;save result in sqrt

            mov      ah,4Ch               ;return control to DOS
            int      21h
Turbo       ENDP                          ;end main procedure
            END                           ;end whole program
```

In this example, **edx** is initially zeroed out since it will form the location for the answer (the square root). The **ecx** register will hold the location of the successively higher odd numbers. It is seeded with the first odd number, one. Upon entering the loop, **ecx** is subtracted from the value contained in the **eax** register. If the result of the subtraction is below zero, the program is ended. If the result of the subtraction is above or equal to zero, **ecx** is incremented to the next odd number and the loop is repeated. After leaving the loop, the square root is stored in *ans*. The square root value obtained in this example is 0D25Eh. Check the answer with the results shown here:

```
 ┌──Watches──────────────────────────────────────────────2──┐
 │edx                    dword 53854 (D25Eh)                 │
 │ecx                    dword 107709 (1A4BDh)               │
 │ebx                    dword 2 (2h)                        │
 │eax                    dword 4294870481 (FFFEA511h)        │
 │sqrt                   dword 53854 (D25Eh)                 │
 │num                    dword 2900272210 (ACDEA452h)        │
 └──────────────────────────────────────────────────────────┘
```

Using Pointers for Accessing and Storing Data

In most assembly language work, you have to make sure that the variable sizes match the register sizes when loading and storing the contents of registers. Generally, you can only load defined byte (db) variables in 8-bit registers, such as **ah** or **dl**. The same holds true for all of the remaining data types. If you have been writing your own assembly language examples, you have probably encountered the assembler error message "data sizes do not match." This is why the multiple precision examples had to hold answers in two registers and store results in two separate variables. Using pointers eliminates the need for separate variables. Pointers allow you to work with mismatched data and register types, as shown in the next example.

```
;TURBO Assembly Language Programming Application
;Copyright (c) Chris H. Pappas and William H. Murray, 1990

;program to show the use of pointers when accessing
;and storing various data sizes

          DOSSEG                    ;use Intel segment-ordering
          .MODEL    small           ;set model size
          .8086                     ;8086 instructions

          .STACK    300h            ;set up 768-byte stack

          .DATA                     ;set up data location
num1      dw        1214h
num2      dd        5532AB12h
num3      dq        123456789FEDCBA0h
num4      dw        0021h
num5      dw        0054h
num6      dw        0076h
num7      dw        0022h
num8      dq        ?
num9      dw        4577h
num10     dw        0BA83h
num11     dd        ?

          .CODE
Turbo     PROC      FAR             ;main procedure declaration
          mov       ax,DGROUP       ;point ds toward .DATA
          mov       ds,ax

;moving dw sized number to 8-bit registers
          mov       al,byte ptr num1 ;moves 14h into al
          mov       ah,byte ptr num1+1 ;moves 12h into ah

;moving dd sized number to 16-bit registers
          mov       ax,word ptr num2 ;moves AB12h into ax
```

```
        mov     bx,word ptr num2+2 ;moves 5532h into bx
;moving dq sized number to 16-bit registers
        mov     ax,word ptr num3 ;moves CBA0 into ax
        mov     bx,word ptr num3+2 ;moves 9FED into bx
        mov     cx,word ptr num3+4 ;moves 5678 into cx
        mov     dx,word ptr num3+6 ;moves 1234 into dx

;storing 16-bit number in a dq variable
        mov     ax,num4          ;put 0021h into ax
        mov     word ptr num8,ax ;put ax in lsb of num8
        mov     ax,num5          ;put 0054h into ax
        mov     word ptr num8+2,ax ;place in num8
        mov     ax,num6          ;put 0076h into ax
        mov     word ptr num8+4,ax ;place in num8
        mov     ax,num7          ;put 0022h into ax
        mov     word ptr num8+6,ax ;place in msb of num8

;multiplying two dw sized numbers and storing results
;in a dd variable using pointers
        mov     ax,num9          ;place 4577h in ax
        mul     num10            ;multiply by 0BA83h
        mov     word ptr num11,ax ;save lsbs in num11
        mov     word ptr num11+2,dx ;save msbs in num11

        mov     ah,4Ch           ;return control to DOS
        int     21h
Turbo   ENDP                     ;end main procedure
        END                      ;end whole program
```

In the first block of code, a *byte ptr* separates a 16-bit number and allows access to either the upper or lower 8 bits. Watch the syntax carefully. In the second block, two *word ptrs* divide a defined double (dd) into two 16-bit numbers. To get to the upper 16 bits, a 2 is added to the displacement in order to skip over two bytes. In the third block, a defined quadword (dq) is divided between four 16-bit registers.

You can save numeric results in the same manner. In the fourth block, information from defined word (dw) variables is packed and placed into a defined quadword (dq). Again, note the syntax.

Finally, the last piece of code multiplies *num9* and *num10*. Recall that the product formed by the **mul** mnemonic (when two words are multiplied together) is stored in the **dx:ax** pair of registers. Rather than storing them in separate variables, this program will pack them into one variable (*num11*), which is a defined double (dd). View the variables from the variable window shown here:

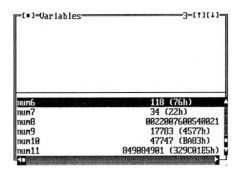

USING A LOOKUP TABLE

A *lookup table,* as the name implies, allows you to look up a value or extract a piece of data from a previously defined table. Lookup tables are often used in high-speed graphics and spelling checker programs. For example, you can enter a whole dictionary into a data segment in the form of a table. If you index the proper amount into the table, you can compare a word with one previously stored in the dictionary. If the word is found, a message such as "correctly spelled" could be printed on the screen. Otherwise, you might see a message such as "the word is not in the dictionary." Depending upon their function, lookup tables can also be called *data tables* or *shape tables.*

Creating a Lookup Table to Find Sine Values

You have already seen that special mathematical functions require the implementation of programmer-created algorithms. Algorithms are not only hard to come by, but hard to implement in assembly language. This is the perfect place to illustrate the use of lookup tables to find hard to determine mathematical values. The following program allows you to obtain the sine values for the angles between 0 and 90 degrees, in increments of 10 degrees:

```
;TURBO Assembly Language Programming Application
;Copyright (c) Chris H. Pappas and William H. Murray, 1990

;program shows how to access a lookup table of data
```

```
        DOSSEG                      ;use Intel segment-ordering
        .MODEL   small              ;set model size
        .8086                       ;8086 instructions

        .STACK   300h               ;set up 768-byte stack

        .DATA                       ;set up data location
table   dw       0,1736,3420,5000,6428,7660,8660
        dw       9397,9848,10000
value   dw       70
answer  dw       ?
ten     db       10

        .CODE
Turbo   PROC     FAR                ;main procedure declaration
        mov      ax,DGROUP          ;point ds toward .DATA
        mov      ds,ax

;example of using value given as index into a lookup table
        mov      ax,value           ;number to look up
        div      ten                ;reduce to an index value
        rol      ax,1               ;multiply by 2, for word index
        lea      bx,table           ;find start of table
        add      bx,ax              ;get index+offset
        mov      dx,[bx]            ;get value from table
        mov      answer,dx          ;move value from dx to answer

        mov      ah,4Ch             ;return control to DOS
        int      21h
Turbo   ENDP                        ;end main procedure
        END                         ;end whole program
```

The data segment shows a table (*table*) containing the sine values for the decimal angles 0 through 90, and accurate to three or four places. Each number in the table has an implied decimal point. For example, the number 1736 represents the sine of 10 degrees and is actually 0.1736. Also, notice that these numbers are stored in decimal format so they are easier to read. In a data dump, however, you will see hexadecimal results. To keep the program simple, the sine value to be looked up is contained in the variable *value*. The answer will be returned to a defined word (dw) variable called *answer*. The *value* moved into the **ax** register at the start of the program will serve as the index into the lookup table after some software conditioning.

First, the number in *value* is divided by ten to produce a simple index into the table. Recall that the table contains sine values for each 10 degrees. Because the program deals with a table using defined words (dw), this index must be multiplied by two since a word is made up of 2 bytes. Instead of using the multiply instruction, a simple rotate left command (**rol**) produces faster results. The value in **ax** is added to the starting location of the *table*, given in **bx**, to produce the total offset into *table*. The **mov** instruction returns the digits 9397 (24B5h) to the **dx** register and that value is finally stored in the variable *answer*.

You gain several advantages by using a lookup table. You obtain a relatively easy program, and the possibility of high precision answers in decimal or hexadecimal (or any other) format. The disadvantages might not be as apparent. The results had to be previously stored in the data segment, limiting the program's flexibility. For example, in the preceding case, if you wanted the sine of 45 degrees, you would have to expand the program to include angle increments of 5 instead of 10. Another disadvantage is that the precision and accuracy of the answer is controlled by the programmer, not by a mathematical function. Errors creep into data entry, especially when data tables are many lines long.

Performing Code Conversions Without a Lookup Table

You can also use a lookup table to convert numbers from ASCII to hexadecimal. However, this example performs the conversion with a simple mathematical operation. ASCII codes are used for almost all information read from keyboards and sent to monitor screens or printers. For example, if a 7 is entered at the keyboard, an ASCII 37h might be read into the **al** register. Likewise, if numbers generated from a program are to be displayed on the screen, they must be in ASCII form, not hexadecimal. Observe the relationship between ASCII and hexadecimal numbers in Table 17-1.

For the numerical ASCII digits between 30h and 39h, merely subtract 30h from each number to form the correct hexadecimal result. For the digits from 41h to 46h, subtract 37h. Remember to use hexadecimal arithmetic when making the subtractions. Also, note that there are many possible ASCII values, and that you can only convert numerical digits in this manner. The following example performs no error checking. In other words, it assumes input in the correct range of acceptable values.

```
;TURBO Assembly Language Programming Application
;Copyright (c) Chris H. Pappas and William H. Murray, 1990

;program to convert ascii digits to hexadecimal numbers

        DOSSEG                  ;use Intel segment-ordering
        .MODEL  small           ;set model size
```

```
            .8086                       ;8086 instructions

            .STACK   300h               ;set up 768-byte stack

            .DATA                       ;set up data location
ascii       db       44h                ;ascii "D"
hexdig      db       ?

            .CODE
Turbo       PROC     FAR                ;main procedure declaration
            mov      ax,DGROUP          ;point ds toward .DATA
            mov      ds,ax

;converting an ascii value to a hexadecimal number
;assume ascii input for 0,1,2,3,4,5,6,7,8,9,a,b,c,d,e,f
            mov      al,ascii           ;ascii number to convert in al
            sub      al,30h             ;see if a number 0-9
            cmp      al,9
            jg       isletter           ;if greater than 9, a letter
            jmp      done               ;quit
isletter:
            sub      al,07h             ;sub 7 and finish conversion
done:
            mov      hexdig,al          ;save result in answer

            mov      ah,4Ch             ;return control to DOS
            int      21h
Turbo       ENDP                        ;end main procedure
            END                         ;end whole program
```

Notice that 30h is subtracted from the contents of the variable *ascii*. This is because the input should fall in the range 30h to 46h. Now, if the result of the subtraction is a number between 0h and 9h, the program is over and the conversion is complete. However, if the **cmp** operation finds a number greater than 09h, it must be a hexadecimal "letter." To complete the conversion of a letter, a 07h (a total of 37h, from ASCII) is subtracted to place the data in the correct range of the hexadecimal digits A through F. For this example, a 0Dh will be returned to the variable *hexdig*.

USING THE BIOS/DOS SYSTEM INTERRUPTS AND ADDRESSING PORTS

The BIOS and DOS interrupts are easy to implement and provide access to powerful screen, cursor, character, and graphics routines. These routines are part of your computer's hardware or DOS operating system. They are actually machine code instructions that are either embedded in ROM (read

Table 17-1.   ASCII and Hexadecimal Equivalents

ASCII	Hexadecimal
30h	0h
31h	1h
32h	2h
33h	3h
34h	4h
35h	5h
36h	6h
37h	7h
38h	8h
39h	9h
41h	0Ah
42h	0Bh
43h	0Ch
44h	0Dh
45h	0Eh
46h	0Fh

only memory) chips or loaded into RAM (random access memory) when you boot your system. As mentioned, they provide software routines for controlling the computer's hardware. When you tap into these routines, you are harnessing the heart of the machine. Appendix B contains a complete list of the available BIOS and DOS interrupts. In the following examples, you will learn how to use the BIOS and DOS routines and achieve spectacular control over your system with relatively simple programs.

Ports serve as effective input and output channels on your computer. You are undoubtedly familiar with serial and parallel ports. There are other ports, too. For example, the keyboard and speaker ports. Ports have unique identification numbers. The following sections explain how to send and receive information from your computer's ports.

Clearing the Screen with an Interrupt

When you send output to the screen, you will often want the screen cleared first. In many cases, this may just require a simple screen clear operation issued from DOS (the **cls** command). At other times, you may want to clear the screen or change screen colors and attributes from within your program. You can easily achieve screen control with BIOS type 10h interrupts. Examine the various BIOS interrupts in Appendix B. When using BIOS or DOS interrupts, remember that the interrupt call is a hexadecimal number and should be entered in a program as **int 10h**. You will notice that all BIOS interrupts are **int 10h** and that only the parameters, contained in various registers, are changed for the different functions. These parameters are almost always entered as decimal numbers—for example, **mov ah,11**. Also remember that an interrupt call from your program merely points to more code—code written by someone else. When you call an interrupt, you are using code previously stored in ROM or RAM by the computer manufacturer or by DOS.

The first example clears your computer screen:

```
;TURBO Assembly Language Programming Application
;Copyright (c) Chris H. Pappas and William H. Murray, 1990

;program uses bios interrupt to clear the screen

        DOSSEG                  ;use Intel segment-ordering
        .MODEL  small           ;set model size
        .8086                   ;8086 instructions

        .STACK  300h            ;set up 768-byte stack

        .CODE
Turbo   PROC    FAR             ;main procedure declaration

;actual code to clear screen
        mov     cx,0000         ;row,column upper-left corner
        mov     dx,2479h        ;row,column lower-right corner
        mov     bh,07           ;normal char attribute
        mov     ah,06           ;scroll active page up
        mov     al,00           ;scroll entire window
        int     10h             ;call bios interrupt
;end of clear screen routine

        mov     ah,4Ch          ;return control to DOS
        int     21h
Turbo   ENDP                    ;end main procedure
        END                     ;end whole program
```

Before calling an interrupt, the various system registers are initialized to the proper values. In this case, **ah** specifies "scroll active page up" when set to 6. The **al** register will blank the entire window when set to 0. The **bh** register contains the value of the attribute used when printing blank characters to the screen. The normal attribute is 7. The **cx** and **dx** registers control the size of the screen window that will be cleared. The **cx** register is divided so that **ch** and **cl** point to the upper-left corner of the window.

Likewise, the **dx** register is divided so that **dh** and **dl** mark the lower-right corner of the window. In this program, setting **cx** to 0000 sets **ch** and **cl** to 0, or the upper-left corner of the screen. The **dx** register is set to 2479h, which places a 24h in **dh** and a 79h in **dl**. This specifies the lower-right corner of the screen. When the interrupt is finally called, the entire screen is cleared. By altering the values in **cx** and **dx**, you can clear any portion of the screen (called a window). Could you find use for such a program? Why not experiment with different window sizes and see what happens.

Turning Off the NUMLOCK Feature

You may want to control the initial setup of your keyboard. Maybe you like to type in all uppercase, or perhaps you would like to have the SCROLL LOCK turned on automatically. Did you know that the IBM PS/2s automatically set the NUMLOCK to ON when the system is booted? This is a problem for many people. If you use the numeric keypad to move the cursor and forget to turn NUMLOCK off, you will have a string of 4s, 8s, 6s, or 2s across your screen. To fix this, the following program sets NUMLOCK to OFF. If the program is stored and called from the *autoexec.bat* file, the whole process will be automatic and NUMLOCK will be turned off when you boot your machine.

To manipulate the keyboard, you must use a technique called a *segment override*. When using a segment override, you will transmit information to the keyboard port. The information you send affects the keyboard status byte at memory location 417h. This status byte is the same for the PC, XT, AT, and PS/2 series computers. Table 17-2 shows the meaning of each bit in the keyboard status byte. If you want to change another feature, just change the bit that affects that feature.

```
;TURBO Assembly Language Programming Application
;Copyright (c) Chris H. Pappas and William H. Murray, 1990

;program will turn off numlock on the keyboard

        DOSSEG                  ;use Intel segment-ordering
        .MODEL   small          ;set model size
        .8086                   ;8086 instructions

        .STACK   300h           ;set up 768-byte stack
```

```
        .CODE
Turbo   PROC    FAR                 ;main procedure declaration

        mov     ax,0                ;prepare to set es to zero
        mov     es,ax               ;move it in
        mov     al,es:[417h]        ;keyboard status byte
        and     al,11011111b        ;prepare to mask numlock
        mov     es:[417h],al        ;return altered information

        mov     ah,4Ch              ;return control to DOS
        int     21h
Turbo   ENDP                        ;end main procedure
        END                         ;end whole program
```

In this example, the status byte is first read to obtain the current information. That information is then masked so that everything but the NUMLOCK information is retained. The altered information is then returned to the same memory location. Notice that the memory location 417h, the keyboard port, is read into the **es** register. The syntax used here is known as a segment override, with **es** being the extra segment. The information from the read information is stored in the **al** register. This data is then "ANDed" with the mask 0DFh or 11011111b. The mask allows all information but the NUMLOCK data to be retained. The information is then rewritten to location 417h. You can use the AND mask technique any time you need to set a particular bit to 0. Similarly, you can use an OR mask to force a bit to 1.

Table 17-2.   Keyboard Bit Information from Port 417h Returned to the **al** Register

Bit	Meaning
0	Right SHIFT key depressed (1)
1	Left SHIFT key depressed (1)
2	CTRL key depressed (1)
3	ALT key depressed (1)
4	SCROLL LOCK active (1)
5	NUMLOCK active (1)
6	CAPS LOCK active (1)
7	INSERT active (1)

If this program were written exclusively for the 80486 or 80386, you could have cleared the NUMLOCK bit with

```
btr al,5
```

instead of using a mask.

Sending Information to the Speaker Port

The next example program manipulates information at the speaker port located at 61h. You can turn on the speaker by sending a 0 to port 61h. By alternating an on-off sequence through bit 1 of this port, you can obtain different frequencies. When the program itself turns the speaker on and off, the frequency of the sound will be determined by the execution speed of the software. The actual frequencies produced by this program are dependent upon the speed of your system; you may have to adjust them to obtain the desired effect.

```
;TURBO Assembly Language Programming Application
;Copyright (c) Chris H. Pappas and William H. Murray, 1990

;program will generate a strange sound from the speaker

        DOSSEG                  ;use Intel segment-ordering
        .MODEL  small           ;set model size
        .8086                   ;8086 instructions

        .STACK  300h            ;set up 768-byte stack

        .DATA                   ;set up data location
temp    dw      0               ;storage

        .CODE
Turbo   PROC    FAR             ;main procedure declaration
        mov     ax,DGROUP       ;point ds toward .DATA
        mov     ds,ax

        mov     dx,0            ;initialize dx to zero
        in      al,61h          ;get speaker port info in al
        and     al,0FCh         ;mask all but lower two bits
more:   mov     temp,00h        ;place zero in scratch variable
        inc     dx              ;increment dx
        cmp     dx,18           ;repeated sound 18 times?
        je      finish          ;if yes, end program
comp:   xor     al,02h          ;xor lower two bits of al
```

```
            mov     cx,temp         ;get frequency from storage
            cmp     cx,250h         ;reached 592 hertz?
            je      more            ;if yes, repeat sequence,
            inc     temp            ;if not, increase frequency
            out     61h,al          ;and output it to speaker
delay1: loop        delay1          ;the time delay
            jmp     comp            ;complete
finish:

            mov     ah,4Ch          ;return control to DOS
            int     21h
Turbo   ENDP                        ;end main procedure
        END                         ;end whole program
```

Information is retrieved from the port with an **in** operation and written
back to the port with an **out** operation. The masking of bit information is
done twice, once with an AND and once with an XOR mnemonic. From the
logic operations of the previous chapter, can you tell what is happening?
Three loops are used to determine the number of times the sound is
repeated, the frequency of the sound, and the time delay used for each
note. In this example, the **dx** register determines how many times the same
sound is repeated (18 times). The variable *temp* holds the frequency information during each trip around the frequency loop. Finally, the one-line
time delay loop simply decrements the **cx** register to zero. Can you determine where the value of **cx** is being generated? Is **cx** always initialized to
the same value?

Printing on the Text Screen

Of all DOS interrupt routines, none is more popular that the DOS interrupt
21h, which allows you to print string information to the screen. When
using this interrupt, remember that the string must terminate with a $
symbol.

```
;TURBO Assembly Language Programming Application
;Copyright (c) Chris H. Pappas and William H. Murray, 1990

;this program prints a message to the text screen using a
;standard dos interrupt

            DOSSEG                  ;use Intel segment-ordering
            .MODEL  small           ;set model size
            .8086                   ;8086 instructions

            .STACK  300h            ;set up 768-byte stack
```

```
         .DATA                       ;set up data location
text     db              'The TURBO Assembler is great!$'

         .CODE
Turbo    PROC    FAR                 ;main procedure declaration
         mov     ax,DGROUP           ;point ds toward .DATA
         mov     ds,ax

         lea     dx,text             ;get location of string
         mov     ah,09h              ;set print parameter
         int     21h                 ;call dos print routine

         mov     ah,4Ch              ;return control to DOS
         int     21h
Turbo    ENDP                        ;end main procedure
         END                         ;end whole program
```

The text to be printed is stored in a db variable called *text*. This string terminates with a $ sentinel contained in the string itself. To use this interrupt, the effective address of *text* is loaded into the **dx** register. The interrupt parameter for printing a string (09h) is placed in the **ah** register, and then the interrupt is actually called. Operating at Turbo speeds, the text string will be printed on the screen at the current cursor location.

Try altering this program so that the screen is cleared before the string is printed. (You will need to incorporate the clear screen code from the first example.)

Viewing the Flag Values in the eflag Register of the 80486 or 80386

The following program is for users of 80486 and 80386 computers. However, with just a little effort, you could alter the program to display the **flags** register of the 80286/8088 computers. This example will use several DOS interrupts to print the contents of the **eflag** register, which contains 13 flag fields. Six of these flags, called status flags, are changed by, and provide necessary information for, arithmetic and logical control decisions. These are **cf** (carry flag), **pf** (parity flag), **af** (auxiliary carry flag), **zf** (zero flag), **sf** (sign flag), and **of** (overflow flag).

- The carry flag (**cf**) is set to 1 when a carry or borrow out is generated by an arithmetic operation. Otherwise, it is reset to 0. The carry flag is also used by shift and rotate instructions and can contain the bit shifted or rotated out of the register.

- The parity flag (**pf**) is used for data communication applications and is set to 1 to generate odd parity or reset to 0 to generate even parity.

- The auxiliary carry flag (**af**) is used in Binary Coded Decimal (BCD) arithmetic and indicates whether there has been a carry out of or borrow into the least significant 4-bit digit of a BCD value.

- The zero flag (**zf**) sets itself to 1 to indicate when the result of an operation is zero.

- The sign flag (**sf**) is set to 1 for a negative result and reset to 0 for a positive result.

- The overflow flag (**of**) indicates whether an operation has generated a carry into the high-order bit of the result but not a carry out of the high-order bit.

Four of the thirteen flags — **tf**, **if**, **df**, and **vm** — are used to direct certain processor operations. The trap flag (**tf**), when set, puts the microprocessor into single-step mode and enables the debugging of a program. The interrupt-enable flag (**if**) enables external interrupts when set to 1 and disables external interrupts when reset to 0. The direction of string operations is controlled by the direction flag (**df**). With **df** reset to 0, (**e**)**si** and/or (**e**)**di** are automatically incremented forward. With **df** set to 1, (**e**)**si** and/or (**e**)**di** are automatically decremented. When the virtual mode flag (**vm**) is set, the 80486/80386 switches from protected mode to virtual 8086 mode. You can set the **vm** flag by using the **iret** instruction, or by using task switches occurring during protected mode execution.

```
;TURBO Assembly Language Programming Application
;Copyright (c) Chris H. Pappas and William H. Murray, 1990

;this program will print out the current 32-bit eflag register
;to the screen
        DOSSEG                  ;use Intel segment-ordering
        .MODEL  small           ;set model size
        .386                    ;80386 instructions

        .STACK  300h            ;set up 768-byte stack

        .DATA                   ;set up data location
tag     db      3 dup (0ah,0dh)
        db      '          reserved        v  r   n'
        db      ' i/o o d I t s '
        db      'z   a   p   c',0ah,0dh
```

```
        db          '***************************m f 0 t'
        db          '    1 f f f f f '
        db          'f 0 f 0 f 1 f',0ah,0dh
        db          '-----------------------------'
        db          '-----------------------------'
        db          0ah,0dh,'$'

        .CODE
Turbo   PROC    FAR                 ;main procedure declaration
        mov     ax,DGROUP           ;point ds toward .DATA
        mov     ds,ax

        lea     edx,tag             ;print eflag labels
        mov     ah,09h              ;dos parameter
        int     21h                 ;dos interrupt

        pushfd                      ;push eflags to stack
        pop     edx                 ;return them in edx register

        mov     cx,32               ;print 32 bits of eflag
more:   rol     edx,1               ;rotate to get one bit
        mov     al,dl               ;prepare to make ascii byte
        and     al,1                ;mask for lower bit only
        or      al,30h              ;convert 1 or 0 to 31 or 30
        push    edx                 ;save edx contents on stack

        mov     dl,al               ;print the ascii byte to screen
        mov     ah,2                ;dos parameter for char print
        int     21h                 ;dos interrupt
        mov     dl,' '              ;print space between each digit
        mov     ah,2                ;dos parameter for char print
        int     21h                 ;dos interrupt
        pop     edx                 ;return contents to edx
        loop    more                ;repeat until cx is 0

        mov     ah,4Ch              ;return control to DOS
        int     21h
Turbo   ENDP                        ;end main procedure
        END                         ;end whole program
```

To view the **eflag** register, you need two operations. First, the **pushfd** command places the **eflag**'s register contents on the computer's stack. Next, the stack is popped into the **edx** register (**pop edx**), and the **eflag**'s contents are returned. You can now observe the contents of **eflag** by studying the **edx** register. This program will create a table on the screen and then print the **eflag** information in binary digits. A binary 1 represents a set flag while a 0 represents a reset flag. To print the bits in this manner you need a routine that will print 1 bit at a time, from the **edx** register, to the text screen. To accomplish this, the contents of **edx** are simply rotated, masked, converted to ASCII, and printed to the screen as character data—1 bit at a time. A space is placed between each bit for clarity. This program uses a loop to print each bit, so it will be repeated 32 times. A header is printed to identify each flag before the flag information is actually sent to the screen. Here is what the screen will look like:

```
C>flag



             reserved            v r  n i/o o d I t s z  a  p  c
****************************m f 0 t  1 f f f f f f 0 f 0 f 1 f
-----------------------------------------------------------------
0 0 0 0 0 0 0 0 0 0 0 0 0 0 0 0 0 0 1 1 1 0 0 1 0 0 1 0 0 0 1 1 0
C>
```

Plotting Dots on the Screen with a System Interrupt

The entire family of IBM personal computers supports at least two graphics modes on color monitors. One is called the medium resolution mode and the other the high resolution mode. The *medium resolution mode* can plot 320 dots horizontally and 200 dots vertically, with four colors present on the screen at any given time. The *high resolution mode* supports 640 dots horizontally and 200 dots vertically, with two colors (usually black and white). Additional modes have been added with the development of EGA and VGA graphics standards. Table 17-3 shows the various graphics modes available for the IBM models 50, 60, 70, and 80, supporting the VGA standard. The following example plots three tiny dots near the center of the 320×200 graphics screen. Each dot is exactly 1 pixel wide—the smallest dot possible in this screen mode. Look carefully; the dots might go unnoticed.

```
;TURBO Assembly Language Programming Application
;Copyright (c) Chris H. Pappas and William H. Murray, 1990

;program to plot dots on medium resolution
;640x200 color graphics screen using a bios interrupt

        DOSSEG                  ;use Intel segment-ordering
        .MODEL  small           ;set model size
        .8086                   ;8086 instructions

        .STACK  300h            ;set up 768-byte stack

        .CODE
Turbo   PROC    FAR             ;main procedure declaration
;routine for plotting three dots near the center of the screen
        mov     ah,00           ;prepare to set screen mode
```

```
        mov     al,04           ;set 320x200 color mode
        int     10h             ;call interrupt

        mov     ah,11           ;set color palette
        mov     bh,00           ;set background color
        mov     bl,01           ;set it to blue
        int     10h             ;call interrupt

        mov     ah,11           ;set color palette
        mov     bh,01           ;select foreground palette
        mov     bl,00           ;green/red/yellow
        int     10h             ;call interrupt

        mov     al,02           ;set dot color to red
        mov     ah,12           ;write dot parameter
        mov     dx,100          ;set for 100 rows down (vert)
        mov     cx,158          ;set for 158 columns (horz)
        int     10h             ;call interrupt
        mov     ah,12           ;write dot parameter
        mov     cx,160          ;plot another
        int     10h             ;call interrupt
        mov     ah,12           ;write dot parameter
        mov     cx,162          ;plot another
        int     10h             ;call interrupt

        mov     ah,4Ch          ;return control to DOS
        int     21h
Turbo   ENDP                    ;end main procedure
        END                     ;end whole program
```

Before any plotting takes place, you need to initialize the medium resolution screen by using the following code:

```
mov     ah,00           ;prepare to set screen mode
mov     al,04           ;set 320x200 color mode
int     10h             ;call interrupt
```

Table 17-4 shows how the values for **ah** and **al** are determined. Next, you need to set the background and foreground colors:

```
mov     ah,11           ;set color palette
mov     bh,00           ;set background color
mov     bl,01           ;set it to blue
int     10h             ;call interrupt
```

With **bh** set to 0, the color selected will form the background color for the screen. Color numbers range from 0 to 15. Table 17-4 shows 16 possible color values that you can use. The background color for this example is blue. You select the foreground palette a bit differently:

Table 17-3.   Seventeen Video Modes (all available on VGA, some on CGA and EGA)

Mode (hex)	Type	Colors	Buffer Start	Number of Pages	Character Format	Box Size	Graphics Screen
0,1	A/N	16	B8000	8	40×25	8×8	320×200
2,3	A/N	16	B8000	8	80×25	8×8	640×200
0*,1*	A/N	16	B8000	8	40×25	8×14	320×350
2*,3*	A/N	16	B8000	8	80×25	8×14	640×350
0+,1+	A/N	16	B8000	8	40×25	9×16	360×400
2+,3+	A/N	16	B8000	8	80×25	9×16	720×400
4,5	APA	4	B8000	1	40×25	8×8	320×200
6	APA	2	B8000	1	80×25	8×8	640×200
7	A/N	mono	B0000	8	80×25	9×14	720×350
7+	A/N	mono	B0000	8	80×25	9×16	720×400
D	APA	16	A0000	8	40×25	8×8	320×200
E	APA	16	A0000	4	80×25	8×8	640×200
F	APA	mono	A0000	2	80×25	8×14	640×350
10	APA	16	A0000	2	80×25	8×14	640×350
11	APA	2	A0000	1	80×30	8×16	640×480
12	APA	16	A0000	1	80×30	8×16	640×480
13	APA	256	A0000	1	40×25	8×8	320×200

* enhanced modes from EGA adapter
+ enhanced modes

```
mov    ah,11      ;set color palette
mov    bh,01      ;select foreground palette
mov    bl,00      ;green/red/yellow
int    10h        ;call interrupt
```

The **bh** register is set to 1 for foreground color selection, while **bl** selects the green/red/yellow palette. You only need to do the three steps for initialization once, unless you want a color change for the whole screen. The remainder of the program uses the "write dot" command three times.

When you use "write dot," the **cx** register contains the horizontal displacement while **dx** contains the vertical. For this plot, you can plot the dots in red by setting **al** to 2. The **cx** register is moved twice for the remaining dots. To draw a line using BIOS interrupts, a program would have to plot a series of dots in the desired direction by using a loop. This is

Table 17-4.   Color Choices for the 640 × 480 Graphics Screen

Number	Color
0	Black
1	Blue
2	Green
3	Cyan
4	Red
5	Magenta
6	Brown
7	White
8	Dark gray
9	Light blue
10	Light green
11	Light cyan
12	Light red
13	Light magenta
14	Yellow
15	Intensified white

usually not a big chore if the line is vertical or horizontal but becomes more taxing if the line is anything else. Very fast algorithms have been developed for plotting lines between two specified screen points.

This program exits in the medium resolution color mode. If you want to switch back to text mode automatically, you need to make two additions. First, you have to write a small piece of code to switch to the text screen. The format would be similar to the code used in the present example for switching to the graphics screen. But you also need a second piece of code to keep your new "set to text mode" routine from returning to text mode before you can view the dots on the screen. Usually, a routine that will wait for a keypress is inserted between the graphics routine and the return to text mode routine.

18

POWER PROGRAMMING: MACROS AND PROCEDURES

Macros, procedures, and object module libraries enable assembly language programmers to call and use previously debugged code. Besides making debugging faster, this also frees you from "reinventing the wheel" each time you create a new program. This chapter illustrates why assembly language programmers develop a bias for one particular technique, such as macros or procedures. It deals with macros, procedures, and object module libraries and also explains the advantages and disadvantages of each. The fourth section suggests how to select the best method for your particular application.

MACROS

Macros are a flexible programming option available for Turbo assembly language programmers. The word "macro" is an assembly language directive that instructs the Assembler to replace macro calls within the body of the program with a copy of the macro code. Once the operation or code is established in a macro, the Assembler inserts the actual macro code into the program in place of the macro name each time a macro is named in a program. Macros are said to execute "in line" since the program flow is uninterrupted. Macros can be created and stored in the actual program or called from a previously established macro library. A *macro library* is an ASCII file of macros that can be called from your program during assembly. Remember, the code in a macro or macro library has not been assembled— it remains in ASCII form. This is one of the ways in which a macro library differs from an object module library that is available at link time. Object module libraries will be explained later in this chapter.

The Framework of a Macro

A macro has three essential parts: a header, a body, and an end (**endm**). The header contains the name of the macro followed by the *macro* directive and any optional arguments that are to be passed to or from the macro. Macros can receive information in the form of arguments or via any global variable or system register. The body of a macro contains the program code—the code that is actually inserted into the program when the macro is called. All macros must end with the **endm** instruction.

As an example, examine the following listing:

```
;TURBO Assembly Language Programming Application
;Copyright (c) Chris H. Pappas and William H. Murray, 1990

;using a macro for a time delay

        DOSSEG                          ;use Intel segment-ordering
        .MODEL  small                   ;set model size
        .8086                           ;8086 instructions

        .STACK  300h                    ;set up 768-byte stack

        .DATA                           ;set up data location
blank   db      2000 dup (' ')

killtime macro  increment
        local   loop1,loop2             ;;loop1 & loop2 are local labels
        push    dx                      ;;save dx & cx values
        push    cx
        mov     dx,increment            ;;pass time increment to dx
loop2:  mov     cx,0FF00h               ;;load cx with 00FF00h
loop1:  dec     cx                      ;;kill time
        jnz     loop1                   ;;if not zero, loop1
        dec     dx                      ;;if cx=0, decrement dx
        jnz     loop2                   ;;if dx not zero, load cx again
        pop     cx                      ;;restore dx & cx values
        pop     dx
        endm                            ;;leave the macro
```

```
        .CODE
Turbo   PROC    far                 ;main procedure declaration
        mov     ax,DGROUP           ;point ds toward .DATA
        mov     ds,ax
        mov     es,ax
```

```
;program will clear the screen by writing 2000 blanks to
;the screen.  By writing these with a different value in bl
;the color of the whole screen can be changed.  The killtime
;macro will hold the color for a specified amount of time.
```

```
        mov     cx,9                ;repeat loop 9 times
        mov     bl,0                ;set background color
repeat: lea     bp,blank            ;write string of blanks
        mov     dx,0                ;move cursor to top left corner
        mov     ah,19               ;write string attribute
        mov     al,1                ;print characters and move cursor
        push    cx                  ;save loop counter
        mov     cx,2000             ;write 2000 blanks
        int     10h                 ;interrupt call
        killtime 10h                ;delay 10 units
        add     bl,16               ;change color of background
        pop     cx                  ;restore loop counter
        loop    repeat              ;do it 9 total times

        mov     ah,4Ch              ;return control to DOS
        int     21h
Turbo   ENDP                        ;end main procedure
        END                         ;end whole program
```

The name of the macro in this example is **killtime**. When the Assembler encounters the name **killtime** in a program, it copies the body of the macro to that location, passing the argument *increment* to the **dx** register. The local declaration prevents multiple calls to a label by creating a unique label each time **killtime** is requested. These unique labels are substituted for loop1 and loop2 automatically. This macro kills time by decrementing the contents of the **dx** and **cx** registers, creating a time delay when the program executes. The **dx** register serves as the course control for time while the **cx** register can fine-tune the delay. The amount of actual delay depends on the clock speed of your computer.

This program changes the background color of the screen nine times by adding a 16 to the **bl** register each time through the loop. The **killtime** macro will determine how long each differently colored screen remains in view. The value of the **killtime** argument was determined experimentally. Depending on the speed of your computer, you may have to adjust the values up or down.

In the following listing, the *.lst* file for this program shows how the macro was expanded within the program code:

```
Turbo Assembler Version 3.0      1/03/91      20:30:14          Page 1

 1
 2                          ;TURBO Assembly Language Programming Application
 3                          ;Copyright (c) Chris H. Pappas and William H. Murray, 1990
 4
 5                          ;using a macro for a time delay
 6
 7                                      DOSSEG
 8  0000                                .MODEL   small
 9                                      .8086
10
11  0000                                .STACK   300h
12
13  0000                                .DATA
14  0000   07D0*(20)      blank   db        2000 dup (' ')
15
16                          killtime macro   increment
17                                      local    loop1,loop2
18                                      push     dx
19                                      push     cx
20                                      mov      dx,increment
21                          loop2:      mov      cx,0FF00h
22                          loop1:      dec      cx
23                                      jnz      loop1
24                                      dec      dx
25                                      jnz      loop2
26                                      pop      cx
27                                      pop      dx
28                                      endm
29
30  07D0                                .CODE
31  0000                    Turbo   PROC      far
32  0000   B8 0000s                     mov      ax,DGROUP
33  0003   8E D8                        mov      ds,ax
34  0005   8E C0                        mov      es,ax
35
36
37
38
39
40  0007   B9 0009                      mov      cx,9
41  000A   B3 00                        mov      bl,0
42  000C   8D 2E 0000r  repeat: lea      bp,blank
43  0010   BA 0000                      mov      dx,0
44  0013   B4 13                        mov      ah,19
45  0015   B0 01                        mov      al,1
46  0017   51                           push     cx
47  0018   B9 07D0                      mov      cx,2000
48  001B   CD 10                        int      10h
49                          killtime 10h
 1   50 001D   52                       push     dx
```

```
1    51 001E  51              push    cx
1    52 001F  BA 000A         mov     dx,10h
1    53 0022  B9 FF00 ??0001: mov     cx,0FF00h
1    54 0025  49      ??0000: dec     cx
1    55 0026  75 FD           jnz     ??0000
1    56 0028  4A              dec     dx
1    57 0029  75 F7           jnz     ??0001
1    58 002B  59              pop     cx
1    59 002C  5A              pop     dx
```

Turbo Assembler Version 3.0   1/03/91 20:30:14   Page 2
prog10-2.ASM

```
60 002D  80 C3 10            add     bl,16
61 0030  59                  pop     cx
62 0031  E2 D9               loop    repeat
63
64 0033  B4 4C               mov     ah,4Ch
65 0035  CD 21               int     21h
66 0037          Turbo       ENDP
67                           END
```

Turbo Assembler Version 3.0   1/03/91   20:30:14   Page 3
Symbol Table

Symbol Name	Type	Value	Cref	(defined at #)	
??0000	Near	_TEXT:0025	#54	55	
??0001	Near	_TEXT:0022	#53	57	
??DATE	Text	"1/03/90"			
??FILENAME	Text	"prog18-2"			
??TIME	Text	"20:30:13"			
??VERSION	Number	0101			
@CODE	Text	_TEXT	#8	#30	
@CODESIZE	Text	0	#8		
@CPU	Text	0101H	#9		
@CURSEG	Text	_TEXT	#13	#30	
@DATA	Text	DGROUP	#8		
@DATASIZE	Text	0	#8		
@FILENAME	Text	prog18-2			
@WORDSIZE	Text	2	#9	#13	#30
BLANK	Byte	DGROUP:0000	#14	42	
REPEAT	Near	_TEXT:000C	#42	62	
TURBO	Far	_TEXT:0000	#31		

Macro Name   Cref
defined at #

Killtime   #16   49

Groups & Segments	Bit	Size	Align	Combine	Class	Cref	(defined at #)	
DGROUP	Group					#8	8	32
STACK	16	0300	Para	Stack	STACK	#11		
_DATA	16	07D0	Word	Public	DATA	#8	#13	
_TEXT	16	0037	Word	Public	CODE	#8	8	#30

30

Note that the macro is included in the source code but that no machine code is generated to the left. When a macro, or macro library, is used by a program, it will be listed in this manner. However, this code is not yet part of your program's executable code. Notice that the code appears again later in the listing. This is because the line **killtime 10h** called for macro insertion. This time machine code is generated to the left. All comments have been removed from the listing file to save space.

The 1 at the left-hand edge of the screen indicates a macro expansion in the listing file. The number sets this line of code apart from regular program code and should be an aid in debugging. Since **killtime** was only replicated once, the local declaration was not actually required. However, notice that loop1 and loop2 were replaced with strange new labels, ??0000 and ??0001, as a result of the local declaration. If **killtime** had been requested again, those values would be ??0002 and ??0003. To prevent programming accidents, you should make all labels within a macro local labels. Double semicolon (;;) comments are used for macros, and prevent comments from being replicated each time the macro is expanded.

A Macro Library

Macros can be entered and used by a single program or placed in a macro library that you can include with any future programs that you write. Many programmers develop a group of useful macros that they use frequently and place them in a library. They can then save time and avoid debugging headaches by calling the library rather than retyping each macro. What follows is a group of useful macros in a macro library called *tmacro.mac*. Enter this code with your Turbo editor and save it to your disk. Do not attempt to assemble this code—macro libraries remain ASCII files for their entire life.

```
blankscreen macro                     ;;blanks screen
        push    ax                    ;;save registers
        push    bx
        push    cx
        push    dx
        mov     cx,0                  ;;set upper corner of window
        mov     dx,2479h              ;;set lower corner of window
        mov     bh,7                  ;;set normal screen attribute
        mov     ax,0600h              ;;interrupt parameters
        int     10h                   ;;call interrupt
```

```
            pop     dx                  ;;restore registers
            pop     cx
            pop     bx
            pop     ax
            endm                        ;;end macro

cursor  macro   spot                ;;moves cursor to (spot)
            push    ax                  ;;save registers
            push    dx
            mov     ah,15               ;;get current screen
            int     10h                 ;;call interrupt & set bx values
            mov     dx,spot             ;;move screen location to dx
            mov     ah,2                ;;set cursor parameter
            int     10h                 ;;call the interrupt
            pop     dx                  ;;restore the registers
            pop     ax
            endm                        ;;end macro

setscreen macro scrmode
            push    ax                  ;;save registers
            mov     ah,00               ;;prepare for screen switch
            mov     al,scrmode          ;;desired screen
            int     10h                 ;;bios interrupt
            pop     ax                  ;;restore registers
            endm                        ;;end macro

drawdot macro   shade
            push    ax                  ;;save registers
            push    cx
            push    dx
            mov     ah,12               ;;write dot parameter
            mov     al,shade            ;;color of dot
            int     10h                 ;;bios interrupt
            pop     dx
            pop     cx
            pop     ax
            endm

numout  macro   value
            local   loop1,printit       ;;prints ascii number to screen
            push    ax                  ;;save registers
            push    bx
            push    cx
            push    dx
            push    di                  ;;save di for future use
            mov     dx,value            ;;number to convert to ascii
            mov     cx,0                ;;zero out cx
            lea     di,mybuffer         ;;address of temp buffer
loop1:  push    cx                  ;;save value of cx
            mov     ax,dx               ;;copy dx into ax, then
            mov     dx,0                ;;zero out dx
            mov     cx,10               ;;convert hex value to this base
            div     cx                  ;;perform division: ax/cx
            xchg    ax,dx               ;;remainder goes in ax
            add     al,30h              ;;convert byte digit to ascii
```

```
        mov     [di],al         ;;save at di mybuffer location
        inc     di              ;;indicate next storage location
        pop     cx              ;;get orig cx
        inc     cx              ;;increment
        cmp     dx,0            ;;check dx for zero
        jnz     loop1           ;;if no, go around again
printit: dec    di              ;;if yes, print digits
        mov     al,[di]         ;;get a character from mybuffer
        push    dx              ;;save dx
        mov     dl,al           ;;prepare to print
        mov     ah,2            ;;dos print char parameter
        int     21h             ;;do it
        pop     dx              ;;restore dx
        loop    printit         ;;next character to print
        pop     di              ;;restore di
        pop     dx              ;;restore registers
        pop     cx
        pop     bx
        pop     ax
        endm                    ;;end macro
```

A technique for clearing the screen was shown in the last chapter as an entire program. Now, you can call an equivalent routine contained in the **blankscreen** macro as often as you like, without having to enter the code repeatedly. The **cursor** macro uses the value in the argument, *spot,* to obtain the vertical **dh** and horizontal **dl** locations for the cursor on the 80×25 text screen. The **setscreen** macro will allow you to switch screens with the use of a BIOS 10H interrupt. The screen value is passed through the argument *scrmode.* If you want to do graphics, the **drawdot** macro accepts the color of the dot in the argument *shade.* The screen coordinates are passed in **cx** (horizontal) and **dx** (vertical). **numout** will be used to place a single ASCII number on the screen. The value to be printed is passed to the macro through the argument *value.* Remember, a number must be converted to an ASCII value before it can be placed on the screen. **numout** requires that a variable, *mybuffer,* be declared in the data segment. It should reserve 4 bytes:

```
4 dup (' ')
```

The following example shows how a macro library can speed up the program development process and shorten the amount of code that you must write:

```
;TURBO Assembly Language Programming Application
;Copyright (c) Chris H. Pappas and William H. Murray, 1990

;program to display a count sequence on the screen
```

```
INCLUDE TMACRO.MAC                  ;get Turbo macro library

        DOSSEG                      ;use Intel segment-ordering
        .MODEL   small              ;set model size
        .8086                       ;8086 instructions

        .STACK   300h               ;set up 768-byte stack

        .DATA                       ;set up data location
text    db       'Incrementing a count on the screen $'
mybuffer db      4 dup (' ')

killtime   macro   increment
        local    loop2,loop1        ;;loop2 & loop1 are local
        push     dx                 ;;save dx & cx values
        push     cx
        mov      dx,increment       ;;pass increment value to dx
loop2:  mov      cx,0FF00h          ;;load cx with 00FF00h
loop1:  dec      cx                 ;;kill time
        jnz      loop1              ;;if not zero, continue
        dec      dx                 ;;if cx=0, decrement dx
        jnz      loop2              ;;if dx not zero, load cx again
        pop      cx                 ;;restore cx & dx
        pop      dx
        endm                        ;;leave the macro

        .CODE
Turbo   PROC     far                ;main procedure declaration
        mov      ax,DGROUP          ;point ds toward .DATA
        mov      ds,ax

        blankscreen                 ;call blankscreen macro
        cursor   0018h              ;center message to screen
        lea      dx,text            ;print the message
        mov      ah,9               ;print parameter
        int      21h                ;call interrupt

        mov      ax,00              ;initialize count to zero
repeat: cursor   0C28h              ;move to center screen
        numout   ax                 ;print number on screen
        killtime 10h                ;wait 10 units of delay
        add      ax,1               ;add a 1 to ax
        cmp      ax,100             ;counted to 100?
        je       done
        jmp      repeat             ;do it again?
done:   blankscreen                 ;blank screen again

        mov      ah,4Ch             ;return control to DOS
        int      21h
Turbo   ENDP                        ;end main procedure
        END                         ;end whole program
```

This program will use several macros; some are contained in the
tmacro.mac library. The program will clear the screen, print the message

Table 18-1.   Color Choices for Dot Colors

0 - Black	4 - Red	8 - Dark Gray	12 - Light Red
1 - Blue	5 - Magenta	9 - Light Blue	13 - Light Magenta
2 - Green	6 - Brown	10 - Light Green	14 - Yellow
3 - Cyan	7 - White	11 - Light Cyan	15 - Intense White

"Incrementing a count on the screen" at the top, and then continuously display a count from 0 to 99 at the center of the screen. The program will terminate operation after reaching 99. To include the macro library in the program, the *INCLUDE* directive is used. Use the *INCLUDE* directive to specify the drive and the complete path to the macro library.

The **blankscreen** macro clears the monitor screen. The **cursor** macro moves the cursor to the first row and then over to column 18h (24 spaces) to center the message. The **numout** macro places the numbers on the screen. When **numout** is called, the digits in the **ax** register are converted to ASCII characters and printed to the screen. Decimal numbers are generated by the **numout** macro, in a complicated process that converts the hexadecimal digits to decimal. Before you leave the program, the screen is once again cleared. If you have the time, assemble the file and examine the *.lst* file. You will be surprised how many lines of code were saved by macros.

The following final example uses the macro library to perform a simple graphics line draw routine. Table 18-1 lists the various color choices that you can use for the dots.

```
;TURBO Assembly Language Programming Application
;Copyright (c) Chris H. Pappas and William H. Murray, 1990

;program to draw a line on the VGA screen

INCLUDE TMACRO.MAC              ;get Turbo macro library
        DOSSEG                  ;use Intel segment-ordering
        .MODEL  small           ;set model size
        .8086                   ;8086 instructions

        .STACK  300h            ;set up 768-byte stack

        .CODE
Turbo   PROC    far             ;main procedure declaration

        blankscreen             ;call blankscreen macro
        setscreen 12h           ;set to 640 x 480 screen
```

```
            mov      dx,0                ;start in upper-left corner
            mov      cx,0
repeat:
            drawdot 12                   ;plot a light red line
            inc      dx                  ;move down and to the right
            inc      cx
            cmp      dx,479              ;at bottom of screen yet?
            je       finish              ;if yes, leave loop
            jmp      repeat              ;if no, do loop again
finish:
            mov      ah,07               ;wait for a key press
            int      21h

            setscreen  3                 ;now return to text screen

            mov      ah,4Ch              ;return control to DOS
            int      21h
Turbo       ENDP                         ;end main procedure
            END                          ;end whole program
```

The **setscreen** macro is used to switch to the 640×480 VGA graphics screen. (Refer to Appendix B, "DOS Interrupt Parameters," for the various screen parameters.) If you are using an EGA or CGA monitor, select the appropriate screen mode and adjust the value in **dx** to the correct length. The **drawdot** macro is placed in a loop for this program. Recall that you can only plot a single dot with this routine. To draw a line, a series of dots are plotted with repeated calls to **drawdot**. To allow you to observe the line before returning to the text screen, a simple DOS interrupt is used to make the program wait for a keypress. Try writing a few macros that allow you to draw a box or filled rectangle. A box is made up of four lines. You can draw a filled rectangle by plotting a series of horizontal lines.

PROCEDURES

All assembly language programs must have at least one procedure. Assembly language programs can contain many procedures, just as C programs can contain many functions. Assembly language procedures can be considered as *near* (intrasegment) or *far* (intersegment). Debugged routines, such as the ones in the previous macro library, can be placed in procedures within the program; the procedure behaves more like a subroutine. You can call these procedures from the main procedure by using the **call** instruction. The following section illustrates both intrasegment and intersegment procedures.

The Framework of a Procedure

In most assembly programs, the placement of the .STACK, .DATA, and .CODE declarations is about the same. In the example programs, the main procedure, called Turbo, always has a far attribute when it is declared. Every additional procedure added to your program code will be structured in a similar manner with either a near or far attribute.

The near or far attribute for a procedure helps determine the type of call instruction generated when that procedure is requested. A path must also be established for the return from the procedure. This path of instructions will differ depending upon the near or far attribute. If the procedure has a near attribute, the **ip** (instruction pointer) will be saved to the stack. If the procedure has a far attribute, both the **cs** (code segment) and the **ip** (instruction pointer) are saved to the stack.

The next example demonstrates the similarity of code used in macros and procedures. The **killtime** macro of the first example is converted into a near procedure, which is also named **killtime**.

```
;TURBO Assembly Language Programming Application
;Copyright (c) Chris H. Pappas and William H. Murray, 1990

;program to blank screen

        DOSSEG                  ;use Intel segment-ordering
        .MODEL  small           ;set model size
        .8086                   ;8086 instructions

        .STACK  300h            ;set up 768-byte stack

        .DATA                   ;set up data location
blank   db      2000 dup (' ')

        .CODE
Turbo   PROC    far             ;main procedure declaration
        mov     ax,DGROUP       ;point ds toward .DATA
        mov     ds,ax
        mov     es,ax

;program will clear the screen by writing 2000 blanks.
;If these are written with a different value in bl,
;the color of the whole screen will be changed.  The killtime
;procedure will hold the color for a specified amount of time.
        mov     cx,9            ;repeat loop 9 times
        mov     bl,0            ;set background color
repeat: lea     bp,blank        ;write a string of blanks
        mov     dx,0            ;set cursor to top left corner
        mov     ah,19           ;write string attribute
        mov     al,1            ;print characters and move
```

```
cursor
        push    cx                      ;save loop counter
        mov     cx,2000                 ;write 2000 blanks
        int     10h                     ;interrupt call
        call    killtime                ;call the near delay procedure
        add     bl,16                   ;change background color
        pop     cx                      ;restore original loop counter
        loop    repeat                  ;do it 9 total times

        mov     ah,4Ch                  ;return control to dos
        int     21h
Turbo   endp                            ;end main procedure

killtime proc   near
        push    dx                      ;save original dx & cx values
        push    cx
        mov     dx,10h                  ;amount of time increment
loop2:  mov     cx,0FF00h               ;load cx with 00FF00h
loop1:  dec     cx                      ;kill time
        jnz     loop1                   ;if not zero, continue
        dec     dx                      ;if cx=0, decrement dx
        jnz     loop2                   ;if dx not zero, load cx again
        pop     cx                      ;restore dx & cx
        pop     dx
        ret                             ;determine path back
killtime endp                           ;end near procedure

        end                             ;end whole program
```

Notice that the **killtime** procedure is listed after the main procedure, unlike the macro that was placed before the main procedure. You should include all additional procedures in this manner. Notice also that the call to the **killtime** routine has been changed from **killtime 10** to **call killtime**. You invoke macros by just using their name; you invoke procedures with the **call** instruction.

A subtle change is the removal of the 10 during the call to the procedure. Arguments cannot be passed to procedures as they were to macros. To get the 10 hexadecimal units of time delay, the 10 is loaded directly in the **killtime** procedure. The **killtime** procedure itself looks like a miniature program.

At this point, there seems to be little difference between a macro and a near procedure. Actually, the differences are tremendous. The next listing is the *.lst* file for this program (all comments have been deleted to fit the listing on the page).

Turbo Assembler Version 3.0   1/03/91   20:35:02   Page 1
prog18-3.ASM

```
1
2     ;TURBO Assembly Language Programming Application
3     ;Copyright (c) Chris H. Pappas and William H. Murray, 1990
4
5
6
7                                    DOSSEG
8     0000                           .MODEL   small
9                                    .8086
10
11    0000                           .STACK   300h
12
13    0000                           .DATA
14    0000   07D0*(20)       blank   db       2000 dup (' ')
15
16    07D0                           .CODE
17    0000                   Turbo   PROC     far
18    0000   B8 0000s                mov      ax,DGROUP
19    0003   8E D8                   mov      ds,ax
20    0005   8E C0                   mov      es,ax
21
22
23
24
25
26    0007   B9 0009                 mov      cx,9
27    000A   B3 00                   mov      bl,0
28    000C   8D 2E 0000r     repeat: lea      bp,blank
29    0010   BA 0000                 mov      dx,0
30    0013   B4 13                   mov      ah,19
31    0015   B0 01                   mov      al,1
32    0017   51                      push     cx
33    0018   B9 07D0                 mov      cx,2000
34    001B   CD 10                   int      10h
35    001D   E8 000A                 call     killtime
36    0020   80 C3 10                add      bl,16
37    0023   59                      pop      cx
38    0024   E2 E6                   loop     repeat
39
40    0026   B4 4C                   mov      ah,4Ch
41    0028   CD 21                   int      21h
42    002A                   Turbo   endp
43
44    002A                   killtime proc    near
45    002A   52                      push     dx
46    002B   51                      push     cx
47    002C   BA 0010                 mov      dx,10h
48    002F   B9 FF00        loop2:   mov      cx,0FF00h
49    0032   49             loop1:   dec      cx
50    0033   75 FD                   jnz      loop1
51    0035   4A                      dec      dx
52    0036   75 F7                   jnz      loop2
53    0038   59                      pop      cx
54    0039   5A                      pop      dx
```

```
55 003A  C3                                    ret
56 003B                         killtime endp
57
58                                      end
```

```
Turbo Assembler Version 3.0     1/03/91    20:35:02        Page 2
Symbol Table
```

Symbol Name	Type	Value	Cref	(defined at #)
??DATE	Text	"1/03/90"		
??FILENAME	Text	"prog18-3 "		
??TIME	Text	"20:35:01"		
??VERSION	Number	0101		
@CODE	Text	_TEXT	#8	#16
@CODESIZE	Text	0	#8	
@CPU	Text	0101H	#9	
@CURSEG	Text	_TEXT	#13	#16
@DATA	Text	DGROUP	#8	
@DATASIZE	Text	0	#8	
@FILENAME	Text	prog18-3	#9	#13
@WORDSIZE	Text	2		
#16				
BLANK	Byte	DGROUP:0000	#14	28
KILLTIME	Near	_TEXT:002A	35	#44
LOOP1	Near	_TEXT:0032	#49	50
LOOP2	Near	_TEXT:002F	#48	52
REPEAT	Near	_TEXT:000C	#28	38
TURBO	Far	_TEXT:0000	#17	

Groups & Segments	Bit Size	Align	Combine	Class	Cref (defined at #)			
DGROUP	Group				#8	8	18	
STACK	16 0300	Para	Stack	STACK	#11			
_DATA	16 07D0	Word	Public	DATA	#8	#13		
_TEXT	16 003B	Word	Public	CODE	#8	8	#16	16

Unlike the previous *.lst* listing, this listing contains no 1's along the left edge of the printout. This is because no macros were expanded in the code. When the **killtime** procedure was called, it was coded just like any other program code. You can call a procedure such as **killtime** frequently by just typing **call killtime**. The actual code for **killtime** only appears once, regardless of the number of calls to the procedure in your program.

Programs written with procedures are often more compact, since procedures, unlike macros, are not expanded with each use. There is a price to be paid for compactness, however. Programs that use procedures instead of macros do not execute in line. Jumping from the main procedure to a subprocedure takes additional time. If this call is made frequently, say within the body of a loop, the difference in time can become quite noticeable.

A Procedure Library

A group of procedures can be assembled into a *procedure library*. This collection of *.obj* routines will be coupled to the user's program at link time. A procedure library must be handled a little differently than a macro library or procedures contained within the program itself. First, these procedures will have a far attribute since they are external to the current code segment. Second, notice that *mybuffer, shade,* and *scrmode* are declared public in the data segment. Third, an **extern** declaration is required for all procedures that are external to this listing. This declaration is required to avoid assembly and link conflicts. These variables are to be shared with the external procedure library. The next example, which demonstrates how to use a procedure library, is similar to an earlier program that used a macro library:

```
;TURBO Assembly Language Programming Application
;Copyright (c) Chris H. Pappas and William H. Murray, 1990

;program to increment a count to the screen

        DOSSEG                  ;use Intel segment-ordering
        .MODEL  small           ;set model size
        .8086                   ;8086 instructions

        extrn   blankscreen:far,cursor:far
        extrn   setscreen:far,drawdot:far,numout:far

        .STACK  300h            ;set up 768-byte stack

        .DATA                   ;set up data location
        public  mybuffer,shade,scrmode
text    db      'Incrementing a count on the screen $'
mybuffer db     4 dup (' ')
shade   db      0
scrmode db      0

        .CODE
Turbo   PROC    far             ;main procedure declaration
        mov     ax,DGROUP       ;point ds toward .DATA
        mov     ds,ax

        call    blankscreen     ;call blankscreen macro
        mov     dx,0019h        ;set location for cursor
        call    cursor          ;center message
        lea     dx,text         ;point to text for printing
        mov     ah,09           ;interrupt parameter
        int     21h

        mov     ax,0            ;initialize to zero
repeat: mov     dx,0C28h        ;set cursor location
        call    cursor          ;move to center screen
```

```
          call    numout            ;print number on screen
          mov     dx,10h            ;put in 10h delay units
          call    killtime          ;call killtime
          add     ax,01             ;increment ax
          cmp     al,100            ;have we reached 100?
          je      done
          jmp     repeat            ;do it again?
done:     call    blankscreen       ;blank screen again

          mov     ah,4Ch            ;return control to DOS
          int     21h
Turbo     ENDP                      ;end main procedure

killtime proc    near
          push    dx                ;save original dx & cx values
          push    cx
          mov     dx,10h            ;time increment value
loop2:    mov     cx,0FF00h         ;load cx with 00FF00h
loop1:    dec     cx                ;kill time
          jnz     loop1             ;if not zero, continue
          dec     dx                ;if cx=0, decrement dx
          jnz     loop2             ;if dx not zero, load cx again
          pop     cx                ;restore dx & cx
          pop     dx
          ret                       ;determine path back
killtime endp                       ;end near procedure
          end                       ;end whole program
```

Notice that the **extern** directive lists the names of each procedure and attaches a far call attribute.

```
extrn   blankscreen:far,cursor:far,
extrn   setscreen:far,drawdot:far,numout:far
```

Compare this first section of main code with that of the macro example. Note that the cursor position is placed in **dx** before the **cursor** procedure is called. This technique solves the problem of passing parameters by passing them in registers that are global in scope. Look at the procedure library. The file name that these procedures are stored under is only required when linking this code with the main program. Here, it is called *tproc.asm*.

```
          dosseg
          .model  small
          .8086

          .code
          public blankscreen,cursor,setscreen,drawdot,numout
          extrn  mybuffer:byte,scrmode:byte,shade:byte
start:
blankscreen proc far               ;clears screen
```

```
        push    ax                  ;save registers
        push    bx
        push    cx
        push    dx
        mov     cx,0                ;set upper corner of window
        mov     dx,2479h            ;set lower corner of window
        mov     bh,7                ;set normal screen attribute
        mov     ax,0600h            ;interrupt parameters
        int     10h                 ;call interrupt
        pop     dx                  ;restore registers
        pop     cx
        pop     bx
        pop     ax
        ret
blankscreen endp

cursor  proc    far                 ;moves cursor to (spot)
        push    ax                  ;save register
        mov     ah,15               ;get current screen
        int     10h                 ;call interrupt, set bx values
        mov     ah,2                ;set the cursor parameter
        int     10h                 ;call the interrupt
        pop     ax                  ;restore the register
        ret
cursor  endp

setscreen proc  far                 ;sets screen mode
        push    ax                  ;save register
        mov     ah,0                ;prepare for screen switch
        mov     al,scrmode          ;desired screen
        int     10h                 ;bios interrupt
        pop     ax                  ;restore register
        ret
setscreen endp

drawdot proc    far
        push    ax                  ;save registers
        push    cx
        push    dx
        mov     ah,12               ;draw dot parameter
        mov     al,shade            ;color value
        int     10h                 ;bios interrupt
        pop     dx
        pop     cx
        pop     ax
        ret
drawdot endp

numout  proc    far                 ;prints number at cursor location
        push    ax                  ;save registers
        push    bx
        push    cx
        push    dx
        push    di                  ;save di, again, for future use
        mov     dx,ax               ;number to convert to ascii
        mov     cx,0                ;zero out cx
```

```
          lea     di,mybuffer     ;address of temp buffer
loop1:    push    cx              ;hold cx, each time through
          mov     ax,dx           ;copy dx into ax, then
          mov     dx,0            ;zero out dx
          mov     cx,10           ;convert hex value to this base
          div     cx              ;perform division: ax/cx
          xchg    ax,dx           ;remainder in ax
          add     al,30h          ;convert byte digit to ascii
          mov     [di],al         ;save in mybuffer location
          inc     di              ;point to next storage location
          pop     cx              ;get cx before conversion
          inc     cx              ;increment
          cmp     dx,0            ;is dx reached zero yet?
          jnz     loop1           ;if no, go around again
printit:  dec     di              ;if yes, let's print digits
          mov     al,[di]         ;get a char from mybuffer
          push    dx              ;save dx
          mov     dl,al           ;prepare to print
          mov     ah,2            ;dos print char parameter
          int     21h             ;do it
          pop     dx              ;restore dx
          loop    printit         ;get next character to print
          pop     di              ;restore di
          pop     dx              ;restore registers
          pop     cx
          pop     bx
          pop     ax
          ret
numout endp

          end     start
```

The program overhead for external procedures is minimal:

```
public blankscreen,cursor,setscreen,drawdot,numout
```

In this case, each procedure in the library is declared public so that it can be shared with other programs. The variables that are being shared are declared as **extrn**, because they will be defined in the host program. Notice that their size **db** is also registered. This will permit the intersegment exchange of information. The remainder of the overhead is standard fare.

The procedure's name is followed by the directive **proc** and a far attribute. Additionally, all procedures end with the **ret** instruction followed by the name of the procedure and the **endp** directive. The body of each procedure has only been modified slightly from its macro counterpart.

At this point, there are two separate programs. You can consider one the host program and the other a procedure library. Each of these must be assembled separately with TASM. Once this is done, the *.obj* files for each can be combined by the Linker. The Borland TASM manuals describe how to do this and how to take advantage of various linker options. The following example is one possible method for linking these files. This method assumes that the Linker and the files to be linked are on the C drive.

```
c:tlink mainfile + tproc
```

Recall that a macro library is a collection of unassembled routines that reside in a source code file, whereas a procedure library is a collection of assembled routines that reside in an object file. Macros are brought in at the time of assembly (TASM), while the procedure library is brought in at the time of linking (TLINK).

OBJECT MODULE LIBRARIES

An *object module library* doesn't differ greatly from a macro library or a procedure library. All three can store debugged code, which can be called by other programs at a future date. Object module libraries are most closely associated with the Linker. Recall that when you link a program, the following menu arguments are possible:

```
TLINK  objfiles, exefile, mapfile, libfiles
```

You have learned how to specify the first three TLINK options. What are those *libfiles*? The *libfiles* option used by TLINK is closest to the procedure library that was used in the last section. Libraries that are called at link time are actually collections of assembled procedures, much like the procedure library. The Assembler package also includes a library manager, TLIB, that you use to help build, edit, and manage library object modules. When you need a particular library, enter its name as a link argument at the *libfiles* parameter. Like macro and procedure libraries, object module libraries can greatly reduce program development time because frequently called procedures have already been written and debugged.

The Librarian, TLIB, supports the following operations:

- Add object files (+)
- Delete object files (−)
- Extract an object module (*)
- Replace an object module (−+ or +−)
- Extract and remove an object module (−* or *−)

The following example shows how to create an object module library with the Librarian. Basically, you will convert the previous procedure library to an object module library. The conversion and management of the procedure library is the job of the Librarian. To find out the options provided with the Librarian, just type

```
c>tlib
```

The following list should appear on the screen:

```
Syntax: TLIB libname [/C] [/E] commands, listfile
     libname      library file pathname
     commands     sequence of operations to be performed (optional)
     listfile     file name for listing file (optional)

A command is of the form: <symbol>modulename, where <symbol> is:
     +              add modulename to the library
     -              remove modulename from the library
     *              extract modulename without removing it
     -+ or +-       replace modulename in library
     -* or *-       extract modulename and remove it

     /C             case-sensitive library
     /E             create extended dictionary
     /PSIZE         set library page to SIZE

Use @filepath to continue from file "filepath".
Use '&' at end of a line to continue onto the next line.
```

For this example, your collection of procedures from the previous example, called **tproc**, will be converted to a library named *turbolib.lib*:

```
c:tlib  turbolib +tproc, turbolib
```

The library name immediately follows the call to TLIB. Next is any module of procedures to be added or deleted from the library. In this case, **tproc**, is to be added. Finally, a listing file can optionally be specified. Libraries default to a *.lib* file extension and listing files default to *.lst*. Once the library has been created, you can add more procedures and routines at any time with the Librarian. To incorporate this library at link time, simply type **turbolib** as the fourth argument in the TLINK specifications.

At first, the object module library doesn't seem very different from a procedure library. It is, however. First, remember that a procedure library is coupled with other object modules at link time, at the *.obj* option. Second, with the Librarian, you can add or subtract new procedures from the library at any time. You cannot do this with a procedure library without going back to the source code. This makes a link library more dynamic than either of the previous methods. Plus, it enables you to add new procedures to an already established library without revealing the contents of the whole library.

If you want to view the contents of *turbolib*, just request the listing file:

```
c>type turbolib.lst
```

The library listing file will return a list of all public procedures used in the library:

```
Publics by module

MYPROC    size = 116
     BLANKSCREEN                CURSOR
     DRAWDOT                    NUMOUT
     SETSCREEN
```

CONTRASTING MACROS, PROCEDURES, AND LIBRARIES

Macros, procedures, and libraries perform many of the same functions. They give you the flexibility to write and debug code once. You can then use that code in any program you like. This makes programming more efficient and more modular. Each type has its own advantages and disadvantages. The proper selection of a macro, procedure, or library can make the difference between small code size and large, or a fast and a slow program.

Advantages and Disadvantages of Macros

The advantages of macros are

- Macros produce fast code since they execute "in line" within a program.
- Macros can pass and receive arguments that affect how they operate.
- You can save macros in a source code library that you can easily edit.
- The programming overhead for macros is simple.
- You can bring macro libraries into your program with a simple *INCLUDE* directive.

The disadvantages of macros are

- Macros make the source code longer since they are expanded each time they are called.
- A macro library reveals your code to any user of the library.

Advantages and Disadvantages of Procedure Libraries

The advantage of procedure libraries is

- Procedures allow source code to remain short, since procedures are not expanded within a program's code.

The disadvantages of procedure libraries are

- Procedures tend to slow program execution. This is because each call to a procedure must leave the "main" code and jump to another location within the program.
- The overhead for procedure use is more involved. Procedures must be declared as near or far, and library files must be marked as external.
- You cannot send parameters to a procedure to alter how it executes.

Advantages and Disadvantages of Object Module Libraries

The advantages of object module libraries are

- Same advantages as for procedure libraries.
- With the Librarian, you can easily add or delete routines from a library.
- Library source code is known only to you.

The disadvantages of object module libraries are the same as those for procedure libraries.

Which method is the best for you? When should you choose a macro over a procedure? When is an object module library better than a procedure library? Here are some recommendations:

- For short pieces of code, use a macro. Their operations are faster, with little increase in code length.
- For infrequently called routines within a program, choose a macro. If routines are not called frequently, code expansion will not seriously affect the program.
- If you are just starting the program creation process, use a macro. Macros tend to be easier to write, edit, and manage.
- For long routines, choose a procedure. Procedures tend to make the source code shorter.
- For frequently called routines within a program, choose a procedure. Procedures do not expand program code each time they are called.
- If the same routines are used frequently in your programs, put them in an object module library for easy access.
- If you are developing a package of routines for commercial use, choose an object module library. You will only need to ship the *.obj* file, thus offering a degree of protection to your source code.

19

BINDING C AND ASSEMBLY LANGUAGE CODE

The Borland C++ package may at first seem to offer several separate and complete products. The C++ compiler is certainly the reason you purchased the software. You also received a Linker, Assembler, Debugger, and Profiler. The preceding chapters have shown how to write code in two distinct ways. First, you learned how to use the Compiler, Linker, Debugger, and Profiler to develop C and C++ code. Second, you learned how to write assembly language programs with the Assembler, Linker, and Debugger.

In this chapter, you will learn how to combine C and C++ and assembly language object code into one working program. You will soon be able to combine your knowledge of C and assembly language to produce programs that are faster and can control hardware features that you can't control with built-in C and C++ functions.

The discussion will focus on calling assembly language code from C. The C code will appear as the main routine and the assembly language code as an external function. However, it is also possible, although not as common, to call C programs from assembly language source code.

USING INLINE ASSEMBLY LANGUAGE

Instead of splicing C and assembly language code together, you can actually write assembly language code in your C source file. This is called *inline code*. Your C++ compiler allows you to insert assembly language code directly into the C or C++ source code. This technique is ideal for simple assembly language routines, such as DOS and BIOS interrupt calls. To use this technique, include the following pragma at the start of your C code to notify the compiler that your program contains assembly language code:

```
#pragma  inline
```

The actual inline assembly language code is included between two braces and starts with the *asm* keyword. For example:

```
asm {
    push    dx                  /*save general registers*/
    push    cx
    push    bx
    push    ax
    mov     cx,0                /*upper corner of window*/
    mov     dx,2479H            /*lower corner of window*/
    mov     bh,7                /*normal screen attribute*/
    mov     ax,0600H            /*BIOS interrupt value*/
    int     10H                 /*call interrupt*/
    pop     ax
    pop     bx
    pop     cx
    pop     dx                  /*restore general registers*/
}
```

Notice that comments are inserted as though they were C comments, even though they are associated with the inline assembly language code. This assembly language routine will clear the text screen with a call to the BIOS interrupt function. This is an adaptation of an assembly language program that was illustrated in Chapter 18, "Power Programming: Macros and Procedures." Additional BIOS and DOS interrupt values are listed in Appendix B, "DOS 10H, 21H, and 33H Interrupt Parameters."

Your C++ compiler must also know the path to the subdirectories in which your assembler is located. You can do this by setting the path command for your system.

The Parallel Port Connection

The next example will demonstrate how to send information to the computer's parallel port with inline assembly language instructions. First, however, you need to know some details concerning the parallel port.

The parallel port on most IBM-compatible computers is a general-purpose 8-bit communications port used to drive a wide range of printers, plotters, and other external devices. The data lines of the parallel port interface respond to one I/O class of assembly code instructions: **out**. You can use data from these lines to control hardware circuits of your own choosing. (The IBM family of PS/2 computers has parallel ports that can be programmed to read 8 bits of data and respond to the assembly language instruction **in**.)

The parallel port is an 8-bit data port, which means that 8 bits of data can be sent to the port. The 8-bit assembly language data type is **byte**, while the corresponding C data type is **char**. Data is written to the output pins when a write (**out**) instruction occurs. The output signals from the parallel port have sink currents of 20 mA and can source 0.55 mA. The high-level output voltage is 5.0 Vdc while the low-level output voltage is 0.5 Vdc. Data is present at pins 2 through 9 and represents the data lines D0 to D7.

Figure 19-1 shows the parallel port D shell connector. Table 19-1 describes the pin assignment for this connector.

Don't be put off by the technical information on ports; the programming is fairly straightforward.

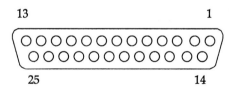

Figure 19-1.   The parallel port D shell connector

Table 19-1.   Pin Assignment for the Parallel Connector

Pin	Description
1	−STROBE
2	Data bit 0
3	Data bit 1
4	Data bit 2
5	Data bit 3
6	Data bit 4
7	Data bit 5
8	Data bit 6
9	Data bit 7
10	−ACK
11	BUSY
12	PE
13	SLCT
14	−AUTO FEED XT
15	−ERROR
16	−INIT
17	−SLCT IN
18 to 25	Ground

The L.E.D. Lights

The example in this section is a complete program that makes two calls to inline assembly language routines. The first routine clears the screen and the second sends an 8-bit value to the parallel port.

The previous section described the parallel port's output as having sink currents of 20 mA and source currents of 0.55 mA. Since the output voltage from the port is TTL compatible (logic 1 is 5.0 Vdc while logic 0 is 0.5 Vdc), the parallel port can directly drive small LED lights.

If you want to wire eight LED lights to your parallel port, you need only a cable that will connect the parallel port to a prototyping board, some hookup wire, and eight LED lights. This example used a 25-pin D shell connector to connect to the parallel port with a ribbon cable terminating in a 24-pin male dip header. It also discarded pin #13 from the D shell connector. The prototyping board was the type that allows DIP chips to be inserted and removed easily. You can find these parts at electronic supply

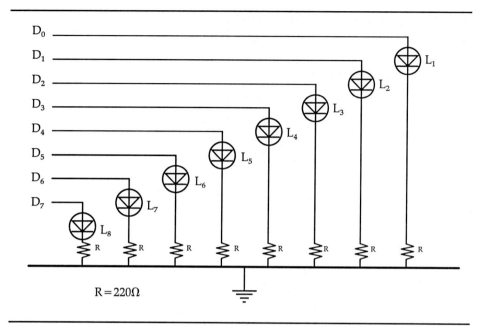

Figure 19-2.   Wiring eight LED lamps to the parallel port

stores throughout the United States. If you purchase connectors that clamp over the ribbon cable, no soldering will be necessary.

The voltages present at the parallel port are lower than that of a car battery and don't present a shock hazard. It is also nearly impossible to damage the computer even if you make wrong connections. You must remember, however, that you are making "live" connections to the computer. Be very careful not to connect the parallel port to any external device or outlet where unsafe voltages are present. Figure 19-2 illustrates the circuit used for this example.

The following C code contains the screen clearing routine, shown earlier in this chapter, and a routine for accessing the parallel port:

```
/*
 *    A C program that demonstrates how to use inline
 *    assembly language to clear the screen and access
 *    the parallel port.  This program will sequentially
 *    light 8 LED lamps connected to data lines D0 - D7
 *    of port 956 (LPT1).
 *    Copyright (c) Chris H. Pappas and William H. Murray, 1990
 */
```

```
#pragma   inline

#include <dos.h>
#include <stdio.h>
#include <math.h>

main()
{
   int i,temp;
   int port=956;

   /*clear the text screen*/
   asm {
      mov      cx,0              /*upper corner of window*/
      mov      dx,2479H          /*lower corner of window*/
      mov      bh,7              /*normal screen attribute*/
      mov      ax,0600H          /*BIOS interrupt value*/
      int      10H               /*call interrupt*/
   }

   for (i=0;i<9;i++) {
      temp=(int) pow(2.0,(double) i);

      /*gain access to the parallel port*/
      asm {
         mov      dx,port        /*place the parallel port number*/
         mov      ax,temp        /*value to be sent to port*/
         out      dx,al          /*send only lower 8 bits*/
      }

      printf("%d\n",temp);
      delay(1000);
   }

   return (0);
}
```

Details of how the separate C and assembly language routines work have been covered in earlier chapters, so further detail on that code will not be included here. However, this program does something far more interesting than just printing numbers to the screen: It sequences the 8-bit values at the parallel port.

With the correct timing sequence, you can create a set of miniature chaser lights. Since each data bit at the parallel port corresponds to an integer power of 2, the numbers 1, 2, 4, 8, 16, 32, 64, and 128 are generated with the **pow** function and sent to the parallel port. (Actually, 256 is also generated and has the effect of turning the sequence off at the completion of the program.)

Why not wire this circuit and experiment with what you can achieve? Writing inline assembly language code makes an efficient use of your professional tools. Try altering the program so that successive pairs of LED lights are sequenced.

WRITING SEPARATE C AND ASSEMBLY LANGUAGE MODULES

Inline assembly language code becomes unmanageable and hard to understand as your program size grows. When you need more complicated assembly language routines, a separate assembly language procedure is often the best solution.

When you use separate assembly language modules, they are treated as an external function and called from the C host program. The assembly language routine must, therefore, be prototyped as a function in the C or C++ host program, along with a list of arguments that are to be passed. The technique for performing this operation will be described in the next sections.

When combining C and assembly language code, you must learn how arguments are passed from the C host program to the assembly language routine.

The New Method of Passing Arguments

There are two methods for passing arguments in C: an older, more complicated method, and a new streamlined method. The old method demands a comprehensive understanding of the computer's stack frame and an assembly language skill for receiving and dealing with the values from the C calling program. The new method puts much less demand on the programmer to understand the computer's architecture. Your compiler uses the new method, but will also permit you to use the older technique. The strongest argument for learning the old technique is that some people are still writing code in that form. If this becomes a problem for you, see Borland's *Programmer's Guide* for information on using the stack frame for passing arguments. The following examples will use the new method of passing arguments with the traditional C calling convention.

An external assembly language function, prototyped in the C host program, might look something like this:

```
int adder(int num1,int num2,int num3);
```

This prototype seems similar to those used for C functions within the host program. The assembly language program can intercept these arguments with the following line of code:

```
adder   PROC    C NEAR   n1,n2,n3:WORD
```

The capital C, a keyword here, tells the program to expect the arguments to be passed from right to left via the stack. The alternate form is to use *PASCAL* instead of *C*. If you use *PASCAL*, the arguments are passed from left to right. The C form of passing arguments is the preferred technique and the one used in all of the examples. The *PASCAL* form is an alternate form employed by Microsoft for calling Windows and OS/2 functions. The procedure is *NEAR* when using the small memory model. If you are using the medium, large, or huge memory model, the procedure would be declared *FAR*. Again, for additional information on these techniques, consult your Borland manuals. The other new feature is listing the arguments and their assembly language data type. Recall that the popular data types in assembly language include **byte**, **word**, and **dword** because you can place them directly in system registers.

A First Look at Argument Passing

This first example uses three separate files. The first is a *make* file named *first*, the second the program named *first.c*, and the third the assembly language module named *task.asm*. You should use *make* files whenever you are linking more than one module. (The *make* utility was explained in Chapter 3, "Getting Started with Borland's Assembler.")

This example passes an 8-bit char, a 16-bit integer, and a 32-bit long value to the assembly language program. The assembly language program performs several operations on these values and returns a 16-bit integer to the C calling program via the **ax** register. In other words, the contents of the **ax** register at the end of the assembly language routine are returned automatically. This value can also be a 16-bit pointer.

The following listing contains all three files, which must be entered separately in your editor before compiling:

THE MAKE FILE (first):

```
first.exe: first.obj task.obj
  tlink c0s first task,first, ,cs

task.obj: task.asm
  tasm task.asm

first.obj: first.c c:\bc\include\stdio.h
  bcc -c first.c
```

THE C PROGRAM (first.c):

```c
/*
 *    A C program that demonstrates how to pass several
 *    data types to an external assembly language routine.
 *    The program uses the new argument passing technique.
 *    Copyright (c) Chris H. Pappas and William H. Murray, 1990
 */

#include <stdio.h>

int task(char,int,long);

main()
{
  char num1=15;
  int  num2=1234;
  long num3=12345678;
  int answer;

  answer=task(num1,num2,num3);
  printf("%d\n",answer);

  return (0);
}
```

THE TASK ASSEMBLY MODULE (task.asm):

```
;TURBO Assembly Language Programming Application
;Copyright (c) Chris H. Pappas and William H. Murray, 1990

;Program accepts several arguments from a C calling program
;and performs mathematical & logical operations with them.
;This is an 80386 program.
```

```
        DOSSEG                  ;use Intel segment-ordering
        .MODEL small            ;set model size
        .386                    ;80386 instructions

        .DATA
little  db      3

        .CODE
        PUBLIC  C task
task    PROC    C NEAR num1:BYTE,num2:WORD,num3:DWORD
        mov     ax,DGROUP
        mov     ds,ax

        mov     edx,0
        mov     eax,num3        ;get 32-bit (long) in eax
        div     WORD PTR num2   ;divide & discard remainder
        and     eax,DWORD PTR num1 ;mask and keep 16 bits
        add     al,little       ;add a small number

        ret                     ;return to calling program
task    ENDP                    ;end main procedure
        END
```

Of particular interest here is the *make* file. The following section of the *make* file is responsible for compiling the C code:

```
first.obj: first.c c:\bc\include\stdio.h
  bcc -c first.c
```

The statement says to compile but not link the C code. The C code is combined with the named header file to produce an object file.

The next section of code assembles the assembly language module to an object file:

```
task.obj: task.asm
  tasm task.asm
```

This is just a simple call to the Assembler to assemble the file.

The final statement controls the Linker. Here, the object modules of the C and assembly language code are linked.

```
first.exe: first.obj task.obj
  tlink c0s first task,first, ,cs
```

Notice in the linker expression a call to the small library. If you wanted the medium library, for example, you would have used *c0m* and *cm*, respectively. Also note that the *c0s* and *cs* files are in the current directory. If your files are in the library subdirectory, use *lib\c0s* and *lib\cs* in the *make* file.

The program code is straightforward and is used primarily to illustrate how values are passed. Incidentally, the answer printed to the screen is 7. Can you figure out why?

A SIMPLE C AND ASSEMBLY LANGUAGE CONNECTION

Earlier in this chapter, you learned how to use inline assembly language code to clear the screen and send information to the parallel port. The next example is a program that functions like that earlier program, but is built with separate assembly language modules. This program uses one external routine to clear the screen and another to send information to the parallel port.

More L.E.D. Lights

Four files are needed to compile the next example. The first is a *make* file named *second*. The next is the C program named *second.c*. The last two files are assembly language routines named *clsscr.asm* and *outport.asm*.

The following listing contains all four files, which must be entered separately in your editor before compiling:

```
THE MAKE FILE (second):

second.exe: second.obj clsscr.obj outport.obj
  tlink c0s second clsscr outport,second, ,maths fp87 cs

clsscr.obj: clsscr.asm
  tasm clsscr.asm

outport.obj: outport.asm
  tasm outport.asm

second.obj: second.c c:\bc\include\dos.h c:\bc\include\stdio.h c:\bc\
  include\math.h
  bcc -c second.c
```

THE C PROGRAM (second.c):

```
/*
 *     A C program that demonstrates how to call an external
 *     assembly language program to access the parallel port.
 *     Program will sequentially light 8 LED lamps connected
 *     to data lines D0 - D7 of port 956 (LPT1).
 *     Copyright (c) Chris H. Pappas and William H. Murray, 1990
 */

#include <dos.h>
#include <stdio.h>
#include <math.h>

void clsscr(void);
void outport(int,int);

main()
{
  int i,temp;
  int port=956;

  clsscr();

  for (i=0;i<9;i++) {
    temp=(int) pow(2.0,(double) i);

  outport(temp,port);

  printf("%d\n",temp);
  delay(1000);
  }

  return (0);
}
```

THE CLSSCR ASSEMBLY MODULE (clsscr.asm):

```
;TURBO Assembly Language Programming Application
;Copyright (c) Chris H. Pappas and William H. Murray, 1990

;program will clear the screen by calling a BIOS interrupt.

        DOSSEG                  ;use Intel segment-ordering
        .MODEL  small           ;set model size
        .8086                   .8086 instructions

        .CODE
        PUBLIC  C clsscr
clsscr  PROC    C NEAR

        mov     cx,0            ;upper corner of window
        mov     dx,2479H        ;lower corner of window
        mov     bh,7            ;normal screen attribute
        mov     ax,0600H        ;BIOS interrupt value
        int     10H             ;call interrupt
```

```
        ret                      ;return to calling program
clsscr  ENDP                     ;end main procedure
        END


THE OUTPORT ASSEMBLY MODULE (outport.asm):

;TURBO Assembly Language Programming Application
;Copyright (c) Chris H. Pappas and William H. Murray, 1990

;program accepts two arguments from C calling program and
;makes access to the specified port.

        DOSSEG                   ;use Intel segment-ordering
        .MODEL  small            ;set model size
        .8086                    ;8086 instructions

        .CODE
        PUBLIC  C outport
Outport PROC    C NEAR temp,port:WORD

        mov     dx,port          ;port id in dx register
        mov     ax,temp          ;value to be sent
        out     dx,al            ;send lower 8 bits to port

        ret                      ;return to calling program
Outport ENDP                     ;end main procedure
        END
```

Notice that the *make* file for this example contains additional libraries in the link command line. The host program looks like the earlier inline example, except for the addition of the function prototypes and actual calls. As you examine the two assembly language modules, notice that the code itself is also identical to the inline assembly language code of the earlier example. Pay particular attention to the function prototypes in the code, and how the arguments are intercepted in the assembly language modules.

A HARDWARE INTERFACE USING C++ AND ASSEMBLY LANGUAGE

The next example again uses the *clsscr.asm* and *outport.asm* files developed in the previous examples. However, this time the interface will be made with C++ in an example that simulates the roll of a die. The C++ program will generate pseudorandom numbers between 1 and 6 and send the numbers to the parallel port's data lines D0 to D2. The binary representation of the decimal numbers is 001, 010, 011, 100, 101, and 110. A die will be

created by arranging 7 LED lights in the pattern shown in Figure 19-3. You
also need a decoding scheme to convert the binary numbers to the correct
LED lighting sequence. The decoding could be done with software or
hardware. The example uses the hardware solution. Figure 19-4 shows the
logic circuit required to decode the binary information.

If you interface this circuit with your computer's parallel port, you will
need a cable to connect the parallel port to a prototyping board, hookup
wire, seven LED lights, a 5 volt power supply, a 7408 (AND gates) chip, and
a 7432 (OR gates) chip. This example used a 25-pin D shell connector to
connect to the parallel port with a ribbon cable terminating in a 24-pin male
dip header. Pin #13 was discarded from the D shell connector. The prototyping board is the type that allows TTL DIP chips to be easily inserted and
removed. All of these parts can be found at electronic supply stores.

Simulating the Roll of a Die

Notice that the following listing contains four files that must be entered and
saved separately. The first file is the *make* file *third*. The next file is the C++

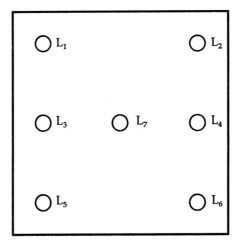

Figure 19-3.   LED layout for an electronic die

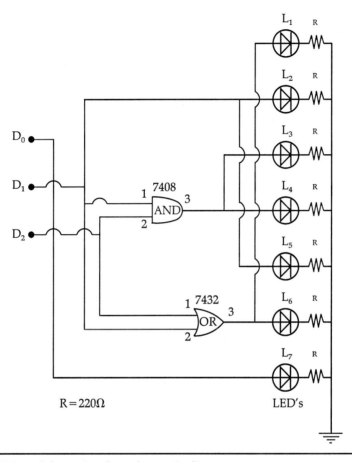

Figure 19-4.   Schematic of an electronic die

program *third.cpp*. The last two files are the familiar assembly language routines *clsscr.asm* and *outport.asm*.

```
THE MAKE FILE (third):

third.exe: third.obj clsscr.obj outport.obj
  tlink c0s third clsscr outport,third, ,cs

clsscr.obj: clsscr.asm
  tasm clsscr.asm
```

```
outport.obj: outport.asm
  tasm outport.asm

third.obj: third.cpp c:\bc\include\dos.h c:\bc\include\stream.h c:\bc\
  include\stdlib.h
  bcc -c third.cpp
```

THE C++ PROGRAM (third.cpp):

```
//
//   A C++ program that demonstrates how to call an external
//   assembly language program to access the parallel port.
//   Program will simulate the roll of a die and light the
//   appropriate LED lamps connected to the parallel port.
//   Port 956 (LPT1) and data lines D0 - D2 are used.
//   Copyright (c) Chris H. Pappas and William H. Murray, 1990
//

#include <dos.h>
#include <iostream.h>
#include <stdlib.h>

void clsscr(void);
void outport(int,int);

main()
{
  char ch;
  int i,temp;
  int port=956;

  clsscr();

  for (;;) {
    cout << "(Q) for quit, (Enter) for roll of die: ";
    cin.get(ch);
    if (ch =='Q' || ch=='q') break;

    for (i=0;i<50;i++) {
      temp=1 + (rand()/3 % 6);
      outport(temp,port);
      delay(20);
      }

    cout << temp << "\n";
  }
  return (0);
}
```

THE CLSSCR ASSEMBLY MODULE (clsscr.asm):

```
;TURBO Assembly Language Programming Application
;Copyright (c) Chris H. Pappas and William H. Murray, 1990

;program will clear the screen by calling a BIOS interrupt.
```

```
        DOSSEG                    ;use Intel segment-ordering
        .MODEL  small             ;set model size
        .8086                     ;8086 instructions

        .CODE
        PUBLIC  C clsscr
clsscr  PROC    C NEAR

        mov     cx,0              ;upper corner of window
        mov     dx,2479H          ;lower corner of window
        mov     bh,7              ;normal screen attribute
        mov     ax,0600H          ;BIOS interrupt value
        int     10H               ;call interrupt

        ret                       ;return to calling program
clsscr  ENDP                      ;end main procedure
        END
```

THE OUTPORT ASSEMBLY MODULE (outport.asm):

```
;TURBO Assembly Language Programming Application
;Copyright (c) Chris H. Pappas and William H. Murray, 1990

;program accepts two arguments from C calling program and
;makes access to the specified port.

        DOSSEG                    ;use Intel segment-ordering
        .MODEL  small             ;set model size
        .8086                     ;8086 instructions

        .CODE
        PUBLIC  C outport
outport PROC    C NEAR temp,port:WORD

        mov     dx,port           ;port id in dx register
        mov     ax,temp           ;value to be sent
        out     dx,al             ;send lower 8 bits to port

        ret                       ;return to calling program
outport ENDP                      ;end main procedure
        END
```

You have already learned how the function arguments are passed from the source code to the assembly language routines. This program generates pseudorandom numbers by calling the C++ **rand** function.

```
temp=1 + (rand()/3 % 6);
```

The random number generator returns values in the range 0 to RAND_MAX. RAND_MAX is defined in *tdlib.h* and is approximately 32,768. The random number generator can also be initialized, or *seeded*, with a call to the **srand** function. True random number generators are difficult to create, and a pseudorandom generator is just a close approximation of the real thing.

Numbers in the range 1 to 6 are generated with the modulo operator. Actually, the random numbers after the modulo operation are in the range 0 to 5. A 1 is added as an offset to these values.

If you have a little technical experience, a whole world of hardware interfacing is open to you. Instead of LED lamps, you can wire the parallel port's data lines to speech synthesizers or digital-to-analog converters. These circuits will allow you to control a wide range of electronic devices.

PASSING ARRAYS FROM C TO ASSEMBLY LANGUAGE

The last example in this chapter will show how to pass two arrays (call-by-reference) to an assembly language routine. The assembly language routine will add each element of each array and produce a final sum that will be returned to the host program. As you examine the following listing, which includes three separate files, notice that the *make* file included specifications that will allow the final program to be examined in the Debugger. The three files include the *make* file *myarray*, the C program *myarray.c*, and the assembly language module *myasm*. You must create each of these files separately with your editor.

```
THE MAKE FILE (myarray):

myarray.exe: myarray.obj myasm.obj
  tlink /v /m /s /l c0s myarray myasm,myarray, ,cs

myasm.obj: myasm.asm
  tasm /zi myasm.asm

myarray.obj: myarray.c c:\bc\include\stdio.h
  bcc -c -v myarray.c
```

THE C PROGRAM (myarray.c):

```
/*
 *    A C program that demonstrates how to pass two arrays
 *    to an external assembly language program.
 *    The assembly language program will add the elements of
 *    both arrays together and return the sum to the C program.
 *    Copyright (c) Chris H. Pappas and William H. Murray, 1990
 */

#include <stdio.h>

int myasm(int array1[],int array2[]);

main()
{
  int array1[10]={2,4,6,8,10,12,14,16,18,20};
  int array2[10]={1,2,3,4,5,6,7,8,9,10};
  int temp;

  temp=myasm(array1,array2);

  printf("%d\n",temp);

  return (0);
}
```

THE ASSEMBLY LANGUAGE MODULE (myasm.asm):

```
;TURBO Assembly Language Programming Application
;Copyright (c) Chris H. Pappas and William H. Murray, 1990

;The program will accept array information from a C host
;program.  Arrays are passed by reference.  The assembly
;language routine will add the elements of both arrays
;together and return the sum.

        DOSSEG                      ;use Intel segment-ordering
        .MODEL  small               ;set model size
        .8086                       ;8086 instructions

        .CODE
        PUBLIC  C myasm
myasm   PROC    C NEAR   array1,array2:WORD

        mov     ax,0                ;initialize ax to 0
        mov     cx,10               ;array size
        mov     bx,array1           ;address of array1
        mov     bp,array2           ;address of array2
more:   add     ax,[bx]             ;value at array1 address
        add     ax,[bp]             ;value at array2 address
        add     bx,2                ;point to next array1 number
        add     bp,2                ;point to next array2 number
        loop    more                ;till all elements summed
```

```
        ret                     ;return to calling program
myasm   ENDP                    ;end main procedure
        END
```

In the previous examples, arguments were passed by value. When array information is passed, it is passed by reference. Thus, the intercepted values are the addresses of the arrays. In assembly language, the addresses can be placed in the **bx** and **bp** registers. You can use indirect register addressing to obtain the array elements. Recall that indirect register addressing places square brackets around the register containing the address. This, in turn, returns the value stored at that address. This program sums the individual elements of each array.

IV

PROGRAMMING FOR WINDOWS

20

AN INTRODUCTION TO WINDOWS CONCEPTS

Borland's C++ or Turbo C++ for Windows compiler gives the C programmer the ability to compile and link Microsoft Windows programs with ease. Windows programming might be of interest to you based on the success of Microsoft's graphics-based operating environment. Windows brings together point-and-shoot control, pull-down menus, and the ability to run programs written especially for Windows, as well as standard programs that run under DOS.

The remaining chapters in this book will concentrate on teaching you how to use the C++ compiler to develop programs for the Windows environment. Because of the limited space, it will not be possible to develop an in-depth study of each Windows topic. For a detailed explanation of Windows concepts, read *Windows Programming: An Introduction*, by Murray and Pappas (Berkeley, CA: Osborne/McGraw-Hill, 1990). This book is devoted exclusively to Microsoft Windows concepts and programming.

To develop programs for Windows, in addition to the Borland C++ compiler, you will need to install Microsoft Windows, version 3.0 or later, on your system.

This chapter was developed to serve as a quick reminder or tour of important Windows concepts and sets the stage for the programs developed in the next several chapters.

WHAT IS WINDOWS?

Windows is an operating environment that runs under MS-DOS. It is a graphics-based multitasking windowing environment that allows programs written specifically for Windows to have a consistent appearance and command structure. This capability makes even new programs easier to master.

Windows provides several built-in routines that allow the easy implementation of pull-down menus, scroll bars, dialog boxes, icons, and many other features of a user-friendly graphical interface. Starting with Windows 3.0, programs can take advantage of new dialog controls, menu types, and "owner-draw controls." By using the extensive graphics programming language a program can easily format and output text in a variety of fonts and pitches.

Windows treats the video display, keyboard, mouse, printer, serial port, and system timers in a device-independent manner. This treatment allows the same program to run identically on a variety of hardware configurations.

Windows is closely related to the OS/2 Presentation Manager operating system, which was developed jointly by Microsoft and IBM. Under OS/2, the Windows-like interface is called the Presentation Manager. In the future, OS/2's Presentation Manager will be the primary development environment for many protected mode graphics-based application programs. Windows will eventually be integrated into the OS/2 environment. At present, while Windows and the Presentation Manager share many design fundamentals, such as the user interface, the application program interface (API) is different.

WINDOWS CAPABILITIES

The Windows operating environment provides many advantages to both users and programmers compared to the MS-DOS environment. Windows has three major capabilities: a graphics-oriented user interface, a multitasking capability, and hardware independence. Individually, none of these capabilities is new in itself, but attempting to combine all three of them into a single microcomputer operating environment is a new concept.

Standardized User Interface

Of the three major capabilities provided by Windows, it is the standardized graphics-oriented user interface that is the most noticeable and certainly the most important for the user. The consistent user interface uses pictures to represent drives, files, subdirectories, and many of the operating system commands and actions. Figure 20-1 shows what a typical Windows window looks like. Programs are identified by captions bars, and many of the basic file manipulation functions are accessed through the program's menus by pointing and clicking with the mouse. Most Windows programs provide both a keyboard interface and a mouse interface. Although most functions of Windows programs can be controlled through the keyboard, using the mouse is often easier for many tasks.

Multitasking

A multitasking operating environment allows the user to have several programs, or several instances of the same program, running concurrently. There are some users who still wonder if multitasking is necessary on a

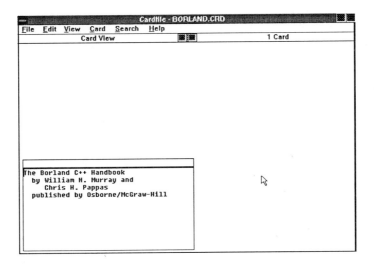

Figure 20-1.   A typical Windows application window

microcomputer. The obvious success of Borland's SideKick, for example, suggests otherwise. Figure 20-2 shows several Windows programs. Each program occupies a rectangular window on the screen. At any time, the user can move the windows on the screen, switch between different programs, change the windows' size, and exchange information from window to window.

Memory Management

Memory is an important shared resource under Windows. With more than one program running at the same time, each program must cooperate to share memory in order not to exhaust the supply. Also, as new programs are started up and old ones are terminated, memory can become fragmented. Windows is capable of consolidating free memory space by moving blocks of code and data in system memory.

Queued Input

Another important shared resource is input from the keyboard and mouse. It is for this reason that many input and output statements under C and

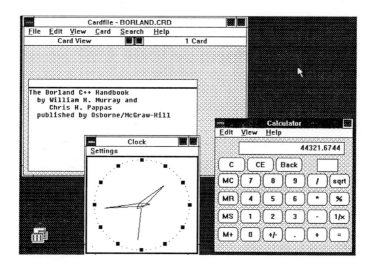

Figure 20-2. Multitasking several applications in the Windows environment

C++, such as **getchar**, should not be used. Windows-specific function calls must be used instead. Under Windows, an application does not make explicit calls to read from the keyboard or mouse input devices. Instead, Windows receives all input from the keyboard, mouse, and timer, in a system queue. It is the queue's job to redirect the input to the appropriate program by copying it from the system queue into the program's queue. At this point, when the program is ready to process any input, it reads from its queue and dispatches a message to the correct window.

Messages

The principal means used to disseminate information in the multitasking environment is the Windows message system. From the program's viewpoint, a message can be seen as a notification that some event of interest has occurred that may or may not need a specific action. These events may be initiated on the part of the user, such as clicking or moving the mouse, changing the size of a window, or making a menu selection. Messages can also be generated by the program itself. For example, a graphics-based spreadsheet could have finished a recalculation resulting in the need to update a displayed bar chart. Here the program would send itself an "update window" message.

Windows, itself, can also generate messages. This occurs in the case of a "close session" message. In this situation Windows informs each program of the intent to shut down. Finally, an additional message source could come from an instrument monitoring program, which indicates that a critical chemical process has reached the specified temperature. Regardless of the source of the message, your program must take the appropriate action.

Device Independence

Another capability provided by Windows is hardware device independence. Windows liberates the programmer from having to account for every possible variety of monitor, printer, and input device available. In the Windows environment, each device driver—whether for a video display, a printer, or whatever—need only be written once. Instead of each software company writing its own complete set, the hardware company writes one driver for the system. There are many drivers with Windows; others are available from the manufacturer.

For the program developer, nothing could make life easier. Your program interacts with Windows rather than with any specific device. It does not need to know what printer is hooked up. The program says to draw a filled rectangle, and Windows worries about how to accomplish the task. By the same token, once developed, each device driver will work with every Windows program.

Dynamic Link Libraries

Much of the functionality of Windows is provided by new dynamic link libraries, called .DLLs, which enhance the base operating system by providing a powerful and flexible graphics user interface. Dynamic link libraries contain predefined functions that are linked with an application program when it is loaded (dynamically), instead of when the .EXE file is generated (statically).

The concept of dynamic libraries did not originate with Windows. For example, C compilers in general depend heavily on libraries to implement standard functions for different systems. The linker makes copies of run-time library functions, such as **getchar** and **printf**, into a program's executable file. Libraries of functions save each programmer from having to re-create a new procedure for a common operation such as reading in a character or formatting output. Programmers can build their own libraries to include additional capabilities such as changing a font and justifying text. Making the function available as a general tool eliminates redundant design.

When a Windows program makes a call to a Windows function, the compiler must generate machine code for a far intersegment call to the function located in a code segment in one of the Windows libraries. This presents a problem, since until the program is actually running inside Windows, the address of the Windows function is unknown!

The solution to this problem is a concept you are already familiar with—*delayed binding* or *dynamic linking*. The C++ Linker allows a program to have calls to functions that cannot be fully resolved at link time. Only when the program is loaded into memory to be run are the far function calls resolved.

WINDOWS FEATURES

Along with the greatly improved performance, memory management, and multitasking capabilities starting with Windows version 3.0, there are many other major changes:

- Direct access to extended memory

- Up to 16 megabytes of virtual memory as a result of swapping memory pages to and from disk

- A palette manager that allows an application to take full advantage of the color capabilities of a device

- Device-independent color icons and bitmaps

- Device-independent cursors and icons that automatically select the appropriate device-specific image from a predefined set of images provided by the program

- An enhanced user interface that allows an application to use new dialog box controls, menu types, "owner-draw" controls, and a wider variety of font selections

- A more adaptable installation procedure

- The Windows help compiler

WINDOWS: CONCEPTS AND TERMINOLOGY

It is possible to break the concepts and terminology of Windows into two major categories: those features of Windows that are visible, such as menus, icons, and so forth; and the behind-the-scenes operations, such as messages, function access, and so on. In order for Windows program developers to communicate effectively with one another, all of the Windows features have been given a name and an associated usage. In this section you will be introduced to the minimum Windows vocabulary necessary to discuss and develop Windows programs.

A Window Defined

To the user, a Windows window is a rectangular portion of the display with a program-independent consistent appearance, that is the visual interface between the user and the program generating the window. To an application, the window is a rectangular area of the screen that is under the control of the program. The program creates and controls everything about the main window, including its size and shape. When the user starts a program, a window is created. Each time the user clicks on a window option, the program responds. Closing a window causes the program to terminate. Just as important as this visual user/application program information exchange, is the role the window plays in representing the fundamental substructure of the Windows system.

For example, while the window itself represents the graphics-oriented user interface, it is also the visible manifestation of both multitasking and hardware independence. It is the visible overlapping of running Windows programs that conveys to the user the true multitasking capabilities of Windows. By partitioning the screen into different windows, the user can direct their input to a specific program within the multitasking environment by using the keyboard or a mouse to select one of the concurrently running programs. Windows then intercepts the user's input and allocates any necessary resources (such as the processor) as needed.

The Visual Interface

Windows programs have certain features and behaviors in common: borders, control boxes, About boxes, and so forth. These give Windows a comforting predictability from program to program. Figure 20-3 illustrates the fundamental components of a window.

The Border

All Windows windows have a *border* around them. The border consists of the lines that frame a window. The border may appear to only delineate one program's screen viewport from another's, but a closer examination of several overlapped Windows programs will reveal something quite different. Not only does the border serve as a screen real estate boundary but it also indicates the active window. By moving the mouse pointer to a border and clicking the left button, the user can change the size of the window.

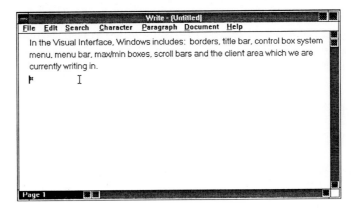

Figure 20-3.   The Windows Visual Interface includes borders, title bar, control box system menu, menu bar, max/min boxes, scroll bars, and client area

The Title Bar

The *title bar* displays the name of the application program at the top of the window. Title bars are located at the top and in the center of the associated window. They can be very useful in remembering which programs are concurrently running.

The Control Box

Windows programs use a *control box,* which is a small square box in the upper-left corner with a single dash in it. Clicking the mouse pointer on the control box will cause Windows to display the system menu.

The System Menu

The system menu is activated by clicking the mouse pointer on the control box and provides standard program options such as "Restore," "Move," "Size," "Minimize," "Maximize," and "Close."

The Minimize Box

The upper-right corner of each Windows application displays two small boxes with arrows. One represents the *minimize box,* which contains a downward pointing arrow and causes the window to be shrunk down to a small picture called an *icon.*

The Maximize Box

The *maximize box,* in the upper-right corner of each window, displays an upward-pointing arrow. The maximize box is used to make an application's window fill the entire screen, thereby covering up any other concurrently running programs.

The Vertical Scroll Bar

Right below each window's maximize box is the *vertical scroll bar,* which has opposite-pointing arrows at its extremes, a shaded colored band, and a transparent window block. The *transparent window block* is used to visually represent the orientation of the currently displayed contents in relation to the overall document (the colored band). The vertical scroll bar is used to select which, of multiple pages of output, you would like displayed. Clicking the mouse on either arrow shifts the display one line at a time. Clicking the mouse on the transparent window block below the UP-ARROW and dragging it causes screen output to be quickly updated to any portion of the program's screen output. One of the best uses for the vertical scroll bar is moving quickly through a multiple-page word processing document.

The Horizontal Scroll Bar

The *horizontal scroll bar* is at the physical bottom of each window. It has opposite-pointing arrows at its extremes, a shaded colored band, and a transparent window block. The transparent window block is used to visually represent the orientation of the currently displayed contents in relation to the overall document (the colored band).

    The horizontal scroll bar is used to select which of the multiple columns of information you would like displayed. Clicking the mouse on either arrow causes the screen image to be shifted one column at a time. Clicking the mouse on the transparent window block to the right of the left-pointing arrow, and dragging it, causes the screen output to be quickly updated to any horizontally shifted portion of the program's screen output. One of the best uses for the horizontal scroll bar is moving quickly through the multiple columns of a spreadsheet program, where the number of columns of information cannot fit into one screen width.

The Menu Bar

Each Windows program usually has a *menu bar* below the title bar. The menu bar is used for making menu and submenu selections. These selections can be made by pointing and clicking on the menu command, or by using a hotkey combination. Hotkey combinations often use the ALT key in conjunction with a bolded and underlined command, as the "F" is in the command File. The menu bar also includes a Help option.

The Client Area

Although the client area description has been saved for last, it actually occupies the largest portion of each window. The *client area* is the primary output area for the program. Managing the client area is the responsibility of the application program. Only the program can output information to the client area.

A Window Class

The fundamental components of a window help define the appearance of an application. Windows that look alike and behave in a similar fashion are said to be of the same *window class.* The windows that you create can take on a variety of different characteristics. They may be of a different size; be placed on different areas of the display; have different text in the caption bars; have different display colors; or use different mouse cursors.

Each window in a Windows program must be based on a window class. Several of these window classes have already been registered by Windows during its initialization phase, and in addition, your program may register its own classes. In order to allow multiple windows to be created based on the same window class, Windows specifies some of a window's characteristics as parameters to the **CreateWindow** function, while others are specified in a window class structure. Also, when you register a window class, the class becomes available to all programs running under Windows.

Windows with a similar appearance and behavior can be grouped together into classes, thereby reducing the amount of information that has to be maintained. Since each window class has its own shareable window class structure, there is no needless replication of the window class parameters. Additionally, two windows of the same class both use the same function and any of its associated subroutines. This also saves time and storage because there is no code duplication. Most important is the consistent performance between like window-classed windows.

Object-Oriented Programming

When you are programming for Windows, you are actually doing *object-oriented programming*. In object-oriented programming, recall that an *object* is an abstract data type that consists of a data structure and the various functions that act on the data structure. Additionally, objects receive messages that can cause them to change. For example, a graphics object is a collection of data that can be manipulated as a whole entity and that is presented to the user as part of the visual interface. In particular, a graphics object implies both the data and the presentation of data. Some examples of graphics objects include menus, title bars, control boxes, and scroll bars. The next section describes several new graphics objects that affect the user's view of an application.

Icons

The icon object is a small graphics symbol used to remind the user of a particular operation, idea, or product. For example, whenever a spreadsheet program is minimized, it could display a very small histogram icon to remind the user that the program is running. Clicking the mouse on the histogram would then cause Windows to bring the program to active status. Windows provides several stock icons including a question mark, exclamation point, asterisk, and upturned palm icon. Developers can create their own device-independent color icon designs. Using the function **Draw-Icon** allows an application to easily place an icon within the client area.

Cursors

Cursors in Windows applications are quite different from the standard DOS variety. A Windows cursor is a graphic symbol, unlike the standard DOS blinking underscore. The graphic symbol changes in response to the movement of the pointing device and helps to reflect the operations currently available. The best example of this is the change in shape of the standard Windows arrow cursor to the small hourglass cursor, which indicates a pause while a selected command is being executed. Incorporated into Windows are several stock cursors: the original diagonal arrow, a vertical arrow, the hourglass, the cross hairs, the I-beam, and several others. You can also create unique cursors of your own.

Carets

Carets are symbols that your program usually places in a window to show the user where input will be received. Carets are easily distinguished from other screen markers due to the fact that they blink. Most of the time mouse input is associated with a cursor and keyboard input with the caret. However, the mouse can move or change the input emphasis of a caret. To help clarify the difference between a cursor and a caret, Windows carets behave most similarly to the standard DOS cursor. One of the carets provided for you automatically when entering a dialog box is the I-beam caret. Unlike icons and cursors, an application must create its own carets using the **CreateCaret** and **ShowCaret** functions. There are no stock carets.

Message Boxes

Another very common graphics object is the Windows message box. Message boxes are pop-down windows that contain a title, an icon, and a message. Here is the standard message box presented when terminating a Windows session:

A single function call to the **MessageBox** function creates, displays, and receives the user's response from the message box. The program needs to supply the message title, the message itself, instructions on which stock icon to use, and whether a stock response is allowed. Stock responses include Okay, Yes/No, Yes/No/Cancel, Ok/Cancel, and Retry/Cancel. Stock icons include IconHand, IconQuestion, IconExclamation, and IconAsterisk.

Dialog Boxes

A dialog box is similar to a message box in the fact that it, too, is a pop-down window. However, dialog boxes are primarily used to receive input from the user rather than to present output to the user. A dialog box allows an application to receive information one field at a time or one box-worth of information at a time, rather than a character at a time. Here is the Windows dialog box that allows the user to change to another subdirectory:

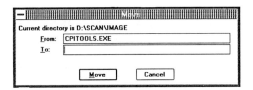

The graphic design of a dialog box is done automatically for you by Windows. The description of the dialog box is normally created by the Dialog Box Editor. Dialog boxes can be used to allow input of text, floats, and integers.

Fonts

A *font* is a graphics object, or resource, that defines a complete set of characters from one typeface, all with a certain size and style, that can be manipulated to give text a variety of appearances. A *typeface* is a basic character design that is defined by certain serifs and stroke widths. Your program can use different fonts, including the standard fonts provided with windows (System, Courier, Times Roman, and so forth), or custom fonts that you define and include in the application program's executable file. Using built-in routines, Windows allows for the dynamic modification of a font including boldface, italics, underline, and changing the size of the font. Windows provides all of the necessary functions for displaying text anywhere within the client area. What is even nicer is the fact that due to Windows device independence, an application's output will have a consistent appearance from one output device to the next.

Bitmaps

A *bitmap* is actually a snapshot of a portion of the display (in pixels) stored in memory. Bitmaps are used whenever an application wants to quickly display a graphics image. Because the object is being transferred directly from memory, it can be displayed faster than executing the code necessary to re-create the image.

Pens

Each time Windows draws a shape on the screen it uses information about the current pen and brush. Pens are used to draw lines and to outline shapes. They have three basic characteristics: line width, style (dotted, dashed, solid), and color. Windows always has a pen for drawing black lines and one for drawing white lines available to each program. New pens can be created. You might want to create a thick light-gray line to outline a portion of the screen, or a dot-dash-dot line for spreadsheet data analysis.

Brushes

Brushes are used to paint colors and fill areas with predefined patterns. Brushes have a minimum size of 8×8 pixels, and like pens, have three basic characteristics: size, pattern, and color.

With their 8×8-pixel minimum, brushes are said to have a pattern, not a style as pens do. The pattern may be anything from a solid color, to hatched, to diagonal, or any other user-definable combination.

Passing Messages

Windows is started just like any normal program running under DOS. While Windows does share the managing of all hardware resources, it concedes its rights to managing the file system of the PC. Windows is therefore totally at home taking charge of the keyboard, video display, mouse, parallel and serial ports, memory, and program execution. It is important to realize that Windows accomplishes all that it does because of its hardware dominance. By taking over the hardware Windows can intercept all user input and distribute that input, as messages, to the appropriate programs. It is only through the total control of the hardware that Windows can ensure that an application can interface with a variety of output devices, thereby creating a *virtual machine.*

With Windows, an application does not write directly to the screen, process any hardware interrupts, nor output directly to the printer. Instead, the program uses the appropriate Windows functions or waits for an appropriate message to be delivered. Program development for Windows must now incorporate Windows' method of processing the program, and the user's view of the program through Windows.

As was said previously, the message system is the underlying structure used to disseminate information in a multitasking environment. From your program's viewpoint, a message is seen as a notification that some event of interest has occurred that may or may not need a specific action. These events may have been initiated on the part of the user, such as clicking or moving the mouse, changing the size of a window, or making a menu selection. However, the signaled event could also have been generated by the program.

The effect of this action is that your program must now be totally oriented toward the processing of messages. It must be capable of awakening, determining the appropriate action based on the type of message received, taking that action to completion, and returning to sleep.

As a result of this new communication, Windows programs are significantly different from their DOS counterparts. Windows provides an application program with access to about 450 function calls. Generally, these function calls are handled by three main modules called the KERNEL, GDI (Graphics Device Interface), and USER modules.

The next section will take a closer look at the message system, examining the format and sources of messages, several common message types, and the ways in which both Windows and your program go about processing messages.

Message Format

The purpose of a message is to notify your program that an event of interest has occurred. Technically, a message is not just of interest to the program, but a specific window within that program. Therefore every message is addressed to a window.

Windows has only one system message queue, but each program currently running under Windows also has its own program message queue. Each message in the system message queue must eventually be transferred by the USER module to a program's message queue. The program's message queue stores all messages for all windows in that program.

The following four parameters are associated with all messages, regardless of their type:

- A window handle (16-bit word)

- A message type (16-bit word)

- One *word* parameter (16-bit word)

- One *long* parameter (32-bit word)

The first parameter specified in a window message is the handle of the window to which the message is addressed. In an object-oriented programming environment, a *handle* is just the identifier of an object, which for the current syntax, is the identifier of the particular window to which the message is addressed.

A handle is a 16-bit unsigned number. Frequently, this handle will reference an object (defined in the form of a data structure) that is located in a moveable portion of memory. What is important to realize is that even though the portion of memory can be moved, the handle remains the same. This allows Windows to manage memory efficiently while leaving the relocation invisible to the program.

Because multiple windows can be created based on the same window class, a single window function could process messages for more than one window within a single program. Under these circumstances, the program would use the handle to determine which window was receiving the message.

The second parameter in a message is its message type. This is one of the identifiers specified in *windows.h*. Under Windows, each message type begins with a two-character mnemonic, followed by the underscore character, and finally a descriptor. The most common type of message an application will process is the window message. Some examples of window messages include WM_CREATE, WM_PAINT, WM_CLOSE, WM_COPY, and WM_PASTE. Other message types include control window messages (BM_), edit control messages (EM_), and list box messages (LB_). When necessary, an application can create and register its own message type. These are called *private message types*.

The purpose for the last two parameters is to provide any additional information necessary to interpret the message. The contents of these last two parameters will therefore vary depending on the message type. Examples of the types of information that would be passed include which key was just struck, the position of the mouse, the position of the vertical or horizontal scroll bar elevators, and the selected pop-up menu item.

Where Do Messages Come From?

Basically, there are four sources for a message. An application can receive a message from the user, from Windows, from the application program, or from other programs. It is through this underlying message structure that Windows is capable of multitasking. Therefore, all messages must be processed by Windows.

Messages from the user include keystroke information; mouse movements; point-and-click coordinates; and any menu selections, such as a font style or the location of scroll bar elevators. Your application program will devote a great deal of time to processing user messages. Messages originating from the user indicate that the person running the program wishes to change the way the program is viewed.

Windows typically originates a message to an application whenever a *state* change is to take effect. An example of this would be when the user clicks on an application's icon, making that program the active program. Here, Windows tells the program that its main window is being opened and that its size and location are being modified, and so forth. Depending on the current state of an application, Windows-originated messages can be responded to or ignored.

In the next chapter, you will learn how to write a simple Windows application. What you will see is that your program is broken down into specific procedures, with each one processing a particular message type for a particular window. One procedure, for example, will deal with resizing the program's window. It is quite possible that the program may want to resize itself. In other words, the source of the message is the program itself.

Currently, most programs written for Windows do not take full advantage of the fourth type of message source: intertask communication. However, this category will become increasingly more important as more and more programs take advantage of this Windows integration capability. To facilitate this type of message, the DDE (Dynamic Data Exchange) protocol has been developed.

Processing Messages

A Windows program will have a procedure for processing each type of message that is of interest to any of its windows. However, different windows will respond differently to messages of the same type. For example, one program may have created two windows that respond to a mouse-button click in two different ways. The first window could respond by changing the background color, while the second window may respond by placing a crosshatch on a spreadsheet. Because the same message can be interpreted differently by different windows, you can see why Windows addresses each message to a specific window within an application.

Not only will the program have a different procedure to handle each message type, but it will also need a procedure to handle each message type for each window! The window procedure is used to group together all the message type procedures for a Windows program.

The Message Loop

A basic fundamental component of all Windows programs will be the message processing loop. Each program will contain procedures to create and initialize windows, followed by the message processing loop, and finally some required closing code. The message loop is responsible for processing a message delivered by Windows to the main body of the program. Here, the program acknowledges the message and then requests Windows to send it to the appropriate window procedure for processing. At this point the window procedure executes the desired action.

The message queue and dispatching priority are two factors that can influence the sequence in which a message is processed. Messages can be sent from one of two queues, either the system queue or the program's message queue. Messages are first placed in the system queue. When this message reaches the front of the queue, it is sent over to the appropriate program's message queue. This dual mode allows Windows to keep track of all messages, while allowing each program to concern itself with only those messages that pertain to it.

Windows normally places messages into the queues as you would expect; first-in-first-out. These are *synchronous* messages. Most Windows programs use this type of dispatching method. However, there are occasions when Windows will push a message to the end of the queue, thereby preventing it from being dispatched. Messages of this type are called *asynchronous* messages. Care must be taken when sending an asynchronous message that overrides the program's normal sequence of processing.

There are three types of asynchronous messages: paint, timer, and quit. A timer message, for example, causes a certain action to take effect at a specified time, regardless of the messages to be processed at that moment. Therefore, a timer message will cause all other messages in the queue to be pushed farther from the front of the queue.

Windows also has asynchronous messages that can be sent to other programs. What is unique about this scenario is that the receiving program doesn't put the message into its queue. Instead, the received message directly calls the called program's appropriate window procedure, where it is executed immediately.

You may be wondering how Windows dispatches messages that are pending for several programs at the same time. Windows settles this issue in one of two ways. One method of message processing that Windows uses is called *dispatching priority*. Each time Windows loads an application it sets the program's priority to zero. Once the program is running, however, the program can change its priority from a −15 to a +15. All things being equal then, Windows would settle any message dispatching contention by sending messages to the highest priority program.

A data communications program is an example of a program that might want to upgrade its priority level. It is possible that your system could be connected long distance to a host computer. Naturally, you are going to want to process the information being sent long distance from the host computer as soon as possible.

Since tampering with an application's priority level is very uncommon, Windows must have another method for dispatching messages to concurrent programs of the same priority level. Besides processing the messages in the queue, whenever Windows sees that a particular program has a backlog of unprocessed messages, it hangs on to the new message while continuing to dispatch other new messages to the other programs.

Resources

Each program that runs under Windows usually includes a unique icon. The concept of icons has already been discussed. These are small graphics symbols used to jog the user's memory as to what program has been loaded and is waiting to be made active.

Some programs may even create their own cursor. For example, a spreadsheet program may choose to have the user point with a small vertical histogram instead of the more typical arrow.

The graphics objects just described — namely, icons and cursors, along with carets, message boxes, dialog boxes, fonts, bitmaps, pens, and brushes — are examples of resources. A *resource* represents data that is included in a program's *.exe* file, although technically speaking it does not reside in a program's normal data segment. When Windows loads a program into memory for execution, very often it will leave all of the resources on the disk. One example of this is when the user first requests to see an application's About box. Before Windows can display the About box it must first access the disk to copy this information from the program's *.exe* file into memory.

Usually, an application defines its resources as read-only and discardable. This allows Windows to discard the resource whenever more memory is required. Should the resource be requested again, Windows simply reads the disk and reloads the data back into memory. Finally, should the user choose to have multiple instances of the same program running concurrently — for example, a word processor — Windows will not only share the program's code, but its resource definitions also.

Utilizing Windows Functions

Windows provides the program developer with roughly 450 functions. Some examples of these functions are **DispatchMessage**, **PostMessage**, **RegisterWindowMessage**, and **SetActiveWindow**. The interface to these functions is through a far intersegment call. This is because Windows treats the function as if it were located in a code segment other than the code segment that the program occupies. Officially called the CALL-based API (Application Program Interface), parameters are passed to the various modules that make up Windows using the stack. Since all Windows modules have code and data segments separate from an application's, Windows functions must be accessed using 32-bit far addresses. This address can be broken down into two components, the 16-bit segment address and the 16-bit offset address.

The Pascal Calling Convention

As you become more and more familiar with Windows source code, you will start noticing function declarations that include the *pascal* modifier. As just discussed, parameters to all Windows functions are passed via the stack. In a C program, for example, function parameters are first pushed onto the stack and then the function is called. Normally, the parameters are pushed from the rightmost parameter first, to the leftmost parameter. Upon return from the function, the calling procedure must adjust the stack pointer to a value equal to the number of bytes originally pushed onto the stack.

In Pascal, however, things look slightly different. While function parameters are still pushed from right to left, it is the called function's responsibility to adjust the stack before the return. It is no longer the job of the calling procedure to adjust the stack. Windows uses this calling convention because it turns out to be more space-efficient. Therefore, the C++ compiler understands that any function declared with the reserved word *pascal* is to use the more efficient calling convention.

The *windows.h* Header

windows.h is a large header file that is very important to Windows programs. This file is included with the C++ compiler and contains over 1200 constant declarations, *typedef* declarations, and over 450 Windows function declarations. One of the main reasons a Windows program takes longer to compile than a regular C or C++ program, is because of the size of the *windows.h* file.

Many of the Windows functions found in the KERNEL, USER, and GDI modules work with their own specified data types and variables to which your program has access. These variables and types are defined in header files. Header files are included in any file that uses the specific functions they refer to by using an *#include* statement.

Many of the parameters used to access the various Windows function calls are defined in *windows.h.* Due to the size and importance of *windows.h,* it is strongly suggested that you print a hardcopy to keep as a convenient reference.

Technically, the *#define* statements found in *windows.h* associate a numeric constant with a text identifier. For example:

```
#define WM_CREATE  0x0001
```

The C compiler will use the hexadecimal constant 0x0001 as a replacement for WM_CREATE during preprocessing. Other *#define* statements may appear a bit unusual. For example:

```
#define NEAR near
```

```
#define VOID void
```

In C++ both *near* and *void* are reserved words. Your programs should use the uppercase NEAR and VOID for one very good reason. Should you decide to port your program over to some other C++ compiler, it would certainly be much easier to change the *#define* statements within the header file than to change all occurrences of a particular identifier!

Windows source code has a style and indentation scheme that will initially look quite peculiar. Officially, this Hungarian style of notation can be credited to the Microsoft programmer Charles Simonyi. Using Hungarian notation, variable names are begun with a lowercase letter or letters that describe the data type of the variable. This variable name prefix is then followed by the name of the variable, which is represented by a meaningful use of upper- and lowercase letters. This approach allows each variable to tag along with it a mnemonic representing the variable's data type. For example:

```
WORD wParam1
```

```
LONG lParam2
```

By prefacing each variable name with a reminder of its data type, you can actually avoid some very common mistakes before compiling your program. The statement

```
Param1 = Param2
```

looks harmless but is incorrect and may go unchecked. However, using Hungarian notation you would undoubtedly catch the following mistake:

```
wParam1 = lParam2
```

Use Table 20-1 as a reference for familiarizing yourself with some of Windows' data types.

Table 20-1. Standard Windows Data Types

Prefix	Data Type Represented
b	BOOL/(integer)
by	BYTE/(unsigned character)
c	character
dw	DWORD/(unsigned long)
fn	function
h	HANDLE/(unsigned integer)
i	integer
l	LONG/(long)
lp	long/(far) pointer
n	short integer
np	near/(short) pointer
p	pointer
s	string
sz	NULL/(0) terminated string
w	WORD/(unsigned integer)
x	short/(when used as the X coordinate)
y	short/(when used as the Y coordinate)

STEPS IN CREATING A WINDOWS PROGRAM

Building a Windows program can involve all or some of the following seven steps:

1. Create the **WinMain** and associated Windows functions in the C or C++ language with the editor.

2. Create optional menu, dialog box, and additional resource descriptions and put them into a resource script file. Use the Borland Programmers Workshop.

3. Create optional cursors, icons, and bitmaps. Use the Borland Programmers Workshop.

4. Create optional dialog boxes. Use the Borland Programmers Workshop.

5. Create any module definitions and place them in the module definition file. Use the C++ editor.

6. Compile and link all C and C++ language sources. Use the C++ compiler.

7. Link the resource file with the executable file.

As you can see, creating an actual Windows program will require the use of some familiar and some new development tools. We'll take a look at some interesting program examples in the following chapters to help you get started.

21

WRITING BORLAND C AND C++ WINDOWS APPLICATIONS

This chapter is devoted to teaching you how to create simple Windows programs with Borland's C++ compiler. To achieve this goal, two templates will be developed: one for C and one for C++. These are called the Simplified Windows Platform (SWP) for C and the Simplified Windows Platform (SWP) for C++. The letters "SWP" will be used to refer to both, and clear indications will be made as to whether it is the C or C++ template that is being referenced.

WHY USE SIMPLIFIED WINDOWS PLATFORM TEMPLATES?

If you have never seen a Windows program, be ready for a giant shock. Even a program such as "Hello, World" utilizes many, many specialized functions and takes several pages to list. This is because Windows always requires a certain amount of overhead just to establish the window and place it on the screen. For many simple situations this overhead remains the same from program to program. If you are just learning how to write Windows programs, having this overhead will allow you to experiment with many graphical functions, without the bother of understanding the details of every specialized function needed just to establish the window.

The SWPs developed for C and C++ will incorporate all of the minimal Windows components necessary to create and display a window (including a main window with a border, a title bar, a system menu, and maximize/minimize boxes); will utilize several GDI functions; and will gracefully exit. These SWPs form the foundations for many simple but exciting Windows programs that you can create on your own. Before getting started, take a moment to look over the Windows data types and structures listed in Tables 21-1 and 21-2. This will help you understand what each Windows function call is passing.

THE COMPILING AND LINKING PROCESS

Before looking at any application code, let us reassure you that building Windows programs follows the same steps you are already familiar with in DOS program development. The C compiler first creates an object file. The object file differs from an ordinary DOS program file in that it contains Windows prolog and epilog code that encompasses each Windows function. The Linker links the object files with the appropriate startup code, libraries, and module definition files. Optionally, your program can utilize the Borland Resource Toolkit to compile the resources for the executable file.

THE SIMPLIFIED WINDOWS PLATFORM

This section will explain the process of putting Windows programs together in C and C++, from both the command line (CL) and the Integrated

Table 21-1.   Frequently Used Windows Data Types

Data Type	Meaning
HANDLE	Defines a 16-bit unsigned integer that is used as a handle
HWND	Specifies the 16-bit unsigned integer used as the handle to a window
LONG	Defines a 32-bit signed integer
LPSTR	Identifies a 32-bit pointer to a character data type
FARPROC	Identifies a 32-bit pointer to a function
WORD	Defines a 16-bit unsigned integer

Table 21-2.   Frequently Used Windows Structures

Structure	Usage
MSG	Specifies the fields of an input message
PAINTSTRUCT	Specifies the paint structure to be used when drawing within a window
RECT	Specifies a rectangle
WNDCLASS	Specifies a window class

Development Environment (IDE). No explanation of individual Windows functions will be discussed in this section—the important Windows functions will be explained later in the chapter. Also note that Appendix C, "Windows Functions," contains the prototypes for important Windows functions.

A Simplified Windows Platform for C

The C code necessary for creating a simple Windows program and placing several GDI shapes on the screen is shown next. Don't panic if this looks like the strangest C code you have ever seen. The C platform basically establishes the Windows window with a series of function calls and draws some familiar shapes on the screen. The *swpc.c* program is shown in the following listing.

```
/* Simplified Windows Platform (SWP) for C Small Model  */
/* (c) William H. Murray and Chris H. Pappas, 1991      */

#include <windows.h>

long FAR PASCAL WindowProc(HWND,unsigned,WORD,LONG);

char szProgName[]="ProgName";

int PASCAL WinMain(HANDLE hInst,HANDLE hPreInst,
                   LPSTR lpszCmdLine,int nCmdShow)
{
```

```
HWND hwnd;
MSG msg;
WNDCLASS wcSwp;
if (!hPreInst)
{
    wcSwp.lpszClassName=szProgName;
    wcSwp.hInstance=hInst;
    wcSwp.lpfnWndProc=WindowProc;
    wcSwp.hCursor=LoadCursor(NULL,IDC_ARROW);
    wcSwp.hIcon=NULL;
    wcSwp.lpszMenuName=NULL;
    wcSwp.hbrBackground=GetStockObject(WHITE_BRUSH);
    wcSwp.style=CS_HREDRAW|CS_VREDRAW;
    wcSwp.cbClsExtra=0;
    wcSwp.cbWndExtra=0;
    if (!RegisterClass (&wcSwp))
       return FALSE;
}
hwnd=CreateWindow(szProgName,"Simplified C Windows Platform",
                  CW_OVERLAPPEDWINDOW,CW_USEDEFAULT,
                  0,CW_USEDEFAULT,0,NULL,NULL,
                  hInst,NULL);
ShowWindow(hwnd,nCmdShow);
UpdateWindow(hwnd);
while (GetMessage(&msg,NULL,0,0))
{
   TranslateMessage(&msg);
   DispatchMessage(&msg);
}
return(msg.wParam);
}


long FAR PASCAL WindowProc(HWND hwnd,unsigned messg,
                           WORD wParam,LONG lParam)
{
   PAINTSTRUCT ps;
   HDC hdc;
   short xcoord;
   POINT polylpts[4],polygpts[5];

   switch (messg)
   {
     case WM_PAINT:
     hdc=BeginPaint(hwnd,&ps);

/*————————— your routines below —————————*/

     /* draw a diagonal line */
     MoveTo(hdc,0,0);
     LineTo(hdc,640,430);
     TextOut(hdc,55,20,"<-diagonal line",15);

     /* draw an arc */
     Arc(hdc,100,100,200,200,150,175,175,150);
     TextOut(hdc,80,180,"small arc->",11);
```

```
/* draw a chord */
Chord(hdc,550,20,630,80,555,25,625,70);
TextOut(hdc,485,30,"chord->",7);

/* draw an ellipse */
Ellipse(hdc,200,200,275,250);
TextOut(hdc,210,215,"ellipse",7);

/* draw a circle with ellipse function */
Ellipse(hdc,400,200,550,350);
TextOut(hdc,450,265,"circle",6);

/* draw a pie wedge */
Pie(hdc,300,50,400,150,300,50,300,100);
TextOut(hdc,350,80,"<-pie wedge",11);

/* draw a rectangle */
Rectangle(hdc,50,300,150,400);
TextOut(hdc,160,350,"<-rectangle",11);

/* draw rounded rectangle */
RoundRect(hdc,60,310,110,350,20,20);
TextOut (hdc,120,310,"<———————rounded rectangle",24);

/* set several pixels on screen to red */
for(xcoord=400;xcoord<450;xcoord+=5)
  SetPixel(hdc,xcoord,150,0L);
TextOut(hdc,455,145,"<-pixels",8);

/* drawing several lines with polyline */
polylpts[0].x=10;
polylpts[0].y=30;
polylpts[1].x=10;
polylpts[1].y=100;
polylpts[2].x=50;
polylpts[2].y=100;
polylpts[3].x=10;
polylpts[3].y=30;
Polyline(hdc,polylpts,4);
TextOut(hdc,10,110,"polyline",8);

/* drawing with polygon */
polygpts[0].x=40;
polygpts[0].y=200;
polygpts[1].x=100;
polygpts[1].y=270;
polygpts[2].x=80;
polygpts[2].y=290;
polygpts[3].x=20;
polygpts[3].y=220;
polygpts[4].x=40;
polygpts[4].y=200;
Polygon(hdc,polygpts,5);
TextOut(hdc,70,210,"<-polygon",9);
```

```
/*———————— your routines above ————————*/
    ValidateRect(hwnd,NULL);
    EndPaint(hwnd,&ps);
  break;
  case WM_DESTROY:
    PostQuitMessage(0);
  break;
  default:
    return DefWindowProc(hwnd,messg,wParam,lParam);
  }
  return(0L);
}
```

After looking at this listing your anxiety level has probably tripled! However, remember that you can use this same template to build your own applications. First, remove the graphics functions (GDI primitives) between the sections marked with "your routines below" and "your routines above" and insert your own routines. This means that without understanding a thing about establishing a window on the screen, you can begin to develop an understanding of individual Windows graphical functions like those shown in the *swpc* program.

The C *swpc* Definition File

C definition files such as *swpc.def* provide important prolog, epilog, and export information for the compiler. The following listing is named *swpc.def*.

```
NAME          SWPC
DESCRIPTION   'SWP for Windows for Borland C'
EXETYPE       WINDOWS
STUB          'WINSTUB.EXE'
CODE          PRELOAD MOVEABLE
DATA          PRELOAD MOVEABLE MULTIPLE
HEAPSIZE      1024
STACKSIZE     5120
EXPORTS       WindowProc
```

The NAME statement defines *swpc* as a Windows program (not a dynamic link library) and gives the module a name. This name should be the same as the program's *.exe* file.

The DESCRIPTION line copies the text into the *.exe* file. Very often this is used to embed additional information such as a release date, version number, or copyright notice.

The EXETYPE specifies the type of executable file (*.exe*) to produce. The STUB statement specifies the name of a program that is to be inserted into the *.exe* file whenever the application is run from the DOS command line by accident.

Both the CODE and DATA segments have been marked "preload" and "moveable," allowing Windows to initially load and relocate them for any dynamic memory allocation requests. The MULTIPLE statement also instructs Windows to create unique data segments for each instance of the application.

The HEAPSIZE statement allocates an amount of extra, expandable, local memory from within the application's data segment. The STACKSIZE has been set to 5120. Larger values may be necessary for applications with large nonstatic variables, or those applications using recursion.

Finally, the EXPORTS statement identifies the application's dynamic link entry point and specifies the name of the procedure, in this case, **WindowProc**.

The C Resource File

For this example, the resource script file, *swpc.rc,* is a dummy file containing only this statement:

/* no resources in SWPC */

Icons, cursors, menus, and dialog boxes add great flare to Windows programs. However, it is impossible to cover every important Windows topic in a limited amount of space. Refer to your Borland C++ compiler documentation and example programs for more detail on their use.

C Program Components for Command-Line Compiling

In order to build Windows programs from the command line, you will need four files. The first three files have already been given: *swpc.c, swpc.def,* and *swpc.rc.* Additionally, you will need a *make* file. The next listing is for the *make* file, called *swpc.mak.*

```
FILE=swpc
LIBPATH=c:\bc\lib
INCPATH=c:\bc\include
```

```
$(FILE).exe: $(FILE).obj $(FILE).def $(FILE).res
  tlink /Tw /n /c $(LIBPATH)\c0ws $(FILE),\
    $(FILE),\
    ,\
    $(LIBPATH)\cws $(LIBPATH)\cs $(LIBPATH)\import,\
    $(FILE)
    rc $(FILE).res

$(FILE).obj: $(FILE).c
  bcc -c -W -I$(INCPATH) $(FILE).c

$(FILE).res:  $(FILE).rc
  rc -r -i$(INCPATH) $(FILE).rc
```

By using macros (such as **file**, **libpath**, and **incpath**), definition files can be easily altered to accommodate a variety of situations. For example, if your Borland C++ library is not located at c:\bc\lib, you can just change **libpath** once to accommodate the alteration. Now look and see how many times **libpath** is used in the definition file. It certainly makes sense to use macros. Next, you will probably develop a habit of *cutting and pasting* when developing new applications. This definition file can be copied and made to function for another program by just changing the program name in **file**.

Once these four files are in place, compiling and linking a C program for Windows is the same as for DOS. Simply type

MAKE -fSWPC.MAK

The *make* file does all of the work. The Borland C compiler compiles *swpc.c* into *swpc.obj*, and then brings in the proper setup code. The link phase is suppressed during compilation by adding the -c option to the command line. The -W option directs the compiler to build a Windows application. The -I option is the path to the necessary include files. As an option, source level debugging can be included by adding the -v option.

The *make* file also adds any necessary resources by calling the resource compiler. The resource compiler compiles the resource file, *swpc.rc*, and produces an *swpc.res* file. The -r option tells the resource compiler not to add the result to the executable file at this time. Later, the resource compiler is called again to add the binary resource file to the executable file.

The linking phase is the most complicated of the group since the Linker must splice information from the *.obj*, *.def*, and *.res* files together with specific library information.

The /Tw option links for a Windows-executable file. The /n option selects no default libraries. The /c option selects lowercase significance in symbols. A /v option can be added to allow for debugging information.

Library path statements direct the Linker to the proper files for linking library information. The *c0ws* (obj understood) is the initialization module for the small C memory model. The *cws* (lib) is the small C memory model run-time library for Windows. The *cs* (lib) is the regular run-time library. Finally, the *import* (lib) provides access to the Borland C++ Windows functions.

The program can now be executed by typing **WIN SWPC**. Figure 21-1 shows the output from this program.

C Program Components for Integrated Development Environment Compiling

When developing Windows code from the Integrated Development Environment you will need to create the *swpc.c, swpc.def,* and *swpc.rc* files shown earlier. You will also need to develop a project file from within the IDE.

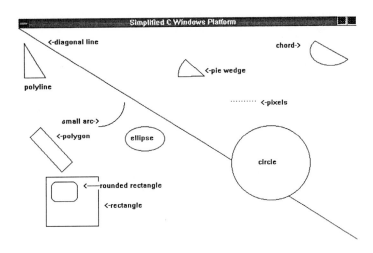

Figure 21-1.   Simplified C Windows platform

Here are the steps necessary for developing a complete program:

1. Get into the Borland C++ IDE by typing **BC** from the DOS prompt.

2. Enter the C source code shown and save as *swpc.c*.

3. Enter the C definition file shown and save as *swpc.def*.

4. Enter the C resource file shown and save as *swpc.rc*.

5. Set the IDE Options to include:

   Compiler, Code Generation = Small Memory Model
   Compiler, Entry/Exit Code = Windows all functions exportable
   Linker, Output = Windows EXE

6. Examine the IDE Application Options:

   Application = Windows App

7. Choose "Project" from the IDE menu. Press ENTER or click "OK" to open a new project and name it *swpc.prj*.

8. Select "Add item" and type **SWPC**. The Name box displays a list of all the *swpc* files that you have entered.

9. Add the three files *swpc.c, swpc.rc,* and *swpc.def* for the program.

10. Close the Project dialog box.

11. Select "Compile" from the menu and click on "Build all" to build the project.

12. If you encounter no errors, exit the IDE by pressing ALT-X or by choosing "File" and clicking on "Quit." Otherwise, open the file with the error and correct.

13. From DOS, type **WIN SWPC**.

DOS will open Windows and automatically execute your program. Figure 21-1, shown earlier, illustrates this program's output.

A Simplified Windows Platform for C++

The C++ code necessary for creating a simple Windows program and placing several GDI shapes on the screen is shown next. The same GDI graphics functions that were used in the C SWP are used here. The C++ platform establishes the Windows window with a series of function calls and takes advantage of C++ classes. The following program listing is named *swpcpp.cpp*.

```
// Simplified Windows Platform (SWP) for C++ Small Model
// (c) William H. Murray and Chris H. Pappas, 1991

#include <windows.h>
#include <stdlib.h>
#include <string.h>

extern "C" {
  long FAR PASCAL WindowProc(HWND hwnd,unsigned messg,
                             WORD wParam,LONG lParam);
}

class Main
{
  public:
  static HANDLE hInst;
  static HANDLE hPrevInst;
  static int nCmdShow;
  static int MessageLoop(void);
};

HANDLE Main::hInst=0;
HANDLE Main::hPrevInst=0;
int Main::nCmdShow=0;

int Main::MessageLoop(void)
{
  MSG msg;

  while(GetMessage(&msg,NULL,0,0))
  {
    TranslateMessage(&msg);
    DispatchMessage(&msg);
  }
  return msg.wParam;
}

class Window
{
  protected:
    HWND hwnd;
  public:
    HWND GetHandle(void) {
    return hwnd;
}
```

```
  BOOL Show(int nCmdShow) {
    return ShowWindow(hwnd,nCmdShow);
  }
  void Update(void)
    UpdateWindow(hwnd);
  }
};

class MainWindow:public Window
{
  private:
    static char szProgName[];
  public:
    static void Register(void)
    {
      WNDCLASS wcSwp;
      wcSwp.lpszClassName=szProgName;
      wcSwp.hInstance=Main::hInst;
      wcSwp.lpfnWndProc=WindowProc;
      wcSwp.hCursor=LoadCursor(NULL,IDC_ARROW);
      wcSwp.hIcon=NULL;
      wcSwp.lpszMenuName=NULL;
      wcSwp.hbrBackground=GetStockObject(WHITE_BRUSH);
      wcSwp.style=CS_HREDRAW|CS_VREDRAW;
      wcSwp.cbClsExtra=0;
      wcSwp.cbWndExtra=0;
      if (! RegisterClass(&wcSwp))
        exit(FALSE);
  }
  MainWindow(void)
  {
    hwnd=CreateWindow(szProgName,
                      "Simplified C++ Windows Platform",
                      WS_OVERLAPPEDWINDOW,CW_USEDEFAULT,
                      0,CW_USEDEFAULT,0,NULL,NULL,
                      Main::hInst,(LPSTR) this);
    if (!hwnd)
      exit(FALSE);

    Show(Main::nCmdShow);
      Update();
  }
};

char MainWindow::szProgName[]="ProgName";

long FAR PASCAL WindowProc(HWND hwnd,unsigned messg,
                           WORD wParam,LONG lParam)
{
  switch (messg)
  {
    case WM_PAINT:
    {
      PAINTSTRUCT ps;
```

```
HDC hdc;
short xcoord;
POINT polylpts[4],polygpts[5];

hdc=BeginPaint(hwnd,&ps);

//————————————your routines below————————————

// draw a diagonal line
MoveTo(hdc,0,0);
LineTo(hdc,640,430);
TextOut(hdc,55,20,"<-diagonal line",15);

// draw an arc
Arc(hdc,100,100,200,200,150,175,175,150);
TextOut(hdc,80,180,"small arc->",11);

// draw a chord
Chord(hdc,550,20,630,80,555,25,625,70);
TextOut(hdc,485,30,"chord->",7);

// draw an ellipse
Ellipse(hdc,200,200,275,250);
TextOut(hdc,210,215,"ellipse",7);

// draw a circle with ellipse function
Ellipse(hdc,400,200,550,350);
TextOut(hdc,450,265,"circle",6);

// draw a pie wedge
Pie(hdc,300,50,400,150,300,50,300,100);
TextOut(hdc,350,80,"<-pie wedge",11);

// draw a rectangle
Rectangle(hdc,50,300,150,400);
TextOut(hdc,160,350,"<-rectangle",11);

// draw rounded rectangle
RoundRect(hdc,60,310,110,350,20,20);
TextOut (hdc,120,310,"<————rounded rectangle",24);

// set several pixels on screen to red
for(xcoord=400;xcoord<450;xcoord+=5)
  SetPixel(hdc,xcoord,150,0L);
TextOut(hdc,455,145,"<-pixels",8);

// drawing several lines with polyline
polylpts[0].x=10;
polylpts[0].y=30;
polylpts[1].x=10;
polylpts[1].y=100;
polylpts[2].x=50;
polylpts[2].y=100;
polylpts[3].x=10;
polylpts[3].y=30;
Polyline(hdc,polylpts,4);
```

```
        TextOut(hdc,10,110,"polyline",8);

        // drawing with polygon
        polygpts[0].x=40;
        polygpts[0].y=200;
        polygpts[1].x=100;
        polygpts[1].y=270;
        polygpts[2].x=80;
        polygpts[2].y=290;
        polygpts[3].x=20;
        polygpts[3].y=220;
        polygpts[4].x=40;
        polygpts[4].y=200;
        Polygon(hdc,polygpts,5);
        TextOut(hdc,70,210,"<-polygon",9);

        //————————————your routines above————————————————

        EndPaint(hwnd,&ps);
      }
      break;

      case WM_DESTROY:
        PostQuitMessage(0);
      break;

      default:
        return DefWindowProc(hwnd,messg,wParam,lParam);
    }
}

int PASCAL WinMain(HANDLE hInst,HANDLE hPrevInst,
                   LPSTR lpszCmdLine,int nCmdShow)
{
  Main::hInst=hInst;
  Main::hPrevInst=hPrevInst; {
  Main::nCmdShow=nCmdShow;

  if (!Main::hPrevInst) {
    MainWindow::Register();
  }

  MainWindow MainWnd;
  return Main::MessageLoop();
}
```

This template can be used to build your own C++ Windows applications. First remove the graphics functions (GDI primitives) between the sections marked with "your routines below" and "your routines above" and insert your own routines. Without a further understanding of how to establish a window on the screen, you can get started by experimenting with many of the simple Windows graphics primitives like those shown in the C++ SWP.

If you compare the C++ SWP with the C SWP shown earlier, you will notice that the same Windows functions are being used. It is just the difference between C and C++ coding that changes the structure of each program.

The C++ *swpcpp* Definition File

C++ definition files, such as *swpcpp.def*, provide important prolog, epilog, and export information for the compiler. The following listing is named *swpcpp.def*.

```
NAME            SWPCPP
DESCRIPTION     'SWP for Windows for Borland C++'
EXETYPE         WINDOWS
STUB            'WINSTUB.EXE'
CODE            PRELOAD MOVEABLE
DATA            PRELOAD MOVEABLE MULTIPLE
HEAPSIZE        1024
STACKSIZE       5120
EXPORTS         WindowProc
```

The NAME statement defines *swpcpp* as a Windows program (not a dynamic link library) and gives the module a name. This name should be the same as the program's *.exe* file.

The DESCRIPTION line copies the text into the *.exe* file. Very often this is used to embed additional information such as a release date, version number, or copyright notice.

The EXETYPE specifies the type of executable (*.exe*) to produce. The STUB statement specifies the name of a program that is to be inserted into the *.exe* file whenever the application is run from the DOS command line by accident.

Both the CODE and DATA segments have been marked "preload" and "moveable," allowing Windows to load and relocate them for any dynamic memory allocation requests. The MULTIPLE statement also instructs Windows to create unique data segments for each instance of the application.

The HEAPSIZE statement allocates an amount of extra, expandable, local memory from within the application's data segment. The STACKSIZE has been set to 5120. Larger values may be necessary for applications with large nonstatic variables or those applications using recursion.

Finally, the EXPORTS statement identifies the application's dynamic link entry point and specifies the name of the procedure, in this case, **WindowProc**.

The C Resource File

For this example the resource script file, *swpcpp.rc,* is a dummy file containing only this:

/* no resources in SWPCPP */

C++ **Program Components for Command-Line Compiling**

In order to build Windows programs from the command line, you will need four files. The first three files have already been given: *swpcpp.cpp, swpcpp .def,* and *swpcpp.rc.* Additionally, you will need a *make* file. The next listing is for the *make* file, called *swpcpp.mak.*

```
FILE=swpcpp
LIBPATH=c:\bc\lib
INCPATH=c:\bc\include

$(FILE).exe: $(FILE).obj $(FILE).def $(FILE).res
  tlink /Tw /x /n /c $(LIBPATH)\c0ws $(FILE),\
    $(FILE),\
    ,\
    $(LIBPATH)\cws $(LIBPATH)\cs $(LIBPATH)\import,\
    $(FILE)
    rc $(FILE).res

$(FILE).obj: $(FILE).cpp
  bcc -c -W -I$(INCPATH) $(FILE).cpp

$(FILE).res:  $(FILE).rc
  rc -r -i$(INCPATH) $(FILE).rc
```

By using macros such as **file, libpath,** and **incpath,** definition files can be easily altered to accommodate a variety of situations. For example, if your Borland C++ library is not located at c:\bc\lib, you can just change **libpath** once to accommodate the alteration. Observe how many times **libpath** is used in the definition file. This shorthand technique will certainly save a lot of typing. It is also possible to develop a habit of cutting and pasting when creating new programs. This definition file can be replicated and made to function for another program just by changing the program name in **file.**

Once these four files are in place, compiling and linking a C program for Windows is the same as for DOS. Simply type

MAKE -fSWPCPP.MAK.

The *make* file does all of the work involved with compiling and linking. The Borland C compiler compiles *swpcpp.c* into *swpcpp.obj*, and then brings in the proper setup code. The link phase is suppressed during compilation by adding the -c option to the command line. The -W option directs the compiler to build a Windows application. The -I option is the path to the necessary include files. As an option, source level debugging can be included by adding the -v option.

The *make* file also adds any necessary resources by calling the resource compiler. The resource compiler compiles the resource file, *swpcpp.rc*, and produces a *swpcpp.res* file. The -r option tells the resource compiler not to add the result to the executable file at this time. Later, the resource compiler is called again to add the binary resource file to the executable file.

The Linker specifications in the *make* file are the most complicated since the Linker must piece information from the *.obj*, *.def*, and *.res* files together with given library information.

The /Tw option links for a Windows-executable file. The /n option selects no default libraries. The /c option selects lowercase significance in symbols. A /v option can be added to allow for debugging information.

Library path statements direct the Linker to the proper files for linking library information. The *c0ws* (obj understood) is the initialization module for the small C memory model. The *cwins* (lib) is the small C memory model run-time library for Windows. The *cs* (lib) is the regular run-time library. Finally, the *import* (lib) provides access to the Borland C++ Windows functions.

Execute your resulting code by typing **WIN SWPCPP**. The screen was shown earlier in Figure 21-1.

C++ Program Components for Integrated Development Environment Compiling

When developing Windows code from the Integrated Development Environment you will need to create the *swpcpp.c*, *swpcpp.def*, and *swpcpp.rc* files shown earlier. You will also need to develop a project file from within the IDE.

Here are the steps necessary for developing a complete program:

1. Get into the Borland C++ IDE by typing **BC** from the DOS prompt.

2. Use the editor to enter the C++ source code and save as *swpcpp.c.*

3. Use the editor to enter the C++ definition file and save as *swpcpp.def.*

4. Use the editor to enter the C++ resource file and save as *swpcpp.rc.*

5. Set the IDE Options to include:

   Compiler, Code Generation = Small Memory Model
   Compiler, Entry/Exit Code = Windows all functions exportable
   Linker, Output = Windows EXE

6. Examine the IDE Application Options:

   Application = Windows App

7. Choose "Project" from the IDE menu. Press ENTER or click "OK" to open a new project and name it *swpcpp.prj.*

8. Select "Add item" and type **SWPCPP**. In the Name box, a list of all the SWPCPP files that you have entered will be displayed.

9. Add the three files *swpcpp.c, swpcpp.rc,* and *swpcpp.def* for the program.

10. Close the Project dialog box.

11. Select "Compile" from the menu and click on "Build all" to build the project.

12. If you encounter no errors, exit the IDE by pressing ALT-X or choosing "File" and clicking on "Quit." Otherwise, open the file with the error and correct it.

13. From DOS, type **WIN SWPCPP**.

DOS will open Windows and automatically execute your program. Refer back to Figure 21-1 to see the screen.

IMPORTANT FEATURES USED WITHIN EACH SWP

Windows utilizes a large number of predefined functions. Paramount to function calls is the use of handles. This section will take a look at handles and functions in order to foster a deeper understanding of how Windows establishes a window on the screen. This will be explained with the help of *swpc.c* presented earlier. The handles and function calls in *swpcpp.cpp* are similar. Refer to Appendix C, "Windows Functions," for important Windows function prototypes.

Handles

Windows uses handles to identify many different types of objects, such as menus, icons, controls, memory allocation, output devices, pens and brushes, windows, and even instances. Windows allows you to run more than one copy of the same application at a time. Windows keeps track of each of these instances by supplying each with its own unique handle.

Usually a handle is used as a simple index into an internal table. By having a handle reference a table element, rather than containing an actual memory address, Windows can dynamically continue to rearrange all resources simply by inserting a resource's new address into the identical table position. If Windows associates a particular application's icon resource with table lookup position 10, then no matter where Windows moves the icon in memory, table position 10 contains the current location.

Windows is very efficient in its management of multiple instances. Some multitasking environments load each instance as if it were an entirely new application. Windows conserves system resources by using the same code for all instances of an application. Only the data segment for each instance is uniquely managed. Also, the first instance of an application has a very important role. The first instance of an application creates all of the objects necessary for the functioning of the application. This can include dialog boxes, menus, and also window classes. What is even more important than each instance of the application reusing these objects is the fact that under most circumstances the same resources are available to all other applications.

Windows Functions

At the highest level, a Windows application can be broken down into two essential components, the **WinMain** function, and the window function.

Windows requires that the main body of your program be named **Win-Main**. This function acts as the entry point for the application and behaves in a similar manner to the **main** function in a standard C program. However, the window function has a unique role. Your Windows applications never directly access any window functions. Instead, your application makes a request to Windows to carry out the specified operation. In order to facilitate this communication, Windows requires a call back function. A *call back function* is registered with Windows, and it is called back whenever Windows wants to execute an operation on a window.

A Closer Look at the WinMain Function

All Windows applications must have a **WinMain** function. **WinMain** is responsible for the following:

- Registering the application's window classes

- Performing necessary initializations

- Creating and starting the application's message processing loop (accessing the application's message queue)

- Upon receiving a **WM_QUIT** message, terminating the program

The **WinMain** procedure receives four parameters from Windows. For the *swpc.c* template, the function looks like this:

```
int PASCAL WinMain(HANDLE hInst,HANDLE hPreInst,
                   LPSTR lpszCmdLine,int nCmdShow)
```

Notice the use of the Pascal calling convention discussed in the last chapter. The first parameter, *hInst*, is passed the instance handle of the application; *hPreInst* contains a null if no previous instance exists (otherwise it returns the handle to the previous instance of the program); *lpszCmdLine* is a long pointer to a null-terminated string that points to the application's parameter line; and *nCmdShow* defines whether the application is to be displayed as a window (SW_SHOWNORMAL) or displayed as an icon (SW_SHOWMINNOACTIVE).

Registering the Window Class

Every window you create for a Windows application must be based on a window class. The windows you create for Windows can have a variety of styles, colors, text fonts, placement, caption bars, icons, and so forth. The *window class* serves as a template that defines these window attributes. Once a window class has been registered, the class becomes available to all programs running under Windows. Because of this, care must be taken to avoid any conflicting names between application window classes.

The window class is a data structure. The file *windows.h* contains a *typedef* statement that defines the structure **WNDCLASS**.

```
typedef struct tagWNDCLASS
  {
    WORD        style;
    LONG        (FAR PASCAL *lpfnWndProc)(HWND,WORD,WORD,LONG);
    int         cbClsExtra;
    int         cbWndExtra;
    HANDLE      hInstance;
    HICON       hIcon;
    HCURSOR     hCursor;
    HBRUSH      hbrBackground;
    LPSTR       lpszMenuName;
    LPSTR       lpszClassName;
  } WNDCLASS;
```

While Windows does provide several predefined window classes, most applications define their own window class. In order to accomplish this, your application must define a structure variable of this type, for example

```
WNDCLASS wcSwp;
```

and then fill the *wcSwp* structure with information about the window class. Table 21-3 explains the various fields within the **WNDCLASS** structure. Some of the fields may be assigned a **NULL**, directing Windows to use predefined values, while others must be given specific values.

The following code section shows how the **WNDCLASS** structure has been defined and initialized for *swpc.c*.

```
char    szProgName[]="ProgName";
        .
        .
        .
  WNDCLASS wcSwp;
```

```
        .
        .
        .
if (!hPreInst)
{
   wcSwp.lpszClassName=szProgName;
   wcSwp.hInstance=hInst;
   wcSwp.lpfnWndProc=WindowProc;
   wcSwp.hCursor=LoadCursor(NULL,IDC_ARROW);
   wcSwp.hIcon=NULL;
   wcSwp.lpszMenuName=NULL;
   wcSwp.hbrBackground=GetStockObject(WHITE_BRUSH);
   wcSwp.style=CS_HREDRAW|CS_VREDRAW;
   wcSwp.cbClsExtra=0;
   wcSwp.cbWndExtra=0;
   if (!RegisterClass (&wcSwp))
     return FALSE;
}
```

For the SWPs, *wcSwp.lpszClassName* is assigned the generic "ProgName." This can be changed for each new window class. When the **WinMain** function is called it will return a value for *wcSwp.hInstance*, indicating the current instance of the application. The *wcSwp.lpfnWndProc* field is given a pointer to the window function that will carry out all of the tasks for the window. In this case the function is called **WindowProc** and must be declared somewhere before the assignment statement.

The next field *wcSwp.hCursor* is assigned the handle to the instance's cursor (IDC_ARROW—this is the standard arrow cursor). Since there is no default icon, *wcSwp.hIcon* is assigned null. Cursors and icons can be added with calls to the **LoadCursor** and **LoadIcon** Windows functions. Assigning a null to *wcSwp.lpszMenuName* indicates that the current application does not have a menu. If a menu is present the menu's name will appear between quotation marks.

The **GetStockObject** function returns a handle to a brush used to paint the background color of the client area of a window created of this class. In this example, the function returns a handle to one of Windows' predefined brushes (WHITE_BRUSH).

The window class style has been set to CS_HREDRAW or CS_VREDRAW. All window class styles have identifiers in *windows.h;* they begin with "CS_". Each identifier represents a bit value. The logical OR operation is used to combine these bit flags. The two parameters used instruct Windows to redraw the entire client area whenever the horizontal or vertical size of the window is changed.

The last two fields, *wcSwp.cbClsExtra* and *wcSwp.cbWndExtra*, are frequently assigned 0. These fields are used to indicate the count of extra bytes

Table 21-3.   **WNDCLASS** Structure Field Definitions

Field Name	Description
style	Defines the class style. Styles can be combined by using the bitwise logical OR operator. Values for the style field include these:

Value	Meaning
CS_BYTEALIGNCLIENT	Using byte boundaries in the X direction, aligns a window's client area.
CS_BYTEALIGNWINDOW	Using byte boundaries in the X direction, aligns a window.
CS_CLASSDC	Assigns a window class its own display context that can be shared by instances.
CS_DBCLKS	Sends a double-click message to a window.
CS_GLOBALCLASS	Defines a global window class.
CS_HREDRAW	If the horizontal size of a window changes, redraws the entire window.
CS_NOCLOSE	Deactivates the Close option on the system menu.
CS_OWNDC	Assigns each window instance its own display context.
CS_PARENTDC	Gives the parent window's display context to the window class.
CS_SAVEBITS	Saves the portion of the screen image that is obscured by a window.
CS_VREDRAW	If the vertical size of a window changes, redraws the entire window.

Field Name	Description
IpfnWndProc	Receives a pointer to the window function that will carry out all of the tasks for the window.
cbClsExtra	Designates the number of extra bytes to allocate for the **WNDCLASS** structure (can be null).

Table 21-3.   **WNDCLASS** Structure Field Definitions (*continued*)

Field Name	Description
cbWndExtra	Designates the number of extra bytes to allocate for all additional structures created using this window class (can be null).
hInstance	Defines the instance of the application registering the window class.
hIcon	Defines the icon to be used whenever the window is minimized (can be null).
hCursor	Similar to hIcon, defines the cursor to be used for the window (can be null).
hbrBackground	Specifies a brush to be used for painting the window's background. This can be the handle to a physical brush or it can be a color value. If a color value is specified it must be one of the following standard system colors listed, and a 1 must be added to the chosen color.
	COLOR_ACTIVEBORDER
	COLOR_ACTIVECAPTION
	COLOR_APPWORKSPACE
	COLOR_BACKGROUND
	COLOR_CAPTIONTEXT
	COLOR_INACTIVEBORDER
	COLOR_INACTIVECAPTION
	COLOR_MENU
	COLOR_MENUTEXT
	COLOR_SCROLLBAR
	COLOR_WINDOW
	COLOR_WINDOWFRAME
	COLOR_WINDOWTEXT
lpszMenuName	A long pointer to a null-terminated string, indicating the resource name of a menu (can be null).
lpszClassName	A long pointer to a null-terminated string, indicating the name of the window class. This name must be unique in order to avoid confusion when sharing a window class among applications.

that have been reserved at the end of the window class structure and the window data structure used for each window class.

Next, examine the following code from *swpc.c.*

```
if (!hPreInst)
{

  if (!RegisterClass (&wcSwp))
    return FALSE;
}
```

From the previous discussion about instances you know that an application only needs to register a window class if it is the first instance. Windows can check the number of instances by examining the *hPreInst* parameter. If this value is null, then this is the application's first instance. Therefore, the first **if** statement fills the **WNDCLASS** structure only for first instances. The last **if** statement takes care of registering a new window class. It does this by sending over a far pointer to the address of the window class structure. The actual parameter's near pointer (*&wsSwp*) is converted to a far pointer by the compiler, since the function **RegisterClass** is expecting a far pointer. If Windows cannot register the window class, possibly due to the lack of memory, the **RegisterClass** will return a 0, terminating the program.

Creating a Window

Regardless of whether this is the first instance of an application or subsequent instances, a window must be created. All windows are of a predefined class type. The previous section illustrated how to, and when to, initialize and register a window class. This section will describe the steps necessary in creating the actual window.

A window is created by making a call to the Windows **CreateWindow** function. While the window class defines the general characteristics of a window, allowing the same window class to be used for many different windows, the parameters to **CreateWindow** specify more detailed information about the window. This additional information falls under the following categories: the window's class, title, style, screen position, parent handle, menu handle, instance handle, and 32 bits of additional information. For *swpc.c,* the template file, this would look as follows:

```
hwnd=CreateWindow(szProgName,"Simplified C Windows Platform",
             CW_OVERLAPPEDWINDOW,CW_USEDEFAULT,
             0,CW_USEDEFAULT,0,NULL,NULL,
             hInst,NULL);
```

The first field *szProgName* (assigned earlier) defines the window's class, followed by the title to be used for the window ("Simplified C Windows Platform"). The style of the window is the third parameter (WS_OVERLAPPEDWINDOW). This standard Windows style represents a normal overlapped window with a caption bar, a system menu box, minimize and maximize icons, and a thick window frame.

The next six parameters (either CS_USEDEFAULT or NULL) represent the initial x and y positions and x and y size of the window, along with the parent window handle and window menu handle. Each of these fields has been assigned a default value. The *hInst* field contains the instance of the program, followed by no additional parameters (null).

Displaying and Updating a Window

To display a window you need to do more than register a window class and create a window from that class. Displaying a window requires a call to the **ShowWindow** function in the form

```
ShowWindow(hwnd,nCmdShow);
```

The second parameter to **ShowWindow**, *nCmdShow*, determines how the window is initially displayed. The value of *nCmdShow* can specify that the window be displayed as a normal window (SW_SHOWNNORMAL), or several other possibilities. For example, substituting *nCmdShow* with the *windows.h* constant SW_SHOWMINNOACTIVE causes the window to be drawn as an icon. Other possibilities include SW_SHOWMAXIMIZED, causing the window to be active and filling the entire display, along with its counterpart SW_SHOWMINIMIZED.

The last step in displaying a window requires a call to the **UpdateWindow** function:

```
UpdateWindow(hwnd);
```

When **ShowWindow** is called with an SW_SHOWNORMAL parameter, the function erases the window's client area with the background brush specified in the window's class. It is the call to **UpdateWindow** that causes the client area to be painted by generating a WM_PAINT message.

The Message Loop

Once an application's window has been created and displayed, the program is now ready to perform its main task; the processing of messages. Remember that Windows does not send input from the mouse or keyboard directly to an application. Instead, it places all input into the application's queue. The queue can also contain messages generated by Windows or other applications. Once the **WinMain** function has taken care of creating and displaying the window, it needs to create a program message loop. This is most frequently accomplished by using a *while* loop:

```
while (GetMessage(&msg,NULL,0,0))
{
  TranslateMessage(&msg);
  DispatchMessage(&msg);
}
```

GetMessage   The **GetMessage** function is responsible for retrieving the next message from the application's message queue, copying it into the **msg** structure, and sending it to the main body of the program. The final three parameters instruct the function to retrieve all of the messages.

Windows is a *nonpreemptive multitasking* system. This means that Windows cannot take control from an application. The application must yield control before Windows can reassign control to another application. In a nonpreemptive multitasking environment, the **GetMessage** function can automatically release control of the processor to another application if the current application has no waiting messages. The current application will pick up execution following the **GetMessage** statement whenever a message finally does arrive in the application's message queue. Sometimes a program has a long job to do, and all other programs running under Windows seem to stop running during this time period. Normally, a Windows application does not care how long it is asleep. An exception might be a data communications application. In this case the application could be written to check the time and take any appropriate actions.

An application can normally return control to Windows any time before starting the message loop. For example, an application will normally make certain that all steps leading up to the message loop have executed properly. This can include making sure each window class is registered and has been created. However, once the message loop has been entered, only one message can terminate the loop. Whenever the message to be processed is WM_QUIT, the value returned is false. This causes the processing to proceed to the main loop's closing routine. The WM_QUIT message is the only way for an application to get out of the message loop.

TranslateMessage   The **TranslateMessage** function call is only required for applications that need to process character input from the keyboard. This can be very useful for allowing the user to make menu selections without using the mouse. Technically, the **TranslateMessage** function creates an ASCII character message (WM_CHAR) from a WM_KEYDOWN and WM_KEYUP message. As long as this function is included in the message loop, the keyboard interface will be in effect.

DispatchMessage   The **DispatchMessage** function is responsible for sending the message to the correct window procedure. By using this function it is easy to add windows and dialog boxes to your application, allowing **DispatchMessage** to automatically route each message to the appropriate window procedure.

The Window Function

Every Windows application must have a **WinMain** function and a window function. Windows applications never directly access any window functions. Instead, each application makes a request to Windows to carry out any specified operations. In order to facilitate this communication, Windows requires a call back function. A call back function is registered with Windows and it is called back whenever Windows wants to execute an operation on a window. The window function itself may be very small, processing only one or two messages, or it may be very complex. Advanced window functions will not only process many types of messages, but will also deal with a variety of application windows.

Initially, this concept of an operating system making a call to the application program can be quite a surprise. For the SWPC template the call back window function takes on the following appearance:

```
long FAR PASCAL WindowProc(HWND hwnd,unsigned messg,
                    WORD wParam,LONG lParam)
{
```

```
   PAINTSTRUCT ps;
   HDC hdc;
   short xcoord;
   POINT polylpts[4],polygpts[5];

   switch (messg)
   {
     case WM_PAINT:
       hdc=BeginPaint(hwnd,&ps);

/*——————————— your routines below ———————————*/
       .
       .
       .    (graphics routines deleted here for brevity)
       .
       .
/*——————————— your routines above ———————————*/

       ValidateRect(hwnd,NULL);
       EndPaint(hwnd,&ps);
     break;
     case WM_DESTROY:
       PostQuitMessage(0);
     break;
     default:
       return DefWindowProc(hwnd,messg,wParam,lParam);
   }
   return(0L);
}
```

Before going any further, it is important to notice that the name of this required window function, for our example, **WindowProc**, must be referenced by name in the *wcSwp.lpfnWndProc* field of the window class structure. **WindowProc** will be the window function for all windows that are created from this window class. The following listing reviews this initialization.

```
       .
       .
       .

if (!hPreInst)
{
   wcSwp.lpszClassName=szProgName;
   wcSwp.hInstance      =hInst;
   wcSwp.lpfnWndProc   =WindowProc;
       .
       .
       .
```

Windows has approximately 220 different messages that it can send to the window function. All of them are identified by names that begin with the letters "WM_". These messages are defined in *windows.h* and are constants that refer to numbered codes. Windows can call the window function for many reasons including window creation, resizing, moving, and being turned into an icon; when a menu item has been selected; when a scroll bar is being moved or changed by a mouse click; when repainting a client area; and when the window is being destroyed.

Like many of the other functions used in Windows, the **WindowProc** function uses the Pascal calling convention. The first parameter to the function, *hwnd*, contains the handle to the window that Windows will send the message. Recall that one window function can process messages for several windows created from the same window class. By using the window handle, **WindowProc** can determine which window is receiving the message.

The second function parameter, *messg*, specifies the actual message as defined in *windows.h*. The last two parameters *wParam* and *lParam* contain additional information related to each specific message. Sometimes the values returned are null and can be ignored; at other times they can contain two byte values and a far pointer or two word values.

WM_PAINT Message   The first thing the window function has to do is to examine the type of the message it is about to process. It must then select the appropriate action to be taken. This selection process is performed by the *switch* statement. The first message that the window function will process is WM_PAINT. The paint procedure prepares the application's client area for updating and obtains a display context for the window. The display context comes equipped with a default pen, brush, and font. It is very important because all of the display functions a Windows application uses require a handle to the display context.

Since Windows is a multitasking environment it becomes quite possible for one application to display its dialog box over another application's client area, thereby creating a display problem whenever the dialog box is closed and removed. Windows takes care of this possible black-hole problem by sending the application a WM_PAINT message, requesting that the application's client area be updated.

Except for the first WM_PAINT message, which is sent by the call to **UpdateWindow** in **WinMain**, additional WM_PAINT messages are sent under the following conditions:

- When resizing a window

- Whenever a portion of a client area has been hidden by a menu or dialog box that has just been closed

- When using the **ScrollWindow** function

- When forcing a WM_PAINT message with a call to the **InvalidateRect** or **InvalidateRgn** functions

Any portion of an application's client area that has been corrupted by the overlay of a dialog box, for example, has that area of the client area marked as invalid. Windows makes the redrawing of a client area extremely efficient by keeping track of the diagonal coordinates of this invalid rectangle. The presence of an invalid rectangle is what prompts Windows to send the WM_PAINT message.

Should the execution of statements invalidate several portions of the client area, Windows will adjust the invalid rectangle coordinates to encapsulate all invalid regions. Windows does not send a WM_PAINT message for each invalid rectangle.

By making a call to **InvalidateRect**, Windows can require the client area to be marked invalid, thereby forcing a WM_PAINT message. By calling **GetUpdateRect**, an application can obtain the coordinates of the invalid rectangle. Calling the **ValidateRect** function validates any rectangular region in the client area and removes any pending WM_PAINT messages.

The processing of the WM_PAINT message ends with a call to the **EndPaint** function. This function is called whenever the application has finished outputting information to the client area. It tells Windows that your program has finished processing all paint messages. This tells Windows that it is now okay to remove the display context.

Terminating an application by selecting the "Close" option from the system menu initiates a WM_DESTROY message, which causes the **PostQuitMessage** function to place a WM_QUIT message in the message queue. The program terminates after retrieving this message. The **DefWindowProc** (default window function) is used to process any WM_PAINT messages not processed by the window function.

WHERE TO GO FROM HERE

Windows offers the programmer an exciting new dimension when developing user friendly applications. In the previous chapter you learned basic Windows terminology and also how to develop simple Windows applications. Use the SWPs developed in this chapter and functions from Appendix C to experiment with other graphics drawing primitives. In the next chapter you'll learn how to integrate icons, cursors, bitmaps, menus, keyboard accelerators, and dialog boxes into your applications.

22

USING THE BORLAND RESOURCE WORKSHOP AND RESOURCE COMPILER

Customizing a Windows application with your own icons, pointers, and bitmaps is a breeze when you use the Borland Resource Workshop (BRW) provided with the Borland C++ compiler package. This workshop, in conjunction with the C++ compiler, gives you a complete environment in which to develop Microsoft Windows applications. In this chapter you will learn how to use this workshop to create your own icons, cursors, menus, and dialog boxes. The workshop can also help you manipulate individual bitmaps, keyboard accelerators, and strings. The icons, cursors, menus, and dialog boxes created separately in this chapter, will be assembled into a presentation-quality bar chart program in Chapter 23.

This chapter concentrates on the fundamentals of using the Borland Resource Workshop provided in the Borland C++ package. If you desire to learn advanced Windows programming concepts, the highly recommended *Windows Programming: An Introduction*, by William H. Murray and Chris H. Pappas (Osborne/McGraw-Hill, 1990) concentrates more on the details of using actual Windows functions.

WINDOWS RESOURCES

Resource files, such as those created with the BRW, are capable of turning ordinary Windows applications, like those of the last chapter, into truly exciting graphical presentations. Developing application icons, cursors, menus, bitmaps, and more, can add graphical flair and make your programs *presentation quality*. Resource files also let you add user-interactive components to your program such as menus, keyboard accelerators, and dialog boxes.

Resource code is stored separately from your main C or C++ program. This ensures that resource information can be loaded into the program on demand, allowing the resource information to be used for several applications and also allowing the application's appearance to be changed without the need to modify the original application code. The BRW allows you to create, edit, and compile these resources.

Resource Types

Application resources fall into several groups. The most important include the keyboard accelerators, bitmaps, cursors, icons, menus, and dialog boxes.

Keyboard Accelerators   An accelerator is a key or key combination you can press as an alternative to clicking the mouse on a menu option. If a keyboard accelerator is added, menu selections can be made without the use of pull-down menus.

Bitmaps   A bitmap is a portion of data used by an application to display graphical information on the screen. Bitmaps can be used to display small graphics images or whole screens. The bitmap editor allows the user to create custom bitmaps. Note that icons and cursors are actually small bitmaps created with their own editors.

Cursors   A screen cursor is used to choose items on the screen or to set the insertion point for data input. A cursor can actually be considered a small bitmap, which allows graphical images to be used as pointing devices on the screen. Cursors use a "hotspot" to identify the tip of the pointing device.

The cursor editor is similar to the bitmap editor in use and appearance.

Icons   Icons are those familiar square boxes at the bottom of your Windows program that represent the applications currently loaded into Windows. By clicking the mouse on an icon, an application can be brought to full screen.

An icon is small bitmap. The icon editor is similar in use and appearance to the bitmap and cursor editors.

Menus   Application menus pop down from the top of the screen. Menus list program options that can be activated with the mouse or hotkey combinations. Menu items can be used to open other menus, dialog boxes, or to take specific actions. Menus allow the user low-level interaction with the program.

The menu editor is used to create menu resources for applications.

Dialog boxes   A dialog box is the main method of obtaining interactive input from the user. Dialog box options are usually chosen from a menu and contain a variety of elements called controls. Dialog box controls include list boxes, scroll bars, data entry fields, and more. The dialog box resource file, created by the dialog box editor, contains all of the information necessary for creating the dialog box on the user's screen.

USING THE BORLAND RESOURCE WORKSHOP (BRW)

Each resource editor is part of the overall Borland Resource Workshop package. The BRW is a completely integrated environment designed to run under Microsoft Windows. It can be entered directly by supplying the path information and typing

C>WIN c:*path*\WORKSHOP

Another technique is to set up a group box under Windows which will allow you to click on the BRW icon to start the workshop.

The BRW is a Windows program with full menu and dialog box support. If the "New" option is selected from the File menu of the BRW, several project types can be selected. By clicking one of the project buttons, shown here, the user can elect to design icons, cursors, dialog boxes, and more.

Creating Icons, Cursors, and Bitmaps

The icon, cursor, and bitmap editors are separate parts of the BRW, but function in an almost identical fashion. In this section we'll describe the editors and then create a custom icon and cursor for a project that will be developed in the next chapter. Icons and cursors are really small bitmaps. Both editors allow for the designing of device-independent color bitmaps. The icons and cursors created with BRW are functionally device-independent in respect to resolution.

This file format allows for the tailoring of a bitmap so that it looks good on each particular display resolution. For example, one icon might consist of four definitions (called DIBs): one designed for monochrome displays, one for CGAs, one for EGAs, and one for VGAs. Whenever the application displays the icon, it simply refers to it by name; Windows then automatically selects the icon image best suited to the current display!

Table 22-1 is a list of each editor's main menu item and the associated options for the item.

Figure 22-1 shows the main editor menus for the icon editor. On the right side of the window is a color palette for selecting the drawing color. Associated with this palette is a color box which shows the currently selected value. A group of editing tools is also visible to the extreme right of the window.

Table 22-1.   Icon, Cursor, and Bitmap Editor Menus and Options

File	New project...
	Open project
	Save project
	Save file As...
	Close all
	Add to project...
	Remove from project
	Preferences...
Exit	Edit Undo
	Redo
	Cut
	Copy
	Paste
	Delete
	Duplicate
	Select all
Resource	New...
	Edit...
	Edit as text...
	View...
	Save resource as...
	Rename...
	Memory options...
	Identifies...
View	Zoom in
	Zoom out
	Actual size
	CGA resolution
	split horizontal
	split vertical
Text	align left
	align center
	align right
	Font
Options	Align
	Size...
	Pattern...
	Brush shape...
	Airbrush shape...
	Pen style...
	Editor options

Table 22-1.   Icon, Cursor, and Bitmap Editor Menus and Options *(continued)*

Cursor	Hide palette
	Hide toolbox
	Set hot spot...
	Test
	Set transparent color...
Window	Tile
	Cascade
Help	Index
	Using help
	Getting started
	Projects
	Resources
	Using the menus
	Error messages
	Resource script
	About Resource Workshop...

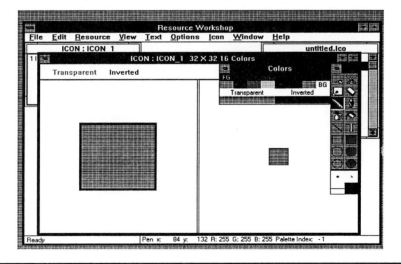

Figure 22-1.   The Icon Editor's design window

A large editing area is provided, on the left, for drawing the icon, cursor, or bitmap. As a matter of fact, the Options menu provides a "Zoom-In" or "Zoom-Out" option to help you draw in this area. Grid lines and a small-view window complement this drawing surface.

A Custom Icon and Cursor

Creating your first icon or cursor is as simple as choosing the "New" option in the File menu. Then select the proper editor (.Ico or .Cur) from the options listed. This will clear the editing area if any previous design is present.

After selecting the icon or cursor size in pixels, you will need to pick a drawing tool from the tools box or use the default drawing pen. Line styles and widths can be selected from the Options menu.

Beginning with Windows 3.0, all resource editors can provide a broad spectrum of painting colors. Click the mouse on the color choice from the palette of colors shown. Now draw the icon, cursor, or bitmap to your program's specification. Be sure to save your final results by selecting the File menu and then either the "Save" or "Save As" option.

Figure 22-2 shows an icon editor window with a completed icon design. This icon will be used in the bar chart project developed in the next chapter. Note that there are actually two renditions of the design. The larger one within the editing area allows you to see easily the image you are creating. The smaller version, to the right, represents the actual size of the design as it would appear in the application window.

Figure 22-3 shows a cursor editor window with a completed cursor design. This cursor will be used along with the previously created icon in the bar chart program of the next chapter.

A word of caution to the beginner. It takes a great deal of patience and experience to create a meaningful icon, cursor, or bitmap. This often requires several trial-and-error attempts. Whenever you come up with a design that looks good, stop and save a copy of it. If you don't, you could easily make one bad change to a good design and ruin all of your previous work.

The first time you select the "Save" option from the File menu, the editor will prompt you for a file name. If you are creating an icon, the file system will automatically append an .ICO file extension. The .CUR file extension is used for cursors. (Note that the file extensions must be .ICO or

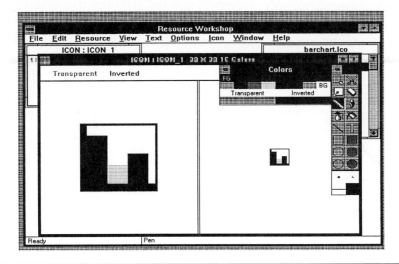

Figure 22-2.   A completed icon in the Icon Editor window

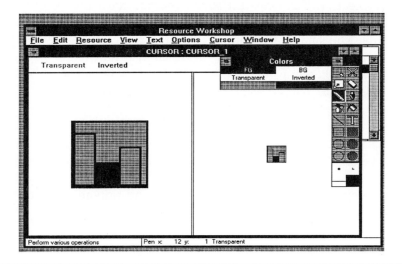

Figure 22-3.   A completed cursor in the Cursor Editor window

.CUR respectively.) If you are creating several possible designs make certain you choose the "Save As" option, *not* "Save." The "Save" option overwrites your original file, "Save As" will allow you to create multiple copies!

When creating cursors an optional hotspot can be selected. This is done by selecting "Hotspot" from the Cursor menu. The hotspot on cursors selects which portion of the cursor (pixel) will be used to return the current screen coordinates. The hotspot on the cursor figure shown in Figure 22-3 is located at the top of the vertical axis.

Once you have selected the "Hotspot" option a very small grid will appear in the drawing box. Simply place the grid on whichever pixel you want to select as the hotspot and click the mouse. The coordinates of the selected hotspot will be added to the display box's list of statistics. Only one hotspot per cursor is allowed.

How to Create Menus

Menus are one of Windows most important tools for creating interactive programs. Menus form the gateway for easy, consistent interfacing across applications. In their simplest form, menus allow the user to make selections by using the mouse to point and click on predefined menu options. Some of these selections are screen color choices, sizing options, and file operations. More advanced menu options allow the user to select dialog boxes from the menu list. Dialog boxes permit data entry from the keyboard and allow the user to enter string, integer, and even real number information in applications. However, before you can get to a dialog box, you typically must pass through a menu!

The menu created in this section will also be used in the bar chart project developed in the next chapter.

Menu Mechanics

In the following sections we will describe what a menu is, what it looks like, how it is created, and the various menu options available to the programmer. Menus are very easy to create and implement in a program.

What Is a Menu?

A menu is a list of options, or names that represent options, that an application can take. In some cases, the items in a menu can even be bitmaps. The user can select an option by using either the mouse, keyboard, or hotkey. Windows, in turn, responds by sending a message to the application stating which command was selected.

Using the Menu Editor

The BRW menu editor lets you design and edit menu resources. The editor is capable of reading menu descriptions contained in resource files (RES), resource script files (RC) and executable files (EXE). It is capable of saving menu information in several formats; the most useful of these are resource files (RES), executable files (EXE), and resource script files (RC). If a header file is available, which describes constants used in a menu's description, the editor can also open the header file. For example, the constant IDM _ABOUT might be identified with 40 in a header file. Under these cases, a symbol value is added at the bottom of the edit window, and the header file is opened. Figure 22-4 shows a menu (BarMenu) being developed in the BRW menu editor.

The menu editor also lets you define different styles and attributes for application menus. These styles and attributes allow you to use checkmarks

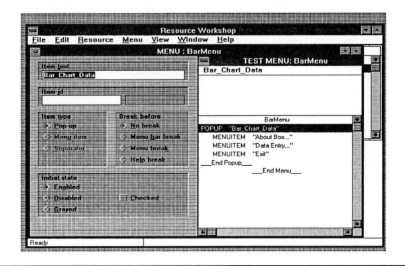

Figure 22-4.   The Menu Editor, showing the creation of *BARMENU*

(checked) to indicate the status of an item, define styles for an item's text (normal or grayed), use separator lines to divide menus (menu bar breaks), align menu items in column format, and assign a help attribute to a menu item. Detailed information for adding these features is discussed in the BRW user's guide.

Menus and the Resource Compiler

By following a set of simple rules, Windows will draw and manage menus for you. In so doing, Windows will produce consistent menus from one application to another. Menus are usually combined with other resource objects associated with a project, but can also be saved separately as resource script files. If you use resource script files the menu information will be combined with your program application at link time forming the final executable (EXE) file. The structure of a simple menu is quite easy to understand. Here is a resource script file, created by the BRW's editor.

```
BARMENU MENU LOADONCALL MOVEABLE PURE DISCARDABLE
BEGIN
  POPUP "Bar_Chart_Data"
  BEGIN
    MenuItem  "About Box...", IDM_ABOUT
    MenuItem  "Data Entry...", IDM_INPUT
    MenuItem  "Exit", IDM_EXIT
  END
END
```

By studying this listing, you can identify a number of additional menu keywords such as *MENU, POPUP,* and *MenuItem.* Brackets ({}) can be used instead of the keywords *BEGIN* and *END,* if you are entering this file from an ASCII editor, instead of through the BRW. It is also easy to identify the menu items that will appear in this menu: "About Box...," "Data Entry...," and "Exit." The three dots following a menu selection inform the user that a dialog box will appear if this option is selected.

Menu Keywords and Options

The name of this program's menu definition is BARMENU. The menu definition name is followed by the keyword *MENU.* This particular example describes the *POPUP* menu, Bar_Chart_Data. This name will appear on the menu bar. Pop-up menus are arranged from left to right on the menu bar. If a large number of pop-up items are used, an additional bar will be provided automatically. Only one pop-up menu can be displayed at a time. An ampersand can be used to produce an underscore under the character that follows it in the selection list. The ampersand allows the menu item to be selected from the keyboard. Our simple menu does not take advantage of this feature, but if the "A" in the "About Box..." choice were preceded with an ampersand, it could be selected with a key combination of ALT-A. With our menu, the item can be selected by positioning the mouse and clicking with the left button. When a pop-up menu is selected, Windows pops the menu to the screen immediately under the selected item on the menu bar. Each *MenuItem* keyword describes one menu item or name, for example, "Data Entry...."

Identification numbers or constants from a header file appear to the right of the menu items. If numbers are present they can be replaced with values identified in header files. For example, IDM_ABOUT 40, IDM_INPUT 50, and IDM_EXIT 70. *IDM* stands for the identification number of a menu item. This form of ID has become very popular, but is not required especially if you create (RES) files directly from the BRW and eliminate script files altogether. What is important, however, is that each menu item have a unique identification associated with it.

Keyboard Accelerators

Keyboard accelerators are most often used by menu designers as a sort of "fast-key" combination for selecting menu items. For example, a menu may have 12 color options for selecting a background color. You could use the menus and point and click the menu for each color, or you could use keyboard accelerators. If a keyboard accelerator is used, the function keys, for example, could be used for color selection without having to pull the menu down at all!

How To Enter Data with Dialog Boxes

In the previous section menus were studied as a means of simple data entry by the user. This section will investigate a more significant means of data entry—the Dialog Box. While data can be entered directly into the application program's window, dialog boxes are the preferred entry form for maintaining consistency among Windows programs.

Dialog boxes allow the user to check items in a window list, set push buttons for various choices, directly enter strings and integers from the keyboard, and indirectly enter real numbers (floats). Starting with Windows 3.0, dialog boxes can also contain *combo boxes*. Combo boxes allow a combination of a single-line edit field and a list box. The dialog box is the programmer's key to serious data entry in Windows programs as well as the programmer's secret for ease of programming, since Windows handles all necessary overhead.

Dialog boxes can be called when selected as a choice from a menu and appear as a pop-up window to the user. To distinguish a dialog box choice from ordinary selections in a menu, ellipsis (...) follow the dialog option name. In the previous section, the "About Box..." and "Data Entry..." menu items referred to dialog box selections. Figure 22-5 shows a completed dialog box (taken from an example that will be developed in the next chapter). The resource script file for this dialog box follows.

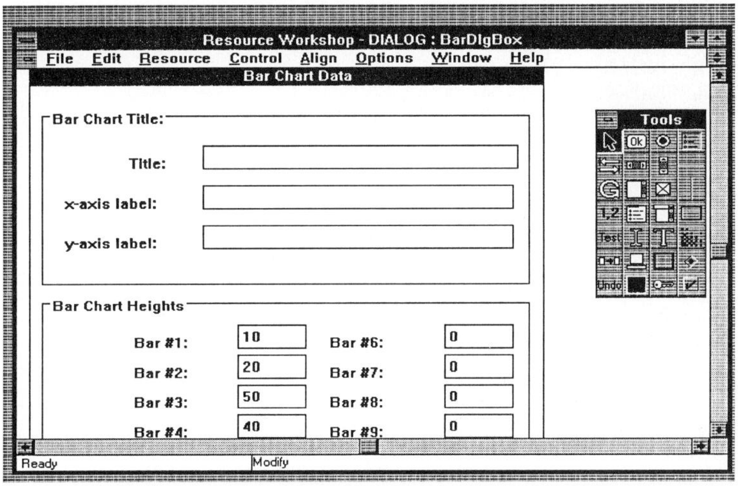

Figure 22-5.   The Dialog Box Editor, showing a complete data entry dialog box

```
BarDlgBox DIALOG LOADONCALL MOVEABLE DISCARDABLE
          42,-10,223,209
          CAPTION "Bar Chart Data"
          STYLE WS_BORDER|WS_CAPTION|WS_DLGFRAME|WS_POPUP
     BEGIN
       CONTROL "Bar Chart Title:",100,"button",
            BS_GROUPBOX|WS_TABSTOP|WS_CHILD,5,11,212,89
       CONTROL "Bar Chart Heights",101,"button",
            BS_GROUPBOX|WS_TABSTOP|WS_CHILD,5,105,212,90
       CONTROL "Title: ",-1,"static",SS_LEFT|WS_CHILD,
            43,35,28,8
       CONTROL "",DM_TITLE,"edit",ES_LEFT|WS_BORDER|WS_TABSTOP|
            WS_CHILD,75,30,137,12
       CONTROL "x-axis label:",-1,"static",SS_LEFT|
            WS_CHILD,15,55,55,8
       CONTROL "",DM_XLABEL,"edit",ES_LEFT|WS_BORDER|WS_TABSTOP|
            WS_CHILD,75,50,135,12
       CONTROL "y-axis label:",-1,"static",SS_LEFT|
            WS_CHILD,15,75,60,8
       CONTROL "",DM_YLABEL,"edit",ES_LEFT|WS_BORDER|WS_TABSTOP|
            WS_CHILD,75,70,135,12
       CONTROL "Bar #1: ",-1,"static",SS_LEFT|
            WS_CHILD,45,125,40,8
       CONTROL "Bar #2: ",-1,"static",SS_LEFT|
            WS_CHILD,45,140,40,8
       CONTROL "Bar #3: ",-1,"static",SS_LEFT|
            WS_CHILD,45,155,40,8
       CONTROL "Bar #4: ",-1,"static",SS_LEFT|
            WS_CHILD,45,170,40,8
       CONTROL "Bar #5: ",-1,"static",SS_LEFT|
            WS_CHILD,45,185,40,8
       CONTROL "Bar #6: ",-1,"static",SS_LEFT|
            WS_CHILD,130,125,40,8
       CONTROL "Bar #7: ",-1,"static",SS_LEFT|
            WS_CHILD,130,140,40,8
       CONTROL "Bar #8: ",-1,"static",SS_LEFT|
            WS_CHILD,130,155,40,8
       CONTROL "Bar #9: ",-1,"static",SS_LEFT|
            WS_CHILD,130,170,40,8
       CONTROL "Bar #10:",-1,"static",SS_LEFT|
            WS_CHILD,130,185,45,8
       CONTROL "10",DM_P1,"edit",ES_LEFT|WS_BORDER|WS_TABSTOP|
            WS_CHILD,90,120,30,12
       CONTROL "20",DM_P2,"edit",ES_LEFT|WS_BORDER|WS_TABSTOP|
            WS_CHILD,90,135,30,12
       CONTROL "50",DM_P3,"edit",ES_LEFT|WS_BORDER|WS_TABSTOP|
            WS_CHILD,90,150,30,12
       CONTROL "40",DM_P4,"edit",ES_LEFT|WS_BORDER|WS_TABSTOP|
            WS_CHILD,90,165,30,12
       CONTROL "0",DM_P5,"edit",ES_LEFT|WS_BORDER|WS_TABSTOP|
            WS_CHILD,90,180,30,12
       CONTROL "0",DM_P6,"edit",ES_LEFT|WS_BORDER|WS_TABSTOP|
            WS_CHILD,180,120,30,12
       CONTROL "0",DM_P7,"edit",ES_LEFT|WS_BORDER|WS_TABSTOP|
            WS_CHILD,180,135,30,12
       CONTROL "0",DM_P8,"edit",ES_LEFT|WS_BORDER|WS_TABSTOP|
```

```
        WS_CHILD,180,150,30,12
  CONTROL "0",DM_P9,"edit",ES_LEFT | WS_BORDER | WS_TABSTOP |
        WS_CHILD,180,165,30,12
  CONTROL "0",DM_P10,"edit",ES_LEFT | WS_BORDER | WS_TABSTOP |
        WS_CHILD,180,180,30,12
  CONTROL "OK",IDOK,"button",BS_PUSHBUTTON | WS_TABSTOP |
        WS_CHILD,54,195,24,14
  CONTROL "Cancel",IDCANCEL,"button",BS_PUSHBUTTON |
        WS_TABSTOP | WS_CHILD,124,195,34,14
END
```

The specifications that make up a dialog box are typically produced with the BRW dialog editor. Again, the BRW dialog editor can read resource files (RES), resource script files (RC), and executable files (EXE). The final results can be saved in several alternate file formats, including those just mentioned.

Dialog Box Concepts

Dialog boxes are actually "child" windows that pop-up when selected from the user's menu. When various items are selected, such as dialog box buttons and check boxes, Windows provides the means necessary for processing the message information.

Dialog boxes can be produced in two basic styles—modal and modeless. Modal dialog boxes are the most popular and are used for the example developed in the next chapter. When a modal dialog box is created, no other options, within the current program, are available until the user ends the dialog box with a "click" on the Okay or Cancel button. The Okay button will process any new information selected by the user, while the Cancel button will return the user to the original window without processing new information. Windows expects the ID values for these pushbuttons to be 1 and 2 respectively. Modeless dialog boxes are more closely related to ordinary windows. A pop-up window can be created from a parent window and allows the user to switch back and forth between the two. The same thing is permitted with a modeless dialog box. Modeless dialog boxes are preferred when a certain option must remain on the screen, such as a color select dialog box.

The Dialog Box Editor

There are two ways to enter dialog box information into a resource file (RES). If you are entering information from a magazine or book listing, it will be easiest for you to use a text editor and simply copy the given menu and dialog box specifications into a resource script file with an (RC) extension. The BRW also provides a text-mode form of data entry for this purpose. If you are creating a new dialog box for your project from scratch, you should use the BRW dialog box editor. This section discusses the fundamentals of using the editor and helps you get started creating simple dialog boxes. The documentation provided with the BRW user's manual will provide additional information for more advanced features and editing.

Why Use a Dialog Box Editor?

One look at the resource script file, shown in an earlier listing, which contains dialog box information, will convince you of the need for a dialog box editor.

Where do all those terms come from? What do all those numbers mean? Without the dialog box editor, you would have to create, size, and place dialog boxes and their associated controls on the screen experimentally. The dialog box editor does all this for you automatically. Unless you want to claim that you, at least once in your life, created a dialog box without the editor, you have no reason not to design dialog boxes without the powerful BRW development environment.

Using the Dialog Box Editor

To use the dialog box editor properly, you must first master the use of files. Dialog box information can be returned from the editor with several file formats, including a (.RES) or (.DLG) extension. The (RES) file is compiled and ready to be linked with the application's source file since it contains information in binary format. The (DLG) file is an ASCII text version of the same information.

If your dialog box information is entered in ASCII form from a book or magazine article, it must be compiled before editing is permitted. The BRW dialog box editor will compile resource script files (DLG and RC). Therefore, the typical dialog box entry process usually involves the creation of the dialog box script file (DLG). Next, that file is read by the BRW dialog box editor and compiled. With the dialog box in view, you can apply any finishing touches you desire before saving the file.

On the other hand, if you are creating a new dialog box for a project from scratch, simply enter the BRW editing environment and select the dialog box option. The dialog box editor can be entered by clicking the "Dialog" option from the BRW's Resource menu. A screen similar to this should appear.

The new dialog box can be named using the File menu. This name will be attached to the dialog box description in the resource file and will be used to access this dialog box from the application program. The screen now contains the initial outline for the new dialog box. This initial dialog box can be moved about the screen and sized to fit your needs. Figure 22-6 shows the initial dialog box moved and sized.

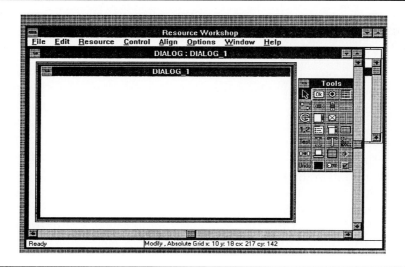

Figure 22-6.   A newly moved and sized initial dialog box

Dialog Editor Features   The dialog box contains eight menus that you can access while you are working on a new dialog box. If you have gotten to this point, you have already used the File menu to initialize and name your new dialog box. The remaining menus include Edit, Resource, Control, Align, Options, Window, and Help. Many of the individual menu items are self-explanatory. Only the most important will be discussed here.

The Edit menu, like other menus, allows you to quickly "Undo" mistakes while in the dialog box creation process. You can also "Select all" followed by "Delete" to start with a clean slate.

Using the Options menu you can make the tools, alignment, and caption windows hidden or visible. This is also useful for things like tabs, tab ID, and item groups. Dialog box features can be tested from the menu option.

The special design windows available in this editor include caption, alignment, and tools windows. The tools window allows you to select various controls, such as radio and push buttons, for inclusion in the final dialog box. Many of these features are augmented when combined with items found in the Control menu.

The Control menu lists fifteen different control options. These controls provide the design interface between the user and the Windows application program and allow you to create push- and radio buttons, list boxes, scroll bars, check boxes, group and combo boxes, text boxes, and more.

Placing Controls   By far, the most important aspect of using the dialog box editor is an understanding of the various controls that are provided for the user. Here is an explanation of the most important controls.

The "Check Box" control creates a small square box, called a check box, with a label to its right. These boxes are usually marked or checked by clicking with the mouse, but can also be selected with the keyboard. Several check boxes usually appear together in a dialog box, allowing the user to check one or more features at the same time.

The "Radio Button" control creates a small circle, called a radio button, with a label to its right. Radio buttons, like check boxes, typically appear in groups. However, unlike check boxes, only one radio button can be selected at a time in any particular group.

The "Pushbutton" control, sometimes simply called a button, is a small rounded rectangular button, which can be sized. A label appears within the button. Pushbuttons are intended for immediate choices such as accepting or canceling the dialog box selections made by the user.

The "Group Box" control creates a rectangular outline within a dialog box to enclose a group of controls that are to be used together. A label appears in the upper-left corner of the group box.

The "Horizontal Scroll Bar" and "Vertical Scroll Bar" controls allow you to create horizontal and vertical scroll bars for the dialog box. These are usually used in conjunction with another window or control that contains text or graphics information.

The "List Box" control creates a rectangular outline with a vertical scroll bar. List boxes are useful when scrolling is needed to select a file from a long directory listing.

The "Edit Text" control creates a small interactive rectangle on the screen in which string information can be entered. The edit box can be sized to accept short or long strings. This string information can be processed directly as character or numeric integer data and indirectly as real number data in the program. The edit box is the most important control for data entry.

The "Static Text" control allows the insertion of labels and strings within the dialog box. These can be used, for example, to label an edit box.

The "Icon" control creates the rectangular space used for the placement of a dialog box icon.

The "Combo Box" is a combination of two elements: a single-line edit field (also called "static text") and a list box. With a combo box, the user has the ability to enter something into the edit box or scroll through the list box looking for an appropriate selection. Windows 3.0 provides several styles of combo boxes.

Controls can be placed in the current dialog box by selecting the appropriate control from the control menu, positioning the mouse pointer in the dialog box, and clicking the mouse button. If the placement is not satisfactory, the mouse can be used for repositioning.

Creating a Dialog Box

In this section, a simple "About" dialog box will be created. About dialog boxes are used to identify the project and the developers, give a copyright date, and more. They usually contain only one pushbutton (OK!), so they are the easiest dialog boxes to design.

Figure 22-7 shows a sized and positioned dialog box outline awaiting the placement of text and button controls. In this dialog box example, only two types of controls will be used, the text and pushbutton controls. To enter text, decide on the type of text alignment and click that control option in the editor's Control menu. Then, use the mouse to position the text box in the dialog window. Clicking the mouse within the box after positioning it will allow you to edit the actual text string. Here is an illustration of this concept:

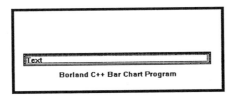

The string to be printed is entered in the Text window, where the word "Text" now appears. The ID value is automatically supplied. Now, place an OK pushbutton in the About box. Select the "Pushbutton" option from the Control menu and place the button on the screen. Click the mouse to set the button's position in the window. Clicking the mouse within the set button allows you to enter text for the button. In this case, type **OK**. Here is the final dialog box showing placement of the pushbutton:

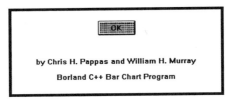

Now you can save the dialog box information by selecting the "Save" option from the File menu. Remember that the dialog box editor will save this file in one of two forms, the (RES) or (DLG) formats. Using the dialog box editor efficiently is a skill learned over a period of time. Large dialog boxes that utilize many controls will initially take hours to design. Again, we urge you to read the detailed information contained in the Help menu and your BRW user's manual. Start with simple dialog boxes and work toward more complicated types.

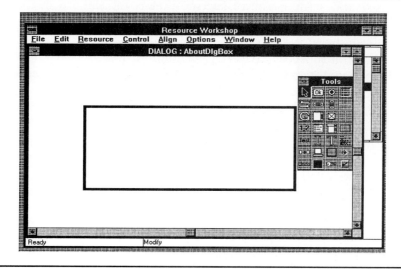

Figure 22-7.   A newly moved and sized dialog box awaiting text and button controls

Examining the Resource Script   It is possible to examine the script file information before saving the dialog box. This is done by selecting the "Edit As Text" option in the Resource menu. You could examine the script file information in this way using the About box we just designed.

```
ABOUTDLGBOX DIALOG DISCARDABLE LOADONCALL PURE MOVEABLE 53, 52,
        180, 80
        STYLE WS_POPUP | WS_DLGFRAME
  BEGIN
    CONTROL "Borland C+ Bar Chart Program" 65535, "STATIC",
        WS_CHILD | WS_VISIBLE | 0x1L, 2, 60, 176, 10
    CONTROL "by Chris H. Pappas and William H. Murray" 65535,
        "STATIC", WS_CHILD | WS_VISIBLE | 0x1L, 2, 45, 176, 10
    CONTROL "OK" 1, "BUTTON", WS_CHILD | WS_VISIBLE | WS_TABSTOP,
        75, 10, 32, 14
  END
```

The name of this dialog box is ABOUTDLGBOX. The editor has affixed various segment values along with size specifications for the box. The various style options further identify the dialog box as one which has a frame and is of a pop-up type. Three controls are listed.

The first and second control specification is for static text. The word "static" identifies the control as a static text box. The remaining specifications establish the text position and type.

The third control specifies an OK pushbutton. The text between the first set of double quotes specifies what will appear within the pushbutton. The labels for the ID values for the pushbutton is a system default.

Remember, you don't have to view this information. The dialog box editor will convert the graphics dialog box you see on the screen directly into a resource file (RES). The only time you will need this information is when you are entering dialog box specifications from a book or magazine.

Both the About box and the data entry box, shown earlier, will be used in the next chapter.

USING THE RESOURCE COMPILER (RC) FROM THE COMMAND LINE

The Resource Compiler can be used directly without the use of the BRW programming environment. This direct use is usually limited to applications taken from books or magazine articles. These are cases where the menu or dialog box resource information is entered in the form of a text file rather than being created directly within the BRW.

The resource file created by the BRW for menus and dialog boxes contains resource information stored in binary format (RES). The resource editor allows you to edit this binary information directly and save the results back into the original file. Another type of optional file is called a resource script file and contains resource information in text format (ASCII). This file has a RC file extension. If only dialog box information is required, you can create a dialog box resource script file, with a DLG file extension. There is also a text file that saves information in ASCII format. Both of these script file types can be created with the resource workshop editor or created with an ASCII text editor. Usually, resource script files are not needed because the workshop editors allow you to edit resource files directly. The only real, but very important, use for resource script files is for reproducing resource information for use in book and magazine article listings, or for creating your own resources from such articles.

Resource Statements

If you opt for resource script files when creating menus and dialog boxes or if you enter resource script files from book and magazine listings, you can use the resource statements shown in Table 22-2.

Defining additional resources for an application is as simple as naming the resource ID followed by a resource compiler keyword, and then the actual file name. Let's suppose we've created a resource script file called MYRES.RC:

```
myicon   ICON   myicon.ico
mycursor CURSOR mycursor.cur
mybitmap BITMAP mybitmap.bmp
```

MYRES.RC is a text file that defines three new resources, named *myicon*, *mycursor*, and *mybitmap*. ICON, CURSOR, and BITMAP, are reserved key-

Table 22-2.   Statements Available for Use with the Resource Compiler

Statement Category	Resource Compiler Statement
Directives	#include
	#define
	#undef
	#ifdef
	#ifndef
	#if
	#elif
	#else
	#endif
Single-line	BITMAP
	CURSOR
	FONT
	ICON
Multiple-line	ACCELERATORS
	DIALOG
	MENU
	RCDATA
	STRINGTABLE
User-defined	Supplied by the user

words defining the type of the resource. These are followed by the actual file names containing the resource information.

There are five additional options that can be included with each single-line statement. These options follow the resource-type keyword and include: (PRELOAD, LOADONCALL) and (FIXED, MOVEABLE, and DISCARDABLE). The first two options define load-options, the latter define memory-options.

Single-line Statement Syntax

```
resourceID resource-type [[load-option]] [[memory-option]]
     filename
```

The PRELOAD option automatically loads the resource whenever the application is run. LOADONCALL only loads the resource when it is called.

If a FIXED memory option is selected, the resource remains at a fixed memory address. Selecting MOVEABLE allows Windows to move the resource to compact and conserve memory. The last choice, DISCARDABLE, allows Windows to discard the resource if it is no longer needed. However, it can be reloaded should a call be made requesting that particular resource. For example, making *mybitmap* LOADONCALL and DISCARDABLE is as simple as entering the following modified single-line statement into the resource script:

```
myicon   ICON   myicon.ico
mycursor CURSOR mycursor.cur
mybitmap BITMAP LOADONCALL DISCARDABLE mybitmap.bmp
```

Compiling Resources

Resource script files must be compiled. This can be done directly from the BRW, as shown earlier in this chapter, or from the command line. The command to run the resource compiler includes the name of the resource script file, the name of the executable file that will receive the compilers binary format output, and any of the optional instructions shown in Table 22-3.

Table 22-3.   Resource Compiler Options

Resource Compiler Option	Description
-r	Instructs the resource compiler to put its output into a file with an .RES file extension, instead of putting it into the executable file.
-d	Defines a symbol for the preprocessor that you can test with the #ifdef directive.
-fo	Renames the .RES file.
-fe	Renames the .EXE file.
-i	Searches the specified directory before searching the directories specified by the INCLUDE environment variable.
-v	Displays messages that report on the progress of the compiler.
-x	Prevents the resource compiler from checking the INCLUDE environment variable when searching for include files or resource files.
-l or lim32*	Causes the resource compiler to compile an application that will use the expanded memory supported by the Lotus Intel Microsoft Expanded Memory Specification, Version 3.2.
-m*	Causes the resource compiler to compile an application using EMS so that multiple instances of the application will use different EMS memory banks.
-e*	Changes the default location of global memory from below the EMS bank line to above the EMS bank line, for a dynamic link library.
-p*	Creates a private dynamic link library that can be called by only one application. This lets Windows load the library above the EMS bank line.
-? or -h	Displays a list of the resource compilers command line options.
-t*	Creates a protected mode only application.
-k*	Keeps segments in .DEF order.

*not valid when -r is also specified

Resource Compiler Syntax

The syntax for using the resource compiler is simple. From the command line, type

```
rc [[compiler options]] filename.rc [[executable filename]]
```

For example, the syntax for invoking the resource compiler with the example resource script described earlier would take one of the following three forms:

```
rc myres
rc myres.rc
rc -r myres.rc
```

The first two examples read the MYRES.RC resource script file, create the compiled resource file MYRES.RES, and copy the resources into the executable file MYRES.EXE. The third command performs the same actions except that it does *not* put the resource into MYRES.EXE. If the third command was executed, the MYRES.RES binary file could be added to the MYRES.EXE file at a later date using the following command structure:

```
rc myres.res
```

This causes the resource compiler to search for the compiled resource file (RES) and place the resource file into the executable file (EXE) of the same file name.

ADDITIONAL RESOURCE INFORMATION

In addition to the information contained in this chapter, the Borland Resource Workshop user's guide provides a wealth of information on each of these topics. While using the BRW, take advantage of the extensive built-in Help engine. Details on the creation of actual Windows resources can be found in the books mentioned in this and earlier chapters and in various magazine articles. Developing serious Windows code is a major undertaking, but don't forget to have fun while learning!

23

DEVELOPING A BORLAND C++ PRESENTATION-QUALITY BAR CHART

In the previous three chapters you have learned the fundamentals of programming with the Windows graphics primitives and how to create Windows enhancements such as icons, pointers, menus, and dialog boxes. In this chapter these individual concepts will be spliced together, yielding a professional-quality presentation graphics bar chart. You will also be introduced to a new Windows 3.0 programming feature, the Palette Manager, and you will learn how to manipulate fonts.

As you have moved from chapter to chapter you have learned the fundamentals necessary for producing a presentation-quality graph. By incorporating menus, dialog boxes, and pointers the presentation-quality application will now take on the glitz and glitter of a commercial program.

You can view the program presented in this chapter as a model that you can further develop. It is complete and just waiting for your individual touches. Enter the code for the program, study what it can do, and then customize the code to suit your needs.

THE PALETTE MANAGER

Before presenting and explaining the code required for the bar chart program in this chapter, it is necessary to explain the features of the Palette

Manager. Windows 3.0 provides a Palette Manager, which serves as a buffer between a user-developed application and an output device such as a color monitor, printer, or plotter. The Palette Manager uses information contained in a program's logical palette and maps it to a system palette used by all Windows applications. When several logical palettes exist, the Palette Manager referees among them. The Palette Manager meets the request of the foreground window first and then attempts to satisfy all subsequent windows.

The Palette Manager was designed for color-intensive applications that are to be device independent. The logical palette, created by your application and managed by the Palette Manager, can be accessed directly or indirectly. When using the direct method, the color is chosen by providing an index into the palette entries. When using the indirect method, a palette-relative RGB value is used. The palette-relative RGB specifications are very similar to the older explicit RGB values.

The Logical Palette Overhead

This section will examine the overhead necessary to create and utilize a logical palette within an application. There are five basic steps that must be accomplished in creating and using a logical palette:

1. Create a *logpalette* data structure.

2. Create the logical palette.

3. Select the palette into the device context.

4. *Realize* the palette (give the logical palette the requested colors).

5. Specify the palette colors (directly or indirectly).

Create the *logpalette* Data Structure

Typically, an application will create a *logpalette* structure in the following manner:

```
#define PALETTESIZE 256
HANDLE   hPal;
NPLOGPALETTE pLogicalPal;
                   .

                   .

                   .

                   .
pLogicalPal=(NPLOGPALETTE) LocalAlloc(LMEM_FIXED,
              (sizeof(LOGPALETTE) +
              (sizeof(PALETTEENTRY)*(PALETTESIZE)))));
pLogicalPal->palVersion=0x300;
pLogicalPal->palNumEntries=PALETTESIZE;
```

The various definitions used in the process are contained in the *windows.h* header file. In this particular case, a *palettesize* of 256 is defined, although larger sizes are permitted when needed. The *logpalette* data structure contains the Windows version number, which in this case is 300 (representing Windows version 3.00).

Create the Logical Palette

The logical palette is created with the use of the **CreatePalette** function.

```
hPal=CreatePalette(pLogicalPal);
```

Select the Palette into the Device Context

The logical palette can be selected into the device context in the following manner:

```
SelectPalette(hdc,hPal);
```

Note that only the **SelectPalette** function can be used to accomplish this task.

Realize the Palette

The selected palette must be realized before it can be used. The **RealizePalette** function is used here.

```
RealizePalette(hdc);
```

Specify the Palette Colors

In an application containing many colors, a cyan color might be specified in the following manner:

```
/*CYAN*/
pLogPal->palPalEntry[4].peRed=0x00;
pLogPal->palPalEntry[4].peGreen=0xFF;
pLogPal->palPalEntry[4].peBlue=0xFF;
pLogPal->palPalEntry[4].peFlags=(BYTE) 0;
```

When using the direct method of specifying colors, an index into the logical palette can be used. **Paletteindex** is a macro that accepts an index value. Note that square brackets are not used here.

```
colorshade=PALETTEINDEX(4);
```

The direct method of specifying colors allows the greatest control over the selected colors but becomes too impractical when the number of colors is large. The indirect method of specifying colors eliminates this problem.
When using an indirect method, a palette-relative RGB color reference is used instead of an index.

```
colorshade=PALETTERGB(0x00,0xFF,0xFF);
```

Palettergb, like **paletteindex**, is also a macro. **Palettergb** accepts three values (RGB), which specify the relative intensities of each of the primary colors. With this technique, output devices supporting a system palette will allow the Palette Manager to map colors from the logical palette. If the output device does not support a system palette, then the color values specified in the palette-relative RGB will be used as explicit RGB colors.

USING FONTS IN AN APPLICATION

Our bar chart program will utilize different fonts, since it will be necessary to label vertical and horizontal axes. There are several ways to create and manipulate fonts in Windows. The **CreateFont** function will be used in this example.

What is a font? A *font* is a complete set of characters of the same typeface and size. Fonts include letters, punctuation marks, and additional symbols. The size of a font is measured in points. For example, 12-point Times Roman is a different font from 12-point Times Roman Italic, 14-point Times Roman, or 12-point Helvetica. A *point* is the smallest unit of measure used in typography. There are 12 points in a pica and 72 points in an inch.

A *typeface* is a basic character design that is defined by a stroke width and a serif (a smaller line used to finish off a main stroke of a letter, as at the top and bottom of the uppercase letter "M"). A font represents a complete set of characters from one specific typeface, all with a certain size and style, including italics and bold. Usually, the system owns all of the font resources and shares them with the application program. Fonts are not usually compiled into the final executable version of a program.

Application programs treat fonts like other drawing objects and manipulate them by using handles.

Windows 3.0 supplies several fonts: System, Terminal, Courier, Helvetica, Modern, Roman, Script, and Times Roman. These are called *GDI-supplied fonts*. These resources are installed from the Fonts disk and become part of the Windows system. With Windows 3.1, True Type font technology is also available to the user.

The CreateFont Function

The **CreateFont** function is of type HFONT as defined in the *windows.h* header file. From the GDI's pool of physical fonts, this function selects the logical font that most closely matches the characteristics specified by the developer in the function call. Once created, this logical font can be selected by any device. The syntax for **CreateFont** is

```
HFONT CreateFont(Height,Width,Escapement,Orientation,Weight,
                 Italic,Underline,StrikeOut,CharSet,
                 OutputPrecision,ClipPrecision,Quality,
                 PitchAndFamily,Facename)
```

With 14 parameters, the **CreateFont** function requires quite a bit of baggage when used by the programmer. Table 23-1 helps explain some of these parameters.

Suppose that the first time **CreateFont** is called, the parameters are set to the following values:

```
Height = 12
Width  = 12
Escapement = 0
Orientation = 0
Weight = FW_BOLD
Italic = FALSE
Underline = FALSE
StrikeOut = FALSE
CharSet = OEM_CHARSET
OutputPrecision = OUT_DEFAULT_PRECIS
ClipPrecision = CLIP_DEFAULT_PRECIS
Quality = DEFAULT_QUALITY
PitchAndFamily = VARIABLE_PITCH ¦ FF_ROMAN
Facename = "Roman"
```

The function will attempt to find a font match to these specifications. This font could be used to print a horizontal string of text to the window.

The second time **CreateFont** is called, the parameters are set to the following values:

```
Height = 12
Width  = 12
Escapement = 900
Orientation = 900
Weight = FW_BOLD
Italic = FALSE
Underline = FALSE
StrikeOut = FALSE
CharSet = OEM_CHARSET
OutputPrecision = OUT_DEFAULT_PRECIS
ClipPrecision = CLIP_DEFAULT_PRECIS
Quality = DEFAULT_QUALITY
PitchAndFamily = VARIABLE_PITCH ¦ FF_ROMAN
Facename = "Roman"
```

The function will attempt to find a font match to these specifications. As you can see, the only values that have changed are Escapement and Orientation. Both of these parameters have angles specified in tenths of a degree. In this case, then, the actual angle is 90 degrees. The Escapement parameter thus rotates the line of text from horizontal to vertical. Orientation rotates each character in the string 90 degrees. This font could be used to print a vertical label in a program.

Table 23-1.   CreateFont Parameters

(int) Height	Desired font height in logical units.
(int) Width	Average font width in logical units.
(int) Escapement	Angle (in tenths of a degree) for each line written in the font.
(int) Orientation	Angle (in tenths of a degree) for each character's baseline.
(int) Weight	Weight of font (0 to 1000): 400 is normal; 700 is bold.
(byte) Italic	Italic font.
(byte) Underline	Underline font.
(byte) StrikeOut	Strike out fonts (redline).
(byte) CharSet	Character set (ANSI_CHARSET, OEM_CHARSET).
(byte) OutputPrecision	How closely output must match the requested specifications (OUT_CHARACTER_PRECIS, OUT_DEFAULT_PRECIS, OUT_STRING_PRECIS, OUT_STROKE_PRECIS).
(byte) ClipPrecision	How to clip characters outside of clipping range (CLIP_CHARACTER_PRECIS, CLIP_DEFAULT_PRECIS, CLIP_STROKE_PRECIS).
(byte) Quality	How carefully the logical attributes are mapped to the physical font (DEFAULT_QUALITY, DRAFT_QUALITY, PROOF_QUALITY).
(byte) PitchAndFamily	Pitch and family of font (DEFAULT_PITCH, FIXED_PITCH, PROOF_QUALITY, FF_DECORATIVE, FF_DONTCARE, FF_MODERN, FF_ROMAN, FF_SCRIPT, FF_SWISS).
(lpstr) Facename	A string pointing to the typeface name of the desired font.

THE BAR CHART

Let's now investigate the presentation bar chart program and the files necessary for the creation of the final executable file. The bar chart program will allow the user to enter up to ten bars via the dialog box. The bar widths are scaled in order that the final figure will fill the entire horizontal axis. Thus, two bars or ten bars will produce the same size horizontal plot. The vertical heights of the bars are also scaled. The value for the largest bar is scaled to the maximum value of the y-axis, with all other values drawn in proportion to this bar. Automatic scaling allows for a wide range of data values, without the need for changing plotting ranges, and so forth.

This program utilizes the power of the Palette Manager in controlling the logical palette. Since the Palette Manager is used, this program will be device independent. Notice from the listings that this example uses the direct method of specifying palette colors with the help of the **paletteindex** macro.

The program allows the user to input three labels. One label is used for the title, which is centered over the bar figure. The remaining two labels are for the vertical axis and horizontal axis. The vertical label is plotted vertically, from top to bottom.

You will have ten files on your disk when the *make* utility is finished:

barchart.mak	barchart.c
barchart.def	barchart.cur
barchart.h	barchart.res
barchart.rc	barchart.obj
barchart.ico	barchart.exe

All of the ASCII files are shown in the next listing—they must be separated into the individual files mentioned. Remember that the icon and cursor are binary files created by the Borland Resource Workshop (BRW), as illustrated in the previous chapter. If you didn't create an icon and a cursor earlier, now is the time to do it.

THE BARCHART MAKE FILE (BARCHART.MAK)

```
FILE=barchart
LIBPATH=c:\bc\lib
INCPATH=c:\bc\include

$(FILE).exe: $(FILE).obj $(FILE).def $(FILE).res
    tlink /Tw /x /n /c $(LIBPATH)\c0ws $(FILE),\
    $(FILE),\,\
    $(LIBPATH)\cws $(LIBPATH)\cs $(LIBPATH)\import,\
    $(FILE)
    rc $(FILE).res

$(FILE).obj: $(FILE).c
    bcc -c -W -I$(INCPATH) $(FILE).c

$(FILE).res:  $(FILE).rc
    rc -r -i$(INCPATH) $(FILE).rc
```

THE BARCHART DEFINITION FILE (BARCHART.DEF)

```
;BARCHART.DEF for Borland C++ Compiling

NAME            barchart
DESCRIPTION     'Borland Bar Chart Program'
EXETYPE         WINDOWS
STUB            'WINSTUB.EXE'
CODE            PRELOAD MOVABLE
DATA            PRELOAD MOVEABLE MULTIPLE
HEAPSIZE        4096
STACKSIZE       9216
EXPORTS         AboutDlgProc    @1
                BarDlgProc      @2
                WindowProc      @3
```

THE BARCHART HEADER FILE (BARCHART.H)

```
#define IDM_ABOUT     40
#define IDM_INPUT     50
#define IDM_EXIT      70

#define DM_TITLE     280
#define DM_XLABEL    281
#define DM_YLABEL    282
#define DM_P1        283
#define DM_P2        284
#define DM_P3        285
#define DM_P4        286
#define DM_P5        287
#define DM_P6        288
#define DM_P7        289
#define DM_P8        290
#define DM_P9        291
#define DM_P10       292
```

THE BARCHART RESOURCE FILE (BARCHART.RC)

```
#include "windows.h"
#include "barchart.h"

BarCursor CURSOR barchart.cur
BarIcon   ICON   barchart.ico

BarMenu   MENU
BEGIN
  POPUP "Bar_Chart_Data"
  BEGIN
    MENUITEM "About Box...",   IDM_ABOUT
    MENUITEM "Data Entry...",  IDM_INPUT
    MENUITEM "Exit",           IDM_EXIT
  END
END
```

```
AboutDlgBox DIALOG LOADONCALL MOVEABLE DISCARDABLE
        50,300,180,80
        STYLE WS_DLGFRAME | WS_POPUP
  BEGIN
    CONTROL "Borland C++ Bar Chart Program",-1,"static",
        SS_CENTER | WS_CHILD,2,60,176,10
    CONTROL "by Chris H. Pappas and William H. Murray",-1,
        "static",SS_CENTER | WS_CHILD,2,45,176,10
    CONTROL "OK",IDOK,"button",
        BS_PUSHBUTTON | WS_TABSTOP | WS_CHILD,75,10,32,14
  END


BarDlgBox DIALOG LOADONCALL MOVEABLE DISCARDABLE
        42,-10,223,209
        CAPTION "Bar Chart Data"
        STYLE WS_BORDER | WS_CAPTION | WS_DLGFRAME | WS_POPUP
  BEGIN
    CONTROL "Bar Chart Title:",100,"button",
        BS_GROUPBOX | WS_TABSTOP | WS_CHILD,5,11,212,89
    CONTROL "Bar Chart Heights",101,"button",
        BS_GROUPBOX | WS_TABSTOP | WS_CHILD,5,105,212,90
    CONTROL "Title: ",-1,"static",SS_LEFT | WS_CHILD,
        43,35,28,8
    CONTROL "",DM_TITLE,"edit",ES_LEFT | WS_BORDER | WS_TABSTOP |
        WS_CHILD,75,30,137,12
    CONTROL "x-axis label:",-1,"static",SS_LEFT |
        WS_CHILD,15,55,55,8
    CONTROL "",DM_XLABEL,"edit",ES_LEFT | WS_BORDER | WS_TABSTOP |
        WS_CHILD,75,50,135,12
    CONTROL "y-axis label:",-1,"static",SS_LEFT |
        WS_CHILD,15,75,60,8
    CONTROL "",DM_YLABEL,"edit",ES_LEFT | WS_BORDER | WS_TABSTOP |
        WS_CHILD,75,70,135,12
    CONTROL "Bar #1: ",-1,"static",SS_LEFT |
        WS_CHILD,45,125,40,8
    CONTROL "Bar #2: ",-1,"static",SS_LEFT |
        WS_CHILD,45,140,40,8
    CONTROL "Bar #3: ",-1,"static",SS_LEFT |
        WS_CHILD,45,155,40,8
    CONTROL "Bar #4: ",-1,"static",SS_LEFT |
        WS_CHILD,45,170,40,8
    CONTROL "Bar #5: ",-1,"static",SS_LEFT |
        WS_CHILD,45,185,40,8
    CONTROL "Bar #6: ",-1,"static",SS_LEFT |
        WS_CHILD,130,125,40,8
    CONTROL "Bar #7: ",-1,"static",SS_LEFT |
        WS_CHILD,130,140,40,8
    CONTROL "Bar #8: ",-1,"static",SS_LEFT |
        WS_CHILD,130,155,40,8
    CONTROL "Bar #9: ",-1,"static",SS_LEFT |
        WS_CHILD,130,170,40,8
    CONTROL "Bar #10:",-1,"static",SS_LEFT |
        WS_CHILD,130,185,45,8
    CONTROL "10",DM_P1,"edit",ES_LEFT | _BORDER | WS_TABSTOP |
        WS_CHILD,90,120,30,12
```

```
         CONTROL "20",DM_P2,"edit",ES_LEFT┊WS_BORDER┊WS_TABSTOP┊
             WS_CHILD,90,135,30,12
         CONTROL "50",DM_P3,"edit",ES_LEFT┊WS_BORDER┊WS_TABSTOP┊
             WS_CHILD,90,150,30,12
         CONTROL "40",DM_P4,"edit",ES_LEFT┊WS_BORDER┊WS_TABSTOP┊
             WS_CHILD,90,165,30,12
         CONTROL "0",DM_P5,"edit",ES_LEFT┊WS_BORDER┊WS_TABSTOP┊
             WS_CHILD,90,180,30,12
         CONTROL "0",DM_P6,"edit",ES_LEFT┊WS_BORDER┊WS_TABSTOP┊
             WS_CHILD,180,120,30,12
         CONTROL "0",DM_P7,"edit",ES_LEFT┊WS_BORDER┊WS_TABSTOP┊
             WS_CHILD,180,135,30,12
         CONTROL "0",DM_P8,"edit",ES_LEFT┊WS_BORDER┊WS_TABSTOP┊
             WS_CHILD,180,150,30,12
         CONTROL "0",DM_P9,"edit",ES_LEFT┊WS_BORDER┊WS_TABSTOP┊
             WS_CHILD,180,165,30,12
         CONTROL "0",DM_P10,"edit",ES_LEFT┊WS_BORDER┊WS_TABSTOP┊
             WS_CHILD,180,180,30,12
         CONTROL "OK",IDOK,"button",BS_PUSHBUTTON┊WS_TABSTOP┊
             WS_CHILD,54,195,24,14
          CONTROL "Cancel",IDCANCEL,"button",BS_PUSHBUTTON┊
             WS_TABSTOP┊WS_CHILD,124,195,34,14
     END


THE BARCHART  APPLICATION FILE (BARCHART.C)

// Presentation Quality Borland C++ Bar Chart Program    //
// (c) William H. Murray and Chris H. Pappas, 1991        //

#include <windows.h>
#include <string.h>
#include <stdlib.h>
#include "barchart.h"

#define maxnumbar 10
#define PALETTESIZE 256
HANDLE hPal;
NPLOGPALETTE pLogPal;

extern "C" {
long FAR PASCAL WindowProc(HWND hwnd,unsigned messg,
                          WORD wParam,LONG lParam);
}

extern "C" {
BOOL FAR PASCAL AboutDlgProc(HWND hwnd,unsigned messg,
                            WORD wParam,LONG lParam);
}

extern "C" {
BOOL FAR PASCAL BarDlgProc(HWND hwnd,unsigned messg,
   WORD wParam,LONG lParam);
}

char szProgName[]="ProgName";
```

```
char szApplName[]="BarMenu";
char szCursorName[]="BarCursor";
char szIconName[]="BarIcon";
char szTString[80]="(bar chart title area)";
char szXString[80]="x-axis label";
char szYString[80]="y-axis label";
int iBarSize[maxnumbar]={10,20,50,40};

class Main
{
  public:
  static HANDLE hInst;
  static HANDLE hPrevInst;
  static int nCmdShow;
  static int MessageLoop(void);
};

HANDLE Main::hInst=0;
HANDLE Main::hPrevInst=0;
int Main::nCmdShow=0;

int Main::MessageLoop(void)
{
  MSG msg;

  while(GetMessage(&msg,NULL,0,0))
  {
    TranslateMessage(&msg);
    DispatchMessage(&msg);
  }
  return msg.wParam;
}

class Window
{
  protected:
    HWND hwnd;
  public:
    HWND GetHandle(void) {
  return hwnd;
  }
  BOOL Show(int nCmdShow) {
    return ShowWindow(hwnd,nCmdShow);
  }
  void Update(void) {
    UpdateWindow(hwnd);
  }
};

class MainWindow:public Window
{
  private:
    static char szProgName[];
  public:
    static void Register(void)
    {
```

```
        WNDCLASS wcSwp;
        wcSwp.lpszClassName=szProgName;
        wcSwp.hInstance=Main::hInst;
        wcSwp.lpfnWndProc=WindowProc;
        wcSwp.hCursor=LoadCursor(NULL,IDC_ARROW);
        wcSwp.hIcon=NULL;
        wcSwp.lpszMenuName=szApplName;
        wcSwp.hbrBackground=GetStockObject(WHITE_BRUSH);
        wcSwp.style=CS_HREDRAW|CS_VREDRAW;
        wcSwp.cbClsExtra=0;
        wcSwp.cbWndExtra=0;
        if (! RegisterClass(&wcSwp))
          exit(FALSE);
    }
  MainWindow(void)
  {
    hwnd=CreateWindow(szProgName,
                      "Borland C++ Bar Chart Program",
                      WS_OVERLAPPEDWINDOW,CW_USEDEFAULT,
                      0,CW_USEDEFAULT,0,NULL,NULL,
                      Main::hInst,(LPSTR) this);
    if (!hwnd)
      exit(FALSE);

    Show(Main::nCmdShow);
      Update();
  }
};

char MainWindow::szProgName[]="ProgName";

// no lParam never used warning
#pragma argsused

BOOL FAR PASCAL AboutDlgProc(HWND hdlg,unsigned messg,
                             WORD wParam,LONG lParam)
{
  switch (messg)
  {
    case WM_INITDIALOG:
      break;
    case WM_COMMAND:
      switch (wParam)
      {
        case IDOK:
          EndDialog(hdlg,TRUE);
          break;
        default:
          return FALSE;
      }
      break;
    default:
      return FALSE;
  }
  return TRUE;
}
```

```
// no lParam never used warning
#pragma argsused

BOOL FAR PASCAL BarDlgProc(HWND hdlg,unsigned messg,
                           WORD wParam,LONC lParam)
{
  switch (messg)
  {
    case WM_INITDIALOG:
      return FALSE;
    case WM_COMMAND:
      switch (wParam)
      {
        case IDOK:
          GetDlgItemText(hdlg,DM_TITLE,szTString,80);
          GetDlgItemText(hdlg,DM_XLABEL,szXString,80);
          GetDlgItemText(hdlg,DM_YLABEL,szYString,80);
          iBarSize[0]=GetDlgItemInt(hdlg,DM_P1,NULL,0);
          iBarSize[1]=GetDlgItemInt(hdlg,DM_P2,NULL,0);
          iBarSize[2]=GetDlgItemInt(hdlg,DM_P3,NULL,0);
          iBarSize[3]=GetDlgItemInt(hdlg,DM_P4,NULL,0);
          iBarSize[4]=GetDlgItemInt(hdlg,DM_P5,NULL,0);
          iBarSize[5]=GetDlgItemInt(hdlg,DM_P6,NULL,0);
          iBarSize[6]=GetDlgItemInt(hdlg,DM_P7,NULL,0);
          iBarSize[7]=GetDlgItemInt(hdlg,DM_P8,NULL,0);
          iBarSize[8]=GetDlgItemInt(hdlg,DM_P9,NULL,0);
          iBarSize[9]=GetDlgItemInt(hdlg,DM_P10,NULL,0);
          EndDialog(hdlg,TRUE);
          break;
        case IDCANCEL:
          EndDialog(hdlg,FALSE);
          break;
        default:
          return FALSE;
      }
      break;
    default:
      return FALSE;
  }
  return TRUE;
}
long FAR PASCAL WindowProc(HWND hwnd,unsigned messg,
                           WORD wParam,LONG lParam)
{
  HDC hdc;
  PAINTSTRUCT ps;
  HFONT hOFont,hNFont;
  HBRUSH hOrgBrush,hBrush;
  static FARPROC lpfnAboutDlgProc;
  static FARPROC lpfnBarDlgProc;
  static HWND hInst1,hInst2;
  static short xClientView,yClientView;
  int i,iNBars,iBarWidth,iBarMax;
  int ilenMaxLabel;
  int x1,x2,y1,y2;
```

```
int iBarSizeScaled[maxnumbar];
char sbuffer[10],*strptr;

iNBars=0;
for (i=0;i<maxnumbar;i++)
{
  if(iBarSize[i]!=0) iNBars++;
}

iBarWidth=400/iNBars;

// Find bar in array with maximum height
iBarMax=iBarSize[0];
for(i=0;i<iNBars;i++)
  if (iBarMax<iBarSize[i]) iBarMax=iBarSize[i];

// Convert maximum y value to a string
strptr=itoa(iBarMax,sbuffer,10);
ilenMaxLabel=strlen(sbuffer);

// Scale bars in array. Highest bar = 270
for (i=0;i<iNBars;i++)
  iBarSizeScaled[i]=iBarSize[i]*(270/iBarMax);

switch (messg)
{
  case WM_SIZE:
    xClientView=LOWORD(lParam);
    yClientView=HIWORD(lParam);
    break;

  case WM_CREATE:
    hInst1=((LPCREATESTRUCT) lParam)->hInstance;
    hInst2=((LPCREATESTRUCT) lParam)->hInstance;
    lpfnAboutDlgProc=MakeProcInstance(AboutDlgProc,hInst1);
    lpfnBarDlgProc=MakeProcInstance(BarDlgProc,hInst2);
    pLogPal=(NPLOGPALETTE) LocalAlloc(LMEM_FIXED,
            (sizeof(LOGPALETTE) +
            (sizeof(PALETTEENTRY)*(PALETTESIZE))));
    pLogPal->palVersion=0x300;
    pLogPal->palNumEntries=PALETTESIZE;

    //BLACK
    pLogPal->palPalEntry[0].peRed=0x00;
    pLogPal->palPalEntry[0].peGreen=0x00;
    pLogPal->palPalEntry[0].peBlue=0x00;
    pLogPal->palPalEntry[0].peFlags=(BYTE) 0;
    //BLUE
    pLogPal->palPalEntry[1].peRed=0x00;
    pLogPal->palPalEntry[1].peGreen=0x00;
    pLogPal->palPalEntry[1].peBlue=0xFF;
    pLogPal->palPalEntry[1].peFlags=(BYTE) 0;
    //RED
    pLogPal->palPalEntry[2].peRed=0xFF;
    pLogPal->palPalEntry[2].peGreen=0x00;
    pLogPal->palPalEntry[2].peBlue=0x00;
```

```
          pLogPal->palPalEntry[2].peFlags=(BYTE) 0;
          //GREEN
          pLogPal->palPalEntry[3].peRed=0x00;
          pLogPal->palPalEntry[3].peGreen=0xFF;
          pLogPal->palPalEntry[3].peBlue=0x00;
          pLogPal->palPalEntry[3].peFlags=(BYTE) 0;
          //CYAN
          pLogPal->palPalEntry[4].peRed=0x00;
          pLogPal->palPalEntry[4].peGreen=0xFF;
          pLogPal->palPalEntry[4].peBlue=0xFF;
          pLogPal->palPalEntry[4].peFlags=(BYTE) 0;
          //YELLOW
          pLogPal->palPalEntry[5].peRed=0xFF;
          pLogPal->palPalEntry[5].peGreen=0xFF;
          pLogPal->palPalEntry[5].peBlue=0x00;
          pLogPal->palPalEntry[5].peFlags=(BYTE) 0;
          //MAGENTA
          pLogPal->palPalEntry[6].peRed=0xFF;
          pLogPal->palPalEntry[6].peGreen=0x00;
          pLogPal->palPalEntry[6].peBlue=0xFF;
          pLogPal->palPalEntry[6].peFlags=(BYTE) 0;
          //WHITE
          pLogPal->palPalEntry[7].peRed=0xFF;
          pLogPal->palPalEntry[7].peGreen=0xFF;
          pLogPal->palPalEntry[7].peBlue=0xFF;
          pLogPal->palPalEntry[7].peFlags=(BYTE) 0;
          //MIX1
          pLogPal->palPalEntry[8].peRed=0x00;
          pLogPal->palPalEntry[8].peGreen=0x80;
          pLogPal->palPalEntry[8].peBlue=0x80;
          pLogPal->palPalEntry[8].peFlags=(BYTE) 0;
          //MIX2
          pLogPal->palPalEntry[9].peRed=0x80;
          pLogPal->palPalEntry[9].peGreen=0x80;
          pLogPal->palPalEntry[9].peBlue=0x80;
          pLogPal->palPalEntry[9].peFlags=(BYTE) 0;

       hPal=CreatePalette(pLogPal) ;
       break;
    case WM_COMMAND:
      switch (wParam)
      {
        case IDM_ABOUT:
          DialogBox(hInst1,"AboutDlgBox",hwnd,lpfnAboutDlgProc);
          break;
        case IDM_INPUT:
          DialogBox(hInst2,"BarDlgBox",
                      hwnd,lpfnBarDlgProc);
          InvalidateRect(hwnd,NULL,TRUE);
          UpdateWindow(hwnd);
          break;
        case IDM_EXIT:
          SendMessage(hwnd,WM_CLOSE,0,0L);
          break;
        default:
          break;
```

```
    }
    break;
case WM_PAINT:
{
    hdc=BeginPaint(hwnd,&ps);
    SelectPalette(hdc,hPal,1);
    RealizePalette(hdc);

    //——————— your routines below ———————

    // Set View Port and Map Mode
    SetMapMode(hdc,MM_ISOTROPIC);
    SetWindowExt(hdc,640,400);
    SetViewportExt(hdc,xClientView,yClientView);
    SetViewportOrg(hdc,0,0);

    // Print Text to Screen
    hNFont=CreateFont(12,12,0,0,FW_BOLD,
                      FALSE,FALSE,FALSE,OEM_CHARSET,
                      OUT_DEFAULT_PRECIS,
                      CLIP_DEFAULT_PRECIS,
                      DEFAULT_QUALITY,
                      VARIABLE_PITCH¦FF_ROMAN,
                      "Roman");
    hOFont=SelectObject(hdc,hNFont);
    TextOut(hdc,(300-(strlen(szTString)*10/2)),
            15,szTString,strlen(szTString));
    TextOut(hdc,(300-(strlen(szXString)*10/2)),
            365,szXString,strlen(szXString));
    TextOut(hdc,(90-ilenMaxLabel*12),
            70,strptr,ilenMaxLabel);
    hNFont=CreateFont(12,12,900,900,FW_BOLD,
                      FALSE,FALSE,FALSE,
                      OEM_CHARSET,
                      OUT_DEFAULT_PRECIS,
                      CLIP_DEFAULT_PRECIS,
                      DEFAULT_QUALITY,
                      VARIABLE_PITCH¦FF_ROMAN,
                      "Roman");
    hOFont=SelectObject(hdc,hNFont);
    TextOut(hdc,50,200+(strlen(szXString)*10/2),
            szYString,strlen(szYString));

    // Draw Coordinate Axis
    MoveTo(hdc,99,49);
    LineTo(hdc,99,350);
    LineTo(hdc,500,350);
    MoveTo(hdc,99,350);
    x1=100;
    y1=350;
    x2=x1+iBarWidth;

    // Draw Each Bar
    for(i=0;i<iNBars;i++)
    {
        hBrush=CreateSolidBrush(PALETTEINDEX(i+1));
```

```
        SelectObject(hdc,hBrush);
        y2=350-iBarSizeScaled[i];
        Rectangle(hdc,x1,y1,x2,y2);
        x1=x2;
        x2+=iBarWidth;
      }
    SelectObject(hdc,hOFont);
    DeleteObject(hNFont);

//———————— your routines below ————————

    EndPaint(hwnd,&ps);
    }
    break;

    case WM_DESTROY:
      PostQuitMessage(0);
    break;

    default:
      return DefWindowProc(hwnd,messg,wParam,lParam);
    }
  return 0L;
}

// no lpszCmdLine never used warning
#pragma argsused

int PASCAL WinMain(HANDLE hInst,HANDLE hPrevInst,
                   LPSTR lpszCmdLine,int nCmdShow)
{
  Main::hInst=hInst;
  Main::hPrevInst=hPrevInst;
  Main::nCmdShow=nCmdShow;

  if (!Main::hPrevInst) {
    MainWindow::Register();
  }

  MainWindow MainWnd;

  return Main::MessageLoop();
}
```

The *barchart.mak* and *barchart.def* Files

As you can see from the *barchart.mak* file listing, this program will also use a cursor, *barchart.cur*, and an icon, *barchart.ico*. The BRW supplied with Borland C++ provides the necessary cursor and icon editors for creating these simple bitmap objects. Refer to the previous chapter for details on creating your own unique cursor and icon. Both the cursor and icon are small bitmaps depicting a bar graph. The *barchart.def* file contains three EXPORTS: **AboutDlgProc**, **BarDlgProc**, and **WindowProc**.

The *barchart.h* Header File

The *barchart.h* header file contains identification information for the menu and dialog items of the main program. Additionally, three ID values are associated with the title, x-axis labels, and y-axis labels. This header file also contains ten unique identification numbers, which will represent the ten input values for bar heights entered from the dialog box by the user. Recall from the previous chapter that these ID values can be utilized by the BRW when creating menus and dialog boxes.

The *barchart.rc* Resource File

The *barchart.rc* file contains information for the cursor (**BarCursor**), the menu (**BarMenu**), and two dialog boxes (**AboutDlgBox** and **BarDlgBox**). This file was created with the BRT dialog box editor and saved as an ASCII file. Remember that it is not necessary to save this information as a text (ASCII) file since the editor will allow you to save the information in binary form. However, if you are entering this program from the book, it would be easiest for you just to type in this resource file as it appears. This is a long listing, so be careful as you type.

The *barchart.c* Program

The *barchart.c* program for this section is built upon the programming concepts presented throughout this book. The data entered by the user in this program will determine the height and number of bars to be plotted. The maximum number of bars is set to ten. The width and height of the bars are scaled to fit and fill the graph. Thus, a two-bar bar chart will have wider bars than one with five bars. The largest bar will be scaled to the chart's maximum height with all other bars being proportionally sized. The user may enter a title, x-axis labels, and y-axis labels for the bar chart. Many parts of this program incorporate the features of the Simplified Windows Platform (SWP) explained in Chapter 21, "Writing Borland C and C++ Windows Applications," so the explanation of the program's operation will concentrate on the additions to this platform.

Data from the Dialog Box

The data for the three bar chart labels are entered through the dialog box. These are passed to the global variables *szTString, szXString,* and *szYString.* Text information is processed with the **GetDlgItemText** function within **BarDlgProc.**

```
case WM_COMMAND:
  switch (wParam)
  {
    case IDOK:
      GetDlgItemText(hdlg,DM_TITLE,szTString,80);
      GetDlgItemText(hdlg,DM_XLABEL,szXString,80);
      GetDlgItemText(hdlg,DM_YLABEL,szYString,80);
          .
          .
            .
```

Integer values representing the bar chart heights can be intercepted in a similar manner with the use of the **GetDlgItemInt** function.

```
iBarSize[0]=GetDlgItemInt(hdlg,DM_P1,NULL,0);
iBarSize[1]=GetDlgItemInt(hdlg,DM_P2,NULL,0);
          .
          .
          .
iBarSize[9]=GetDlgItemInt(hdlg,DM_P10,NULL,0);
```

Processing the Bar Height Data

Examine the code that starts in the **WindowProc** procedure. The global data array, *iBarSize[],* is examined for the first zero value. This value represents the end of data entry. By counting the number of nonzero entries, the number of bars (*iNBars*) can be determined.

```
iNBars=0;
for (i=0;i<maxnumbar;i++)
  {
  if(iBarSize[i]!=0) iNBars++;
  }
```

There are 400 data points, out of 640, available horizontally. The width of each bar (*iBarWidth*) can be determined by dividing 400 by *iNBars*.

```
iBarWidth=400/iNBars;
```

The next step is to scan the array for the bar with the maximum height (*iBarMax*). This is done in a simple loop.

```
// Find bar in array with maximum height
iBarMax=iBarSize[0];
for(i=0;i<iNBars;i++)
  if (iBarMax<iBarSize[i]) iBarMax=iBarSize[i];
```

This maximum value is also converted into a string and pointed to by *strptr* in order to label the maximum y value in the final plot.

```
// Convert maximum y value to a string
strptr=itoa(iBarMax,sbuffer,10);
ilenMaxLabel=strlen(sbuffer);
```

Knowing the height of the largest bar will allow all other bar heights to be adjusted proportionally. These will be placed in a new array, *iBarSize-Scaled[]*. The maximum vertical height for bars is 270, out of 480 pixels.

```
// Scale bars in array. Highest bar = 270
for (i=0;i<iNBars;i++)
  iBarSizeScaled[i]=(float) iBarSize[i]*(270.0/iBarMax);
```

Now skip down to the code contained under WM_PAINT. You will notice that the MM_ISOTROPIC mapping mode is used. Windows allows several different mapping modes, dependent upon individual needs, as shown in Table 23-2.

```
    case WM_PAINT:
      hdc=BeginPaint(hwnd,&ps);
      SelectPalette(hdc,hPal,1);
      RealizePalette(hdc);

//——————— your routines below ———————

      // Set View Port and Map Mode
      SetMapMode(hdc,MM_ISOTROPIC);
      SetWindowExt(hdc,640,400);
      SetViewportExt(hdc,xClientView,yClientView);
      SetViewportOrg(hdc,0,0);
```

The default mapping mode is MM_TEXT, which allows drawing in pixel coordinates for the screen. Under MM_TEXT, point (0,0) is in the upper-left corner of the screen. MM_ISOTROPIC allows you to select the

Table 23-2.   Mapping Modes

Value	Meaning
MM_ANISOTROPIC	Arbitrary units with arbitrarily scaled axes
MM_HIENGLISH	Logical unit mapped to 0.001 inch Positive x is to the right Positive y is up
MM_HIMETRIC	Logical unit mapped to 0.01 millimeter Positive x is to the right Positive y is up
MM_ISOTROPIC	Arbitrary units with equally scaled axes
MM_LOMETRIC	Logical unit mapped to 0.1 millimeter Positive x is to the right Positive y is up
MM_LOENGLISH	Logical unit mapped to 0.01 inch Positive x is to the right Positive y is up
MM_TEXT	Logical unit mapped to device pixel Positive x is to the right Positive y is down
MM_TWIPS	Logical unit mapped to 1/20 of printer's point Positive x is to the right Positive y is up

extent of both the x- and y-axes. The mapping mode is changed by calling the function **SetMapMode. SetWindowExt** sets the height and width of the client (application) area to 640 × 400. These are logical sizes, which Windows adjusts (scales) to fit the physical display device. The display size values are used by the **SetViewportExt** function and were returned earlier by WM_SIZE.

The section of code devoted to printing labels actually creates two fonts, using the **CreateFont** function explained earlier.

```
// Print Text to Screen
hNFont=CreateFont(12,12,0,0,FW_BOLD,
                  FALSE,FALSE,FALSE,OEM_CHARSET,
                  OUT_DEFAULT_PRECIS,
                  CLIP_DEFAULT_PRECIS,
                  DEFAULT_QUALITY,
                  VARIABLE_PITCH | FF_ROMAN,
                  "Roman");
hOFont=SelectObject(hdc,hNFont);
TextOut(hdc,(300-(strlen(szTString)*10/2)),
        15,szTString,strlen(szTString));
TextOut(hdc,(300-(strlen(szXString)*10/2)),
        365,szXString,strlen(szXString));
TextOut(hdc,(90-ilenMaxLabel*12),
        70,strptr,ilenMaxLabel);
hNFont=CreateFont(12,12,900,900,FW_BOLD,
                  FALSE,FALSE,FALSE,
                  OEM_CHARSET,
                  OUT_DEFAULT_PRECIS,
                  CLIP_DEFAULT_PRECIS,
                  DEFAULT_QUALITY,
                  VARIABLE_PITCH | FF_ROMAN,
                  "Roman");
hOFont=SelectObject(hdc,hNFont);
TextOut(hdc,50,200+(strlen(szXString)*10/2),
        szYString,strlen(szYString));
```

The first is a variable-pitch Roman font for printing horizontal labels, while the second is the same font rotated 90 degrees for plotting the vertical y label.

Finally, the x-axis and y-axis are drawn in black, and the bars are plotted.

```
// Draw Each Bar
for(i=0;i<iNBars;i++)
  {
  hBrush=CreateSolidBrush(lColor[i]);
  SelectObject(hdc,hBrush);
  y2=350-(int) iBarSizeScaled[i];
  Rectangle(hdc,x1,y1,x2,y2);
  x1=x2;
  x2+=iBarWidth;
  }
```

Notice that the bars are drawn by subtracting the bar size from 350. This is required since the origin for the chart is in the upper-left corner of the window. The **Rectangle** function is used to draw each bar and fill it with the current color. For each pass through the loop, the 1 value will be the x2 value of the previous bar while x2 will be incremented by the bar width, *iBarWidth*.

Figure 23-1 shows the default bar chart. Four bars and label locations are shown. By clicking on the Bar_Chart_Data menu item and selecting the "About box" option, the About box shown in Figure 23-2 can be viewed. Likewise, if the "Data Entry box" option is selected, the Data Entry box in Figure 23-3 will be presented to the user. Instead of accepting the defaults, a new bar chart will be formed with the data shown in Figure 23-4. The results are shown in Figure 23-5.

USING THE WINDOWS DEBUGGER

Not everything works as planned, and Borland realized this would happen during the creation of Windows applications. A Windows version of the Debugger is included with the Borland C++ compiler. The Windows program Debugger and the application are run under Windows.

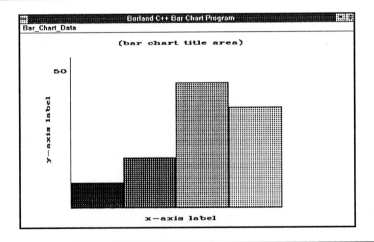

Figure 23-1. The default bar chart window

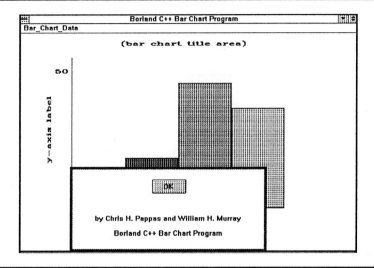

Figure 23-2.   The About box selected from Bar_Chart_Data

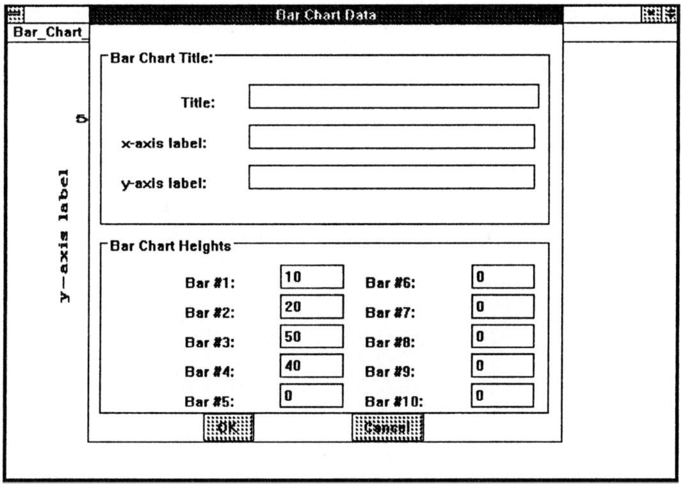

Figure 23-3.   The Data Entry dialog box selected from Bar_Chart_Data

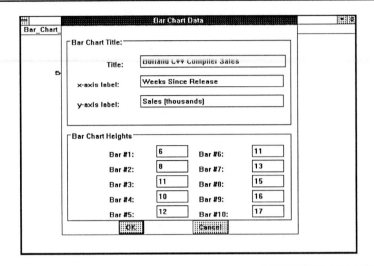

Figure 23-4.   Entering data for a custom bar chart

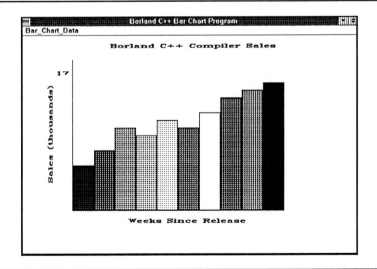

Figure 23-5.   A custom bar chart

In order to prepare your application for debugging, symbolic debugging information must be included on the compile and link lines by using the v option. Here is an example:

```
FILE=barchart
LIBPATH=c:\bc\lib
INCPATH=c:\bc\include

$(FILE).exe: $(FILE).obj $(FILE).def $(FILE).res
  tlink /Tw /x /n /v /c $(LIBPATH)\c0ws $(FILE),\
  $(FILE),\,\
  $(LIBPATH)\cws $(LIBPATH)\cs $(LIBPATH)\import,\
  $(FILE)
  rc $(FILE).res

$(FILE).obj: $(FILE).c
  bcc -c -W -v -P- -I$(INCPATH) $(FILE).c

$(FILE).res:  $(FILE).rc
  rc -r -i$(INCPATH) $(FILE).rc
```

The Debugger can be started by typing

C>WIN TDW BARCHART.EXE

You can also start the Debugger from within Windows with the Run option or select it from the File Manager. The application name can be specified once you are in the Debugger.

All of the standard Debugger options covered earlier in this text are available to you. You can open Watch windows, set breakpoints, and so forth.

A TEMPLATE FOR OBJECTWINDOWS C++ PROGRAM DEVELOPMENT

ObjectWindows is an optional and alternate way of writing Windows applications. If you choose to use ObjectWindows with your Borland C++ or Turbo C++ for Windows compilers, we suggest that you install all files to the suggested default subdirectories.

Windows contains the essential elements for support of an object-oriented programming language such as C++. In Chapters 20 through 23 you have used a message-based approach when communicating with Windows functions in either C or C++. This traditional programming approach, originally designed for the C language, has been a favorite with programmers since the introduction of Windows. Borland has added another optional, but important, tool to their integrated C++ development environment. Borland's ObjectWindows provides a powerful object-oriented library to the standard Windows programming environment. ObjectWindows is a complete collection of objects that describe standard Windows features. By using the properties of inheritance, you can now take advantage of pre-written code that performs the repetitive work required to write Windows applications.

ObjectWindows makes your C++ development cycle shorter in length, applications easier to write, and errors easier to debug. All of the Windows features that you have used in Chapters 20 through 23 can be applied to programs written with Borland's ObjectWindows for C++.

ObjectWindow libraries can be accessed in any of three ways: from the command line with the Borland command-line compiler (BCC), from the integrated text mode environment with Borland C++ (BC) or from the integrated Windows environment with Borland's Turbo C++ for Windows (TCW). If you chose TCW, everything from design to execution can be done directly under Microsoft Windows.

Before starting this chapter you may decide a little brush up is in order for object-oriented terminology. We suggest a review of the material in Chapter 14, "Introduction to Object-Oriented Programming," before you continue.

OBJECTWINDOWS' THREE OBJECT-ORIENTED FEATURES

In Chapter 14 you learned that a true object-oriented language can boast of three important features: abstraction, encapsulation, and message response. ObjectWindows provides class libraries which enable the Windows programmer to take advantage of these object-oriented features.

Abstraction

ObjectWindows provides object member functions that abstract many of Windows hundreds of function calls. Also, since many parameters for Windows functions can be stored in the data members of interface objects, ObjectWindows places related Windows function calls into groups. ObjectWindows' groups can then supply parameters to other related functions in the same group. This streamlines the overall programming approach. For example, WMCommand and WMSize are related functions which share the (*TMessage& Message*) parameter.

Encapsulation

Borland coined the term "interface object" to refer to ObjectWindows' objects, because of the way they interface with the visual components of

Windows. Borland also named the visual components of a Window "interface elements." Interface objects contained in ObjectWindows instruct Windows how to generate interface elements. ObjectWindows provides the objects for defining the behavior of Windows properties and the data storage necessary for their use.

Message Response

Windows is a message-based environment. With the standard Windows programming techniques, shown in earlier chapters, it is possible to directly communicate with Windows functions via messages. There are hundreds of messages that Windows. must be able to intercept and process. Message processing in standard Windows applications is frequently based on the use of case statements. Examine the bar chart program in Chapter 23, "Developing a Borland C++ Presentation-Quality Bar Chart," and find case statements, such as:

```
        .
        .
        .
case WM_SIZE:
        .
        .
case WM_CREATE:
        .
        .
case WM_COMMAND:
        .
        .
case WM_PAINT:
        .
        .
case WM_DESTROY:
        .
        .
        .
```

With ObjectWindows, Windows messages are processed by objects designed for the task. Specifically, ObjectWindows turns Windows messages into object member function calls. Programs will now have a unique object member function to respond to each Windows message a program might generate or encounter. For example, if Windows generates a message such

as mouse movement, mouse button click, or a key press, a member function
will respond to the Windows message. For example, WM_SIZE and
WM_COMMAND are now handled by the member functions **WMSize**
and **WMCommand**.

AN OBJECTWINDOWS OBJECT

Various ObjectWindows libraries, found in the OWL library subdirectory,
contain a collection of objects that can be used by programmers. The
member prototypes are described in the header files found in the OWL
include subdirectory. The gateway to all necessary object header files is
OWL.h. In other words, OWL.h gives your program access to all other
object headers. For example, the **TWindow** class is prototyped in *windows.h*,
in the OWL subdirectory. **TWindow** appears in every Windows application
in this and the next chapter. Here is how **TWindow** appears in *windows.h*:

```
class _EXPORT TWindow:public TWindowsObject
{
public:
  TWindowAttr Attr;
  PTScroller Scroller;
  HANDLE FocusChildHandle;
  TWindow(PTWindowsObject AParent,LPSTR ATitle,PTModule
          AModule = NULL);
  TWindow(HWND AnHWindow);
  virtual  TWindow();
  virtual BOOL AssignMenu(LPSTR MenuName);
  virtual BOOL AssignMenu(int MenuId);
  virtual BOOL Create();
  virtual classTypeisA() const
    {return windowClass;}
  virtual Pchar nameOf() const
    {return "TWindow";}
  static PTStreamable build();
protected:
  virtual LPSTR GetClassName()
    {return "OWLWindow";}
  virtual void GetWindowClass(WNDCLASS _FAR & AWndClass);
  virtual void SetupWindow();
  virtual void WMCreate(RTMessage Msg)=[WM_FIRST +
                                        WM_CREATE];
  virtual void WMActivate(RTMessage Msg)=[WM_FIRST +
                                          WM_ACTIVATE];
```

```
    virtual void WMMDIActivate(RTMessage Msg)=[WM_FIRST +
                                         WM_MDIACTIVATE];
    virtual void ActivationResponse(WORD AMsg,WORD Activated,
                                  BOOL IsIconified,HWND
                                  OtherWindowHandle);
    virtual void WMHScroll(RTMessage Msg)=[WM_FIRST +
                                         WM_HSCROLL];
    virtual void WMVScroll(RTMessage Msg)=[WM_FIRST +
                                         WM_VSCROLL];
    virtual void WMPaint(RTMessage Msg)=[WM_FIRST + WM_PAINT];
    virtual void Paint(HDC PaintDC, PAINTSTRUCT _FAR &
                        PaintInfo);
    virtual void WMSize(RTMessage Msg)=[WM_FIRST + WM_SIZE];
    virtual void WMMove(RTMessage Msg)=[WM_FIRST + WM_MOVE];
    virtual void WMLButtonDown(RTMessage Msg)=[WM_FIRST +
                                         WM_LBUTTONDOWN];
    TWindow(StreamableInit) : TWindowsObject(streamableInit) {};
    virtual void write (Ropstream os);
    virtual Pvoid read (Ripstream is);
private:
    virtual const Pchar streamableName() const
      {return "TWindow";}
};
```

Use this listing as a reference and turn to your Borland ObjectWindows
reference. Now examine the description of **TWindow**'s properties and components. Do you notice any similarities between the **TWindow** components
and message-based Windows functions used in Chapters 20 through 23?
Now, repeat the same steps for the **TApplication** prototype. **TApplication**
is another important object class that will be use repeatedly in our examples.

In the next sections, you'll learn how several important objects form the
foundation in establishing a Microsoft Windows window.

A TEMPLATE FOR SUCCESS, *swpo.cpp*

In Chapter 21, "Writing Borland C and C++ Windows Applications," you
began working with a simplified Windows program, using standard Windows programming techniques. This program contained the minimum
amount of program code required to create and display a window on the
screen. This code, developed for both C and C++, also provided the window with a border, title bar, system menu, and maximize/minimize boxes.

In this section you'll learn about another template that performs a similar feat, but one that is built with the use of ObjectWindows. The template is named *swpo.cpp*. SWPO stands for Simplified Windows Platform with ObjectWindows. SWPO also contains all of the Windows' components necessary to create and display a window on the screen—that is, a main window with a border, title bar, system menu, and maximize/minimize boxes.

If you are working with the examples for this chapter, enter the three pieces of code given in the next listing, and save them as *swpo.rc, swpo.def,* and *swpo.cpp* respectively.

```
THE RESOURCE FILE (save as SWPO.rc):
// no resources in this application

THE DEFINITION FILE (save as SWPO.def):
NAME            SWPO
DESCRIPTION     'SWPO with Objects for Windows with Borland C++'
EXETYPE         WINDOWS
CODE            PRELOAD MOVEABLE DISCARDABLE
DATA            PRELOAD MOVEABLE SINGLE
HEAPSIZE        1024
STACKSIZE       5120

THE APPLICATION FILE (save as SWPO.cpp):
// Simplified Windows Platform With Objects (SWPO) for C++
// Using Borland's ObjectWindows
// (c) William H. Murray and Chris H. Pappas, 1991

#include <owl.h>

class TMainWindow:public TWindow
{
public:
  TMainWindow(PTWindowsObject AParent,LPSTR ATitle);
  virtual void Paint(HDC hdc,PAINTSTRUCT& ps);
};

typedef TMainWindow* PMainWindow;

class TSWPO:public TApplication
{
public:
  TSWPO(LPSTR name,HANDLE hInstance,HANDLE hPrevInstance,
        LPSTR lpCmd,int nCmdShow)
        :TApplication(name,hInstance,hPrevInstance,
        lpCmd,nCmdShow) {};
  virtual void InitMainWindow(void);
};

void TMainWindow::Paint(HDC hdc,PAINTSTRUCT&)
{
//---your variables and graphics functions below---
```

```
//---your variables and graphics functions above---
}

TMainWindow::TMainWindow(PTWindowsObject AParent,LPSTR ATitle)
            :TWindow(AParent,ATitle)
{
  Attr.X = 0;
  Attr.Y = 0;
  Attr.W = 639;
  Attr.H = 479;
}

void TSWPO::InitMainWindow(void)
{
  MainWindow=new TMainWindow(NULL,
                 "An Object Template For Success!");
}

int PASCAL WinMain(HANDLE hInstance,HANDLE hPrevInstance,
                   LPSTR lpCmd,int nCmdShow)
{
  TSWPO SWPO("SWPO",hInstance,hPrevInstance,
             lpCmd,nCmdShow);
  SWPO.Run();
  return (SWPO.Status);
}
```

If you are working from within the integrated environment (compiling from within Borland C++ or Turbo C++ for Windows) remember to set your include and library directories. For example, if you chose the default setting during setup:

```
(Include):    c:\borlandc\owl\include;
              c:\borlandc\classlib\include;
              c:\borlandc\include
(Libraries):  c:\borlandc\owl\lib;
              c:\borlandc\classlib\lib;
              c:\borlandc\lib
```

Your project file, created from within the integrated environment must include:

swpo.cpp
swpo.def
swpo.rc
owlws.lib
tclassws.lib

With this accomplished, compile and run the *swpo.cpp* program template. What appears on the screen? If your compilation is successful you

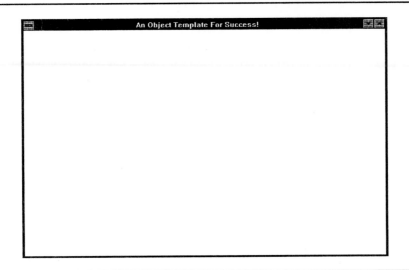

Figure 24-1.   Establishing a window in Microsoft's Windows with Borland's
ObjectWindows for C++

should see a blank window and the message "An Object Template For
Success!" in the title bar, as shown in Figure 24-1.

This template program, *swpo.cpp,* contains the essential objects for placing a window on the screen. It should be used as the foundation of any
graphics program you wish to develop or experiment with.

The template makes use of Borland's ObjectWindows libraries, however,
it is still possible to make ordinary message-based function calls as you did
in earlier Windows chapters. This mix-and-match approach gives you the
best of both programming worlds.

Resource files for dialog boxes, menus, icons, cursors, and other window
attributes will not change in the ObjectWindows environment. (Chapter 25,
"Developing C++ ObjectWindows' Applications with Resources," discusses
this in greater detail.) At this point, you may not understand how the
various objects work, but you'll have to admit that the results are similar to
those produced by *swpc.c* and *swpcpp.cpp* from Chapter 21. If you compare
listings, also notice that the resulting window was obtained with

about one third the number of program lines as found in those earlier listings!

Understanding the Use of Objects in the SWPO Template

With object-oriented code, you have learned that programs do not take a top-down programming approach. An important section of ObjectWindows code appears on the last eight lines of the SWPO template. WinMain is the entry point for Microsoft Windows! A Pascal calling sequence is used for parameter passing.

```
int PASCAL WinMain(HANDLE hInstance,HANDLE hPrevInstance,
                   LPSTR lpCmd,int nCmdShow)
{
  TSWPO SWPO("SWPO",hInstance,hPrevInstance,
             lpCmd,nCmdShow);
  SWPO.Run();
  return (SWPO.Status);
}
```

As you study different ObjectWindows applications, these previous lines will not change much in terms of structure and location within each application. Figure 24-2 shows a diagram of ObjectWindows' class hierarchy, which should aid you in understanding how the various ObjectWindow classes are utilized.

One requirement necessary in program development is that each program that uses objects must define a new class that is derived from **TApplication**, the ObjectWindow class. **TApplication** describes the behavior that all applications must adhere to. The first line of code, in the previous listing, states that **TSWPO** must be an instance of **TApplication**. "SWPO" is the Name data member passed to the constructor. Next, Run initiates a series of steps that starts and executes the new program under Windows. Finally, the object's Status data member is returned.

TSWPO, as you have learned, is derived from **TApplication**. In the next listing, notice that it will also typically contain the definition for at least one virtual member function. In this case, **InitMainWindow**. Find that definition in the next listing.

```
class TSWPO:public TApplication
{
public:
  TSWPO(LPSTR name,HANDLE hInstance,HANDLE hPrevInstance,
           LPSTR lpCmd,int nCmdShow)
       :TApplication(name,hInstance,hPrevInstance,
                     lpCmd,nCmdShow) {};
  virtual void InitMainWindow(void);
};
```

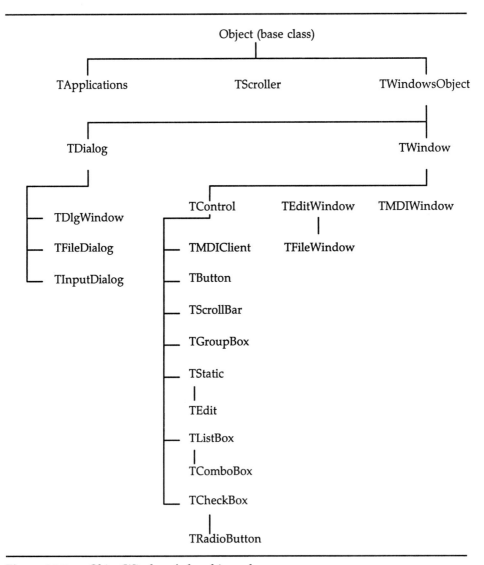

Figure 24-2.   ObjectWindows' class hierarchy

InitMainWindow is the virtual member function responsible for building a new main window object. Windows are initialized when an application is started.

The **TWindowsObject** serves as the parent or base class for all interface objects, such as, dialog boxes, controls, and windows.

The **TWindow** class is a window class that can be used to create instances for the main, child, and pop-up windows. **TMainWindow** is derived from the **TWindow** class and will serve as the main window for our application. Notice in the next listing that **Paint** is declared as a virtual member function of this class.

```
class TMainWindow:public TWindow
{
public:
  TMainWindow(PTWindowsObject AParent,LPSTR ATitle);
  virtual void Paint(HDC hdc,PAINTSTRUCT& ps);
};
```

If you examine the full program listing you will also notice that the main window object, **TMainWindow**, is stored in the MainWindow. MainWindow is a data member of the main window object. The next section of code serves as the constructor for the object.

```
void TSWPO::InitMainWindow(void)
{
  MainWindow=new TMainWindow(NULL,
              "An Object Template For Success!");
}
```

The *NULL* parameter used in the constructor indicates a main window is to be established while the second parameter serves as the window's title bar text. **TApplication** was vital in establishing the main application window, **TWindow** (or a derivative such as **TMainWindow**) plays an equally important role in manipulating window features such as sizing, moving, or painting.

The **Paint** member function is passed to the device context handle, *hdc*, and the *PAINTSTRUCT&* parameter. Now you can experiment with numerous Windows graphics functions from within this member function.

```
void TMainWindow::Paint(HDC hdc,PAINTSTRUCT&)
{
//---your variables and graphics functions below---
```

```
TextOut(hdc,200,250,"Hello ObjectWindows C++ World",29);

//---your variables and graphics functions above---
}
```

If you add the **TextOut** function call to the original SWPO C++ code, as shown in the previous listing, you should see results such as those shown in Figure 24-3, when the program is executed.

Recall that **Paint** was originally inherited from **TWindow**. **Paint** is called (receives a message) anytime the window must be updated. Updating a window is required when a window is, for example, sized or moved. A new update message will be generated by Windows each time this occurs.

EXPERIMENTING WITH THE *swpo.cpp* TEMPLATE

In this section, we'll look at three simple Windows applications that can directly employ the *swpo.cpp* template created in the previous section. The

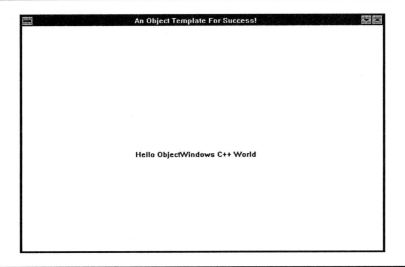

Figure 24-3. A new "Hello World" message

first program will allow you to draw a damped sine curve on the screen with damping envelope. The next two programs will allow you to manipulate and experiment with various font parameters. If you have Windows 3.1 installed on your computer, you can also develop applications using the new TrueType font technology.

If you are building these applications from within the Borland C++ or Turbo C++ for Windows environment, remember to set your include and library directories. For example, using the setup defaults:

```
(Include):      c:\borlandc\owl\include;
                c:\borlandc\classlib\include;
                c:\borlandc\include
(Libraries):    c:\borlandc\owl\lib;
                c:\borlandc\classlib\lib;
                c:\borlandc\lib
```

A project file, created from within the integrated environment must include:

(your program name).*cpp*
(your program name).*def*
(your program name).*rc*
owlws.lib
tclassws.lib

If the compiler cannot find the *owlws.lib* or *tclassws.lib,* a large number of errors will be reported at link time, even though your program compiled successfully.

Using the SWPO to Draw a Mathematical Curve

The SWPO template gives the programmer the freedom to experiment with all of the GDI graphics primitives, within the framework of an ObjectWindows program. Many of these GDI graphics primitives were discussed in Chapters 20 through 23. Additional GDI primitives can be found in Appendix C, "Windows Functions."

The first example will draw a mathematical curve simply by inserting the following statements in *swpo.cpp* at the indicated points. Be sure to also add an include line, #include <math.h>, at the top of the program in order to bring the math functions and constants into your application.

```
//---your variables and graphics functions below---
  HPEN hNewPen,hOldPen;
  double y;
  int    i,x;

  // create a red pen
  hNewPen=CreatePen(0,1,0x0000FFL);
  hOldPen=SelectObject(hdc,hNewPen);

  // draw one side of damping envelope
  MoveTo(hdc,100,240);
  for (i=0;i<500;i++)
  {
    y=180.0*(exp(-i*0.01));
    LineTo(hdc,i+100,240-(int) y);
  }

  //draw other side of damping envelope
  MoveTo(hdc,100,240);
  for (i=0;i<500;i++)
  {
    y=180.0*(exp(-i*0.01));
    LineTo(hdc,i+100,240-(int) -y);
  }

  TextOut(hdc,250,30,"A Damped Sine Wave",18);

  // select default pen
  hOldPen=SelectObject(hdc,hOldPen);
  DeleteObject(hNewPen);

  // draw x & y coordinate axes
  MoveTo(hdc,100,50);
  LineTo(hdc,100,430);
  MoveTo(hdc,100,240);
  LineTo(hdc,600,240);
  MoveTo(hdc,100,240);

  // draw damped sine wave
  for (i=0;i<500;i++)
  {
    y=180.0*(exp(-i*0.01))*sin(M_PI*i*(1440.0/500.0)/180.0);
    LineTo(hdc,i+100,240-(int) y);
  }
//---your variables and graphics functions above---
```

Compile and execute the new code. This program will draw a damped sine wave on the screen, similar to Figure 24-4.

The *swpo.cpp* template gives the user a plug-and-play ability with regards to GDI graphics primitives. You have already used most of these GDI graphic functions in earlier chapters. It is simply a matter of replicating the *swpo.cpp* code, inserting the GDI functions and any associated variables, and compiling and then running the application.

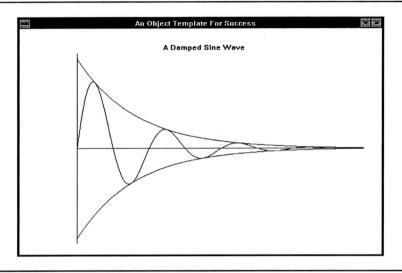

Figure 24-4.   A damped sine wave and envelope are drawn in the window

If you want to save this new program code under a different name, *damp.cpp* for example, be sure to create the files *damp.rc, damp.def,* and *damp.prj.*

Using the SWPO to Experiment with Text Fonts

In this example, that we'll use the same *swpo.cpp* template to create a program allows us to change the size of text fonts on the screen. Chapter 20, "An Introduction to Windows Concepts," discussed font definitions and terminology. You might recall that the bar chart program, in Chapter 23, "Developing a Borland C++ Presentation-Quality Bar Chart," used the CreateFont function to set font parameters for the bar chart graph. Here we'll simply print a string several times, while changing the height property of the font. In addition to the code, shown in the next listing, you'll have to add an include line, #include <string.h>, at the start of the program.

Add these code insertions to *swpo.cpp,* in the location shown.

```
//---your variables and graphics functions below---
  static LOGFONT lf;
  HFONT hNFont;
  static char szTextString[]="Wow! Better than my handwriting.";
  short i,ypos;
  lf.lfWeight=FW_HEAVY;
```

```
lf.lfCharSet=OEM_CHARSET;
lf.lfPitchAndFamily=FF_SCRIPT;
ypos=0;
for (i=1;i<10;i++)
{
   lf.lfHeight=6+(6*i);
   hNFont=CreateFontIndirect(&lf);
   SelectObject(hdc,hNFont);
   TextOut(hdc,0,ypos,szTextString,strlen(szTextString));
   ypos+=11*i;
}
//---your variables and graphics functions above---
```

Compile and execute the new code. This program will draw several rows of the same message on the screen. Each time the string is drawn, it will be in a larger point size, as shown in Figure 24-5.

This example uses a bold script font from the OEM character set. The first time around the loop, a point size of 12 is requested. The second time, 18, and so on. Windows will attempt to supply you with the point size requested or select the closest size based on internal calculations.

This program can also be saved under a different name, perhaps *font1.cpp*. If you use this name, be sure to create the text files *font1.rc* and

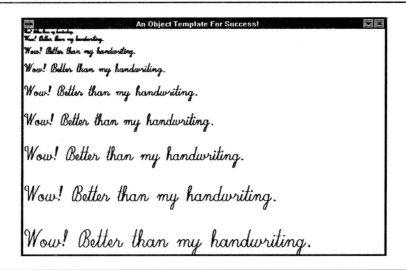

Figure 24-5.   The SWPO as a template for font experimentation: a string is printed several times, each in a different point size

font1.def. While you're in the Borland integrated environment, create a project file, *font1.prj.* These extra files can be similar to those used for SWPO.

If you are running under Windows 3.1 or later, you can experiment with the new TrueType font technology. For example, try setting the *lfFaceName* field to Courier, Arial, Times New Roman, or Symbol.

Using the SWPO to Rotate Text Fonts

There are times in graphing when it is necessary to be able to rotate strings of characters and/or individual characters. Consider the case where a vertical axis label is needed. The string must be rotated 90 degrees to make it vertical. Each character in the string must also be rotated by 90 degrees. The string rotation parameter is called *escapement,* while the character rotation parameter is called *orientation.*

In the next example, a string is rotated around a common point in 45 degree increments. Windows allows the angles to be changed one tenth of a degree at a time. Values are expressed as the angle value multiplied by 10: 900 means 90 degrees while 455 means 45.5 degrees.

This example will also need the *string.h* include statement at the start of the program.

```
//---your variables and graphics functions below---
  int i;
  static LOGFONT lf;
  HFONT hNFont;
  static char szTextString[]="    Windmills of my mind!";
  lf.lfWeight=FW_HEAVY;
  lf.lfCharSet=OEM_CHARSET;
  lf.lfPitchAndFamily=FF_MODERN;
  lf.lfHeight=25;
  lf.lfEscapement=0;
  lf.lfOrientation=0;
  for (i=1;i<9;i++)
  {
    hNFont=CreateFontIndirect(&lf);
    SelectObject(hdc,hNFont);
    TextOut(hdc,320,240,szTextString,strlen(szTextString));
    lf.lfEscapement+=450;
    lf.lfOrientation+=450;
  }
//---your variables and graphics functions above---
```

Compile and execute the new code. This program will draw the same string, rotated about a center point in the window. Your results should be similar to Figure 24-6.

Figure 24-6.   Font rotation where both escapement and orientation are changed. Escapement rotates the position of the string, while orientation rotates the characters within the string

The programming is fairly direct. A call is made to the function, **Create-FontIndirect**, during each pass through the *for* loop. Notice how escapement and orientation are incremented.

Save this new program code under the name, *font2.cpp*. Also create the files *font2.rc, font2.def,* and *font2.prj* as you did in the previous example.

Again, if you are running under Windows 3.1 or later, experiment by setting the *lfFaceName* field to Courier, Arial, Times New Roman, or Symbol. Using TrueType font technology will yield outstanding results.

TOWARD MORE ADVANCED WORK

This chapter has developed a basic object-oriented template for use in experimenting with simple Windows functions, such as the GDI graphics functions. In order to develop more robust applications you'll need to add resources such as icons, cursors, menus, and dialog boxes. Chapter 25 will show you how to do this within the ObjectWindows framework.

25

DEVELOPING C++ OBJECTWINDOWS' APPLICATIONS WITH RESOURCES

In the previous chapter, a template was created to aid in the development of C++ ObjectWindows' applications. That template forms the foundation of the applications developed in this chapter. These applications include various Windows resources: You'll learn how to combine resources with the template code in order to produce Windows applications that have a professional appearance. In order to build and execute these examples you must have a Borland's C++ compiler and ObjectWindows' libraries installed on your system. Naturally, Windows 3.0 or later must be present for program execution. It will also be possible for you to develop the applications directly under Windows by using Turbo C++ for Windows.

Borland's Resource Workshop, covered in Chapter 22, "Using the Borland Resource Workshop and Resource Compiler," allows you to create many resource items such as customized icons, cursors, bitmaps, menus, keyboard accelerators, and dialog boxes. Resources can be used individually or together depending upon your application's needs. You might want to take the time to review Chapter 22 in order to understand how the resources for this chapter were created.

As you explore this chapter, you will find that it is relatively easy to extend the SWPO template to include these powerful resources. The first application, *Draw25*, will teach you how to include a custom cursor, icon, two menus, and a group of keyboard accelerators in an application. The second application, *Pie25,* is a professional graphics program using a custom cursor, menus, and two dialog boxes.

draw25, DEVELOPING A CUSTOM ICON, CURSOR, MENU, AND GROUP OF KEYBOARD ACCELERATORS

The *draw25* program will draw an ellipse centered in the window. The menu will allow the ellipse to be sized or the background color of the window to be changed to one of twelve colors. The background colors can be selected from the menu or from a corresponding function key that has been selected as a keyboard accelerator. Because of the added resource information, you will need seven files in your directory before building the final project. Using the Borland C++ integrated development environment (IDE), these files are: *draw25.prj, draw25.def, draw25.h, draw25.ico, draw25.cur, draw25.rc,* and *draw25.cpp.* In this section, we will examine the makeup and contents of each file and take a close look at the important elements.

The *draw25.prj, draw25.def,* and *draw25.h* files

The project file, *draw25.prj,* is created from within the IDE of the Borland C++ compiler. Simply select the "Project" menu option, name the new project, and add the following items to the project file:

```
DRAW25.cpp
DRAW25.def
DRAW25.rc
owlws.lib
tclasss.lib
```

The ObjectWindows' libraries, *owlws.lib* and *tclasss.lib,* changed names several times while this product was in development. If your application doesn't link properly, check the library subdirectories to make sure they are the same. Your compiler should be set to develop Windows applications. Also, be sure your include and library directories point to the following locations:

```
(Include):      c:\borlandc\owl\include;
                c:\borlandc\classlib\include;
                c:\borlandc\include
(Libraries):    c:\borlandc\owl\lib;
                c:\borlandc\classlib\lib;
                c:\borlandc\lib
```

The *draw25.def* file is typical of the definition files you have encountered in the other chapters that dealt with Windows programs.

```
NAME          DRAW25
DESCRIPTION   'A Simple Menu Program with ObjectWindows'
EXETYPE       WINDOWS
CODE          PRELOAD MOVEABLE DISCARDABLE
DATA          PRELOAD MOVEABLE MULTIPLE
HEAPSIZE      4096
STACKSIZE     9216
```

The header file, *draw25.h,* contains the constants needed for menu ID values. We use IDM_ to represent the identification of a menu item.

```
// draw25.h header file
// size information
#define IDM_SMALL     201
#define IDM_MEDIUM    202
#define IDM_LARGE     203
// background colors
#define IDM_BLACK     101
#define IDM_WHITE     102
#define IDM_RED       103
#define IDM_ORANGE    104
#define IDM_YELLOW    105
#define IDM_GREEN     106
#define IDM_BLUE      107
#define IDM_MAGENTA   108
#define IDM_LTGREEN   109
#define IDM_LTBLUE    110
#define IDM_LTRED     111
#define IDM_LTGRAY    112
```

As you can see from the header file, three ellipse sizes (small, medium, and large) can be selected from one menu and twelve background colors from the second menu.

The *draw25.ico* Icon

The icon for this application is created in the icon editor of the Borland Resource Workshop. The icon is saved as *draw25.ico*. Information on the icon is also added to the *draw25.res* (compiled resource file), as you will see when we examine this file. Figure 25-1 shows the icon we designed for the application.

The *draw25.cur* Cursor

The cursor for this application is created with the help of the cursor editor in the Borland Resource Workshop. The cursor is saved as *draw25.cur*. Information on the cursor is also added to the *draw25.res* (compiled resource file). Figure 25-2 shows the cursor designed for the application.

The *draw25.rc* Menu and Keyboard Accelerators

The resource script file, shown next, contains menu and accelerator key information. This file was returned by the Borland Resource Workshop by

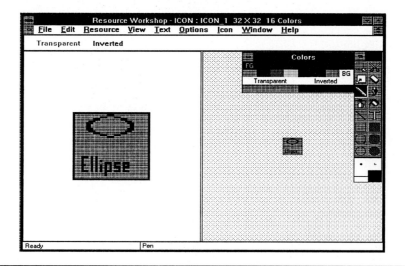

Figure 25-1.   The *draw25* icon is created in the Borland Resource Workshop

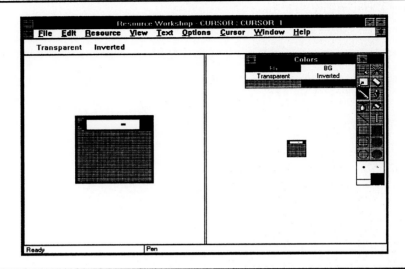

Figure 25-2.   The *draw25* cursor created in the Borland Resource Workshop

requesting a script file (*rc* extension). It should also be saved as a compiled resource file by requesting a file with an *res* extension.

In this example, the twelve function keys (F1...F12) are used as accelerator keys for color selection. When the application is run, background colors can be selected from the menu or simply by hitting a function key. For example, pressing F3, will change the window's background color to red.

```
#include "windows.h"
#include "draw25.h"
CURSOR_1 CURSOR draw25.cur
ICON_1   ICON   draw25.ico
Alteration MENU
{
  POPUP "&Ellipse_Size"
  {
    MENUITEM "&small",          IDM_SMALL
    MENUITEM "&Medium",         IDM_MEDIUM
    MENUITEM "&LARGE",          IDM_LARGE
  }
  POPUP "Ba&ckground_Colors"
  {
    MENUITEM "BLAC&K\tF1",      IDM_BLACK
    MENUITEM "&WHITE\tF2",      IDM_WHITE
    MENUITEM "&RED\tF3",        IDM_RED
    MENUITEM "&ORANGE\tF4",     IDM_ORANGE
    MENUITEM "&YELLOW\tF5",     IDM_YELLOW
```

```
    MENUITEM "GREE&N\tF6",        IDM_GREEN
    MENUITEM "&BLUE\tF7",         IDM_BLUE
    MENUITEM "&MAGENTA\tF8",      IDM_MAGENTA
    MENUITEM SEPARATOR
    MENUITEM "Lt GR&EEN\tF9",     IDM_LTGREEN
    MENUITEM "Lt BL&UE\tF10",     IDM_LTBLUE
    MENUITEM "Lt RE&D\tF11",      IDM_LTRED
    MENUITEM "Lt GR&AY\tF12",     IDM_LTGRAY
  }
}
Alteration ACCELERATORS
{
  VK_F1,   IDM_BLACK,    VIRTKEY
  VK_F2,   IDM_WHITE,    VIRTKEY
  VK_F3,   IDM_RED,      VIRTKEY
  VK_F4,   IDM_ORANGE,   VIRTKEY
  VK_F5,   IDM_YELLOW,   VIRTKEY
  VK_F6,   IDM_GREEN,    VIRTKEY
  VK_F7,   IDM_BLUE,     VIRTKEY
  VK_F8,   IDM_MAGENTA,  VIRTKEY
  VK_F9,   IDM_LTGREEN,  VIRTKEY
  VK_F10,  IDM_LTBLUE,   VIRTKEY
  VK_F11,  IDM_LTRED,    VIRTKEY
  VK_F12,  IDM_LTGRAY,   VIRTKEY
}
```

Examine the previous code and identify the menu and keyboard accelerator names.

Remember as you enter this text file, that this resource script file, *draw25.rc*, should be compiled with the Borland Resource Workshop to produce *draw25.res*, the compiled resource file.

The *draw25.cpp* Application Code

The *draw25.cpp* code contains many items of interest. As you enter the following code, notice the additions that have been made to the SWPO template of the previous chapter.

```
// A Simple Menu Application created with Borland's C++
// with ObjectWindows and added resources. The base template
// for this application is the Simplified Windows Platform
// With Objects (SWPO) for C++
// (c) William H. Murray and Chris H. Pappas, 1991

#include <owl.h>
#include <windows.h>
#include "draw25.h"

static WORD wSize=25;
```

```
static WORD wColor;
static int wColorValue[12][3]={0,0,0,          //black
                               255,255,255,    //white
                               255,0,0,        //red
                               255,96,0,       //orange
                               255,255,0,      //yellow
                               0,255,0,        //green
                               0,0,255,        //blue
                               255,0,255,      //magenta
                               128,255,0,      //lt green
                               0,255,255,      //lt blue
                               255,0,159,      //lt red
                               180,180,180};   //lt gray

class TMainWindow:public TWindow
{
public:
  TMainWindow(PTWindowsObject AParent,LPSTR ATitle);
  virtual void WMCommand(TMessage& Message)=
                        [WM_FIRST+WM_COMMAND];
  virtual void Paint(HDC hdc,PAINTSTRUCT&);
  virtual void GetWindowClass(WNDCLASS& WndClass);
};

typedef TMainWindow* PMainWindow;

class TDraw:public TApplication
{
public:
  TDraw(LPSTR name,HANDLE hInstance,HANDLE hPrevInstance,
        LPSTR lpCmd,int nCmdShow)
    :TApplication(name,hInstance,hPrevInstance,
                  lpCmd,nCmdShow) {};
  virtual void InitMainWindow(void);
};

void TMainWindow::GetWindowClass(WNDCLASS& WndClass)
{
  TWindow::GetWindowClass(WndClass);
  WndClass.style=0;
  WndClass.hbrBackground=CreateSolidBrush(0x00808080);
  WndClass.hCursor=LoadCursor(GetApplication()->hInstance,
                              "Cursor_1");
  WndClass.hIcon=LoadIcon(GetApplication()->hInstance,
                          "Icon_1");
}

void TMainWindow::WMCommand(TMessage& Message)
{
  HMENU hmenu;
  switch (Message.WParam)
  {
    case IDM_SMALL:
      wSize=25;
      break;
    case IDM_MEDIUM:
```

```
          wSize=50;
          break;
        case IDM_LARGE:
          wSize=100;
          break;
        case IDM_BLACK:
        case IDM_WHITE:
        case IDM_RED:
        case IDM_ORANGE:
        case IDM_YELLOW:
        case IDM_GREEN:
        case IDM_BLUE:
        case IDM_MAGENTA:
        case IDM_LTGREEN:
        case IDM_LTBLUE:
        case IDM_LTRED:
        case IDM_LTGRAY:
          hmenu=GetMenu(HWindow);
          CheckMenuItem(hmenu,wColor,MF_UNCHECKED);
          wColor=Message.WParam;
          CheckMenuItem(hmenu,wColor,MF_CHECKED);
          SetClassWord(HWindow,GCW_HBRBACKGROUND,CreateSolidBrush
                    (RGB(wColorValue[wColor-IDM_BLACK][0],
                         wColorValue[wColor-IDM_BLACK][1],
                         wColorValue[wColor-IDM_BLACK][2])));
          break;
        default:
          break;
    }
    InvalidateRect(HWindow,NULL,TRUE);
}


void TMainWindow::Paint(HDC hdc,PAINTSTRUCT&)
{
//---your variables and graphics functions below---
Ellipse(hdc,320-(wSize*2),200-wSize,
        320+(wSize*2),200+wSize);
TextOut(hdc,240,50,"Variations on an ellipse",24);
//---your variables and graphics functions above---
}


TMainWindow::TMainWindow(PTWindowsObject AParent,
                         LPSTR ATitle)
            :TWindow(AParent,ATitle)
{
  Attr.X = 0;
  Attr.Y = 0;
  Attr.W = 639;
  Attr.H = 479;
  AssignMenu("Alteration");
}


void TDraw::InitMainWindow(void)
{
  MainWindow=new TMainWindow(NULL,
                             "New Sizes and Colors");
```

```
    HAccTable=LoadAccelerators(hInstance, "Alteration");
}

int PASCAL WinMain(HANDLE hInstance,HANDLE hPrevInstance,
                   LPSTR lpCmd,int nCmdShow)
{
  TDraw Draw("Draw",hInstance,hPrevInstance,
             lpCmd,nCmdShow);
  Draw.Run();
  return (Draw.Status);
}
```

The first group of resources to be added to this application are the icon and cursor bitmaps. Icon and cursor resources are easy to add with the **LoadCursor** or **LoadIcon** functions. Notice the inclusion of both in the following section of the **GetWindowClass** member function.

```
             .
             .
             .
    WndClass.hCursor=LoadCursor(GetApplication()->hInstance,
                          "Cursor_1");
    WndClass.hIcon=LoadIcon(GetApplication()->hInstance,
                          "Icon_1");
             .
             .
             .
```

The next resource to be added are the menus and keyboard accelerators resources. Menu items are processed in the member function **WMCommand**. **WMCommand** responds to WM_COMMAND messages. The case statement for changing ellipse size, *wSize,* is straightforward. The case statements for the color selection are of immediate importance to us because they require additional work before they can be used.

```
      case IDM_BLACK:
      case IDM_WHITE:
      case IDM_RED:
      case IDM_ORANGE:
      case IDM_YELLOW:
      case IDM_GREEN:
      case IDM_BLUE:
      case IDM_MAGENTA:
      case IDM_LTGREEN:
      case IDM_LTBLUE:
      case IDM_LTRED:
      case IDM_LTGRAY:
```

Regardless of which color was just selected, via the case statement, the **GetMenu** function will be called to return the menu handle. Observe this in the next block of code.

```
        .
        .
        .
hmenu=GetMenu(HWindow);
CheckMenuItem(hmenu,wColor,MF_UNCHECKED);
wColor=Message.WParam;
CheckMenuItem(hmenu,wColor,MF_CHECKED);
        .
        .
        .
```

The structure of this code can be conveniently used for related menu items, but it requires that the items have sequential identification numbers (which our color values do). Menus also permit listed items to be checked or unchecked. The function **CheckMenuItem** has the ability to place or remove a check mark next to the specified menu item. It is customary to remove a previously placed check (MF_UNCHECKED) mark before placing a new check mark (MF_CHECKED). The sequence is to remove the old value, retrieve the new color value from the menu, and place the new check mark next to it.

The function **SetClassWord** uses this information to change the background color.

```
        .
        .
        .
SetClassWord(HWindow,GCW_HBRBACKGROUND,CreateSolidBrush
        (RGB(wColorValue[wColor-IDM_BLACK][0],
            wColorValue[wColor-IDM_BLACK][1],
            wColorValue[wColor-IDM_BLACK][2])));
        .
        .
        .
```

The handle for this function is the menu handle, *HWindow*. The second value, called the index, is selected from seven possible options: GCW_CBCLSEXTRA, GCW_CBWNDEXTRA, GCW_HBRBACKGROUND, GCW_HCURSOR, GCW_HICON, GCW_HMODULE, and GCW_STYLE. These options permit the replacement of the given parameter in the WND-CLASS structure at the beginning of each program. The option

GCW_HBRBACKGROUND sets a new handle to a background brush. The third value in the function specifies the replacement value. For this example, the replacement value is derived from the color value, *wColor*. Suppose a red background was selected by the user. In that case, *wColor* will be passed the ID value of 103. Also notice that the color black has an ID value of 101. The black ID number is subtracted from the red ID number, leaving a result of 2. The value of 2 is used as an index into the *wColorValue* array. The RGB color values for red, in the array, correspond to [2][0], [2][1], and [2][2]. Now you know why the values must be sequential.

The accelerator keys are loaded into the application code when the **InitMainWindow** member function is run.

```
           .
           .
           .
    HAccTable=LoadAccelerators(hInstance, "Alteration");
           .
           .
           .
```

The function **LoadAccelerators** is used to load or return the handle of the specified accelerator table. Keyboard accelerator keypresses are sent directly to the window and are not posted in the message queue.

The remainder of the program is just the familiar SWPO code discussed in the previous chapter. Adding resource information to ObjectWindows code can be very simple and straightforward.

Testing the *draw25* Application

With all seven of the previously discussed files in place, load the project file while in the Borland C++ IDE and select the "Compile" option from the menu. If your compile and link are successful, leave the Borland IDE and enter Windows to execute the application. Alternately, if you use Turbo C++ for Windows, compile and link the application while running under Windows. Select the "Run" menu option to execute the application directly.

The large ellipse option is shown in Figure 25-3 with a white background color.

Figure 25-4 shows the color menu options. A light gray background is present in this figure. For this figure, the small ellipse option was selected.

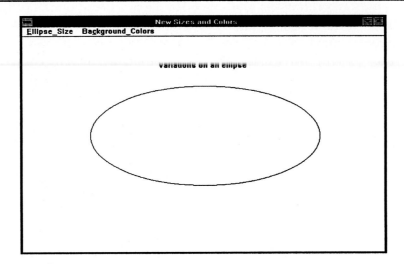

Figure 25-3. The selection and display of the large ellipse option in *draw25*

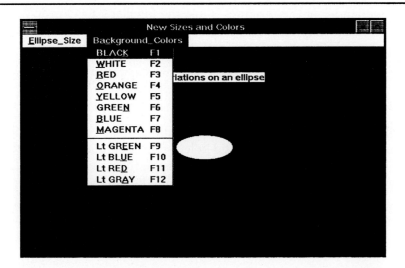

Figure 25-4. The selection of a light gray background and the small ellipse option

As we end the discussion for this example, we have a programming challenge to get you started with resources: Add a third menu option to the program that will allow you to select an ellipse, circle, or rectangle.

pie25, PRESENTATION-QUALITY GRAPHICS WITH A CUSTOM ICON, CURSOR, MENU, AND TWO DIALOG BOXES

The *pie25* program will draw a presentation-quality pie chart on the screen. In addition to the cursor resource, the pie chart program provides a menu with three options that allow the user to view an About box, enter pie chart data, or terminate the application. The inclusion of dialog box resources provides the ultimate touch for entering data into an application.

This application requires six files in your directory before building the final project from the Borland C++ integrated development environment (IDE). These files are: *pie25.prj, pie25.def, pie25.h, pie25.cur, pie25.rc,* and *pie25.cpp.*

The *pie25.prj, pie25.def,* and *pie25.h* files

Create the project file, PIE25.prj, from within the IDE of the Borland C++ compiler. Do this by selecting the "Project" menu option, naming the new project, and adding the following items to the project file:

```
PIE25.cpp
PIE25.def
PIE2525.rc
owlws.lib
tclasss.lib
```

As mentioned earlier, compile for a Windows executable file and be sure your include and library directories point to the following locations before starting the compile operation:

```
(Include):    c:\borlandc\owl\include;
              c:\borlandc\classlib\include;
              c:\borlandc\include
```

```
(Libraries):     c:\borlandc\owl\lib;
                 c:\borlandc\classlib\lib;
                 c:\borlandc\lib
```

The *pie25.def* file is similar to those of past Windows applications and does not warrant further discussion. Only the name and description have changed in this listing.

```
NAME            PIE25
DESCRIPTION     'A Presentation Quality Pie Chart With Objects'
EXETYPE         WINDOWS
CODE            PRELOAD MOVEABLE DISCARDABLE
DATA            PRELOAD MOVEABLE MULTIPLE
HEAPSIZE        4096
STACKSIZE       9216
```

The *pie25.h* header file contains constants for each menu and dialog box option. The values DM_P1 through DM_P10 are used to identify up to ten pie slice values.

```
#define IDM_ABOUT    40
#define IDM_INPUT    50
#define IDM_EXIT     70
#define DM_TITLE    280
#define DM_P1       281
#define DM_P2       282
#define DM_P3       283
#define DM_P4       284
#define DM_P5       285
#define DM_P6       286
#define DM_P7       287
#define DM_P8       288
#define DM_P9       289
#define DM_P10      290
```

Enter these three files and save them in the directory that you'll use to compile your final application.

The *pie25.ico* Icon

The icon for this application is created in a unique manner. Instead of creating an icon from within the icon editor of the Borland Resource Workshop, the icon is created dynamically as the application is executed. As you know, graphics can be scaled to fit a resized window. By taking this concept to an extreme, an icon is a very small resized window. The icon for this application is the current pie chart being viewed, but in miniature. You may or may not like this technique since an attempt is also made to miniaturize the chart title.

The *pie25.cur* Cursor

The cursor for this application is created in the cursor editor of the Borland Resource Workshop. The cursor is saved as *pie25.cur* and also added to the *pie25.res* (compiled resource file). Figure 25-5 shows the cursor designed for the application.

The *pie25.rc* Menu and Dialog Box Resource File

The *pie25.rc* resource file contains information for the pointer (PieCursor), menu (PieMenu), and two dialog boxes (AboutDlgBox and PieDlgBox). Figure 25-6 shows the Data Entry dialog box.

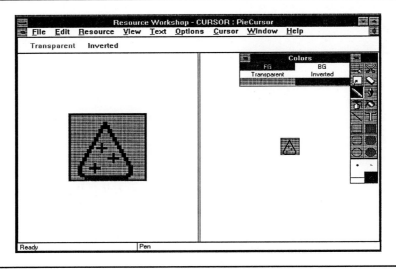

Figure 25-5.   The *pie25* cursor created in the Borland Resource Workshop

Here is the About box used with the *pie25* presentation graphics:

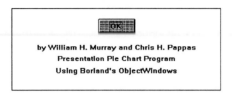

The *pie25.rc* file, shown in the next listing, was created by designing the menu and dialog boxes within the Borland Resource Workshop and saving the file in both a script (*rc* extension) and compiled (*res* extension) format. If you are entering this code directly from the IDE editor, simply load the *pie25.rc* file into the Borland Resource Workshop and select the compiled format (*res* option) when saving the final version. If you do this, your dialog boxes will look exactly like ours. If you are creating your own custom dialog boxes for this application, you must have a fairly clear idea of how you want to represent items such as the various data fields. The various CONTROL values that you see in the next listing determine the position, size, and more of dialog box items. The positional values are calculated by the Workshop.

```
#include "pie25.h"
#include "windows.h"
PieCursor CURSOR pie25.cur
PieMenu MENU
```

Pie Chart Information

Pie Chart Title:

Title: [   ]

Pie Chart Slice Sizes

Slice #1:	10	Slice #6:	0
Slice #2:	20	Slice #7:	0
Slice #3:	30	Slice #8:	0
Slice #4:	40	Slice #9:	0
Slice #5:	0	Slice #10:	0

OK   Cancel

Figure 25-6.   The data entry box used with *pie25*. Up to ten pie slices and a chart title can be specified from this dialog box

```
BEGIN
  POPUP "Pie_Chart_Input"
  BEGIN
    MENUITEM "About...", IDM_ABOUT
    MENUITEM "Input...", IDM_INPUT
    MENUITEM "Exit",     IDM_EXIT
  END
END
AboutDlgBox DIALOG 50,300,180,80
BEGIN
  CONTROL "Presentation Pie Chart Program",-1,
          "static",SS_CENTER,3,45,175,10
  CONTROL "by William H. Murray and Chris H. Pappas",-1,
          "static",SS_CENTER,3,34,175,10
  CONTROL "OK",IDOK,"button",
          BS_PUSHBUTTON|WS_TABSTOP|WS_CHILD,75,10,32,14
  CONTROL "Using Borland's ObjectWindows",-1,"STATIC",
          SS_CENTER|WS_GROUP,3,57,175,8
END
PieDlgBox DIALOG 72,40,175,163
CAPTION "Pie Chart Information"
BEGIN
  GROUPBOX "Pie Chart Title:", 100, 7,0,130,30
  GROUPBOX "Pie Chart Slice Sizes", 101, 7,31,161,106
  CONTROL "Title: ", -1, "static", SS_LEFT|WS_CHILD, 10,15,22,8
  CONTROL "", DM_TITLE, "edit", ES_LEFT|WS_BORDER|
          WS_TABSTOP|WS_CHILD, 35,12,95,12
  CONTROL "Slice #1:", -1, "static", SS_LEFT, 10,50,31,8
  CONTROL "Slice #2:", -1, "static", SS_LEFT, 10,65,31,8
  CONTROL "Slice #3:", -1, "static", SS_LEFT, 10,80,31,8
  CONTROL "Slice #4:", -1, "static", SS_LEFT, 10,95,31,8
  CONTROL "Slice #5:", -1, "static", SS_LEFT, 10,110,31,8
  CONTROL "Slice #6:", -1, "static", SS_LEFT, 96,50,31,8
  CONTROL "Slice #7:", -1, "static", SS_LEFT, 96,65,31,8
  CONTROL "Slice #8:", -1, "static", SS_LEFT, 96,80,31,8
  CONTROL "Slice #9:", -1, "static", SS_LEFT, 96,95,31,8
  CONTROL "Slice #10:", -1, "static", SS_LEFT, 96,110,33,8
  CONTROL "10", DM_P1, "edit", ES_LEFT|WS_BORDER|
          WS_TABSTOP|WS_CHILD, 45,46,30,12
  CONTROL "20", DM_P2, "edit", ES_LEFT|WS_BORDER|
          WS_TABSTOP|WS_CHILD, 45,61,30,12
  CONTROL "30", DM_P3, "edit", ES_LEFT|WS_BORDER|
          WS_TABSTOP|WS_CHILD, 45,76,30,12
  CONTROL "40", DM_P4, "edit", ES_LEFT|WS_BORDER|WS_TABSTOP|
          WS_CHILD, 45,91,30,12
  CONTROL "0", DM_P5, "edit", ES_LEFT|WS_BORDER|WS_TABSTOP|
          WS_CHILD, 45,106,30,12
  CONTROL "0", DM_P6, "edit", ES_LEFT|WS_BORDER|WS_TABSTOP|
          WS_CHILD, 135,46,30,12
  CONTROL "0", DM_P7, "edit", ES_LEFT|WS_BORDER|WS_TABSTOP|
          WS_CHILD, 135,61,30,12
  CONTROL "0", DM_P8, "edit", ES_LEFT|WS_BORDER|WS_TABSTOP|
          WS_CHILD, 135,76,30,12
  CONTROL "0", DM_P9, "edit", ES_LEFT|WS_BORDER|WS_TABSTOP|
          WS_CHILD, 135,91,30,12
  CONTROL "0", DM_P10, "edit", ES_LEFT|WS_BORDER|WS_TABSTOP|
```

```
        WS_CHILD, 135,107,30,12
   PUSHBUTTON "OK", IDOK, 20,144,33,14
   PUSHBUTTON "Cancel", IDCANCEL, 118,144,34,14
END
```

Note that IDOK and IDCANCEL are identification values provided by the *windows.h* header file.

The *pie25.cpp* Application Code

This pie chart will use a dialog box for user input. Specifically, the data entry dialog box will prompt the user to enter up to ten numbers which will define the size of each pie wedge. These integer numbers are then scaled in order to make each "pie slice" proportional in the 360 degree pie chart. Slices are colored in a sequential manner. The sequence is defined by the programmer and contained in the global array *lColor[]*. The program also allows the user to enter a title for the pie chart which is centered just above the pie figure. You may wish to continue the development of this example by adding a legend, label, or value for each pie slice.

Enter the following C++ code and save the file as *pie25.cpp*.

```
// Program will draw a Presentation Quality Pie Chart
// with Borland's C++ with ObjectWindows and added
// resources. The base template for this application
// is the Simplified Windows Platform with Objects (SWPO)
// Save as pie25.cpp
// (c) William H. Murray and Chris H. Pappas, 1991

#include <owl.h>
#include <math.h>
#include <windows.h>
#include <string.h>
#include <dialog.h>
#include "pie25.h"

#define radius      180
#define maxnumwedge 10

char szProgName[]="ProgName";
char szApplName[]="PieMenu";
char szCursorName[]="PieCursor";
char szTString[80]="(bar chart title area)";
unsigned int iWedgesize[maxnumwedge]={10,20,30,40};
long lColor[maxnumwedge]={0x0L,0xFFL,0xFF00L,0xFFFFL,
                          0xFF0000L,0xFF00FFL,0xFFFF00L,
                          0xFFFFFFL,0x8080L,0x808080L};
short xClientView,yClientView;
```

```
class TPieDialog:public TDialog
{
public:
  TPieDialog(PTWindowsObject AParent,LPSTR AName);
  virtual void WMCommand(TMessage& Message)=
                        [WM_FIRST+WM_COMMAND];
};

TPieDialog::TPieDialog(PTWindowsObject AParent,LPSTR AName)
          :TDialog(AParent,AName) {};

class TMainWindow:public TWindow
{
public:
  TMainWindow(PTWindowsObject Parent,LPSTR ATitle);
  virtual void About(TMessage& Message)=[CM_FIRST+IDM_ABOUT];
  virtual void PieInput(TMessage&)=[CM_FIRST+IDM_INPUT];
  virtual void Paint(HDC hdc,PAINTSTRUCT& ps);
  virtual void WMSize(TMessage& Message)=[WM_FIRST+WM_SIZE];
  virtual void GetWindowClass(WNDCLASS& WndClass);
};

typedef TMainWindow* PMainWindow;

class TPIE24:public TApplication
{
public:
  TPIE24(LPSTR name,HANDLE hInstance,HANDLE hPrevInstance,
         LPSTR lpCmd,int nCmdShow)
  :TApplication(name,hInstance,hPrevInstance,
                lpCmd,nCmdShow) {};
  virtual void InitMainWindow(void);
};

void TPieDialog::WMCommand(TMessage& Message)
{
  switch(Message.WParam)
  {
    case IDOK:
      GetDlgItemText(HWindow,DM_TITLE,szTString,80);
      iWedgesize[0]=GetDlgItemInt(HWindow,DM_P1,NULL,0);
      iWedgesize[1]=GetDlgItemInt(HWindow,DM_P2,NULL,0);
      iWedgesize[2]=GetDlgItemInt(HWindow,DM_P3,NULL,0);
      iWedgesize[3]=GetDlgItemInt(HWindow,DM_P4,NULL,0);
      iWedgesize[4]=GetDlgItemInt(HWindow,DM_P5,NULL,0);
      iWedgesize[5]=GetDlgItemInt(HWindow,DM_P6,NULL,0);
      iWedgesize[6]=GetDlgItemInt(HWindow,DM_P7,NULL,0);
      iWedgesize[7]=GetDlgItemInt(HWindow,DM_P8,NULL,0);
      iWedgesize[8]=GetDlgItemInt(HWindow,DM_P9,NULL,0);
      iWedgesize[9]=GetDlgItemInt(HWindow,DM_P10,NULL,0);
      EndDialog(HWindow,TRUE);
      break;
    case IDCANCEL:
      EndDialog(HWindow,FALSE);
      break;
```

```
    }
}

void TMainWindow::PieInput(TMessage& )
{
  GetModule()->ExecDialog(new TPieDialog(this,
                                        "PieDlgBox"));
  InvalidateRect(HWindow,NULL,TRUE);
  UpdateWindow(HWindow);
}

void TMainWindow::WMSize(TMessage& Message)
{
  xClientView=LOWORD(Message.LParam);
  yClientView=HIWORD(Message.LParam);
}

void TMainWindow::About(TMessage&)
{
  GetApplication()->ExecDialog(new TPieDialog(this,
                               "AboutDlgBox"));
}

void TMainWindow::GetWindowClass(WNDCLASS& WndClass)
{
  TWindow::GetWindowClass(WndClass);
  WndClass.hCursor=LoadCursor(GetApplication()->
                             hInstance,szCursorName);
  WndClass.hIcon=LoadIcon(GetApplication()->
                         hInstance,szProgName);
}

void TMainWindow::Paint(HDC hdc,PAINTSTRUCT& )
{
//---your variables and graphics functions below---
  HMENU     hMenu;
  HBRUSH    hOrgBrush,hBrush;
  unsigned int iTotalWedge[maxnumwedge+1];
  int       i,iNWedges;
  iNWedges=0;

  for (i=0;i<maxnumwedge;i++)
  {
    if(iWedgesize[i]!=0) iNWedges++;
  }

  iTotalWedge[0]=0;

  for (i=0;i<iNWedges;i++)
    iTotalWedge[i+1]=iTotalWedge[i]+iWedgesize[i];

  TextOut(hdc,(310-(strlen(szTString)*8/2)),
          15,szTString,strlen(szTString));
  SetMapMode(hdc,MM_ISOTROPIC);
  SetWindowExt(hdc,500,500);
  SetViewportExt(hdc,xClientView,-yClientView);
```

```
    SetViewportOrg(hdc,xClientView/2,yClientView/2);

    for(i=0;i<iNWedges;i++)
    {
      hBrush=CreateSolidBrush(lColor[i]);
      SelectObject(hdc,hBrush);
      Pie(hdc,-200,200,200,-200,
          (short) (radius*cos(2*M_PI*iTotalWedge[i]/
          iTotalWedge[iNWedges])),
          (short) (radius*sin(2*M_PI*iTotalWedge[i]/
          iTotalWedge[iNWedges])),
          (short) (radius*cos(2*M_PI*iTotalWedge[i+1]/
          iTotalWedge[iNWedges])),
          (short) (radius*sin(2*M_PI*iTotalWedge[i+1]/
          iTotalWedge[iNWedges])));
    }
//---your variables and graphics functions above---
}

TMainWindow::TMainWindow(PTWindowsObject AParent,
                         LPSTR ATitle)
          :TWindow(AParent,ATitle)
{
  Attr.X = 0;
  Attr.Y = 0;
  Attr.W = 639;
  Attr.H = 479;
  AssignMenu("PieMenu");
}

void TPIE24::InitMainWindow(void)
{
  MainWindow=new TMainWindow(NULL,
                             "Pie Chart with ObjectWindows");
}

int PASCAL WinMain(HANDLE hInstance,HANDLE hPrevInstance,
                   LPSTR lpCmd,int nCmdShow)
{
  TPIE24 PIE24("PIE24",hInstance,hPrevInstance,
               lpCmd,nCmdShow);
  PIE24.Run();
  return (PIE24.Status);
}
```

The *pie25.cpp* program for this section allows the user to develop a pie chart with up to ten slices. As we have already mentioned, *pie25.cpp* allows the user to input the data on pie slice sizes, directly from a dialog box. Additionally, the user may enter the title of the pie chart.

Several virtual member functions will aid us in processing messages. Notice in particular, **WMCommand**, **About**, **PieInput**, **Paint**, **WMSize**, and **GetWindowClass**.

The data entry dialog box is created when requested by the **PieInput** member function.

```
        .
        .
        .
GetModule()->ExecDialog(new TPieDialog(this,
                                       "PieDlgBox"));
InvalidateRect(HWindow,NULL,TRUE);
UpdateWindow(HWindow);
        .
        .
        .
```

Modal dialog classes descend from class **TDialog**, which descends from **TWindowsObject**. **ExecDialog** is used to safely create dialog boxes. **ExecDialog** checks with **ValidWindow** to be sure the dialog box was drawn successfully in the window. If successful, the **Execute** member function from **ExecDialog** is called. When execution is completed successfully, **ExecDialog** will remove the dialog box from memory.

When the dialog box is closed, **InvalidateRect** and **UpdateWindow** send a repaint message to the window. The About dialog box is created in a similar manner.

The current pie chart values are retrieved from the dialog box with the help of **WMCommand**. When the IDOK statement is executed, the new chart label and slice values will be read into the appropriate variables. If IDCANCEL is selected, the original values will be used to repaint the window.

```
        .
        .
        .
case IDOK:
  GetDlgItemText(HWindow,DM_TITLE,szTString,80);
  iWedgesize[0]=GetDlgItemInt(HWindow,DM_P1,NULL,0);
  iWedgesize[1]=GetDlgItemInt(HWindow,DM_P2,NULL,0);
  iWedgesize[2]=GetDlgItemInt(HWindow,DM_P3,NULL,0);
  iWedgesize[3]=GetDlgItemInt(HWindow,DM_P4,NULL,0);
  iWedgesize[4]=GetDlgItemInt(HWindow,DM_P5,NULL,0);
  iWedgesize[5]=GetDlgItemInt(HWindow,DM_P6,NULL,0);
  iWedgesize[6]=GetDlgItemInt(HWindow,DM_P7,NULL,0);
  iWedgesize[7]=GetDlgItemInt(HWindow,DM_P8,NULL,0);
  iWedgesize[8]=GetDlgItemInt(HWindow,DM_P9,NULL,0);
  iWedgesize[9]=GetDlgItemInt(HWindow,DM_P10,NULL,0);
  EndDialog(HWindow,TRUE);
        .
        .
        .
```

When the user selects the data entry item (a dialog box) from the program's menu, they are allowed to enter a pie chart title and the data for the pie slices. This information is accepted when the OK pushbutton is selected. The title is returned as a text string with the **GetDlgItemText** function. Numeric information is returned with the **GetDlgItemInt** function. This function translates the "numeric" string information entered by the user into a short integer which can be a signed or unsigned number. Notice that this function requires four parameters. The handle and ID number are self-explanatory. The third parameter, which is NULL in this case, is used to flag a successful conversion. The fourth parameter is used to indicate signed and unsigned numbers. In this case, a zero states that the dialog box is returning unsigned numbers. These numbers are saved in the global array *iWedgesize[]* for future use.

The member function **WMSize** is used in determining the size of the client or application window.

```
        .
        .
        .
  xClientView=LOWORD(Message.LParam);
  yClientView=HIWORD(Message.LParam);
        .
        .
        .
```

Windows sends a message, which is processed by **WMSize**, any time the window is resized. For this example, the size will be returned in two variables, *xClientView* and *yClientView*. This information will be used by **Paint** to scale the pie chart to the window. It will also produce a miniature icon of the window when the "Minimum" option is selected from the main menu.

Except for gathering data, the real work in this program is done under **Paint**. First, the pie chart title is printed to the screen using the coordinates for the default mapping mode. The title is centered using a simplistic approach that assumes a default character set eight pixels wide.

```
        .
        .
        .
  TextOut(hdc,(310-(strlen(szTString)*8/2)),
         15,szTString,strlen(szTString));
        .
        .
        .
```

Next, the mapping mode is changed to MM_ISOTROPIC. The default
drawing mode is MM_TEXT, which draws in "pixel" coordinates. Under
MM_TEXT, point (0,0) is in the upper-left corner of the screen.
MM_ISOTROPIC allows us to select the extent of both the x and y axes.

```
        .
        .
        .
SetMapMode(hdc,MM_ISOTROPIC);
SetWindowExt(hdc,500,500);
SetViewportExt(hdc,xClientView,-yClientView);
SetViewportOrg(hdc,xClientView/2,yClientView/2);
        .
        .
        .
```

The mapping mode is changed by calling the function **SetMapMode**.
When the function **SetWindowExt** is called, with both parameters set to
500, the height and width of the client or application area are equal. These
are logical sizes, which Windows adjusts (scales) to fit the physical display
device. The display size values are used by the **SetViewportExt** function.
The negative sign for the −y coordinate specifies increasing y values from
the bottom of the screen. It should be no surprise that these are the values
previously obtained by **WMSize**. Additionally, for this example, we wish to
center the pie chart on a traditional x,y coordinate system, with the center
of the pie chart at (0,0). The **SetViewportOrg** function will do this for us.

Before actually plotting the pie wedges, we must return to the beginning of the WindowProc procedure to gain an understanding of how the
pie wedges are scaled to fit a complete circle. Several pieces of code play an
important role.

```
        .
        .
        .
iNWedges=0;
for (i=0;i<maxnumwedge;i++)
{
  if(iWedgesize[i]!=0) iNWedges++;
}
iTotalWedge[0]=0;
for (i=0;i<iNWedges;i++)
  iTotalWedge[i+1]=iTotalWedge[i]+iWedgesize[i];
        .
        .
        .
```

This first nugget of code determines how many wedges or pie slices have been requested. Since the total number of wedges to be plotted will be greater than 0 (or else we don't have a chart to plot at all!), the array *iWedgesize[]* can be scanned for the first 0 value. For each non-zero value returned the number of wedges, *iNWedges*, will be incremented. Thus, when we leave this routine, *iNWedges*, will contain the number of wedges for this pie chart.

Next, a progressive total of wedge values will be returned to the *iTotalWedge[]* array. These values will help determine where one pie slice ends and the next begins. For example, if the user entered 10, 20, 30, and 40 for wedge sizes, *iTotalWedge[]* would contain the values 0, 10, 30, 60, 100. Take a minute and make sure you understand how these values were determined.

The values contained in *iTotalWedge[]* are needed in order to calculate the beginning and ending angles for each pie wedge. The **Pie** function accepts nine parameters. The first parameter is the handle, and the next four specify the coordinates of the bounding rectangle. In this case, for the mapping mode chosen, they are *−200, 200, 200,* and *−200*. The remaining four parameters are used to designate the starting x,y pair and the ending x,y pair for the pie arc. To calculate x values, the cosine function is used and to calculate y values, the sine function is used. For example, the first x position is determined by multiplying the radius of the pie by the cosine of *2*pi*iTotalWedge[0]*. The *2*pi* value is needed in the conversion of degrees to radians. The y value is found with the sine function in an identical manner. Those two values (x,y) serve as the starting coordinates for the first slice. The ending coordinates are found with the same equations, but using the next value in *iTotalWedge[]*. In order to scale each of these points to make all slices proportional and fit a 360 degree pie, each coordinate point is divided by the grand total of all individual slices. This total is the last number contained in *iTotalWedge[]*.

A **for** loop is repeated in order to draw and fill all slices. This loop will index through all *iNWedge* values. Since we are using trigonometric functions, the *math.h* header file is included at the start of this program.

Testing the *pie25* Application

With the six *pie25* files in place, load the project file while in the Borland C++ IDE and select the "Compile" option from the menu. If the compile and link are successful, leave the Borland IDE and enter Windows to

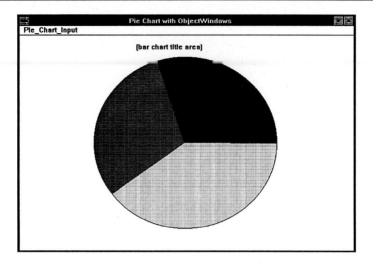

Figure 25-7.   The default pie chart drawn by *pie25*

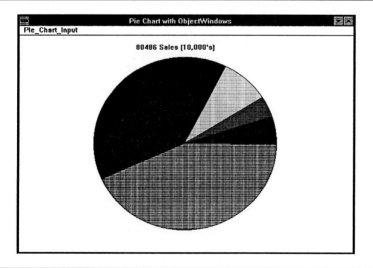

Figure 25-8.   A custom pie chart drawn by entering a title and slice values in a
data entry dialog box

execute the application. You may alternately choose the integrated environment of Turbo C++ for Windows. In this case, once the application is
compiled and linked, just click on the "Run" menu option to execute the
application.

Figure 25-7 shows the default pie chart.

Figure 25-8 is a unique pie chart application. Remember, don't believe
everything you see in a chart!

V

APPENDIXES

EXTENDED ASCII TABLE

Decimal	Hexadecimal	Symbol	Decimal	Hexadecimal	Symbol
0	0		20	14	¶
1	1	☺	21	15	§
2	2	☻	22	16	▬
3	3	♥	23	17	↨
4	4	♦	24	18	↑
5	5	♣	25	19	↓
6	6	♠	26	1A	→
7	7	●	27	1B	←
8	8	◘	28	1C	∟
9	9	○	29	1D	↔
10	A	◙	30	1E	▲
11	B	♂	31	1F	▼
12	C	♀	32	20	
13	D	♪	33	21	!
14	E	♫	34	22	"
15	F	☼	35	23	#
16	10	►	36	24	$
17	11	◄	37	25	%
18	12	↕	38	26	&
19	13	‼	39	27	'

Decimal	Hexadecimal	Symbol	Decimal	Hexadecimal	Symbol
40	28	(	76	4C	L
41	29	)	77	4D	M
42	2A	*	78	4E	N
43	2B	+	79	4F	O
44	2C	,	80	50	P
45	2D	-	81	51	Q
46	2E	.	82	52	R
47	2F	/	83	53	S
48	30	0	84	54	T
49	31	1	85	55	U
50	32	2	86	56	V
51	33	3	87	57	W
52	34	4	88	58	X
53	35	5	89	59	Y
54	36	6	90	5A	Z
55	37	7	91	5B	[
56	38	8	92	5C	\
57	39	9	93	5D	]
58	3A	:	94	5E	^
59	3B	;	95	5F	_
60	3C	<	96	60	`
61	3D	=	97	61	a
62	3E	>	98	62	b
63	3F	?	99	63	c
64	40	@	100	64	d
65	41	A	101	65	e
66	42	B	102	66	f
67	43	C	103	67	g
68	44	D	104	68	h
69	45	E	105	69	i
70	46	F	106	6A	j
71	47	G	107	6B	k
72	48	H	108	6C	l
73	49	I	109	6D	m
74	4A	J	110	6E	n
75	4B	K	111	6F	o

Decimal	Hexadecimal	Symbol	Decimal	Hexadecimal	Symbol
112	70	p	148	94	ö
113	71	q	149	95	ò
114	72	r	150	96	û
115	73	s	151	97	ù
116	74	t	152	98	ÿ
117	75	u	153	99	Ö
118	76	v	154	9A	Ü
119	77	w	155	9B	¢
120	78	x	156	9C	£
121	79	y	157	9D	¥
122	7A	z	158	9E	Pt
123	7B	{	159	9F	ƒ
124	7C	¦	160	A0	á
125	7D	}	161	A1	í
126	7E	~	162	A2	ó
127	7F		163	A3	ú
128	80	Ç	164	A4	ñ
129	81	ü	165	A5	Ñ
130	82	é	166	A6	ª
131	83	â	167	A7	º
132	84	ä	168	A8	¿
133	85	à	169	A9	⌐
134	86	å	170	AA	¬
135	87	ç	171	AB	½
136	88	ê	172	AC	¼
137	89	ë	173	AD	¡
138	8A	è	174	AE	«
139	8B	ï	175	AF	»
140	8C	î	176	B0	░
141	8D	ì	177	B1	▒
142	8E	Ä	178	B2	▓
143	8F	Å	179	B3	│
144	90	É	180	B4	┤
145	91	æ	181	B5	╡
146	92	Æ	182	B6	╢
147	93	ô	183	B7	╖

Decimal	Hexadecimal	Symbol	Decimal	Hexadecimal	Symbol
184	B8	⌐	220	DC	▄
185	B9	╢	221	DD	▌
186	BA	║	222	DE	▐
187	BB	╗	223	DF	▀
188	BC	╝	224	E0	α
189	BD	╜	225	E1	β
190	BE	╛	226	E2	Γ
191	BF	┐	227	E3	π
192	C0	└	228	E4	Σ
193	C1	┴	229	E5	σ
194	C2	┬	230	E6	μ
195	C3	├	231	E7	τ
196	C4	─	232	E8	φ
197	C5	┼	233	E9	Θ
198	C6	╞	234	EA	Ω
199	C7	╟	235	EB	δ
200	C8	╚	236	EC	∞
201	C9	╔	237	ED	∅
202	CA	╩	238	EE	∈
203	CB	╦	239	EF	∩
204	CC	╠	240	F0	≡
205	CD	═	241	F1	±
206	CE	╬	242	F2	≥
207	CF	╧	243	F3	≤
208	D0	╨	244	F4	⌠
209	D1	╤	245	F5	⌡
210	D2	╥	246	F6	÷
211	D3	╙	247	F7	≈
212	D4	╘	248	F8	°
213	D5	╒	249	F9	•
214	D6	╓	250	FA	·
215	D7	╫	251	FB	$\sqrt{}$
216	D8	╪	252	FC	^{n}
217	D9	┘	253	FD	^{2}
218	DA	┌	254	FE	■
219	DB	█	255	FF	(blank)

B

DOS 10H, 21H, AND 33H INTERRUPT PARAMETERS

This appendix contains the most popular DOS, BIOS, and MOUSE interrupts and parameters.

SCREEN CONTROL WITH BIOS-TYPE 10H INTERRUPTS

Syntax: INT 10H (when the following parameters are set to the required values)

INTERFACE CONTROL OF THE CRT

AH Value	Function	Input	Output
AH = 0	Set the mode of display	AL = 0	40 × 25 color text
		AL = 1	40 × 25 color text
		AL = 2	80 × 25 color text
		AL = 3	80 × 25 color text
		AL = 4	320 × 200 4-color graphics
		AL = 5	320 × 200 4-color graphics
		AL = 6	640 × 200 2-color graphics
		AL = 7	80 × 25 monochrome text
		AL = 13	320 × 200 16-color graphics
		AL = 14	640 × 200 16-color graphics
		AL = 15	640 × 350 monochrome graphics
		AL = 16	640 × 350 16-color graphics
		AL = 17	640 × 480 2-color graphics
		AL = 18	640 × 480 16-color graphics
		AL = 19	320 × 200 256-color graphics
AH = 1	Set cursor type	CH =	Bits 4-0 start of line for cursor
		CL =	Bits 4-0 end of line for cursor
AH = 2	Set cursor position	DH =	Row
		DL =	Column
		BH =	Page number of display (zero for graphics)
AH = 3	Read cursor position		DH = row
			DL = column
			CH = cursor mode
			CL = cursor mode
			BH = page number of display
AH = 4	Get light pen position		AH = 0, switch not down/ triggered
			AH = 1, valid answers as follows:
			DH = row
			DL = column
			CH = graph line (0-199)
			BX = graph column (0-319/639)

AH Value	Function	Input	Output
AH = 5	Set active display page	AL =	New page value (0-7) modes 0 and 1 (0-3) modes 2 and 3
AH = 6	Scroll active page up	AL =	Number of lines, 0 for entire screen
		CH =	Row, upper-left corner
		CL =	Column, upper-left corner
		DH =	Row, lower-right corner
		DL =	Column, lower-right corner
		BH =	Attribute to be used
AH = 7	Scroll active page down	AL =	Number of lines, 0 for entire screen
		CH =	Row, upper-left corner
		CL =	Column, upper-left corner
		DH =	Row, lower-right corner
		DL =	Column, lower-right corner
		BH =	Attribute to be used

HANDLING CHARACTERS

AH Value	Function	Input	Output
AH = 8	Read attribute/ character at cursor position	BH = AL = AH =	Display page Character read Attribute of character
AH = 9	Write attribute/ character at cursor position	BH = CX = AL = BL =	Display page Count of characters to write Character to write Attribute of character
AH = 10	Write character at cursor position	BH = CX = AL =	Display page Count of characters to write Character to write

GRAPHICS INTERFACE

AH Value	Function	Input	Output

AH − 11	Select color palette	BH =
		 BL =
			Palette ID (0-127)
			 Color for above ID
			 0−background (0-15)
			 1−palette
			   0−green(1), red(2), yellow(3)
			   1−cyan(1), magenta(2),
			     white (3)

AH = 12	Draw dot on screen	DX = CX = AL =	Row (0-199) Column (0-319/639) Color of dot
AH = 13	Read dot information	DX = CX = AL =	Row (0-199) Column (0-319/639) Value of dot

ASCII TELETYPE OUTPUT

AH Value	Function	Input	Output
AH = 14	Write to active page	AL = BL =	Character to write Foreground color
AH = 15	Get video state	AL = AH = BH =	Current mode Number of screen columns Current display page
AH = 16	(Reserved)		
AH = 17	(Reserved)		
AH = 18	(Reserved)		
AH = 19	Write string	ES:BP = CX = DX = BH = AL = 0	Point to string Length of string Cursor position for start Page number BL = attribute (char,char, char...char) cursor not moved

AH Value	Function	Input	Output
		AL = 1	BL = attribute (char,char, char...char) cursor is moved
		AL = 2	(char,attr,char,attr...) cursor not moved
		AL = 3	(char,attr,char,attr...) cursor is moved
AH = 1A	R/W display combination code		
AH = 1B	Return functional-ity state informa-tion		
AH = 1C	Save/restore video state		

SPECIFICATIONS AND REQUIREMENTS FOR THE DOS 21H INTERRUPT

Syntax: INT 21H (when the following parameters are set to the required values)

AH Value	Function	Input	Output
AH = 0	End of program		(similar to INT 20H)
AH = 1	Wait and display key-board character with CTRL-BREAK check		AL = character entered
AH = 2	Display character with CTRL-BREAK check	DL =	Character to display
AH = 3	Asynchronous character input		AL = character entered
AH = 4	Asynchronous character output	DL =	Character to send
AH = 5	Character to write	DL =	Character to write
AH = 6	Input keyboard character	DL =	0FFH if character entered, 0 if none
AH = 7	Wait for keyboard character (no display)		AL = character entered

AH Value	Function	Input	Output
AH = 8	Wait for keyboard character (no display— CTRL-BREAK check)		AL = character entered
AH = 9	String display	DS:DX =	Address of string; must end with $ sentinel
AH = A	Keyboard string to buffer	DS:DX =	Address of buffer. First byte = size, second = number of characters read
AH = B	Input keyboard status		AL—no character = 0FFH character = 0
AH = C	Clear keyboard buffer and call function	AL =	1,6,7,8,0A (function #)
AH = D	Reset default disk drive	None	None
AH = E	Select default disk drive		AL = number of drives DL—0 = A drive 1 = B drive, and so forth
AH = F	Open file with unopened FCB	DS:DX =	Location AL = 0FFH if not found AL = 0H if found
AH = 10	Close file with FCB	DS:DX =	Location (same as AH = 0FH)
AH = 11	Search directory for match of unopened FCB. DTA contains directory entry	DS:DX =	AL = 0FFH if not found AL = 0H if found Location
AH = 12	Search (after AH = 11) for other files that match wildcard specifications		(same as AH = 11H)
AH = 13	Delete file named by FCB	DS:DX =	Location (same as AH = 11H)
AH = 14	Sequential read of open file. Number of bytes in FCB (record size)	DS:DX =	Location AL = 0 transfer OK AL = 1 end of file AL = 2 overrun DTA segment AL = 3 EOF/partial read

AH Value	Function	Input	Output
AH = 15	Sequential write of open file. Transfer from DTA to file, with FCB update of current record	DS:DX =	Location AL = 0 transfer OK AL = 1 disk full/ROF AL = 2 overrun DTA segment
AH = 16	Create file (length set to zero)	DS:DX =	Location (same as AH = 11H)
AH = 17	Rename file	DS:DX =	Location AL = 0 rename OK AL = 0FFH no match found
AH = 18	(DOS internal use)		
AH = 19	Drive code (default)		AL−0 = A drive 1 = B drive, and so forth
AH = 1A	Set Data Transfer Add	DS:DX =	Points to location
AH = 1B	File Allocation Table	DS:DX =	Address of FAT DX = number of units AL = record/alloc. unit CX = sector size (same as AH = 1B)
AH = 1C	Disk drive FAT information	DL =	Drive number: 0 = default 1 = A 2 = B
AH = 1D	(DOS internal use)		
AH = 1E	(DOS internal use)		
AH = 1F	(DOS internal use)		
AH = 20	(DOS internal use)		
AH = 21	Random read file	DS:DX =	Location of FCB (same as AH = 14H)
AH = 22	Random write file	DS:DX =	(same as AH = 21H)
AH = 23	Set file size	DS:DX =	Location of FCB AL = 0 if set AL = 0FFH if not set
AH = 24	Random record size	DS:DX =	Location of FCB
AH = 25	Set interrupt vector (change address)	DS:DX = AL =	Address of vector table Interrupt number
AII = 26	Create program segment	DX =	Segment number

AH Value	Function	Input	Output
AH = 27	Random block read	DS:DX =	Address of FCB
			AL—0 read OK
			1 EOF
			2 wrap around
			3 partial record
AH = 28	Random block write	DS:DX =	Address of FCB
			AL—0 write OK
			1 lack of space
AH = 29	Parse file name	DS:SI =	Point to command line
		DS:DI =	Memory location for FCB
			AL = bits to set options
AH = 2A	Read date		CX = year (80 to 99)
			DH = month (1 to 12)
			DL = day (1 to 31)
AH = 2B	Set date		CX & DX (same as above)
			AL—0 if valid
			0FF if not valid
AH = 2C	Read time		CH = hours (0-23)
			CL = minutes (0-59)
AH = 2D	Set time		CX & DX (same as above)
			AL—0 if valid
			0FF if not valid
AH = 2E	Set verify state	DL =	0
		AL =	0 = verify off
			1 = verify on
AH = 2F	Get DTA	ES:BX =	Get DTA into ES
AH = 30	Get DOS version		AL = version number
			AH = sub number
AH = 31	Terminate and remain resident		AL = exit code
			DX = memory size in paragraphs
AH = 32	(DOS internal use)		
AH = 33	CTRL-BREAK check	AL =	0, request state
		AL =	1, set the state
			DL = 0 for off
			DL = 1 for on

AH Value	Function	Input	Output
AH = 34	(DOS internal use)		
AH = 35	Read interrupt address	AL =	Interrupt number ES:BX point to vector address
AH = 36	Disk space available	DL =	Drive (0 = default, 1 = A, 2 = B, and so forth) AX = sectors/cluster (FFFF if invalid) BX = number of free clusters CX = bytes per sector DX = total number of clusters
AH = 37	(DOS internal use)		
AH = 38	Country dependent information (32-byte block)	DS:DX	Location of memory Date/time Currency symbol Thousands separator Decimal separator
AH = 39	Make directory	DS:DX =	Address of string for directory
AH = 3A	Remove directory	DS:DX =	Address of string for directory
AH = 3B	Change directory	DS:DX =	Address of string for new directory
AH = 3C	Create a file	DS:DX =	Address of string for file AX = file handle
		CX =	File attribute
AH = 3D	Open a file	DS:DX = AL =	Address of string for file 0 = open for reading 1 = open for writing 2 = open for both AX returns file handle
AH = 3E	Close a file handle	BX =	File handle
AH = 3F	Read a file or device	BX = CX = DS:DX =	File handle Number of bytes to read Address of buffer AX = number of bytes read
AH = 40	Write a file or device	BX = CX =	File handle Number of bytes to write

AH Value	Function	Input	Output
		DS:DX =	Address of buffer
			AX = number of bytes written
AH = 41	Delete a file	DS:DX =	Address of file string
AH = 42	Move file pointer	BX =	File handle
		AL =	Pointer's starting location
		CX:DX	Number of bytes
		DX:AX	Current file pointer
AH = 43	Set file attribute	AL = 1	
		CX =	Attribute
		DS:DX =	Address of file string
AH = 45	Duplicate file handle	BX	File handle
			AX = returned file handle
AH = 46	Force duplicate file handle	BX	File handle
			CX = second file handle
AH = 47	Current directory	DL =	Drive number (0 = default, 1 = A drive, 2 = B drive)
		DS:SI =	Buffer address DS:SI returns address of string
AH = 48	Allocate memory	BX	Number of paragraphs
			AX = allocated block
AH = 49	Free allocated memory	ES	Segment of returned block
AH = 4A	Set block	ES	Segment block
		BX	New block size
AH = 4B	Load/execute program	DS:DX	Location of ASCIIZ string (drive/path/file-name)
			AL−0 =load and execute 3 = load/no execute
AH = 4C	Terminate (exit)	AL	Binary return code (all files closed)

AH Value	Function	Input	Output
AH = 4D	Retrieve return code		AX returns exit code of another program
AH = 4E	Find first matching file	DS:DX	Location of ASCIIZ string (drive/path/file-name)
			CX = search attribute
			DTA completed
			(AH = 4EH called first)
AH = 4F	Next matching file		
AH = 50	(DOS internal use)		
AH = 51	(DOS internal use)		
AH = 52	(DOS internal use)		
AH = 53	(DOS internal use)		
AH = 54	Verify state	none	AL−0 if verify off
			1 if verify on
AH = 55	(DOS internal use)		
AH = 56	Rename file	DS:DX =	Address of string for old information
		ES:DI =	Address of string for new information
AH = 57	Get/set file date/time	AL	00 (return)
			01 (set)
		BX	File handle
		DX and CX	Date and time information
AH = 59	Extended error code	BX =	DOS version (3.0 = 0)
			AX = error code
			BH = class of error
			BL = suggested action
			CH = where error occurred
AH = 5A	Create temporary file		CX = file attribute
			CF = Set on error
			AX = error code
		DS:DX =	Points to string
AH = 5B	Create a new file		(same as above)

Note: For DOS versions above 2.0, use AH = 36H + for file management.

MOUSE CONTROL FUNCTIONS ACCESSED THROUGH INTERRUPT 33H

Syntax: INT 33H (when the following parameters are set to the required values)

AH Value	Function	Input	Output
AX = 0	Install flag and reset	BX = CX = DX =	If AX = 0 and BX = −1 Mouse support not available AX = −1, then BX = number of supported mouse buttons
AX = 1	Show pointer	BX = CX = DX =	Does nothing if already visi- ble, otherwise increments the pointer-draw flag by 1 Shows pointer image when pointer-draw flag = 0
AX = 2	Hide pointer	BX = CX = DX =	Does nothing if already hid- den, otherwise decrements the pointer-draw flag. Value of −1 hides image
AX = 3	Get position and button status	BX = CX = DX =	For 2- or 3-button mice, BX returns which button pressed: 0 leftmost, 1 rightmost, 2 center button. Buttons 3-15 reserved. CX = x coordinate; DX = y coordi- nate of pointer in pixels
AX = 4	Set pointer position	CX = DX =	New horizontal position in pixels New vertical position in pixels For values that exceed screen boundaries, screen maximum and minimum are used
AX = 5	Get button press information	BX =	Button status requested, where 0 = leftmost, 1 = rightmost, 2 = center button.

AH Value	Function	Input	Output

			AX—bit 0 (leftmost) = 0 or 1
			    bit 1 (rightmost) = 0 or 1
			    bit 2 (center) = 0 or 1
			If 0 button up, and if 1 button down.
			BX = number of times button pressed since last call
			CX = horizontal coordinate of mouse
			DX = vertical coordinate of mouse

AX = 6	Get button release information	BX =	Button status requested, same format as for AX = 5 above. AX, BX, CX, and DX as above. If 0 button up, if 1 button down
AX = 7	Set minimum and maximum horizontal position	CX = DX =	Minimum virtual-screen horizontal coordinate in pixels Maximum virtual-screen horizontal coordinate in pixels
AX = 8	Set minimum and maximum vertical position	CX = DX =	Minimum virtual-screen vertical coordinate in pixels Maximum virtual-screen vertical coordinate in pixels
AX = 9	Set graphics pointer block	BX = CX = DX = ES =	Pointer hot-spot horizontal coordinate in pixels Pointer hot-spot vertical coordinate in pixels Address of screen/pointer masks Segment of screen/pointer masks
AX = 10	Set text pointer	BX = CX = DX =	Pointer select value Screen mask value/hardware cursor start scan line Pointer mask value/hardware cursor stop scan line

AH Value	Function	Input	Output
			BX = 0 select software text pointer
			BX = 1 select hardware cursor
			CX and DX bits map to:
			0-7 character
			8-10 foreground color
			11 intensity
			12-14 background color
			15 blinking
AX = 11	Read mouse motion counters	BX = CX = DX =	CX = horizontal count
			DX = vertical count
			Range −32,768 to +32,768 read in mickeys
AX = 12	Set user-defined subroutine	CX = DX = ES =	Call mask
			Offset of subroutine
			Segment of subroutine CX word bit map:
			0 pointer position changed
			1 leftmost button pressed
			2 leftmost button released
			3 rightmost button pressed
			4 rightmost button released
			5 center button pressed
			6 center button released
			7-15 reserved = 0
			Following values loaded when subroutine is called:
			AX = condition of mask
			BX = button status
			CX = pointer horizontal coordinate
			DX = pointer vertical coordinate
			SI = last vertical mickey count read
			DI = last horizontal mickey count read
AX = 13	Light pen emulation on	BX = CX =	Instructs mouse driver to emulate a light pen

AH Value	Function	Input	Output
		DX =	Vertical mickey/pixel ratio Ratios specify number of mickeys per 8 pixels
AX = 14	Light pen emulation off	BX = CX = DX =	Disables mouse driver light pen emulation (same as AX = 13)
AX = 15	Set mickey/pixel ratio	CX = DX =	Horizontal mickey/pixel ratio (Same as AX = 13)
AX = 16	Conditional off	CX =	Left column coordinate in pixels
		DX =	Upper row coordinate in pixels
		SI =	Right column coordinate in pixels
		DI =	Lower row coordinate in pixels Defines an area of the screen for updating
AX = 19	Set double speed threshold	BX = DX =	Doubles pointer motion Threshold speed in mickeys/ second
AX = 20	Swap user-defined sub-routine	CX = DX = ES =	Call mask Offset of subroutine Segment of subroutine Sets hardware interrupts for call mask and subroutine ad-dress, returns previous values CX word call mask: 0 pointer position changed 1 leftmost button pressed 2 leftmost button released 3 rightmost button pressed 4 rightmost button released 5 center button pressed 6 center button released 7-12 reserved = 0 Following values loaded when subroutine is called: AX = condition of mask BX = button status CX = pointer horizontal coordinate

AH Value	Function	Input	Output
			DX = pointer vertical coordinate
			SI = last vertical mickey count read
			DI = last horizontal mickey count read
AX = 21	Get mouse state storage requirements	BX = CX = DX =	Gets size of buffer in bytes needed to store state of the mouse driver
			BX = size of buffer in bytes
AX = 22	Save mouse driver state	BX = CX = DX = ES =	Saves the mouse driver state
			Offset of buffer
			Segment of buffer
AX = 23	Restore mouse driver state	BX = CX = DX = ES =	Restores the mouse driver state from a user buffer
			Offset of buffer
			Segment of buffer

C

WINDOWS FUNCTIONS

This appendix contains an alphabetical list of frequently used Windows functions. For a complete listing of Windows function prototypes, examine the *windows.h* header file supplied with your copy of the Borland C++ compiler.

short AddFontResource(lpFilename)

Function Will add the *lpFilename*-specified font to the list of available fonts, thereby making them available for the application to use.

Parameters *lpFilename* (LPSTR) contains a character string that names the font resource file.

Value Returned The return value contains the number of fonts loaded; otherwise, the function returns a 0.

Notes Memory conservation can be accomplished by an application removing any unused font resources as soon as possible.

BOOL Arc(hDC,x1,y1,x2,y2,x3,y3,x4,y4)

Function   Draws an elliptical arc with the center of the arc bounded by the rectangle defined by *x1*, *y1* and *x2*, *y2*. The arc begins at *x3*, *y3* and ends at *x4*, *y4*.

Parameters

hDC (HDC) identifies the device context.

x1 and *y1* (short) define the logical X and Y coordinates of the upper-left corner of the bounding rectangle.

x2 and *y2* (short) define the logical X and Y coordinates of the lower-right corner of the bounding rectangle.

x3 and *y3* (short) define the logical X and Y coordinates of the arc's starting point.

x4 and *y4* (short) define the logical X and Y coordinates of the arc's ending point.

Value Returned   A nonzero value is returned if the function is success-ful; otherwise, a zero is returned.

Notes   The width and height of the rectangle must not exceed 32,767 units.

HDC BeginPaint(hWnd,lpPaint)

Function   Gets the window ready for painting and using the *lpPaint* parameter, which points to a paint structure and fills the structure with information about the painting to be performed.

Parameters

hWnd (HWND) indicates the window to be repainted.

lpPaint (LPPAINTSTRUCT) points to a *paintstruct* structure that will receive the painting parameters.

Value Returned   Returns the device context for the specified window.

Notes   BeginPaint must be called in response to a WM_PAINT message.

void CheckDlgButton(hDlg,nIDButton,wCheck)

Function   Places or removes a check mark from a button control, or changes the state of a three-state button.

Parameters

hDlg (HWND) specifies the dialog box containing the button.

nIDButton (int) defines the button control to be modified.

wCheck (WORD) defines the action to be performed. A nonzero value causes a check mark to be placed next to the button. A zero value removes the check mark. With a three-state button: 2 grays the button; 1 checks the button; 0 removes a check mark.

Value Returned   None.

Notes   The function sends a BM_SETCHECK message to the button control of the specified dialog box.

BOOL CheckMenuItem(hMenu,wIDCheckItem,wCheck)

Function   Using the pop-up menu pointed to by the *hMenu* parameter, this function either positions a check mark next to a menu item or removes the check mark from a previously selected menu item.

Parameters

hMenu (HMENU) identifies the pop-up menu.

wIDCheckItem (WORD) indicates which menu item is to be checked or unchecked.

wCheck (WORD) can be any combination of options combined using the logical OR operation. These include MF_CHECKED, MF_UN-CHECKED, MF_BYPOSITION, or MF_BYCOMMAND. The *wCheck* parameter defines how to modify the menu item, along with a specification of how to locate the item.

Check Options	Description
MF_CHECKED	Causes a check mark to be placed next to the selected menu item.
MF_UNCHECKED	Removes the check mark from a previously selected menu item.
MF_BYPOSITION	Uses the *wIDCheckItem* parameter and indicates that the position of the menu item has been given. The first menu item begins at position 0.
MF_BYCOMMAND	Causes the *wIDCheckItem* parameter to contain the menu item ID. MF_BYCOMMAND is the default option.

Value Returned The return value indicates the previous state of the selected menu item (MF_UNCHECKED or MF_CHECKED).

Notes Top-level menu items cannot be checked. The *wIDCheckItem* parameter can specify a menu or submenu item.

void CheckRadioButton(hDlg,nIDFirstButton, nIDLastButton,nIDCheckButton)

Function This function will check the radio button identified by the *nIDCheckButton* parameter while simultaneously removing any previous check marks from all radio buttons referenced by the *nIDFirstButton* to the last radio button defined by *nIDLastButton*.

Parameters

hDlg (HWND) specifies the dialog box.

nIDFirstButton (int) is an integer value indicating the first radio button in the selected group.

nIDLastButton (int) is an integer value indicating the last radio button in the selected group.

nIDCheckButton (int) is an integer value indicating the radio button that is to be checked.

Value Returned   None.

Notes   The function sends a BM_SETCHECK message to the radio-button control referenced by the ID in a given dialog box.

BOOL Chord(hDC,x1,y1,x2,y2,x3,y3,x4,y4)

Function   Draws a chord using the selected pen, with a fill pattern based on the selected brush. A chord is defined as an area bounded by the intersection of an ellipse and a line segment.

Parameters

hDC (HDC) specifies the device context on which the chord will be drawn.

x1 (short) defines the upper-left corner X coordinate of the bounding rectangle.

y1 (short) defines the upper-left corner Y coordinate of the bounding rectangle.

x2 (short) defines the lower-right corner X coordinate of the bounding rectangle.

y2 (short) defines the lower-right corner Y coordinate of the bounding rectangle.

x3 (short) defines the X coordinate of one end of the line segment.

y3 (short) defines the Y coordinate of one end of the line segment.

x4 (short) defines the X coordinate of the opposite end of the line segment.

y4 (short) defines the Y coordinate of the opposite end of the line segment.

Value Returned   A nonzero value is returned if the arc is drawn. A zero value indicates that the arc was not drawn.

Notes   *x1, y1, x2,* and *y2* define the rectangle bounding the ellipse that is part of the chord. *x3, y3, x4,* and *y4* define the line that intercepts the ellipse.

HBRUSH CreateBrushIndirect(lpLogBrush)

Function   Uses the data structure pointed to by *lpLogBrush* to create a logical brush. The *logbrush* data structure defines the intended brush's style, color, and pattern.

Parameters   *lpLogBrush* (LOGBRUSH FAR *) is a pointer to a *logbrush* data structure.

Value Returned   If successful, the value returned is to the created logical brush; otherwise, a null is returned.

Notes   A BS_INDEXED style will guarantee that the first eight indexed brushes will be unique for any selected device.

HWND CreateDialog(hInstance,lpTemplateName, hWndParent,lpDialogFunc)

Function   The *lpTemplateName* data structure defines the size, style, and any controls associated with the modeless dialog box the function will create. The *hWndParent* parameter specifies the owner window of the dialog box, with *lpDialogFunc* pointing to the message processing function that will handle any messages received by the dialog box.

Parameters

hInstance (HANDLE) specifies the instance of the module whose executable file owns the resource.

lpTemplateName (LPSTR) is a pointer to a null-terminated character string naming the dialog box template.

hWndParent (HWND) is a handle to the window that owns the dialog box.

lpDialogFunc (FARPROC) is a procedure-instance address for the dialog function. The dialog function address must have been created by using the **MakeProcInstance** function. The callback function must use the Pascal calling convention and be declared FAR using the following form:

```
HWND FAR PASCAL DialogFunc(hWnd,wMsg,wParam, lParam)
HWND hwnd;          /* identifies message receiving
                       dialog box                    */
unsigned wMsg;      /* indicates the message number  */
WORD wParam;        /* specifies 16 bits of additional
                       message-dependent information */
DWORD lParam;       /* specifies 32 bits of additional
                       message-dependent information */
```

Value Returned   A successful return contains a valid identifier to the dialog box. A −1 is returned if the function call was unsuccessful.

Notes   This function is used only if the dialog class is used for the dialog box. This is the default class used whenever no explicit class is given in the dialog box template. The function must not call *DefWindowProc*, but must process all unwanted messages internally by the dialog-class window function.

You should use the WS_VISIBLE style for the dialog box template if the dialog box should appear in the parent window during creation.

You should use the **DestroyWindow** function to delete a dialog box created by the **CreateDialog** function.

HWND
CreateDialogIndirect(hInstance,lpDialogTemplate, hWndParent,lpDialogFunc)

Function   The *lpDialogTemplate* data structure defines the size, style, and any controls associated with the modeless dialog box the function will create. The *hWndParent* parameter specifies the owner window of the dialog box, with *lpDialogFunc* pointing to the message processing function that will handle any messages received by the dialog box.

Parameters

hInstance (HANDLE) specifies the instance of the module whose executable file owns the resource.

lpDialogTemplate (LPSTR) is a pointer to a dialog box template structure.

hWndParent (HWND) is a handle to the window that owns the dialog box.

lpDialogFunc (FARPROC) is a procedure-instance address for the dialog function. The dialog function address must have been created by using the **MakeProcInstance** function. The callback function must use the Pascal calling convention and declared FAR using the following form:

```
HWND FAR PASCAL DialogFunc(hWnd,wMsg,wParam,lParam)
HWND hwnd;      /* identifies the message receiving the
                   dialog box                         */
unsigned wMsg; /* indicates the message number  */
WORD wParam;    /* specifies 16 bits of additional
                   message-dependent information */
DWORD lParam;  /* specifies 32 bits of additional
                   message-dependent information */
```

Value Returned   A successful return contains a valid identifier to the dialog box. A −1 is returned if the function call was unsuccessful.

Notes   **CreateDialogIndirect** sends a WM_INITDIALOG message to the dialog function before displaying the dialog box, allowing the dialog function to initialize the dialog box controls.

This function is used only if the dialog class is used for the dialog box. This is the default class that is used whenever no explicit class is given in the dialog box template. The function must not call *DefWindowProc*, but must process all unwanted messages internally by the dialog-class window function.

You should use the WS_VISIBLE style for the dialog box template if the dialog box should appear in the parent window during creation.

You should use the **DestroyWindow** function to delete a dialog box created by the **CreateDialog** function.

HFONT CreateFont(nHeight,nWidth,nEscapement,nOrientation, nWeight,cItalic,cUnderline,cStrikeOut,cCharSet, cOutputPrecision,cClipPrecision,cQuality, cPitchAndFamily,lpFacename)

Function   Creates a logical font that can be selected as the font for any device. The logical font that is created is based on the options that follow.

Parameters

nHeight (short) defines the logical font's height in one of three ways:

nHeight > 0	Transforms the height into device units and matches it with the cell height of the available fonts
nHeight = 0	Selects a reasonable default size
nHeight < 0	Transforms the height into device units and matches the absolute value against the character height of the available fonts

The font mapper follows these precedents for height comparisons: it first looks for the largest font that does not exceed the requested font size. If there is no such font available then it looks for the smallest font available.

nWidth (short), using logical units, defines the average width of the characters in the font. When *nWidth* contains a zero value, the aspect ratio of the device will be matched with the digitization aspect ratio of the available fonts to select the best match.

nEscapement (short), using tenths of a degree increments, defines the angle of each line of text output in the specified font, relative to the bottom of the page.

nOrientation (short), using tenths of a degree increments, specifies the angle of each character's baseline relative to the bottom of the page.

nWeight (short) indicates the preferred weight of the font in the range of 0 to 1000. A value of 0 selects the default weight, with a value of roughly 450 defining a normal weight, and 750 representing bold.

cItalic (BYTE) indicates if the font is italic or not.

cUnderline (BYTE) indicates if the font is underlined or not.

cStrikeOut (BYTE) indicates if the characters in the font are struck out.

cCharSet (BYTE) indicates which character set is desired. Two values (ANSI_CHARSET and OEM_CHARSET) are predefined. Others may be purchased through specific font manufacturers.

cOutputPrecision (BYTE) indicates the preferred output precision. This specifies just how closely the output must match the requested font's characteristics. There are four choices:

OUT_CHARACTER_PRECIS
OUT_DEFAULT_PRECIS
OUT_STRING_PRECIS
OUT_STROKE_PRECIS

cClipPrecision (BYTE) indicates the preferred clipping precision. Clipping precision references just how each character that extends beyond the clipping region is to be "clipped." There are three choices:

CLIP_CHARACTER_PRECIS
CLIP_DEFAULT_PRECIS
CLIP_STROKE_PRECIS

cQuality (BYTE) selects the preferred output quality. This parameter selects just how carefully the graphics device interface (GDI) must attempt to match the logical font with the actual physical fonts provided for the requested output device. There are three possible match conditions:

DEFAULT _ QUALITY
DRAFT _ QUALITY
PROOF _ QUALITY

cPitchAndFamily (BYTE) selects the pitch and family of the font. There are three pitch choices:

DEFAULT _ PITCH
FIXED _ PITCH
VARIABLE _ PITCH

There are six possible font families.

FF _ DECORATIVE
FF _ DONTCARE
FF _ MODERN
FF _ ROMAN
FF _ SCRIPT
FF _ SWISS

lpFacename (LPSTR) is a 30-character maximum, null-terminated string that identifies the name of the font. If there is a question about the available typefaces, the **EnumFonts** function can be invoked to list the fonts.

Value Returned   A successful return contains a value identifying the created logical font. A null value indicates an unsuccessful creation.

Notes   It is important to understand that the **CreateFont** function does not create a new font. All it does is to match, as closely as possible based on the matching parameters specified, your preference with the actual physical fonts available.

HFONT CreateFontIndirect(lpLogFont)

Function   Creates a logical font based on the parameters specified in the *lpLogFont* data structure.

Parameters   *lpLogFont* (LOGFONT FAR *) is a pointer to a *logfont* data structure defining the logical font's characteristics.

Value Returned   Null is returned if the function was unsuccessful; otherwise, the value returned identifies the created logical font.

Notes   **CreateFontIndirect** is identical in purpose to **CreateFont**, with the exception that the "matching" parameters are stored in a data structure pointed to by *lpLogFont* rather than being explicitly declared. For a complete analysis of the various font-matching options, see the Parameters section of the **CreateFont** function.

HBRUSH CreateHatchBrush(nIndex,rgbColor)

Function   Creates a logical brush with the defined color and hatch pattern. Once created, the brush can then be selected as the current brush for any device.

Parameters

nIndex (short) selects one of the following hatch styles for the brush:

HS_BDIAGONAL	45-degree left-to-right cross-hatching (upward)
HS_CROSS	Horizontal and vertical cross-hatching
HS_DIAGCROSS	45-degree cross-hatching
HS_FDIAGONAL	45-degree left-to-right cross-hatching (downward)
HS_HORIZONTAL	Horizontal cross-hatching
HS_VERTICAL	Vertical cross-hatching

rgbColor (DWORD) selects an RGB color for the color of the hatch lines to be drawn.

Value Returned   The value returned identifies the logical brush that has been created. An unsuccessful attempt will return a null.

HMENU CreateMenu( )

Function   Creates a menu. While the created menu is initially empty, it can be filled by using the **ChangeMenu** function.

Parameters   None.

Value Returned   Identifies the newly created menu. A null value indicates an unsuccessful attempt.

HPALETTE CreatePalette(lpLogPalette)

Function   Creates a logical color palette.

Parameters   *lpLogPalette* (PALETTE FAR *) is a pointer to a *logpalette* data structure.

Value Returned   Specifies a logical palette if the function was successful; otherwise, it is null.

HBRUSH CreatePatternBrush(hBitmap)

Function   Using the *hBitmap* parameter, creates a logical brush with the selected pattern.

Parameters   *hBitmap* (HBITMAP) points to a previously created bitmap, with a minimum-sized pattern fill bitmap of 8×8.

Value Returned   Identifies either the created logical brush or a null for an unsuccessful attempt.

Notes   Once created, the brush pattern can be selected for any device that supports raster operations. Logical pattern brushes can be deleted with a call to **DeleteObject** without affecting the bitmap used to create the brush, thereby allowing the bitmap to be used to create other pattern brushes.

HPEN CreatePen(nPenStyle,nWidth,rgbColor)

Function   Creates a logical pen based on the style, width, and color selected.

Parameters

nPenStyle (short) selects the pen style from a list of six possibilities:

Constant	Pen Style
0	Solid
1	Dash
2	Dot
3	Dash-dot
4	Dash-dot-dot
5	Null

nWidth (short) defines the pen's width in logical units.

rgbColor (DWORD) selects an RGB color for the pen.

Value Returned   Either identifies that the logical pen is successful or returns a null.

Notes   Any pen created with a physical width greater than 1 pixel will always have either a solid or null style.

HPEN CreatePenIndirect(lpLogPen)

Function   Creates a logical pen based on the parameters stored in the data structure pointed to by lpLogPen.

Parameters   *lpLogPen* (LOGPEN FAR *) is a pointer to a *logpen* data structure.

Value Returned   Identifies either a valid logical pen or null for an unsuccessful attempt.

Notes   See the **CreatePen** function section for an explanation of the pen's possible appearances.

HRGN CreatePolygonRgn(lpPoints,nCount,nPolyFillMode)

Function   Creates a polygon region.

Parameters

lpPoints (LPPOINT) is a pointer to a *point* data structure that identifies the X and Y coordinates of one angle of the polygon.

nCount (short) identifies the number of elements in the array.

nPolyFillMode (short) selects either an alternate or winding polygon-filling mode.

Value Returned   Either identifies that the new region is successful or returns null.

HMENU CreatePopupMenu( )

Function   Creates and returns a handle to an empty pop-up menu. Using the **InsertMenu** and **AppendMenu** functions, an application can add items to the pop-up menu.

Parameters   None.

Value Returned   Specifies the newly created menu if successful, null otherwise.

HRGN CreateRectRgn(x1,y1,x2,y2)

Function   Creates a rectangle.

Parameters

x1 (short) is the upper-left corner X coordinate.

y1 (short) is the upper-left corner Y coordinate.

x2 (short) is the lower-right corner X coordinate.

y2 (short) is the lower-right corner Y coordinate.

Value Returned   Returned value identifies the newly created rectangular region; otherwise, an unsuccessful attempt will return a null.

Notes   The width and height of the rectangle, defined by the absolute value of $x2-x1$ and $y2-y1$, must not exceed 32,767.

HRGN CreateRectRgnIndirect(lpRect)

Function   Creates a rectangle. This function is identical to the **CreateRectRgn** function, except that its parameters are passed in a RECT data structure rather than being explicitly defined.

Parameters   *lpRect* (LPRECT) is a pointer to a *rect* data structure containing the upper-left and lower-right limits for the rectangular region to be created.

Value Returned   Returned value identifies the newly created rectangular region; otherwise, an unsuccessful attempt will return a null.

Notes   The width and height of the rectangle must not exceed 32,767.

HRGN CreateRoundRectRgn(x1,y1,x2,y2,x3,y3)

Function   Creates a rounded rectangular region.

Parameters

x1 (int) identifies the logical X coordinate of the upper-left corner of the region.

y1 (int) identifies the logical Y coordinate of the upper-left corner of the region.

x2 (int) identifies the logical X coordinate of the lower-right corner of the region.

y2 (int) identifies the logical Y coordinate of the lower-right corner of the region.

x3 (int) identifies the width of the ellipse that will be used to draw the rounded corners.

y3 (int) identifies the height of the ellipse that will be used to draw the rounded corners.

Value Returned   A nonzero value indicates that the region was successfully drawn. A zero value indicates an unsuccessful draw.

HBRUSH CreateSolidBrush(rgbColor)

Function   Creates a logical brush using the selected color.

Parameters   *rgbColor* (DWORD) selects an RGB color for the brush.

Value Returned   If successful the return value identifies the newly created solid brush; otherwise, a null return indicates an unsuccessful creation attempt.

HWND CreateWindow(lpClassName,lpWindowName, dwStyle,x,y,nWidth,nHeight,hWndParent,hMenu, hInstance,lpParam)

Function   This frequently invoked Windows function creates either an overlapped, pop-up, or child window specifying the window's class, title, and style and can even set the window's initial position and size. If the window to be created has an owning parent or menu, this is also defined.

The function also sends the necessary messages, WM_CREATE, WM_GETMINMAXINFO, and WM_NCCREATE, to the window. If the WS_VISIBLE style option has been selected, all necessary window messages are sent to activate and visually display the window.

Parameters

lpClassName (LPSTR) points to a null-terminated character string naming the window's class.

lpWindowName (LPSTR) points to a null-terminated character string identifying the window by name.

x (int) defines the initial X coordinate position for the window.

Window Type	Description
Overlapped or Pop-Up	X coordinate of the window's upper-left corner in screen coordinates. If the value is CW_USEDEFAULT, Windows selects the default upper-left X coordinate.
Child	X coordinate of the upper-left corner of the window in the client area of its parent window.

y (int) defines the initial Y coordinate position for the window.

Window Type	Description
Overlapped or Pop-Up	Y coordinate of the window's upper-left corner in screen coordinates. If the value is CW_USEDEFAULT, Windows selects the default upper-left Y coordinate.
Child	Y coordinate of the upper-left corner of the window in the client area of its parent window.

nWidth (int) using device units, defines the width of the window.

Window Type	Description
Overlapped	Either the window's width in screen coordinates or CW_USEDEFAULT. If the latter, Windows selects the width and height for the window.

nHeight (int), using device units, defines the height of the window.

Window Type	Description
Overlapped	Either the window's height in screen coordinates or CW_USEDEFAULT. If the latter, Windows ignores *nHeight*.

hWndParent (HWND) specifies the parent window for the window that is about to be created. Overlapped windows must not have a parent (*hWndParent* must be null). A valid parent handle must be passed when creating a child window.

hMenu (HMENU), depending on the window's style, specifies a menu or a child-window identifier.

Window Type	Description
Overlapped or Pop-Up	Identifies the menu to be used with the window. A null value specifies the use of the class menu.
Child	Contains a child-window identifier. This is determined by the application and is to be unique for all child windows of the same parent.

hInstance (HANDLE) specifies the instance of the module to be identified with the window.

lpParam (LPSTR) is a pointer to the value passed to the window through the *lParam* parameter of the WM_CREATE message.

Value Returned   Either a valid new window identifier, if successful, or a null.

Notes   The following seven tables provide an alphabetical listing of window control classes (Table C-1), window styles (Table C-2), and control styles (Tables C-3 through C-7).

Table C-1.   Possible Control Classes

Class	Description
BUTTON	This identifies a small rectangular child window displaying a button the user can turn on or off with a mouse click. Buttons usually change display appearance when selected and deselected. BUTTON Control Styles BS_AUTOCHECKBOX BS_AUTORADIOBUTTON BS_AUTO3STATE BS_CHECKBOX BS_DEFPUSHBUTTON BS_GROUPBOX BS_LEFTTEXT BS_PUSHBUTTON BS_RADIOBUTTON BS_3STATE BS_USERBUTTON
EDIT	This identifies a small, rectangular child window in which the user can enter text from the keyboard. Input focus can be changed by clicking the mouse button or using TAB. Edit control classes allow the user to repeatedly select the input focus, make entries, backspace over mistakes, and reenter information. The user inserts text whenever the control display exhibits a flashing caret. EDIT Control Styles ES_AUTOHSCROLL ES_AUTOVSCROLL ES_CENTER

Table C-1.   Possible Control Classes (*continued*)

Class	Description
EDIT (*continued*)	ES_LEFT ES_MULTILINE ES_NOHIDESEL ES_RIGHT
LISTBOX	This identifies a list of character strings. Most frequently used when an application needs to present a list of names, such as available file names, from which the user can select. Options are selected by moving the mouse and clicking on the selected item. This causes the item to be highlighted and a notification of the choice to be passed to the parent window. Whenever the list is long, LISTBOX controls can be used in conjunction with SCROLLBAR controls. LISTBOX Control Styles LBS_MULTIPLESEL LBS_NOREDRAW LBS_NOTIFY LBS_SORT LBS_STANDARD
SCROLLBAR	The SCROLLBAR control displays a stretched rectangular box containing a page position reference, sometimes called a "thumb," along with direction arrows at both ends. The user selects a position within the list by sliding the thumb up or down the bar. SCROLLBAR controls are identical in appearance to scroll bars used in ordinary windows; however, they may appear anywhere within a window. Automatically associated with the SCROLLBAR controls is a SIZEBOX control. This small rectangle allows the user to change the size of the window. SCROLLBAR Control Styles SBS_BOTTOMALIGN

Table C-1.   Possible Control Classes (*continued*)

Class	Description
SCROLLBAR (*continued*)	SBS_HORZ SBS_LEFTALIGN SBS_RIGHTALIGN SBS_SIZEBOX SBS_SIZEBOXBOTTOMRIGHTALIGN SBS_SIZEBOXTOPLEFTALIGN SBS_TOPALIGN SBS_VERT
STATIC	The STATIC control class defines a simple text field, box, or rectangle, which is most frequently used to identify, box, or separate other controls. It therefore outputs or inputs information. STATIC Control Styles SS_BLACKFRAME SS_BLACKRECT SS_CENTER SS_GRAYFRAME SS_GRAYRECT SS_ICON SS_LEFT SS_RIGHT SS_SIMPLE SS_USERITEM SS_WHITEFRAME SS_WHITERECT

Table C-2.   Possible Window Styles

Style	Description
WS_BORDER	Creates a bordered window.
WS_CAPTION	Adds a title bar to the bordered window.
WS_CHILD	Creates a child window. Not to be used with WS_POPUP style windows.

Table C-2.   Possible Window Styles (*continued*)

Style	Description
WS_CHILDWINDOW	Creates a child window of the WS_CHILD style.
WS_CLIPCHILDREN	Used when creating the parent window. The WS_CLIPCHILDREN window style prohibits drawing of the parent window within the area occupied by any child window.
WS_CLIPSIBLINGS	Used with the WS_CHILD style only. This style clips all other child windows whenever a particular child window receives a paint message. Without this, it would be possible to draw within the client area of another child window.
WS_DISABLED	Creates an initially disabled window.
WS_DLGFRAME	Creates a double-bordered window without a title.
WS_GROUP	Used only by dialog boxes. This window style defines the first control of a group of controls. The user can move from one control to another by using the direction keys.
WS_HSCROLL	Creates a window with a horizontal scroll bar.
WS_ICONIC	Used with the WS_OVERLAPPED style. WS_ICONIC creates a window that is initially displayed in its iconic form.
WS_MAXIMIZE	Creates a window of maximum size.
WS_MAXIMIZEBOX	Creates a window that includes a maximize box.
WS_MINIMIZE	Creates a window of minimum size.
WS_MINIMIZEBOX	Creates a window that includes a minimize box.
WS_OVERLAPPED	Creates an overlapped window.
WS_OVERLAPPEDWINDOW	Uses the WS_CAPTION, WS_OVERLAPPED, WS_THICKFRAME, and WS_SYSMENU styles to create an overlapped window.
WS_POPUP	Not to be used with WS_CHILD style. Creates a pop-up window.
WS_POPUPWINDOW	Uses the WS_BORDER, WS_POPUP, and WS_SYSMENU styles to create a pop-up window.

Table C-2.   Possible Window Styles (*continued*)

Style	Description
WS_SYSMENU	Used only with windows including title bars. Creates a window with a system-menu box displayed in its title bar. When used with a child window, this style creates only a close box instead of the standard system-menu box.
WS_TABSTOP	Used only by dialog boxes. Indicates any number of controls the user can move by using TAB. Successive presses of TAB move through the controls specified by the WS_TABSTOP style.
WS_THICKFRAME	Creates a thick-framed window that can be used to size the window.
WS_VISIBLE	Creates a window that is automatically displayed. Can be used with overlapped and pop-up windows.
WS_VSCROLL	Creates a window with a vertical scroll bar.

Table C-3.   BUTTON Class Control Styles

Style	Description
BS_AUTOCHECKBOX	Identical in usage to BS_CHECKBOX, except that the button automatically toggles its state when the user selects it by clicking the mouse button.
BS_AUTORADIOBUTTON	Identical in usage to BS_RADIOBUTTON, except that when the button is selected, a BN_CLICKED message is sent to the application, removing check marks from any other radio buttons in the group.
BS_AUTO3STATE	Identical to BS_3STATE, except that the button automatically toggles its state when the user selects it by clicking the mouse button.

Table C-3.   BUTTON Class Control Styles (*continued*)

Style	Description
BS_CHECKBOX	Defines a small rectangular button that can be checked. The check box is shown in bold when it is selected. Any associated text is printed to the right of the button.
BS_DEFPUSHBUTTON	Defines a small elliptical bold-bordered button. Usually used to identify a user default response. Any associated text is displayed within the button.
BS_GROUPBOX	Defines a rectangular region bounding a button group. Text is displayed within the rectangle's upper-left corner.
BS_LEFTTEXT	Forces text to be displayed on the left side of the radio or check box button. Can be used with the control styles BS_3STATE, BS_CHECKBOX, or BS_RADIOBUTTON.
BS_PUSHBUTTON	Defines a small elliptical button containing the specified text. This control sends a message to the parent window whenever the user clicks the button.
BS_RADIOBUTTON	Defines a small circular button with a border that is shown in bold when it has been selected with a mouse button click. The parent window is also notified via a message. A subsequent click produces a normal border, and another message is sent to the parent window indicating the change.
BS_3STATE	Identical to BS_CHECKBOX, but the button can be grayed as well as checked. The grayed state is a visual reminder that the current check box has been disabled.
BS_USERBUTTON	Defines a user-designated button. The parent window is notified when the button is clicked, sending a request to paint, invert, and disable the button.

Table C-4.   EDIT Class Control Styles

Style	Description
ES_AUTOHSCROLL	Automatically scrolls text to the right ten characters whenever the user enters data at the end of a line. When the user presses ENTER the text scrolls back to the left edge border.
ES_AUTOVSCROLL	Automatically scrolls text up one page when the user presses ENTER at the last line.
ES_CENTER	Centers text.
ES_LEFT	Uses flush-left text alignment.
ES_MULTILINE	Provides multiple-line editing control. When used in conjunction with the ES_AUTOVSCROLL style, scrolls text vertically when the user presses ENTER. If ES_AUTOVSCROLL style is not specified, it beeps when the user presses ENTER, and no more lines can be displayed. A similar condition exists when used with the ES_AUTOHSCROLL style. If selected, the style will allow the user to remain on the same line, shifting text to the left. When deactivated, text not fitting on the same line within the window causes a new line to be created. ES_MULTILINE styles can include scroll bars.
ES_NOHIDESEL	Overrides the default action, preventing the edit control from hiding the selection whenever the control loses the input focus, and does not invert the selection when the control receives the input focus.
ES_RIGHT	Uses flush-right text alignment.

Table C-5.   STATIC Class Control Styles

Style	Description
SS_BLACKFRAME	Defines a box with a black frame.
SS_BLACKRECT	Defines a black-filled rectangle.
SS_CENTER	Takes the given text and centers it within a simple rectangle. All text is formatted. Any text not fitting on one line is automatically wrapped to the next line, with the next line also being automatically centered.

Table C-5.   STATIC Class Control Styles (*continued*)

Style	Description
SS_GRAYFRAME	Defines a gray-framed box.
SS_GRAYRECT	Defines a gray-filled rectangle.
SS_ICON	Automatically sizes and displays an icon within the dialog box.
SS_LEFT	Similar to SS_CENTER except the text displayed within the rectangle is aligned flush left. This includes auto word-wrap and next line flush-left alignment.
SS_RIGHT	Similar to SS_CENTER except the text displayed within the rectangle is aligned flush right. This includes auto word-wrap and next line flush-right alignment.
SS_SIMPLE	Defines a rectangle that will display a single line of flush-left aligned text.
SS_USERITEM	Defines a user-defined item.
SS_WHITEFRAME	Defines a white-framed box.
SS_WHITERECT	Defines a white-filled rectangle.

Table C-6.   LISTBOX Class Control Styles

Style	Description
LBS_MULTIPLESEL	Allows for the selection of any number of strings, with the string selection toggling each time the user clicks or double-clicks on the string.
LBS_NOREDRAW	The LISTBOX display is not updated when changes are made.
LBS_NOTIFY	Whenever the user clicks or double-clicks on a string, the parent window receives an input message.
LBS_SORT	Sorts the strings in the LISTBOX alphabetically.
LBS_STANDARD	Sorts the strings within the LISTBOX alphabetically, sending a message to the parent window whenever the user clicks or double-clicks on a string. The LISTBOX contains a vertical scroll bar and borders on all sides.

Table C-7.   SCROLLBAR Class Control Styles

Style	Description
SBS_BOTTOMALIGN	Used in conjunction with SBS_HORZ style. Scroll bar alignment is along the bottom edge of the rectangle defined by x, y, nWidth, and nHeight, using the system default scroll bar height.
SBS_HORZ	Defines a horizontal scroll bar. The height, width, and position of the scroll bar will be determined by the **CreateWindow** function if neither SBS_BOTTOMALIGN nor SBS_TOPALIGN style is requested.
SBS_LEFTALIGN	Used in conjunction with SBS_VERT style. Here the left edge of the scroll bar is aligned with the left edge of a rectangle defined by x, y, nWidth, and nHeight, using the system default scroll bar height.
SBS_RIGHTALIGN	Used in conjunction with SBS_VERT style. Here the right edge of the scroll bar is aligned with the right edge of a rectangle defined by x, y, nWidth, and nHeight, using the system default scroll bar height.
SBS_SIZEBOX	Defines a size box. The size box will have the height, width, and position given by the **CreateWindow** function if neither the SBS_SIZEBOXBOTTOMRIGHTALIGN nor the SBS_SIZEBOXTOPLEFTALIGN style is selected.
SBS_SIZEBOXBOTTOMRIGHTALIGN	Used in conjunction with the SBS_SIZEBOX style. Here the lower-right corner of the scroll bar is aligned with the lower-right corner of a rectangle defined by x, y, nWidth, and nHeight, using the system default scroll bar height.

Table C-7.   SCROLLBAR Class Control Styles (*continued*)

Style	Description
SBS_SIZEBOXTOPLEFTALIGN	Used in conjunction with the SBS_SIZEBOX style. Here the upper-left corner of the scroll bar is aligned with the upper-left corner of a rectangle defined by *x, y, nWidth*, and *nHeight*, using the system default scroll bar height.
SBS_TOPALIGN	Used in conjunction with SBS_HORZ style. Scroll bar alignment is along the top edge of the rectangle defined by *x, y, nWidth*, and *nHeight*, using the system default scroll bar height.
SBS_VERT	Defines a vertical scroll bar. The height, width, and position of the scroll bar will be determined by the **CreateWindow** function if neither the SBS_RIGHTALIGN nor the SBS_LEFTALIGN style is requested.

HWND CreateWindowEX(dwExStyle,lpClassName, lpWindowName,dwStyle,x,y,nWidth,nHeight, hWndParent,hMenu,hInstance,lpParam)

Function   Creates an overlapped, pop-up, or child window with an extended style. Otherwise, the function is identical to the **CreateWindow** function.

Parameters

dwExStyle (DWORD) defines the extended style of the window being created. Can be set to WS_EXDLGMODALFRAME; this causes the window to be drawn with a modal dialog frame.

lpClassName (LPSTR) points to a null-terminated character string naming the window's class.

lpWindowName (LPSTR) points to a null-terminated character string identifying the window by name.

dwStyle (DWORD) specifies the style of window being created.

x (int) defines the initial X coordinate position for the window.

Window Type	Description
Overlapped or Pop-Up	X coordinate of the window's upper-left corner in screen coordinates. If the value is CW_USEDEFAULT, Windows selects the default upper-left X coordinate.
Child	X coordinate of the upper-left corner of the window in the client area of its parent window.

y (int) defines the initial Y coordinate position for the window.

Window Type	Description
Overlapped or Pop-Up	Y coordinate of the window's upper-left corner in screen coordinates. If the value is CW_USEDEFAULT, Windows selects the default upper-left Y coordinate.
Child	Y coordinate of the upper-left corner of the window in the client area of its parent window.

nWidth (int), using device units, defines the width of the window.

Window Type	Description
Overlapped	Either the window's width in screen coordinates or CW_USEDEFAULT. If the latter, Windows selects the width and height for the window.

nHeight (int), using device units, defines the height of the window.

Window Type	Description
Overlapped	Either the window's height in screen coordinates or CW_USEDEFAULT. If the latter, Windows ignores *nHeight*.

hWndParent (HWND) specifies the parent window for the window that is about to be created. Overlapped windows must not have a parent (*hWndParent* must be null). A valid parent handle must be passed when creating a child window.

hMenu (HMENU), depending on the window's style, specifies a menu or a child-window identifier.

Window Type	Description
Overlapped or Pop-Up	Identifies the menu to be used with the window. A null value specifies the use of the class menu.
Child	Contains a child-window identifier. This is determined by the application and is to be unique for all child windows of the same parent.

hInstance (HANDLE) specifies the instance of the module to be identified with the window.

lpParam (LPSTR) is a pointer to the value passed to the window through the *lParam* parameter of the WM_CREATE message.

Value Returned   A valid new window identifier if successful; otherwise, returns a null.

Notes   See the **CreateWindow** function for window control classes, window styles, and control styles.

BOOL DeleteDC(hDC)

Function   Deletes the designated device context.

Parameters   *hDC* (HDC) identifies the device context.

Value Returned   For a successful delete, a nonzero value is returned; otherwise, the return value is zero.

Notes   If the device context to be deleted is the last device context for a given device, the device is notified with all subsequent system storage resources used by the device being released.

BOOL DeleteMenu(hMenu,nPosition,wFlags)

Function   Deletes an item from the menu.

Parameters

hMenu (HMENU) specifies the menu to be changed.

nPosition (WORD) defines the menu item to be deleted.

wFlags (WORD) defines how the *nPosition* parameter is to be interpreted. The default is MF_BYCOMMAND, but it can also be set to MF_BYPOSITION.

Value Returned   TRUE if the function is successful, FALSE otherwise.

Notes   MF_POSITION specifies the position of the menu item, with the first item being numbered 0. However, if MF_BYCOMMAND is specified, *nPosition* specifies the ID of the existing menu item.

BOOL DeleteObject(hObject)

Function   Deletes a logical font, pen, brush, bitmap, or region from memory.

Parameters   *hObject* (HANDLE) represents a handle to the object (font, pen, brush, bitmap, or region).

Value Returned   A successful delete returns a nonzero value; otherwise, a zero is returned indicating that the handle was not valid.

Notes   To delete an object selected into a device context, the device context must be deleted first, followed by the deletion of the object itself.

BOOL DestroyMenu(hMenu)

Function   Destroys and frees any system memory associated with the menu pointed to by *hMenu*.

Parameters   *hMenu* (HMENU) defines the menu to be deleted.

Value Returned   A nonzero value is returned for a successful menu deletion; otherwise, a null is returned.

BOOL DestroyWindow(hWnd)

Function   Destroys the designated window. This complicated process of destroying a window involves possibly hiding or permanently closing the window. Also, messages are sent to the window to deactivate it or remove its input focus. Destroying the window additionally involves sending a message to flush the associated message queue. Messages sent include WM_DESTROY and WM_NCDESTROY.

Parameters   *hWnd* (HWND) indicates the window to be destroyed.

Value Returned   A nonzero value is returned for a successful menu deletion; otherwise a null is returned.

Notes   Should the parent window have any children, the associated child windows will be destroyed first, followed by the owning parent window.

int DialogBox(hInstance,lpTemplateName,hWndParent, lpDialogFunc)

Function   Creates a modal dialog box.

Parameters

hInstance (HANDLE) specifies the instance of the module whose executable file contains the dialog box template.

lpTemplateName (LPSTR) points to a null-terminated character string naming the dialog box template.

hWndParent (HWND) specifies the window that owns the dialog box.

lpDialogFunc (FARPROC) contains the current procedure-instance address of the dialog function. The callback function must use the Pascal calling convention and be declared FAR using the following form:

```
HWND FAR PASCAL DialogFunc(hWnd,wMsg,wParam,lParam)
HWND hwnd;     /* identifies the message receiving the
                  dialog box                          */
unsigned wMsg;/* indicates the message number  */
WORD wParam;   /* specifies 16 bits of additional
                  message-dependent information */
DWORD lParam; /* specifies 32 bits of additional
                  message-dependent information */
```

Value Returned   Values returned by an application's dialog box are not processed by the application; instead they are processed by Windows. The return value is −1 if the function fails.

Notes   The size, style, and controls for the dialog box are referenced by the *lpTemplateName* parameter. Care should be taken since the **DialogBox** function first calls **GetDC** to obtain the display context. If the Windows display context cache has been filled by making calls to **GetDC**, **DialogBox** could accidentally access some other display context.

int DialogBoxIndirect(hInstance,hDTemplate, hWndParent,lpDialogFunc)

Function   Similar to the **DialogBox** function in that it will create a modal dialog box. However, instead of explicitly defining each parameter, the *hDTemplate* parameter points to a *dlgtemplate* data structure containing the equivalent information.

Parameters

hInstance (HANDLE) specifies the instance of the module whose executable file contains the dialog box template.

hDTemplate (HANDLE) identifies a *dlgtemplate* data structure.

hWndParent (HWND) specifies the window that owns the dialog box.

lpDialogFunc (FARPROC) contains the current procedure-instance address of the dialog function. The callback function must use the Pascal calling convention and be declared FAR using the following form:

```
HWND FAR PASCAL DialogFunc(hWnd,wMsg,wParam,lParam)
HWND hwnd;      /* identifies message receiving
                   dialog box                    */
unsigned wMsg; /* indicates the message number  */
WORD wParam;   /* specifies 16 bits of additional
                   message-dependent information */
DWORD lParam;  /* specifies 32 bits of additional
                   message-dependent information */
```

Value Returned   Values returned by an application's dialog box are not processed by the application; instead, they are processed by Windows. The return value is −1 if the function fails.

Notes   The size, style, and controls for the dialog box are referenced by the *lpTemplateName* parameter. Care should be taken since the **DialogBox** function first calls **GetDC** to obtain the display context. If the Windows display context cache has been filled by making calls to **GetDC**, **DialogBox** could accidentally access some other display context.

LONG DispatchMessage(lpMsg)

Function   Sends a message from the MSG data structure pointed to by *lpMsg*. The message is sent to the window function of the designated window.

Parameters   *lpMsg* (LPMSG) is a pointer to a *msg* data structure. This structure contains message information from the Windows application queue.

Value Returned   The return value is determined by the window function. Generally, the returned value is not used; however, its meaning is dependent on the message that is actually being dispatched.

Notes   The *msg* data structure must only contain valid message values.

BOOL DrawIcon(hDC,x,y,hIcon)

Function   Draws an icon on the selected device.

Parameters

hDC (HDC) represents the device context for a window.

x (int) defines the logical upper-left corner X coordinate of the icon.

y (int) defines the logical upper-left corner Y coordinate of the icon.

hIcon (HICON) specifies the icon to be drawn.

Value Returned   A nonzero value is returned for a successful menu deletion; otherwise, a null is returned.

Notes   Subject to the current mapping mode of the device context, the icon's upper-left corner will be placed at the location represented by the X and Y coordinates.

int DrawText(hDC,lpString,nCount,lpRect,wFormat)

Function   Draws formatted text within a rectangle. The text tabs are expanded as needed, as left, right, or center aligned, with each line of text broken as necessary to make certain that all lines fit within the defined area.

Parameters

hDC (HDC) specifies the device context.

lpString (LPSTR) is a pointer to the string to be drawn. However, if the *nCount* value is −1, the string pointed to must be null-terminated.

nCount (int) represents the number of bytes the string occupies. When *nCount* is −1, the **DrawText** function assumes *lpString* is null-terminated. Under these conditions the function automatically computes the character count.

lpRect (LPRECT) is a pointer to a *rect* data structure containing the diagonal coordinates (logical units) for the rectangle the text must fit within.

wFormat (WORD) indicates the type of formatting to use. The values can be combined using the logical OR operation:

DrawText Formats	Description
DT_BOTTOM	Selects single-line, bottom-justified text.
DT_CALCRECT	For single-line text the right side of the rectangle will be modified to contain the entire string. For multiple-line text the rectangle width remains as defined; however, the height of the rectangle is modified to accommodate the entire text. Both modes return the resulting height of the rectangle.
DT_CENTER	Centers the text.
DT_EXPANDTABS	Expands the tabs.
DT_EXTERNALLEADING	Incorporates the font's external leading into the line height. Normally, this is not included.
DT_LEFT	Aligns text flush left.
DT_NOCLIP	Draws without clipping.
DT_NOPREFIX	Ignores processing of prefix characters. When left on, the **DrawText** function uses the & character to indicate that the string should be underlined. && signals the printing of a single &.
DT_RIGHT	Aligns text flush right.
DT_SINGLELINE	Defines a single line, ignoring all carriage returns and linefeeds.
DT_TABSTOP	Defines tab stops with the high byte of the *wFormat* parameter representing the number of characters for each tab stop.
DT_TOP	Selects single-line top-justified text.
DT_VCENTER	Selects vertically centered single-line text.

DT_WORDBREAK   Activates word breaking. Allows text to be
                                     broken between lines to accommodate string
                                     length in respect to the rectangular perimeter.

Value Returned   The returned value represents the height of the text.

Notes   **DrawText** uses the selected device context's font, text color, and
background color for drawing the text. All formatting assumes multiple
lines unless DT_SINGLELINE is specified.

BOOL Ellipse(hDC,x1,y1,x2,y2)

Function   Draws an ellipse.

Parameters

hDC (HDC) specifies the device context.

x1 (short) defines the upper-left corner X coordinate of the rectangle.

y1 (short) defines the upper-left corner Y coordinate of the bounding
rectangle.

x2 (short) defines the lower-right corner X coordinate of the bounding
rectangle.

y2 (short) defines the lower-right corner Y coordinate of the bounding
rectangle.

Value Returned   A nonzero value indicates a successful ellipse creation;
otherwise, a zero value indicates an unsuccessful attempt.

Notes   The width and height of the rectangle must not exceed 32,767
units.

BOOL
EnableMenuItem(hMenu,wIDEnableItem,wEnable)

Function   Enables, disables, or grays a menu item.

Parameters

hMenu (HMENU) identifies the menu.

wIDEnableItem (WORD) identifies the menu or pop-up menu item to be checked.

wEnable (WORD) specifies the action to take. The options can be logically ORed together:

Option	Description
MF_BYCOMMAND	Indicates that the *wIDEnableItem* parameter contains the menu item ID
MF_BYPOSITION	Indicates that the *wIDEnableItem* parameter contains the position of the menu item
MF-DISABLED	Disables the menu item
MF_ENABLED	Enables the menu item
MF_GRAYED	Grays the menu item

Value Returned   The returned value represents the previous state of the menu item.

Notes   The WM_SYSCOMMAND message can be used to enable or disable input to a menu bar.

void EndDialog(hDlg,nResult)

Function   Terminates a modal dialog box sending the result to the **Dialog-Box** function. However, the **EndDialog** function does not immediately terminate the dialog box. Initially, it sets the appropriate flag, which in turn directs the dialog box to terminate as soon as the dialog function is completed.

Parameters

hDlg (HWND) specifies the dialog box to be destroyed.

nResult (int) defines the value to be returned from the dialog box to the **DialogBox** function originally creating it.

Value Returned   None.

Notes   The dialog function can call the **EndDialog** function at any time.

void EndPaint(hWnd,lpPaint)

Function   Indicates that the painting for a given window is complete.

Parameters

hWnd (HWND) specifies the window that has been repainted.

lpPaint (LPPAINTSTRUCT) is a pointer to a *paintstruct* containing the retrieved information given by the **BeginPaint** function call.

Value Returned   None.

Notes   A call to **EndPaint** must be made for each call to the **BeginPaint** function. While a call to **BeginPaint** can hide the caret, making a call to **EndPaint** will display the caret.

int FillRect(hDC,lpRect,hBrush)

Function   Using the specified brush, fills a rectangle.

Parameters

hDC (HDC) specifies the device context.

lpRect (LPRECT) is a pointer to a *rect* structure containing the coordinates of the rectangle that will be filled with the specified brush.

hBrush (HBRUSH) selects the brush used to fill the rectangle.

Value Returned   The function returns an integer value that has no usage and is therefore ignored.

Notes   The rectangle cannot be filled unless a brush has been previously created by calling **CreateSolidBrush, CreatePatternBrush,** or **Create-HatchBrush**. The filled rectangle is brushed up to and including the upper border and left border. The bottom border and right border are left un-painted.

BOOL FillRgn(hDC,hRgn,hBrush)

Function   Paints a region using the selected brush pattern.

Parameters

hDC (HDC) specifies the device context.

hRgn (HRGN) marks the region to be filled using logical coordinates.

hBrush (HBRUSH) selects the brush to be used for filling the region.

Value Returned   A nonzero value indicates a successful outcome. A zero indicates an unsuccessful attempt.

BOOL FloodFill(hDC,x,y,rgbColor)

Function   Fills an area of the display surface bounded in the *rgbColor*. Painting begins at the X and Y coordinates specified.

Parameters

hDC (HDC) specifies the device context.

x (short) specifies the logical X coordinate of where the painting is to begin.

y (short) specifies the logical Y coordinate of where the painting is to begin.

rgbColor (DWORD) selects the RGB color value to be used to indicate the color of the border boundary.

Value Returned   A nonzero value means a successful fill; otherwise, a null is returned.

Notes   Not all device contexts support **FloodFill**.

int FrameRect(hDC,lpRect,hBrush)

Function   Using the specified brush, draws a border around the specified rectangle.

Parameters

hDC (HDC) specifies the device context.

lpRect (LPRECT) is a pointer to a *rect* structure containing the coordinates of the rectangle that will be filled with the specified brush.

hBrush (HBRUSH) selects the brush used to fill the rectangle.

Value Returned   The function returns an integer value that has no usage and is therefore ignored.

Notes   The rectangle cannot be filled unless a brush has been previously created by calling **CreateSolidBrush**, **CreatePatternBrush**, or **Create-HatchBrush**. The frame border is always drawn one logical unit in width and height.

BOOL FrameRgn(hDC,hRgn,hBrush,nWidth,nHeight)

Function   Draws a border around the specified region using the selected brush, with the defined width and height.

Parameters

hDC (HDC) specifies the device context.

hRgn (HRGN) specifies the region to be enclosed with a border.

hBrush (HBRUSH) selects the brush used to fill the rectangle.

nWidth (short), using logical units, expresses the width of the border to be drawn in vertical brush strokes.

nHeight (short), using logical units, expresses the height of the border to be drawn in horizontal brush strokes.

Value Returned   A nonzero value indicates a successful attempt; otherwise, a zero is returned.

void FreeProcInstance(lpProc)

Function   Frees the specified function from the data segment in which it was bound.

Parameters   *lpProc* (FARPROC) is the procedure-instance address of the function about to be freed.

Value Returned   None.

Notes   *lpProc* must point to a function that was previously created using the **MakeProcInstance** function. An unrecoverable error condition can occur if an attempt is made to call the function after it has been freed.

DWORD GetBkColor(hDC)

Function   Returns the current background color of the specified device.

Parameters   *hDC* (HDC) specifies the device context.

Value Returned   Indicates the current RGB background color value.

short GetBkMode(hDC)

Function   Returns the background mode for the specified device.

Parameters   *hDC* (HDC) specifies the device context.

Value Returned   Indicates the current background mode (transparent or opaque).

Notes   The background mode is important because it is used with text, hatched brushes, and nonsolid pen styles.

DWORD GetBrushOrg(hDC)

Function   Returns the current brush origin for the specified device context.

Parameters   *hDC* (HDC) specifies the device context.

Value Returned   Returns the origin of the current brush with the high-order word indicating the device unit's Y coordinate and the low-order word indicating the device unit's X coordinate.

Notes   The initial brush origin is always set at 0,0.

BOOL GetCharWidth(hDC,wFirstChar,wLastChar,lpBuffer)

Function   Using the current font, returns the widths of individual characters in consecutive groups of characters.

Parameters

hDC (HDC) specifies the device context.

wFirstChar (WORD) using the current font, specifies the first character in a consecutive group of characters.

wLastChar (WORD) using the current font, specifies the last character in a consecutive group of characters.

lpBuffer (LPINT) is a pointer to the buffer that will receive the width of each character in a group of characters.

Value Returned   A nonzero value indicates a successful function call; otherwise, zero is returned.

Notes   Any character not defined for the current font will be given a default character width, which is usually based on a blank space character.

void GetClientRect(hWnd,lpRect)

Function   Copies the coordinates of a window's client area into the *lpRect* data structure.

Parameters

hWnd (HWND) specifies the window associated with the client area.

lpRect (LPRECT) is a pointer to a *rect* structure.

Value Returned   None.

Notes   The returned coordinates represent the upper-left and lower-right corners of the client area. Client coordinates are relative to the window's upper-left corner, 0,0.

DWORD GetCurrentPosition(hDC)

Function   Retrieves the logical coordinates of the current position.

Parameters   *hDC* (HDC) specifies the device context.

Value Returned   Represents the current position, with the high-order word containing the Y coordinate and the low-order word containing the X coordinate.

void GetCursorPos(lpPoint)

Function   Returns the current cursor position using screen coordinates.

Parameters   *lpPoint* (LPPOINT) is a pointer to a *point* data structure receiving the cursor's screen coordinates.

Value Returned   None.

Notes   The current mapping mode of the window containing the cursor has no effect on the screen coordinates returned.

HDC GetDC(hWnd)

Function   Returns a handle to a display context for the client area of the specified window.

Parameters   *hWnd* (HWND) specifies the window whose display context is to be returned.

Value Returned   Indicates the display context if it is a nonzero value. An unsuccessful call returns a null.

Notes   The returned value can be used for subsequent GDI function calls that draw in the client area.

LONG GetDCOrg(hDC)

Function   Returns the translation origin for the specified device context.

Parameters   *hDC* (HDC) specifies the device context.

Value Returned   Contains the final device coordinate translation origin, with the high-order word containing the Y coordinate and the low-order word containing the X coordinate.

Notes   The returned coordinates represent the offset used by Windows to translate device coordinates into client coordinates for any points in an application's window. This is relative to the physical origin of the display screen.

HWND GetDlgItem(hDlg,nIDDlgItem)

Function   Returns the handle of the control contained in the specified dialog box.

Parameters

  hDlg (HWND) specifies the dialog box that contains the control.

  nIDDlgItem (int) represents the integer ID of the item being retrieved.

Value Returned   Indicates the given control. If no control exists, as specified by *nIDDlgItem,* a null is returned.

Notes   The function can also be used with any parent-child window pair, not just dialog boxes.

unsigned GetDlgItemInt(hDlg,nIDDlgItem,lpTranslated,bSigned)

Function   Translates the text of a control of the specified dialog box (or parent-child window pair) into an integer value.

Parameters

hDlg (HWND) specifies the dialog box that contains the control.

nIDDlgItem (int) represents the integer ID of the item being translated.

lpTranslated (BOOL FAR *) is a pointer to a Boolean variable receiving the translated flag.

bSigned (BOOL) identifies whether the retrieved value is signed.

Value Returned   Represents the translated value of the dialog box item text.

Notes   The function translates numeric characters into their equivalent signed or unsigned values. Translation skips over leading blanks and continues until either the end of the string is reached or a non-numeric character is encountered.

If a minus sign is encountered, the value returned is a signed number; otherwise, it is unsigned. A value greater than 32,767 (signed) is returned as a zero. The same is true for an unsigned value greater than 65,635. The function sends a WM_GETTEXT message to the control.

int
GetDlgItemText(hDlg,nIDDlgItem,lpString,nMaxCount)

Function   Retrieves the text associated with the specified control into a string, returning the number of characters copied.

Parameters

hDlg (HWND) specifies the dialog box that contains the control.

nIDDlgItem (int) represents the integer ID of the item being translated.

lpString (LPSTR) is a pointer to the buffer receiving the copied text.

nMaxCount (int) represents the maximum number of characters (in bytes) to be copied to *lpString*. A string longer than the value specified will automatically be truncated.

Value Returned   Returns the actual number of characters copied. A zero value indicates no text was copied.

short GetMapMode(hDC)

Function   Returns the current mapping mode.

Parameters   *hDC* (HDC) specifies the device context.

Value Returned   Represents the current mapping mode.

BOOL GetMessage(lpMsg,hWnd,wMsgFilterMin, wMsgFilterMax)

Function   The function takes a message from the application's message queue and places it in the *msg* data structure. Control is yielded if no messages are available.

Parameters

lpMsg (LPMSG) is a pointer to an *msg* structure containing message information supplied by the Windows application queue.

hWnd (HWND) specifies the window whose messages are to be retrieved. If the parameter is null, the function will retrieve any message for the window that belongs to the calling application.

wMsgFilterMin (unsigned) is an integer value indicating the lowest message to be examined.

wMsgFilterMax (unsigned) is an integer value indicating the highest message to be examined.

Value Returned   A nonzero value indicates some message other than WM_QUIT was retrieved. A zero value indicates that the message retrieved was WM_QUIT.

Notes   Using the WM_KEYFIRST and WM_KEYLAST constants will retrieve only keyboard input-related messages. The WM_MOUSEFIRST and WM_MOUSELAST constants can filter out and retrieve only those mouse-related messages.

DWORD GetMessagePos( )

Function   Returns the screen coordinate mouse position after the last message was obtained by a call to **GetMessage**.

Parameters   None.

Value Returned   The low-order word contains the X coordinate, the high-order word the Y coordinate.

Notes   By making a call to the **GetCursorPos** function instead of **GetMessagePos**, an application can obtain the current position of the mouse instead of the time the last message occurred.

DWORD GetNearestColor(hDC,rgbColor)

Function   Returns the closest physical color to a specified logical color that the requested device can represent.

Parameters

hDC (HDC) specifies the device context.

rgbColor (DWORD) identifies an RGB color value specifying the color to be matched.

Value Returned   Represents the solid RGB color closest to the rgbColor request that the device is capable of producing.

DWORD GetNearestPaletteIndex(hPalette,rgbColor)

Function   Returns the index specifier of the entry in the logical palette that most closely matches an RGB color value.

Parameters

hPalette (HPALETTE) specifies the logical palette.

rgbColor (DWORD) identifies an RGB color value that specifies the color to be matched.

Value Returned   The logical-palette index that most nearly matches the RGB value.

short GetObject(hObject,nCount,lpObject)

Function   Assigns the logical data information defining a logical object to the buffer pointed to by *lpObject*.

Parameters

hObject (HANDLE) specifies a logical font, pen, brush, or bitmap.

nCount (short) represents the number of bytes to be copied to the buffer.

lpObject (LPSTR) is a pointer to a *logfont, logpen, logbrush,* or *logbitmap* data structure that will receive the logical object information.

Value Returned   Specifies the number of bytes actually retrieved. If null, some error condition has occurred.

Notes   If the logical information being retrieved involves a bitmap, the function will only return the width, height, and color format bitmap information. To retrieve the actual bitmap, a call must be made to **GetBitmapBits**.

WORD GetPaletteEntries(hPalette,wStartIndex, wNumEntries,lpBuffer)

Function   Copies the RGB color values and flags contained in a range of entries in a logical palette to a buffer.

Parameters

hPalette (HPALETTE) specifies the logical palette.

wStartIndex (WORD) defines the first entry in the logical palette to be copied.

wNumEntries (WORD) defines the number of entries in the logical palette to be copied.

lpBuffer (LPSTR) is a pointer to a buffer to receive the palette entries.

Value Returned   The number of entries copied. It is zero if the function failed.

DWORD GetPixel(hDC,x,y,)

Function   The RGB color value of the point specified by x and y and within the clipping region is returned.

Parameters

hDC (HDC) specifies the device context.

x (short) defines the logical upper-left corner X coordinate of the point to be inspected.

y (short) defines the logical upper-left corner Y coordinate of the point to be inspected.

Value Returned   Contains the RGB color value of the point referenced. A -1 value indicates the point was not within the clipping region.

Notes   Not all device contexts support this function.

short GetPolyFillMode(hDC)

Function   Returns the current polygon filling mode (alternate or winding).

Parameters   *hDC* (HDC) specifies the device context.

Value Returned   Alternate, for alternate polygon filling mode, or winding, for winding polygon filling mode.

short GetROP2(hDC)

Function   Returns the current drawing mode.

Parameters   *hDC* (HDC) specifies the device context.

Value Returned   Specifies the previous drawing mode.

Notes   The current drawing mode determines how the selected pen or interior color will be combined with the color already on the display.

int GetScrollPos(hWnd,nBar)

Function   Returns the current position of the specified scroll bar thumb.

Parameters

hWnd (HWND) identifies the window containing the standard scroll bar.

nBar (int) identifies the scroll bar to examine using one of the following values:

Value	Definition
SB_CTL	Returns the position of a scroll bar control, assuming that *hWnd* points to a window handle of a scroll bar control

SB_HORZ	Returns the position of a window's horizontal scroll bar
SB_VERT	Returns the position of a window's vertical scroll bar

Value Returned   Identifies the current position of the scroll bar thumb.

Notes   The returned value is a relative value depending on the current scrolling range. For example, a range of 0 to 50 would yield a mid-position value of 25.

void GetScrollRange(hWnd,nBar,lpMinPos,lpMaxPos)

Function   Returns the current minimum and maximum scroll bar positions for the defined scroll bar.

Parameters

hWnd (HWND) specifies the window that has a standard scroll bar or scroll bar control.

nBar (int) identifies the scroll bar to examine using one of the following values:

Value	Definition
SB_CTL	Returns the position of a scroll bar control, assuming that *hWnd* points to a window handle of a scroll bar control
SB_HORZ	Returns the position of a window's horizontal scroll bar
SB_VERT	Returns the position of a window's vertical scroll bar

lpMinPos (LPINT) is a pointer to an integer variable that will receive the scroll bar's minimum position value.

lpMaxPos (LPINT) is a pointer to an integer variable that will receive the scroll bar's maximum position value.

Value Returned   None.

Notes   The default range for a standard scroll bar is 0 to 100.

HANDLE GetStockObject(nIndex)

Function   Returns the handle to a predefined stock font, pen, or brush.

Parameters

nIndex (short) identifies the type of stock object to be returned.

Value	Definition
BLACK_BRUSH	Black brush
DKGRAY_BRUSH	Dark gray brush
GRAY_BRUSH	Gray brush
HOLLOW_BRUSH	Hollow brush
LTGRAY_BRUSH	Light gray brush
NULL_BRUSH	Null brush
WHITE_BRUSH	White brush
BLACK_PEN	Black pen
NULL_PEN	Null pen
WHITE_PEN	White pen
ANSI_FIXED_FONT	ANSI fixed system font
ANSI_VAR_FONT	ANSI proportional system font
DEVICE_DEFAULT_FONT	Device-dependent font
OEM_FIXED_FONT	OEM-supplied fixed font
SYSTEM_FONT	System-dependent fixed font

Value Returned   Identifies the selected logical object, or a null if the function call was unsuccessful.

Notes   DKGRAY_BRUSH, GRAY_BRUSH, and LTGRAY_BRUSH objects should not be used as background brushes for any window not using CS_HREDRAW and CS_VREDRAW styles. This can lead to misalignment of brush patterns when the window is sized or moved.

DWORD GetSysColor(nIndex)

Function   Returns the color value of the specified display object.

Parameters   *nIndex* (int) indicates the display object whose color is to be returned.

Value Returned   Represents the RGB color value of the selected object.

Notes   Monochrome displays usually interpret various colors as shades of gray.

int GetSystemMetrics(nIndex)

Function   Returns the system's metrics. The measurements represent the widths and heights of various display elements.

Parameters

nIndex (int) identifies the system measurement that is to be retrieved.

Index	Description
SM_CXSCREEN	Screen width
SM_CYSCREEN	Screen height
SM_CXFRAME	Width of sizeable window frame
SM_CXVSCROLL	Width of arrow bitmap on vertical scroll bar
SM_CYVSCROLL	Height of arrow bitmap on vertical scroll bar
SM_CXHSCROLL	Width of arrow bitmap on horizontal scroll bar
SM_CYHSCROLL	Height of arrow bitmap on horizontal scroll bar
SM_CYCAPTION	Height of caption
SM_CXBORDER	Width of nonsizeable window frame
SM_CYBORDER	Height of nonsizeable window frame
SM_CXDLGFRAME	Width of WS_DLGFRAME styled window
SM_CYDLGFRAME	Height of WS_DLGFRAME styled window
SM_CXHTHUMB	Width of horizontal scroll bar thumb
SM_CYVTHUMB	Height of horizontal scroll bar thumb
SM_CXICON	Icon width
SM_CYICON	Icon height

Index	Description
SM_CXCURSOR	Cursor width
SM_CYCURSOR	Cursor height
SM_CYMENU	Single-line menu bar height
SM_CXFULLSCREEN	Full-screen client area window width
SM_CYFULLSCREEN	Full-screen client area window height
SM_CYKANJIWINDOW	Kanji window height
SM_CXMINTRACK	Minimum window tracking width
SM_CYMINTRACK	Minimum window tracking height
SM_CXMIN	Window minimum width
SM_CYMIN	Window minimum height
SM_CXSIZE	Title bar bitmap width
SM_CYSIZE	Title bar bitmap height
SM_MOUSEPRESENT	Nonzero when mouse hardware is installed
SM_DEBUG	Nonzero for a Windows debugging version
SM_SWAPBUTTON	Nonzero when the left and right mouse buttons are swapped

Value Returned   Indicates the specified system metric.

Notes   The function can also indicate whether the Windows version being used is capable of debugging, if a mouse is present, and if so, if the left and right buttons have been swapped.

WORD GetTextAlign(hDC)

Function   Returns the status of the text-alignment flag.

Parameters   hDC (HDC) specifies the device context.

Value Returned   The returned value can be one or a combination of the following:

TA_BASELINE   Selects alignment along the X axis and the baseline of the selected font within the bounding rectangle

TA_BOTTOM	Selects alignment along the X axis and the bottom of the bounding rectangle
TA_CENTER	Selects alignment along the Y axis and the center of the bounding rectangle
TA_LEFT	Selects alignment along the Y axis and the left side of the bounding rectangle
TA_NOUPDATECP	Notes that the current position is not updated
TA_RIGHT	Selects alignment along the Y axis and the right side of the bounding rectangle
TA_TOP	Selects alignment along the X axis and the top of the bounding rectangle
TA_UPDATECP	Notes that the current position is updated

Notes   By using the logical AND operation, a particular flag's value can be checked. A zero value indicates that the flag was not set.

short GetTextCharExtra(hDC)

Function   Returns the current intercharacter spacing.

Parameters   hDC (HDC) specifies the device context.

Value Returned   Indicates the current intercharacter spacing.

Notes   The intercharacter spacing is defined in terms of logical units.

DWORD GetTextColor(hDC)

Function   Returns the current text color.

Parameters   hDC (HDC) specifies the device context.

Value Returned   Returns an RGB color value.

Notes   The returned color value indicates the color used for the foreground color of characters output by the call to the **TextOut** function.

DWORD GetTextExtent(hDC,lpString,nCount)

Function   Calculates the height and width of a line of text.

Parameters

hDC (HDC) specifies the device context.

lpString (LPSTR) is a pointer to a text string whose height and width are to be calculated.

nCount (short) indicates the number of characters in the text string.

Value Returned   Represents the height and width of the text string: the high-order word for the height, the low-order word for the width.

Notes   For those devices that use kerning for character placement, the sum of the extents of the individual characters may not equal the extent of the entire string.

short GetTextFace(hDC,nCount,lpFacename)

Function   Copies the typeface name of the desired font into a buffer.

Parameters

hDC (HDC) specifies the device context.

nCount (short) indicates the buffer size in bytes.

lpFacename (LPSTR) is a pointer to the buffer to receive the name of the typeface.

Value Returned   Either the number of bytes copied into the buffer, or a null for an unsuccessful attempt.

BOOL GetTextMetrics(hDC,lpMetrics)

Function   Places the metrics for the selected font into the *textmetrics* data structure pointed to by *lpMetrics*.

Parameters

hDC (HDC) specifies the device context.

lpMetrics (LPTEXTMETRIC) is a pointer to a *textmetric* structure.

Value Returned   A nonzero value for a successful function call; otherwise null.

DWORD GetViewportExt(hDC)

Function   Retrieves the X extent and Y extent of the selected device's context viewport.

Parameters   *hDC* (HDC) specifies the device context.

Value Returned   The X and Y extents are returned using device units. The high-order byte is used for the Y extent, and the low-order byte indicates the X extent.

DWORD GetViewportOrg(hDC)

Function   Returns the X coordinate and Y coordinate of the viewport origin associated with the specified context.

Parameters   *hDC* (HDC) specifies the device context.

Value Returned   Using device coordinates, the returned high-order byte contains the Y coordinate, and the low-order byte contains the X coordinate.

HDC GetWindowDC(hWnd)

Function   Returns the window's display context.

Parameters   *hWnd* (HWND) identifies the window to be used in determining the display context.

Value Returned   Either contains the display context for the specified window or, if unsuccessful, returns a null.

Notes   Display contexts are very important because they allow painting anywhere in a window. The painting includes title bars, menus, and scroll bars. The origin of the context is always the upper-left corner of the window, not the client area. Once painting beyond the client area is complete (which is not recommended), a call to *ReleaseDC* must be made releasing the display context.

BOOL InsertMenu(hMenu,nPosition,wFlags, wIDNewItem,lpNewItem)

Function   Inserts a new item at the position specified, moving other items down.

Parameters

hMenu (HMENU) specifies the menu to be changed.

nPosition (WORD) specifies the menu item ID if *wFlags* is set to MB_BYCOMMAND. If *wFlags* is set to MB_BYPOSITION, this parameter identifies the position of the existing menu item. The first item is numbered 0. A −1 value causes the new item to be inserted at the end of the list.

wFlags (WORD) defines how *nPosition* is to be interpreted.

wIDNewItem (WORD) defines either the command ID or the menu handle of the pop-up menu.

lpNewItem (LPSTR) defines the content of the new menu item.

Value Returned   TRUE if the function was successful, FALSE otherwise.

Notes   Whenever the menu changes, the application should call **Draw-MenuBar.**

void InvalidateRect(hWnd,lpRect,bErase)

Function   Invalidates the client area within the specified rectangle by adding the rectangle to the window's update region.

Parameters

hWnd (HWND) specifies the window whose update region is about to be modified by the specified rectangle.

lpRect (LPRECT) is a pointer to a *rect* structure containing coordinates of the rectangle to be used for adding to the update region. A null value will cause the entire client area to be added to the update region.

bErase (BOOL) indicates whether the background in the update region will be erased.

Value Returned   None.

Notes   If the update region is not empty and there are no other application queue messages for that window, Windows will send a WM_PAINT message.

void InvalidateRgn(hWnd,hRgn,bErase)

Function   Adds the current update region of the specified window to the given region in the client area, thereby invalidating it.

Parameters

hWnd (HWND) specifies the window whose update region is about to be changed.

hRgn (HRGN) specifies the region (in client area coordinates) that is to be added to the update region.

bErase (BOOL) defines whether the background within the update region is to be erased. A nonzero value erases the background. When it is zero, the background remains unchanged.

Value Returned   None.

Notes   When the update region is not empty and there are no application queue messages pending, Windows sends a WM_PAINT message.

void InvertRect(hDC,lpRect)

Function   Inverts the contents of the specified rectangle.

Parameters

hDC (HDC) specifies the device context.

lpRect (LPRECT) is a pointer to a *rect* structure containing the logical coordinates of the rectangle to be inverted.

Value Returned   None.

Notes   On color monitors the color inversion depends on how colors are generated for the display. Monochrome monitors invert the image by making white pixels black and black pixels white. Two calls to the function will restore the original colors of the rectangle. A nonzero value indicates a successful inversion, zero unsuccessful.

BOOL InvertRgn(hDC,hRgn)

Function   Inverts the contents of the specified region.

Parameters

hDC (HDC) specifies the device context.

lpRgn (HRGN) contains the logical coordinates of the region to be inverted.

Value Returned   None.

Notes   On color monitors the color inversion depends on how colors are generated for the display. Monochrome monitors invert the image by making white pixels black and black pixels white. Two calls to the function will restore the original colors of the region. A nonzero value indicates a successful inversion, zero unsuccessful.

void LineDDA(x1,y1,x2,y2,lpLineFunc,lpData)

Function   Calculates all of the points in a line defined by the X and Y coordinates.

Parameters

x1 (short) identifies the logical X coordinate of the starting point.

y1 (short) identifies the logical Y coordinate of the starting point.

x2 (short) identifies the logical X coordinate of the ending point.

y2 (short) identifies the logical Y coordinate of the ending point.

lpLineFunc (FARPROC) is the procedure-instance address of the application-defined function.

lpData (LPSTR) is a pointer to the application-defined data.

Value Returned   None.

Notes   The callback function must use the Pascal calling convention with the FAR option.

BOOL LineTo(hDC,x,y)

Function   Draws a line using the current pen from the current position up to, but not including, the point indicated by *x* and *y*. The current position is then set to *x,y*.

Parameters

hDC (HDC) specifies the device context.

x (short) defines the logical X coordinate of the ending point for the line.

y (short) defines the logical Y coordinate of the ending point for the line.

Value Returned   Nonzero for a successful line draw, zero otherwise.

HCURSOR LoadCursor(hInstance,lpCursorName)

Function   Loads the selected cursor from the executable file associated with the module pointed to by *hInstance*.

Parameters

hInstance (HANDLE) specifies the instance of the module whose executable file contains the cursor to be loaded. When the parameter is null, the function can be used to load a predefined Windows cursor, with *lpCursorName* being one of the following:

IDC_ARROW	Selects the standard Windows arrow cursor
IDC_CROSS	Selects the standard Windows crosshair cursor
IDC_IBEAM	Selects the standard Windows I-beam text cursor
IDC_ICON	Selects the standard Windows empty icon
IDC_SIZE	Selects the standard Windows four-pointed arrow
IDC_UPARROW	Selects the standard Windows vertical arrow cursor
IDC_WAIT	Selects the standard Windows hourglass cursor

lpCursorName (LPSTR) is a pointer to a null-terminated character string naming the cursor.

Value Returned   Either specifies the selected cursor or returns a null if the specified cursor does not exist.

Notes   Using the low-order word of *lpCursorName*, the function can be used to load a cursor created by a call to the **MakeIntResource** function.

POINT MakePoint(lInteger)

Function   Converts a long value containing the X and Y coordinates of a particular point into a *point* structure.

Parameters   *lInteger* (LONG) is the long integer containing the points to be converted.

Value Returned   Identifies the *point* data structure created.

FARPROC MakeProcInstance(lpProc,hInstance)

Function   Creates the procedure-instance address.

Parameters

lpProc (FARPROC) is a procedure-instance address.

hInstance (HANDLE) specifies the instance associated with the specified data segment.

Value Returned   Either points to the function or contains a null if unsuccessful.

Notes   The created address points to prologue code that is actually executed before the function itself. This procedure allows the current instance of the function to access variables and data structures in that particular instance's data segment.

int MessageBox(hWndParent,lpText,lpCaption,wType)

Function   Creates and displays a window containing application-supplied messages, caption, icons, and push buttons.

Parameters

hWndParent (HWND) specifies the window that owns the message box.

lpText (LPSTR) is a pointer to the null-terminated message string that will be displayed.

lpCaption (LPSTR) is a pointer to a null-terminated string that will be used for the caption in the dialog box. When it is null the caption displayed will be "Error!"

wType (WORD) identifies the contents of the dialog box and can be any single value or logically ORed combination listed.

Value Returned   A zero return value indicates there is insufficient memory to create the message box. A successful creation will cause one of the following menu items to be returned by the dialog box:

IDABORT	Abort button was pressed.
IDCANCEL	ESC key or cancel button was pressed. If the message box doesn't have a cancel button, pressing ESC will be ignored.
IDIGNORE	The ignore button was pressed.
IDNO	No button has been pressed.
IDOK	OK button was pressed.
IDRETRY	Retry button was pressed.
IDYES	Yes button was pressed.

Notes   The following table contains an alphabetical list showing the possible contents of a dialog box.

Indentifier	Description
MB_ABORTRETRYIGNORE	Indicates the message box has three buttons: ABORT, RETRY, and IGNORE.

Indentifier	Description
MB _ APPLMODAL	Indicates the user must respond to the message box; this is the default. (**Note:** This does not prevent the user from switching to other applications—see MB _ SYSTEM MODAL.)
MB _ DEFBUTTON1	Indicates the first button is the default.
MB _ DEFBUTTON2	Indicates the second button is the default.
MB _ DEFBUTTON3	Indicates the third button is the default.
MB _ ICONASTERISK	Means an asterisk icon will be displayed in the message box.
MB _ ICONEXCLAMATION	Means an exclamation point icon will be displayed in the message box.
MB _ ICONHAND	Means a hand icon will be displayed in the message box.
MB _ ICONQUESTION	Means a question mark icon will be displayed in the message box.
MB _ OK	Indicates the message box has one push button, labeled OK.
MB _ OKCANCEL	Indicates the message box has two push buttons, labeled OK and CANCEL.
MB _ RETRYCANCEL	Indicates the message box has two push buttons, labeled RETRY and CANCEL.
MB _ SYSTEMMODAL	Suspends all applications due to the seriousness of the event that is about to occur; the user must respond to the message box and cannot switch to other tasks.
MB _ YESNO	Indicates the message box has two buttons, labeled YES and NO.
MB _ YESNOCANCEL	Indicates the message box has three push buttons: YES, NO, and CANCEL.

DWORD MoveTo(hDC,x,y)

Function   Moves the current position to the X and Y coordinates specified.

Parameters

hDC (HDC) specifies the device context.

x (short) identifies the logical X coordinate of the new location.

y (short) identifies the logical Y coordinate of the new location.

Value Returned   Contains the coordinates of the previous position. The high-order word contains the Y coordinate, the low-order word the X coordinate.

Notes   A call to **MoveTo** affects many other functions that use the current position.

void OffsetRect(lpRect,x,y)

Function   Using the signed X and Y offset values, the function moves the indicated rectangle.

Parameters

lpRect (LPRECT) is a pointer to a *rect* structure that contains the rectangle about to be moved.

x (int) indicates how much to move the rectangle left (negative value) or right.

y (int) indicates how much to move the rectangle up (negative value) or down.

Value Returned   None.

Notes   The coordinates of the rectangle must not be greater than 32,767 or less than −32,768 units.

short OffsetRgn(hRgn,x,y)

Function   Using the signed X and Y offset values, the function moves the indicated region.

Parameters

hRgn (HRGN) identifies the region about to be moved.

x (int) indicates how much to move the region left (negative value) or right.

y (int) indicates how much to move the region up (negative value) or down.

Value Returned   Indicates the new region's type:

COMPLEXREGION	Identifies a region with overlapping borders
ERROR	Indicates that the region handle is not valid
NULLREGION	Indicates that the region is empty
SIMPLEREGION	Indicates that the region does not have any over-lapping borders

Notes   The coordinates of the region must not be greater than 32,767 or less than $-32,768$ units.

DWORD OffsetViewportOrg(hDC,x,y)

Function   Modifies the specified viewport origin relative to the current values.

Parameters

hDC (HDC) specifies the device context.

x (short) indicates how many device units to add to the current origin's X coordinate.

y (short) indicates how many device units to add to the current origin's Y coordinate.

Value Returned   Contains the previous viewport origin expressed in device coordinates. The high-order word contains the Y coordinate, the low-order word the X coordinate.

Notes   The new viewport origin is calculated by adding the current origin to the X and Y values.

DWORD OffsetWindowOrg(hDC,x,y)

Function   Modifies the specified window origin relative to the current values.

Parameters

hDC (HDC) specifies the device context.

x (short) indicates how many device units to add to the current origin's X coordinate.

y (short) indicates how many device units to add to the current origin's Y coordinate.

Value Returned   Contains the previous window origin expressed in device coordinates. The high-order word contains the Y coordinate, the low-order word the X coordinate.

Notes   The new window origin is calculated by adding the current origin to the X and Y values.

BOOL PaintRgn(hDC,hRgn)

Function   Paints the specified region with the selected brush.

Parameters

hDC (HDC) specifies the device context.

hRgn (HRGN) specifies the region to be filled.

Value Returned   Zero value for an unsuccessful paint. Nonzero value for a successful paint.

COLORREF PALETTEINDEX(nPaletteIndex)

Function   Accepts an index to a logical color palette entry and returns a palette entry specifier.

Parameters   *nPaletteIndex* (int) defines an index to the palette entry containing the color to be used for a graphics operation.

Value Returned   Returns the value of a logical palette index specifier.

BOOL Pie(hDC,x1,y1,x2,y2,x3,y3,x4,y4)

Function   Draws a pie-shaped wedge using the selected pen and then fills the wedge with the selected brush. Drawing takes place in a counter-clockwise direction.

Parameters

hDC (HDC) specifies the device context.

x1 (short) identifies the logical X coordinate of the upper-left corner of the bounding rectangle.

y1 (short) identifies the logical Y coordinate of the upper-left corner of the bounding rectangle.

x2 (short) identifies the logical X coordinate of the lower-right corner of the bounding rectangle.

y2 (short) identifies the logical Y coordinate of the lower-right corner of the bounding rectangle.

x3 (short) identifies the logical X coordinate of the starting point for the arc.

y3 (short) identifies the logical Y coordinate of the starting point for the arc.

x4 (short) identifies the logical X coordinate of the ending point for the arc.

y4 (short) identifies the logical Y coordinate of the ending point for the arc.

Value Returned   A nonzero value indicates the wedge was successfully drawn. A zero value indicates an unsuccessful draw.

Notes   The width and height of the rectangle specified must not exceed 32,767. Pie does not use the current position, nor does it update the current position after the wedge is drawn.

BOOL Polygon(hDC,lpPoints,nCount)

Function   Draws a polygon consisting of two or more points connected by lines.

Parameters

hDC (HDC) specifies the device context.

lpPoints (LPPOINT) is a pointer to an array of *point* structures containing the vertices of the polygon.

nCount (short) indicates the number of elements in the array.

Value Returned   A nonzero value indicates a successful draw; otherwise, the result is zero.

Notes   Polygon does not use the current position, nor does it update the current position after the polygon is drawn. The polygon is drawn using the current polygon filling mode. In alternate mode, the current pen is used to draw lines from the first point through subsequent points, with the interior filled using the current brush. While in winding mode, the current pen is used to draw a border that is computed using all of the points. The interior is also filled using the current brush.

BOOL Polyline(hDC,lpPoints,nCount)

Function   Draws a set of connected line segments.

Parameters

hDC (HDC) specifies the device context.

lpPoints (LPPOINT) is a pointer to an array of *point* structures containing the points to be connected.

nCount (short) indicates the number of elements in the array.

Value Returned   A nonzero value indicates a successful draw; otherwise, the result is zero.

Notes   Polyline does not use the current position, nor does it update the current position after the polyline is drawn.

BOOL PtInRect(lpRect,Point)

Function   Identifies whether the referenced point is inside the selected rectangle.

Parameters

lpRect (LPRECT) is a pointer to a *rect* structure identifying the rectangle.

Point (POINT) is a pointer to a *point* structure indicating the point to be checked.

Value Returned   A nonzero value indicates that the point lies within the selected rectangle. A zero return value indicates that the point is not within the designated rectangle.

BOOL PtInRegion(hRgn,x,y)

Function   Using X and Y as point coordinates, indicates whether the point lies within the specified region.

Parameters

hRgn (HRGN) specifies the region that is to be examined.

x (short) indicates the logical X coordinate of the point to be checked.

y (short) indicates the logical Y coordinate of the point to be checked.

Value Returned   A nonzero value indicates the point lies within the selected region. A zero return value indicates the point is not within the designated region.

int RealizePalette(hDC)

Function   Maps to the system palette entries in the logical palette currently selected for a device context.

Parameters   *hDC* (HDC) specifies the device context.

Value Returned   The returned value identifies the number of entries changed in the system palette.

Notes   When **RealizePalette** is called, Windows guarantees that it will display all the colors it requests, up to the maximum number simultaneously available on the display, and displays additional colors by matching them to available colors.

BOOL Rectangle(hDC,x1,y1,x2,y2)

Function   Using the selected pen, draws a rectangle; then fills the interior with the selected pen.

Parameters

  hDC (HDC) specifies the device context.

  x1 (short) is the upper-left corner X coordinate.

  y1 (short) is the upper-left corner Y coordinate.

  x2 (short) is the lower-right corner X coordinate.

  y2 (short) is the lower-right corner Y coordinate.

Value Returned   Returned value identifies the newly created rectangular region or an unsuccessful attempt returns a null.

Notes   The width and height of the rectangle, defined by the absolute value of $x2 - x1$ and $y2 - y1$, must not exceed 32,767.

int ReleaseDC(hWnd,hDC)

Function   Releases the device context, allowing it to be used by other applications.

Parameters

hWnd (HWND) is a handle to the window whose device context is about to be freed.

hDC (HDC) specifies the device context.

Value Returned   A nonzero value for a successful release; otherwise, a null is returned.

Notes   For every call that is made to **GetWindowDC** or **GetDC** retrieving a common device context, a call to **ReleaseDC** must be made.

BOOL RemoveMenu(hMenu,nPosition,wFlags)

Function   Deletes an item with an associated pop-up menu from the menu specified.

Parameters

hMenu (HMENU) specifies the menu to be changed.

nPosition (WORD) defines the position of the menu item to be removed. The first menu item is at position zero.

wFlags (WORD) must be set to zero.

Value Returned   TRUE for a successful deletion, otherwise FALSE.

Notes   Whenever a menu changes, the application should call **Draw-MenuBar**.

BOOL RestoreDC(hDC,nSavedDC)

Function   Restores the device context specified.

Parameters

hDC (HDC) specifies the device context.

nSavedDC (short) identifies the device context that is to be restored. When the parameter is assigned a -1, the function will restore the most recently saved device context.

Value Returned   A nonzero value for a successful restore, zero otherwise.

Notes   The device context is restored by copying the information saved on the context stack by previous calls to the **SaveDC** function. Since the context stack can contain the state information for more than one device context, care must be taken when a call is made to **RestoreDC**. When the device context referenced by *nSavedDC* is not the top of the stack, the function will permanently delete the state information stored for all device contexts between the top and the *nSavedDC* context reference.

DWORD RGB(cRed,cGreen,cBlue)

Function   Selects an RGB color based on the supplied preferences combined with the color capabilities of the selected output device.

Parameters

cRed (BYTE) identifies the intensity for the red color.

cGreen (BYTE) identifies the intensity for the green color.

cBlue (BYTE) identifies the intensity for the blue color.

Value Returned   Indicates the RGB color that has been selected.

Notes   Each color field's intensity can be a value from 0 to 255 (inclusive). Three zero parameters select the color black. All three parameters being assigned 255 will select white.

BOOL RoundRect(hDC,x1,y1,x2,y2,x3,y3)

Function   Using the current pen, draws a rectangle with rounded corners. The interior of the rectangle is then painted using the selected brush.

Parameters

hDC (HDC) specifies the device context.

x1 (short) identifies the logical X coordinate of the upper-left corner of the rectangle.

y1 (short) identifies the logical Y coordinate of the upper-left corner of the rectangle.

x2 (short) identifies the logical X coordinate of the lower-right corner of the rectangle.

y2 (short) identifies the logical Y coordinate of the lower-right corner of the rectangle.

x3 (short) identifies the width of the ellipse that will be used to draw the rounded corners.

y3 (short) identifies the height of the ellipse that will be used to draw the rounded corners.

Value Returned   A nonzero value indicates the rectangle was successfully drawn. A zero value indicates an unsuccessful draw.

Notes   The width and height of the rectangle, defined by the absolute value of $x2-x1$ and $y2-y1$, must not exceed 32,767. **RoundRect** does not use the current position, nor does it update the current position after the rectangle is drawn.

short SaveDC(hDC)

Function   Saves the state of the current device context.

Parameters   *hDC* (HDC) specifies the device context.

Value Returned   Identifies the saved device context. A zero value indicates an error has occurred.

Notes   The saved device context state is pushed onto the device context stack and can be restored by invoking the **RestoreDC** function.

HANDLE SelectObject(hDC,hObject)

Function   Selects a logical object for the specified device context.

Parameters

hDC (HDC) specifies the device context.

hObject (HANDLE) specifies the logical object to be selected and may be any one of the following functions:

Object	Function Name
Bitmap	CreateBitmap
	CreateBitmapIndirect
	CreateCompatibleBitmap
Brush	CreateBrushIndirect
	CreateHatchBrush
	CreatePatternBrush
	CreateSolidBrush
Font	CreateFont
	CreateFontIndirect

Object	Function Name
Pen	CreatePen
	CreatePenIndirect

Region	CombineRgn
	CreateEllipticRgn
	CreateellipticRgnIndirect
	CreatePolyRgn
	CreateRectRgn
	CreateRectRgnIndirect

Value Returned   Identifies the object being replaced by *hObject* of the same type. Otherwise, if an error has occurred, a null is returned.

Notes   Selected objects become defaults used by many GDI functions that write text, draw lines, fill interiors, and clip output to selected devices. Device contexts can have up to five objects selected, with only one being used at a time. Each call to **SelectObject** causes the GDI to allocate space for that object in the data segment. **DeleteObject** should always be called whenever a selected object (font, pen, or brush) is no longer needed to conserve memory. Also, bitmaps can only be selected into one device context at a time.

HPALETTE SelectPalette(hDC,hPalette)

Function   Selects the logical palette specified by the *hPalette* parameter as the selected logical palette of the device context identified by *hDC*. The new palette replaces the previous palette.

Parameters

hDC (HDC) specifies the device context.

hPalette (HPALETTE) specifies the logical palette to be selected.

Value Returned   Returns the identifier of the logical palette being replaced by *hPalette*. Otherwise, a null is returned.

Notes   An application can select a logical palette for more than one device context.

long SendDlgItemMessage(hDlg,nIDDlgItem,wMsg, wParam,lParam)

Function   Sends a message to a dialog box's control.

Parameters

hDlg (HWND) specifies the dialog box that contains the control.

nIDDlgItem (int) identifies the dialog item that is to receive the message.

wMsg (unsigned) identifies the message value.

wParam (WORD) identifies any additional message information.

lParam (long) can be used for additional message information.

Value Returned   If the controller identified is invalid, the function returns a null. Otherwise, the return value represents the outcome of the function. A successful return value is generated by the control's window function.

Notes   Using **SendDlgItemMessage** is the same as obtaining a handle to the specified control and then calling **SendMessage**.

long SendMessage(hWnd,wMsg,wParam,lParam)

Function   Sends a message to single or multiple windows.

Parameters

hWnd (HWND) specifies the window that will be sent the message. If the parameter is FFFF (hexadecimal), the specified message will be sent to all pop-up windows currently in the system. The message is not sent to any child windows.

wMsg (unsigned) identifies the message value.

wParam (WORD) identifies any additional message information.

lParam (long) can be used for additional message information.

Value Returned   Depends on the message sent.

Notes   If the receiving window is part of the same application, the window function is called immediately. When the receiving window is part of some other task, Windows will switch to the task and then call the appropriate window function, sending the message. Note that the message is not placed in the destination task's application queue.

DWORD SetBkColor(hDC,rgbColor)

Function   Sets the current background color to the color specified. The function will choose the nearest logical color of the device if no direct match exists.

Parameters

hDC (HDC) specifies the device context.

rgbColor (DWORD) selects an RGB color for the new background color.

Value Returned   Contains the previous RGB background color. A return value of 80000000 (hexadecimal) indicates an error has occurred.

Notes   When the background mode is opaque, the background color is used to fill the gaps between styled lines, hatched lines in brushes, and character cells. The graphics device interface (GDI) also uses the background color for converting bitmaps from color to monochrome or vice versa.

short SetBkMode(hDC,nBkMode)

Function   Sets the background mode.

Parameters

hDC (HDC) specifies the device context.

nBkMode (short) selects the background mode:

OPAQUE   Background color is used to fill the gaps between
                         styled lines, hatched lines in brushes, and character
                         cells

TRANSPARENT   Leaves the background unchanged

Value Returned   Returns the previous background mode (OPAQUE or
TRANSPARENT).

Notes   The function tells the GDI whether to remove the existing background colors on the device surface before drawing text, hatched brushes,
or any nonsolid pen style.

DWORD SetBrushOrg(hDC,x,y)

Function   Sets the origin for all selected brushes into the specified device
context.

Parameters

hDC (HDC) specifies the device context.

x (short) identifies the logical X coordinate of the new origin.

y (short) identifies the logical Y coordinate of the new origin.

Value Returned   Indicates the previous origin of the brush. The high-
order word contains the Y coordinate, the low-order word the X coordinate.

Notes   The original brush origin is always set to the 0,0 coordinate.

HCURSOR SetCursor(hCursor)

Function   Sets the system cursor shape.

Parameters   *hCursor* (HCURSOR) specifies a previously loaded (**LoadCursor**) cursor resource.

Value Returned   Identifies the cursor resource defining the previous cursor shape. A zero value indicates that there was no previous shape.

Notes   The cursor shape should only be set when the cursor is in the client area or when it is capturing all mouse input.

void SetCursorPos(x,y)

Function   Sets the system cursor to the position specified.

Parameters

x (int) identifies the new screen X coordinate of the cursor.

y (int) identifies the new screen Y coordinate of the cursor.

Value Returned   None.

Notes   The cursor should only be moved when it is in the window's client area.

void SetDlgItemInt(hDlg,nIDDlgItem,wValue,bSigned)

Function   Sets the text of a control in the specified dialog box to the string represented by the integer value given by *wValue*.

Parameters

hDlg (HWND) specifies the dialog box containing the control.

nIDDlgItem (int) defines the control to be modified.

wValue (unsigned) indicates the value to be set.

bSigned (BOOL) indicates whether the integer value is signed.

Value Returned   None.

Notes   The function converts the *wValue* parameter to a string consisting of decimal digits. It then copies the string to the control. The function also sends a WM_SETTEXT message to the specified control.

void SetDlgItemText(hDlg,nIDDlgItem,lpString)

Function   Sets the text of a control in the dialog box.

Parameters

hDlg (HWND) specifies the dialog box containing the control.

nIDDlgItem (int) defines the control to be modified.

lpString (LPSTR) is a pointer to a null-terminated string that will be copied to the control.

Value Returned   None.

Notes   The function sends a WM_SETTEXT message to the specified control.

short SetMapMode(hDC,nMapMode)

Function   Sets the mapping mode of the selected device context.

Parameters

hDC (HDC) specifies the device context.

nMapMode (short) selects one new mapping mode from the following:

MM_ANISOTROPIC	Maps logical units to arbitrary units with arbitrarily scaled axes
MM_HIENGLISH	Maps each logical unit to 0.001 inch
MM_HIMETRIC	Maps each logical unit to 0.01 millimeter
MM_ISOTROPIC	Maps logical units to arbitrary units with equally scaled axes
MM_LOMETRIC	Maps each logical unit to 0.1 millimeter
MM_LOENGLISH	Maps each logical unit to 0.01 inch
MM_TEXT	Maps each logical unit to 1 device pixel
MM_TWIPS	Maps each logical unit to 1/20 of a printer's point or approximately 1/1440 inch

Value Returned   Represents the previous mapping mode.

Notes   The mapping modes HIENGLISH, HIMETRIC, LOENGLISH, LOMETRIC, and TWIPS are used most frequently for applications drawing in physically meaningful units such as millimeters or inches. MM_TEXT mode permits the use of device-specific pixels whose size may vary from one device to another. MM_ISOTROPIC enables a 1:1 aspect ratio, which is most useful in maintaining the exact shape of an image. MM_ANISOTROPIC mode allows for independent adjustment of the X and Y coordinates.

WORD SetPaletteEntries(hPalette,wStartIndex, wNumEntries,lpColors)

Function   Sets RGB color values and flags in a range of entries in a logical palette.

Parameters

hPalette (HPALETTE) specifies the logical palette.

wStartIndex (WORD) identifies the first entry in the logical palette to be set.

wNumEntries (WORD) identifies the number of entries in the logical palette to be set.

lpColors (LPSTR) points to the first number of an array of *paletteentry*.

Value Returned   Indicates the number of entries set in the logical palette. A zero is returned if the function has failed.

Notes   When the logical palette is selected into a device context, the changes will not take effect until a call is made to **RealizePalette**.

DWORD SetPixel(hDC,x,y,rgbColor)

Function   Sets the color of the pixel indicated by *x* and *y*.

Parameters

hDC (HDC) specifies the device context.

x (short) specifies the logical X coordinate of the point to be set.

y (short) specifies the logical Y coordinate of the point to be set.

rgbColor (DWORD) indicates the RGB color to be used to paint the pixel.

Value Returned   Indicates the actual RGB color the pixel was painted. A −1 return value indicates an error condition. The color value returned could be different than the color specified if no direct match exists.

Notes   The point specified must be in the clipping region.

short SetPolyFillMode(hDC,nPolyFillMode)

Function   Sets the polygon fill mode.

Parameters

hDC (HDC) specifies the device context.

nPolyFillMode (short) selects the new filling mode. Can be either alternate or winding.

Value Returned   Indicates the previous filling mode. A null value indicates an error has occurred.

Notes   Alternate and winding modes only differ for those polygons with overlapping complex forms. Alternate mode fills every other enclosed region within the polygon; winding mode fills all regions.

void SetRect(lpRect,x1,y1,x2,y2)

Function   Creates a new rectangle by assigning the *rect* data structure pointed to by *lpRect* to coordinates specified.

Parameters

lpRect (LPRECT) is a pointer to a *rect* structure that will be assigned the new end points.

x1 (int) is the upper-left corner X coordinate.

y1 (int) is the upper-left corner Y coordinate.

x2 (int) is the lower-right corner X coordinate.

y2 (int) is the lower-right corner Y coordinate.

Value Returned   None.

Notes   The width and height of the rectangle, defined by the absolute value of $x2-x1$ and $y2-y1$, must not exceed 32,767.

void SetRectRgn(hRgn,x1,y1,x2,y2)

Function   Creates a rectangular region.

Parameters

hRgn (HANDLE) specifies the region.

x1 (short) is the upper-left corner X coordinate of the rectangular region.

y1 (short) is the upper-left corner Y coordinate of the rectangular region.

x2 (short) is the lower-right corner X coordinate of the rectangular region.

y2 (short) is the lower-right corner Y coordinate of the rectangular region.

Value Returned   None.

Notes   Unlike **CreateRectRgn**, **SetRectRgn** does not use the local memory manager. Instead, the function uses the space allocated for the region. *x1*, *y1*, *x2*, and *y2* indicate the minimum size of the allocated space.

short SetROP2(hDC,nDrawMode)

Function   Sets the current drawing mode.

Parameters

hDC (HDC) specifies the device context.

nDrawMode (short) selects from one of the following drawing modes:

R2_BLACK	The pixel is always black.
R2_NOTIMERGEPEN	The pixel is the inverse of the R2_MERGEPEN color.
R2_MASKNOTPEN	The pixel is a combination of the colors of the display and the inverse of the pen.
R2_NOTCOPYPEN	The pixel is the inverse of the pen color.
R2_MASKPENNOT	The pixel is a combination of the colors of the pen and the inverse of the display.
R2_NOT	The pixel is the inverse of the display color.
R2_XORPEN	The pixel is a combination of the colors in the pen and in the display.

R2_NOTMASKPEN	The pixel is the inverse of the R2_MASKPEN color.
R2_MASKPEN	The pixel is a combination of the colors in both the pen and the display.
R2_NOTXORPEN	The pixel is the inverse of the R2_XORPEN color.
R2_NOP	The pixel remains unchanged.
R2_MERGENOTPEN	The pixel is a combination of the display color and the inverse of the pen color.
R2_COPYPEN	The pixel is the pen color.
R2_MERGEPENNOT	The pixel is a combination of the pen color and the inverse of the display color.
R2_MERGEPEN	The pixel is a combination of the pen color and the display color.
R2_WHITE	The pixel is always white.

Value Returned   Specifies the previous drawing mode.

Notes   The drawing mode is for raster devices only and is not available on vector devices. The drawing modes represent the binary raster operations representing all of the possible binary Boolean functions AND, OR, and XOR as applied to two variables, along with the unary NOT operation.

int SetScrollPos(hWnd,nBar,nPos,bRedraw)

Function   Sets the current position of a scroll bar thumb.

Parameters

hWnd (HWND) specifies the window whose scroll bar will be set.

nBar (int) identifies which scroll bar thumb is to be set:

Value	Definition
SB_CTL	Sets the position of a scroll bar control, assuming that *hWnd* points to a window handle of a scroll bar control

| SB_HORZ | Sets the position of a window's horizontal scroll bar |
| SB_VERT | Sets the position of a window's vertical scroll bar |

nPos (int) identifies the new position within the valid scrolling range.

bRedraw (BOOL) indicates whether the scroll bar should be redrawn. A nonzero value indicates the scroll bar should be redrawn. If zero, it is not redrawn.

Value Returned   Indicates the previous position of the scroll bar thumb.

void SetScrollRange(hWnd,nBar,nMinPos, nMaxPos,bRedraw)

Function   Sets the minimum and maximum position values for the selected scroll bar.

Parameters

hWnd (HWND) specifies the window whose scroll bar will be set.

nBar (int) identifies which scroll bar thumb is to be set:

Value	Definition
SB_CTL	Sets the position of a scroll bar control, assuming that *hWnd* points to a window handle of a scroll bar control
SB_HORZ	Sets the position of a window's horizontal scroll bar
SB_VERT	Sets the position of a window's vertical scroll bar

nMinPos (int) sets the minimum scrolling position.

nMaxPos (int) sets the maximum scrolling position.

bRedraw (BOOL) indicates whether the scroll bar should be redrawn. A nonzero value indicates the scroll bar should be redrawn. If zero, it is not redrawn.

Value Returned   None.

Notes   If **SetScrollRange** is called right after **SetScrollPos**, *bRedraw* should be set to zero to prevent the scroll bar from being drawn twice.

void
SetSysColors(nChanges,lpSysColor,lpColorValues)

Function   Sets the system colors.

Parameters

nChanges (int) defines the number of system colors to be set.

lpSysColor (LPINT) is a pointer to an array of integers that specify the elements to be changed. The following is a list of valid system color indexes:

Value	Definition
COLOR_ACTIVEBORDER	Active window border index
COLOR_ACTIVECAPTION	Active window caption index
COLOR_APPWORKSPACE	MDI (multiple document interface) application background color index
COLOR_BACKGROUND	Desktop index
COLOR_CAPTIONTEXT	Text in caption, scroll bar arrow box, or size box index
COLOR_INACTIVEBORDER	Inactive window border index
COLOR_INACTIVECAPTION	Inactive window caption index
COLOR_MENU	Menu background index
COLOR_MENUTEXT	Text in menus index
COLOR_SCROLLBAR	Scroll bar gray area index
COLOR_WINDOW	Window background and thumb box index
COLOR_WINDOWFRAME	Window border and caption text background index
COLOR_WINDOWTEXT	Text in window index

Value Returned   None.

Notes   The function sends a WM_SYSCOLORCHANGE message to all windows, informing them of the color change(s). Windows is instructed to repaint the affected portions of all visible windows.

WORD SetTextAlign(hDC,wFlags)

Function   Sets the text alignment flag for the specified device context.

Parameters

hDC (HDC) specifies the device context.

wFlags (WORD) selects a mask affecting the horizontal and vertical alignment from the following list:

TA_BASELINE	Selects alignment along the X axis and the baseline of the selected font within the bounding rectangle
TA_BOTTOM	Selects alignment along the X axis and the bottom of the bounding rectangle
TA_CENTER	Selects alignment along the Y axis and the center of the bounding rectangle
TA_LEFT	Selects alignment along the Y axis and the left side of the bounding rectangle
TA_NOUPDATECP	Notes that the current position is not updated
TA_RIGHT	Selects alignment along the Y axis and the right side of the bounding rectangle
TA_TOP	Selects alignment along the X axis and the top of the bounding rectangle
TA_UPDATECP	Notes that the current position is updated

Value Returned   Indicates the alignment with the high-order word containing the vertical alignment and the low-order word containing the horizontal alignment.

Notes   Only one of the two flags that alter the current position can be chosen for the *wFlags* parameter.

short SetTextCharacterExtra(hDC,nCharExtra)

Function   Sets the amount of intercharacter spacing.

Parameters

hDC (HDC) specifies the device context.

nCharExtra (short) selects the amount of extra space to be added to each character.

Value Returned   Indicates the amount used for the previous intercharacter spacing.

Notes   When the current mapping mode is not set to MM_TEXT, the *nCharExtra* parameter is translated to the nearest pixel.

DWORD SetTextColor(hDC,rgbColor)

Function   Sets the text color.

Parameters

hDC (HDC) specifies the device context.

rgbColor (DWORD) selects an RGB color value to be used for text output.

Value Returned   Indicates the previous RGB color value used for text color.

Notes   **SetBkColor** is used to set the background color.

short SetTextJustification(hDC,nBreakExtra,nBreakCount)

Function   Justifies text using the *nBreakExtra* and *nBreakCount* parameters.

Parameters

  hDC (HDC) specifies the device context.

  nBreakExtra (short) selects the total amount of extra space to be added to the line of text.

  nBreakCount (short) selects the number of break characters in the line.

Value Returned   Indicates the outcome of the function. A value of 1 indicates a successful call; otherwise, a zero value is returned.

Notes   The break character used to delimit words is the ASCII 32 or blank space character. By calling **GetTextMetrics** the current font's break character can be obtained.

DWORD SetViewportExt(hDC,x,y)

Function   Sets the X and Y extents of the viewport of the selected device context.

Parameters

  hDC (HDC) specifies the device context.

  x (short), using device units, identifies the X extent of the viewport.

  y (short), using device units, identifies the Y extent of the viewport.

Value Returned   Contains the previous viewport extents with the high-order word containing the previous Y extent and the low-order word containing the previous X extent. A null return value indicates an error has occurred.

Notes   When one of the mapping modes HIENGLISH, HIMETRIC, LO-ENGLISH, LOMETRIC, TEXT, or TWIPS is in effect, subsequent calls to **SetWindowExt** or **SetViewportExt** are ignored.

DWORD SetViewportOrg(hDC,x,y)

Function   Sets the viewport origin of the specified device context.

Parameters

    hDC (HDC) specifies the device context.

    x (short), using device units, indicates the X coordinate of the origin of the viewport.

    y (short), using device units, indicates the Y coordinate of the origin of the viewport.

Value Returned   Contains the previous viewport origins with the high-order word containing the previous Y origin and the low-order word containing the previous X origin. A null return value indicates an error has occurred.

Notes   The viewport origin identifies the point in the device coordinate system that the GDI uses to map the window origin.

DWORD SetWindowExt(hDC,x,y)

Function   Sets the X and Y extents of the window of the selected device context.

Parameters

    hDC (HDC) specifies the device context.

    x (short), using device units, identifies the X extent of the window.

    y (short), using device units, identifies the Y extent of the window.

Value Returned   Contains the previous window extents with the high-order word containing the previous Y extent and the low-order word containing the previous X extent. A null return value indicates an error has occurred.

Notes   When one of the mapping modes HIENGLISH, HIMETRIC, LO-ENGLISH, LOMETRIC, TEXT, or TWIPS is in effect, subsequent calls to **SetWindowExt** or **SetViewportExt** are ignored.

DWORD SetWindowOrg(hDC,x,y)

Function   Sets the window origin of the specified device context.

Parameters

hDC (HDC) specifies the device context.

x (short), using device units, indicates the X coordinate of the origin of the window.

y (short), using device units, indicates the Y coordinate of the origin of the window.

Value Returned   Contains the previous window origins with the high-order word containing the previous Y origin and the low-order word containing the previous X origin. A null return value indicates an error has occurred.

Notes   The window origin identifies the point in the device coordinate system that the GDI uses to map the window origin.

void SetWindowPos(hWnd,hWndInsertAfter,x,y,cx,cy,wFlags)

Function   Changes the size, position, and ordering of child, pop-up, and top-level windows.

Parameters

hWnd (HWND) specifies the window to be positioned.

hWndInsertAfter (HWND) specifies the window from the window manager's list that is to precede the positioned window.

x (int) identifies the X coordinate of the window's upper-left corner.

y (int) identifies the Y coordinate of the window's upper-left corner.

cx (int) specifies the new window's width.

cy (int) specifies the new window's height.

wFlags (WORD) can be any one of the following values:

SWP_DRAWFRAME	Draws a frame around the window
SWP_HIDEWINDOW	Hides the window
SWP_NOACTIVATE	Doesn't activate the window
SWP_NOMOVE	Ignores the *x* and *y* parameters and does not move the window
SWP_NOSIZE	Ignores the current *cx* and *cy* values and does not change the window's size
SWP_NOREDRAW	Doesn't redraw
SWP_NOZORDER	Ignores the *hWndInsertAfter* value, retaining the current ordering
SWP_SHOWWINDOW	Displays the specified window

Value Returned   None.

Notes   When SWP_NOZORDER is not specified, Windows will place the window in the position following the window specified by *hWndInsert-After*.

void ShowScrollBar(hWnd,wBar,fShow)

Function   Hides or displays a scroll bar.

Parameters

hWnd (HWND) specifies the window containing the scroll bar.

wBar (WORD) identifies whether the scroll bar is a control or part of a window's nonclient area. It can be any one of the following values:

SB_CTL	Sets the position of a scroll bar control, assuming that *hWnd* points to a window handle of a scroll bar control
SB_HORZ	Sets the position of a window's horizontal scroll bar
SB_VERT	Sets the position of a window's vertical scroll bar

fShow (BOOL) identifies whether or not Windows hides the scroll bar. If *fShow* has a zero value the scroll bar is hidden; otherwise, it is not hidden.

Value Returned   None.

Notes   **ShowScrollBar** does not destroy a scroll bar's position and range when it hides the scroll bar. A call to **SetScrollBar** will.

BOOL TextOut(hDC,x,y,lpString,nCount)

Function   Writes a character string to the selected display.

Parameters

hDC (HDC) specifies the device context.

x (short) identifies the logical X coordinate of the string's starting point.

y (short) identifies the logical Y coordinate of the string's starting point.

lpString (LPSTR) is a pointer to a null-terminated string that is to be drawn.

nCount (short) identifies the number of characters in the string to be drawn.

Value Returned   A nonzero value indicates the string was successfully drawn; otherwise, a null is returned.

Notes   The current position is not used or updated by **TextOut**. All character origins are defined to be at the upper-left corner of the character position.

BOOL TrackPopupMenu(hMenu,wFlags,x,y,cx,hWnd)

Function   The function displays a "floating" pop-up menu.

Parameters

hMenu (HMENU) specifies the pop-up menu to be displayed.

wFlags (WORD) is not used and must be set to zero.

x (int) defines the horizontal position in screen coordinates of the left side of the menu on the screen.

y (int) defines the vertical position in screen coordinates of the top of the menu on the screen.

cx (int) defines the width in screen coordinates of the pop-up menu. A value of zero causes Windows to calculate the width based on the widest menu item.

hWnd (HWND) identifies the window that owns the pop-up menu.

Value Returned   TRUE for a successful call, otherwise FALSE.

int UpdateColors(hDC)

Function   The function updates the client area of the device context by matching the current colors in the client area to the system palette on a pixel-by-pixel basis.

Parameters   *hDC* (HDC) specifies the device context.

Value Returned   Return value is not used.

Notes   This function typically updates a client area faster than redrawing the area. This can result in the loss of some color information.

void UpdateWindow(hWnd)

Function   Updates the client area of the specified window by sending a WM_PAINT message.

Parameters   *hWnd* (HWND) is a handle to the window to be updated.

Value Returned   None.

Notes   The WM_PAINT message is sent directly to the window function of the selected window, bypassing the application queue.

void ValidateRect(hWnd,lpRect)

Function   Validates the client area within the given rectangle by removing the rectangle from the update region of the selected window.

Parameters

hWnd (HWND) is a handle to the window whose update region is about to be modified.

lpRect (LPRECT) is a pointer to a *rect* structure containing the client coordinate rectangle to be removed from the update region.

Value Returned   None.

Notes   The function automatically validates the entire client area.

void ValidateRgn(hWnd,hRgn)

Function   Validates the client area within the given region by removing the region from the update region of the selected window.

Parameters

hWnd (HWND) is a handle to the window whose update region is about to be modified.

hRgn (HRGN) specifies the region that defines the area to be removed from the update region.

Value Returned   None.

Notes   The region coordinates are assumed to be in client coordinates.

void WaitMessage( )

Function   Yields control to all other applications when the current application has no other tasks to execute.

Parameters   None.

Value Returned   None.

INDEX

A

A Special Diskette Offer

A diskette is available containing all of the program listings in this book. To use the diskette, you will need a computer with the Borland C++ compiler properly installed and running.

Send a check or money order, in U.S. currency, for **$30** for the 5.25-inch or 3.5-inch diskette, to the address below. Please allow three weeks for personal checks to clear. No purchase orders, please. All foreign orders (outside North America) must have a check drawn on a U.S. bank in U.S. currency for **$35** for the 5.25-inch or 3.5-inch diskette. Foreign orders will be sent air mail.

_ _

Please send me the program listings included in the *Borland C++ Handbook* by Pappas and Murray. Enclosed is a money order or check, for $30 ($35 foreign orders) in U.S. funds, which covers the cost of the diskette and all handling and postage. Sorry, no purchase orders can be accepted! This coupon may be copied.

Check one:

5.25-inch 360K format: _____

3.5-inch 1.44M format: _____

Name: _____

Address: _____

City: _____ State: _____ Zip: _____

Country: _____

Mail to: Nineveh National Research
         NEW Borland C++ Diskette Offer
         P.O. Box 2943
         Binghamton, NY 13902

*This is solely the offer of the authors. Osborne **McGraw-Hill** takes No responsibility for the fulfillment of this offer.*

Osborne McGraw-Hill

Computer Books

(800) 227-0900

Bookmarker Design — Lance Ravella

Tear off for Bookmark

▼

You're important to us...

We'd like to know what you're interested in, what kinds of books you're looking for, and what you thought about this book in particular.

Please fill out the attached card and mail it in. We'll do our best to keep you informed about Osborne's newest books and special offers.

◄ *YES, Send Me a FREE Color Catalog of all Osborne computer books*
To Receive Catalog, Fill in Last 4 Digits of ISBN Number from Back of Book
(see below bar code) 0-07-881 _ _ _ − _

Name: _____ Title: _____

Company: _____

Address: _____

City: _____ State: _____ Zip: _____

I'M PARTICULARLY INTERESTED IN THE FOLLOWING *(Check all that apply)*

I use this software
- ☐ WordPerfect
- ☐ Microsoft Word
- ☐ WordStar
- ☐ Lotus 1-2-3
- ☐ Quattro
- ☐ Others _____

I use this operating system
- ☐ DOS
- ☐ Windows
- ☐ UNIX
- ☐ Macintosh
- ☐ Others _____

I rate this book:
- ☐ Excellent   ☐ Good   ☐ Poor

I program in
- ☐ C or C++
- ☐ Pascal
- ☐ BASIC
- ☐ Others _____

I chose this book because
- ☐ Recognized author's name
- ☐ Osborne/McGraw-Hill's reputation
- ☐ Read book review
- ☐ Read Osborne catalog
- ☐ Saw advertisement in store
- ☐ Found/recommended in library
- ☐ Required textbook
- ☐ Price
- ☐ Other _____

Comments _____

Topics I would like to see covered in future books by Osborne/McGraw-Hill include:

_____

IMPORTANT REMINDER
To get your FREE catalog, write in the last 4 digits of the ISBN number printed on the back cover (see below bar code) 0-07-881 _ _ _ − _

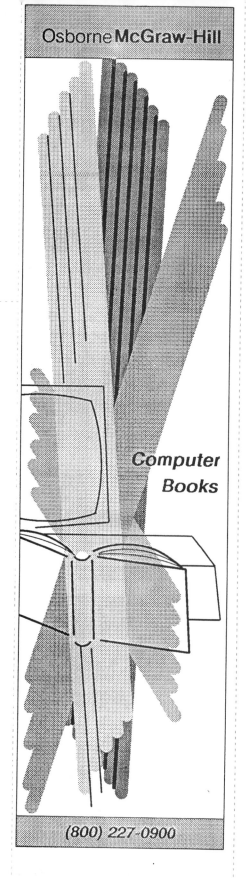
Osborne McGraw-Hill

Computer
Books

(800) 227-0900

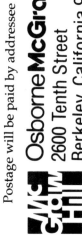